بسم الله الرحمن الرحيم ۰ الحمد لله رب العالمين ۰ الرحمن الرحيم ۰ مالك يوم الدين ۰ إياك نعبد وإياك نستعين ۰ اهدنا الصراط المستقيم ۰ صراط الذين أنعمت عليهم غير المغضوب عليهم ولا الضالين ۰

IN THE NAME OF ALLAH, THE MOST GRACIOUS, THE EVER MERCIFUL.

ALL PRAISE BELONGS TO ALLAH, LORD OF ALL THE WORLDS, THE MOST GRACIOUS, THE EVER MERCIFUL, MASTER OF THE DAY OF JUDGMENT.

THEE ALONE DO WE WORSHIP AND THEE ALONE DO WE IMPLORE FOR HELP.

GUIDE US IN THE RIGHT PATH— THE PATH OF THOSE ON WHOM THOU HAST BESTOWED *THY* BLESSINGS, THOSE WHO HAVE NOT INCURRED DISPLEASURE, AND THOSE WHO HAVE NOT GONE ASTRAY.

Revelation, Rationality, Knowledge and Truth

Mirza Tahir Ahmad

1998
ISLAM INTERNATIONAL PUBLICATIONS LTD.

Revelation, Rationality, Knowledge and Truth

by: *Mirza Tahir Ahmad*
   (Supreme Head of the worldwide
   Ahmadiyya Muslim Community)

First Published in U.K. in 1998

Published by:
   Islam International Publications Limited
   "Islamabad"
   Sheephatch Lane,
   Tilford, Surrey
   GU10 2AQ
   United Kingdom

Printed at:
   The Bath Press
   Lower Bristol Road
   Bath BA2 3BL

British Library Cataloguing in Publication Data:

Ahmad, Mirza Tahir
   Revelation, Rationality, Knowledge and Truth
   1.   Koran – Hermeneutics 2. Revelation (Islam)
        3. Rationalism
   I.   Title
   297. 2' 115

ISBN 1 85372 640 0

Dedication

I dedicate this book to
Hazrat Mirza Ghulam Ahmad[as],
the Founder of the Ahmadiyya Muslim Jamaat,
who authored his two outstanding
philosophical/religious works,
"Brahin-e-Ahmadiyyah"
and
"The Philosophy of the Teachings of Islam"
during the last two decades of the previous century. They
dispelled darkness and filled the age with the light of
Divine wisdom which radiated from his pen.
Their brilliance was not confined to that century alone.
They were to remain outstanding works of unique greatness
for the centuries to come.

I owe this achievement of my life to my late mother,
Maryam,
whose prayers always stood by my side,
though she could not.
Blessed be her soul.

Contents

PART IV

PART V

PART VI

PART VII

INDEX

Throughout the book, full-page illustrations are numbered as I.1, I.2, I.3 etc. The coloured illustrations are given in plates 1 to 8 except the first two which are not numbered.

Publisher's Note

PLEASE NOTE that in referencing the Holy Quran we have counted verse بِسْمِ اللهِ الرَّحْمٰنِ الرَّحِيْم *In the name of Allah, the Most Gracious, the Ever Merciful* as the first verse of the Chapter in which it appears. Some publishers of the Holy Quran however, begin counting the verses after the verse بِسْمِ اللهِ الرَّحْمٰنِ الرَّحِيْم Should the reader not find the relevant verse under the number given in the book, it would be found in the adjacent lower number. For instance, the reader would find the referred verse under 143 instead of 144.

Many translators add explanatory words in their translation which is not found in the Quranic text. But they see to it that the reader is not misled to consider them as the words of the Quran. Maulawi Sher Ali Sahib has italicized such words.

The name Muhammad or his titles – the Holy Prophet or the Founder of Islam, is generally followed by the symbol ˢᵃ for the salutation *Ṣal-Lallāho 'Alaihi wa Sallam* meaning *May peace and blessings of Allah be upon him.*

The names of most other prophets and Messengers of God are followed by the symbol ᵃˢ for *'Alaihis-Salām* meaning *on whom be peace.* The actual salutations have not been set out in full, in most cases, for the sake of brevity. Muslim readers should treat the full salutation as implicit.

System of Transliteration

In transliterating Arabic words, the system adopted by the Royal Asiatic Society has been followed:

ا   at the beginning of a word, pronounced as *a, i, u* preceded by a very slight aspiration, like *h* in the English word 'honour'.

ث   *th,* pronounced like *th* in the English word 'thing'.

ح *ḥ,* a guttural aspirate, stronger than h.

خ *kh,* pronounced like the Scotch *ch* in 'loch'.

ذ *dh,* pronounced like the English *th* in 'that', 'with'.

ص *ṣ,* strongly articulated s.

ض *ḍ,* similar to the English *th* in 'this'.

ط *ṭ,* strongly articulated platal t.

ظ *ẓ,* strongly articulated z.

ع *'a,* a strong guttural, the pronunciation of which must be learnt by the ear.

غ *gh,* a sound approached very nearly in the *r 'grasseyé'* in French, and in the German *r.* It requires the muscles of the throat to be in the 'gargling' position whilst pronouncing it.

ق *q,* a deep guttural *k* sound.

ء *a',* a sort of catch in the voice.

Short vowels are represented by *a* for ﹷ (like *u* in 'bud'); *i* for ﹻ (like *i* in 'bid')' *u* for ﹹ (like *oo* in 'wood'); the long vowels by *ā* for ﺍ or آ (like *a* in 'father'); *ī* for ﻰ (like ee in 'deep'); *ai* for ﻰﹷ (like *i* in 'site'); *ū* for ﻭﹹ (like oo in 'root'); *au* for, ﻭ ﹷ (resembling *ou* in 'sound').

The consonants not included in the above list have the same phonetic value as in English.

There are, however, some proper nouns that have not been spelt according to the above rules of transliteration in our earlier literature. We have left them unchanged. The same applies to the titles like Hazrat. When a reference is given to an earlier book, we always follow the transliteration employed in that book. Many extensively used proper nouns have been spelt differently by different authors. We spell them as follows: the Quran, Muhammad, Ahmad.

Since the word 'Surah' is now accepted in English to indicate one of the 114 Chapters of the Holy Quran, we prefer to use Surah when referring to the Quran and chapter when referring to sections of this or any other book. We hope this will avoid any possible confusion to the reader.

Acknowledgements

*T*HE LIST OF THOSE who have helped me during the writing of this book and after it was finished is long. But their memories are printed on my heart with loving care.

At different stages, different people were involved. Most of them could do no more than make an effort to faithfully translate the original Urdu version. Their labour was not altogether lost. Every time I critically examined any translation, invariably new ideas were born to be incorporated in the book. Also, after every critical examination of their translations, I decided to change the sequence of the discussions to a better one. Thus I journeyed from version to version which was a climbing spiral like the path of evolution. Hopefully, with this final version, I have reached the summit.

During all these stages, there were so many scholars and technocrats who were involved, not for the work of translation, but in things which I could not have handled alone. For instance, I needed to retrieve certain passages from books or articles I had read during the last forty years of my life. They were so varied that they belonged to all the subjects discussed in my work, which the reader can realize are not a mere few. Libraries had to be combed by scholars belonging to different continents and cities.

From Rabwah, the headquarters of the Ahmadiyya Muslim Community, many learned scholars were involved in retracing the religious references.

From America, it was Professor Malik Masood Ahmad and his team who were required to trace many references which belonged mainly to *Scientific American* and *American Scientist* of the last twenty years or so. His team was selected from Ahmadi scholars from all over

America whose names are difficult to produce in this short acknowledgement. But he was specifically helped by Dr Salahuddin and Jawad Malik, his son.

Dr Salahuddin in particular did a great job in finding lost references. I had not remembered the titles of the articles or the years of their publication. All he had to work with was a general idea of the subject matter I had retained in my memory. Amazingly, he retrieved everything and to my pleasant surprise, my memory of what had been said was precise.

In London, it was Mrs Saleha Safi who performed the major role of reference hunting. Assisted by her daughter, Sophia Safi Mahmood, she performed amazing feats of retracing various books which contained the desired references. Then there were those girls and boys and women and men in London, who volunteered themselves for various tasks and did the job with dedicated diligence. It is impossible to mention them all, but I should be excused if I produce a list of just some names which I specially remember.

AT THE TOP OF THE LIST I must mention Farina Qureshi and her peerless contribution in organizing and directing a scholarly team to help her detect and pinpoint the areas needing my special attention. In this respect, Farida Ghazi's participation outshone every other member of her team, except for Farina of course. Farina has been extremely humble in this service she rendered. As a rule she refrained from suggesting specific amendments or improvements which a passage required. It was rarely that I wanted her and her team members to suggest amendments in some specific place; they humbly complied but their suggestions were not always accepted. I must pay compliment to the largeness of their heart that they always accepted my decision with good grace. It was during this exercise of trying alternative suggestions that they also realized, like I had so often done, how difficult it was to change an expression without altering the entire chain of links leading up to it. We immensely enjoyed this game which proved a much welcome diversion. In short, no appreciation on my part can do justice to their contribution to help me improve the quality of my work. A full mention of this team is made in the preface which follows.

OF THOSE WHO HAVE HELPED ME with this book, many are listed below. My memory may have failed me in remembering them all. To them I render my loving apologies.

1. Munir Ahmad Javed, Private Secretary, London.
2. Munir-ud-Din Shams, London.
3. Farina Qureshi, London.
4. Mansoora Hyder, London.
5. Farida Ghazi, London.
6. Mahmood Ahmad Malik, Islamabad, UK.
7. Professor Amatul Majid Chaudhary, Islamabad, UK.
8. Basit Ahmad, London.
9. Fowzia Shah, London.
10. Musarrat Bhatti, Northampton.

The above list has been specifically chosen from a longer list of many who helped at different stages of this work. But the participation of those who are named above has been so persistent and important in its nature that I cannot feel at rest without specially mentioning them. Munir Javed, number one on the list, played a pivotal role in implementing my plan to allocate different roles to different scholars. Munir-ud-Din Shams has earned a special place because of his persistent hard labour which amazed me at how much he could take. Many mentioned above worked for days and nights without any rest, and without informing me of their amazing sacrifices. I had to keep an eye on them somehow, peeping across the screen which they had built to hide their labour from my eyes. However, I had my own ways of knowing what was happening. At times I had to specially order them to have a little rest and a little food before they could drop exhausted, having reached the tether of their tolerance.

11. Muzaffar Ahmad Malik, Islamabad, UK.

Muzaffar Malik requires special mention because it was he who was entrusted with the job of the final printing and to negotiate with various presses to strike the best bargain. In the final preparation of the camera ready copy, his work has been conspicuous.

12. Bashir Ahmad, Private Secretary's Office London.
13. Pir Muhammad Alam, Private Secretary's Office London.

Two voluntary workers, Bashir Ahmad and Pir Muhammad Alam, played a highly essential role of taking care of all the scholars who helped me during their presence in the office. When they worked the whole night, both Bashir Sahib and Pir Sahib did the same to fulfil their odd requirements during their work. Occasionally they also took care in serving them food despite their complete silence of how hungry they were at times.

Following is the list of some scholars in Rabwah who were contacted from time to time by Munir Ahmad Javed whenever some material was required to which these scholars had access:

14. Maulvi Dost Mohammad, Rabwah.
15. Syed Abdul Haye, Rabwah.
16. Hafiz Muzaffar Ahmad, Rabwah.
17. Habibur Rehman Zirvi, Asst. Librarian, Rabwah.

18. Professor Ch. Mohammad Ali, Rabwah.

There is one who did not participate in the work, yet I owe him so much for the service he rendered. I am speaking of Professor Raja Ghalib Ahmad of Lahore who insisted that a final chapter may please be added on the issue of the finality of prophethood. This chapter virtually pays him a standing ovation: 'how right you were Raja Sahib!'

Mansoora Hyder has performed an additional task which was highly essential but at the same time, extremely painstaking. All the references given in this book have been checked by her with minute attention so that every dot, comma, word and spelling is exactly the same as in the original excerpt. This required the collection of a mini-library which only deals with our references. This she has done to perfection. To my knowledge she had to chase some original books to which reference was given in certain articles. She did not abandon the pursuit till she actually got the required book in her hand. For this stupendous task she must be applauded here, a compliment due to her.

During references to original Chinese works and their available translations the irreplaceable services of Usman M. Chou had to be acquired. He is a great scholar whose translation of the Holy Quran has found great acclaim from a large number of Chinese scholars. Without his help we could not have ascertained the exact meaning of many Chinese expressions which are slightly mistranslated in old classical literature.

I must also express my profound acknowledgement to Uzma Aftab Ahmad Khan. She is a professionally trained lady for examining literary works in search of small flaws and errors which often find their way undetected into them.

She excels in this task of critically examining them before they are finally approved for publication. My team and I were pleased to notice that she has really an extraordinarily sharp eye. Without her assistance and diligent work we may not have noticed that many expressions had to be further elaborated and many a sequence had to be reordered. Her professional services which she offered completely voluntarily have left me particularly obliged.

In the last chance for bug detection given to us by the press, it was Fowzia Shah who performed an excellent work. It seems she is a born bug detector. How can I thank her enough!

The index for this book was painstakingly prepared by Munawar Ahmed Saeed of Washington DC. His team of dedicated assistants include his son Ahmed Muneeb Saeed, Fouzan Pal, Jawad A. Malik, Mazher Ahmad and Fizan Abdullah. Considering the magnitude of the task and the very little time they had at their disposal, they have done an excellent job, Masha Allah.

The Artists

As for the cover design, Noma Saeed from America made many attempts to pictorially display the contents. Unfortunately, her long laborious task was declined by the professionals from the press. They strongly advised the cover images to be an artist's impression of the contents, portrayed by his brush instead of a computer. This wise counsel was finally adopted. The services of many artists from London were incorporated, the chief among them being Hadi Ali Chaudhary and Ch. Abdul Rashid, a prominent architect who excels in giving pictorial expression to abstract ideas, and Syed Fahim Zakria of Birmingham. They were assisted by a team of artists of their choice.

Many artists were involved in various artistic projections contained within the book, but Safdar Hussain Abbasi and Hadi Ali Chaudhary have particularly rendered invaluable services, excelling above all others in the fine quality of the work they have produced. The other artists are Musarrat Bhatti, Farida Ghazi, Fahrija Avdić and Tahira Osman.

One person must also be mentioned without naming him, that is what he himself desired, when he offered me a large amount of money to be spent on the preparatory expenses. All he requested was that he and his parents, and his family should be remembered by me in my prayers. I have decided to mention this so that all others who would like to join me in my prayers, may do so.

Also, my daughter Faiza Luqman deserves my special gratitude. Throughout the writing of this book, she has always wholeheartedly and untiringly taken care of such helpers who worked odd hours and needed meals. For her silent, but dearly appreciated service, I especially owe her my thanks.

ALLAH bless all whose names are mentioned above, and also those whose names have not been mentioned but their participation is remembered by me with personal gratitude – Ameen.

Mirza Tahir Ahmad

PREFACE

I T ALL BEGAN in Zurich in 1987 with a suggestion by the late Masud Jhelumi, the then Missionary in charge of the Ahmadiyya Mission Switzerland, to Professor Dr Karl Henking, Professor of Ethnology, University of Zurich. He requested the Professor to invite the Head of the Worldwide Ahmadiyya Muslim Community to deliver a lecture on Islam – a topic on which no religious scholar had ever addressed the University.

The first response by the Professor was rather negative. In his opinion the students of the University were least interested in religion. In fact most took pride in being atheists with scant respect for any religion. After a few days however, the Professor himself suggested to Masud that if the title were changed to Rationality as the main theme, while Revelation could also be added by way of comparison, to show how the two play a role severally in leading to Knowledge and Eternal Truth, perhaps such a topic could attract students. He was proved right by subsequent events.

On Thursday, the 14 June 1987 at 8.15 p.m., the proposed lecture was delivered under the title *Rationality, Revelation, Knowledge, Eternal Truth*. The students, evidently intrigued by the title, thronged Oule (the great auditorium) which became filled to capacity so that additional arrangements had to be made in another hall with provisions for relaying the proceedings through television screens and loudspeakers.

Incidentally, this was the same auditorium where Sir Winston Churchill had delivered his historic address on 9 September 1946 entitled *Let Europe Arise*. It was this lecture, in fact, which created the blueprint for the present-day European Common Market. At that time he was no longer the Prime Minister of Great Britain, but his greatness did not lie in the office he had occupied, it was the office which was made greater when he occupied it. His lecture was epoch-making.

When the time for my address started on the fixed date, I began with a few introductory remarks in English. They were followed by the main address, originally written by me in Urdu and rendered into excellent German by Sheikh Nasir Ahmad. He took some seventy-five minutes to deliver the written speech. Finally the audience were invited to ask questions. As the questions were addressed to me, Sheikh Nasir Ahmad began to perform the role of interpreter. It was altogether a very refreshing experience. The session had advanced to two and a half hours, yet the interest of the students was still alive until the session had to be closed at 10.45 p.m. because the hall had to be vacated according to the University schedule.

That was how the seed of this book was first sown. It was a mere seed, in the first place, because most of the points covered by my notes could not be incorporated in the article from which the translation was made. Again the translation which Sheikh Nasir Ahmad had prepared could not be read to the end, because of the shortage of time.

Many attempts were made during the subsequent years to translate the full Urdu manuscript, which had been much enlarged by me later, into English. It took some years for these attempts to be exhausted and abandoned at last. The topic was so varied that no single scholar could translate all the subjects covered by it even to his own satisfaction. Some groups of scholars also tried their hand together but to no avail.

Finally, despite my heavy engagements, it was considered essential that I should myself dictate most of the book anew. Basit Ahmad, currently on the Board of Editors of the *Review of Religions*, volunteered his services for the task. He managed to prepare many generations of dictated material on his laptop computer, but none could satisfy us because the time lapse between our meetings was often too long so that a coherent work without repetitions could not be produced. Moreover, every time a new dictation was given, new ideas were inserted and quite a few amendments were also made which required relevant changes in other chapters as well. He had put in so much labour continuously for two years, without complaint, that it began to hurt me to see him suffer pointlessly. He had to be relieved yet his highly precious service immensely helped to advance the cause further. Every version displayed a definite improvement on the previous one.

After Basit, a group of ladies opted for the resumption of the work. Thus it continued to progress bit by bit but could not develop into a coherent work with uninterrupted flow.

I was left in the end with no option but to rewrite most of the manuscript in my own hand, a task which took me the better part of last year with many intervening breaks because of other pressing engagements. In the end, all it needed was a competent person to scrutinize it from the beginning to the end in search of such lapses and repetitions as may have remained undetected. This laborious but highly essential task was excellently performed by Mrs Farina Qureshi, assisted by a team of dedicated workers with varied experience in literary work. With their combined effort, under her exacting supervision, they pointed out to me some discrepancies which had escaped my notice. Thus I was in a position to remove the wrinkles and press the manuscript into its final shape.

The team consisted of Mrs Farida Ghazi, Mrs Mansoora Hyder, Professor Amatul Majid Chaudhary, Mrs Saleha Safi, Mr Munir-ud-Din Shams, Mr Mahmood Ahmad Malik – the computer typist and Mr Munir Ahmad Javed. These names have also been included in the long list of extremely dedicated honorary workers to whom I owe my most sincere gratitude.

THE BOOK was finally ready for publication after a seemingly interminable long wait of ten years since its initial beginning at Zurich. But for Professor Dawkins, an eminent British zoologist who authored the famous book entitled *The Blind Watchmaker* this work could have been published long ago. In his outstanding work he has actually rewritten Darwin, overly advocating his theories to disprove the existence of any deity other than the blind principle of natural selection.

Unfortunately, my attention was drawn to this book rather late, only after I had almost completed the task of the final retouching of my book. All the same, I was compelled by this information to delay its publication until such time as I could read this book and examine his arguments in depth. Having done so, I have now added a full new chapter in this book on Professor Dawkins' fantastic theory of creation without a creator. Evidently, every creation requires a creator. You cannot believe in the Mona Lisa and deny Leonardo da Vinci. Yet this exactly is the blunder which Professor Dawkins has committed. While believing in creation he denies the existence of a Creator, clumsily trying to replace Him with Darwin's natural selection. That is what is least expected of him as an eminent biologist. He should have known that the Darwinian principles are not creative principles.

This discussion will be carried out in full in the chapter *The 'Blind Watchmaker' who is also Deaf and Dumb*. Here we only consider it appropriate to point out that the title Professor Dawkins has given to his book would perhaps be more relevant if it were changed into *Mr Bat, the Watchmaker par Excellence*. The blind watchmaker of Professor Dawkins' book is evidently not a man but only an idea. Mere ideas cannot make things, particularly a clock. But bats, as described by Professor Dawkins, are more worthy of and better equipped for constructing clocks. They have minds, they can hear sounds and voices in a manner which no other animal can. They can virtually see in total darkness. They can distinguish between infinitesimal sonar variations which even the most sophisticated and advanced man-made sonar systems cannot.

A bat can hear the slightest movement of the cogs and springs of a watch which even the keenest ear of a human watchmaker cannot.

Enough of titles. We find ourselves at pains to strongly disagree with him, but we should be pardoned to describe his theory as absolutely devoid of substance. All the same Professor Dawkins enjoys wide fame all over the world. It is so because most of his fans are drawn from a new generation of scientists who are atheists first and scientists after. They must have always been perplexed at the colossal mysteries of nature and wondered how they could have been created without a conscious, intricate designer. In Professor Dawkins they must have found their champion who twisted the issues so dextrously that even some advanced students of natural science were also deceived into believing that their problem was solved. But he deceived only those who wanted to be deceived deep within. Had they examined Professor Dawkins' presentation of natural selection with unprejudiced open minds, they could have most certainly discovered the flaws, the discrepancies and the contradictions which his thesis contained. Perhaps they wanted to take refuge in the obscurities created by him because in God they shall not believe.

We have had some experience of those who are predetermined in their dogmas in all fields of faith and belief. The present work is in fact not directly addressed to them nor could we entertain a genuine hope in their conversion. The address is to the general reader who is not already committed to any scientific or unscientific dogma. Professor Dawkins' bit by bit theory is in fact no surprise because even Darwin, as early as 1859, in his great work *The Origin of Species,* mentioned this theory himself during his discussion on the intricacies of an eye as an organ. There he clearly confesses that the intricate mechanism of an eye can in no way be explained by his own theory of natural selection. Following is the confession of Darwin in his own words:

> 'To suppose that the eye, with all its inimitable contrivances for adjusting the focus to different distances, for admitting different amounts of light, and for the correction of spherical and chromatic aberration, could have been formed by natural selection, seems, I freely confess, absurd in the highest possible degree.'[1]

Having said that he carves a path of retreat by building his bit by bit theory which has now become the mainstay of Professor Dawkins' arguments in favour of natural selection being the only creator. However, Darwin's bit by bit theory was based on such conjectures as have already been proved absolutely wrong. If anything, they are positively counter-productive. Thus Darwin continues after his honest confession mentioned above:

> 'Yet reason tells me, that if numerous gradations from a perfect and complex eye to one very imperfect and simple, each grade being useful to its possessor, can be shown to exist; if further, the eye does vary ever so slightly, and the variations be inherited, which is certainly the case; and if any variation or modification in the organ be ever useful to an animal under changing conditions of life, then the difficulty of believing that a perfect and complex eye could be formed by natural selection, though insuperable by our imagination, can hardly be considered real.'[1]

Thus the much exaggerated bit by bit theory was primarily suggested by Darwin himself, and that too, specifically in relation to the eye. But how false he is proved in the light of the most modern researches which have revealed a highly advanced mechanism in the most rudimentary and ancient specimens of eyes.

Their deep sea studies have revealed that the most ancient specimens of eyes as found in the earliest species of marine life are highly developed masterpieces of such visionary systems as perplex the most modern manufacturer of optical instruments. This is no place to go into another detailed discussion but we refer the reader to the article *Animal Eyes with Mirror Optics*[2] by Michael F. Land which appeared in *Scientific American* about twenty years before the publication of this book. We specifically draw the readers' attention to page 93 of that article which describes the eye of the *Gigantocypris*. The miracle of the creation of its two unique eyes with two absolutely precision-made reflectors, instead of the customary spherical eyes which need lenses for focusing, is a marvel of the highest degree. This is exactly what was needed in the dark world of oceans at such depths where this animal dwells. It has to put to maximum advantage the extremely dim light bordering upon total darkness. This could not have been made possible but for the pre-existence of a most sophisticated designer with perfect know-how who could conceive and manufacture this rudimentary yet absolutely precise optical instrument. The entire article covers so many real examples of some of the most ancient eyes which are fascinatingly purpose-built. Each of these shatters to bits and pieces the so-called bit by bit theories of Professor Dawkins and those of his great master Charles Darwin. We did not mention all this in our book which is already packed with similar examples, but having referred here to Darwin's speculative argument in favour of his bit by bit theory concerning the construction of an eye, this reference becomes essentially contradictory to what he speculated. A perusal of that article should convince even the most sceptical of naturalists that there is more to the making of an eye than actually meets the eye. But if scepticism is based on a predetermined bias, nothing can be done for it! We hope our chapter on Professor Dawkins' much celebrated book will help those who did not agree with him yet were overawed by his image.

We beg the scientist as well as the non-scientist to read not only the chapter on Professor Dawkins but our entire work which was written before it. The reader would discover that even without mentioning his book, our work provided enough satisfactory answers to all the questions specifically raised by the Professor. The main theme of the book however, is far wider than the limited discussions we have referred to above. It relates to the Quranic treatment of all the various issues the book contains – a treatment so fascinating yet so rational that it dazzles the human intellect. It is to this that the reader should concentrate his attention. On his way he may also encounter the mysteries of life and the solution to those mysteries which the Quran offers.

We promise the reader that he will be amply rewarded and that his study will assist him by ushering him into the majestic presence of his Lord – the Creator, the Master of the universe.

REFERENCES

1. DARWIN, C. (1985) *The Origin of Species*. Introduction by Burrow, J. W. Penguin Classics, England, p.217
2. LAND, M.F. (December, 1978) *Animal Eyes with Mirror Optics*. Scientific American, p.93

PART I

INTRODUCTION WITH
A HISTORICAL PERSPECTIVE

T
HE STUDY of the history of religious and secular thought reveals that throughout the ages great philosophers, sages and religious leaders held different views about the comparative values of reason, logic and revelation. As such, they can be divided into various groups.

There are those who emphasize the role of rationality to a degree that they consider it as the only valid means of discovering truth. For them, the only conclusion worthy of acceptance is the one which can be derived through dialectical logical reasoning based on observed facts. Hence, they believe that truth (in whatever form they define it) can only be reached through the faculty of reasoning.

There are thinkers who believe in the phenomenon of Divine guidance which, according to them, plays a definite role in enlightning the human mind, providing it with answers to many unresolved questions.

Again there are those who believe that truth can be reached entirely through inner experiences referred to as 'inspiration'. They consider it to be attainable through a deep search within oneself, as if its blueprint had been imprinted upon every human soul. They delve deep within themselves, and through an introspective study attain a fundamental understanding of nature and how it works.

Another mode of reaching truth shared both by the religious and secular schools of enquiry is mysticism. Mystification of life seems to be a common tendency shared by believers and non-believers alike. Mystics may belong to all the categories mentioned above and their methodology could be philosophical or religious. Their distinguishing mark is that they enjoy being cryptic.

Then there are pseudo-philosophers who use words and phrases that are too elusive for the common man to understand. Thus they hide their views behind the mystic screen of their verbosity. There are others however, who have truly scientific minds but are mystics all the same, as were Pythagoras and Averroes. They burrow deep in search of the seed of truth and do not remain content with hovering on the surface of things. To keep track of them with concentration of mind is always rewarding.

In religion, we find mystics of different hues and colours. There are those who, whilst accepting and fulfilling the outward observances required by the form of religion, strive to find deeper meaning below the surface. Also, there are some who overemphasize the inner meaning at the cost of the external form, sometimes doing away with the observances altogether.

But followers of religions founded upon revelation do not always remain confined to discussions within the boundaries of revelational truths. In the later stages of each religion we also find such debates, as are difficult to be defined as entirely religious in nature. The same age-old questions are again revived within a new framework. What is reason? What part does it play in human affairs, and where does revelation stand in relation to logic and reason?

It is universally observed that the interplay of various ideas at later stages of a religion's history tends to revert to the confusion which prevailed prior to their advent. It happens because man's influence on religion has always been to break it into factions and to partially revert it to the older mythical ideas and philosophies. It has seldom led to a reunification of differing schools of thought born through the degenerating processes that divide and split religions. This degeneration seems to be irreversible.

RELIGIONS which begin with the firm faith in the Unity of God, gradually decay into numerous idolatrous schisms. There are occasional attempts made by man to reconstitute the unity of religious understanding among the people and to re-establish the Unity of God. Alas, such efforts gain only limited success. As a whole, the process is never reversed, unless it is Divinely aided and guided.

We cannot discuss here in detail all the varying views propounded by past philosophers and sages, but we shall give a brief account of the assessment of revelation, rationality and their interrelationship made by various prominent intellectuals of the past.

What is eternal truth, and what is knowledge? What is the relationship, if any, between the two? Does revelation provide knowledge which in turn leads to eternal truth, or could both be attainable through rationality alone?

These, and many other similar questions have been agitating the minds of philosophers, religious divines and secular thinkers since time immemorial. But before we begin a careful in-depth study, it would be appropriate perhaps to further elaborate the nature of eternal truth as understood by different thinkers.

All believers in God who advocate the cause of eternal truth, understand it to be an unchangeable reality in relation to the past, present and future. As such, primarily, it is to God with His attributes that they refer as Truth Eternal. However, when secular philosophers discuss the same issue, they do not always discuss it in relation to God. Their discussion generally revolves around certain values such as truth, honesty, integrity, faith, loyalty etc. The prime question which agitates the minds of the philosophers is whether there exists any unchangeable reality even in the face of changeable circumstances. The merit of a given truth itself is many a time challenged as such. One often begins to wonder whether truth would not acquire different meanings in different situations.

ANOTHER ASPECT of the same question relates to the concept of truth as applicable to the hidden realities behind the screen of what appears. For instance, if we treat the light of the sun as an independent reality we may be wrong. More than the light itself it is the causative reality of radiation which works behind all its manifestations, light being just one of them. The hidden universal truth is the radiation which may or may not vibrate at the spectrum which humans see as light. From this angle, nothing seems to be eternal about the sun's luminosity. But if, as suggested above, the reason why the sun radiates is perfectly understood, then wherever that reason is found to be at work, it will produce the same result and as such, it could be referred to as the 'eternal' truth which commands the laws of radiation and luminosity. With this illustration it becomes quite evident that the term 'eternal' does not always indicate a state of unbroken, unceasing continuity. Here it only applies to a causative phenomenon, which whenever present will always produce the same results.

In this simple understanding of eternal truth, relating to the external realities, the phenomenon of gravity could be rightly referred to as eternal truth. However, it should be well understood that any minute variation in the application of gravitational pull does not in any way challenge the unchangeable fundamental reality of gravity.

It becomes evident from the preceding discussion that although all eternal truths give rise to certain knowledge, all types of knowledge, however, cannot be defined as eternal. Knowledge can be defined as a perception of something which is safely stored in the mind as a reliable piece of information. All such pieces of information put together build a storehouse of human knowledge. How can we gain certain knowledge, and how can we determine which specific knowledge is false and which is true?

Again, by what means can we categorize knowledge as transient truth, substantial truth, eternal truth, conditional truth etc.? It is only the human faculty of reasoning and rationality which ruminates these facts as they are fed into the brain, turns them over and over again and permutates them into various possible combinations. This mental process of sorting out the right from the wrong, the definite from the indefinite, is the mechanism of rationality.

The question arises as to how far this method of analysing the constituents of knowledge is reliable. When we reach this stage of our comprehension of rationality, other intriguing questions also begin to raise their heads. We know, for instance, that the human mind has no consistency in relation to its own findings. We know for certain that whatever is considered rational in one age may not necessarily be considered rational in another. We know, without doubt, that the faculty of reasoning has been progressively developing and maturing ever since man emerged from the domain of the animal kingdom into the world of humans. From that time onward, the collective experience as it is amassed in the form of knowledge and truth in the human mind continued to improve the faculty of his reasoning and the quality of his rational appraisals.

As physical exercise improves muscle power, so also the mental, rational and retentive faculties develop and gain strength with mental exercise. It is this exercise perhaps which may also have contributed to a progressive evolutionary increase in the brain mass of animals.

This realization of the progressive advance of our mental faculties though welcome on one count, is rather unwelcome on another. It puts to question the very reliability of our mental rational deductions during different stages of our development.

Is it not likely that the same facts fed to the human brain at different stages of its development may have resulted in different conclusions? If the objective realities appear different when observed from different vantage points, if the conclusions drawn by the unbiased human mind also differ in different ages, then will it be justified to adjudge them as only justified truths? With our faculties of deductive logic and reasoning alone at any point in time, we cannot pronounce any knowledge we possess to be absolute truth.

The issues we are about to discuss are concerning the instruments which may lead to knowledge and the manner in which any knowledge could be ascertained as truth. If all human vantage points are actually placed on a moving platform, with constant change in the angle of vision, how can any knowledge or piece of information we obtain be declared, with any certainty, to be the truth? There is one vantage point, that of God the Creator, which is eternal and constant. Hence, if the existence of an Omniscient, Omnipotent, Omnipresent God is proved and if He is Eternal, Infallible, Transcendent, All-Powerful and Possessor of absolute attributes — then and only then could the possibility of gaining knowledge of eternal truth through Him arise. But this hypothesis is only conditional on the premise that not only does such a Supreme Being exist, but that He also communicates with humans. It is this communication of God with humans which is called revelation in religious terminology.

To discuss issues of such great import, purely on a secular and rational basis is not an easy task. Add to this the question of revelation as having played any significant role in human guidance, and the task will become all the more challenging. Yet this is the task we have undertaken, with the full realization of all the complexities involved.

The reader is most humbly requested to make an effort to remain alert. Once he familiarizes himself with the intricacies of the philosophical and rational jigsaw, he will be amply rewarded with the ultimate pleasure of watching the pieces of this jigsaw fall into the right places.

In application to religion, this view has given birth to a school of sociologists and modern thinkers who consider the birth and development of religion to be a reflection of man's developing power of reasoning. The implication of this is that man's comparatively primitive intellect in the remote past led to the creation of many godly images, which, with the passage of time, gave birth to the idea of a single deity, referred to as God, Allah, Parmatma etc. If accepted, this theory would lead to the conclusion that the development of religion at every cross-section of its history corresponded to man's changing intellectual capabilities.

This is a diametrically opposed view to the one held by various religions of the world, who all believe in the Divine origin of religion. According to this view, religion is directly taught to man by the One, Eternal, All-Wise God. They see polytheism, which dominates many periods of human history, merely as a degenerative process – a process which invariably follows monotheism after it is established by the messengers of God. A further discussion on these issues will follow later.

Nearly all major religions profess belief in an invisible God Who can and does communicate with man. They claim that God chooses human representatives and that the communication they receive from Him is the only dependable means of attaining true knowledge. They maintain that it is not possible to establish any truth with complete certainty, if it is based solely upon man's experiences and his rational deductions.

All that has been briefly summed up above is addressed more elaborately in the following chapters.

INDIVIDUAL VERSUS SOCIETY

REEDOM is a prerogative of all living things, man being no exception. Liberty is the most cherished fruit of life. Man is the epitome of liberty which is ingrained in him. His very texture is woven with the yarn of liberty. Yet, amazingly, we find all man-made institutions shaped to work against the liberty of man in the final analysis.

A careful study of the history of progressive growth of traditions, customs and legislation is sufficient to prove this assertion. The evolution of the state when viewed from an unbiased, detached angle of perception will appear no more than an institutionalized journey of man towards progressive self-imposed slavery. To resolve this dilemma requires a deeper understanding of the factors which are responsible for this step by step transition from freedom to bondage.

One thing must be noted at the outset, that man by nature will bow to the authority of society only when he is driven by selfish motives; otherwise he will have to be coerced into submission. But to socialise is not a prerogative of man alone. As the animal kingdom moves from lower to higher orders, there appears to be a gradual transition from a chaotic to a more disciplined, organized and centralized animal society. Sometimes we notice it as a trend, where necessity must have taught the animals to live together in their common interest of survival. Sometimes, to our utter amazement, we find social order and meticulous discipline ingrained even in such animal species as are not very highly placed in the ladder of evolution. No gradual evolutionary influences can be traced in their highly disciplined order which seem to have erupted as such in their final perfected form. All that we can infer from the study of their institutionalized existence is that it is naturally ingrained in them.

Take for example the case of certain insects. Where would one place in the ladder of evolution the society of honey-bees? What could possibly have preceded them if they had slowly evolved step by step? Where would one find the evidence of a gradual stage-by-stage development of a long line of insects culminating in the creation of honey-bees? Likewise, when we examine the case of termites and some of the other species of ants belonging to the order of insects, we experience similar problems.

Without any trace of gradual evolution, they are all precisely made to perform specific functions with an ingrained discipline which they follow meticulously. With them it is an inviolable law etched upon their RNA and DNA. By comparison they put to shame even the most strictly regimented and disciplined communist societies. They are all exceptional solitary cases of organized creative wonders which show no traceable history of a crude elementary beginning, gradually evolving into higher complex societies.

We can safely conclude from this that life as such offers two types of disciplines for us to study. One appears to be spontaneous, as though born out of nothingness in a sudden outburst of God's creative wonders. The scientists, however, may refer to it as a host of mutative changes all taking place simultaneously in one single moment. This hypothetical proposition is of course scientifically unentertainable.

The second type of development of social orders in the animal kingdom is much more generalized and progressive in nature; though the results are not so dramatic as the previously mentioned examples. Even dogs and wolves and wildebeests exhibit this positive trend of living together in societies in the interest of class survival. Whatever the reason, we also find a similar trend in the flocking together of birds of the same feather. Likewise shoals of fish, turtles and sea urchins display similar tendencies. This bonding together, therefore, is common to life.

With discipline, authority is born and leadership emerges. A vague precept of crime and punishment begins to creep into the society at every level. For man to have evolved as a social animal, therefore, is not a solitary accident but is in conformity with a predesigned plan of behaviour shared equally by most other animals to a lesser or greater degree.

How the institution of society developed all over the world simultaneously is a question which requires a lengthy discussion. We intend only to deal with a few important features of social development among humans which are directly related to the subject under discussion.

Individual liberty has always been intrinsically at odds with the restraints imposed by society. A deeper understanding of the dilemma presented by this equation is most essential for a better comprehension of the forces which finally determine the boundaries of individual liberty on the one hand and the rising power of the society on the other. Individual-family relationship, individual-clan relationship and individual State relationship are all examples of how life can be studied in its institutionalized conduct. If man is by nature free and loves freedom, then why at all bow to any social authority is the prime question which has to be addressed first.

Whenever a social, racial, economic or political order evolves, it always evolves around an unwritten understanding of give and take between the society and the individuals which collectively make the society. No individual will ever readily surrender his freedom but only on the understanding that in the bargain he gains more than what he has lost.

Primarily, it is individual security which he bargains for at the cost of some personal freedom. On the one hand he surrenders some of his rights to whatever institution he becomes a member of and, on the other, he gains some guaranteed protection and such assistance as would make his individual existence easier and more comfortable.

It is interesting to note that in the beginning of the formation of society at all levels, individuals always emerged as beneficiaries. This is what we find as a natural trend in the animal kingdom. This is also true of human societies at their rudimentary level. But human societies as they grow more organized, tend to become lopsided in the distribution of power between them and the individual. The larger the ratio between the membership of the society and the ruling few grows, the greater becomes the danger of misappropriation and exploitation of power by the ruling minority.

Although theoretically it is possible for the individual to gain some value in exchange for every loss of his liberty, it does not always happen in accordance with what should normally be expected. The prime principle of individual liberty is gradually and progressively sacrificed at the altar of society. It often happens that the society as it grows, becomes more authoritative and less mindful of the ultimate interest of the individual.

On this subject we shall have a more comprehensive discussion later, when we take up the issue of Marxism.

Here the purpose is merely to determine the basic cause of this degenerative process. Why should not an individual feel more comfortable and better protected in a more developed and powerful society? Among animals we never come across a decadent and degenerative trend in their social conduct. Why should human society alone fall short of its expectations in relation to its responsibilities towards the rights of the individual?

One dividing line between animals and humans which distinctly separates them is the powerful tendency in man to defraud, cheat and break the laws of nature. In this game the humans outpace all other animals by a phenomenal margin. Animals too, sometimes appear to cheat but it is always a strategy on their part, and not a deception in the criminal sense. There is no breach of trust in their case such as we observe among the humans. They live a normal and simple disciplined life within the gamut of natural laws which control and command them. If they do ever seem to cheat they do so only intuitively, as governed by their genetic pulses which lie outside the definition of crime.

This in fact is a by-product of the gift of freedom of choice. Animals are strictly governed by intuitive and instinctive laws and have little choice in the matters of right and wrong. In fact no right or wrong exists for them.

It is humans alone who can wilfully ignore their responsibilities and usurp the rights of other members of society knowing it to be wrong. So the individual freedom in relation to the collective responsibility man owes to any institution is undermined and sabotaged by his propensity to break laws, commit frauds and act wrongfully, yet hoping to run away with whatever he can. Hence when Karl Marx observed that man is a corrupt animal, he was very right indeed – only he had no right to exclude himself. Nor had he any right to exclude the socialist leadership which was to be built upon the bricks of immorality. This has been the tragedy of human society throughout the ages. No institution is exempt from this. This inevitable built-in flaw in the individual social relationship promotes the tendency among systems towards ever increasing legislation.

Apparently, every new law is aimed at protecting the right of the individual on the one hand, and the right of the society on the other, from unjustified trespass into each other's exclusive domains of rights and prerogatives. But unfortunately because of the corruption in man, the legislators fail to remain loyal to the principles of absolute justice. During the collective process of legislating, many a time the individual will be deprived of his fundamental rights at the hands of the very institutions which were created to defend them.

We do not propose here to take up the issues of religious societies at length, but from the secular viewpoint of social philosophy, religion should also be briefly mentioned. The sociologists as a class do not treat religion as a Divine phenomenon. Hence, from their vantage point religion is just another expression of the social behaviour of man.

If their view of the development of the institution of religion is right, then all religious societies should be viewed as occupying a unique position among the human social systems. They would be perceived as symbols personified of fraud committed both against the society and the individual. Evidently, in that case, all founders of religions should be classified as prime crooks who wilfully deceive the common masses in the name of gods of their own creation as implied in the sociologist's theory. Some crooks indeed!

They, according to the sociologist's view, legislate themselves on behalf of God to keep the simple unsuspecting common people chained to the so-called Divine laws. Thus, in the name of God it is a fraudulent religious hierarchy which rules to its own advantage. This is the sociologist's perception of a religious society. Karl Marx also seems to be in full agreement with this view of religion as an opiate concocted to keep the labouring multitudes forever doped, lest they should wake up to the awareness of their merciless exploitation by the bourgeoisie. The name of this potent opiate which keeps the proletariat drugged is the code of morality advocated by all religions. As such, morality is always linked to the idea of God which commands and trims human behaviour in His name.

ISLAMIC SCHOOLS OF THOUGHT

THE ISLAMIC POINT OF VIEW can be presented from two different perspectives: first by analysing the work of various Muslim thinkers, and second by attempting to directly assess the Quranic stance in the light of the *Sunnah* which comprises both verbal instructions as well as the practice of the Holy Prophet[sa]. The authenticity of the former's understanding of Islam becomes more and more dubious with the passage of time. It is so because they are inclined to turn progressively more dogmatic in their inferences which may not always be rational and justified. Otherwise what they call Islamic is of course initially based on their study of the fundamentals of Islam. Those who draw their inferences from the Quran and the *Sunnah* can only be treated as a separate category if they strictly adhere to the principle of rationality. Such an analytical study of the major issues will be made later in this book. Presently, we turn our attention to the former and discuss the thought processes of early Muslim scholars, sages and philosophers in the era that led to the formation of many different schools of Islamic thought. Two distinctive influences were at play during the early period of Islamic history:

1) The most powerful and predominant was the influence of the Quran and the *Sunnah*, which had revolutionized the concept of knowledge and broadened the horizon of study and investigation to unsurpassed dimensions.

2) A growing interest in Greek philosophy and sciences, as well as the study of classical philosophy of India, Persia and China, had also a role to play in the

development of Muslim thought. This paved the way for various alien philosophers to become the focus of Muslim attention independently or in conjunction with Islamic teachings.

Because of this interest in various alien philosophies and a desire to interrelate them with Quranic revelations, new schools of thought developed. These schools are called Islamic for the simple reason that Islamic thought, education and beliefs had primarily cradled them. Hence, the philosophies foreign to Islam interplayed with their previously held views, founded solely on the basis of the Quranic studies. Despite the fact that they were branded as un-Islamic because of their flexible accommodating attitude by some of the narrow-minded scholars, there is no shadow of doubt that these great scholars remained essentially Muslim. Their association with secular branches of knowledge was seldom at the cost of their faith. In this regard, everyone has the right to decide for himself whether, after an appropriate study of the Holy Quran and the *Sunnah,* any philosophical point of view presented by such thinkers is to be accepted as Islamic or not. However, the conclusions they draw always remain open to question. Some may find them in accordance with the Islamic teachings and some may not. Yet it does not give anyone the right to suspect their intentions. It is the right of every seeker of truth to form his own conclusions after sincerely attempting to understand the Quran and the *Sunnah* in depth. So also is the right of others to disagree with him, but neither has the authority to deprive the other of his fundamental right to believe in whatever he may and believe himself to be true.

We will now briefly introduce a few of the varied schools of Islamic thought which arose because of different conclusions they drew from the study of the same sources.

However, it should be remembered that every school that claims to be based on the Holy Quran and *Sunnah* ought to be carefully evaluated with direct reference to the evidence they quote in their support. Of the various ideologies and points of view thriving in the age of Muslim domination, not all could be described as Islamic in character. Some of them were partially contradictory or even diametrically opposed to each other. This however does not divest them of the right to be referred to as Islamic by their proponents.

Asháriyyah

The *Asháriyyah* school of thought is indebted to Imam Abul Hassan 'Alī Bin Ismā'īl Ál-Áshárī (260-330 AH) for giving it its distinctive style among the other prevalent schools of thinking. This was an era when some Muslim scholars of the period were rapidly inclining towards rationalism, a need was thus felt to react against this trend. At the head of this reactionary movement was the famous Imam Ismā'īl Ál-Áshárī. It is ironic that Ál-Áshári's own teacher, Al-Jubbāī (d. 303 AH), was one of the leading rationalist scholars of the time. Imam Áshárī not only voiced his disagreement with the rationalist, but also powerfully revealed the inadequacies of any system placing total reliance upon rationality for the discernment of truth.

For the *Asháriyyah*, rationality led neither to the acquisition of certain knowledge nor to eternal truth, rather they considered that it led to greater doubt and contradictions. The *Ásha'irah* stressed that real knowledge applied only to the recognition and acceptance of revelation as the only means to reach eternal truth because the ultimate source of truth is God Himself. Therefore the only way to attain it is through Divine revelation.

In their reaction against rationality, some *Ásha'irah* went to such extremes as to reject any explanation of

21

Quranic verses supported by human logic. They went so far as to totally deny any figurative interpretation of the Holy Quran. Imam Áshárí himself was a skilled logician. The arguments he forwarded against the use of rationality were, interestingly, themselves based on rationality. One of his famous public debates against his own teacher, 'Allāmah Al-Jubbāī, highlights this point.

'What is your opinion about the salvation of three brothers: a believer, a non-believer and a child?' Áshárí questioned Al-Jubbāī.

'The believer will go to heaven, the non-believer will go to hell, but the child will neither go to heaven nor to hell, because none of his acts are worthy of reward or punishment', Jubbāī replied.

Áshárí commented, 'The child could argue with God, "If You had given me some time, I would have done some good deeds. So why should I be deprived of heaven?" '

Jubbāī retorted, 'God could reply, "I knew that if you had grown older you would do bad deeds. Thus your death at this early age is really a favour, because you have been saved from hell." '

Áshárí replied, 'At this stage the non-believer will interrupt and will blame God for not granting him death at the same age as the child so that he could be saved from bad deeds.'

It is worthy of note that Áshárí while arguing against rationality was himself employing all the weaponry of the rationalists. Thus it is not correct to say that he was totally against rationality. The followers of this school of thought, such as Imam Ghazāli and Imam Rāzi, relied heavily on rational arguments to resolve their problems and establish their beliefs. Possibly the excessive reaction against reliance on rationality was due to a fear that new philosophies, which were being introduced to the realm of

Islam, might jeopardise the Islamic viewpoint. It was suspected that the use of reason might lead to movements that would ultimately deviate from the true Islam. Hence, all such movements with rationalistic leanings were dubbed as *Ilhādī* or innovative, which is a derogatory term because it implies deviation from the right path. The concern of the rigid orthodoxy was reflected in the terms they used to describe the founders of the rationalist movements. They referred to them as Muʻtazilah or those who had strayed from the true path and become *Ilhādī.*

Another group known as Maturidiyya believed that revelation should be first accepted as such and then logical explanations required to support it should be sought. They believed that revelation strengthened faith while logical explanations provide further satisfaction to that faith. The *Ásháriyyah* did not reject logical explanations entirely, but considered them superfluous; if they were available, then well and good, otherwise whatever was received through revelation was quite sufficient, even without the props of logic and rationality.

On the right wing of the *Ásháriyyah* movement another sect came into being, known as Sulfia (the blind followers of well-established scholars of old). According to them, revelation should be accepted without question. No philosophical or logical explanation was permitted as they feared this would lead to deviation from the correct path.

Muʻtazilah

The Muʻtazilahs on their part did not reject revelation to be the most reliable instrument for leading one to the truth. They, however, emphasized that the real message of revelation could not be properly understood without the use of reasoning. Thus they gave reason preference over revelation only in the sense that whenever the two appeared to clash, rationalistic understanding must prevail, not as an alternative to revelation, but as a genuine clarification of the revealed message. They held the view that it becomes very difficult to get to the truth of the Holy Quran and the *Sunnah* without rationally deciphering the various similes, metaphors and symbols that are extensively used therein. For example they pointed out that expressions such as God's hand and face must be interpreted to mean His power and grace and so on. Ál- Áshárī in turn stressed that such references in the Quran represented real attributes of God whose precise nature was not known, albeit he agreed that no physical features were meant by such terms.

Although the Mu'tazilah movement appears to resemble in character the European schools of thought from the ninth to the seventeenth centuries, it did not take the *Ilḥādī* (innovative) turn which European rationalism had taken during its progressive decline. The Mu'tazilah always drew upon the original Islamic sources of the Holy Quran and the *Sunnah* to support their arguments, always remaining comfortably close to them — never permitting themselves to drift far apart.

Today there is very little apparent difference between Mu'tazilah and *Ásháriyyah* viewpoints. Although the historical perspective portrayed above has left its mark on the scholarly pursuits of the contemporary generation of Muslim scholars, the sharp divisions of the past are no longer clearly defined. The scholars of today seem to advocate their personal views more than the views of any previous sectarian schools of thought. However, the remnants of past conclusions are still discernible. They are the product of a gradual compromise that developed between the different schools over the ages. Among them are those who are decidedly medieval in their attitudes but they do not quote exclusively from any previous school to support their viewpoint. They jump from one to the other in search of any scholar belonging to any school of thought who can be quoted in their favour. For them the boundaries between different medieval sects disappear but medievalism itself continues to exist, guiding their path. The same is true to a degree of the so-called modernists. Whenever it suits their purpose they will not hesitate to quote any of the earlier scholars in their favour but they feel free to innovate in other areas of their personal views.

Sufism

Sufism was quite popular in Turkey, Iran and in the countries to the east of Amu Darya, an area historically referred to as the Trans-Oxus. Many Muslims from the former USSR were followers of Sufism, which has played a very important role in keeping Islam alive in their countries during the Tsarist as well as the Communist era.

The point most forcibly stressed by Sufism was that beneath the form of religion, there operates an underlying spirit of revelation which must be given preference over the form. What the Sufis understood to be the underlying spirit was simply the ultimate goal which all religions strive for. The ultimate goal was identified as the love of God and communication with Him. Hence, to them, if you reach this goal somehow with or without adherence to the form, the purpose will be served and that is all that is required. All the Sufis however, did not abandon the form altogether and kept subjecting their lives in accordance with the laws of Islamic *Sharī'ah* as they understood them. Yet they would spend most of their efforts not engaged in formal worship but repeating certain attributes of God day in and day out to help focus their attention entirely to the memory of God. Such practices, at times, drifted close to the yogic practice discussed in the section on Hinduism. Sometimes new ways and modes of remembrance were innovated by different Sufi saints, which, finally, got almost entirely divorced from the well-established *Sunnah* of the Holy Founder[sa] of Islam. Yet the followers of such Sufi sects adhered to them more passionately and vehemently than to the Quranic teaching itself. Thus, new schools of Sufism cropped up at different times and in different countries of the Muslim world.

The purpose of this exercise is not to go into a detailed account of the development of Sufi thought — or the schisms which appeared among the Sufis later on — but one thing which most clearly distinguishes Sufism in Islam from all other similar practices is the unshakeable belief of the Sufis in the continuity of revelation or their communion with God. In fact, all the eminent Sufis in Islam have claimed to be in constant communication with God and many a revelation bestowed upon them has been recorded in authentic books. Yet there are some among the Sufis who have broken all ties with the fundamentals of Islam. To them the purpose of religion is only to lead man to God and the forms of worship have become redundant for those who have already achieved this purpose. They introduced certain mental and spiritual exercises with the claim that they were sufficient to establish a sort of communication between man and God which is sometimes described as an awareness of oneness with Him. It did not take long for music and drug addiction to find their way into this school of Sufism, to break them loose from reality to drift aimlessly into a world of delusion. However, all Sufi movements did not start their journey with innovations, though, very often they were led to them during their decadence later on.

There are four major well-established and highly revered sects of Sufism which also deviated from the path of *Sharī'ah* with the passage of time. Yet as for their founders, their loyalty to the Holy Quran and the *Sunnah* remained unquestionable and uncompromising. These major sects are *Chishtiyyah, Soharverdiyyah, Qadiriyyah and Naqshbandiyyah* — which are further divided into many other sub-sects. They all stress the importance of abstinence and austerity to facilitate the attainment of truth. Initially, these practices were not a substitute for the traditional Islamic observances, but were carried out in addition to them.

Gradually the Sufi understanding of the creation-creator relationship began to be influenced by such philosophies as were alien to Islam. For instance, the influence of classical Greek philosophy can be traced in some Sufi sects. The Greek notion of pantheism was adopted in a modified form by some Sufi sects, though strongly opposed by others. The opponents of pantheistic tendencies stress that there is a clear and distinct separating line between God and His creation. According to them though the creation bears a stamp of the Creator and reflects Him, yet it is not diffused with His identity. By contrast, some other factions believe that because the whole universe is a manifestation of God, there can be no clear distinction between the Creator and the creation. For them, creation cannot be separated from God because His attributes are inseparable from the nature of all that He has created. No separating line can be drawn. Hence God is the universe and the universe is God. Yet He has His own independent Will, which works like the natural properties in matter.

At first sight this view of the universe may appear to be entirely pantheistic, in which God is everything and everything is God. But a significant difference should be noted. The pantheistic notion of God is not one that recognizes an externally existing Conscious Creator, a Being who communicates with man through revelation, who takes interest in their trials, tribulations and joys and offers them guidance. The Muslim Sufis, in contradiction to the classical pantheistic view continued to believe in the independent identity of God who, though reflected in His creation, was also the Creator.

As for the Sufis' temperament, they were seldom inclined to fierce, strongly worded debates. They often practised moderation in their belief, while respecting and tolerating views opposing their own. The same cannot be said of the orthodoxy which grew progressively jealous. Hence most sufi sects had to encounter extreme hostility at the hands of the orthodox clergy. Very often there arose a countermovement from among the orthodoxy. Every Sufi sect had to encounter similar experiences of extreme hostility from time to time. The Sufis who adhered to the pantheistic concept of God were specifically targeted by the mainstream clergy for their wrath. At times they were even condemned to death and brutally murdered. Their protestations that their pantheistic philosophy in no way compromised the unity of an independent Supreme Creator were of no avail and they were roundly condemned for claiming to share godhead with God. Hence the orthodoxy often resorted to perpetrating crimes of persecution against them.

The case of the renowned Sufi, Mansoor Al-Ḥallāj, would serve a befitting example of how such Sufis were treated for their alleged proclamation of being God themselves. He was condemned to hang by the neck for shouting in ecstasy *'Anal-Ḥaq, Anal-Ḥaq'* (I am the Truth, I am the Truth). The orthodoxy understood this to mean that he was claiming to be God himself, whereas he had proclaimed in his sublime spiritual ecstasy, simply a total annihilation of himself. What he meant was that he mattered naught; all that mattered was He (God). Mansoor Al-Ḥallāj climbed the gallows with his head held high, not the least daunted by his imminent death. Nor could his shouts be drowned in the tumult of abuses which were hurled at him; they rose loud and clear and high *'Anal-Ḥaq, Anal-Ḥaq'* until his soul departed to the fountainhead of his life on high.

Another Sufi sect was born on the issue of whether the external universe was a fact or merely an impression of the mind. This in fact was an age-old question which was even addressed by Plato and Aristotle. It could not come to a conclusion then, nor could it be concluded by the Sufis. Still it is a live debate among philosophers. No contemporary philosopher can ignore it because neither time nor space can be visualized without the coming into play of the human mind. A mad man's imagination seems as real to him as a scientist's observation of the laws of nature in action. Examined from such angles, these problems appear to be insoluble.

Again, every person's impression of the external universe is different from that of others. However, some perceived images of the elementary world around us and the understanding of their properties are often shared by most observers. For example, most people would agree about the definition of an article as simple as a chair or a table. Yet there are numerous other common things about which people may not necessarily agree with each other. For instance, the colour of things may appear different to people with different eyesight. Similarly, all faculties which we possess are not shared equally by everyone else. Sense of smell differs, so also the sense of heat or cold varies with

29

every person. Moreover, a change in the point of observation will present a different visual percept to the same observer. Hence the perception of the same thing by the same observer will vary with the change in point of perception. Add to this, different moods and different states of health, the problem would be immensely multiplied. No objective truth would seem to completely agree with the subjective truth which people fathom within their brains. In short, subjective impressions cannot always be related to the outer world in exactly the same way. This, in the opinion of some philosophers, deprives the viewer of the possibility of ever achieving absolute certainty in relation to whatever he perceives.

The aspect of uncertainty and unreliability of impressions as mentioned above, gave birth to another Sufi sect which totally denied the outer existence of things and claimed that eternal truth was merely a subjective notion. Those who were more extreme among them totally denied the existence of any external physical form, including their own. Thus, an intellectual movement that started with an attempt at an extra fine discernment of detail and perception of outside reality ended up in utter madness. Yet there was a strange magic in this madness, that sometimes spellbound the wisest of the logicians and the academics of their time.

An interesting episode is related about a renowned Sufi leader of this sect, who was summoned to the court of a king to hold a debate with some of the outstanding scholars of his time. But to the amazement and chagrin of all, the outcome of the debate turned out to be exactly the opposite of what they had expected. Within a few exchanges of arguments and counter-arguments the great academics were driven out of their depth, gasping for their breath and groping for words. None could succeed in

 matching the intricacies of the Sufi's ethereal logic. At this point, the king was struck with a brilliant idea and ordered the warden of the elephants' house to have the most ferocious of his elephants brought to the palace grounds. This particular elephant happened to be stricken with a madness no less than that of the Sufi. The only difference perhaps was that in the Sufi's mind the outer reality did not exist. But the elephant wanted to destroy all outward reality himself. From the one end the Sufi was pushed into the open and from the other the elephant was let loose. The Sufi without losing his breath, ran for his life forthwith.

Observing this, the king shouted from the balcony of his palace, 'Don't run away O Sufi, from this phantom elephant. He is only a figment of your imagination!'

'Who is running away?' shouted back the Sufi. 'It is only a figment of your imagination.'

Thus ended the predicament of the Sufi but not the debate itself. It still rages on.

The Spanish School of Islamic Thought

We have already discussed the controversy regarding the superiority of revealed truth, vis-à-vis observational truth. Some thinkers give preference to revelation over logic, and some others do the vice versa. Ibne Rushd (known in the West as Averroes), one of the greatest Muslim thinkers of all-time, proposed the idea that the above views express parallel realities and should be treated separately. Revealed truth should be accepted as such and the knowledge gained from observation and experiment should be accepted for what it is. For him, it was not necessary to seek a correlation between the two,

31

nor was there any need to search for contradictions and attempts to resolve them.

This was the age when Muslim scientists were making rapid progress in Spain in their pursuit of scientific knowledge. They did so undeterred by the fact that some religious scholars of the older schools were issuing edicts of *Ilḥād* (innovation) against them. Ibne Rushd may have thought it better not to get involved in such controversies, lest it should impede the progress of science.

What he evidently avoided was the danger of finding contradictions between religion and science. A true believer in Islam and a scientist dedicated to the truth without prejudice as he was, this policy served the cause of both religion and science in Spain admirably for a long time to come. The danger of contradiction between the revealed truth and the observed truth was never squarely confronted. Hence the issue of preferences never arose seriously. This 'no-conflict policy' remained predominant in Spain for many centuries, thanks largely to the prudence of Ibne Rushd.

When we re-examine the possible issues of controversy in the afterglow of what followed, we can say with certainty that the age was not yet ripe for such issues to be addressed. The possibility of defective or partial perception or even a complete misunderstanding of the observed facts could not be ruled out.

For example, in medieval times the ideas adopted by Muslim scientists about the universe were not really based on the Holy Quran or *Ḥadith,* but were, for the greater part, influenced by the prevailing ignorance of that age. The religious scholars as always happens, considered their own views to be Islamic and as such final, while there was little they could understand of the true Quranic views in the context of the prevailing knowledge.

On such a matter in Spain, there does not appear to have been any dialogue between scientists and religious scholars. There was no forum for the transfer of knowledge between these two groups, nor any debates about the comparative merits of their respective beliefs. Consequently, there were no Galileos in Spain who had to choose between life and truth. The scientists and their contemporaries did not even attempt to explain to the religious scholars their compulsion to call a spade a spade when they saw one, nor did they find it necessary to prove to them that their interpretation of the Holy Quran was wrong because it contradicted the known scientific facts of the time.

As a result, there developed two parallel movements which gradually grew further apart with the passage of time. It so happened at last that Islamic knowledge took a completely different course from that of the philosophical and scientific channels of thought, never to cross their path. They were like two streams running in parallel without interrupting each other's flow.

Consequently, the Islamic nation of Andalusia (the title of the Muslim Empire in Spain), outpaced other Islamic countries in most fields of scientific research. Further to its advantage, Spain enjoyed a long and seldom broken period of relative peace, safe from the attacks of invaders such as Ghengis Khan and Halākū Khan. This period of Islamic history in Andalusia could be rightly considered as the golden age of Rationalism. With the expulsion of Muslims from Andalusia, the great era of Muslim domination came to an end. All ties of Islam with the Spanish people were severed. If ever a tragic retrogression of intellectual and scientific advancement took place anywhere in the world, it took place in the land of Andalusia. And what a tragic retrogression it was. As the gates were opened at the southern end of Andalusia for the exodus of Islam, out went along with it wisdom, knowledge, fair play, truth and light in all its spectra, perhaps for centuries not to return. But the light flooded out not in the direction of the journey of the Muslim expatriates. Spain was once again plunged into the utter darkness of the pre-Islamic era. The world of Islam elsewhere did not fare better either. There, the darkness was to grow from within. It was the darkness of religious prejudices, bigotry, narrow-mindedness, arrogance, egoism and mutual jealousies, which began to rage like hellfire. It began to rise like a column of smoke spreading far and wide screening the light of heaven out. Thus the land beneath was covered by progressive shadows of darkness which grew and thickened over the years.

As for the inhabitants of northern Europe, it was a different story altogether. That which was lost to the people of Spain turned out to be their gain. And what a gain it was. The same Queen Isabella and King Ferdinand who had thrown the Muslims out of the country did not take long to turn their wrath upon the Jews under the ever growing influence of a bigoted, despotic Christian priesthood. As the southern gates of Andalusia were opened to flood out the Muslims, the northern gates were opened wide for a large-scale exodus of the Jews. Among them were highly knowledgeable people, great scholars, scientists and intellectuals who excelled in many professions. They had mastered many skills during the seven centuries of the beneficent Muslim rule. They had gained excellence in all fields of human occupation such as industry, trade, scientific research, architecture, sculpture, surgery and many other similar areas. A persistent well-organized scheme of persecution banished the Jews out of the country, after dispossessing them of all their belongings. It were they who carried the torches of knowledge all the way from Muslim Andalusia to the South of France and beyond. The philosophies of Aristotle and Plato began to reach Europe through the Muslim philosophers of Spain. The healing genius of Avicenna, the greatest physician ever known to the world till his time, and the wisdom of Averroes who combined in himself secular and religious philosophies and sciences also began to dawn upon the European horizon. Thanks largely to the exodus of the Jews, their great works were transported across and translated into various European languages by scholars. In fact, it was they who laid the foundation of a new era of enlightenment in Europe, known as the Renaissance.

The Plight of the Muslim World

Turning our gaze to the post-Spanish era we observe the same gloomy view fraught with tragedy hanging over the entire world of Islam. From then on, Muslim countries other than Spain lost their interest in the secular sciences and their quest for investigation and research which they themselves had once promoted and advanced to such high levels of excellence.

This unfortunate trend proved counterproductive not only in the field of science, but also in the field of religion itself. The Muslim *Ummah* (the Muslims as a people) further split and broke into schisms and factions. The noble doctrine of the unity of God became the victim of this destructive suicidal trend. Cracks began to appear in the image of God itself which began to be interpreted so differently as though they were talking of different gods rather than One. Their search for knowledge was not quenched however, only their preferences were changed.

They continued to debate the issues of right and wrong with the same vehemence as before while the subject

35

of discussion had changed. Yet they remained engrossed in the same questions which for centuries had agitated them. Instead of the serious issues of fundamental practices, their jurisprudence remained occupied by trivialities such as the eating of the flesh of crows. Riots are reported to have erupted on this issue between the supporters of the two opposing views. The polemics which resulted grew progressively more complicated and involved. It is a tribute to their intellect that they could really build mountains out of molehills — a tribute which at the same time was reflective of an utter lack of common sense. Senseless intellectualism is the name for what they did!

Some of the other so-called "highly important" questions which kept agitating their minds also stirred their blood to a pitch of high frenzy. Among them was a question as banal as that the case of a dog which may have fallen into a well. How many bucketfuls would have to be drained out before the remaining water became clean for the purpose of ablution, was the all-important question which engaged the attention of great scholars of that time. Let alone a dog, if a Mullah accused of heresy, by the clerics of another school, fell into a well of theirs, the question would acquire far more serious implications. How many buckets would have to be hauled would become a complex mathematical exercise. Many may have preferred that well to be filled with earth, having turned into the burial pit of the same Mullah. Such was the time and such were the tales built on the realities of their mad intolerance.

Bizarre as they may appear, seldom were they altogether false. The jurisprudence of that period must have gone beserk! They were involved in such meaningless debates as made as mockery of the holiest of the Muslim religious practices such as "Salāt" — the formal prayer.

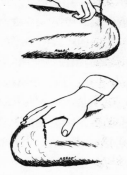 The Muslims always recite the fundamental article of faith during the sitting posture of the second *Rak'at* of their prayers. During this declaration some raise their index fingers and some do not. But jurists of that period were sharply divided on this issue. They were bent upon punishing the finger which had offended their sensibility. Raised or not raised, the offending wretch must be chopped off, was their unanimous verdict. They differed on everything else but not on this. To go to the wrong mosque was a grave risk indeed. The entry was no problem of course but it was the exit which posed real problems. They might have to walk out with one finger less than the five Allah had bestowed upon them!

A third small issue was related to the saying of *"Ameen"*, which is recited after the recitation of Surah *Fātiḥah* by the Imam. The 'vital' point under discussion was whether it should be said aloud or quietly. It was quite likely for the 'loudists' to be beaten if they had blurted *Ameen* loudly in a mosque where it was considered a serious crime. A silent *Ameen* among the loudists was no less provocative.

The most prominent among such doctrinal differences which acquired deadly dimensions was concerning the creation or the non-creation of the Holy Quran. The holders of these opposite views had no doubt whatsoever that disagreement on such vital issues was punishable by death. But it all hung on the great dispenser of justice — chance. If the king was on the side of eternalists, the holders of the contrary doctrine were not only murdered, but even burnt alive in their homes. When chance took the swing to the other side, the persecutors became the persecuted. Many a time, the long dead and buried were not spared the punishment either. They were dug out from their graves and publicly hung, for the living to learn their lesson. But what lesson could one draw anyway? Which side of the see-saw was safer remained the unanswered question. For those involved in these trivial broils with such seriousness, their life upon earth was turned into hell. And the threat of hell after death, hurled at them by their opponents, did not have to wait to be reached till after death!

The centuries of darkness of the medieval ages began to cast their deadly shadows far and wide, and the world of Islam which had emerged from darkness to light as the sun of Islam rose from the deserts of Arabia, was plunged once again into the abyss of ignorance. The vision of Islam began to flicker and change colours like distant stars seen through dark, gloomy nights with the change in the vantage point and the shifting of the angle of vision. The image of Islam lost its lustre and constancy.

The two major channels of enlightenment which could turn the darkness of ignorance into knowledge seemed to be shut forever. Neither was there clarity or integrity of vision left, nor was there any hope entertained for revelation from on high. To them both windows were closed. What a tragic end indeed.

However, some centuries later, the sun of secular knowledge began to rise once again but this time from the West. The transmitters of light from the East looked westward hoping to catch a glimpse of that which they had themselves bestowed upon the West some interminably long centuries ago it seemed.

EUROPEAN PHILOSOPHY

WHEN THE SUN of secular enlightenment finally set upon Andalusia, its radiant face rose from the horizon of France to smile upon what lay of Europe beyond. It lit up the entire Continent from South to North, and from East to West. A glorious day of knowledge broke which was to dominate Europe for centuries to come. The age of the Renaissance had begun.

But few in Europe realize today how much they owe to Muslim Spain for that great dawn of enlightenment called the Renaissance. Many outstanding philosophers, mathematicians, scientists, astronomers and physicians from Andalusia are but obliterated memories for Europe, buried in the forlorn graveyards of oblivion.

With the dawn of the Renaissance as the darkness was dispelled, reason and rationality began to dispossess the blind faith of the territories which it had long held under its mighty sway. To keep a balance between the secular philosophies on the one hand, and faith and belief on the other was not an easy task. It was no trivial challenge for the priest-ridden society of that age to defend their faith against the new philosophical invasion by reason and rationality. They had inherited an image of Christianity which largely under Pauline influence had disintegrated into mythical dogmas. It was no longer the same Divine light which had illuminated Christ.

Even before the Renaissance, some European intellectuals had attempted to maintain a balance between reason and faith. E.J. Scotus in the ninth century AD had set the noble example of bringing about a measure of truce between faith and reason. He maintained that truth cannot be reached through reason alone, but reason and faith had a part to play together. He suggested that in the beginning religious beliefs were founded on rational grounds. Convictions cannot be born out of mere conjectures. There has to be some logical basis for the building of convictions. Whether it is done advertently or inadvertently, for every conviction, as it is born, there has to be some rational basis. In short, Scotus believed that true faith should not be equated with myth. It should be understood to have been founded on some solid, rational platform. In the beginning when faith took root in the human mind, it could not have happened without some reason and logic to support it, he assumed. Yet with the passage of time, that link must have faded out and was no longer observable. From then on faith appeared to be suspended in mid-air without the pillars of reason to support it. Yet its firmness and tenacity which have stood the test of time are indicative that it could not have reached this high level of conviction altogether without reason or logic.

In conclusion, Scotus advises that the validity of one's faith should be examined from time to time according to the dictates of rationality. If the two appear to be conflicting then one must follow reason. Thus reason will always hold an edge over faith.

This attitude is best illustrated in Newton's (1642-1727) treatment of the Trinity. As long as he did not consciously and scientifically examine his inherited religious views, he continued to remain a devotee of the doctrine. But when at a later stage he decided to put his faith to the test of reason and

NEWTON

rationality, he was left with no option but to reject the dogma of Trinity which in his view had failed the test of reason.

Thus he became the all-time greatest victim of the prejudices of the Christian church sacrificed at the altar of the cross. As a tribute to the genius of Newton, he was elected as a Fellow of the "College of the Holy and Undivided Trinity", University of Cambridge, a post which he held for many years. In 1675 however, he was given the choice to either vacate his seat and keep his convictions, or to compromise his convictions and assert his orthodoxy under oath one last time in ordination.

But the "Holy and Undivided Trinity" itself stood in his way. His stubborn refusal to subscribe to the doctrine of Trinity cost him not only his fellowship, but also the handsome stipend of £60 a year. No small amount indeed, judging by the value of money in those days. He was dispossessed of his fellowship and chair from the university on the charge of heresy. The charge of heresy was levelled against him only because in Newton's eyes worshipping Christ was idolatry, to him a fundamental sin. R.S. Westfall writes on Newton:

> 'He recognized Christ as a divine mediator between God and humankind, who was subordinate to the Father Who created him.'[1]

> 'The conviction began to possess him that a massive fraud, which began in the fourth and fifth centuries, had perverted the legacy of the early church. Central to the fraud were the Scriptures, which Newton began to believe had been corrupted to support trinitarianism. It is impossible to say exactly when the conviction fastened upon him. The original notes themselves testify to earlier doubts. Far from silencing the doubts, he let them possess him.'[2]

Hence, his faith in the Unity of God and rejection of the Trinity was based on his unbiased, honest investigation into the validity of Christian beliefs. There is many a note written in his own hand on the margins of his personal Bible:

'Therefore the Father is God of the Son (when the Son is considered) as God.'[3]

Thus concludes Westfall:

'... almost the first fruit of Newton's theological study was doubt about the status of Christ and the doctrine of the Trinity.' [3]

WHEN during the Renaissance interest was renewed in this age-old question of faith versus rationality on a wider basis, it fell to the lot of Rene Descartes (1596-1650) to keep the flag of belief held high. The issue with him was not Christianity versus reason, it was a more straightforward issue of belief in the existence of God in an age of philosophical wanderings of the mind.

An exceptionally clear-headed logician as he was, he not only believed in God but was the first amongst the philosophers to boldly take up the issue of reason, leading to God. Fortunately for him, he refused to be drawn into a debate on the rationale of Trinity. What he proved was simply the existence of one Supreme Being. Perhaps it was this rejection on his part of the then prevalent Christian dogma, which lost him an honourable place among the believing intellectuals of that age. J. Gutman explains this situation in his book *Philosophy*.[4] Here Descartes is not mentioned as a revelational theist, which he was, but he is merely spoken of as one who is purported to be a revelational theist. This treatment was meted out to him entirely because of his rationalistic disregard for Christianity's distinctiveness.

Unfortunately, a rebellion against God, as such, did not hurt the sensibility of the Christian priests as much as the public denouncement of Christianity. It is a great tragedy that a philosopher and a mathematician of such an exceptionally high status as Descartes was not paid the homage due to him. It should be remembered that he was not merely a theoretical philosopher, he was also an outstanding geometrist who took the work of Pythagoras (c. 580-500 BC) on geometry to such heights as it had never scaled before. His solid contribution to geometry which comprised many pioneering works will always be remembered with heads bowed to his greatness.

Another mark of his greatness lies in the fact that he was the first to introduce the trend of mathematical argumentation into philosophy. His concept of truth and absoluteness begins with his journey of self-consciousness. His test of truth is related to the first impression one receives after hearing or observing something. He asserted that anything which fails to pass the criterion of truth immediately is worthy of doubt. In other words, anything one could believe to be true without any dialectical argumentation was acceptable as evident truth. Applying this logic to self-consciousness, the following is a paraphrase of his argument: because I think I am — and I accept this simple statement without supporting it with any logical deduction — so most certainly I am.

As such this becomes the first and the prime evident truth. A simple and charming phrase he coined in this regard was Cogito, ergo sum meaning 'I think, therefore I am.'[5] The second truth which he recognized after the first truth was the truth of the existence of God. He mathematically calculated that the very idea of such an

43

existence was enough evidence of His existence just as the sum of the three angles of a triangle are most certainly equal to the sum of two right angles.

Whether his philosophical proof of the existence of God was acceptable or not to the generations of philosophers who followed him, at least they were all profoundly influenced by him. Thus, in the subsequent generations of thinkers, logic was freely employed for or against the belief in the existence of God. Dialectical materialism was also born as a subsequent development of the same trend.

This line of thinking continued into the seventeenth century when John Locke, Berkeley and Hume demarcated the boundary of phenomenon and reason as having no common borders with faith and belief. While subscribing to this philosophy, Locke did not specifically rule out the validity of faith and belief but left them alone for the believers to have faith in whatever way they chose. It was left to a later generation of European philosophers to deny the existence of God on the basis of logic — Rousseau and Nietzsche being most prominent among them.

NIETZSCHE declared God to be dead in his own dramatic style. Rousseau, on his part, advocated the synthesis of a new religion in place of revealed religions. He stressed the need for a religion based on a study of human nature and human experiences. He proposed that the human mind itself should create a civic code or rule of life. Rousseau seems to be among the first of the European philosophers who openly rebelled against the philosophy to have anything to do with the belief in God. It was an age when religion was profoundly and advertently affected by the rationalist movement.

This generation of philosophers was followed by Utilitarians like Mill and Sidgwick. Essentially they believed in the choice of advantage. Whatever was to one's advantage, one should have free unrestrained access to it. But when it came to a clash between egoism and altruism they advised recourse to reason for arbitration between them.

This means that during the pursuit of pleasure when it comes to making a choice between extreme selfishness and selfless sacrifice of one's own interest, reason should arbitrate between the two. A verbose philosophy indeed, meaning nothing in substance. Those given to pleasure would hardly need advice from Bentham, Mill, Sidgwick etc. to stop short at the border of moderation and desist from leaping into the domain of utter selfishness. For them the choice between egoism and altruism would be out of the question. Who would stand in need of arbitration of reason in the area of his sensual desires? A person given to lustful and carnal pleasures needs no counsel. He pursues this course knowing full well the pros and cons of it.

THE UTILITARIANS were followed by a generation of philosophers, who left a deep mark on the history of European philosophy. Locke, Berkeley and Hume known as Empiricists stand at the head of the movement. Many a generation of philosophers was to be influenced by them. Their philosophy can be summed up in the simple statement: one should believe only in the conclusion drawn from experimental observation which is demonstrable. They believed that only pure reason and signs gave birth to ideas which were worthy of acceptance — the ideas which could be retried through scientific experimentation with unfailing consistency. A better definition of science cannot be visualized.

Hume was followed by Immanuel Kant (1724-1804) who was deeply stirred and influenced by Hume's realistic philosophy. Hence the realism of Kant owes much to the

45

empiricism of Hume. Agnostic as he was, he was wise enough to realize the indispensability of morality. He was perhaps the pioneer in the suggestion that morality should be deduced from reason alone. He divided reality into phenomenal reality and noumenal reality. He believed that scientific investigation cannot go beyond phenomenon. As such he ruled out that the existence of God could be proved through the instrument of phenomenal investigation. His system is usually referred to as a transcendental idealism.

This in turn gave birth to Hegel's absolute idealism. Many a new phrase was coined during this prolific period of the growth of his philosophy, such as the logical positivism, existentialism and objectivism. Yet no new dramatic chapter was added to the philosophies of Plato and Aristotle, who reigned supreme as the undisputed masters till the end of time. Even the smart clichés of dialectical materialism and scientific socialism were but other names for what we find freely discussed in the works of Aristotle. It should not be forgotten however, that the European philosophers were no less indebted to their Muslim forerunners of Andalusia and Baghdad, than they were to their Greek masters. This was the period when Hegel's absolute idealism ruled supreme. Yet most of the Europeans little realised the fact that it was no more than the continuity of the idealism of Plato. If we understand Hegel correctly, for him subjectivism was inseparably related to the outside realities. This means that he did not deny objective realities altogether, but laid emphasis on the supremacy of ideas.

In the Islamic school of thought, the objectivist Sufis were a different tale altogether. They carried their subjectivism to such dizzy heights as the European philosophers could not have dreamt of. These Sufis could as well be referred to as illusionists.

*A*S FAR AS the issue of revelation leading to knowledge is concerned, no such discussion is found in the works of European philosophers of any generations. Among the believers in the existence of God, Descartes continued to hold fast to his belief that reason must be placed before faith. He believed in God because his reason supported his belief, hence there was no contradiction in him. Voltaire and Thomas Paine maintained that in the development of human civilization, reason had played a far more significant role than faith. In metaphysical philosophy, abstract forms of existence beyond the material world have been the subject of discussion, but the question of revelation has never been examined with any seriousness.

Despite the philosophical interest of that age, in judging the comparative merits of faith versus rationality, they somehow remained silent on the issue of revelation having played any part in leading man to truth and knowledge. At best, their interest remained revolving around the existence of God, only philosophically. No quest was ever made to find out any traces of evidence in the universe which could lead to the proof of His existence. The validity of revelation from on high was never examined seriously. By comparison, the modern attempts to trace messages from aliens are taken far more seriously. Such attempts are already institutionalized and funded by great world powers.

As we get closer to the modern period, from the time of Bentham, Mill and Sidgwick we find an ever increasing reliance on rationality, while faith is gradually waived to a position of lesser significance. The ultimate victim of this emphasis on rationality has been the belief in God. Thus, rationality gained dominance slowly and gradually, like the appearance of a long, northerly dawn interrupted only by an occasional flurry of aurora.

The rationalists gave preference to reason over all other means of attaining knowledge and truth. Yet among the rationalists too, we find both believers in Christianity as well as non-believers. It was the latter, however, who consistently gained the upper hand. During the age of rationalism, the Church had to defend Christianity somehow with whatever logical arguments it could muster. But this proved a strategic mistake on its part, to be lured into the battleground of reason and rationality.

The most prominent theists of this period were Kierkegaard, Jaspers and Marcel. Of them, it was Kierkegaard who first rang the bell of alarm warning the Church not to commit suicide by entering the arena of logical debate between faith and reason. Referring to Kierkegaard's efforts to salvage faith from the onslaught of reason, Coppleston writes in 'Contemporary Philosophy':

> 'For Kierkegaard, however, this procedure was simply a dishonest betrayal of Christianity. The Hegelian dialectic is an enemy within the gates; and it is not the business of any Christian writer or preacher to dilute Christianity to suit the general educated public. The doctrine of the Incarnation was to the Jews a stumbling-block and to the Greeks foolishness, and so will it always be. For the doctrine not only transcends reason but is repugnant to reason: it is the Paradox *par excellence,* and it can be affirmed only by faith, with passionate inwardness and interest. The substitution of reason for faith means the death of Christianity.'[6]

What Kierkegaard did not further elaborate was that the converse was also true. It nearly implied that the Christian faith was completely empty of reason and rationality. It could be adhered to only if one withdraws into the shell of obstinate rejection of reason. The moment the tortoise dares to stick his neck out, his head would be plucked by rationality, waiting for just such an opportunity. Yet Kierkegaard believed that he could keep both his Christianity and reason simultaneously. Perhaps he knew how to have his cake and eat it too!

Berkeley and Hegel remained consistently adamant that reason must be given preference over sensory experience. God to them was mainly a description invented to fill a void for a logical gap. Thus the debate continued to rage among the believing European philosophers and the non-believing ones. It raged on, until its fire was extinguished by burning itself out. All that was left, were the ashes of faith in caskets of agnosticism and atheism.

As for the believing Jewish philosophers, their strategy was much less vulnerable. They believed in the historicity of their faith. The victorious past of Judaism over its Gentile antagonists was sufficient for them to keep their cinders alive. To debate the issue between faith on the one side and reason on the other, was just irrelevant.

Among the atheists, Nietzsche, Sartre, Merleau-Ponty, Camus and Marx were a category in themselves. None believed in generalizations. As such, it was not possible for them to universalize subjectivity. The subjective experience of each person has a uniqueness about it which cannot be exactly shared by others.

We believe that here it is important to devote a sub-section to Marxism. However much we may differ with this philosophy, it cannot be denied that it has universally earned for itself a permanent place which will always be treated with respect by an enormously large number of people all over the world.

MARX

MARX (1818-1883), among the atheist philosophers of the ninteenth century, should be treated separately in his own right. To him the denial of God is not merely incidental, it is an integral component of his philosophy, with which religion is absolutely incompatible. With him, humans are like elements interacting with each other under the socio-economic laws which govern them. They must be set free from the religious interference which distracts their natural course. To Marx, revelation and inspiration lie beyond the vocabulary of philosophical thought.

Next to him is Nietzsche, with his own special domineering personality. His sabre-like pen impales God as his prime victim, until he pronounces Him dead; or, so he thought. In fact he knew no God, other than the God of the Christian dogma and it was Him that his sword of reason had murdered. Thus, Kierkegaard is proved so right in his warning to the priests to maintain a sullen silence about the divine mystery of Trinity; rather than invite trouble by venturing to defend it with instruments of reason.

Most of the atheist European philosophers of that age were, in fact, driven to the denial of God largely by the Christian Church, which had mystified God's image to the extent of absurdity. Among other atheist philosophers, Sartre (1905-1980) is perhaps the most interesting and playful. He knows how to coin simple phrases with profound ideas. At the helplessness of man in his freedom to shift for himself in a Godless universe, he exclaims:

'... man is condemned to be free.'[7]

By this he means that the responsibility to make choices for himself, which lies on every human shoulder, is a challenge extremely difficult to meet. There is no one else to help him or guide his steps in the dreary wilderness of existence. Commenting on the episode of Abraham[as], he explains the presence of angels as a psychic phenomenon. To him, that Divine revelation which the angels brought to Abraham[as] was no more than the anguish of his soul. Wrong as we may consider Sartre's explanation, we must pay homage to his fiery outburst of desperation and vengefulness. This applies far more befittingly to Sartre himself who may have suffered pangs of anguish and exasperation in the emptiness of his Godless philosophy. Revelation is the anguish of the soul, is indeed a profoundly revealing statement from the vantage point of an atheist — if atheists ever admit to possessing souls. Bernard Shaw is close to Sartre, but not quite, when he defines revelation as 'inner voices' — at best, a smart remark of a dramatist lacking the depth and force of Sartre's reflection! All said and done, Sartre fails to distinguish between inspiration and revelation, terms that simply do not exist in his philosophy; what does exist is the agony of soul — a tongue of fire that leaps out in occasional outbursts of desperation. No revelation descends from on high, whatever rises, rises from the depth of human frustration.

Hegel (1770-1831) is another agnostic whose interest in denial is not as strong and committed. His philosophy is not directly related to religious issues. Among his outstanding contributions is his attempt to create a bridge between subjectivity and objectivity.

It was he who first presented the dialectical conflict between the ideas of one generation and the ideas of the following generation. This is the well-known Hegelian theory of dialectical struggle between thesis and anti-thesis. He simply believed in contrariety of ideas. This means that ideas which are contrary to each other, but not contradictory, are constantly locked in a dialectical struggle for supremacy.

This results in his thesis that superior ideas are inevitably born out of the preceding dialectical processes. This in turn results in the birth of another anti-thesis born out of the preceding theses. Thus it goes on and on until a stabilized thesis is ultimately reached which demonstrates a positive and lasting understanding of the nature of objective reality.

He used this method to establish the role of logic for attaining knowledge. However, this dialectical method of reaching truth is only possible within systems that are factual and not abstract. The final outcome of this struggle of ideas is what he referred to as the absolute idea. This was Hegel's concept of ultimate reality on universal truth. To him history is nothing but the movement of thought, the integration of theses and anti-theses into syntheses. In Lenin's words Hegel believed that:

> 'Life gives rise to the brain. Nature is reflected in the human brain. By checking and applying the correctness of these reflections in his practice and technique, man arrives at objective truth.'[8]

For him any ideological theory that was not related to the realm of physical experience was not worthy of serious consideration. Thus, any discussion of its significance was only of academic interest.

Implementing Hegel's philosophy, it was Marx who experimented on giving man a new code of life based purely on man's reasoning. A purely secular exercise to begin with, it soon began to demand respect from society. A sort of man-made politico-economic religion was born, founded on the denial of God. Marxist scholars were in basic agreement with the Hegelian point of view, and rejected the notion of eternal truth. They did not accept the objective truth to be absolute. It was always relative to a particular time and circumstance.

Among the socialist thinkers, Engels accepted the idea of absolute truth, and thus met with Bogdanov's disapproval. By and large, to the Communist philosophers, truth is the name of knowledge obtained by objective study, subject to a given time and state of affairs. Within these

ENGELS

specifics, truth is knowledge, and knowledge is truth. As such, knowledge could be defined as a constantly changing objective truth, corresponding to ever-changing environments.

It did not take long before this materialist philosophy turned into an ordained way of life. Marx became the chief apostle of this Godless religion as well as its oracle. To him we must turn now for an in-depth study because it was the stupendous power of his idea and not the mere mechanism of dialectical materialism which was to change the face of the earth.

In the spectrum of conflict of human ideas and beliefs, religion stands at one extreme, with its emphasis on the role of revelation as the most valid guiding principle. Marxism stands at the other end with its total denial of revealed truth. Between these two occur various philosophies — some closer to one, some to the other. But negation of all that religion stands for is never found so total and absolute anywhere except in the Marxist philosophy of dialectical materialism and scientific socialism.

Marx, among all the European philosophers, seems to be the most clear-headed, matter-of-fact, yet idealistic without confessing his idealism — extremely cunning in his philosophical strategy against God and religion. To him neither God nor revelation mean anything, so also, inspiration has no place in his philosophy. He would not agree with Hegel's idealism which precedes objective realities and participates in their activation.

In Hegel's philosophy, the idea is born first and material changes are brought about later under its influence. Thus, when they grow to a certain stage of maturity and become pregnant with new ideas, they in their turn are subjected to new trials of verification. Thus they move on, wave after wave, transferring the subjective realities into observable, demonstrable objective truths.

Marx is clever enough to suspect the tiger in the bush. If the subjective ideas turn into objective realities as Hegelian philosophy would require, then the subjective ideas must precede the objective reality. This would create a dangerous cause and effect chain. Ideas must require a preceding consciousness which cannot be conceived without life. As such, this would ultimately lead to God, as the Prime Mover, who can bring about objective changes with the instrument of idea. Perhaps it is for this reason that Marx does not openly subscribe to the Hegelian idealism. Yet, with a subtle twist in the sequence of cause and effect, he transforms Hegelian philosophy into that of his own. He puts matter before the idea. This dialectical struggle does not begin with ideas, but with matter which is governed by autonomous natural laws. As such, dialectical materialism must reach its logical conclusion, with or without the help of ideas. Sheer matter will carve its own course by working upon life and shaping its destiny. This philosophy preconceives the non-existence of God, Who has to be dislodged from the driving seat of human affairs. It is only man who is entitled to take command of his own affairs with full responsibility.

Thus Marx's dependence on reason and logic is as total as his rejection of God and Divine revelation. Absolute idealism versus dialectical materialism are but questions of arrangement. Which precedes which, is the only issue to be determined.

This leads us to another important question which, when properly resolved, will help us better understand Marx's hidden intentions. How could he ever envision the smooth and flawless working of any system without morality? He was far too intelligent to miss the point, but he was also intelligent enough to be able to perceive the link between morality and God. Man by nature is not a moral animal. On the contrary he is the most corrupt animal under the firmament of heaven. All attempts to make man moral emanate from a belief in God, but Marx knew full well that belief in God was incompatible with his philosophy. Everything that leads or may lead to God was taboo. He had to choose between the two options: either to promote morality within Communism to safeguard its interest and run the risk of leading the Communist world back to God, or to shun the risk and accept instead the possible threat to the system itself. Perhaps he hoped that the impending terror of punishment would adequately offset the absence of moral training among the custodians of Communist rule.

In this, however, he has been proved utterly wrong. Man is a corrupt animal, corrupt indeed even beyond the reach of the merciless retribution of a totalitarian regime to straighten him.

The Marxist philosophy of dialectical materialism leaves no room for God. It was for the same reason that Lenin launched a fierce campaign

LENIN

55

against those who dared to plead the cause of morality albeit within the framework of Communism.

So in Marxism there is neither room for revelation from on high, nor for any code of ethics based on revelation. Marx must have deemed it essential to banish morality from human affairs because of its implied potential to lead to God.

Another potent reason why he may have rejected morality could be the fear that morality would stand in the way of uninhibited proletarian revolution. The proletariat were tied to their bourgeois masters, in the name of moral obligation. Such ties must be shattered and the masses must be set free to do whatever they could to rebel against their despotic usurpers. No moral obligation must be permitted to stand in the way. They should feel free to kill, murder, rob, burn and destroy to annihilate the bourgeois order of economic and political domination. Thus he perceived morality as an arch-enemy of his Godless system.

Despite this matter-of-fact level-headedness of Marx, he is still full of inconsistencies. He lays the foundation for his projected ideas so soundly and firmly on reason and analysis, that it is hard indeed to suspect him of the crime of inherent contradictions. Yet contradictions run deep in Marxism. The total rejection of morality on the one hand, and the launching of a revolutionary movement founded entirely on the moral phenomenon of sympathy, on the other, is one such example of inconsistency.

But that is not all. The sympathy for the cause of the miserable, if carried beyond all boundaries of justice and fair play leading to cruelty to others, is where the contradiction becomes more glaring. If there is no justice in human affairs and you start a movement in the name of justice to rehabilitate it, you cannot violate the very principle upon which your movement is resting. It would be like severing the very bough upon which one is perched.

Again, an advocate of a system which holds no brief for sentiments and moral considerations, seems at odds with himself when he expects total commitment of loyalty to a system which is essentially amoral. There is another contradiction in Marx which lies in his well-calculated and well-planned scheme to help the proletariat topple the despotic domination of the bourgeoisie. Call it scientific socialism or dialectical materialism, if this philosophy is correct then it should not require any outside assistance of humans manipulating and guiding its steps.

Another important point to be observed is that Marx's dialectical materialism was clearly influenced by Darwin's monumental work *The Origin of Species*. In fact, a deeper study reveals that dialectical materialism is merely another name for Darwin's struggle for existence, extended into human affairs.

The supply of food and means of sustenance continue to dominate the life of Homo sapiens as they had ever dominated the earlier animal species before man. The same principle of the survival of the fittest continues to operate as it ever operated before. There is no choice or option for life to take a different course, other than the one dictated by this law. This is scientific. If Marxist philosophy does not possess this equality of finality and precision, then his doctrine cannot be entitled as scientific. Dialectical materialism would lose its significance as an inevitable natural phenomenon.

EXAMINE now how different the case of Darwinian evolution is from that of dialectical materialism. The Darwinian principle of evolution predominates everything else in shaping life and carving its path. It needs no ideological campaign in its favour or external assistance to advance its cause. On the contrary, it has the potential to frustrate and destroy any outside attempt to obstruct its passage. If Darwin had not been born, if none had unravelled the mystery of evolution, the reality of evolution would have remained unchanged. The absence of Darwin could not make the smallest dent upon its inevitability.

The laws of nature do not depend upon the human understanding of their implementation. The perception of man has no part to play in the reality of their existence. Whether anyone understands them or not, the gigantic wheel of nature would continue to roll on.

How different is the case of dialectical materialism! Had Marx and Lenin not been born, a Communist revolution in Russia or anywhere else in the world could not have taken place. At that point in Russian history, She was ripe for revolution with or without Lenin. The only difference that Lenin made was to ride the crest of the imminent storm when it broke, loose, and exploited it to the advantage of scientific socialism. In the case of the Darwinian precept of evolution however, no advocate is ever needed to further its cause, no designer is required to assist the process of natural history.

When we compare Hegel's philosophy with that of Marx, the central question which emerges is this: Do ideas precede objective changes in the material world, or is it the objective changes themselves which give birth to ideas as they roll on? If Marx is right, then he need not have launched an intellectual and idealistic campaign to bring about a Communist revolution. Anything contrary to the inevitable scientific conclusion could not have taken place.

If Communism were indeed a law unto itself like the law of evolution, then even the most powerful ideas together would not have impeded the advance of Communism even if they had colluded to do so. Here is the case of another contradiction in Marx. Apparently he pleads in the precedence of dialectical materialism over the idea, but in practice he leans entirely upon the power of idea to make it work.

If his vision were based on sound scientific principles, then it would bring about the inevitable transfer of economic and political power from the hands of a few to the hands of the numerous, as its logical conclusion. But the circumstances which created Marx and which created Lenin have no inevitability about them. For Marx to have been born with just the right faculties of head and heart and to win the support of a highly intellectual, influential and wealthy friend like Engels was not a natural outcome of dialectical materialism.

Again, his failure to bring about such a revolution in Germany, which according to his philosophy was an ideal arena with all the factors present to bring about a proletariat revolution, is proof enough that dialectical materialism by itself was not sufficient to change the political and economic face of the world.

The success of Lenin on the other hand, in a comparatively much less industrialised country than Germany, is yet another proof to support the proposition that the Russian revolution was merely coincidental and not a direct consequence of Marxism. It was a misfortune of Russian history that Lenin was available during that critical period when reaction to the Tsar's despotic, selfish and evil rule, coupled with the frustration of defeat in the First World War, created the opportune moment for Lenin to pounce upon.

RUSSIA was ripe for revolution anyway. Indeed, Russia was ripe for any revolution. Had it not been the Communist revolution, it could have been any other. All that was needed was a leader of Lenin's status. It was a mere accident that in Lenin, Russia found the revolutionary leader who happened to be a scientific socialist pupil of Marx. He, who condemns exploitation in severest terms emerges himself as the worst exploiter of Russian History. It was Lenin who dictated history in Russia and not dialectical materialism.

Apart from contradictions, Marx can also be blamed for at least one gross omission — his science of socialism completely ignores the factor of the mind from its computations.

Mind is the seat of ideas which has its own distinct identity apart from that of the brain. The brain is the material abode of mind, but the mind which occupies and dwells in the abode is not material. If the brain can be likened unto a computer, then the mind could be conceived as its operator. A clever idea is born when the mind manipulates the computeral brain. Even if any two material brains were to be one hundred per cent alike, if different minds operated them, the ideas thus born out of them will not be identical.

All the human scientific, social, economic and political progress is taking shape under the sway of the mind. The powerful nations of the world exercise their authority over the weaker nations merely because of their accumulated superior power of the mind. It is the same resources of the mind at the disposal of the bourgeoisie which make them most formidable in their absolute command of power. The doctrine of dialectical materialism however, does not take this most powerful factor into account.

It was a mistake on the part of Marx to believe that the accumulated wealth in a capitalist system is the sum total of conserved labour which the capitalists exploited. This conserved energy, he believed, comes from the unpaid dues of the exploited labour and the interest accrued from the idle capital deposited in the banks. Thus the proletariat majority is robbed by the bourgeois few. But sheer labour in itself cannot accumulate wealth without being wedded to the superior power of the mind. This in fact is conveniently ignored by Marx. The progressive scientific inventions which have revolutionised the input-output ratio of labour versus production are essentially the product of mind.

The labour in many a third world country continues to toil and sweat, yet their output is nothing compared to that of the labour in the highly developed industrial countries. Superior tools and highly mechanised productive units and modern technology, when wedded to labour, make all the difference. It is this superior potential achieved with the faculty of the mind which enhances productivity. Otherwise, labour is labour, whether in England or in Bangladesh, in the Pacific Islands or the African jungles; why then is some labour rewarded far more than the labour employed elsewhere? Evidently, it is the mind which plays a decisive role in this unequal reward. It should be remembered here that the power of the mind is a natural factor which can be played for good or evil depending on who employs it.

As labour aided by the mind becomes far more productive, so also is the case of capitalism which when rightly aided by superior mind becomes formidable. This power of capitalism does not flow automatically from the accumulation of wealth into fewer hands. The accumulation of wealth in fewer hands can only be made possible if the power of the mind is working on its side. If the power of the mind is evil Mafias will begin to be created. Against such Mafias the entire might of the proletariat will stand no chance of succeeding.

The number of such Mafias, once begun, forever multiplies extending their domain over every territory of human interests. In due time, they become ever more powerful, dictating terms to the high and low alike. In finance, in commerce, in politics, in business, in the pleasure industry, in health and in sickness, in the progressively expanding travel industry, in computers and electronics, everywhere, these Mafias will cast their evergrowing and deepening ominous shadows.

Hence it is the power of the mind, good or bad which ultimately governs the material world. The mechanism of dialectical materialism has no dominant role to play in shaping the destiny of man. Alas, the mind which has emerged to control world affairs is evil — an inevitable consequence of the rejection of God.

It is not a distinctive feature of Marxism alone that morality is denied any role in human affairs. That which Communists do openly, the capitalists do with a masterly hypocrisy. Their politics, trade and economics are no less devoid of morality, rendering them equal partners in crime with their counterparts across the border. The chance, that the proletariat in Communist states stand against their oppressors is as little as the one enjoyed by the multitudes in the capitalist world.

The Mafias created by power of evil minds in capitalism are no less horrendous then the ones operating among the Communist world when the helpless have-nots cross the path of their ruling class. It is this factor upon which we must concentrate now. Why should the erstwhile have-nots of a Communist hierarchy suddenly forget about all their miseries and suffering of the past, and begin to command the destiny of the masses with stony hearts and iron claws? What morals would govern them? What pangs of conscience would reproach them? When there is no morality, there are no pangs of conscience. It is this heartless mechanism of a merciless system in operation which is responsible for the ultimate failure of Communism.

A deep, careful examination of all absolute regimes would reveal a strange inherent paradox. It makes no difference whether they are built around a totalitarian philosophy of Communism or Fascism, or emerge as a dictatorial expression of power by a capitalist despot. They all have one thing in common: they cannot afford to be moral, because without merciless oppression they cannot survive, and morality cannot coexist with cruelty. Thus they thrive on the absence of morality, yet it is the very same absence of morality which brings about their ultimate downfall.

Mere ruthlessness is not sufficient to protect any totalitarian or despotic regimes. The power of cunning, scheming, plotting, conspiring minds is no less essential for their survival than ruthlessness is. It is the unholy wedlock between corrupt minds and merciless hearts which gives birth to all dictatorial regimes. It helps them to survive for a while but always deserts them in the end. The same factors of conspiracy and moral destitution become the ultimate cause of their downfall. In fact nothing good or bad happens in human affairs as a result of an inevitable inbred system. The two most important factors which shape human destiny are the factor of mind and the factor of morality. Their strength or weakness, their virtue or vice, decide the fate of every man-made plan. Hence, Marx is wrong on both counts. Remove the factors of mind and morality from scientific socialism and what is left is neither scientific nor social. The proletariat, however massive they may swell, are no match whatsoever when confronted with the united might of evil minds. Woe for the age when the might of evil mind colludes with his ego to rule the world. Hence little difference would it make whether the world were ruled by the mindless, amoral mechanism of materialism, or by the evil-minded immoral Mafia of capitalism. Yet there is a difference, and a vast difference for that matter which exposes the inadequacies and inherent flaws of Marxism. In capitalism there is always a measure of freedom which every individual of the society enjoys. It is this freedom which promotes the ultimate cause of the whole society as such. There is no freedom in Communism. An ever-increasing depression of gloominess continues to grow and penetrates every fibre of Communist society. It depresses all their potentials except in the areas where the state itself is compelled to promote them.

ANOTHER DILEMMA which Marxism faces is that morality cannot be defined in partisan terms. A society which is taught and trained in rejecting all moral obligations with respect to others, is very unlikely to fulfil its obligations to itself. Once given to immorality, always given to immorality, is the general pattern of human behaviour. The same applies to the Communist command system. Immorality seems to strengthen the grip of the corrupt upon the system which they operate. The more corrupt they become, the more callous and merciless they must grow to perpetuate their command.

Morality and immorality cannot be channelled exclusively in any single direction. It is not possible for the Communist hierarchy to treat the Communist world with morality, even if they so decide, while they are trained to treat the non-Communist world and non-Communist interests without the least moral obligations. This single factor was sufficient and powerful enough to bring about the downfall of the Communist dictatorship in the long run.

The popular cliché that 'Dictatorship corrupts and absolute dictatorship corrupts absolutely' applies perfectly to the Communist command. The immoral cannot survive without having recourse to cruelty, oppression and a blatant disregard of justice. As hatred begets hatred, so does immorality breed immorality. This state of progressive disregard of moral values at the highest level of Communist hierarchy is bound to end up in an absolutely immoral dictatorship. The absolute immoral dictatorship cannot remain confined for long within a small selective circle of their command. For their group survival, it is essential that corruption must also prevail in all adjacent levels of decision making. Thus the arid patches of immorality begin to grow bigger and wider, spreading in all planes.

However, the case of the absolute authority of a prophet of God, is vitally different from that of the mundane authorities. The prophet's authority is confined by a strict moral religious code which even he cannot violate otherwise the very edifice of his authority would crumble. It should also be noted here that the Divinely revealed moral code is always consistent and possesses the quality of making its adherents consistent in their conduct. Hence, it is the revealed truth alone which has the potential to cure man of his intrinsic ills. No man-made code of conduct based purely on human reason can work this miracle, even when aided with merciless coercion. The main difference between secular dictators and the absolute authority of a prophet, is that while secular dictators are entirely free from any obligation to a legislative code, the prophets are strictly governed by a Divine Book of moral teachings which simultaneously and equally applies to all their followers. It is this difference which sets their roles poles apart.

Any Communist regime brought to power can never be unsaddled by the revolt of the proletariat. The power they command is total and merciless. Mercy or mere moral jargon has no place in the dictionary of Marxism. Stalin was a paragon of the Marxist amoral code of conduct. Mass murders of the proletariat themselves at the altar of Marxism, during the absolute dictatorial regime of Stalin, can be pronounced as pride of performance only from the vantage point of Communist philosophy.

Alas the genius of Marx failed to identify the inherent weakness of his dialectical materialism. The hand of Communism even if it were mightier than the furies of a desert would still not have succeeded in levelling the highs and lows of the human society.

Every stormy sea is returned to calm after the turbulent elements of nature have run their course, presenting a picture of rippleless stability. So does a vast duneless desert of sand create the illusion of perfect peace and tranquillity. The Marxists' concept of stability and peace in the human society is closest to the scenario just presented. But little do the Marxists realize that such scenes of tranquillity in nature present no more than a picture of death. Where there is absolute levelling there is no interplay between the forces of nature, but what the Marxists also forget is the fact that the perfectly calm sea or a deathly still desert, do not share the human freedom of choice to cheat or to defraud and to create artificial ups and downs when there are no natural ups and downs left. Moreover, it is impossible for man to propose a system which can remove every element of high and low from human society. Drops of water may look alike and particles of sand may also be shaped as perfect facsimiles of each other, but humans are not made like that.

In Marxist philosophy, it is the human particles which make the Communist utopia of tranquillity. If each citizen of a Communist state is provided equal economic opportunities, each is fed with the same quantity of bread, butter and meat; if all that man lives for or desires is made available to him, exactly in accordance with his requirements, then no human vice born out of greed should ever germinate. In such an economically levelled society there seems no need left for anyone to rob, steal or cheat, or to even attempt to accommodate wealth, which would not be able to buy him anything beyond the provisions made by the state. Such a society should ultimately be rid of all crimes because greed, the most powerful causative factor of crime, would seem to have been uprooted.

When this state of equal opportunities, equal needs and equal fulfilment of needs is guaranteed, provided of course, that each member of the society puts in his share of labour to his capacity, only then the Communist dream of perfect stability could possibly come true. Such a society will need no state to govern its affairs. This, in short, is the utopia of Marx's materialism.

The latest trends of political and economic developments in the world, however, have already exploded this materialist myth. But no outside decree is needed to destroy Marx's garden of Eden. The rejection of morality is in itself enough to guarantee its ultimate destruction.

There are other inherent flaws in Marx's regimentational philosophy. Apart from the fact that it provides no moral code for guiding its members to discharge their responsibilities with honesty, an emphatic denial of God and the assertion that there will be no life after death hence no accountability, emboldens the functionaries of the party to absolute indiscipline and selfishness. An utter state of selfishness ensues where no holds are barred in pursuance of one's personal desires and ambitions. One feels free to do whatever one may to satiate one's greed. The corrupt always gang up to protect their class interest. They can always find means to escape exposure and consequent punishment, by joining hands with others of the same ilk. Perhaps it is this inbred propensity towards selfish behaviour in man which led Marx to conclude that man is an immoral animal. But little did he realize then, that it would be the same propensity which would ultimately bring about the demolition of the Communist empire.

The rejection of morality is not the only hurdle which prevents the realization of Marx's dream of a stateless society. Equal access to opportunities is not enough to achieve the goal of a stateless society, nor are the greeds confined only to the fulfilment of economic requirements. Where is the answer to the greed for capturing the source of power which runs supreme in every dictatorial system? Again, where is the scientific guarantee in the system for blocking the passage of jealousies, hatred and revenge in relation to the capturing of power? Marx's scientific philosophy does not even touch this issue.

To reach the utopia, one has to pass through the hazards of a society which knows no morals and no mercy. Long before a stage of perfect levelling of economic and political society is reached, the immorality in man would have demolished the very edifice of the Communist vision of life.

In the light of this, when we reinvestigate the problems leading to the collapse of the Communist empire, we cannot fail to identify the moral failure of its functionaries to be the main culprit. It was the corruption of the Communist world which is largely to be blamed for the downfall of the Communist empire of the U.S.S.R. Thus, the failure of the system was underwritten in the Communist charter when morality was banished from it.

On the one hand there is the revealed truth and on the other, the so-called truth reached entirely through the agency of human reason. The merits of the two philosophies are not too difficult to examine. The Divine proclamation invariably claims that justice and fair play in human affairs cannot be established without their absoluteness. Moral corruption and a code of ethics based on absolute justice cannot go hand in hand. Absolute truth is the essence of all morality, and absolute morality is the essence of all truth. Hence without the rehabilitation of absolute values in man, no dream of a heaven upon earth can be envisioned. This has always been the universal pronouncement of all ages.

Marx rose to defy this age-old philosophy founded on revelation. He rejected it outright and made the counterclaim that man stands in no need of Divine guidance — nor according to him, does any God exist. Hence it is for man to carve his own path to the ultimate realization of his dream of heaven upon earth. Thus, he carved a path guided entirely by his own intellect, completely devoid of Divine guidance.

Looking at the Marxist vision of a stateless society once again, another fundamental flaw which has already been hinted at comes to light. It is assumed without foundation that if the society is economically levelled, the root cause of crime will be destroyed; hence no state power will be needed to combat crime. The greed in man, however, is certainly not limited to the area of his economic activity. Even if the objectives of Marxism are entirely achieved there is much more to the greed of man than meets the Marxist eye.

Human psyche gives birth to so many desires and ambitions that any solution proposed to solve problems without taking them into account would be inadequate.

Inequalities in man are not only economic. They may belong to his physical or mental aptitudes and other faculties of head and heart. His innate desire to rule, to conquer, to govern, to dominate, to love and to be loved, are but a few areas which provide a fertile soil for the seed of greed to take root in.

Beauty is one thing that cannot be shared equally by all men and women, nor can physical fitness and health be doled out to them in equal measures. The faculties of hearing and sight, of taste and touch; the likes and dislikes, cravings and aversions, even artistic aptitudes, the taste for music and passion for art, the literary pursuits and the lack of interest in what bookworms would relish and devour, are but a few examples of variants which nature has itself produced over a long course of evolution. No proponents of scientific socialism can ever do away with them. They have to be accepted as *fait accompli*. The problem is that it is this diversity itself which is the ultimate root cause of all the corruption in human society. All social maladies are born out of them. The only valid solution to discipline such tendencies lies in the Divinely revealed moral codes, which in turn cannot work without the belief in God. Remove God and revealed truth from human affairs and there will be no peace left whatsoever.

This in-depth comparison between the Godless philosophy of Marxism and the belief in revealed truth serves to clarify the case in point. On the one hand there is man's reason alone, unaided by Divine guidance, striving to resolve all human problems by itself. On the other, there is the Divinely revealed truth which emphasizes the role of absolute moral measures to combat immorality in man.

A critical review of the former leads one to the only logical conclusion, that reason by itself is totally inadequate for guiding human steps to peace and tranquillity. A study of religious history reveals that peace and tranquillity were only achieved when Divine messengers fought heroic battles against the immorality in man. It was through a course of toil, sweat and blood, that islands of a near peaceful human society were ever created in the midst of the raging ocean of crime and sin. No doubt they were always reclaimed by the seas of temptation. But even so, the level of human morality was invariably raised a notch or two. Had it not been so, and had there been no Divinely generated movements for the moral rearmament of man, society would be a hundred times worse than it is today. There is no doubt left, therefore, in the indispensability of revelation and revealed truth.

REFERENCES

1. WESTFALL, R.C. (1993) *The Life of Issac Newton.* Cambridge University Press, Cambridge, p. 124
2. WESTFALL, R.C. (1993) *The Life of Issac Newton.* Cambridge University Press, Cambridge, p. 122
3. WESTFALL, R.C. (1993) *The Life of Issac Newton.* Cambridge University Press, Cambridge, p. 121
4. GUTMAN, J. (1963) *Philosophy A to Z.* Grosset & Dunlap Inc, New York.
5. KIERNAN, T. (1966) *Who's Who In The History of Philosophy.* Vision Press, New York, p. 54
6. COPLESTON, F. (1956) *Contemporary Philosophy.* Studies of Logical Positivism and Existentialism. Burns, Oates and Washbourne Ltd., London, pp.154-155
7. SARTRE, J. (1975) *Existentialism and Humanism.* Eyre Methuen Ltd., London, p.34
8. LENIN, V, I. (1963) *Collected Works.* Vol.38, Philosophical Notebooks. Foreign Languages Publishing House, Moscow, p.201

GREEK PHILOSOPHY

IN MATTERS OF REVELATION AND RATIONALITY, it is difficult to find many Greek philosophers fitting into the genuine description of a prophet who combines in him a perfect balance of the two. Socrates is an exception.

Socrates, (470-399 BC) being a class unto himself, occupies a unique position in the history of Greek philosophy which fails to mention anyone other than him to belong to that class. There must have been prophets before and after him but of them we can only infer from some oblique references by Socrates himself. For instance, he is known to have said that he is not the only one from God who has been the recipient of revelation; there have been great men before who did the same to serve the cause of goodness. Again, he warns Athenians not to put him to death otherwise they would never see the like of him again, except if God so desires to teach the right path to the Athenians by sending someone else.

This chapter is largely devoted to Socrates and what he stood for, because he manifests a perfect balance of revelation and rationality; but it is impossible not to mention Plato and Aristotle when one talks of Greek philosophy. It is indeed they who pioneered a new mode which has become almost eternal, but they certainly owed their greatness to their revered master.

It was Socrates who had introduced into philosophical discussions of the time, the elements of knowledge, truth and rationality with emphasis so powerful that some biographers describe him as having brought high-flown ethereal philosophies from the heavens down to earth. We believe that the converse is true; the philosophical babble of the sophists before him were the acts of earthly men. It is knowledge, truth and rationality which lift human thoughts to sublime loftiness. That is why though Plato and Aristotle left a most profound and rich heritage for us concerning all philosophical discussions, there is nothing like the lasting noble influence of Socratic integrity which went largely into the making of Plato and Aristotle. The philosophies of Plato and Aristotle are but briefly dealt with, just by way of introduction.

Both Plato and Aristotle give priority to rationality in the understanding of the universal scheme of things. What is the relationship between rationality and the external world? How is knowledge attained and what is eternal truth? On these questions, the two great philosophers offer divergent views.

With Plato it is incorrect to consider the perceptions of the external world as the ultimate truth because a superficial study of any external matter is not sufficient to gain true knowledge of its inner nature. Plato believes that hidden within every external phenomenon is a deeper, invisible world of meaning that cannot be reached by mere superficial analysis.

PLATO

Plato accepts the existence of an unseen realm, governed by a Supreme Conscious Being with numerous other subordinate agents working under Him for the maintenance of the whole system of creation. However, he does not appear to believe that revelation plays any role in providing knowledge of the unknown. For him, it is through an interaction between rationality and intellectual inspiration alone that true knowledge is acquired. This interplay of intellect and inspiration can sometimes result in fascinating or even strange consequences. The outcome of this process may result in leaps of knowledge rather than step by step advancement. New ideas may be created but they are always related to the thought processes of man. Their value, according to Plato, depends on the quality and level of rationality of the perceiving mind.

For Plato, rationality demands an intensive search being carried out to penetrate into the deepest recesses of all categories of natural phenomena. By arranging the data thus gained into an intellectual orderly form, man is able to attain truth. According to him:

> 'Because of the presence in him of something like a divine spark, he can, after suitable preparation, fix his intellectual gaze on the realities of the unseen world and, in the light of them, know both what is true and how to behave. He will not attain this result easily — to get to it will involve not only immense intellectual effort, including the repeated challenging of assumptions, but also turning his back on everything in life that is merely sensual or animal. Yet, despite this, the end is attainable in principle, and the man who arrives at it will exercise the most important part of himself in the best way that is open to him.'[1]

Thus for Plato, knowledge can be attained merely through the faculties of observation and rationality, aided sometimes by the faculty of inspiration and intuition. Truth is the knowledge gained as a result of this exercise. In short, Plato held that the apparent world is only a façade while the truth, which lies hidden behind, could be quite different from what is observed. This means that however hard we may try, we cannot completely comprehend the nature of any external fact, because all external facts or objects are constantly changing. Thus an observation made at any given time could differ from that made at another.

> 'Plato held that the idea is an ideal, a non-sensible goal to which the sensible approximates; the geometer's perfect triangle "never was on sea or land," though all actual triangles more or less embody it. He conceived the ideas as more real than the sensible things that are their shadows and saw that the philosopher must penetrate to these invisible essences and see with the eye of his mind how they are linked together. For Plato they formed an orderly system that was at once eternal, intelligible, and good.'[2]

In contrast to Plato, Aristotle gives priority to the external observable reality. For him any understanding gained by man at any particular moment is to be taken as the truth. It seems as though for Aristotle the external world was itself the eternal truth. Aristotle was also persuaded of the existence of ideas towards which all the 'various physical forms' are moving. In sharp

ARISTOTLE

contrast to Plato, he perceived matter to be an independent eternal reality and presents a view of continuous evolution in which no External Conscious Being has a hand to play. He considers this evolution to be dependent only upon the natural propensities latent within matter itself.

That should not be taken to mean that Aristotle does not believe in God, the Creator. On the contrary, he believed in a Supreme Being Who was responsible for the entire chain of cause and effect and could be referred to as the Ultimate First Cause. However, as we trace the idea of

God discussed by Socrates, Plato, and Aristotle, we see a gradual change in relation to their concept.

SOCRATES seems to have a very personalized and intense relationship with the Supreme Being. His very personality is built on the pattern of the messengers of God. Plato represents the first generation of his pupils, who are also charged to a substantial degree with the Socratic spirit. In their philosophic and scientific discussions there is an inevitable stamp of spirituality. But in the transitional period, from Plato to Aristotle, we notice a perceptible decline in the idea of God playing a live and active role in the phenomena of nature. In Aristotle we do not detect any evidence that he believed in any form of communication between God and man.

Although the idea of eternal truth is not explicitly mentioned or explored in Aristotelian philosophy, an analysis of his work allows us to attribute a notion of eternal truth to him. This notion is linked to the constant motion of matter and its natural propensity to evolve towards an ideal state. According to this philosophy, matter progresses to an ideal form towards which it has always been evolving.

It becomes clear that to Aristotle, whatever one observes at any given time can be classed as a fact at that particular moment. The conclusion derived from such facts, as compiled by reason, can be called knowledge. This knowledge, when verified from different angles of observation, should be considered the truth.

Among the early philosophers Aristotle stands out because of the unbroken continuity of his influence over many an era of philosophical thought. Even today, there is no branch of philosophy which is altogether free from the influence of his dominating intellect.

We may conclude by pointing out that among most Greek philosophers, even when they believed in God, revelation was not specifically mentioned as an essential instrument for the transfer of knowledge from God to man. Rationality wedded to observation and human examination is all that is accepted as the most reliable means of gaining knowledge and truth.

This brief reference to Greek philosophy does not cover all the major Greek philosophers who have made an indelible mark on the history of human thought. The main purpose of this exercise is to present a brief review on the concept of rationality, revelation and truth, as found in the works of Greek philosophers whose words and fame have become eternal. It is here that we must introduce Socrates in his full image.

Socrates, the noblest of all Greek philosophers who presents no contradiction between his ideas and personal righteous deeds, is portrayed by many modern writers in a strange dusky light of contradiction. An outstanding moral teacher, largely seen today through the reflective mirror of Plato, Xenephon and some others of his contemporaries, Socrates is not as yet placed where he truly belongs. Of Xenephon it must be said, that being himself a believer in the polytheistic mythology of the Athenians, he was largely responsible for attributing to Socrates the belief in many gods. That is why in all that is written on Socrates today, one repeatedly finds contradictory references to him as believing in many gods as well as in One, Who is the Creator of the universe. Every fibre of his monotheist personality throbs with the life and spirit of a devotee to One God.

His belief in the Unity of God was unshakeable; his defiance of the plurality of Greek mythology was uncompromising. Virtue, knowledge, truth and eradication of all contradictions from one's person, were the subjects of his lifelong dedication. His whole life was in itself a holy war against evil, ignorance, arrogance, and duality in man. He believed in absolute justice and answerability; he believed in life after death and the consequent punishment or reward. Readily he gave up his life with such peace of mind and tranquillity of soul, on the altar of his conviction in the Unity of God, as behoves any great prophet of God.

But that was not all that there was to his supreme sacrifice. To compromise with falsehood — even with the faintest of its shades — was not in the grain of Socrates. He would have smilingly given up his life, rejecting any unjustified pressure upon him by society to change even the smallest of his convictions under the threat of death. It is this great Greek philosopher of a prophet, who is paradoxically described as 'the father of Western Philosophy'.

Whatever was there common between him and the philosophical pursuit of the western philosophers, is prominent only by its total absence. Virtue, humility, absolute justice, firm belief in the Unity of God, accountability of humans both here and in the hereafter can be summed up as the main body of his philosophy. Could he be the father of the philosophies of Descartes, Hegel, Engels and Marx? If so, all genetic marks of his paternal stamp must have been totally wiped out by the passage of time. Could their negation of morality be traced back to him with any sense of justice? No — certainly not.

His was a different world. His was a world of Prophets. He believed in Divinely revealed dreams; he believed in revelation; he believed in knowledge to be truth, and truth to be knowledge. He believed that no knowledge is trustworthy but that bestowed upon man by God Himself.

He was charged with the mission of delivering a Divine message to the people of Greece. To him this life was only a preparatory stage for the life to come. It was the human soul which mattered to him. It was this soul which was decreed to be delivered and transferred to the hereafter. This was his philosophy, call it Divine wisdom if you will, but certainly not a secular philosophy as portrayed by modern intellectuals.

Repeated attempts have been made to pluck him away from the comity of prophets to that of mere philosophers. Many modern writers, great as they may be in their learning, are miserably confused about his true identity. They have wasted bookfuls of material on him to try to place him where he does not belong.

Some renowned scholars have seriously attempted to remove an imaginary contradiction in him which actually did not exist. For them the contradiction was between his belief in Divine revelation and his profession of rationality. If rationality and Divine revelation ever posed a paradox, it was always posed by all the prophets of God, Socrates being no exception. Every true prophet and all the founders of great religions simultaneously believed in Divine revelation and rationality, holding fast to both with absolute tenacity. They saw no contradiction between the two. Had they seen any, true as they were, they must have rejected either the idea of God or the idea of rationality, or both perhaps. To them, the idea of rationality and God could not belong to opposite camps. Hence those who see a parallax in Socrates' beliefs and his rationality must be suffering from diplopia themselves. Let them read Socrates once again and all that is written of him by authentic sources. They are bound to discover a new person in him who can never simultaneously be separated from his adherence to God and his rational philosophy. They must notice the fact that central to all the important material on him is his obsession that people do not pay proper attention to the importance of virtue and do not understand its real meaning.

The dilemma of contradiction is between the real image of Socrates and the unreal one — which is being transposed upon him — and is largely responsible for the distortion of some significant terms used in the source material. Whether one such term *arete* really means virtue or whether it has a secular connotation, is one of the questions which needs to be addressed. In the view of W.K.C. Guthrie:

> 'We know now that the word "virtue" attaches false associations to the Greek *arete*, which meant primarily efficiency at a particular task.'[3]

It is this, according to Guthrie which jarred the sensibilities of the 'practical' Athenians. The word 'practical' reveals a glaring contradiction in Guthrie's understanding of *arete* because if his definition is correct then it is Socrates who emerges to be the most practical man in Athens, not his critics: who were interested only in 'political ability' and 'moral obligations'.

> 'One of the things about Socrates which irritated the sensible, practical Athenian was that he would insist on turning the talk to such humble and apparently irrelevant people as shoemakers and carpenters, when what they wanted to learn about was what constituted political ability or whether there was such a thing as moral obligation.'[3]

It is evident from this statement that in the eyes of Guthrie, Socrates was not at all interested in 'virtue' as a moral term. All that he was really interested in was a common artisan's know-how of his trade and a clear

81

understanding of the purpose for which he was working. He must understand for instance, what a ladder stands for and to serve what purpose a ladder is to be built. This is the secular philosophy of Socrates as seen by Guthrie. The only theme which occupied him was the purpose and trade of an artisan. That is how he visualized Socrates roaming the streets of Athens, addressing the common people and teaching them how to achieve excellence in arts and crafts. He completely misses the main thrust of Socrates' philosophy, whom he would allow no interest in virtue and piety.

One thing is certain about Socrates — whatever he indulged in was *arete.* So if at the same time he is condemned by society for not discussing morality it can only mean that according to them *arete* had no connotation of moral sense. We protest against this allegation of the author which is most certainly wrong. Athenian society never blamed Socrates for not discussing morality. Quite to the contrary, the Athenians condemned him of overmuch indulgence in his brand of morality which they considered tantamount to corrupting the youth of Athens. Thus, by ridding *arete* of any moral sense, Guthrie denies Socrates his status as a moral teacher. By this rather devious method he has attempted to change the facts of history. But all that he succeeds in is the creation of a parallax between an imaginary personality of Socrates, which the author himself imposes on him, and the real one that he possessed. Anyone who knows Socrates presented by the writings of Plato and some of his other contemporaries, cannot accept this baseless conjecture of the author. It is but common knowledge that what irritated Athenian society was not what the author proclaims. Socrates pleaded the Unity of God and waged a holy war against immorality. That was all the mission of Socrates and all that *arete* meant to him.

These are the facts which must be understood in relation to the meaning of *arete*.

AGAINST GUTHRIE, *arete* is rightly translated by many other scholars as 'virtue' with all its connotations. When Socrates talks of such small things as the nature of the instruments of arts and crafts, and the manner in which they work, and further speaks of a clearly defined purpose that every art and craft must fulfil, he is most certainly talking in cryptic terms referring all the time to humans. Otherwise he would not deny the artisans the knowledge of their own trade and would not condemn them of utter ignorance. What he in fact describes is the human ignorance to discern the nature of Divine knowledge which lies deep beneath the surface of every human occupation, yet humans remain oblivious to it. With this ignorance no human is entitled to be called human, just as an artisan is not worthy of being called an artisan if he does not possess the know-how of his trade or the purpose of building an artifact. It is to this human ignorance that Socrates strives to draw the attention of man.

It is the Divine purpose of their creation which Socrates believes humans cannot attain merely with their own efforts. They do not know how to carve their lives to suit the purpose for which they are created. Of that they know nothing, claiming all the same that they are all-knowledgeable. This is what he considers to be utter ignorance. This exercise of discovering the purpose of one's existence is what *arete* stands for. But this cannot be achieved without perfect humility and absolute admission of one's ignorance. Only then is man ready to be helped by God with step by step guidance from ignorance to knowledge. The only knowledge known to Socrates is that which is revealed by Him; the rest is ignorance.

This exactly is also the message of the Quran, which attributes all knowledge to God so that even the angels admit their ignorance before him. They beseech:

سُبْحَنَكَ لَا عِلْمَ لَنَا اِلَّا مَا عَلَّمْتَنَا اِنَّكَ اَنْتَ الْعَلِيْمُ الْحَكِيْمُ*

2: 33

… Holy art Thou! No knowledge have we except what Thou hast taught us; surely, Thou art the All-Knowing, the Wise.[4]

The Quran repeatedly reminds humans that no knowledge of the right path can be granted them unless they profess total dependence upon Him and implore His help to guide their steps:

اِيَّاكَ نَعْبُدُ وَاِيَّاكَ نَسْتَعِيْنُ * اِهْدِنَا الصِّرَاطَ الْمُسْتَقِيْمَ* 1:5-6

Thee alone do we worship and Thee alone do we implore for help.
Guide us in the right path.[5]

It is this same lesson in humility which is so forcefully delivered by Socrates, indicating that man cannot acquire knowledge without admitting his ignorance and realizing that he needs Divine help to show him the path.

Thus, cryptically, he is alluding to man all the time while he speaks apparently of a hypothetical artisan. He sees man as suffering from the conceit that he is knowledgeable while as long as he considers himself to be knowledgeable, he cannot ever become conscious of his need to learn. This symbolism helps Socrates to fulfil his prophetic mission which was to awaken his fellow countrymen to an awareness of moral, spiritual and Divine purpose of human creation which cannot be understood or pursued without succour from Him.

Most humans move like pawns, not aware of why they move and who the Mastermind is, behind the hand that moves them. Such oblivious men can neither know their obligations to their Creator nor to their fellow human beings. To impress upon man the gravity of this situation, Socrates reminds him of life after death when he will be finally held accountable for all his deeds during his life on earth. This, the life after death, is certainly not what the secular philosophers talk about. This is the main mission and occupation of the prophets of God. We only wish that Guthrie had remembered what he himself had written about the character of Socrates in the same book. Of particular significance are the following words he claims that Socrates uttered just before his death:

> 'It is probable that many, if not most, of those who disapproved of him had no wish to see him die, and would have been more than content if he could have been persuaded to leave Athens...'[6]

He rejected this suggestion point blank and responded by saying:

> '...that he had all his life enjoyed the benefits which the laws of Athens conferred on her citizens, and now that those same laws saw fit that he should die, it would be both unjust and ungrateful for him to evade their decision. **Besides, who could tell that he was not going to a far better existence than that which he had known hitherto?**'[6]

Many other highly competent scholars have also researched the true and full translation of *arete*. One of the most prominent among them is Gregory Vlastos who strongly rejects attempts to treat it merely as an artisan's term. Explaining the original Greek word in its various possible connotations, he emphasizes that, in Socratic usage the word *arete* must be equated with piety and virtue in every form of goodness that they may refer to:

> 'Any lingering doubt on this point in my readers' mind may be resolved by referring them to the fact that whenever he brings the general concept under scrutiny — as when he debates the teachability of *aretē* in the *Protagoras* and the *Meno* — he assumes without argument that its sole constituents or "parts" (μόρια, μέρη) are five qualities which are, incontestably, the Greek terms of moral commendation par excellence: *andreia* ("manliness," "courage"), *sōphrosynē* ("temperance," "moderation"), *dikaiosynē* ("justice," "righteousness"), *hosiotēs* ("piety," "holiness"), *sophia* ("wisdom").'[7]

Thus Vlastos is very rational in his stance that it is far more important to search *aretes'* intended central meaning which Socrates himself consistently portrays and highlights.

To this intended meaning of *arete* another great scholar, Christopher Janaway, refers when he states that Socrates:

> '...was concerned with questions of ethics, in particular with defining the virtues (justice, wisdom, courage, piety, temperance). This is how Socrates is portrayed by Plato in the early dialogues, and is how he makes Socrates describe himself in the *Apology*.'[8]

> 'Central propositions in Socrates' ethics are: virtue is knowledge; all the virtues are one; virtue is happiness...
> 'Socrates also believes that no one who has knowledge of good and bad can lack any of the virtues — with such knowledge one must also be courageous, holy, temperate, and just. Finally, he

thinks that the perfectly virtuous person is bound to be happier — to have greater well-being in fact — than someone who lacks virtue.'[9]

We fully accept Janaway's understanding of Socrates' ethics.

What Socrates is describing is a law which relates profoundly to human psyche and has to be accepted in its totality. The knowledge that a thorny bush could be the only safe place against a vicious beast would certainly make a sensible man accept the comparatively lesser evil of thorny pricks and, as long as he is protected, the suffering which the thorns cause will, by comparison appear to him as pleasure. While Socrates does not deny the physical suffering of a truly knowledgeable person, what he emphasizes is that whatever action is deemed suitable by a truly knowledgeable person is the only action in which he will find peace. It is as true today as it was then. It explains the optional acceptance of suffering, by godly people, in which they find happiness. For them the converse of losing God's favour is unbearably painful. Likewise, dignified men who prefer to die in 'pain' rather than live in comfort by sacrificing their principles, certainly die 'happily' with the realization of their moral victory. They smilingly accept physical suffering rather than the spiritual disgrace which to them is far more punishing.

Vlastos has dedicated a long chapter, *Socratic Piety,* to resolve an imaginary contradiction in Socrates' views and his experience. It is a scholarly yet an apologetic attempt on his part to prove that in reality no such contradiction exists. His philosophy is thoroughly rational throughout, as Vlastos sees it, but his experience of revelation and his belief in a Superior Being Who guides his life is the contradiction which must be removed. Thus, he quotes Socrates himself to bring this point home. Of his perfectly rational attitude, Socrates is known to have said:

> 'Not now for the first time, but always, I am the sort of man who is persuaded by nothing in me except the proposition which appears to me to be the best *when I reason* (λογιζομέμῳ) about it.'[10]

Despite his emphasis on reason he appears to Vlastos to be a superstitious man when it comes to his personal experience. Thus he writes:

> 'And yet he is also committed to obeying commands reaching him through supernatural channels.'[10]

To support his contention, Vlastos quotes Socrates during his trial:

> 'To do this has been commanded me, as I maintain, by the god through divinations and through dreams and every other means through which divine apportionment has ever commanded anyone to do anything.'[10]

Having postulated this, Vlastos has written a long discourse on absolving Socrates of what he himself admits of his spiritual experience. Through an involved logic, he finally assumes that Socrates did not genuinely believe in what appears to be his personal confession. Yet despite all his scholarly effort, Vlastos fails to achieve this purpose. Read again for instance the above quoted passage by Vlastos beginning with the words

> 'To do this has been commanded me, ...'[10]

and note that the word God used by Socrates is in the singular, yet the author prefers to write it with a small 'g'.

This statement of Socrates, concerning his personal experience of Divine dreams, revelations and specific commands in other forms, is so powerful and so completely at one with the universal experience of Divine prophets that it leaves no room for doubt that he means exactly what he says. A large number of Quranic verses fully support Socrates when they speak of all the prophets before the Holy Founder of Islam[sa] having shared with him all the different modes of Divine revelation.

Vlastos further builds his contradiction theory by raising the question:

> 'Should this incline us to believe that Socrates is counting on two disparate avenues of knowledge about the gods, rational and extra-rational respectively, yielding two distinct systems of justified belief, one of them reached by elenctic argument, the other by divine revelation through oracles, prophetic dreams and the like?'[11]

ONE IS AMAZED to note how imaginary contradictions can be built between what Socrates believed and what he actually experienced. He is known, of course, to have criticized the so-called Greek gods and disparaged the reliability of their revelation through oracles, but whenever he spoke of his personal experience he never ridiculed, even once, his own Divine revelation or dreams. The author has done no justice to him by adding 'through oracles' after 'divine revelation'. The personal Divine revelation of which Socrates has spoken, as quoted above, has no mention whatsoever of any 'oracles'. Invariably when he speaks of his personal experience he speaks of 'God' in singular, with capital G, and not of 'gods'. When he mentions the poets' visions, as though they were god-given, he only uses such expressions as a figure of speech, not meaning them to be actually 'God-given':

'Yes, what the inspired poet puts into his poem is a wonderful, god-given thing; but *it isn't knowledge* — it can't be knowledge for it is mindless.'[12]

His criticism that 'it is not knowledge — it can't be knowledge for it is mindless', is absolutely in accordance with the common practice of poetic expressions. No doubt there is a sort of magic in some poetry as though God were speaking through the poet's tongue, but a sensible man would not take this too seriously. For Socrates to speak of a poet as 'god-possessed,' may also have referred to the Athenians' superstitious views of people being possessed by 'gods'. Such expressions are poles apart from the language which Socrates uses for himself. He is never **God-possessed** but is only addressed by Him as a humble servant of His.

He makes it clear that the poetic experiences which may seem Divine are certainly not so. Whatever their import, they can at best be described as inspiration, not Divine Revelation:

'I soon perceived that *it is not through knowledge* that poets produce their poems but through a sort of inborn gift and in a state of inspiration...'[13]

However, the conclusion drawn by Vlastos from the same passage drives the reader out of his mind, rather than the poet he refers to as being driven 'out of his mind':

'...when the god is in him the poet is "out of his mind," ἔκφρων...'[13]

Again he absolves Socrates of irrationality by declaring:

'Socrates has disarmed the irrationalist potential of the belief in **supernatural gods** communicating with human beings by **supernatural signs**.'[14]

We respectfully yet strongly disagree with him when he assumes that the same applied to Socrates' own experiences. Only two pages after what he has concluded about the nature of the supernatural commands of others, the author has to admit that the God of Socrates was different:

> 'Because, as we saw earlier, unlike their gods, Socrates' god is invariantly good, incapable of causing any evil to anyone in any way at any time. Since to deceive a man is to do evil to him, Socrates' god cannot be lying.'[15]

Further, in the same chapter, he rightly attributes a concept of worship to Socrates which was distinctly opposed to the so-called worship of the Athenians. The worship of Athenians according to him was:

> '...an art of commercial exchanges between gods and men.'[16]

Their worship had to be rebuffed because they, the Athenians, make gods appear dependent on them by whatever is offered at their altar, but the God of Socrates — who is wrongly referred to as "gods" by the author:

> '... stand in no need of gifts from us, while we are totally dependent on their gifts to us...'[16]

Evidently, Socratic treatment of Athenian worship is with reference to their polytheistic godhead which may be referred to in plural, but it should be remembered here that the word 'god', whenever used in plural by Socrates, does not always indicate the Athenian gods which were just a product of their fancy. A careful study of Socrates reveals that by the term 'gods', he sometimes refers to angels or any other spiritual form of life above men and under God.

However when he speaks of his own experience, he totally discards the plurality and begins to refer to one God.

> 'I believe that no greater good has ever come to you in the city than this service of mine to **the god**.'[17]

(Note the singleness of *God* in relation to the mission bestowed to *him*.)

His religio-political philosophy was always at one with the universal trend of Divine teachings. No prophet of God is recorded in history to have risen in revolt against the law of the land, but when the state interfered with his obedience to God, he unhesitatingly rejected the state power without fear and followed the dictates of God.

The same was the philosophy of Socrates. He was absolutely loyal to the state but when loyalty to the state contradicted his loyalty to God, the only conclusion he drew for himself was to discard the lesser loyalty for the sake of the higher one which was due only to the Creator. Addressing the senate which was about to convict him to death, he spoke of this with unperturbed composure and dignity:

> '... Men of Athens, I honor and love you; but I shall obey God rather than you, and while I have life and strength I shall never cease from the practice and teaching of philosophy ...' [18]

(Note that Jowett always writes 'God' with a capital 'G' when he relates Him to Socrates.)

When the Athenians offered him release from the death penalty on the condition that he should stop 'corrupting' the youth of Athens by instigating them to defy the Athenian gods and obey his own, Socrates refused them outright. There is a long discourse on this issue between him and Meletus, his chief prosecutor. During this, Meletus insists that his defiance of Athenian gods, despite his assertion that he believed in one God, is tantamount to absolute atheism and as such he must be condemned to death. Socrates' obedience to God stood higher than his obedience to the law of Athens. He stood by it and was felled for it, but before his death delivered to the people of Athens this prophetic warning in the following words:

> '... you may think, but for yours, that you may not sin against the God, or lightly reject his boon by condemning me. For if you kill me you will not easily find another like me,...'[19]

Having said that he goes on building the case of his innocence with incontrovertible logic, clinching the issue finally by an argument which will for ever pay tribute to his greatness. Jowett quotes him as saying:

> '...not even the impudence of my accusers dares to say that I have ever exacted or sought pay of any one; they have no witness of that. And I have a witness of the truth of what I say; my poverty is a sufficient witness.'[19]

He also invokes his past conduct to stand witness by his side and to bear testimony to the truth of his present behaviour.

Then referring to a past incident which singled him out as the only person who dared to oppose the might of the entire senate he declared:

> '...I cared not a straw for death, and that my only fear was the fear of doing an unrighteous or unholy thing. For the strong arm of that **oppressive power** did not frighten me into doing wrong...'[20]

Socrates, would not demean himself like many so-called nobles in his place might have done. So he goes on to elaborate:

'I have seen men of reputation, when they have been condemned, behaving in the strangest manner: they seemed to fancy that they were going to suffer something dreadful if they died, and that they could be immortal if you only allowed them to live; ...'[21]

'Do not then require me to do what I consider dishonorable and impious and wrong, especially now, when I am being tried for impiety on the indictment of Meletus.'[21]

What follows indicates that despite his unshakeable belief in Unity, he also believed in some god-like figures to whom he attributes a different and nobler sense, which does not apply to the so-called gods of Athenians. He speaks of them exactly in the same sense as 'angels' are referred to in other Divinely revealed religions. Thus his belief in gods in the sense of angels was certainly not contradictory to his belief in one God. When he commits his cause finally, it is not to them — the gods of Athens — that he commits it. He commits his cause to the people of Athens and to God:

'And to you and **to God I commit my cause**...'[22]

Even to the minutest detail, Socrates is just like any other Prophet mentioned in the Holy Quran and other scriptures. He condemned suicide as an offence against God because he treated life as His gift of which He remained the sole Master. In Phaedo, he is reported to have spoken at length with powerful arguments against the legality of suicide which he considered absolutely unpardonable. Thus, he pronounces his judgment on the issue of suicide:

'...there may be reason in saying that a man should wait, and not take his own life until God summons him, as he is now summoning me.'[23]

His discourse continued until he was interrupted by Crito from whose gestures he understood that he wanted to say something. He dismissed him and all that he wanted to say on behalf of the attendant who was to administer him the poison. The attendant had suggested that if he talked too much it would weaken the effect of the poison and he would be obliged to drink it two or three times. He showed scant respect with regards to the suggestion and the discomfort which his discourses could have caused him. 'Let him mind his business' answered Socrates 'and be prepared to give the poison two or three times.'

'And now I will make answer to you, O my judges,' — here he only refers as judges to those of his admirers who had gathered around him during his last moments — 'and show that he who has lived as a true philosopher has reason to be of good cheer when he is about to die, and that after death he may hope to receive the greatest good in the other world.'[24]

Thus he continued to teach the Divine philosophy to the people of Athens until he put the opiate to his lips. Even as life was slowly ebbing out, as long as he had strength to speak, he continued to discharge his Divine commission never ceasing, before death silenced him at last.

Thus came to an end the life of one of the most glorious prophets of God who lived in the fifth century BC (a contemporary of Buddha[as]). Like Buddha, he never wrote his scriptures but they were recorded by his contemporaries and committed to writing later in the form of his *Dialogues*. Buddha too was accused of atheism because he denied the gods of the Brahmans.

The greatest service he did to philosophy is summed up by Chambers Encyclopaedia in the following words:

'Socrates, in bringing down philosophy from the skies to the common life of men (as Cicero put it), was only carrying out in a conspicuous and earnest way one of the new intellectual tendencies of his age.'[25]

'He was indifferent to luxury and even to ordinary comfort; but he was by no means an ascetic.'[25]

As for the nature of his Divine Revelation, the author of the above-quoted article, states:

'There has been much discussion about the "divine sign" (δαιμόνιον) of which Socrates used to speak as a supernatural voice which frequently gave him guidance, according to Xenophon telling him to act or not to act, according to Plato only restraining him from action, never instigating. Later writers, especially in Christian times, speak of it as a daemon, genius or attendant spirit. **For this there is no authority whatever** in Plato and Xenophon.'[25]

'… he seems to have had certain vivid presentiments which he took for special divine monitions; and it is possible, as has been suggested, that he was subject to occasional hallucinations of hearing, such as may occur even in quite sane and healthy persons.'[25]

Socrates' revelation is thus respectfully dismissed as hallucination.

In reality, there is no contradiction in Socrates. Whatever contradiction there is, has to be in the mind of the author who apparently defended Socrates by suggesting that his hallucinations were not all that bad as those of psychic people suffering from mental aberrations. Hallucinations can also sometimes be experienced by sane healthy persons as in the case of Socrates.

What sympathy, what a condescending attitude to Socrates by some modern writer who has faith in Socrates but has no faith in his belief in God. However condescending that remark may be, it is no tribute to the greatness of Socrates who does not stand in need of any apology. Did not the same misfortune befall all the prophets of God before or after him? *Each of them was accused of hallucination by the society he addressed* though not as politely as the author of the said article has treated Socrates. All such accusers knew full well that the prophets they accused of such mental aberrations were neither frail in mind nor weak of moral health. They were the wisest people of their time, sound of head and heart, respected as such by the society in which they grew from the age of their childhood to that of full maturity. None of them is accused of behaving in any manner like a soothsayer prior to their claim to prophethood; none is ever reported even after that to act as though he were hallucinating. Hallucinations are always unpredictable, disjointed and incoherent. The voices that some hallucinators hear do seem to address them as though they were from God but they never reveal to them any philosophy or way of life which can be shared and practised by others. There is no logic in what they hear and no logic in what they say. Hallucinations never give birth to rationality.

To mix up hallucination with prophecy is but a morbid attempt to discredit Divine revelation. The experience of the prophets of God is essentially different! Truth, wisdom and rationality are their distinctive features while the hostile society they confront symbolizes dogma, falsehood and superstition. The message that the prophets deliver is always based on sound moral code. They breathe wisdom, they exude piety, they advocate rationality, they preach morality, justice, moderation, understanding, kindness, patience, service and sacrifice. Is this the prophetic message delivered to them during their maddest moments of 'hallucination'? What hallucination indeed! One only wishes that their accusers had remembered their own hallucinatory experiences while they were stricken, for instance, by a severe attack of septic fever or typhoid. Do they ever remember a wise code of life bestowed upon them during those temporary derangements which could stand the test of time and deliver a new message to mankind to be taken seriously by them?

Rationality and hallucination never cohabit healthy minds. How we wish that whoever accused him of hallucination had further elaborated his statement by quoting from his own experience. Had a sane person ever learnt an exceptionally sound philosophy of life through his occasional outbursts of delusion? How we wish the author had remembered that all the wisdom and all the piety and all the rationality and faith, which Socrates displayed, he had learnt from the so-called voices of his 'hallucination'! If his faith in revelation is to be rejected as based on hallucination, then all his philosophy of life, and all his wisdom must also be rejected by the same token. He can never be separated from his rationality.

We accept the whole of Socrates. Noble was his character, noble his vision, noble was the life he led. Such as he are never forged by hallucinations. Peace was with him when he was born, peace was with him while he lived, peace was with him when he died smilingly — while the throng of his admirers bitterly wailed and cried and sobbed around him. Athens had never seen the departure of a soul as noble as that of Socrates.

Allah be pleased with him! May He shower His choicest blessings upon him; but woe to his murderers. Athens will never see the like of him again!

REFERENCES

1. *The New Encyclopaedia Britannica.* Vol 24, 15th ed.
2. *The New Encyclopaedia Britannica.* Vol 25, 15th ed.
3. GUTHRIE, W.K.C. (1950) *The Greek Philosophers.* Methuen & Co, p.72
4. Translation of 2:33 by Maulawi Sher Ali.
5. Translation of 1:5-6 by Maulawi Sher Ali.
6. GUTHRIE, W.K.C. (1950) *The Greek Philosophers.* Methuen & Co, p.79
7. VLASTOS, G. (1991) *Socrates, Ironist and Moral Philosopher.* Cambridge University Press, Cambridge, p.200
8. GRAYLING, A.C. (1995) *Philosophy — A Guide Through The Subject.* Oxford University Press, Oxford, p.360
9. GRAYLING, A.C. (1995) *Philosophy — A Guide Through The Subject.* Oxford University Press, Oxford, p.364
10. VLASTOS, G. (1991) *Socrates, Ironist and Moral Philosopher.* Cambridge University Press, Cambridge, p.157
11. VLASTOS, G. (1991) *Socrates, Ironist and Moral Philosopher.* Cambridge University Press, Cambridge, p. 167
12. VLASTOS, G. (1991) *Socrates, Ironist and Moral Philosopher.* Cambridge University Press, Cambridge, p.168
13. VLASTOS, G. (1991) *Socrates, Ironist and Moral Philosopher.* Cambridge University Press, Cambridge, p.169
14. VLASTOS, G. (1991) *Socrates, Ironist and Moral Philosopher.* Cambridge University Press, Cambridge, pp. 170-171
15. VLASTOS, G. (1991) *Socrates, Ironist and Moral Philosopher.* Cambridge University Press, Cambridge, p. 173
16. VLASTOS, G. (1991) *Socrates, Ironist and Moral Philosopher.* Cambridge University Press, Cambridge, p.174
17. VLASTOS, G. (1991) *Socrates, Ironist and Moral Philosopher.* Cambridge University Press, Cambridge, p.175
18. JOWETT, B. (1989) *Plato, The Republic And Other Works.* Anchor Press, New York, p. 459
19. JOWETT, B. (1989) *Plato, The Republic And Other Works.* Anchor Press, New York, pp.460-461
20. JOWETT, B. (1989) *Plato, The Republic And Other Works.* Anchor Press, New York, p.462
21. JOWETT, B. (1989) *Plato, The Republic And Other Works.* Anchor Press, New York, p.464

22. JOWETT, B. (1989) *Plato, The Republic And Other Works*. Anchor Press, New York, pp.464-465
23. JOWETT, B. (1989) *Plato, The Republic And Other Works*. Anchor Press, New York, pp.493-494
24. JOWETT, B. (1989) *Plato, The Republic And Other Works*. Anchor Press, New York, p.495
25. *Chambers Encyclopaedia* (1970) New Revised Edition Volume XII Roskilde-Spahi. International Learning Systems Corporation Limited, London, p.673

PART II

In the second part we have included some important world religions which are generally misunderstood as Godless mere philosophies or idolatrous religions, followed by The Question of Suffering. Many of their followers are themselves unclear as to their true nature. This category contains the following:

Hinduism

Buddhism

Confucianism

Taoism

Zoroastrianism

The Question of Suffering

HINDUISM

INDUISM is a class in itself in the comity of religions. To find in Hindu literature evidence of revelation as understood in traditional Divine religions is a difficult task. This is so, mainly because on the one hand the concept of revelation is wholly confined to the Vedic teachings, while on the other, God is mentioned to have manifested Himself in human form to instruct mankind.

Though in Christianity too, Jesus[as] is described in a manner somewhat similar to that of Krishna[as], the similarity however is superficial. In the personification of Jesus Christ, God the father remains in command of the universe, and a manifestation of His sonship somehow displays itself in the human image of Jesus. Again in the case of Christianity, there is a third person entitled the Holy Ghost who is neither Christ, nor God the father, but is an integral part of the Trinity in its own right.

Hinduism however, is not clear concerning the manifestation of Brahmâ in the person of Krishna. Did he rule the heavens and the earth from his heavenly seat even when Krishna remained on earth, or was it Krishna who as God personified governed the universe during his human phase? Or was Krishna merely an apparition or icon while God remained in command in the heavens like He ever was? Questions such as these remain unanswered.

Again as far as revelation is concerned, Christianity is completely at one with the belief of traditional religions concerning the nature of revelation from on high. In Hinduism, however, the mode of revelation is not shared by traditional religions. To fulfil the role of an exemplar, God manifests Himself in human form. He does not have to employ a messenger to fulfil this task.

The case of the ancient rishis who are said to be the recipients of the Vedas is different. "Rishi" is a Hindu term for a religious divine who severs all ties with the material world and submits completely to the will of God. Despite the fact that the Vedas are believed to be Divine teachings, there is no clear account of the rishis having received revelation as a well-defined verbal message. The question whether the inspiration of rishis can genuinely be entitled as revelation will perhaps forever remain moot. What we know from Hindu sources is based entirely on their belief. Although different ages are mentioned by different scholars, they are unanimous in their claim that the rishis are the most ancient of all human beings.

This description of Hinduism is in all probability born out of human fancy. Man always interpolates, misconstrues or misappropriates Divine teachings after the prophets have come and gone. No wonder then that the messages of the Hindu prophets were also distorted by the future generations of those who followed. When we suggest that the Vedas must have been interpolated, we do not mean that all the Vedic teachings underwent a complete man-made transformation. This is never permitted to happen to Divine scriptures by God. There is always retained some of the original truth, untouched and unadulterated. It is in the light of this that a careful study of every religion at its source is always rewarding. A careful scrutiny of the source material of Hinduism reveals it to be no different from other Divinely revealed religions in fundamentals.

With a slight twist in the kaleidoscope, the perception changes dramatically. Enough evidence can be presented from the *Mahabharat* and *Bhagavad Gita* that Krishna[as] never claimed Godhead for himself, nor did he ever claim immortality. Krishna[as] can easily be identified as just another prophet of God, no different from those who appeared before or after him throughout the recorded history of religion.

As portrayed in his authentic biographies, Krishna[as] is known to have been born on earth, around 1458 BC, like any other human child, to Basudeba and his wife Deboki. They named him Kinai (Kinhai). The name "Krishna" was given to him later, meaning "the enlightened one". He is known to have led an ordinary child's life with an exceptional flare of the supernatural (which is also related concerning many other prophets of God by their followers). He lived like humans, acted like humans and attended the call of nature like humans. During his childhood, he occasionally took childish licences, like stealing a kilo or two of butter, or at least that is what is claimed by the Hindu analysts. We believe however that it was no crime on his part, children who are kind of heart do similar things in their own right for the sake of their poorer playmates. Such a child in the circumstances described generates love rather than abhorrence. All this is but human, in no way different from the birth and lifestyle of other prophets of God. He grew up to a strong adulthood and acquired and displayed outstanding qualities of leadership. In the battlefield he led great armies to epoch-making victories. In ordinary life, he rose to the exalted position of a great spiritual exemplar and performed his role as a reformer, the like of which had seldom been seen in India. He admonished people to become righteous and to eschew evil. To him it is important to destroy evil-minded people who want to wipe out religion and to promote Godlessness.

As far as his physical description goes, we do find some oddities. The image of Lord Krishna as portrayed by Hindu artists depicts him as having four arms instead of two and is also shown bearing wings. He is often portrayed standing with a flute pressed against his lips. Again, some comely maidens rather colourfully dressed are shown to throng around him. These are *gopis*. *Gopi* is a term applied to such womenfolk who tend the cows. It is a term similar to that of a shepherdess. It should be remembered here that the title of Krishna himself was that of *Gao'pal* which means "the tender of cows". This, when read together with the Biblical accounts of Israelite prophets as shepherds tending the sheep of the house of Israel, makes the similarity between the two abundantly clear. As India was a country of cows instead of that of sheep, the common people are referred to as cows. Hence for Krishna to be entitled a tender of cows, is quite understandable. Likewise, reference to his disciples as gopis presents no mystery either.

Other episodes woven around the image of Krishna can also be read as parables and allegories rather than matter-of-fact statements. As regards the image of Krishna possessing four arms and wings, it can be symbolically interpreted to mean that highly ranked servants of God are gifted with extra faculties. The Holy Quran too, mentions wings in relation to the Holy Prophet[sa] of Islam. He is enjoined by God to lower his wing of mercy over the believers. Similarly, when angels are mentioned as bearing different numbers of wings, it is their attributes which are referred to, and not physical wings.

But it often happens that religious allegories and parables are taken too literally by the followers of religions and thus their underlying significance is altogether missed. The image of Lord Krishna and what is shown to be around him, is no exception.

Krishna is also called *Murli Dhar* which means a flute player. The flute here, is evidently a symbol of revelation because the tune that the flute emits is not emitted by the flute itself. It only transmits that which is being breathed into it. Hence, it was Lord Krishna himself who has been depicted as a flute played by God. Whatever tune God played into him he most faithfully transmitted to the world. Thus the reality of Krishna can be seen as no different from that of any other messenger of God who, as a faithful custodian of Divine messages, passes them on to the world unchanged. The flute thus becomes a most expressive symbol of the integrity of prophets assuring the world that they say nothing from themselves, other than what has been revealed to them from on high.

LET US NOW TURN to another fundamental feature of Hinduism, which is shared only by a few other religions, the most well-known among them being Buddhism. We refer to the doctrine of reincarnation. This doctrine is entwined with two other Hindu beliefs relating to the eternity of the soul and that of the matter on the one hand, and the eternity of the Supreme God and other lesser gods on the other. According to this philosophy, life on earth is not generated as a completely new creation. Every living thing that exists, though not eternal in itself, is composed of eternal constituents. The mother earth to them is only a mixing laboratory where soul and parts of matter are moulded together to give birth to a myriad of living forms. Thus they believe in the creative faculties of God only as those of an apothecary or a pharmacist. He does not possess the power of a Creator who can create something out of nothing.

Their vision of the universe envisages three levels of existence. The first and the highest is occupied by Brahmâ the chief god, along with many other lesser ones. They perform various functions in the universe for which they are suitably equipped. Some are responsible for maintaining the raising of clouds or the creating of thunderbolts. Some others are responsible for the administration, maintenance and command of natural phenomena. They enjoy a measure of comparative freedom within their own respective domains and seldom come to clash with each other. But when they do, woe to the universe. Storms are raised in heaven and furies are let loose upon the earth. It always pays to be on the right side of these gods or goddesses, otherwise their displeasure could cost the mortals most dearly. There are gods and goddesses of wealth, there are gods and godesses of fertility, there are gods and goddesses of health, longevity and what not. The mythical gods who occupy this level enjoy eternity.

The second, or the middle order of existence comprises soul and matter. It is they who, when combined together, make the lowest order of existence which relates to life on earth. According to this Hindu philosophy, it is Brahmâ, the supreme among gods, who alone possesses the power to bind souls to matter for the creation of life on Earth.

How and when this exercise began and to what purpose, is discussed at length in the Hindu philosophical literature with reference to the Vedic teachings. They believe that the beginning of life on earth did not take place in the manner as prescribed by the modern scientists. It did not originate with the appearance of the most rudimentary organisms and bio-units, in the primordial soup of the oceans or upon the surface of rocks a billion years ago. Thus writes Professor J. Verman, in his book *The Vedas*:

'... those scholars whose minds have been fed with the spurious Darwinian theory of evolution, find it difficult to understand this secret of revelation. However, we have overwhelming evidences to show that man's earlier stage was a better one, and there is no ground to believe that the pre-historic men were necessarily primitive. The Vedic rishis were not simple minded people. They were poets, visionaries, and spiritualists, all the three in one. Their students who too were rishis by their own rights, were capable of understanding the real import of the mantras the moment they heard them... we are also told that there was a gradual deterioration of the psycho mental powers of the people. The generation of the seers also started disappearing.'[1]

Thus according to his understanding of the Divine scheme of things, the earth is created eternally, again and again and yet again, so also is the life on earth. At the birth of every new earth, a new world is born. In the beginning of the creation of the world, Brahmâ reveals the Vedas, the constitution of the universe, to the rishis, on the basis of which they prepare laws to govern the actions of other men on earth. So life began with the human beings rather than with other forms of life preceding them.

Another passage from the same book further elaborates the role of the four rishis sitting on the roof of the world and what they were to bequeath to the future generations of man:

'... four seers, viz. Agni, Vaayu, Soorya and Angiraa, who were really men of great intellectual excellence and spiritual eminence, being moved by the soothing and enchanting scenes of the creation, while looking around from the roof of the world, from the holy region of the celebrated Maanasarovara lake in Trivishtapa (modern Tibet), the land of the gods, across the Himalayas, the prime source of the great rivers like Ganga, Sindhu, Shatadru and Brahmaputra, surrounded by the majestic snow-capped peaks and the fascinating natural phenomena, their hearts filled with ecstasy and rapture, their senses sublimated, their souls elevated and exalted, their minds filled with quest for knowledge, in a poised receptive state of awareness, went deep into meditation and exerted themselves. Then they saw into the spheres of reality, different from the physical universe and heard the divine eternal, speech-potent sound from within, and had simultaneously, the vision of the truth...'[2]

Thus, the Vedic teachings as understood by the Hindu pundits, would have us believe that life did not evolve, but devolved. Human generations which were to be born in a distant future from the time of the great four pioneer rishis were destined to deteriorate in all their faculties in comparison to the earliest men. This declining graph in human faculties also covers their moral behaviour. In the Hindu philosophy of Karma and reincarnation, it certainly augers ill for the future of the human race. According to Professor Verman:

'Destroying future life means, preparing to be born among species of living beings inferior to human beings. This is the fruit of action, this is the punishment for bad actions. The punishment comes in the form of deprivation of the various human faculties and organs of sense and actions. This is the doctrine of karma, and this is the system how the divine jurisprudence functions; this is called the rule of law in nature.'[3]

We believe that by attributing this doctrine to the Vedic teachings, the Hindus have done no justice to the honour of the Vedas. If such statements are to be taken seriously, the story of the origin of life will have to be rewritten altogether. In the new vision of the origin of species, Karma would certainly play the most pivotal role.

The struggle for existence, survival of the fittest and the genetic mutations which the evolutionists so fervently talk about, would be rejected outright as mere figments of science fiction without an iota of substantial evidence to support it. The only key that would remain to unlock the riddle of life would be Karma.

Following this cue we can safely infer that life began its journey with the creation of holy men of the highest order, but as future generations were born, they began to deteriorate mentally, physically and spiritually. It did not take them very long to fill the earth with sin. With sin, comes Divine punishment and they rapidly began to lose their human status. They must have been deeply dismayed and shocked to watch the transformation of humans into animals of the lower order, but they had only to blame their own sins. The law of Karma must operate and the sins must take their toll. Hence it should not have been an uncommon experience with them to witness the birth of numerous new animal species instead of normal human babies during the course of reproduction.

But perhaps this is not how the Hindu religious scholars envisage the origin of species and how Karma operates. In the absence of a clear-cut statement on this point, one can only attribute to them some possible interpretations within the framework of their overall belief. Perhaps they envision the unfolding of the mysteries of life on earth in a different pattern. As man began to deteriorate during his journey away from the time of the four rishis, his reproductive faculties began to dwindle and an epidemic of sterility broke out. Rapidly the number of humans began to reduce and surprisingly a myriad of various animal species began to spring forth from the surface of earth.

The earth split open here and there, as the elephants and the lions erupted. So also appeared the cats, the dogs,

111

the hyenas and the wolves. From water emerged the fish in all shapes and colours, in multiple measure and sizes while the turtles did not lag far behind. Suddenly the insects invaded the animal kingdom, like locusts appearing from nowhere. Underneath such visible forms of life, the invisible kingdom of bacteria and viruses must have proliferated far more rapidly. But alas, despite all the attempts and warnings of the four rishis, man refused to submit and continued to rebel against the Vedic teachings. As a natural consequence of their sin, reincarnation of humans into lower forms of animal species must have run amok as if with a spirit of vengeance.

Finding no more space on the flat surface of the earth or in the depth of oceans, man began to be born within the human gut as well. What of the roundworms, the flatworms, the tapeworms and the threadworms — who would not even take pity on infants — there were an untold number of other viral or bacterial guises in which the erstwhile humans must have invaded the human body in the blood stream, in the capillaries, in the cellular tissue of flesh and the vital organs. The lymph would not be spared, or the bone marrow for that matter. What an ingenious plan to have man punished by his own hands. Yet, he would not see.

An extremely interesting scheme of things no doubt, in support of which Professor Verman claims to possess 'overwhelming evidence'! The only little snag we find in this scheme is the fact that humans continue to become more sinful with the passage of time, yet they are not diminishing in number. On the contrary, their population is exploding.

This takes us back to the ancient time when life just began with the creation of four rishis and a myriad of common men. If man was at his best in spiritual and social conduct at the time, then there was no question of his transmigration into the lower species after that generation had died. The scheme of Karma guarantees that as long as this state of piety was maintained by man, no animal species could have been created. They could only be created as a result of punishment to a sinful generation of humans.

PROFESSOR VERMAN seems to have an answer to this dilemma. Human generations, as they moved away from the pious generation of the rishis, began to disintegrate in their character. Evidently therefore, the moment man became sinful, the gates for the creation of other animal species were flung wide open. From then on, there was no dearth of sinful human souls to be condemned to the rank of subhuman species during their reincarnation.

But such a scheme could only work if the total population of humans at that time were a billion or more times greater than their number today. The total number of animals belonging to all the species of life runs into trillions upon trillions upon trillions. Hence, it can be safely inferred that all these animals from bacteria upwards must have been human once. That being so, the human population, at the time of the great holy rishis must have been astronomical, defying all calculations. In such a case, this earth had to be a billion times more massive than it is today to accommodate the entire human populace of God-fearing ancient followers of Vedic Dharma.

Incidentally, scientists also inform us that the land of Tibet, where the four great rishis are related to be sitting at the beginning of time, was not yet created. It came into being much later — a billion years ago, as a result of continental drift and the subsequent collision between their plates. This clash of claims, between the geologists and the Vedic authorities, casts some shadow of doubt on the scenario of the four rishis, serenely watching the world go by from their lofty post on the Tibetan high planes. But of course the Hindu scholars, like Professor Verman, have a right to dismiss this geological yarn to be as hollow and devoid of sense as the theory of evolution. This too, should be chucked into the rubbish bin of scientific hallucinations into which the theory of evolution had been earlier dumped.

Turning again to the issue of the human populace, which sprang from the holy loins of the great rishis, it must have swelled to enormous dimensions because it was they who were to be the great-forefathers of all the animal species to follow. It would be their sinful souls who would be demoted to the rank and file of the lower animal kingdom. The size of the human population at that time had to comprise the total number of animal species which were to be born after. One is indeed confounded to visualize such a colossal number of humans squirming, wiggling-waggling like mountains of worms on the surface of this tiny planet Earth. All that could be surveyed from any rooftop anywhere, call it Tibet or the Himalayas, would be humans, humans everywhere, and not a morsel to eat.

Re-examining the issue of Karma, let us now return to a purely academic discussion. The fate of every generation of life hinges entirely upon the Karma of its previous generation. The soul in itself is a neutral entity; so also is the matter to which it is bonded. As such the real question which Hindu sages try to resolve, relates to the wisdom behind the creative policy of God. If He is a just God, they argue, why should He display partiality to some over others? It is to answer this apparently unanswerable question, that they present the philosophy of the eternal unending circle of deeds and corresponding rewards or punishments. For the transmigration of souls it is this priniciple which works as an ongoing circle of cause and effect, crime and punishment, goodness and reward. As against this view, the image of God perceived by other major religions of the world is that of an All-Powerful Supreme Being, who can create at His own Will whatever He pleases. As such, He is the Supreme proprietor of all creation, enjoying absolute liberty to dispose of them as He pleases. His hands are free. He can make whatever He likes. The principle of justice in relation to the choice of His creation does not apply. However, by virtue of being All-Wise, All-Fair and All-Powerful, He provides to perfection all that is needed by any animal species, internally and externally. Thus an amoeba could be as happy and content within his tiny insignificant domain as a great king sitting on his majestic throne.

Such is not the freedom which can be justifiably enjoyed by the supreme god of Hindu mythology. Not being their creator, he has no right to interfere with the freedom of the soul and matter subjecting them to his slavery. There is also the question of choice at every act of creation. Why should one be made better than another, or placed higher in the order of creation? Why should one be born in the stately palace of a king or be delivered in the gloomy emptiness of a pauper's shack?

It is this dilemma which necessitates the provision of some manner of justification for God in relation to His multifarious scheme of creation. The Hindu philosophy resolves this question by suggesting that God never takes an arbitrary decision in His capacity as a Creator. Contrary to the rest of the world's religions, they see the earth as a place of punishment and reward. The conduct of life on earth, according to this philosophy, will directly bear upon the future shape to be granted to it in its next incarnation. The supreme god Brahmâ adjudges every act of life during its sojourn on earth. The future rests upon its own Karma.

Life and death are interwoven as parts of an eternal scheme of goodness and reward, crime and punishment. But the problem is that, when the soul is picked by God from its abode in space and brought down to Earth to be bonded with matter in the form of some species of life, it is at that instant that a term of imprisonment is imposed upon it without a previous Karma. It is this first imprisonment which constitutes a glaring violation of justice and fair play on the part of God Himself, justly warranting His own incarnation into the lowest forms of animal species.

Returning to the discussion of how Karma works, it should be understood that it is an extremely intricate scheme which takes into account even the minutest variations in the good or bad conduct of life on earth. These variations could help God to pronounce a punishment to be harsher or milder or a reward to be lesser or greater.

Every crime would not necessarily result in the transformation of every sinful human into another animal. A person who was a king during his previous incarnation for instance, could be turned into a poorly beggar during the next. Likewise, a beggar could be transformed into a Royal Highness during his next incarnation, all depending upon their respective bad or good conduct in the sight of God, during their previous term of life on earth.

As already explained, depending on the merit of each case a species can be transmigrated into any other during its reincarnation. A human in his previous incarnation could as well be turned into a worm in his next. An unpleasant surprise indeed, but one should thank one's own sinful stars for that.

Where does the chain begin? That is the real question — an insoluble eternal enigma. If every reincarnation requires a previous incarnation then how would the chain begin? Surely, it cannot be done by simply pushing the cause and effect chain further back in time. This would require all life forms with their respective Karmas to be eternal. A proposition which even the most zealot of the Hindu pundits could not endorse because the eternity of animal life would render the act of creation redundant and meaningless. The only other alternative is to perceive Karma, and its consequences in the form of a chain which is linked together in a circle. But this is not possible either, because even such an unending circle of Karmas and their resultant reward or punishment, cannot be possible without a beginning and an end. An eternal circle of cause and effect can only be logically entertained if it comprises identical links. If there is a change in the nature of links, the beginning and the end can immediately be identified. Links which show for instance, a downward or upward trend of deterioration or improvement cannot be organized into an eternal circle.

Let us return our gaze once again to the Vedic scenario of the beginning of life and the origin of species. If it is a circular chain, as the Hindu theologians insist, then after the deterioration has reached its maximum, the chain must become unidentifiable from the links which mark its beginning. After the human species has been wiped out from the face of the earth, all that is left is the animal life of lower order, constantly sliding down the scale because of their persistent sinfulness. The only task left now would be to link them to a new beginning of life on earth, so that the circle is completed. Life on earth according to the Vedic teachings, as we have already seen, always begins with the four rishis reclining on the Tibetan roof of the world. How on earth could the vermin and insects and centipedes and rats and skunks (the end products of the sinful humans), be hooked on to the lofty start of life in the holy personages of the four rishis to complete the circle! The circle of transmigration we have just described, can neither be linked onto its beginning nor can it be described as eternal, because eternity demands an unbroken continuity.

If the end of the chain has to be linked on to this beginning, the consequences are too horrendous for anyone to visualize. Imagine a serpent sitting coiled with its tail held in its mouth. No sane observer can call it an eternal circle with no beginning, no end. A tail is a tail, even if securely pressed under the teeth. This circle will have a head and it will have a tail; it will have a beginning and it will have an end. No man with the slightest respect in his heart for the great rishis (four in number) would permit himself to envision their rebirth out of a tail made up of the lowliest forms of animal existence.

We do sincerely hope that no Hindus, educated or uneducated, subscribe to this bizarre fantasy of an eternal circle. Nature debunks this notion absolutely. There is not the least evidence to support it.

The issue of Karma should also be examined from another angle. The term Karma applies to all actions for which the actor is answerable, i.e. he will be rewarded if the action is good, and punished if it is bad. This requires that the Divine Will must be clearly expressed, regarding the goodness or badness of actions, otherwise no one can know as to what God approves or disapproves. It is for this specific purpose that the four great rishis are placed in the beginning of mankind. If Vedic teachings had not been revealed to them, humans could not learn what was good or bad for them, hence they could not be held accountable for their Karmas. Thus the principle of Karma can only be applicable to humans alone, who are provided with a clear charter of do's and don'ts by the pioneer four rishis.

When it comes to animals, other than humans, the problem becomes rather complicated. Do all species have their own well-defined books based on Divine law? If not, how would they conduct themselves and how could their Karma be adjudged? Will their intuitive behaviour replace the Divine teachings? If it is the intuitive behaviour which fills the void of Divine teaching among animals, then how can they exercise any free choice?

Again, in humans, the Divine teachings are vouched through the human agency (the four rishis were no doubt human). But it is somewhat difficult for one to perceive the office of prophethood being discharged by animals. Every species has its own limited sphere of understanding, with a specific ingrained way of life. If prophets are to be sent to them, they must be sent separately to each species. If animal rishis are to be born among them they have to be born equally among the lions, the brown bears, the white bears, the hyenas, the reptiles, the fishes of all sorts and the birds of all feathers. Can one imagine for instance a prophet crow or a rishi wolf?

But that is not all. If instincts replace the Divine teachings and works as the animal code of life, then the same question of choice in relation to the instinctive animal behaviour will have to be raised and answered. Can they accept or reject instinctive trends? It is instinctive to a horse to eat grass or grain, could a horse possibly defy this Divine injunction? In case he chooses to be wicked, can he possibly change his diet from vegetable to flesh, thus blatantly violating the Divine law of instinct? In such a case, of course that horse could justifiably be punished by God for being a wicked horse. Perhaps the most likely punishment for him during his next incarnation would be a transformation into a donkey or a dog. What if that donkey also persists in the misconduct which was responsible for his degenerate birth and chooses to remain carnivorous, relishing dog meat more than green grass. What would be his next incarnation one wonders — maybe he would be turned into a dog, left at the mercy of other wicked donkeys — God knows best.

We are building this hypothetical scenario, only to bring to the surface the underlying absurdities in the philosophy of reincarnation, based on the current Hindu understanding of Vedic teachings. It is farthest from our intention to hurt anyone's sensibilities.

The same hypothetical illustration applies to the entire animal kingdom. If a lion, for instance, will be adjudged goody-goody and noble only if he remains true to his instinct, then his disregard for the sanctity of life will be a sure sign of his nobility. If on the other hand he abandons eating flesh, showing a wanton disregard of his noble instinct, then such a beastly vegetarian lion is likely to be demoted during his reincarnation to, maybe, a carrion eating vulture. Thus the beasts of the jungle could only be adjudged gentlemen by God, if they continue to follow their ungentlemanly instincts.

It should have become apparent by now, that in no way can intuitive animal behaviour be treated as a Divine code of life, as long as the animals are deprived of the freedom of choice. If, however, the advocates of The Vedas insist that the instinctive animal behaviour is a substitute for a Divine law, then all animals must be promoted to the human rank during their next reincarnation because they follow their instincts meticulously — much better than humans ever follow Divine laws. It is an extremely dangerous proposition. It would lead inevitably to the total extinction of non-human life, culminating in a most gigantic explosion of human population, pushing man back to the beginning of time. Will there be any food for them to survive, or will they turn to cannibalism as a last resort? Allah knows best.

To the good fortune of the human race, however, no plan of Karma can conceivably work among the non-human animals. Once condemned to be animals, souls can in no way regain their lost human heights ever again. Thus the scheme of Karma would swing the fate of man from one extreme to another. Which of the two would he opt for if ever he were to make a choice? Neither, of course, if he has an iota of wisdom. Not to be is the only sensible option.

We consider it proper to observe here that the Hindu doctrine of transmigration of the soul also offers a third option, but only for the insignificant few. Such humans as lead a life of perfection, like the four ancient rishis for instance, are not recycled immediately, but there is a long intervening period of relief for their souls. This is the vision of Hindu Nirvana or heaven. But this period of rest, even if it runs into millions of years, must come to an end. At last, such souls having enjoyed their Nirvana must return to earth for reincarnation.

But this critical appraisal of Hindu mythology has been carried too far afield. The Hindu religious scholars may claim the right to divorce their faith from reason as has been often done by the followers of some other religions. In that case, despite anything proved to the contrary, they would still maintain that somehow a balance is juggled by God between various animal species, and they are all judged by some invisible system of Karma.

Each individual belonging to any species of life is judged in accordance with its Karma. If a man misconducts himself, he would also be transmigrated into an animal of a lower order during his next visit to earth. Likewise, an animal with good conduct could be raised to the status of a human in his next incarnation. A well-behaved dog for instance, could be born into the house of his earlier master as the master himself, while the wicked master could be reborn in his own house as a dog to his new human master (ex-dog).

It is evident that this philosophy has its internal logic. Although God appears to be an absolute dictator Who despite having no right subjugates free soul and free matter to an eternal chain of slavery, He does so on the basis of a system of justice. He presses soul and matter together, always as a reward or a punishment for their Karma in their previous earthly sojourn. Also as already mentioned, there remains a chance, however thin, for a soul to gain Nirvana which is a temporary deliverance from material bondage. Hence what we despise as death could in fact be a great benefactor which liberates the soul from body, its corporal partner. For how long shall the separated couple enjoy their deliverance from each other, is a question which will be decided in relation to their conduct during their wedded life on earth. If they had conducted themselves ideally – the physical body taking good care of the soul and the soul discharging its responsibilities to the physical body – the longer would be their reward of separation. No different would be the fate of married couples. The noblest among them who have the ideal relationship as husband and wife, most satisfied with each other's pleasant loving company, would no doubt be awarded the Nirvana of the highest order. This means that their souls will be separated not only from their bodies but also from each other for an extremely long time bordering on eternity. The sinful couples, however, may be despatched to earth soon after they both finally die, to yet another even longer spell of each other's company of sinful carnal pleasures! Good Heavens! What a Hell on Earth and what a Heaven in heavens!

TO A SCIENTIST, the Hindu philosophy of life, death, and eternity may appear devoid of sense and reason, yet it cannot be denied that this philosophy has a special charm about it which keeps many a modern man and woman enchanted by it, without bothering about its rationale. The most powerful attraction it possesses lies in the hope that one would return to this miserable earthly life again. Man is the strangest of all the living paradoxes. All his life he continues to complain against the strings of miseries attached to life, hoping for death to sever them, yet how he longs to return to the same earthly dungeon again!

The imprisonment of life and the bondage of sorrow are in fact one and the same thing. How can deliverance from sorrow be possible without death? Yet how he yearns at the same time to pay an unlimited number of visits to the same wretched abode. Evidently, the charm of this philosophy lies in the universal love of life ingrained in the fibre of the living.

Yet, those infatuated by this promise of another tomorrow, should not forget that human society as a whole has substantially deteriorated in moral and religious conduct. For such as these to entertain the hope to be reborn as humans yet again, is a dream most unlikely to be fulfilled. If the Vedic philosophy of Karma is right then most probably the majority of the humans of today will be reborn tomorrow as monkeys, wild boars, crocodiles or mere worms. To live again is good indeed but will it be worth the risk at such a price?

Returning to the issue of the four rishis – the recipients of the Vedas – if one accepts the time scale in which they are fitted, they must have been born aeons before life began on earth, in an age when the earth's atmosphere was empty of oxygen. What Karma preceded their promotion to the rank of rishis, is the question. Who could survive in an oxygen-free atmosphere generation after generation after generation and what did they feed upon is no less an important question. All that polluted the oceans and the air was rudimentary forms of viruses and bacteria. Either the first generation of these holy men survived on this staple food or maybe human life began on earth not with holy men but with holy viruses and pious bacteria. If the time calculations regarding the appearance of the four rishis or other holy men on earth is erroneous, if they did not appear on earth as early as maintained by some scholarly pundits then the beginning of life on earth and the Vedas had to have happened much later. Their appearance upon earth could not be possible before the Tibetan archipelago came into being. In fact the entire Indian subcontinent was shaped similar to what we find it today, some time between twenty million and forty million years ago. Although India had been carved into a sub-continent around one hundred and sixty million years ago it had yet to begin its merger with the rest of Asia. It was this merger which in fact was responsible for the eruption of the Himalayas and other great mountains including the Tibetan archipelago. It matters little when exactly Tibet was created within this time scale. The evidence of fossil remains proves beyond a shadow of doubt that life had begun some eight hundred million years before the creation of the Indian subcontinent. Whoever and whatever they were who sat on the top of the Tibetan plateau could not have been human because humans appeared on earth much later. At that time the most advanced form of life that had evolved was dinosaurs. Evidently one cannot conceive a dinosaur rishi by any stretch of one's imagination. Hence, if the Vedic teachings in their interpolated form as we find them today are to be taken literally, then the rishis and their holy companions must have landed on earth from some alien planet. But this solution, if at all worthy of being called a solution, would create a far more intricate and utterly absurd problem to solve. The story of Karma will have to begin not with the four rishis but with the weird and varied forms of life emanating and evolving from the first bio-units on earth a billion years ago.

An unprejudiced appraisal would clearly reveal that the doctrines of Karma and reincarnation are the products of a decadent age of Hindu philosophy. It must have happened when the Hindu theologians attempted to find answers philosophically to the enigma of life and death, reward and punishment, by themselves, without enlightenment from on high. Still, it is not impossible to trace the elements of Divine revelation in the Vedas. The elements of ignorance which we find therein today must have been the product of human interpolation from that which was interpolated into the Vedas by the human hand.

Before ending this discourse, we would like to examine the nature of yoga, and where it fits into the vast intricate network of Hindu philosophy. It is of special interest to the main subject of discussion, because it is widely claimed that through deep contemplation, a yogi can reach the fountainhead of knowledge and truth within himself. However, it is not at all easy to determine with any measure of certainty whether the yogic system is Hindu in origin or Buddhist. It is an instrument of learning which at least Lord Krishna is never reported to have employed.

But that is not all there is to yoga. Apart from its meditational value, yoga is also a highly developed physical science, which attempts to promote the latent qualities of human physique to their maximum. Miraculous deeds are reported to have been performed. It is even claimed that through yoga one can reach a state of almost perfect hibernation, whereby the metabolism is brought to a near standstill and life seems to hang by its finest thread. Some yogis, having mastered the art of yoga, are said to have lived for days submerged under water. Some reports even speak of their uncanny ability to de-materialise at one place and materialise at another. Some exaggeration indeed!

Yet some other special powers developed through yogic practices, cannot be waived off as mere exaggeration. For instance, some yogis are known to have held their breath for so long, that an ordinary man would die many a death during the same period without breathing. Again, yoga is a form of exercise which helps to improve the quality of human physique in every sphere of its functions. It is also acclaimed as an excellent remedy for the alleviation of physical and psychic tensions. We have briefly discussed the yogic potential for improving the physical qualities of man and developing some latent possibilities in him, which otherwise would remain dormant. The same can also be spiritually enhanced by disciplining the human ways and conduct of life.

Now we explore these possibilities with reference to the yogic system. The yogis claim that they can reach the fountainhead of inner truth merely through the instrument of contemplation and inspirational yogic practices. How far they are right or wrong, is only a matter of opinion. Unless an inner truth, discovered with the help of yogic practice, is presented to the world as a solution for human problems, one is not in a position to accept or reject this claim. The maximum that can be granted in this regard is the fact that yoga in itself is an excellent code of exercise.

REFERENCES

1. VERMAN, J. (1992) *The Vedas*. Oxford & IBH Publishing Co. PVT. LTD, New Delhi, p. 6
2. VERMAN, J. (1992) *The Vedas*. Oxford & IBH Publishing Co. PVT. LTD, New Delhi, p. 4
3. VERMAN, J. (1992) *The Vedas*. Oxford & IBH Publishing Co. PVT. LTD, New Delhi, p.24

BUDDHISM

THE GENERAL IMPRESSION that prevails in the world about Buddhism is that it is a philosophy of life which, though counted among religions, does not prescribe to the existence of God. This impression is only partially correct. Even in contemporary Buddhism, it is wrong to say that none of the Buddhists believe in God or gods. Although the predominant sects, Mahayans and Theravadins, are known to believe only in the ultimate inherent wisdom in man which Buddha[as] perfected, they too believe in many superstitions and demonic figures which substitute God for them. This impression of the Buddhists' negation of God is also wrong on another count. An exploration of early Buddhist sources as we shall demonstrate, reveals ample proof that Buddhism began like any other Divinely revealed faith with its emphasis on the Unity of God.

BUDDHA - As presented by the Buddhist religion

As for the position of Buddha (563-483 BC) among the Buddhists, although he is not directly worshipped as a deity, there is very little difference between the veneration shown to the Buddha by the Buddhists and the manner of worship of God found in other religions. They revere him and pay homage to him, bow to his images and statues and prostrate before them like the adherents of any other idolatrous religion in the world.

In fact, despite the denial of God by most Buddhists, deep within their hearts there seems to be lurking a desire to worship something. It is this which is manifested in their veneration of Buddha. The same unquenchable innate thirst for God etched deep upon the human soul urges them to worship Him, or something, if not Him. So it is to fill this void that the Buddhists worship the Buddha without formally recognizing him to be a god.

It must also be mentioned here that in the Tibetan form of Buddhism not only is the existence of superhuman deities or demons a part and parcel of their faith, but also they certainly believe in communication with them. The selection of a new Panchen Lama for instance, requires many rites and rituals to be performed, to obtain guidance from gods as to which one of the newborn Tibetan children should be the future Panchen Lama.

Among the so-called atheistic Buddhist sects, it is commonly alleged that Buddha himself denied the existence of God. They support their claim by pointing at the hostility shown to Buddha by the contemporary Hindu pundits. That hostility, they maintain, was largely due to the contempt shown by Buddha to their gods. The Buddhists in general do not bother to analyse the real factors at work which generated misunderstandings leading to the persecution of Buddha. It is quite sufficient for them to believe that Buddha must have rejected the idea of God in totality.

However, as we shall presently establish by re-examining some facts of history and some important relevant passages in the Buddhist sacred literature, it can be clearly shown that Buddha[as] is absolved from all such allegations. Yet it must be said, at the very outset, that the historical evidence to which the adherents of both view points refer, is in itself meagre. This difficulty, however, can be offset to a large degree by having recourse to other circumstantial evidence.

The Buddhist philosophy, teachings and practices remained to be transmitted only verbally for almost five hundred years after Buddha, except in the case of inscriptions on the rocks and stupas made during the illustrious reign of Ashoka (273-232 BC). Ashoka, it should be remembered, appeared some three hundred years after his spiritual master, Buddha[as]. This fact in itself is of vital importance because these writings can certainly serve the purpose of judging Buddha's philosophy and way of life from the vantage point of Ashoka. Moreover, at a time when nothing of Buddhism was committed to writing, it was Ashoka alone who left behind a written account of what he understood to be Buddha's teachings. Again, his authority as a true representative of Buddha has never been challenged. What remains therefore, is simply a case of different interpretations.

As far as the story of Buddha is concerned, although it too was committed to writing many centuries after his demise, it has been unanimously accepted by all researchers without serious disagreement. This knowledge seems to have been passed on from generation to generation. Hence the personality of Buddha and his lifestyle appear to have a continuity, beginning from Buddha himself to the present day.

From this, it is reasonable to conclude, that an understanding of Buddha and Buddhism which accords with these two sources i.e. the life of Buddha and the writings on the stupas, should have the stronger claim to acceptance. Against this, such views as are clearly at variance with them may safely be rejected. However, if the early sources seem to contradict each other, caution has to be applied in accepting one and rejecting the other.

A close examination of Buddha's biography reveals that in his lifestyle, he was not any different from other prophets of God, who appeared in different parts of the world. There is a universality about the character and style of prophets which can also be discerned in the life of Buddha.

Coming to the issue of the fundamental beliefs of Buddhism, the problems begin with different interpretations of what he is known to have said or done. We disagree with the commonly held view that Buddha was an atheist. We maintain that Buddhism was a Divinely revealed religion. We emphasize the fact that the founder of Buddhism was certainly not an atheist, but was a man commissioned by God Himself, to deliver His message in the style that all other messengers were raised.

Most scholars who write about Buddhism are out of their depth in trying to justify the placing of Buddhism among the great religions of the world. To do that they have to change the universally accepted definition of religion so that it also accommodates Godless philosophies and religions. Why should a code of conduct which starts its journey with a denial of God be admitted into the comity of religions, is the question. As far as our view is concerned, no such objection can be raised on this count. We on our part reject the premise that Buddhism had no Divine origin. To support our contention we shall have recourse to the same well-established sources as the Buddhists themselves rely on and demonstrate that our interpretations have a stronger basis for acceptance. We repeat that Buddhism is no oddity among religions; on the contrary, its fundamental characters are at one with the rest of the Divinely revealed faiths.

The erroneous popular belief in the Godless origin of Buddhism was spread largely by the Western scholars of the eighteenth and nineteenth centuries. Their knowledge of Buddhism was largely based on the translations of Buddhist literature from the Pali language by Buddhist scholars who had permitted their own biased, godless philosophy to influence their translations. Few among them understood the Pali language, which is the language of the source material. Moreover, instead of drawing their own inferences directly from a study of reliable Buddhist sources, they leaned entirely on the beliefs about Buddhism prevailing among the major Buddhist sects.

CONTRARY TO this general trend of Western scholars, a solitary voice in India was raised by Hazrat Mirza Ghulam Ahmad[as] of Qadian (1835-1908), who presented a diametrically opposed view. He maintained that Buddha[as] had firm belief in the existence of God who Himself had raised him as His messenger with a specific mission to perform. He demonstrated that Buddha[as], like all other prophets of God, also believed in the existence of Satan, as well as in heaven and hell, in angels and in the Day of Resurrection. Hence, the allegation that Buddha[as] did not believe in God is pure fabrication. What Buddha rejected was *Vedanta* (i.e. doctrines and beliefs found in the Hindu sacred books, the Vedas). He rejected the belief in corporeal manifestations of gods as found in Hinduism. He was severely critical of the Brahmans and regarded them to have corrupted their Divine teaching through their distorted interpretation.

The voice of Hazrat Mirza Ghulam Ahmad[as] was not to remain solitary for long. Soon, other voices from among the second generation of Western scholars and researchers on Buddhism began to follow suit. The most prominent among them was the great French scholar Dr Gustav Le Bon (1841-1931) who writes:

> Unfortunately, the study of Indian monuments has been completely neglected by European scholars. The specialists of Indian studies, through whom we

have come to learn of Buddhism, had never visited India. They had only studied this religion in books; an unfortunate twist of fate made them chance upon the works of philosophical sects written five or six centuries after the death of Buddha, these being absolutely alien to the religion practised in reality. The metaphysical speculations which had so astonished Europeans by their profoundity were in fact nothing new. Ever since the books of India have been better known, these have been found in the writings of philosophical sects which had developed during the Brahmanic period.*[1]

So far, Dr Le Bon seems to be perfectly right in his criticism, but as is apparent from the following text, he himself committed the same mistake of not deriving the concept of true Buddhism, strictly as it is presented by the writings on the stupas — which never mention Buddhism as polytheistic. In the words of Dr Le Bon:

It is not in the books, but in the monuments that one should study what Buddhism used to be. What the monuments tell us differs strangely from what certain books teach us. The monuments prove that this religion, which modern scholars want to see as an atheistic cult, was, on the contrary, the most polytheistic out of all the cults.*[2]

It is this last part of his statement which is false as will be presently shown.

After Dr Le Bon, another renowned scholar, Arthur Lillie drew a completely different conclusion from his careful study of the inscriptions on Ashoka's stupas. He amply quotes them in his book, *India in Primitive*

---

* Both these passages have been faithfully translated from Dr Le Bon's original book which is in French.

Christianity. It should be noted that these inscriptions were not etched solely on the stupas which were specifically built for this purpose, they were also discovered upon the faces of huge rocks situated on highways and trade routes. We present below two examples of such inscriptions from Lillie's translations.

On the Eastern bank of the river Katak, twenty miles from Jagan Nath, there is a rock by the name of Pardohli upon which is written:

'Much longing after the things (of this life) is a disobedience, I again declare; not less so is the laborious ambition of dominion by a prince who would be a propitiator of heaven. Confess and believe in God (Is'ana) who is the worthy object of obedience. For equal to this (belief), I declare unto you, ye shall not find such a means of propitiating heaven. Oh strive ye to obtain this inestimable treasure.'[3]

Is'ana, mentioned in this inscription is the name of ShivDevta – God. (See *The Sanskrit/English Dictionary* by Shivram Apte).

On the seventh Stupa the same writer quotes:

'Thus spake Devanampiya Piyadasi: "Wherefore from this very hour, I have caused religious discourses to be preached, I have appointed religious observances that mankind, having listened thereto, shall be brought to follow in the right path, and give glory to God* (Is'ana)." '[4]

From these references it becomes obvious that the early sources portray Buddha[as] as a dedicated believer in God (may He bless his soul).

---

* The usage of the word God in singular is highly significant.

The second source material in order of credibility and authenticity, is such Buddhist literature as came into being five hundred years after Buddha. This too contains enough evidence to indicate that Buddha was neither an atheist nor an agnostic but was indeed a believer in God. We specifically refer to the *Theravada* texts known as *Tripitaka (Three Baskets),* which as the name suggests, are divided into three sections. The first part is called *Vinaya-Pitaka (Rules of Conduct),* the second is called *Sutta-Pitaka (Discourses on Truth)* and the third is called *Abhidhamma-Pitaka (Analysis of Religion).*

In *Sutta-Nipta* there is *The Chapter on Going to the Far Shore,*[5] in which the goal of conquering death is expressed. Buddha explains that birth and death do not mean anything to those who have overcome their ego thus becoming at one with God. These passages may have been misunderstood and confused with the Brahman concept of *Mukti* (redemption), but it is not right. Buddha clearly speaks of only those who have already reached the other side of the barrier here on earth before their death. This simply means that according to him, no man could have access to the hereafter, unless he had experienced it during his life here on earth, a teaching close to the Quranic precept. He preached that by being at one with God, man rises above life and death and becomes eternal.

At the end of the chapter, Pingiya, a follower of Buddha describes the excellence of his master which becomes instrumental in converting him to Buddhism. Having already expressed that he was enfeebled by old age and close to dying, Pingiya concludes his discussion with the following statement:

'Assuredly I shall go to the immovable, the unshakeable, the likeness of which does not exist

anywhere. I have no doubt about this. Thus consider
me to be one whose mind is so disposed.'[6]

This illustrates the hope and expectation of a disciple
of Buddha, that after his death he will meet his Lord, who is
described as immovable, unshakeable and without likeness.
This is a description of God in full agreement with that
found in other scriptures.

There is another interesting account giving further
information about Buddha's beliefs found in *Sutta-Pitaka*
—the second part of the *Tripitaka* texts, subdivided into
five books containing many of the Buddha's dialogues. The
president of the Pali Text Society of London, Mrs T.W.
Rhys Davids has translated some of these dialogues into
English and her translation can be found in a series of
books entitled *Sacred Books of the Buddhists.* Dialogue
number thirteen of the second volume entitled *Tevigga
Sutta,* deals specifically with the question of how man can
be led to God.

In response to this question, Buddha first rejects the
suggestion that anyone among the Hindu clergy of his time
was capable of leading man to God, then he answers the
question as he understood it himself. The background of
how and where this dialogue took place is quite interesting.

It is said that once upon a time there used to be a
famous Brahman village by the name of Manasâkata. This
village was situated at a most scenic spot of the country
beside a beautiful river. Its fame had reached far and wide
because it was the centre of Brahmanic religious
controversy. Five of these Brahmans were especially
distinguished and led the school of their respective religious
ideology. It so happened that Buddha also alighted by the
same river along with his chosen disciples. The news
spread and people began to pay him visits to enlighten
themselves on Buddha's doctrine and hear about Buddhism

from his own lips. Once, Vâsettha and Bharadvaga of the same village, while taking a walk after their bath in the river, began to debate a religious doctrine. Neither of the two could convince the other of the correctness of the opinions of their respective gurus. Vâsettha, the young Brahman, suggested that it should be taken to the court of Buddha. This agreed upon they proceeded to present the issue to Buddha seeking his wise council. During the meeting, Bharadvaga, the young Brahman, remained silent and Vâsettha asked the questions. Before responding to the question, Buddha posed some counterquestions.

First he asked, 'Did any Brahmans versed in the Three Vedas, ever see Brahmâ face to face?' The answer was 'No'. Then Buddha asked Vâsettha if any of the Brahmans or their pupils of the previous seven generations had seen Brahmâ, and the answer was again, 'No'. Then Buddha asked them if they themselves claimed that they had ever seen Brahmâ. Again the answer was, 'No'. Then he asked Vâsettha that if a man, born and brought up in Manasâkata was asked the way to Manasâkata, would that man be in any doubt or difficulty in answering that question. Vâsettha answered:

'Certainly not, Gotama! And why? If the man had been born and brought up in Manasâkata, every road that leads to Manasakâta would be perfectly familiar to him.'

At this point Buddha expounded:

'That man, Vâsettha, born and brought up at Manasakâta might, if he were asked the way to Manasakâta, fall into doubt and difficulty, but to the Tathâgata,' (the fully enlightened one, meaning himself), 'when asked touching the path which leads to the world of Brahmâ, there can be neither doubt nor difficulty. For Brahmâ, I know, Vâsettha, and

the world of Brahmâ, and the path which leadeth
unto it. Yea, I know it even as one who has entered
the Brahmâ world, and has been born within it!'[7]

Buddha's argument was that the residents of
Manasâkata should clearly know the roads leading to
Manasâkata. Any claimant belonging to God, must also
know the path leading to Him, but it would only be possible
if he had come from God and had known Him personally.
But the answers to the counter questions of Buddha clearly
showed that none of the gurus had either seen God or had
any personal knowledge of Him. Hence, the identity of God
was completely outside and beyond their understanding. Up
to this point of the dialogue, Buddha's arguments may have
been misunderstood by some to mean that Buddha was
declaring there was no God because nobody had met Him.
Indeed, the translator in her introduction has suggested that
the whole line of argument followed in this discourse is:

'... only an *argumentum ad hominem.* If you want
union with Brahmâ — which you had much better
not want — this is the way to attain to it.'[8]

But this analysis of the discourse shows a total failure
on the part of the author to understand what Buddha
positively proves. It illustrates how some researchers have
been influenced by the beliefs of the Buddhist monks who
had misread Buddha's heroic campaign against his
contemporary order of the Brahmans. What he categorically
rejected were their superstitious beliefs in godlike figures,
which they had neither seen nor heard from. But Buddha's
answer did not end there. He went on to claim that for the
Tathâgata, there could be no such difficulty in pointing out
the way to God. He went on to claim that he himself was
the one who could lead man to God because he had been in
communion with Him and had come from Him.

It should by now have become obvious that Buddha did have faith in the existence of one Supreme God and it was from Him that he claimed to have come. He knew Him better than the villagers of Manasâkata knew their own village or the roads leading to it. Here Buddha asserts for himself a life of constant communion with God, a state which stands higher in order of nearness to Him than mere revelation. Many great prophets have made similar claims of witnessing a life of eternity with Him here on earth, even before death transports them to the otherworldly life. They, all the Divine messengers, share this eternal state of communion with Him, Buddha being no exception. Buddha referred to God as Brahmâ, because this was a familiar term to the Hindus, who applied it to the Supreme God among their gods. As the dialogue continues, the position is made even clearer.

> 'When he had thus spoken, Vâsettha, the young Brahman, said to the Blessed One:
> 'So has it been told me, Gotama, even that the Samana Gotama knows the way to a state of union with Brahmâ. It is well! Let the venerable Gotama be pleased to show us the way to a state of union with Brahmâ, let the venerable Gotama save the Brahman race!'[9]

Having heard Vâsettha, Buddha does not reject his prayer and aspirations with reference to Brahmâ as unreal and meaningless; a definite proof of his approval of whatever he spoke of the Brahmâ and His communion with His chosen ones.

For people who respond to the call of God, irrespective of their caste, the path to God is made easy for them. For one who fears God, all human passions such as anger, jealousy, prejudice etc., cease to dominate him. When one transcends them, one is likely to imitate Godly attributes and acquire them. This whole dialogue is worthy of special attention by those who want to understand Buddha's attitude towards Him.

So why should Buddha have been misunderstood by his own followers? An answer to this question may lie in earlier Buddhist history and the conflict between the newly emerging religion of Buddha and the older religious order of Brahmanism. They attributed to Buddha their own views, not a rare phenomenon with religious clergy, or they might have misunderstood him in good faith. When Buddha waged war against the prevalent idolatry, to which the Brahmans of the time were entirely dedicated, he was accused of denying the existence of God. This propaganda, carried out by a powerful class of Brahmans, was so loudly proclaimed that the voice of Buddha was drowned in their tumultuous antagonism.

Considering the difficulties of communication and lack of writing facilities, it is not at all unlikely that this propaganda not only found favour with the Hindus, but also influenced the followers of Buddha. Ultimately, they themselves began to believe that Buddha's rejection of the Hindu gods was total. Thus Gotama Buddha's denial of the gods of the Brahmans was overgeneralized and led many to maintain that he did not believe in any God.

As far as their allegiance to Buddha is concerned, it remains untouched. They had accepted Buddha as an all-wise teacher, so kind, so loveable, so humane. We are talking of an age when literacy was at its lowest level. The common people would often make their decisions on hearsay, hence the followers of Buddha themselves could have been carried away by this Brahmanic propaganda. But it created little effect upon their loyalty to him. For them it was sufficient that Buddha was the perfect source of wisdom. As such they revered him and continued to follow him with all their heart, as their beloved and all-wise master. Slowly and imperceptibly, however, this so-called Godless master of theirs began to be revered as God himself.

It had not happened for the first time in the history of religions. How often oracles had been transformed into gods and humans raised to the level of deities! In the case of Buddha however, all the forms of their love and attention remained centred upon Buddha as a human paragon of perfection and he was not literally raised to the mythical concept of godly figures. For them, it was sufficient to place the Brahmans on one end of the spectrum and Buddha on the other. To them the Brahmans stood as oracles of legends and myths, while Buddha personified truth, wisdom and rationality. Thus, gradually Buddhism acquired a character where the belief in a legendary god had no role to play. Whatever the urge in human nature there is for believing in God, it was progressively filled with the image of Buddha. So Buddha, who in the eyes of his followers of the fourth century, had started his journey as just a source of absolute wisdom, began to rise to a status much higher than can be filled by an ordinary secular philosopher. In his case, he did not remain a mere symbol of mundane wisdom for long, but began to command such high respect and veneration as is commanded by God, or gods, among religions.

We are not talking here of a short period of a few years. It might well have taken centuries for the shadow of atheism to have cast its ominous spell over a large part of the Buddhist world. Again, it may also have taken centuries for the Buddhists to ultimately build a god out of Buddha, without naming him so. The manner in which we suggest the transformation of Buddhists took place from believing in God to a Godless people, is not merely conjecture. A study of Buddhist sources, as we have demonstrated, fully supports the view that Buddha[as] was a believer in One Supreme Creator. What he rejected was polytheism. This is the true image of Buddha which survived untarnished for the first three centuries despite the best efforts of his enemies. Here we take the reader's mind once again to the age of the great Buddhist monarch Ashoka, who ruled a vast Buddhist empire which extended beyond the boundaries of India covering the whole of Afghanistan. It is he who possesses the most authentic and unquestionable authority on the teachings and the ways of Buddha's life. There is no shadow of doubt that what he portrayed Buddha to be was simply a messenger of God who founded his teachings upon Divine revelation. Whatever he conveyed to mankind was only what he was commissioned to, by their Supreme Creator. It is this verdict of Ashoka which is indelibly etched upon the rocks of history.

Asceticism or Escapism

Renunciation of the world and the severing of worldly ties is considered as the ultimate means in Buddhism for the complete liberation of self from anguish and misery. It takes an ascetic to understand the problems associated with the conflicts between the soul and the mundane temptations of life. Unless one is endowed with exceptional qualities of patience and resolution, this challenge seems insurmountable. But in this lies the only hope offered by Buddhism. A total renunciation of all that life is made of and a total withdrawal from the allurements of life is the only path to Nirvana, the eternal peace.

The complete denial of all passions is therefore claimed by the Buddhists to be the absolute truth. The greed for material wealth, for power, or even for the love of others, when unfulfilled, results in the agony and frustration of the deprived. Similarly, hatred also plays havoc with one's peace of mind. All these forces weaken the spiritual powers of man. This also emphasized that because man's intrinsic nature cannot be changed and his lust for evermore cannot be stilled, full contentment and satisfaction can never be achieved without severing all ties with matter.

This for the Buddhists is a starting point upon a long journey of denial to reach the ultimate goal of redemption. He has to deny all that life requires for its comfortable existence in a material sense. It is a struggle of denial relating to all the five senses. A denial of what the eyes require, and what the ears crave for, a denial of touch, taste and smell, a denial of all which agitates human hearts. They seek to avoid all dangers of addiction by avoiding all situations in which there is a threat to man becoming involved and enslaved by material influences. In short, the Buddhist concept of peace through denial is simply another name for escapism. To live is the problem, to die is the solution.

Rather than attempting to struggle and conquer the baser motivations and to bring them under the command of the soul, the soul is advised to beat a retreat and vacate the arena of life on earth. All that is born out of desire to satisfy one's ego, is lowly, materialistic, ignoble and should be sacrificed for the sake of the ultimate good of the same ego. The peace achieved through such an escape amounts to little more than death i.e., the negation of life.

Peace can be of two types. Death can also be classed as peace; to draw a line between peace and death is not an easy task. For instance, a compromise with defeat and resignation to a state of dishonour can serve as a case in point. The contentment of victory and the calm of surrender, though similar, are in reality poles apart. One is life and the other is death. The identification and classification of religions, at times, becomes difficult because of this attendant confusion. Each religion seemingly invites to the same ultimate goal of peace and contentment. Yet there are some which prefer a peaceful surrender to death rather than to die for a noble cause and there are those who raise the banner of a holy war to be fought against evil at all costs. All challenges to absolute morality are taken on bravely and roundly defeated. The calm that ensues is the true Nirvana.

Religions such as the decadent form of Buddhism admonish their adherents to find peace in the haven of escape. They teach escapism from all temptations which may lure them to their natural desires, urges and cravings. A Buddhist would withdraw to the safety of his inner self – a state described vaguely by some as an emptiness – by others as something which is eternal and possesses the qualification of being without substance. Are they talking of God? One may wonder! But opinions differ. Most believe that it is a state shared and understood only by those who reach it. If it is not an ultimate return to God, and most Buddhist scholars will refrain from admitting the existence of God in any form, then the only valid definition for this emptiness is absolute annihilation and total death.

In short, all natural urges related to the five senses which constitute life are denied with a finality for gaining absolute peace or Nirvana. Of course, all the adherents cannot reach that goal simultaneously, but all true adherents are required to continue to endeavour to achieve it step by step, as they advance to the precipice of annihilation.

To illustrate this point further, let us relate an episode which we find so befitting in helping the reader to understand the specific point we are raising. There used to be a beggar in Kashmir, who was half mystic and half beggar. He begged for the barest necessities of his life and no more. He was often found lost in contemplation and reverie, delving deep into his own self in search of something. Once a sage walked past him and suddenly noticed that he was no longer the same person, because he was bubbling with joy and dancing with ecstasy.

'Baba why this great transformation? You do not seem to be the same pauper any more. Whatever have you achieved?' were the questions. 'Have you chanced upon a treasure?'

'Yes,' was the answer. 'A priceless, peerless treasure! Why should not one exult at the fulfilment of all one's desires?'

Having received this reply, the sage inquired, 'You are clothed in the same rags and tatters, covered from head to foot in dust like you ever were, how then can you claim that all your desires are fulfilled?'

The beggar dismissed him with a wave of his hand, staring at him with a gaze of profound wisdom and said, 'Remember this, that one's desires are only fulfilled when he is left with no desires. Such is my great moment of liberation. Off you go and leave me to dance.'

A beautiful answer, leaving the sage absolutely nonplussed. But looking at it once again, one is bound to admit that the answer of the beggar was as beautiful as it was empty. No change had taken place beyond the confines of his limited personal world. The world around was the same miserable world of sorrow, suffering and pain. The world around him was the same world of tyranny, oppression and despotism. He still needed something to live by – food, water and air were as indispensable to him as they ever were. Of desires one may get rid, but not of needs.

Whatever change was brought, was brought about within himself. But who knows whether it had come to stay forever. Maybe it was just a brief moment of triumph. Maybe on a chilly night with freezing cold, he would desire to have some warmth around, some clothes, some shelter, some hearth. Maybe if he fell ill, he would feel the need of a healer and pray for one. With what surmounting resolve would he conquer such challenges of the hard realities of life? Only a Buddhist sage would know the answer. It was only a subjective feeling of fulfilment and no more. In truth it was an absolute resignation to the state of helplessness – call it peace or call it death, by whatever name you may, it is not entitled to be called true Nirvana.

The search for peace through complete denial of all that relates to life and supports it, seems to have taken hold in both the major Indian religions, Hinduism and Buddhism. This is tantamount to denying the struggle for existence and the survival of the fittest. In application to the human pursuit of peace, this can only mean surrender and acceptance of defeat.

Here we are not discussing the teachings of the founders of Hinduism or Buddhism, but are merely examining the philosophies that have resulted after thousands of years of decadence. Both have moved far away from their Divine origin. In fact they have followed the same course as is followed by mysticism or Sufis in other major religions of the world. In their case, the latter do not break their ties with a belief in God; instead within the framework of a Divine religion, they carve their own domain of subjective spiritual experiences which result from inspiration rather than revelation.

In the case of yogic philosophy in Hinduism and Buddhism, both are completely broken away from their traditional teachings without a trace of the original to be found in them. As against revelation, which was the ultimate source of enlightenment of Buddha, the emphasis during the later ages kept shifting from revelation to inspiration, contemplation and reverie. In a strange way, despite the fact that Buddhism at its beginning was at complete odds with Hinduism, both joined forces later in the philosophy and practices of yoga.

It is amazing that the first mention of yogic teachings is only found in the *Tantras,* the so-called religious documents, which were compiled at least five hundred years after Buddha[as]. These documents were only for the eyes of a few who comprised the supreme Buddhist hierarchy and were kept under strict secrecy from the common people. To doubly reassure their secrecy they were written in such cryptic language and terminology as would be impossible for an ordinary person to understand. Much later, the contents of the *Tantras* became accessible to scholars who were horrified to find this so-called sacred literature to be extremely profane and indecent. There are mentions of demons and frightful phantom images. They are also full of vulgar language speaking of obscene and sexual desires in a manner as jars the human sensibilities. As such, the yogic teachings as contained in the *Tantras* have no connection whatsoever with the holy words of Buddha[as].

Maybe all the talk of demonic nonsense and sexual vulgarity are symbols and allegories. Perhaps no living monks share the secret of such cryptic language. Maybe the Buddhist hierarchy of two thousand years ago were the only people who invented this jargon and understood its meaning. But they are long dead and with them has died the age of the *Tantras.* Yoga however, has outlived the cryptic in the *Tantras.* There are scholars who still understand and implement the subtle science of yoga contained in the *Tantras.*

It is hard indeed to draw a clear-cut line between the yoga as understood and practised in Hinduism and the yoga as understood and practised in Buddhism. If there are any minor differences, they merely belong to nomenclature. Call them Hindu hermits or Buddhist ascetics, the reality of their withdrawal from the world, for the sake of God, will not change. Give them any name possessing the same meaning, it would not make the slightest difference to their holy identity. Whatever they find and whatever they consider enlightenment to be, neither has ever been able to change the face of the world with their subjective experiences. It is a dishonour for Buddha[as] and Krishna[as] to be counted in this category. They were revolutionaries – like all other prophets of God, whose philosophy of the spiritual and moral revolution sprang forth from the fountainhead of revelation. They gave a call for a noble struggle against falsehood and evil. They sounded the bugle for a heroic strife in life which was not just subjective. It was an outward, outgoing holy war, which came into headlong clash with the forces of darkness. A dire struggle for the survival of the fittest ensued. The life histories of Buddha[as] and Krishna[as] clearly present them as belonging to this category. They are only warriors, not suicidal escapists. Their faiths were products of revelation. Their teachings gave birth to inspirations, but were not born out of them.

The understanding of the majority of present day Buddhists appears to be that their religion is just a wisdom, *budhi,* discovered by Buddha through meditation. All that is claimed of their philosophy is that it was an inspiration of Buddha.

From the vantage point of those who believe in God, inspiration is nothing but a psychic experience in which many a time one feels spiritually elated. During this phase of elation, one experiences a sense of peace which seems to be the very ultimate of tranquillity. Returning from this ecstatic state to normal life, one has a strong impression of having gained something which might well have been the very purpose of life – the goal which mankind is striving to reach.

This psychological experience is all that they can boast of as spiritual enlightenment and redemption from the bondage of matter. Even at its very best, it cannot change any objective realities or reform the wicked people. It cannot transfer a jot from the world of the unknown to the world of the known – it cannot change darkness into light. Never has inspiration been able to retrieve the unknown events buried in the graves of history, nor has it ever been able to leap into the future to catch a glimpse of events to come.

If the philosophy of absolute self-negation is followed to its logical conclusion, it will inevitably lead to the extinction of the human race. To ascribe this inspirational jibberish to the Divinely enlightened wisdom of Buddha[as] does him no honour; this is not the Divine cup of revelation from which he drank deep and became immortalised!

REFERENCES

1. LE BON, G., GUIMET, E. (1992) *Mirages Indiens:de Ceylan au Népal, 1876-1886.* Chantal Edel et R. Sctrick, Paris, p.241

2. LE BON, G., GUIMET, E. (1992) *Mirages Indiens:de Ceylan au Népal, 1876-1886.* Chantal Edel et R. Sctrick, Paris, p.240

3. LILLIE, A. (1909) *India in Primitive Christianity.* Kegan Paul, Trench, Trübner & Co, London, p.85

4. LILLIE, A. (1909) *India in Primitive Christianity.* Kegan Paul, Trench, Trübner & Co, London, p.86

5. NORMAN, K.R., (1992) *The Group of Discourses* (Sutta-Nipata). Vol II. The Pali Text-Society, Oxford, pp.112-129

6. NORMAN, K.R., (1992) *The Group of Discourses* (Sutta-Nipata). Vol II. The Pali Text Society, Oxford, p.129

7. MAX MÜLLER, F. (1881) *The Sacred Books of the East.* Vol. XI, Clarendon Press, Oxford, p.186

8. MAX MÜLLER, F. (1992) *Dialogues of The Buddha I.* The Pali Text Society, Oxford, p.299

9. MAX MÜLLER, F. (1881) *The Sacred Books of the East.* Vol. XI, Clarendon Press, Oxford, p. 186

CONFUCIANISM

ONFUCIANISM is a treasure house of profound wisdom. A study of this religion reveals that rationality, revelation and knowledge go hand in hand in leading man to truth. Although many Chinese consider it to be a religion on the pattern of other Divinely revealed religions of the world, there are others among them who view it as a mere philosophy. In Japan, for instance, Confucianism has no geography of its own. The followers of Taoism, Shintoism and Buddhism equally believe in Confucianism as a philosophy compatible with their own. Hence they coexist in a diffused form, unheard of in the case of other religions of the world.

When we speak of Confucianism being treated as a mere philosophy, we particularly have in mind the question of the existence of God. Few followers of Confucius (550-478 BC) today have a clear belief in any Divine existence. Yet they believe in the world of spirits and souls, and some even practise ancestor worship. However we believe that a reappraisal of the currently popular understanding of Confucianism is vital.

Examining the early texts upon which Confucianism is founded, there is no doubt that this religion too is squarely built on a sound belief in the existence of God. It owes much of its philosophy and wisdom to revelation, rather than to the contemplations of wise men.

The extent to which this religion has deviated from its original course can be measured by the currently popular spirit-worship, so commonly found among the adherents of Confucius today. In the source material of Confucius however, there is not the slightest hint of any such superstitious beliefs and practices. Evidently therefore, as happened in the case of other religions, Confucianism also drifted away from its original sources with the passage of time. Many superstitions and erroneous practices crept into it at the cost of the belief in one Supreme God. A tragedy, alas, which is repeated only too often.

As for ancestral worship, they do not treat them as gods or saints, yet, many beg favours from them. But in Japan this worship does not have the same meaning as understood elsewhere. It is merely an expression of respect and loyalty to the memory of the dead. Not everyone begs for things from the souls of the dead, and do not treat them as independent gods. A perfect symmetry and coordination in the laws of nature prove beyond a shadow a doubt that if this universe is created, it must have been created by a single Supreme Being. There is not an iota of trace of two or three creative hands at work in nature. It is quite logical to conclude from this that the deep innate desire to believe in something must have been created for the purpose of creating a linking bridge between the Creator and the creation. When this communion is not established the absence of Divine revelation leaves a void which must somehow be filled by that fundamental urge. It is that urge that creates gods for itself whether they are souls, spirits, ghosts or other ethereal beings. Hence to believe in superstitions is not accidental. The phantom figures of gods found among the superstitious people are like the images of ghosts born during the absence of light.

This decadent trend gradually pushes the image of God out of the arena of religious beliefs. The belief in God requires reformation in one's conduct and consequent accountability, while the spirits, ghosts and other ethereal beings demand no submission to any moral religious code.

FROM an in-depth study of classical Confucian literature, it is not difficult to prove that Confucianism is not a man-made philosophy at its origin. It did embrace the idea of one immortal God, from Whom its teachings originated and Who is believed to govern the universe. "Heaven" is a manifestation of that God, and as such sometimes He Himself is referred to as Heaven. Confucianism considers true knowledge to consist of understanding the attributes of God and adopting them in one's own conduct. This brings man closer to eternal truth and serves as a source of knowledge for his benefit.

The history of Confucianism and Taoism goes as far back as the time of Fu Hsi, (pronounced as Foo She) (c. 3322 BC), who was both a king and a great sage. Once, in a vision, he saw a horse dragon rising from the Yellow River which had a diagram on its back. This is not the only incident of Chinese history regarding a prophet learning things through his vision. Prophet Yu (c. 2140 BC) is also recorded benefitting from Divine revelation. In the vision of Fu Hsi he had the opportunity to study the diagram. The diagram consisted of eight sets of three male and female lines. The combination of these trigrams into upper and lower pairs provides sixty-four hexagrams. The significance of each hexagram is depicted by its name and is related to the particular arrangement of male and female lines. It is reported of a sage, King Wan (c. 1143 BC), that he was the first to write down the interpretations of these hexagrams. His son, Cheu Kung (c. 1120 BC), added to these explanations and later Confucius added his commentary to it in the form of appendices. This was the development of Fu Hsi's vision into the *Book of Changes* known as *I Ching (or Yi King)*.

An understanding of the principles of this theory (the theory of the eight trigrams) influenced the growth of many a science and discipline in Chinese life pertaining to all fields of human interest. It is said that in China this philosophy played a vital role in the development of agriculture, industry, medicine, economy, politics and many other fields of knowledge. One Chinese scholar, Chou Chih Hua, writes in his book *Acupuncture and Science*[1], that the theory of eight trigrams has the same relationship with Chinese medicine as mathematics has with European science. According to the book *History of Medicine of China*[2], Fu Hsi, the prophet who formulated the theory of the eight trigrams through revelation, also discovered the science of medicine and acupuncture. However, some believe that this knowledge was developed in a later period by the sage King Huang Ti, who in turn had derived his knowledge from the *I Ching*.

Master Sun's *Art of War*, which also uses the *I Ching*, is famous in the military world. Military people throughout the ages have given importance to this book, which has been translated into six different languages. Chinese logicians and the various ancient classical schools of thought also based their theories on the principles outlined in the *Book of Changes*. To a minor degree the *Book of Changes* has also influenced the Western world, where the *I Ching* has gained in popularity, although some use it only as a kind of oracle for fortune telling.

According to Confucianism, formal academic study is not essential for the attainment of truth. God Himself is Truth, so whatever He creates He blesses it with this same quality central to His own identity. Thus human nature and eternal truth have become synonymous in Confucianism.

Mencius (372-289 BC) was a Chinese philosopher, theorist and educationalist. He was also a very religious man and a prominent personality among the followers of Confucius. He left a great impression on Chinese philosophy, so much so that some consider him to be a prophet. Explaining a way of reaching eternal truth, he is reported to have said:

> 'Benevolence, righteousness, propriety, and knowledge are not infused into us from without. We are certainly furnished with them. *And a different view* is simply from want of reflection. Hence it is said, "Seek and you will find them. Neglect and you will lose them."'[3]

Here, the external source being denied by Mencius is not revelation. Rather, he points out that our moral qualities, which are an essential element of our being, do not come to us from outside. Mencius expressed the view that sensory experience does not give us a new message by itself. In the mirror of sensory experience, the human mind can see the external images of its inner nature. Thus he does not deny the benefit of objectivity, what he denies is its independent potential in leading man to truth. All the same he admits that objective experience can be greatly helpful in guiding us to the innate fountainhead of eternal truth. Mencius further expounded that nature, by which he means the entire cosmos, itself is not eternal but created for us by "Heaven" and "Heaven" is a sensible Creator. Explaining this, Mencius said:

> 'It is said in the *'Book of Poetry'*:
> "Heaven, in producing mankind,
> Gave them their *various* faculties and relations with *their specific* laws.
> These are the invariable rules of nature for all to hold,
> And *all* love this admirable virtue." '[4]

The term "Heaven", as understood by Mencius is a Conscious Being and it is interchangeable with our term of

God. Heaven may be seen to symbolize the active and conscious creative principles of God. Thus he says:

> 'This is illustrated by what is said in the 'Book of Poetry,'—
> "Be always studious to be in harmony with the ordinances *of God*,
> So you will certainly get for yourself much happiness;" '[5]

Classical Confucianism, undoubtedly, presents man as a creation of God rather than just a product of unconscious nature. For Confucius, the ultimate goal in attaining knowledge of one's own nature is to attain harmony with God, and this is the ultimate of man's vision of heaven. This belief is quite similar to the Quranic teaching in presenting man as having been created according to God's attributes.

$$\text{فِطْرَتَ اللهِ الَّتِىْ فَطَرَ النَّاسَ عَلَيْهَا} \quad 30:31$$

> ... and follow the nature (attributes) of Allah after which He fashioned all mankind...[6]

Confucius further propounded that man has to make a conscious effort to first gain knowledge of this image of God, latent within his nature, and then to develop within himself attributes that accord with this image. If he does not make this conscious effort, then there is no guarantee that man's moral development will, as a matter of course, be in the image of God.

According to Confucian understanding, knowledge as an entity does not exist in isolation from man's actions and character (his virtue, dignity and propriety). The two are deeply linked, as the following reference reveals:

> 'The Master (Confucius) said,

"When a man's knowledge is sufficient to attain,
and his virtue is not sufficient to enable to hold,
whatever he may have gained, he will lose again.
When his knowledge is sufficient to attain, and he
has virtue enough to hold fast, if he cannot govern
with dignity, the people will not respect him.
When his knowledge is sufficient to attain, and he
has virtue enough to hold fast; when he governs also
with dignity, yet if he try to move the people
contrary to the rules of propriety:- full excellence is
not reached." '7

It is also evident that Confucius was convinced that
man's Creator has great influence over him and that He
alone was worthy of his worship. This is revealed by the
following tradition:

'Wang-sun-Chiâ saying, (to the Master Confucius):
"What is the meaning of the saying, It is better to
pay court to the furnace than the southwest corner?"
The Master said, "Not so. He who offends against
Heaven (God) has none to whom he can pray." '8

To offend against the creative principles of God is to
act contrary to the inner nature of man, which God has
designed to be a reflective mirror of His own attributes. The
one who turns away from God has none else to turn to.

The above quotes serve to illustrate that at its source,
Confucianism cannot be treated as a man-made philosophy.
At its core, it contained the essential belief in an externally
existing Creator, whose ways are to be revered and
emulated. They further illustrate that mere knowledge,
devoid of the essential ingredients of seeking God and
putting into practice His ordinances, was considered to be
of no value.

Furthermore, as will become evident from the quotes
furnished below, Confucianism presents God (or Heaven)

as a Being Who takes an active interest in the welfare and development of mankind. The necessity of upholding the value of Truth is established by God, through His choice of suitable people to establish truth for the guidance of man.

The Chinese sages can be considered to be the equivalent of prophets as mentioned in the Quran or the Bible, i.e. men who are representatives or messengers of God. We find this similarity expressed in a statement attributed to Confucius.

> 'The Master was put in fear in K'wang.
> 'He said, "After the death of King Wăn, was not the cause of truth lodged here *in me* (Confucius)?
> If Heaven had wished to let this cause of truth perish, then I, a future mortal, should not have got such a relation to that cause. While Heaven does not let the cause of truth perish, what can the people of K'wang do to me?" '[9]

Here Confucius expresses his complete conviction that the eventual transcendence of truth was assured by an unchanging decree of God in whose safe hand he was a mere instrument. God does not allow those He has directly guided to perish without having accomplished their task of establishing truth, even though they may stand alone against seemingly all-powerful odds. This is exactly the picture given of the prophets in the Bible and the Quran. Those who are worthy to be chosen for such tasks are men who have excelled in emulating God's attributes.

> 'Confucius said, "Great indeed was Yaou as a sovereign. It is only Heaven that is great, and only Yaou corresponded to it. How vast was his virtue! The people could find no name for it." '[10]

In other words, through emulating God, his qualities became so great that people could not find adequate words to describe him:

> '*Chang* said, "I presume to ask how it was that *Yaou* presented *Shun* to Heaven, and Heaven accepted him; and that he exhibited him to the people, and the people accepted him." '[11]

Again these verses make it clear that Heaven is not the cosmos, nor the inner micro-universe of a person, but an active and conscious being, synonymous with the term God. As Heaven chooses sages according to certain criteria, so God chooses the prophets. Our proposition that Chinese sages are considered to have the same qualities as those of the prophets of the Bible and the Quran, has been well served by the references presented above.

A further study of the Confucian text illustrates that revelation was not only a means of establishing the true philosophy of life, but was also of practical value in guiding man's actions in everyday life. We have already mentioned Fu Hsi's vision and its application in a practical way to many aspects of Chinese civilization — an influence that lasted for many millennia. Below we present some other examples where revelation played a role in influencing the material well-being of a nation:

> ' "... When the king speaks, *his words* form the commands *for them;* if he do not speak, the ministers have no way to receive their orders." The king on this made a writing, and informed them, saying, "As it is mine to secure what is right in the four quarters *of the empire,* I have been afraid that my virtue is not equal *to that of my predecessors,* and therefore have not spoken. *But* while I was respectfully and silently thinking of the *right* way, I dreamt that God gave me a good assistant, who should speak for me." He then

161

minutely described the appearance of the person, and caused search to be made for him by means of a figure throughout the empire. Yuě, a builder in the country of Foo-yen, was found like.

On this the king raised and made him his prime minister, keeping him also at his side.

He charged him, saying, 'Morning and evening present your instructions to aid my virtue...' '[12]

Here, it is claimed that the King had no way of knowing how, or by whom, his difficulties of government could be overcome, but he was granted an answer by God through a dream.

Again it is related of the great Sage, king Wǎn:

'God said to king Wǎn,
'Be not like those who reject this and cling to that;
Be not like those who are ruled by their likings and desires;"
So he grandly ascended before others to the height [of virtue].
The people of Meih were disobedient,..."
'God said to king Wǎn,
"I am pleased with your intelligent virtue,
Not loudly proclaimed nor pourtrayed,
Without extravagance or changeableness,
Without consciousness of effort on your part,
In accordance with the pattern of God."
'God said to king Wǎn,
"Take measures against the country of your foes.
Along with your brethren,
Get ready your scaling ladders,
And your engines of onfall and assault,
To attack the walls of Ts'ung." '[13]

This illustrates the process by which God chooses His servants, who are to represent His cause. First, God guided and instructed King Wǎn, who responded by putting His advice into practice and thus rose in status in the eyes of God.

The concluding verses of the above quote are reminiscent of David in the Bible who was also a prophet and a king. Just as David was given permission to attack his enemies, who sought to wipe out the cause of truth, so too was King Wăn. A comparative study of religious history reveals other similarities between the experiences of King Wăn and the Prophet King David[as], but we shall not enter into this lengthy discussion here.

With the help of the references quoted above, it should become amply clear that in the Chinese religions and philosophies, revelation has a significant place and is an important means of attaining the truth. Many other examples from the Chinese classics also demonstrate that Confucianism cannot be considered merely a man-made philosophy of life, which has no belief in an external God. On the contrary, God is an intrinsic part of this faith and whatever was received through dreams and visions, is most definitely attributed to communication from God.

REFERENCES

1. CHOU, C.H. [year unknown] *Acupuncture and Science*. 1st ed. Shi-Wei Typographic Co., Ltd., Taiwan

2. ZHENG, M.Q., LIN, P.S. [year unknown] *History of Medicine of China*. Shang Wu Printing and Publishing House, Taiwan, pp.2-3

3. LEGGE, J. (1985) *The Four Books*. The Great Learning, The Doctrine of the Mean, Confucian Analects and the Works of Mencius. 2nd ed, Culture Book Co., Taiwan, p.862

4. LEGGE, J. (1985) *The Four Books*. The Great Learning, The Doctrine of the Mean, Confucian Analects and the Works of Mencius. 2nd ed, Culture Book Co., Taiwan, p. 863

5. LEGGE, J. (1985) *The Four Books*. The Great Learning, The Doctrine of the Mean, Confucian Analects and the Works of Mencius. 2nd ed, Culture Book Co., Taiwan, p. 544

6. Translation of 30:31 by the author.

7. LEGGE, J. (1985) *The Four Books*. The Great Learning, The Doctrine of the Mean, Confucian Analects and the Works of Mencius. 2nd ed, Culture Book Co., Taiwan, pp. 354-355

8. LEGGE, J. (1985) *The Four Books*. The Great Learning, The Doctrine of the Mean, Confucian Analects and the Works of Mencius. 2nd ed, Culture Book Co., Taiwan, pp. 152-153

9. LEGGE, J. (1985) *The Four Books*. The Great Learning, The Doctrine of the Mean, Confucian Analects and the Works of Mencius. 2nd ed, Culture Book Co., Taiwan, pp. 231-232

10. LEGGE, J. (1985) *The Four Books*. The Great Learning, The Doctrine of the Mean, Confucian Analects and the Works of Mencius. 2nd ed, Culture Book Co., Taiwan, p. 632

11. LEGGE, J. (1985) *The Four Books*. The Great Learning, The Doctrine of the Mean, Confucian Analects and the Works of Mencius. 2nd ed, Culture Book Co., Taiwan, p. 793

12. LEGGE, J. (1865) *The Chinese Classics*. Vol. III, Part I, The Shoo King. Trübner Co., London. pp.248-252

13. LEGGE, J. (1871) *The Chinese Classics*. The She King, Part III. Decade of King Wăn Book I, Vol. IV, Part II, Trübner and Co., London. pp. 452-454

CONFUCIUS
(As depicted by Chinese literature)

I.1

LAO-TZU
(As presented in Chinese literature)

I.2

TAOISM

ALL CHINESE RELIGIONS are derived from the same ancient source of spiritual and religious experiences of the great Chinese sage prophet Fu Hsi. In the subsequent ages, many a great sage and thinker pondered over the works of Fu Hsi and studied them in-depth. Based on their study they presented to the Chinese people new philosophies, sciences, religions and moral teachings. Among them are King Wăn, his son Cheu Kung and Lao-tzu, all held in great esteem by the Chinese people of all ages. The way of life presented by Lao-tzu (6th century BC), a contemporary of Confucius, is known as Taoism.

In Taoism, eternal truth is embodied in a being known as Tao whose attributes are spiritual and holy rather than material. Tao can be aptly defined as a personification of eternal virtues. They are precisely the same attributes as ascribed to God in Islam and other Divinely revealed religions. Taoism teaches man to completely submit to Truth (Tao), and to strive to modulate Tao. Tao is the model, and Taoism is the way to gain nearness to this model.

The same is the treatment in the Holy Quran regarding the relationship between God and man:

2:139 *صِبْغَةَ اللهِ وَمَنْ أَحْسَنُ مِنَ اللهِ صِبْغَةً وَّنَحْنُ لَهُ عٰـبِدُوْنَ

The hues of God! And who is more beautiful in hues than God? – and Him alone do we worship.[1]

165

In Islam God is described and introduced through His attributes and the goal set for Muslims is to emulate them to modulate their lives. The description of Tao, presented by Lao-tzu, is quite similar to the attributes of God mentioned in the Quran. He writes:

'The great Tao is vast. He is on the left and He is on the right. All creatures depend upon Him, and the care of them tires Him not. He brings creation to completion, without seeking reward. He provides for all His creation, but requires nothing for Himself, so He may be considered small. All creatures turn to Him for their needs, yet He keeps nothing for Himself, thus He may be named 'the Supreme'. He does not consider Himself great and because of this He is truly Great.' [2]

Again we have another description:

'Looked for but not visible, such a Being may be colourless. Listened for but not heard, such a Being may be called Silent. Grasped for but not caught, such may be called Concealed. No one can comprehend the ultimate source of these three qualities, but they are found in one Being. Though not luminous yet below Him there is no darkness. Being infinite He cannot be described. All His shapes keep returning to nothingness, thus we can say He is Shapeless; His image is without form. He is beyond comprehension (being the rarest of things). Try to reach His beginning, no beginning can be seen. Seek His end, no end can be perceived. Therefore, follow the ancient ways and improve your present.' [3]

Also, in another verse the description of Tao runs as follows:

'He is indivisible and His true nature cannot be grasped. All creation originates from Him. He existed before heaven and earth were created. He is One and alone without form or sound. He exists independently without any support. Nothing changes in Him. He is in constant motion, but never tires. He can be called the Begetter of the universe.'[4]

The description of Tao given in the above passages is also found in different verses of the Quran, which when read together, reproduce everything covered by the above quotes. The image of God thus described in the Holy Quran, is summed up by the founder of the Ahmadiyya Muslim Community, the late Hazrat Mirza Ghulam Ahmad[as] of Qadian (India), in the following words:

'He is near yet far, distant yet close... He is highest of high, yet it cannot be said that there is anyone below Him farther than He. He is in heaven, but it cannot be said that He is not on Earth. He combines in Himself all the most perfect attributes and manifests the virtues which are truly worthy of praise.'[5]

It is pertinent to note that Chinese philosophy had its roots in religion, but with the passage of time its religious origin was obscured. Its followers adhered to the philosophy itself but thought it unnecessary to have any direct link with the source which had nourished it in the past. Consequently, the image of God was gradually impersonalised and the followers of Tao ceased to cultivate a personal relationship with Him as a Supreme Conscious Living Being.

IN SHORT, like Confucianism, Taoism too at its source believed undoubtedly in a living, personal God to be the Eternal Truth. In the original works of Taoism or Confucianism, it was not considered sufficient just to gain an intellectual understanding of Tao, but the entire goal of life was set to mould one's character and actions according to the concept of Tao.

However, in the source material of Taoism, as quoted above, the belief in Tao as an eternal intelligent creator has over the ages been obscured. But the idea of revelation itself is still retained, though only under the guise of inspiration. A conspicuous shift from Divine revelation to inspiration without a Divine origin, marks the trend among the spiritual thinkers of the later ages until no trace of Divinity is left in their writings. Inspiration to them became purely an internal phenomenon, which through deep contemplation and meditation could lead to the fountainhead of truth within oneself.

To delve deep into one's nature can of course lead to the discovery of inner truth, but the Tao experience of inspiration as quoted in the authentic Taoist works is not entirely internal. With them inspiration has its own limitations — it cannot lead to objective truth which lies beyond the reach of the person who undergoes an inspirational experience.

The very foundation of Taoism is based on the great vision of Fu Hsi. The definition of inspiration however extended, can in no way be applied to that vision. When interpreted, it comprises such fountainheads of knowledge as were to give birth to many highly evolved and complex Chinese philosophies and sciences much later in time.

This is sufficient to illustrate the case in point. Inspirations cannot give birth to prophecies; no way can they lead to such future events as stand witness to the existence of an All-Knowing Supreme God by their realizations.

REFERENCES

1. Translation of 2:139 by the author.
2. DAN, L (1969) *The Works of Lao Tzyy*. Truth and Nature. The World Book Company, Ltd. Taipei, Taiwan, China. Ch.34, p.17
3. DAN, L (1969) *The Works of Lao Tzyy*. Truth and Nature. The World Book Company, Ltd. Taipei, Taiwan, China. Ch.14, p.6
4. DAN, L (1969) *The Works of Lao Tzyy*. Truth and Nature. The World Book Company, Ltd. Taipei, Taiwan, China. Ch.25, p.12
5. *Al-Waṣiyyat. Roohānī Khazāin*, 1984 edition, Vol.20, p.310

ZOROASTRIANISM

IN PERSIAN HISTORY, the most noteworthy contribution to religious philosophy is made by Zoroastrianism. According to this philosophy, not only are truth and goodness eternal, but falsehood and evil also share eternity with them. Both have separate gods who have their own independent orders of management. There is a god of goodness, Ahura Mazda, also known as the god of light and there is a god of evil, Ahraman, also known as the god of darkness; each has his own well-defined role to play. All activity within the universe results from the collision and interaction of these two combatant gods, who are eternally locked in a grim battle of survival and supremacy.

The powers of the god of goodness are constantly endeavouring to dominate those of the god of evil. Like a see-saw, the outcome of this struggle is always changing sides sometimes in favour of goodness and sometimes in favour of evil. Thus Zoroastrian philosophy presents a simple explanation for the coexistence of evil and suffering, goodness and happiness, by attributing their origin to two different sources. All the ills in the world — pain, grief, distress, ignorance and suffering — are believed to ensue when the god of evil gains the upper hand.

It should be noted that what Zoroaster[as]* (c. sixth century BC) really taught was that the force of good and evil

---

* Zoroaster, a great Prophet of Persia, is understood by many Zoroastrians to be a dualist. Many others insist he was a monotheist. His name is spelt and pronounced differently. We have adopted Zoroaster, the English version, with which most people are familiar. Nietzsche, however, refers to him as 'Zarathustra'. In this context we have used his term with his spelling but the person is the same.

coexist to enable man to exercise his free will. Thus, man would ultimately be judged in accordance with his good or bad intentions and deeds. Zoroaster[as] also taught that the universe was created by the god of light and that the forces of good will ultimately prevail.

One can safely deduce from an in-depth study of Zoroastrianism that what was later referred to as an independent God of darkness, was only identical to the concept of a devil found in traditional religions like Judaism, Christianity and Islam. It seems that at some stage the followers of Zoroaster[as] began to misunderstand his philosophy of good and evil, and took them to be the manifestation of two independent, conscious supreme beings who coexisted eternally. This is the essence of the Zoroastrian concept of dualism. A second glance at Zoroastrian philosophy can lead a careful observer to the conclusion that it is only a matter of different terminology which creates a false parallax between them.

The role ascribed to Satan in other religions is ascribed to Ahraman in Zoroastrianism. Most likely the adherents of Zoroastrians of later ages got the concept of Satan mixed up with the idea of an independent god of evil, believed to be the supreme master of the forces of darkness. This one blunder on their part led to yet another blunder. Ahraman, the 'God of Evil', is portrayed as sharing eternity with the One and Only Supreme Creator.

It is hard to identify the age when this erroneous belief crept into Zoroastrian doctrines but one thing is certain that Cyrus (c. 590-529 BC), an exemplary pupil of Zoroaster[as], was far from being a dualist. The lofty position he held in Zoroastrianism was even higher than that held by Ashoka in Buddhism.

To judge Zoroastrianism through the mirror of Cyrus, therefore, would be no less reliable than judging Buddhism through the mirror of Ashoka. The monotheism of Cyrus can be proved from the tribute paid to him in the Old Testament (Isaiah 45:1-5). It is impossible to conceive "the God of Israel" to have praised Cyrus in such high terms if he were a dualist. Thus spoke prophet Isaiah:

> "Thus says the LORD to His anointed,
> To Cyrus, whose right hand I have held—
> To subdue nations before him
> And loose the armor of kings,
> To open before him the double doors,
> So that the gates will not be shut:
> 'I will go before you
> And make the crooked places straight;
> I will break in pieces the gates of bronze
> And cut the bars of iron.
> I will give you the treasures of darkness
> And hidden riches of secret places,
> That you may know that I, the LORD,
> Who call *you* by your name,
> *Am* the God of Israel.
> For Jacob My servant's sake,
> And Israel My elect,
> I have even called you by your name;
> I have named you, though you have not known Me.
> I *am* the LORD, and *there is* no other;
> *There is* no God besides Me..."[1]

Cyrus the great is also remembered in the Cyrus legend as a tolerant and ideal monarch who was called 'father of his people' by the ancient Persians. In the Bible an outstanding homage is paid to him as the liberator of the Jews captive in Babylonia.

In short, the figure of Cyrus has survived throughout history as a man of exceptional qualities. He built a vast empire the like of which was seldom created by other warriors of heroic fame. Among the emperors, he is the

173

only one who escaped censure by all the historians who ever wrote about great men of history. None could ever find a speck of a blemish in his character as a man or in his conduct as a monarch. He became the epitome of the greatest qualities expected of a ruler. In wars he was bold and dauntless, in conquest magnanimous. His unshakeable belief in the Unity of God must have sprung from Zoroaster[as] himself.

Zoroastrianism in all its features is closest to Judaism and Islam. Hence its precept of goodness and evil, light and darkness had to be the same as it was in Judaism and Islam. 'Ahraman' is very likely therefore, another name for Satan and no more.

THE ONLY QUESTION which remains to be resolved is, why do the Zoroastrians find the idea of duality so fascinating that once it took root into their doctrine, it continued to flourish securing a permanent place for itself? It must have happened during the phase of intense philosophical activity when the question of evil and suffering specifically bothered their thinkers. This is a problem which has been plaguing man since time immemorial. Many religious intellects in different ages have offered different explanations to justify their belief in a good God. In Athens too, during the same general age, this question had engaged the attention of many ethical, religious or secular thinkers. For them it was not too difficult to resolve the question, because the majority of Athenians believed in mythical gods for whom it was not rare to tell lies or play tricks upon humans or even gods. The concept of such trickster gods is fully endorsed by the Illiad of Homer.

Yet among them, there was born in 470 BC a monotheist philosopher whose name was Socrates. He was a prophet among philosophers and a philosopher among prophets. He believed in the unshakeable Unity of God. Of His absolute goodness he did not entertain the slightest doubt. This is what he pronounced during his last speech before the Athenian senate. He believed in God, the possessor of absolute goodness, not merely through his intellectual and metaphysical exercise, he believed because he had personally known Him as such, right from the early days of his childhood. Nay, he was brought up in the very lap of God with His personal love and care. This was Socrates who also tackled this question with profound logic but it is a logic largely spent on proving the impossibility of any evil originating from God. When it came to the issue of evil and suffering in the world, he dismissed them as human errors, logically impossible to have emanated from Him. He had to be good, He was good and He could not be anything but good. Hence, evil must have been generated by earthly people, God having no share in their defiled practices. His answer was simple but left room for others to assail him philosophically so that ultimately he could be driven to an indefensible position. The Zoroastrian thinkers in Iran however, could not be satisfied with this answer. They probed the question and further enquired as to who those evil men were and who had created them. If it were God, He had to be ultimately responsible. Thus to break His ties with evil altogether, the Zoroastrian intellects must have devised the existence of another creator beside Him. One was referred to as the god of goodness and the other as the god of evil; both enjoyed their godhead in their exclusive areas of light and darkness.

Incidentally, it should also be mentioned here that all Zoroastrians do not subscribe to this so-called Zoroastrian doctrine of duality. There are those, though small in number today, who strongly defend the cause of Unity within Zoroastrianism. Most of these unitarians must have been powerfully pulled towards Islam as it entered Persia. It should be remembered that apart from duality and the consequent fire worship, the rest of the Zoroastrian faith is much closer to Islam than to any other faith.

In Zoroastrianism, God – referred to as Ahura Mazda – is described exactly in the same terms and with the same attributes as in all other major religions. Thus by blaming all the evil and suffering upon the scapegoat Ahraman, the Zoroastrian thinkers thought they had ultimately resolved the dilemma. But it was not to be so. Socrates, also a contemporary of theirs, might have heard of it or thought of it himself, yet he rejected it and faithfully adhered to the Unity of God. This Zoroastrian excuse, though it seems to solve one problem, creates an even more defiant one. To that we shall turn later but presently it must be remembered that evil in itself has no independent existence which needs to be created.

In reality however, evil is only another name for the absence of goodness. Its absence only becomes conspicuous when light and shade play hide and seek. Yet shade is not a substantial thing. It is only light that matters and seems to create shadows. Shadows however are not created by light but are the name for its absence. They are born whenever light is obstructed. There was no need therefore for the Zoroastrians of later ages to create a devil of their own by the name of Ahraman. Likewise it is goodness alone which needs to be created, sin will by itself appear whenever goodness is eschewed. Thus if Ahraman is the god of darkness, he himself is the outcome of the negation of light and virtue, and not a creator of them.

In the light of what has passed, we can safely conclude that Zoroaster[as] believed in the God of goodness and in Him alone. He was a recipient of revelation from Him. For him knowledge and eternal truth were directly bestowed by revelation, not merely deduced through logic or inspiration.

Returning once again to the Zoroastrian solution of the dilemma of the existence of suffering and evil, let us examine this philosophy once again in depth. How did suffering come into being? Whatever is the meaning of suffering? If there was a separate god who contrived evil and another who fashioned goodness, then what will be the final outcome of their strife to gain victory over the other? Who will win and why? Although the Zoroastrians seem to entertain the hope of a final victory of goodness, their philosophy does not offer any explanation as to why the power of goodness must prevail. If the two gods are independent, but one is weaker than the other, then the powerful God must have annihilated the weaker since time immemorial. Thus with the passage of time goodness should have finally prevailed over the forces of evil. Since this is not the case, both the gods could have been equally balanced in their respective powers, engaged in an endless game of see-saw. In that case the hope for the ultimate victory of goodness over evil is impossible to entertain.

Another important question to which we feel the need to return, is the question of suffering. As has already been demonstrated, the dualist philosophy of Zorastrianism despite its apparent advantage fails to resolve the dilemma. Dualism when examined in depth is found to be absolutely inadequate in solving the mystery of suffering in the scheme of creation by a Benignant Creator. This question we propose to take up in the following chapter independently on its own merit.

REFERENCE

1. *The Holy Bible* (1982) The New King James Version. Thomas Nelson Publishers, Nashville. Isaiah 45:1-5

THE QUESTION OF SUFFERING

WHEN WE EXPLORE the history of evolution in search of the causative factors which gave birth to the sensory organs as life evolved, we can safely conclude that right from the beginning they have always been the sense of loss and gain. We identify the journey of evolution to be a long procession of some obscure realisation of gains and losses which gradually evolved the sensory organs to register the presence of pleasure and pain, comfort and suffering. If we look back at the lower forms of life, at the first few rungs of the ladder and compare them with the higher forms of life near the top, it is not difficult to recognize that in real terms the evolution is the evolution of consciousness. Life is constantly spiralling up from a lesser state of consciousness to a higher state with continuously sharpening faculties of awareness.

The awareness of gain and loss is rather vague and obscure in the beginning, and we cannot locate a definite seat for this awareness in the anatomy of rudimentary organisms. But we know from their reactions to the surrounding elements and situations that they do possess some defused sense of awareness. It is this diffused inexplicable sense which is employed somehow by the Creator to initiate the sense of perception in life. This sense of perception gradually developed and created its own seats in the organism of life. It is these seats which got precipitated ultimately into what we know now as sensory organs. The creation of the brain was not a separate and unrelated incident. No development of sensory organs could be meaningful without a corresponding development of a central nervous system and a simultaneous evolution of the brain, which could decipher the messages transmitted by the sensory organs. Evidently therefore, the brain developed as an essential counterpart of the system of perception. The more evolved the consciousness becomes, the more intense grows the sense of loss and gain felt by specific nerve centres which translate the awareness of loss as suffering, and gain as pleasure, to the mind through the brain.

The less developed the consciousness, the smaller is the awareness of suffering. The same goes for happiness. Thus, the sensory provisions for the recognition of suffering and happiness are indispensable to each other. It is quite likely that if the level to which suffering can be experienced is reduced, its opposite number, the capacity to feel pleasure and happiness, will also be lowered to the same degree. The two seem to participate equally in propelling the wheel of evolution; both possess equal significance. One cannot be done away with alone without the other, thus nullifying the entire creative plan of evolution.

We understand from the Holy Quran, that God did not create suffering as an independent entity in its own right, but only as an indispensable counterpart of pleasure and comfort. The absence of happiness is suffering, which is like its shadow, just as darkness is the shadow cast by the absence of light. If there is life, there has to be death; both are situated at the extreme poles of the same plane, with innumerable grades and shades in between. As we move away from death, we gradually move towards a state of life which is happiness; as we move away from life, we move away with a sense of loss and sorrow towards death. This is the key to understanding the struggle for existence, which in turn leads to a constant improvement in the quality of life and helps it to achieve the ultimate goal of evolution. The principle of the "survival of the fittest" plays an integral role in this grand scheme of evolution.

This phenomenon is mentioned in the Holy Quran in the following verse:

تَبَـٰـرَكَ الَّذِىْ بِيَدِهِ الْمُلْكُ وَهُوَ عَلَىٰ كُلِّ شَىْءٍ قَدِيْرٌ * إِلَّـــــذِىْ

خَلَقَ الْمَوْتَ وَالْحَيَـٰـوةَ لِيَبْلُوَكُمْ أَيُّـــكُمْ أَحْسَنُ عَمَلًا وَهُـــوَ

الْعَزِيْزُ الْغَفُوْرُ * 67:2-3

Blessed is He in whose hand is the kingdom, and He has power over all things;
It is He Who has created death and life that He might try you — which of you is best in deeds; and He is the Mighty, the Most Forgiving.[1]

The answer to the question 'Why is there suffering?' is clearly implied in this verse in its widest application.

The profound philosophy of life and death, the innumerable shades in between, and the role they play in shaping life and improving its quality are all covered in the above verse. It is the very scheme of things that God discloses here. We know that life is only a positive value, and death merely means its absence, and no sharp border exists separating one from the other. It is a gradual process, the way life travels towards death and ebbs out, or from the other direction we view death travelling towards life gaining strength, energy and consciousness as it moves on. This is the grand plan of creation, but why has God designed it so? *'That He might try you – which of you is best in deeds'*, is the answer provided by the Holy Quran.

It is the perpetual struggle between life and death that subjects the living to a constant state of trial, so that all who conduct themselves best survive and gain a higher status of existence. Herein lies the philosophy and the machination of evolution as described in the verses above. It is this constant struggle between the forces of life and the forces of death which provide the thrust to the living to perpetually move away from death or towards it. It may result either in the improvement or deterioration in the quality of existence in the wide spectrum of evolutionary changes. This is the essence and spirit of evolution.

Suffering could only be considered objectionable if it were created as an independent entity with no meaningful role to play in the scheme of things. But without the taste of suffering or an awareness of what it means, the feeling of relief and comfort would also vanish. Without an encounter with pain and misery, most certainly, joy and happiness would lose all meaning. Indeed the very existence of life would lose purpose, and the steps of evolution would stop dead in their tracks.

Thus in the evolution of our five senses, the awareness of loss and gain has played an equally essential role like the two wheels of a wagon; remove one, and the other would also lose its meaning. The very concept of the wagon would be grounded. The struggle between life and death, which produces suffering, is also the means of creating pleasure. It is the primary motivating force which fuels the carriage of evolution to move forward eternally.

During the long history of evolution, disease has arisen from various causes, directly or indirectly related to developmental changes. Environmental variations, the struggle for existence, mutations and accidents, have all jointly or severally played their part. Disease, defects and shortcomings all have a role to play in effecting improvement. This is how various animal species went on evolving unconsciously it seems, but certainly with a direction, which appears to follow a consciously designed course towards greater consciousness.

LET US NOW try to conceive another scheme in which the element of suffering is set aside by the application of a hypothetical rule: all forms of life must be equally provided with an equal share of happiness with no portion of suffering at all. Perhaps then we shall be able to eliminate suffering altogether from afflicting life. There would be absolute equality and everyone would be placed on a level platform, but how and where should we introduce this new scheme? Alas! Wherever we attempt to introduce it in the long chain of evolution, we are bound to come across insurmountable problems. These new rules either have to be introduced at the very beginning of creation or not at all. To apply absolute equality at any following stage would be impossible without creating insoluble contradictions. We shall thus need to return to the point where life started.

We must go back all the way in the history of life; all the way to the very beginning and start to build the ladder of evolution anew, rung by rung. But try as we may, we are bound to get stuck at the very first step, the starting point of life. We would not be able to take a single step forward because an equal distribution of happiness and total absence of suffering would entirely eliminate the impetus for evolution. There would be no struggle for existence, no natural selection, no survival of the fittest. Not a single progressive step would be taken by the first, most rudimentary forms of life.

Picture the stage of life represented by the three earliest life units known to man, i.e. bacteria with nuclei, bacteria without nuclei and pyro-bacteria (born by the energy of fire). In this imaginary system there would be no competition for food or survival, because all are equally provided for; there would be no suffering either. As a consequence, in that hypothetical revised plan of creation, life would certainly remain stationary and stagnant, forever fixed at its earliest rudimentary form. The creation of man would remain a far cry from the point of its ancient beginning. Therefore the real question is whether to choose a system with suffering as its integral part, perpetually spiralling evolution in the greater interest of life, or to abandon the plan altogether for the fear of unavoidable suffering. In the final analysis therefore, the only question we are left with is, 'To be or not to be'?

The rudimentary forms of life, if they had a brain to think, would much rather wish 'not to be' than 'to be' in such meaningless drudgery of existence.

Suffering is also associated with the idea of retribution and punishment. Glimpses of retribution can be witnessed in the animal kingdom only in a narrow and limited application. They can be observed in the behaviour of many animals of land, sea and air. Elephants and buffaloes are notorious for their propensity towards revenge. This gradually developing trait of life is inevitably linked up to the gradual synthesis of choice. To do something or not to do something can either be an intuitive compulsion or a calculated decision of mind. We are not yet certain about how far the element of choice plays a role in animal conduct, but we know that choice begins to play a vital role in the decision-making process of humans. Whether one moves towards light or darkness, towards life or death, is most often a conscious decision on the part of man. If therefore, as a natural consequence of man's wilful actions, a reward is provided or penalty exacted, none else is to be blamed but man himself.

Sometimes people may suffer without realizing that they themselves are to be blamed — that there is a general principle of retribution operative in nature known as nemesis. They may have earned that suffering advertently

I.3

I.4

or inadvertently, without identifying the cause. It is so because every fault does not result in an immediate punitive consequence. It often happens that nature executes justice against transgression imperceptibly.

However this is not the whole problem. It is far too complex, vast and intricate and needs to be further illustrated with the help of specific scientific examples, hypothetical or real. There are some very difficult cases to explain, like those of children born with certain congenital defects. Why are they made to suffer? It cannot be said that it is through any fault of theirs. If there is any fault it might have been of their parents, yet that may not have been intentional on their part. In this context the term "fault" should be understood in its widest application, covering even accidental occurrence of congenital diseases. Such faults are far from being conscious crimes. Whatever the nature of the particular cause of some defect, one thing is certain that the poor innocent child who is born with any disadvantage is not responsible for the cause of this suffering in any way.

The solution to the understanding of this problem lies in the realization that all suffering cannot be categorized as punishment, nor all happiness as reward. There is always a small percentage of individuals who will seem to suffer as though without justification. However, a closer more careful examination of such cases would reveal that there is no question of wilful injustice involved. They are merely an unavoidable by-product of the wide plan of creation, but they also play a meaningful role in the general advancement of human society.

One must not forget that 'cause and effect' is one thing and 'crime and punishment' is quite another, however closely they may seem to resemble each other. It is correct to say that a crime may work as a cause and every punishment that may ensue would be an effect of that causative crime. But it is not correct to claim that every suffering is a punishment of some crime committed before. It is wrong to say that all healthy babies are healthy because they are rewarded for some act of goodness of their parents. So also it is wrong to maintain that every unhealthy baby is punished for an unidentified crime of its parents or forefathers. Health and disease, ability and disability, fortune or misfortune, congenital advantages or disadvantages are themselves but indispensable to the grand scheme of things, in which they play a causative role. They are distinctly apart from the phenomenon of crime and punishment, goodness and reward. As we have discussed above, suffering, like happiness, is an essential prerequisite for life to evolve and in the course of evolution it is not related to the phenomenon of crime and punishment at all. Suffering in its causative role produces a wide spectrum of useful effects which amply justify its existence.

Suffering has been a great teacher, cultivating and culturing our conduct. It develops and refines sensibilities, teaches humility and in more than one way, prepares humans to be able to turn to God. It awakens the need for search and exploration and creates that necessity which is the mother of all inventions. Remove suffering as a causative factor in developing man's potential and the wheel of progress would turn back a hundred thousand times. Man may try his hand at altering the plan of things, but frustration would be all he will achieve. Thus, the question of apportioning blame for the existence of suffering upon the Creator should not arise. Suffering, to play its subtle creative role in the scheme of things, is indeed a blessing in disguise.

The secret of all scientific investigation and discovery lies in a constant quest for the relief of pain and discomfort.

The motivation behind scientific exploration and discovery is based less on a desire to gain luxuries than on a need to escape pain. Luxury itself is, after all, a further extension of the same tendency to move away from a state of discomfort to a state of comparative ease.

Let us once again examine the scenario of the 'innocent sufferers', the newborn babies with congenital defects or those falling ill at a later age with typhoid or some other disabling disease, rendering them blind, deaf and dumb, or even partially or totally paralysed for life. Worse still may be the case of those, whose central nervous system is damaged by mishaps during birth, resulting in mental disorders. Is the question valid: Why this particular child, A or B? Why not another, say for instance C or D? Would not the same question repeat again and yet again: Why C or D? Why not E or F and so on? The only valid question therefore, would be: Why anyone at all? Hence the only option the Creator is left with is either to create all babies equally healthy or equally unhealthy. This leads us to the realization that the health of a baby itself is merely of relative value. Perhaps it is hard to find any two babies equally gifted with the health of mind and heart and all the physical organs alike. To resolve the question of suffering, there is another valid question to be raised against the Creator. If one child is born with pinhole eyes and a large ugly nose and other disproportionate features, will he not suffer all his life comparing his disadvantages with the advantages of other more fortunate fellow human beings?

Inequality of health and looks will continue to irritate most individuals and will even agonise some at finding themselves to be at a disadvantage in comparison to others. Does it not warrant in the name of absolute justice and fair play that God should create every human exactly alike in health and looks? Widen the area of comparison by bringing into play the faculties of head and heart and disposition and the contrast between those who have advantages and those who have disadvantages will become even more pronounced. In the absence of extreme cases even the mild cases will appear offensive to the sense of justice. One has to begin somewhere to create variety and diversity to break the monotony. Wherever there is variety and diversity, comparative suffering and happiness are bound to be generated. To object against the plan of things in the name of compassion for disabled children is one thing, but to replace the plan with a more just and compassionate viable plan is quite another. One may try one's hand at altering the scheme for aeons of time but one will still not be able to replace the plan of God's creations for a better one. In other words, we shall be again reverting to the question of why any disease and suffering at all; why should they be inevitable? One answer to this question, we have already given above.

LET US EXAMINE the same question from yet another perspective: from the viewpoint of an atheist as well as from the viewpoint of a believer in God.

For the atheist, strictly logically speaking, there should be no problem to be resolved — there should be no question to be answered. They do not owe their existence to any creator, and no creator is accountable before them if they find any distortion in the random unrolling of creation. For every suffering, every misery, every unequal distribution of happiness, nothing but chance is to be blamed and that realization ends the age-old debate. Chance being the creator, or nature, as we may call it, being unconscious, deaf and dumb, blind and chaotic cannot be blamed for any flaw in what is born out of chaos. The outcome of chance, without a creator, has to be blind and disorderly, without reason, without design, without direction.

For those who believe in God, the Creator, there should be no problem either, because they see enough direction, balance and purpose in creation, to submit to the wisdom of the plan in its totality. An odd thorn jutting out here and there from a most artistically arranged, colourful and fragrant bouquet of flowers will not provide sufficient cause for the rejection of the bouquet, or will it?

If the atheist's scepticism is correct, then death seems to be the only solution for the drawn out misery of the innocent sufferers. If the believer's scenario of creation is right, then death again acquires the role of a redeemer, but in a completely different way. For them, death acts only as a gateway to the life after death, which will usher the innocent sufferers into an era of unlimited reward. If they could only dream of what rewards were waiting for them in the Hereafter as compensation for their transient misery on earth, they would smilingly jog along despite suffering as though it were mere pinpricks or an odd thorn on the way to an eternal life of comfort and happiness.

Some people may not accept this and may still insist that they are not satisfied because there is no God and no life of reward or punishment after death. For them there is no value in this answer. If so, then the question should not be discussed at all. The question, they should remember, can only be discussed in relation to the role of God as Creator. The question of morality, the right and wrong of something, arises only with the belief in the existence of God. If there is God, then the suggestion of a possible compensation presented above cannot be dismissed merely with a scornful chuckle. If there is no God, then we cannot blame Him or anyone else for any chance suffering that we may encounter. We must then take life and all that pertains to it merely as an accident without meaning, without direction, without goal. Suffering has to be accepted as a part of nature, as something that cannot be done away with and cannot be run away from. Either way, one must learn to live with suffering.

Of course, suffering is a vital constituent of the motive force of evolution. However the question of balance between suffering and the pleasure derived from the consciousness of existence, remains to be decided. If, in this simple equation, suffering offsets the deep-rooted satisfaction born out of the awareness of one's existence, then most people would rather die than live to suffer. If most of those who suffer would much rather lose conscious identity of existence than compromise with unhappiness, then the very wisdom of such a plan would be called into question. But that, which we actually observe in real life, is exactly the opposite of what is suggested above. Life dearly clings to the very awareness of its existence, sometimes even at the price of immense misery and unhappiness. That is the predominant rule with minor exceptions too insignificant by comparison.

Again we should remember that the perspective of suffering is variable. It constantly keeps changing when viewed from different angles of observation. Those who are healthy themselves perceive the state of a subnormal child as that of extreme suffering, but those who are placed at an even lower level of deprivation than the subnormal child in question may look up to him with envy.

ON A MUCH WIDER CANVAS, each form of life is either superior or inferior to the forms of life below or above it respectively. Throughout the process of evolution our awareness of values has kept changing as they evolved from lower to higher orders. The stages that occur in the upward spiralling course of evolution, when

190

looked down upon from a higher vantage point, appear to be at a disadvantage. The higher forms of life cling dearly to the greater awareness of values which they have gained over millions of years of evolution. Any reversal or loss of such values and faculties would inevitably result in suffering, which by itself is indispensable for the promotion of the same values. Consider the state of worms in comparison to some higher forms of life, and compare yet again the state of those higher forms of life in comparison to the more advanced animal species placed even higher in the ladder of evolution. They all are certainly not equally gifted. The worms that thrive on the product of organic decay and filth could not by any means perceive themselves to be at par with the freely roaming wild horses, grazing in prairies on tender grass. Yet they cannot perceive themselves at a disadvantage either. Theirs are two different worlds, different faculties, different requirements and different aspirations — if aspirations could be attributed to worms at all!

Thus this imbalance does not suggest that they have been the target of any injustice. Visualize, for instance, the case of a few happy healthy worms. They all seem to be perfectly adjusted to their environment which in turn is well adjusted to them. They are fully content with the faculties they are provided with, and are incapable of yearning for things beyond the scope of their senses. Yet, if a human child were to be offered to exchange his suffering state of life with that of a happy contented worm, would he not rather die than to accept this option of living the lowly existence of a worm?

The very awareness of one's life and the higher status one occupies in the grades of life is sufficient in most cases to offset the disadvantage of suffering. It transpires that suffering is after all a relative state. The source of suffering is embedded in the sense of deprivation. It is the awareness of loss of some familiar cherished values which generate a sense of pain. It can only happen when one has already tasted the pleasure of such values or has observed others enjoying them. The loss of such values once enjoyed or the knowledge of others possessing them, while one cannot, are two powerful factors which generate pain. But the lack of such values, the nature of which one does not perceive cannot cause suffering. What is pain after all, if not mere signals of a variety of losses? Despite the fact that we cannot always relate all our varied encounters with pain to specific bereavements, an in-depth study would always reveal that every sense of pain is inseparably connected with a corresponding sense of loss.

The creation and evolution of sensory organs owe their existence to interminably long encounters with loss or gain. They are the two most potent creative factors created by God. All the five senses which we possess are the products of our awareness of them, as discussed before, which during a billion years of our evolution, gradually materialised into sensory perceptive mechanisms. Suffering and happiness could not by themselves have created the mechanism of consciousness. To register their presence without such mechanisms, they themselves would cease to be. How then can nothingness create anything? Unconsciousness cannot design and create consciousness even in trillions of years. It has to be a conscious Creator to endow death with consciousness and create life out of it. The Most Masterly Creator seems to have employed pain and pleasure in an, as yet, unknown manner to create the very organs which perceive them. Remove the pain as an instrument in the making of this masterpiece of creative wonder and life will be rendered into a senseless mass of vegetation, not even aware of itself. Are a few odd cases of misery and deprivation too big a price to pay for the prodigious marvel of consciousness?

Let us remind the reader that Islam defines evil only as a shadow created by the lack of light. It is not a positive existence in itself. We can imagine a source of light (a lamp or the sun), but we cannot imagine any object as a source of darkness. The only way in which an object becomes a source of darkness is through its ability to obstruct light. Likewise, it is only the absence of goodness that constitutes evil. The grades of evil are only determined by the opacity of the obstructing medium.

Likewise, it is the awareness of possession which constitutes happiness. Any loss or threat of loss to possession constitutes pain or agony. But they must coexist in an equation of positive and negative poles. Remove one, and the other will disappear. Hence no one on earth can interfere with the creative design of pain, pleasure, goodness and evil and succeed in altering the plan of things. It is beyond the reach of human compassion to efface suffering without effacing life itself.

REFERENCE

1. Translation of 67:2-3 by the author.

PART III

Secular Viewpoints Examined

The Concept of God Among
the Aborigines of Australia

SECULAR VIEWPOINTS EXAMINED

THE THEORY OF religious development presented by sociologists and their concept of how belief in God developed, is primarily based on their understanding of social psychology. Having observed the general tendency of man in his social behaviour, they seem to have concluded that man reveres whatever he fears and also adopts a controlled, respectful attitude to what he likes or stands in need of. Their understanding of the 'give and take' motives behind social order is extended to their understanding of religion, incorporating within it the motives of fear and greed.

They believe that ancient man in his naivety, as he stood just a step beyond the dividing line between humanoid and human being, confused and bewildered by all that he saw around him. Thus he failed to comprehend the true nature of things as he ventured to find answers to many a puzzling question. In the hazy light of the dawn of man's intellect, nature's wondrous powers so impressed him that he presumed natural phenomena to be manifestations of superpowers which were beyond his comprehension, yet were capable of influencing his life.

Consequently, he assigned to such forces the status of deities. Seeing the devastating effects of storms and hurricanes, he bowed to them in fear, lest they should strike him down. Yet again, when he saw the light of day and experienced the creative powers of the sun, he formed a beneficent impression of gods of his imagination. Seeing these manifestations through the reflective mirror of natural phenomena he could conceive them either as fearsome or benign. Thus, the dark forces of nature appeared hostile and scary such as the tidal waves and tempests and the rainstorms which brought lightning, thunder and floods in their wake.

The dangerous animals did not lag behind either, and the beasts of the jungle, the wildcats, the serpents and the scorpions also claimed their share among the assembly of the imaginary gods with evil powers. Benign manifestations of nature such as cool gentle breeze and winds laden with moisture, bringing pleasant life-supporting rains appeared on the other hand to be controlled by benign gentle deities. To the early man in his primitive thinking, they all appeared to be gods or agents of gods with differing temperaments, moods and characteristics. All such gods of his fancy were to be paid homage to, lest one should earn their wrath or lose their favour. The celestial wonders, the glorious sun, the moon and the stars with their mysterious constellations, won even more profound reverence from them in due course. Thus his rudimentary ideas of gods began to spiral upwards and gods were classified and arranged in ascending or descending order.

Although today one may criticize early man as over-credulous, the sociologists maintain that this credulity on his part was a natural outcome of his befogged mental faculties as yet unperfected. This in short, is the widely held view of the origin of religion and its subsequent evolution by most of the eminent sociologists.

It is further argued that this primitive thought process eventually evolved to produce the idea of a single Creator. They insist that the image of one God was gradually evolved out of the belief in many gods, but not at their cost. They coexisted in an uneasy equation, struggling for supremacy, permanently locked in a grim battle. Gradually, as the universal clock ticked on, various religions came into being, developing around one concept or another, worshipping one God or many. Little did they realize in their ignorance that they were in effect, worshipping, mere conjectures. It were they who created gods — no God created them. Thus a simple primitive thought process developed, multiplied and proliferated, growing in complexity and generating much bewilderment and confusion around a myriad images of superhuman masters.

This atheistic view of religion has gone one step further in imputing to the founders of religion the act of deliberate falsehood and deception. They claim that at a later stage of its growth, religion no longer remained a jumble of superstitions of the common people. An organized clergy began to evolve. At this stage, the idea of revelation was deceitfully introduced, as a contrivance to further abet the deception of the priestly class. This elite group of religious hierarchy claimed for themselves a special status as the chosen recipients of messages from on high and acquired the exclusive role of the channel of communication between god/gods and men. Many such claimants arose in time, each claiming a close relationship with the powerful supernatural forces shaping the destiny of man.

This is what the sociologists saw reflected in Greek mythology and in the beliefs and practices of many a primitive religion. The genuine search by early man for the solutions to the complex mysteries of nature surrounding him, thus ended in a conscious attempt on the part of the religious hierarchy to deceive and defraud people in the name of god/gods.

Man's evolving consciousness also took another simultaneous and parallel course. According to the sociologists, as his understanding of the surrounding physical world improved, so his treatment of the images of God began to exhibit revision and adjustment. The

199

inanimate objects like idols and statues, which were previously treated as gods themselves, now began to be conceived only as channels leading to real gods who dwelt in the skies. Thus, they were gradually turned into vehicles through which *the gods* from on high expressed their varying moods of wrath and pleasure. The concept of 'gods' was thus slowly lifted from a commonplace physical palpable entity to a rare rarefied and abstract idea. The same process developed further to give birth to a more complicated system of divine hierarchy in which each god was given a particular place in relation to others, and was assigned a specific role to play in the cosmos. It was this categorization and classification of gods which culminated in the creation of one Supreme God, held to be above all others. This is how the sociologists visualize how God could have been created by human mind. In other words, were they to be assigned the task of manufacturing God, this is how they would go about it, given of course, the vast span of time required for it.

They founded their theory on the presupposition that no God exists, hence their conjecture is not based on any real investigation, but is a natural expression of an atheist's mind. It is this pre-fixed judgement of theirs which they proclaim to be an impartial intellectual enquiry. They somehow fail to notice the flaws and contradictions in the manner they theorize and co-relate the imagined facts of history. The history of the human thought of the early period of man's development is unrecorded, obscure and virtually non-existent. We are only entitled to call 'history' whatever we find as evidence from the relics of the past, indicating the lifestyle of that age. This history began as early as some two hundred or more thousand years in the past, while the actual history of religious development began hardly some thousands of years ago. Thus all they have to build their theories upon are suppositions. Their attempted projection into the minds of the ancients is no more than a fictional leap upon the wings of fancy. The orientation of this leap is prefixed in the direction of atheism. Their inferences are not corroborated by the evidence of human nature – the only reliable instrument for assessing thought processes.

DO WE REALLY worship what we fear? And does greed invariably make us inclined to fall prostrate to objects in an act of worship? Neither of these two factors can build even the most rudimentary religion. Fear simply makes one run away from the object of terror. One can imagine of course, such helpless miserable targets of torture who can not run away beseech their tormentors, begging them for mercy but not worshipping them. The same when released would abuse their erstwhile tormentors in the foulest terms and vilest language. The concept of worship would not even remotely cross his mind. We have yet to read a spy tale in which an MI5 agent is motivated by terror to begin to worship his KGB tormentor. The fear of God which we find mentioned in Divinely revealed religions has nothing to do with the idea of terror related to beasts and other fearsome objects. The threat of Divine punishment is merely used as a deterrent against crime, preventing people from transgression against themselves. In the primitive society of man, no promise of such punishment could be born merely out of their fear of the beasts of the jungle or the thunderstorms. No such fear or threat of punishment from the beasts of jungle or tempestuous forces of nature is ever known to have stayed the hand of ancient societies from committing aggression. Police officers, traffic wardens and magistrates are feared and hated, but never worshipped! In the most ancient times too, the fear of a vicious lion would make a savage run for

201

his life rather than to fall prostrate before him, begging for mercy and extolling him for his grandeur and majesty. The bolts of lightning, torrents of rain, or the blazing radiation of hot summer sun could only

motivate early man to run for shelter or devise protective measures. Can a sociologist really believe that during a severe thunder storm the ancient man instead of seeking cover would jump out of his cave to fall prostrate to the angry forces of nature in spate. The mention of sun-worship and star-worship does not in any way relate to a gradually developing idea of worship through fear or greed. There is no evidence whatsoever of a course of evolution leading man from worship of small earthly objects to a gradually developing form of worship related to more powerful and loftier imaginary beings.

The sociologists merely talk of evolution without adopting scientific methods to prove their hypothesis. When the scientists talk of evolution, they trace the entire course of stage by stage advancement of life, through a traceable trail extending back to a billion years. Is there an iota of proof that similar evolutionary processes did take place in relation to the development of the image of God? Which superstitious idolatrous societies ever evolved into monotheistic religions? None whatsoever.

Yet the sociologists would insist that it was the rudimentary faculty of perception in man which culminated in the creation of God. As mentioned before they doggedly persist in maintaining that the fear of the unknown did play its part in building godly images; darkness played its tricks, and the dangers lurking under the cover of ignorance began to command respect. The ancients began to worship the snake, the scorpion, the puma, the tiger and the lion. Earthquakes shook the earth, lightning rent the trees asunder and the storms raged wild and merciless, so the idea of God started to evolve. It evolved from the worship of natural phenomenon to the worship of material objects that struck terror in their hearts. It evolved from the worship of the inanimate to the worship of the animals, from the worship of scorpions and snakes to the worship of cats and other beasts of the jungle. Even monkeys were turned into gods. They could not reach the lofty cradles of lightning, and could not understand the nature of forces which created them, but they were terrified of them all the same.

They must have viewed every mighty phenomenon as an expression of the wrath of some god of terror sitting behind the curtains of clouds. So their rudimentary minds, simple as they were, began to weave the yarn of superstitions. They invented teachings and rules of conduct to please despotic gods, or to escape their wrath at least. Temples were built, sacrifices were offered and the ideas of right and wrong began to take shape. A host of rituals and rites cropped up and finally scriptures were compiled. An over-inflated tribute, indeed, to their rudimentary primitive understanding! Or more aptly perhaps a tribute to the intellect of sociologists who built such lofty Divine castles in the air on behalf of the primitive men of rudimentary understanding.

They have failed to discern the marked differences between the pagan faiths and the Divinely revealed religions of the world. They have also failed to notice that the high priests, priestesses and oracles found among the ancient mythical cults never claimed to have received a new code of life based on revelation. Likewise, the validity of their claims to mediumship was never put to question, because their authority was traditionally handed down to them by their predecessors and was accepted as such by the society. They were never challenged to produce Divine signs in support of their claim, and felt free to concoct gimmicks in their support. Thus the credulous were further impressed by their supposed access to gods, which was no more than a ruse. The false gods were thus supported by false claimants.

The following points are worth noting about the above category of seers, which contrast with the case of the Divinely appointed founders of the world's great religions. Their distinctive features can be summed up as follows:

1) The idolatrous priests are recognized within an already established temple.

2) They do not introduce a new religious doctrine which is controversial to the old established order and challenges its validity. Nor do they endeavour to change the values and conduct of the society. They always support beliefs and practices of the old system and never oppose the popular myths and superstitions.

3) Most often they are an accepted part of the prevailing political system and do not challenge the religious ideologies of the rulers. One may find, however, exceptional instances of rebellion by religious leaders against the monarchs of their time. In such cases it is necessitated by an urge for revenge against their excessive interference in their affairs. Sometimes it is motivated by their ambition to assume greater political control. Yet these are exceptions. The rule is that the corrupt idolatrous leadership most often serves the cause of a popular myth and philosophy firmly rooted in a strong power base.

How essentially different is the case of the Divinely appointed prophets, the upholders of the Unity of God who founded great religions of the world such as Judaism,

Christianity, Islam and Zoroastrianism etc. If we examine the lives of Moses[as], Jesus[as] or Muhammad[sa] and other similar prophets who claimed Divine origin, we shall invariably discover that none among them ever represented a well-established and popular religious order. Theirs was a lone voice of revolution. Invariably they based their claims on revelation and advocated a new philosophy demanding a completely different way of life. They preached values which were at odds with the prevailing customs and practices. They always emerged as harbingers of a new order and dared to challenge the prevailing religious authorities of the time. They appeared at a time when the dominant religions of the age had already split into sects and schisms, and fought among themselves for gaining greater domination over the ignorant masses. In such an age, as described, it was the emergence of a new Divine messenger which resulted in a state of forged unity among his opponents, who for the time being forgot their own differences and mustered their forces to put up a joint colossal resistance against the newly introduced Divine order. They presented a united front of opposition, exhibiting violent hostility. The Divine messenger on his part had no human support whatsoever. He was backed neither by the bulk of the common folk nor by any power group of the society. He was not championed by any political power. He was left alone, abandoned and rejected.

Such were the men who arose to confront the adulterous societies which always grow out of a wild proliferation of superstitious trends. The ushers of the new order always pleaded belief in the Unity of God and attempted to stamp out idolatry in every form, under every guise. Whatever unity their opponents could forge among themselves was only forged in opposition to the prophets, while within themselves they remained as deeply split as they ever were. If the upholders of the Unity of God were mere fabricators then theirs was an impossible task. No fabricators can ever persist in pursuance of such goals as lie visibly beyond their reach. The faith of such as these has to be deeply founded on the reality of God, or they must perish and be wiped out of existence. If there is no God then claimants like them should simply have been dismissed by society as raving mad. There is no third option. If not insane, how could they hold on to their beliefs so tenaciously as to sacrifice all they had for an unreal unfruitful cause. But they cannot be waived off as insane because the insane keep moving hither and tither in their ravings. As for the prophets, the society shows a violent reaction as though the ground under their feet had erupted. No human support by the rich or the poor, the powerful or the weak is ever known to have come to their aid against the united wrath of their violent opponents. The nobility of their message, the dignity of their conduct and their unshakeable faith in their final victory at the hour of utter desolation always stood witness to their truth.

Theirs was a case of extreme sacrifice, not of greed. Whatever they possessed, they lost in the cause of their noble goal. Not only they, but also those who continued to join them crossing all the hurdles, treading the same path of absolute sacrifice. Accusing fingers could not discourage people such as these.

The theory that ascribes the creation of imaginary gods to man's ignorance, may be partially true in certain phases of human history of ignorance and immaturity. The exploitation of the ignorant masses by the priestly classes is not denied at all. But to suggest that this process generated a continuous evolutionary flow of ideas, leading eventually to the belief in One God, is what we categorically deny. The facts of history do not support the evolution of Unity from the growth of idolatrous superstition. It is a figment of the sociologists' wayward fancy.

History does not produce any evidence to support the theory of progressive transformation of polytheism to monotheism. No transitional stages are witnessed in which communities moved from worshipping many gods to the worship of One. On the contrary, it is the sudden and abrupt appearance of one great man which sets into motion a train of events causing great upheavals and tribulations, requiring enormous sacrifices from those who chose to follow him.

THE HOLY QURAN rejects this hypothesis. It categorically proclaims the opposite to be true. All the major religions of the world invariably began their journey with belief in Unity. The proposition of evolution can neither be proved with reference to history nor to the working of human psyche.

The character of prophets is like an open book which defies allegations of hidden intentions and secret designs. There is no phase in their earlier life before their claim to prophethood which could justify the accusation that they had planned to fake their prophetic claim at a later stage. No such evidence is at all found in the lives of the great advocates of God's Unity, like Abraham[as], Moses[as] and Prophet Muhammad[sa].

By the time of Abraham[as], the lofty belief of Noah[as] in the Unity of God was already degenerated by his distant progeny into the earthly myths of many gods. Abraham[as] once again launched a gigantic struggle for the restoration of Unity. It prevailed at last, and the torch of Unity was held aloft by his progeny and others who followed him for many a generation to come.

The old fateful trend of decadence set in eventually with the same disastrous consequences. Within a few hundred years from the time of Abraham[as], the House of Israel reverted to the evil practice of idol worship. This continued until the time of Moses[as]. Although Moses[as] was an outstanding champion of the cause of Unity among prophets, idolatry kept infiltrating and defiling the faith of his followers during the subsequent centuries. This again proves beyond a shadow of doubt that to move away from Unity is a downhill task. Left to himself, man would always slide down the ladder to the lowly ground of idolatry — a ground which breeds the vermin of superstition and polytheism.

Another example quoted by the Holy Quran is that of 'Baitul Ḥarām'(بيت الحرام) in Mecca, the House of God built by Abraham[as], dedicated only to the cause of His Unity. But alas, it did not take the idols very long to re-enter this illustrious House of God. Except for the name everything else was changed. It was ultimately occupied by no less than three hundred and sixty idols representing each day of the lunar year, filling its chambers from wall to wall. There was room for all of them, but no room for God.

Is this the evolutionary process the sociologists talk so much about? Is this the way they believe idolatry evolved into the idea of a single Supreme Being? Is this how the image of God is ultimately created by man as he advances from his primitive mental state to a more developed one? Nay, certainly not! The history of religions unanimously rejects this arbitrary sociologist conclusion. It clearly demonstrates that belief in the Unity of God always descends from Him. It never ascends to Him through a natural upward spiralling trend of progressive idol worship.

If a transition from many gods to one did ever occur, then the history of religion should have attested to it. But not a trace of it is found in the established history of world religions. Monotheistic societies do slowly degenerate into the polytheistic ones; the opposite never occurs.

IT is extremely difficult for pious people to bequeath their piety to subsequent generations for a long time. Seldom does it happen that the righteousness of the forefathers runs deep and long into the following generations. A vast majority of the first generation, ushered into light, never returns to the previous state of darkness. Faith however, gradually weakens over successive generations. It does not happen overnight. It is a long slow process of decadence set in after the demise of a prophet which ultimately erodes the hard-earned belief in the Unity of God. Whenever belief dwindles, superstitions begin to encroach and take over. Firm faith in a single Omnipotent God splinters into fragments of a shattered image of Godhead. Oracles begin to be concocted from temple to temple and a dishonest religious clergy feels free to deceive the common masses.

Without exception, all religions emphasize the role of morality in human affairs. They may differ in other features, but not with regard to their stress on morality. It is a universal trend found everywhere in all ages. To accuse religion of siding with the rich and the powerful, may be justified to some extent only in the context of a decadent age. In the light of the early history of religion as it is unfolded with the advent of a prophet, this accusation is simply not entertainable. Morality as taught by the prophets, always works on the side of justice and fair play, waging a noble war against immorality and the exploitation of the weak and the destitute. It always strengthens the hands of the oppressed against the oppressor and those of the hunted against the hunter.

Where on earth did religious morality ever support the cause of the exploiter against the exploited? Search the entire early history of the dawn of religions and you will not find a single such example. It always legislated in favour of the weak and the poor. Genuine implementation of this legislation is guaranteed and impregnated by belief in an All-Knowing God. The believer can never escape His knowledge of whatever He does or intends to do. No man-made law enjoys this advantage in relation to its implementation. It invariably fails to protect the system which they legislate, because of the absence of awareness in the mind of the criminal that he is being watched by the law-makers. Legislation alone, however much fortified with the threats of punishment, cannot stay the hand of the criminal. Its influence does not reach the breeding ground of crime — the hidden soil of secret intentions. The criminal always seeks shelter in his hope that like his intentions, his act of crime will also escape the eye of the law. To seek protection in the lap of falsehood is another major abettor of crime. Man's propensity and impetuous tendency to commit crime is directly proportional to his hope of escaping detection. Hence, legislation alone can never succeed in uprooting social evils, because it lacks the vital prerequisite of reaching the dark abysses where crimes are nurtured. Most evils are perpetrated behind the smokescreen of imagined invisibility and unaccountability. However advanced the techniques of detection may become, they can never shake the confidence of the criminal in his calculated hope of escaping detection because he plans and plots safely hidden from the sight of law, couched in the secret chambers of his heart.

It is only a sound belief in the existence of God and accountability, which can frustrate and defeat all crimes in the offing. This and largely this, has been the purpose of moral legislation on the part of religion. Morality, in fact, is virtually essential for the survival of religion itself. When moral standards are lowered, religion is the first to suffer. Dishonesty and immorality corrode even the most powerful man-made edifices of law and constitution. The spiritual edifices of religion are likewise corroded and turned to dust by the dry rot of immorality. Like termites, it razes to the ground the lofty moral structures of great religions.

This is the key to the understanding of decadence at all levels of religious beliefs and practices. The Unity of God is split and continues to be splintered because of the lowering standards of morality. Idolatry begins to replace the Unity of God, and idols occupy the houses of God turning them into temples. Deep below such destructive phenomenon, one will always find the worms of dishonesty at work. Dishonesty becomes a deadly poison when it works at the level of leadership, but no deadlier poison can be conceived than dishonesty when it works at the level of religious leadership. In the name of God, they play havoc with the peace of His creation. God ceases to play any substantial role in the affairs of men. His emptied throne is occupied by the pseudo-gods of religious hierarchy.

It would be much wiser therefore, to judge religions at their nascent stage rather than later, when through human interpolation they become mere ruins of their noble beginning. Their beginning is noble but also humble. The attitude of the society towards religions when they are found in their pristine purity is that of extreme hostility and rejection. The noblest living example of religious teachings are the prophets themselves. It is they who are rejected and ridiculed and made the target of merciless hostility.

The same goes for the early believers whose integrity, dedication and willing sacrifice in the cause of truth finds no parallel in the later period. How ironical it is that noble men such as these are not acceptable to a society as long as they live. After they have departed the arena of life on

211

earth, they are revered, even beyond the status they actually occupied. They are raised to the status of godlike figures; even their graves are worshipped. This strange inconsistency in the attitude of the society gradually grows among those who inherit their faith without paying the price of sacrifice. They corrode the noble values of religion surreptitiously and work beneath the surface like worms. Unity of God always works in two planes. All advocates of His Unity are inseparably bound to Him, as well as among themselves, together. Again, on the other plane, Unity exists between the Creator and His creation.

In the established history of prophethood, no prophet is ever found to reject and malign the prophets before him. The same attitude of oneness is extended into the future. Of course warnings are issued against 'false prophets' who are clearly recognizable, by their ungodly character, but the advent of genuine Divine messengers is always mentioned with love and respect. This applies invariably to all upholders of Unity belonging to all ages. Unity of God forges them into one brotherhood. Corrupt religious patriarchs do not possess this distinctive feature. They preach division while beating the drum of Unity. The love of Unity binds His prophets so powerfully together that to offend one is tantamount to offending the other. It becomes the strongest symbol of Unification between God and His chosen servants on the one hand, and between the chosen servants, mutually, on the other.

Unity also manifests itself as a universal link between Him and every other form of existence. The Unity of the Creator unites Him with His creation, unifying them in apparent or subtle ways. Alas, that in relation to both these integrals of Unity, disintegration begins to take place with the passage of time. This eventually prepares the soil upon which the Tree of Evil thrives.

The first signs of disruption appear when the arrogant priesthood of later periods begins to raise the status of their human prophets beyond the inviolable line of Unity, assigning to them some of the exclusive Divine attributes, which they never, ever, claimed for themselves. An over-exaggerated love of the past prophets becomes the new faith of this degenerate religious society. Hyperbolical eulogies are showered upon them, new human gods are in the making, new mortals are immortalised. Little do they realize that they and the entire society which follows them must pay heavily for this blatant inconsistency. Blind love of past prophets becomes the soul and spirit of their religion but only after the soul and spirit of the prophet's message is completely destroyed and shattered by this new class of their pseudo-devotees. Prophets always come to destroy sin but their love is exploited to promote it. This, they trust, would absolve them of whatever sins they may have committed. The same love of a dead prophet will enliven them to a life worse than death. They feel safe with God, whose Unity they offend, as long as they continue to bow their heads to the godliness of His human partners. This opens such floodgates of moral corruption which once opened can never be shut again by human efforts. Sin is invariably emboldened by the love of sinless prophets.

THE SAME decadent clergy shamelessly advocate hatred, bloodshed, terrorism and destruction of fundamental human rights in the name of their love of God. They create a chasm between God and humans thus securing for themselves a position of command in His absence. From them on, it is they who issue decrees without receiving them from on high. They virtually capture godhead without admitting it in so many words. To them God matters not; what matters is they themselves. It is their wrath which society must fear; from then on, it is their pleasure they must always seek. This becomes the new criterion for punishment and reward. Whoever dares to disagree with the pseudo-gods is condemned to hell, whoever agrees is rewarded with eternal paradise. God must dispose what they propose. About the morals of the common people they care not. All they care for is their own ego and the authority with which they command the masses. Courtesy, culture, a sense of justice and fair play are all mercilessly slaughtered at the altar of their rigid dogmas. This is the price the societies must always pay whenever they violate the Unity of God in one sense or another.

Like an injured serpent, they begin to raise their vengeful head against Divine interference. Their virtual worship of past prophets is a ruse of course; their real intention hidden behind this facade has always been the worship of their own egos. But the dilemma is that such a Godless society abounds in pseudo-gods like them. There can be no unity without the Unity of God. Petty rivalries among the priestly class begin to take their toll. They divide and split into new sects and schisms holding the banners of ideological differences.

An atrocious struggle for gaining ascendancy over the masses ensues. All they really care for is the number of their flock. As for the morals of the people they lead, they could not care less. They exercise no positive influence over their daily life and moral responsibilities to the society. They only know how to excite their emotions to a state of frenzy in generating hatred against the rival sects but they never till and turn the soil of their hearts to sow the seeds of love and sacrifice. A society such as this offers an ideal ground for idolatry to take root therein. Unconditional submission to their authority in matters of faith and doctrine is all they demand. The submission to the will of

God with regard to the life they lead is of no consequence. They may rob or steal, they may maim or kill, they may hoard wealth or build castles with lies, deception, cheating and fraud. They may do whatever they will, as long as they do not change their loyalties to their own priests and do not prostrate to their rivals; everything else about them is just fine and acceptable. The centre of their worship shifts from God to prophets, from prophets to their own wretched egos. Thus the corrupt mortals emerge in their new role of demigods.

The case of the ignorant masses who follow them is no less pitiable. All they know on earth is that God is priest and priest is God. They are incapable of challenging his authority in the matter of faith. A diametrical change in the orientation of submission takes place. It becomes impossible for them to know the difference. The will of the priest, to them, becomes the will of God. It remains so only as long as the priest does not cross the path of their self-interest. The moment he ventures to do so he loses his authority over them and is no longer treated as an object worthy of submission. In the domain of his personal interests, no member of an immoral society such as this knows any God other than himself. Homage is paid to the pseudo-gods of priests only as long as they do not clash with the egos of those they lead. Thus the journey from monotheism to polytheism turns a full circle. Ego worship is the only logical destination of a religious society in decadence.

In all promiscuous societies, as mentioned above, the sudden appearance of a Divine Warner, is always treated as a most annoying interference. Such exactly was the treatment meted out to Jesus[as] when he appeared among the sheep of the House of Israel. But in their attitude to him, they should be referred to as wolves rather than sheep.

215

However, his attitude to them was like that of a loving shepherd who cares for each sheep of his flock.

One can easily visualize how deceptively their passage is eternally blocked. The virtual idolization of prophets works as the most formidable stumbling block in the path of later prophets who must always appear as humans. Even without idolization, the hyperbolical praises showered upon them and attributions to them of supernatural powers should be sufficient cause for the rejection of all genuine prophets who will never come in this grand style. Hence, a crisis of identity will always block their passage.

Without prophets, faith in God is but another name for atheism. Their daily pattern of behaviour and conduct of life reflects everything but God. He seems to have abandoned them, like a nest from which the bird has flown away forever, never to return.

Such also were the challenges confronted by Jesus Christ[as]. The Jewish society of his time was passing through a similar spiritual and moral crisis. The rabbis and the Pharisees and the Sadducees had all become pseudo-gods and no room was left for accommodating the Divine. It is no small wonder, therefore, that the lone, humble voice of Jesus[as] raised in the name of God, was not drowned in the tumultuous uproar of the hostile protests.

This, in short, is the tale of the origin, rise and fall of religions. But a new beginning is always made after every fall to rehabilitate the Unity of God yet again. It always originates in Heaven, and descends with revelation. It never erupts from the earth below, rising heavenwards like curly columns of smoke of human confusion ultimately resolving into a belief in Unity. Instead the Unity of God only descends from on high to raise the fallen man yet again to the celestial heights of nearness to Him.

THE CONCEPT OF GOD AMONG
THE ABORIGINES OF AUSTRALIA

SO FAR we have attempted to disprove the currently popular theories of Western sociologists, who by a strange logic of their own, have tried to prove that the idea of God is a creation of man rather than man being His creation. Their so-called evidence in support of their theory is nothing but mere conjecture. How far the study of the evolution of mind over a billion years of biotic evolution would support this bizarre hypothesis is a subject of inquiry in itself and requires an in-depth study. On the other hand, an unbiased study of the history of religions reveals that belief in God is not a product of human superstition. Was it God Who created man, or was it man who created God, is the vital question we have already discussed with reference to the history of some major monotheistic religions.

Now, we propose to critically examine the sociologists' concept of a gradual evolution of the idea of God, with reference to the Aborigine religions of Australia. This study will further demonstrate the inherent flaw in the sociologists' manner of enquiry. Their enquiry invariably begins with the preconception that there is no God. No fair-minded person can adjudge such an enquiry as scientific, where the verdict is already passed before the enquiry has begun. It is this inherent contradiction which becomes manifestly exposed when the sociologists come face to face with the irrefutable reality of Australian evidence. Before constituting any enquiry, its principles have to be clearly laid down. But no such attempt has ever been made by the sociologists to define them and the purpose of the enquiry.

217

The only principle they know is their conviction that there is no God. The purpose of their enquiry is simply to investigate why people worship God or godly images while they do not exist. Hence the growth of superstitions culminating in the creation of gods is the only subject of their enquiry.

Having said that, let us now draw the attention of the reader to the history of religion in Australia. It is a continent whose culture, social and religious history can be traced back to at least twenty-five thousand years. Many scholars extend it to forty thousand years or beyond. According to some researchers, however, this period could extend even to a past as remote as one hundred and thirty thousand years of unbroken, unadulterated and undisturbed growth of religion.

The Australian continent is not only unique in having been completely broken off from the rest of the world, it is also unique in containing within it hundreds of social islands, each comprising tribes that remained entirely isolated from each other. It is known that between five hundred to six hundred such tribal units had their own independent history of social and religious development, throughout an age of twenty-five to forty thousand years, in complete isolation from each other except for occasional marginal contacts at the boundaries of their territories.

Such contacts were not only brief, but also ineffectual in transferring their ideologies, beliefs, myths and superstitions to each other. It was not only the language barriers which stood in the way, but also their traditional aversion to socialize and communicate with outsiders, which had created an impassable barrier in the way of transfer of information from one to the other.

If the sociologist's view which begins with the negation of God has any substance in it, then in each of the

Aboriginal tribes we should have discovered the same universal trend of worshipping objects of nature gradually evolving into belief in one Supreme God. What we discover, however, to the utter chagrin of the sociologist is a completely different story.

In all the tribes of Australia, without exception, there exists a belief in one Supreme Power, who is the first cause of all creation. Their descriptions differ on minor points and their terminology varies slightly, but according to the consensus of the sociologists and anthropologists, they all invariably believe in the existence of that ultimate first cause called 'High Gods' — another name for Allah, God, Brahma and Parmatama etc.

The central idea of one eternal Supreme Creator remains unadulterated by whatever other superstitions they may have entertained. The superstitions change from tribe to tribe, but not their belief in one God. Nowhere in Australia could the sociologists find any evidence of a gradual evolution of the idea of God. The views prevailing among the different tribes differ only in description. The Wiimbaio tribe, for instance, believed that while engaged in the process of the creation of earth, God remained close at hand but having finished His work He ascended back to the loftiness of the constellations. Similarly, the Wotjobaluk tribe believed Bunjil to be a Supreme Being, who once lived on the earth as a great man but eventually ascended to the sky.[1]

The sociologists, when referring to these beliefs, very often forget to inform the reader that these and all the other five hundred or more tribes, did believe in the eternity of the Creator; whether He took human form or not is only incidental and not central to the issue. Again, what is central to their belief is the fact that the earth and whatever

219

it contained did not eternally coexist with the Supreme
Creator.

Many anthropologists dispute the origin and purpose
of the concept of God amongst the Aborigines. They doubt
that the Australian High Gods*, is the same as the Supreme
Being known elsewhere among traditional religions,
because it is difficult for them to believe that savages or
inferior people, as the primitive Australians were, could
hold such advanced conceptions.

The utter absurdity of their position is self-evident.
Because they could not believe something to have
happened, so it could not have happened, is the crux of
their argument. This further exposes their prejudicial
attitude. If a society as primitive as the Aborigines of
Australia is found to have believed in one God, right from
the beginning of their history, then there is nothing left for
sociologists but to admit ideas of God did not evolve from
primitive superstitious myths. Instead all we have from
them is a childish sulky response: we cannot believe
because it could not have happened.

In an attempt to avoid this embarrassment, E.B. Tylor
has discovered another evasive excuse to discredit the
Australian evidence. In his article *Limits of Savage Religion*
in the *Journal of Anthropological Institute* (1891), he
proposes the novel idea that High Gods is the product of
influences from the Christian missionaries on Australian
religion. An absurd proposition, as it is, it is completely
belied by the facts of history.

A.W. Howitt, another evolutionist, roundly disproves
Tylor's claim pointing out that in some tribes in the South-

---

* The term 'High Gods' is not plural as it appears. In Aborigine
terminology it invariably refers to a Single Supreme Creator. It is out
of respect perhaps that He is referred to in plural.

East of Australia, the belief in One Eternal God certainly preceded the arrival of any missionaries or indeed any Western settlers, among them. Strangely, even he fails to notice that the bizarre idea of Christian missionaries sowing the suggestion of the Unity of God should have been dismissed outright because no trace of Trinity is found anywhere in the entire continent of Australia in the image of God which the Aborigines universally revere.

Nevertheless, despite the range and extent of Howitt's empirical studies, Howitt himself seems reluctant to push his own research to its logical conclusion. While he can readily admit in his book, published in 1904, that the Aborigines believed in an All-Father who was:

'...evidently everlasting, for he existed from the beginning of all things, and he still lives. But in being so, he is merely in that state in which, these Aborigines believe, everyone would be if not prematurely killed by magic.'[2]

Thus Howitt attempts to escape the inescapable evidence of Divinity in their belief by confusing the issue. He claims:

'It cannot be alleged that these Aborigines have consciously any form of religion.'[3]

Here is another example of a desperate attempt on the part of the evolutionists to escape the inevitable. The points Howitt has raised are not only inconclusive but are also irrelevant to the subject of discussion. The simple question which any sociologist must have addressed was: how could a primitive society, like that of the Aborigines, which was split into hundreds of sub-tribes with no means of communication among them, conceive the same idea of One Supreme Eternal Being independently? Again, they should have answered the question as to what legitimacy is left, in view of this, to their theories of an evolutionary development of the idea of God.

As for Howitt, even if we accept his tall claim that all Aborigines believed that if they were not killed by magic they could have evolved into something like the Creator Himself, it offers no haven of escape to him. In no way does it support the sociologists' myth of evolution of the idea of God. One is amazed how a scholar of Howitt's reputation could confuse the two distinctly separate issues. The theory of ultimate evolution of belief in one God, from the primitive superstitious beliefs in many gods, has nothing whatsoever to do with the hypothetical discussion of the possible evolution of men into gods, had death not terminated their span of life. At best this Aboriginal view could be likened unto a similar discussion in the Old Testament in relation to the story of Adam and Eve and the Serpent. God, according to the serpent, had denied Adam and Eve access to the fruit of the forbidden tree, lest they should become like the Creator Himself, sharing eternity with Him. This similarity between the primitive Aborigines' view with the Judeo-Christian beliefs brings their faith even closer to the comity of traditional religions. One really wonders how Howitt could fail to register this evident similarity.

Obviously, it is the Aborigine way to draw a clear-cut line between the Creator and the created. The message delivered is simply this: the Creator is not only Eternal in relation to the past, He is also Everlasting in relation to the future. He is the only One who possesses these attributes. No man can ever achieve eternity in relation to the future because every man is mortal. This brings them in line with all the Unitarian religions which share the same belief that God alone is Eternal and Everlasting.

In his enthusiasm to discredit the Aborigines of having any religion at all, he further argues that there are no signs of worship or sacrifice among them. This observation of Howitt has no relevance to the contention under review. Whether he calls their faith a religion or not, when he admits that they did believe in the existence of a Supreme Eternal Creator, he succeeds only in discrediting the sociologists' theory of gradual evolution of the idea of God.

As for the validity of his claim that there is no evidence of the Aborigines offering worship or sacrifice in any form to the High Gods in whom they believed, it cannot be accepted at its face value. It should be noted here that some of their religious practices have been completely misunderstood by most Western scholars. What they refer to as the habit of dreaming by the Aborigines, is not what the Aborigines themselves believe them to be.

THE AUTHOR has had the opportunity of meeting one of their knowledgeable leaders to verify from them the real significance of their dreams. It is important because one finds dreams mentioned in almost all Western literature written on Aborigines. It took some effort on the part of the author to ultimately persuade that leader to discuss matters of faith, which he was obviously reluctant to share with a non-Aborigine. This reluctance, it transpired, was largely due to the misunderstanding and misrepresentation of their beliefs by many a foreigner who had probed into this area of Aborigine life and history. This is what the author gathered from his conversation with him after a favourable rapport was established.

Dreams to them are merely a means of communication from God. Through dreams they are foretold of many important events in their lives. They have a system of religious hierarchy, comprising leaders who are well versed in the science of interpretation of dreams. Such leaders have no outside contact and access to them by the non-Aborigine is barred. When the dreams are presented to them, the dreamer himself has often no idea as to the message they carry. The interpreter however can read the underlying message and, most often than not, he is proved right. It is the subsequent events which testify to his truth as well as to the validity of the institution of dreams.

Thus, a clear line has to be drawn between their religious beliefs and practices on the one hand and their rituals and superstitions on the other, which are of no real significance anyway. Superstitions and superstitious practices vary from tribe to tribe and there is no common heritage found among all the Aborigines. The issue of dreams is radically different. Like their belief in one God, their reliance on dreams as a means of Divine instruction is shared by all invariably. The dreams very often follow their contemplation on matters of grave importance. Hence, it is not unlikely that this contemplation is just another name for prayers. It has to be so because their contemplation, unlike that among the Buddhists, results in such dreams as are answers to them. In relation to their dreams the Aborigines also have a strong and well-defined discipline, the breach of which is punishable.

To dub them as a religionless people therefore is far from justified. As far as their belief concerning death 'caused by magic' is concerned, in this context, it does not have the same meaning as understood elsewhere in the world. There are no theatrical magicians among the Aborigines, like those who operate elsewhere in the world. They certainly do not believe that every death which occurs among them, occurs because of a spell cast by an evil person through magical chanting. In this case magic is far more likely to refer to satanic influences, which symbolize darkness as against light in the spiritual sense. For magic to mean sin in Aborigine terminology is so apparent that it is hard to understand how the anthropologists and sociologists fail to recognize it. Death is considered to be the result of magic which works in the case of every mortal without exception. Only 'High Gods' is an exception to this rule. None else shares eternity with Him. By no means does it signify that death is caused in every case only by the acts of some magicians casting their spell on the living. Death is a universal phenomenon applicable to all living forms alike, everywhere in the world, Australia being no exception. Aborigines knew it well and however naive one may consider them to be, it is impossible to attribute to them the utter stupidity of considering every death to be the outcome of sorcery.

In view of this, the significance of magic can only be understood in two possible ways. First it may refer to sin as the ultimate cause of all spiritual death, as understood in other Divine religions elsewhere in the world. If this is the case, then they must have received the idea from the same source that enlightened the People of the Book to the existence of an Eternal God.

Alternatively, a second simpler meaning of magic which could reasonably be attributed to them would be that whatever they found to be inexplicable, for which they had no answer, was relegated to the realm of magic, meaning simply a mystery. Hence, the universality and inevitability of death, which marks the demarcation line between the finite and infinite, the Creator and the created, is a mystery spoken of as 'magic' by Aborigines. However, the term magic is not confined to this connotation alone. Whatever else they found to be inexplicable in their day-to-day experience was also referred to as magic.

Again, the eternal conflict between light and darkness, as depicted in somewhat material terms in the Zoroastrian religion, could as well be the underlying philosophy in the so-called superstitious practices of the Aborigine. Their well-established practice of trying to shun the shadow of a moving object may have the same significance as darkness representing sin or Satan.

But the dreams and whatever they understand by them, have nothing to do with their superstitions; they are two unrelated phenomena. The dreams are a part of the central core of their belief in God and the means of receiving communication from Him. According to them, from time immemorial, they have been witnessing the signs of an All-Knowing Supreme Being who takes a live interest in the affairs of what He creates. Thus the Aborigines have a genuine cause of complaint against the Western researchers who dismiss their religious experience as unworthy of being called religious because they deem them too primitive and ignorant. Their efforts to distort the image of the Aboriginal faith must have stemmed from the fear lest this recognition should discredit their own previously held theories.

One Aborigine who particularly impressed the author was a highly educated gentleman who had converted to Christianity, or so it seemed, before his access to higher education. By profession he was an engineer. In the beginning of the dialogue, he was evidently reluctant to share his knowledge of the religious beliefs and practices of the Aborigine. Surprisingly, despite his conversion to Christianity, he still remained Aborigine deep at heart. After a long persuasive effort on the part of the author when he became convinced of his sincerity and genuine concern for the cause of the Aborigine, he gradually began to thaw. The sorrow in his eyes was as deep and profound as the ancient history of Aborigine civilization. He told the author that it was seldom that outsiders could actually gain

Innumerable boundaries between Australian tribes separated them into complete isolation from each other. The languages differed and inter-communication in any form was strictly avoided. Yet in each tribe the concept of One God remained common.

I.5

I.6

access to the elite hierarchy of the Aborigines. The knowledge they have acquired is mostly peripheral. He showed particular disgust at the manner the Aborigines' experience of dreams was treated and portrayed by the Western researchers.

A tradition of the Holy Prophet[sa], is worthy of note here because it speaks of Divine dreams to be one-fortieth part of prophethood.[4] Though this profound observation indicates that universally it is true dreams with which prophethood begins, they ultimately pave the path for verbal revelation from God, which may, when He so pleases, commission the recipient to be His Messenger.

Returning to the subject of the conclusion drawn by the Western researchers, one must admit that all are not alike in their negative attitude to the spiritual experiences of the Aborigines. Among them are scholars who possessed the clear vision and boldness to admit that Aborigines did have a well-defined faith in a Single Supreme God. Andrew Lang in *The Making of Religion*[5], argued that 'High Gods' was an authentic Aborigine idea, and because there were very few myths around the 'All-Fathers', Lang justifiably concluded that the myths were born after the idea of the 'High Gods.'

Peter Wilhelm Schmidt, a German Roman Catholic priest, in his twelve volume *Ursprung der Gottesidee*, written between 1912 and 1925, also supported Lang and asserted that myth came after the idea of 'High Gods'. Schmidt's work was first published in French between 1908 and 1910 in *Anthropos*, a new journal founded by Schmidt himself. A reprint was circulated separately under the heading, *L'origine de Dieu. Etude Historico-Critique et Positive. Premiere Partie. Historico Critique (Vienna 1910)*, a second enlarged German edition appeared in 1926. Here, Schmidt explained the coexistsence of myth and religion in the concept of the High Gods, by arguing that the original idea of High Gods had become mixed up with the later growth of superstitious gibberish.

However, there are some anthropologists who continue to insist that the idea of High Gods was the product of myths. Among them is the leading figure of Raffaele Pettazzoni in *Dio*, (1922) but it is surprising to note that his argument is not at all supported by the evidence consistently found in all the main Aboriginal tribes. For him to extend his conclusions drawn from the mythical traditions of only one particular tribe to all the Aborigines of Australia is neither honest nor logical.[6]

Most Aboriginal tribes do not share the same myths as mentioned by him. As for their belief in God, they all subscribe to the idea of One Supreme, Conscious, Eternal Cause of creation. Moreover, despite the great name of Pettazzoni as an anthropologist, his insistence that the coexistsence of myths and the idea of One Supreme Creator must mean that the superstitions preceded the more highly developed idea of God — is unentertainable without the least evidence to support it. He has not even attempted to connect the development of their myths to the idea of a Supreme God through an evolutionary process.

The theory of the evolutionary growth of the idea of God from myths and superstitions is simply not relevant to the Australian evidence. There is no evidence whatsoever of nature worship under the influence of awe and wonder. No such step by step worship practices can be traced in the Aboriginal religious practices, ultimately leading to the more advanced belief in God. One has to agree therefore with Andrew Lang that the myth definitely followed and did not precede the idea of One God.

The myths among Aborigines are scattered unrelated pieces of superstitions which can be justifiably related to the simple wanderings of the mind of a primitive unlettered people to discover some meaning in what they observed. This attempt on their part is no different from the universal human trend.

Man has always been wondering about the nature of the heavens, the sun, the moon and the constellations. Many a time this wonderment has resulted in the creation of myths. Among the idolatrous people, their imaginary gods are ultimately dressed in the robes of myths. This, however, is not the case with the Aborigines. Their myths are neither related to the idea of worship, nor are they built around the figures of gods, as we find elsewhere. According to them the idea of God is separate and independent, the images of other forms of existence occupying the heavenly bodies and constellations are not gods. Hence it is made more difficult to agree with Pettazzoni when he argues that the High Gods is a product of mythological imagination.

The problem with the rationalist anthropologists and sociologists is basically the same as shared by all other secular scholars. If they accept the Australian evidence, they would ultimately have to admit that the idea of a Supreme Eternal Creator had not evolved, hence it must have descended in its perfected form from God Himself. Otherwise it could not be possible for the most primitive simple-minded dweller of Australia to conceive that idea with such unanimity without any inter-communication. Hence the denial of this evidence by some sociologists and anthropologists, merely because it does not agree with their concept of things, is no compliment to their scholarly image and their integrity. It is a relief however to learn that among them there are many happy exceptions. There are certainly some who exhibit enough maturity and honesty of purpose to accept the evidence as fact. Yet they too continue to explore some avenues of escape to hide behind the mist of obscure, shady explanations.

Such is the case of F. Graebner. While accepting that the 'great god' was certainly a Creator for the Aborigines and a

> '... first cause of, at least, everything which is important for men ...,'

he goes on to argue:

> 'But Preuss is perhaps right in doubting that so abstract an idea as the first cause could have been capable, among primitive men, of producing a figure which is always so full of life.'[7]

Like Howitt, Graebner is reluctant to commit himself to the view that the Aborigines could have perceived the attributes of a Supreme Being all by themselves, yet he lacks the moral strength to draw the inevitable conclusion. A prefixed atheistic bias is evident.

In some tribes of Australia, the idea of one High Gods is found intermixed with some mythical figures around him such as wives, children etc. This does not cast any doubt on our claim that the image of High Gods of the Aborigines is no different from that of God elsewhere in the conventional monotheistic religions. The scholars who discovered the prevalence of such myths have highlighted some of their distinctive features, which help the reader to draw a clear line of demarcation between them and God, with whom they are claimed to be related. It is a mistake to ascribe the same meaning to the so-called Aboriginal myths as normally related to the word 'myth' elsewhere in the world. Elsewhere, the myths are always created around the figures of gods in idolatrous religions, while among the Aborigines no such 'gods' are either worshipped or revered. Whatever myths the sociologists may refer to were certainly not created around the figure of their High Gods. For only a few tribes to entertain such myths is in itself a proof that their existence is not indicative of a universal belief among the Aboriginal tribes. No creative power is ever attributed to them nor are they believed to share eternity with Him. They are all creations none of which has ever created anything. They have to be created themselves because they are not eternal. It is likely that these myths were conceived haphazardly by some religious elders of later ages.

Speaking of the same, Eliade, while paraphrasing T.G.H Strehlow, takes up the case of another tribe of the Western Aranda and shows that according to them:

> '... the earth and the sky had always existed and had always been the home of Supernatural Beings. The western Aranda believe that the sky is inhabited by an emu-footed Great Father (Knaritja), who is also the Eternal Youth *(altjira nditja)*. He has dog-footed wives and many sons and daughters. "They lived on fruits and vegetable foods in an eternally green land, unaffected by droughts, through which the Milky Way flowed like a broad river...".'[8]

They have an Eden-like place where only trees, fruits and flowers flourish. All these sky-dwellers are seen as ageless and beyond death.

Despite the fact that these sky-beings display two essential characteristics of supremacy, that of immortality and chronological precedence (i.e. they came before the totemic heroes), Strehlow rightly refuses to acknowledge their significance in the development of Australian religion. He cannot accept these sky-beings as supreme because they did not shape or create life themselves.[9]

Strehlow's argument is irrefutable because the mythical forms referred to are described as immortal but not eternal in their relation to the past, while the High

Gods, is both eternal and immortal. Moreover, no power of creation whatsoever is attributed to these mythical figures, hence they cannot be perceived as sharing Divinity with High Gods, the only Creator. Again it is quite likely that this belief may have been wrongly categorized as mythical. It may well have been a slightly changed version of the paradise concept common to all major Divinely revealed religions. The description of the Supreme Dweller of paradise being emu-footed and that of His wife and children as dog-footed are the only foreign elements to the concept of paradise found elsewhere, otherwise the same Eden-like gardens, eternally green, abounding in fruits and vegetables, with no fear of drought etc., are very close to metaphoric description of paradise presented by the Holy Quran.

The complete absence of animals other than the 'Children of God' is also significant. The concept of paradise in other major religions is likewise empty of animal life. The dwellers are only the pious people who are also described metaphorically as 'Children of God'. Had it been a myth created by the simple minds of Aborigines, it is unlikely that they should have altogether excluded the animals from their vision of paradise. In other areas of the world we often find mythical concepts involving the presence of some animals. Yet, in the image of paradise common to the major religions, animals are conspicuous by their absence.

THE HISTORY of evolution of society and religious ideas is not shaped by any single factor. It is far too intermixed and the mutual flow of ideas from one region to the other is so frequent that it becomes difficult to disentangle one from the other and determine the direction of influence with any certainty. To trace a single thread of thought process from beginning to end in a sequential order is indeed an extremely challenging task.

The debate as to who influenced whom goes unabated. Was it Buddhism, for instance which mothered Christian ideology or was it Christianity which influenced Buddhism, is one of the many unresolved questions. But what we find in Australia is a completely different story of a unique singularity. If evidence of the Australian religious experience had supported the sociologists' view, one wonders what their attitude would have been. Would they not have raised a storm and shouted 'eureka' at the top of their voice in exultation and pride! But with the hard realities of the unadulterated religious history of the Aborigines staring them in the eye, it is deplorable to watch how desperately they still struggle to escape the inevitable. We particularly speak of such naturalists as are in a state of shock because they had no faith in God the Creator. As such they were absolutely certain that the history of the Aborigines would support their convictions and testify to their theories that the idea of God had gradually evolved over thousands of years. But what they have discovered is so different and exasperating. Why exasperating, one may ask, when they are just in search of truth? Why be so profoundly disappointed at the truth being at variance with their own previously held views? It is so because the rejection of any argument which may lead to God is with them predetermined. Any discoveries contrary to this must either be discarded or misinterpreted. Secularism to them is synonymous with the negation of God. Whatever excuses they offer, however, to save the face of their 'secular' theories, serve only to expose their unscientific attitude further. Prejudice is no prerogative, it seems of the religious clergy alone. Non religious thinkers and philosophers can also have their fill of it whenever it suits their purpose. A

233

draught full of this hemlock invariably drowns their faculty of logic and sense, justice and fair play. Under this influence they behave more like dogmatic religious zealots, than as secular thinkers, as they purport themselves to be.

But whatever argument they muster in support of their erstwhile view can in no way ressurrect it from the ruin it has already met. All their high-flown theories of a God progressively created by human imagination came to a disastrous crash on the Australian continent. They are in utter dismay and disarray confounded by the fall. To put them together again can be done neither by kings nor clowns. Their case is reminiscent of Milton's *Paradise Lost.* Only, no reason or logic will ever help them salvage the wreckage and regain what they have forever lost. Little could Milton imagine that his drama would one day be played in real life, with men for actors. Their paradise lost would not be 'God Himself', but a god of their own creation. What do we care if they lose him forever, and what do they care if God cares for them naught!

REFERENCES

1. ELIADE, M. (1973) *Australian Religions. An Introduction.* Cornell Uni Press, Ithach, p.4

2. ELIADE, M. (1973) *Australian Religions. An Introduction.* Cornell Uni Press, Ithach, p.13

3. ELIADE, M. (1973) *Australian Religions. An Introduction.* Cornell Uni Press, Ithach.

4. Musnad Al-Imam Ahmad Bin Hanbal (1983) Vol.4. Al-Maktab-Al-Islami. Beirut, p.10

5. LANG, A. (1898) *The Making of Religion.* Longmans, Green & Co., London.

6. ELIADE, M. (1973) *Australian Religions. An Introduction.* Cornell Uni Press, Ithach.

7. ELIADE, M. (1973) *Australian Religions. An Introduction.* Cornell Uni Press, Ithach, p.24

8. ELIADE, M. (1973) *Australian Religions. An Introduction.* Cornell Uni Press, Ithach, p.30

9. ELIADE, M. (1973) *Australian Religions. An Introduction.* Cornell Uni Press, Ithach, pp.32-33

PART IV

THE NATURE OF REVELATION

WHAT IS REVELATION? Is revelation merely a term used to describe the conscious or subconscious exploration of one's inner world, or is its source an external being, whose knowledge transcends that of humans?

Even people who believe in revelation differ in their understanding of its nature. For example the majority of today's Buddhists, Confucianists and Taoists consider their founders' experiences to have arisen purely from within their conscious or subconscious minds. As mentioned earlier they believe that truth exists within every soul as a part of nature. Inspiration to them is the instrument of contact with the fountainhead of this eternal truth. Other religions hold the view that revelation is an experience arising from an external source — an Everlasting, All-Wise God.

If we widen the scope of our study, we observe that many authentic cases of revelation are also reported outside the domain of religion. For instance, there are many interesting cases of highly complex information conveyed through revelation to some scientists.

In 1865 a German chemist, Fredrich August Kekule, was struggling to solve a problem in chemistry that had baffled all researchers. One night Kekule had a dream in which he saw a snake with its tail held in its mouth. This dream instantly put him on the right track leading to the solution of the perplexing question. Thus was unravelled the secret of the molecular behaviour in certain organic compounds, a discovery which created a revolution in the understanding of organic chemistry. He interpreted this dream to mean that in the benzene molecule, carbon atoms bond together to form a ring structure. This knowledge gave birth to the huge and highly developed field of synthetic organic chemistry producing a vast new range of synthetic materials. The contemporary pharmaceutical industry has become growingly dependent on synthetic drugs. Mankind is indeed indebted to that one dream through which Kekule resolved that problem.

Elias Howe was the first person to mechanize the process of sewing. He too received the answer to a problem that had frustrated him for a long time through a dream. In his dream he saw himself surrounded by savages, who threatened to kill him unless he designed a sewing machine. Being unable to respond he was tied to a tree and the savages started to attack him with arrows and spears. It surprised him to see eyelets on their spearheads. On waking from this dream, he immediately realized the solution, which led him to invent the prototype of the sewing machine that was to dramatically revolutionize the sewing industry. Through his dream he understood that he should consider placing the eye of the needle in its point.

It was this idea which helped him resolve a seemingly impossible task. It is difficult to visualize the sorry state in which man would find himself today without the blessing of this dream. What a revolution was created indeed by this revelation!

In view of many such experiences, one of the possible explanations that comes to mind is that revelation is a phenomenon arising from the subconscious. When the conscious mind is tired of pondering over intriguing problems before falling to sleep, it transfers those problems to the subconscious. During sleep the subconscious keeps reflecting on the data fed into it, and finally computes the much needed solution. Sometimes the solutions may be perceived through visions and sometimes heard in the form of verbal messages. This being so, would it mean that all types of revelation, in whatever manner they appear, are really messages from the subconscious without exception?

In the cases described above, it may well be argued that all the necessary pieces of information needed for the resolution of those problems were already in the conscious mind, the subconscious only proving to be a more powerful tool for synthesizing such information in some mysterious manner. Is this then the sum total of the entire human experience of inspirational revelation or are there other forms that lie beyond the scope of mental processes alone?

The major religions of the world believe that their prophets and also many other holy men received revelation from an external source called God. Others consider this to be a mistaken inference and do not accuse them of wilful fraud, since they could genuinely have mistaken a purely internal experience for a message received from an external source. But if this was so, then the foundations of all the so-called Divine religions would be on very shaky ground. The truth of such claims could only be proved if ample external evidence supports it.

As it would be too extensive and laborious a task to verify the truth of all such claimants individually, we shall only attempt to apply this criterion to the Holy Quran. The foundation of most major religions rests in the belief that there is a Supreme Creator Who, having created man, never abandoned him and continued to take interest in his affairs. It is He Who imparts guidance through His messengers, whenever and to whomsoever He pleases. He reveals knowledge of His existence and expresses His will to mankind to shape their lives in accordance with His instruction. If this is true then revelation will have to be treated as an independent source of knowledge, distinct from mere psychic inspiration, and rationality would occupy only a second place compared to it.

From the vantage point of the human mind, revelation seems to be an internal experience taking place within the sphere of the human psyche. For this reason Divine messages may well be confused with other similar experiences of the subconscious. Nearly all people at one stage or another of their life have some encounter with the workings of the psyche. The human psyche has a built-in mechanism which can create illusions and visions sometimes so clear that they appear to be real to the person who experiences them.

Such experiences belong to a wide range which can be categorized in brief as dreams, verbal messages, musical sounds, images and impressions. In the case of the deranged or those whose minds are in a high state of excitement, their experiences can be so intense that they may create horrifying hallucinations which could drive them mad. Raging fevers can also produce similar states of mental excitement. Apart from this, there are experiences of a completely different nature which generate orderly, soothing and comforting dreams and visions, pacifying the mind and ridding it of many a lurking fear and premonition which sometimes people suffer from without identifying the cause. Again there are messages delivered in clearly heard distinct voices which sometimes are delivered by human or angelic apparitions, or in the voices of unseen persons. If they too could be explained as products of human mind and psyche, all spiritual experiences would be relegated to the realm of psychic phenomenon!

Where then, is room for revelation and Divinely revealed visions? That is the all-important question, which should be clearly addressed and answered. Man's mind is provided with all the mechanisms needed to receive or create such impressions. But God also, whenever He deems it fit, may directly operate this psychic mechanism. To find an answer to this vital question, one needs to examine it at greater length – a task which can be made easier by dividing it into subcategories.

Inspiration

As the subconscious mind can stir up hallucinations and ravings, so also it is capable of creating orderly and meaningful visions and messages. The mind in its inner recesses may go on ruminating on a subject without being conscious of it and eventually develop an answer previously unknown to the conscious mind. It goes on working on a problem until it gets an answer which it can transmit to the higher conscious level of the mind through dreams, visions etc. The results obtained by this process are always within the scope of the available data, which has already been fed to the mind. This process may not necessarily require the influence of an outside agency to be activated. Even a criminal may develop an ingenious plan to commit crime through this process of subconscious inspiration. But it should not be forgotten that the results of inspiration are always related to the data available to the human mind, and can never step beyond it.

Psychic Experiences other than Hallucinations

Hallucinations resulting from madness or the use of drugs, are created because man's mind becomes overexcited and the same subconscious machinery within man is consequently worked up. In such cases, the results produced are disjointed. Most often an outside observer can easily tell that such visions are merely the scattered segments of one's fancy comprising incoherent ravings or fearsome visions. The outside observer can also easily recognize the state of utter confusion and desperation which usually accompanies such disorders. But apart from this it is also possible for the subconscious mind to spin meaningful well-organized images with a message to deliver. Also it is possible for the subconscious to communicate with the conscious mind as though purposefully. What remains to be determined is the possibility of any outside agency influencing the human mind by employing its internal mechanism.

Wide scale research and experimentation by parapsychologists carried out on a scientific basis has proved this to be possible. The mind of one person can activate another person's mind and direct it to think in accordance with his command. Research into such phenomenon is now being carried out at many universities and, according to the result of such studies, it is not only possible, but it commonly happens in everyday life that sometimes automatically and sometimes through conscious attempts, the ideas of a person can be transmitted to another person's mind without the employment of any material medium.

Hypnotism

A hypnotist can concentrate on the minds of others and create impressions which are in fact planted upon them by the hypnotist himself. As commonly observed in psychic healing, the purpose of hypnotism is to bring the hidden secrets of a subject's mind to the surface, or to encourage the power of his mind to heal him.

It so happens that many a time a deranged patient has lost the courage to confront his own disturbing thoughts. He buries them deep, but not deep enough. They lie somewhere between the conscious and the subconscious mind in a restless state. With a little help from the outside, he ultimately musters enough strength to throw them to the surface and get rid of them. This phenomenon can be likened to any small object lodged under the skin which, unless removed, may cause insufferable agony and restlessness. The job that the knife of a surgeon performs is carried out by a hypnotist's suggestion in the case of a psychic patient.

Telepathy

Telepathy is another mode of paranormal communication which does not employ any suggestion. Without the agency of any known scientific medium, one person's thoughts are transferred to another, without verbal or visual contact. It happens like two tuning forks of the same frequency. If one is resonated, the other would also begin to resonate.

If hypnotism and telepathy work in reality — and there is much evidence that they do — then why cannot God employ the same mechanism for transmitting His command to humans? Why should He not be able to employ the same to convey His will to man?

Other Experiences of Subconscious

Dreams are a truly universal phenomenon shared by people of all countries and all ages, yet dreams do not belong to one category alone. Dreams in most cases are a product of human psyche. The way the subconscious deals with the daily inflow of data reflects the concerns and problems that a particular person is facing. Today the study of dreams has gone far beyond the Freudian era of theorization. Much research is being carried out with the help of advanced electronic equipment.

However, from the religious point of view, there are two types of dreams — those which are generated by

245

psychic factors, and those which are of Divine origin and carry a deeper significance. They may portend future mishaps or bring glad tidings. They may reveal information of which the viewer had no knowledge whatsoever prior to that particular dream. Such dreams bring to a sharper focus the probability of the existence of an invisible, conscious, transcendent, External Being who can, if He so pleases, communicate with humans on whatever subject He chooses.

Enough evidence from religious experiences can be quoted to prove the case in point. But those who do not believe in religion will find it difficult to accept such evidence as valid. This is so because if one accepts the proposition that a Superhuman Conscious Agency can activate the human mind, it would be tantamount to the belief in the existence of God – a fact to which a large number of secular thinkers and scientists are extremely allergic.

The second problem is that in most religions this phenomenon is spoken of with such an air of the supernatural, the bizarre and the fantastic, that it is hard for scientists to subscribe to their credulity. The dramatization of the spiritual experiences of the past saints and prophets on the part of their followers does not serve their cause or the cause of truth for that matter. It only succeeds in obscuring and befogging the reality of such Divine Communications to an extent that no clear separating line can be drawn between the yarn of human fancy and the noble reality of spiritual experiences.

Among Divine Books, the Holy Quran by virtue of being free from interpolation, deals with spiritual issues and experiences in natural and rational terms, rejecting the demand of the non-believer for the supernatural. When studied in the light of the Quranic account, miracles and signs never violate the laws of nature.

The well known miracle of Moses[as] for instance, though believed by the People of the Book to be of a supernatural character, is presented in the Quran in a simple, rational, matter-of-fact style. Yet it would take more than a cursory glance to fathom its underlying meaning. It is not cryptic yet the real intent eludes particularly those who read it with preconceived ideas of a supernatural event. Here we illustrate the Quran's treatment of this miracle.

قَالَ اَلْقُوْاْ فَلَمَّا اَلْقَوْا سَحَرُوْا اَعْيُنَ النَّاسِ وَاسْتَرْهَبُوْهُمْ وَجَآءُوْ بِسِحْرٍ عَظِيْمٍ * وَاَوْحَيْنَآ الْـى مُوْسَى اَنْ اَلْقِ عَصَاكَ فَاِذَا هِـىَ تَلْقَفُ مَا يَاْفِكُوْنَ * فَوَقَعَ الْحَقُّ وَبَطَلَ مَا كَانُوْا يَعْمَلُوْنَ *

7:117-119

He replied, 'Throw ye.' And when they threw, they enchanted the eyes of the people, and struck them with awe and brought forth a great magic.
And We inspired Moses, *saying,* 'Throw thy rod', and lo! it swallowed up whatever they feigned.
So was the Truth established, and their works proved vain.[1]

Here the Quran speaks of an incident in which the magicians of the Pharaoh are described to have cast their spells, not on the ropes they threw, but on the eyes of the spectators, a clear description of mesmerism. No breach of any laws of nature is involved at all. To counter this mesmeric illusion, God employed His superior will through Moses[as] to shatter the spell cast by the magicians. Hence the Quran does not claim that the staff of Moses[as] had actually devoured the ropes; it only pronounces that the staff of

Moses[as] swallowed what the magicians had fabricated – that is the false images of ropes turned into snakes.

The same episode is covered in another Surah which throws more light on what actually happened:

قَالَ بَلْ اَلْقُوْا فَإِذَا حِبَالُهُمْ وَعِصِيُّهُمْ يُخَيَّلُ إِلَيْهِ مِنْ سِحْرِهِمْ أَنَّهَا تَسْعَىٰ*فَاَوْجَسَ فِيْ نَفْسِهِ خِيْفَةً مُّوْسَىٰ*قُلْنَا لَا تَخَفْ اِنَّكَ اَنْتَ الْأَعْلَىٰ * 20:67-69

Moses said *to them*: 'You throw your cast first', and lo their cords and staves appeared to him as though they were moving (like snakes) under the influence of their spell, as if they ran *about*.
At this, Moses conceived fear.
We (God) said: 'Fear not, it is you who will emerge victorious.'[2]

In this verse, the Quran speaks of Moses[as] himself having been influenced by the psychic powers of the magicians. This implies that Moses[as] could not have broken the spell of the magicians by the power of his own mind when he threw his staff. Psychologically it is impossible for the mind to break the spell of a mesmerizer who has already succeeded in subjugating it. Hence it could not have been Moses who countered the magicians' spell with his own will.

It was this aspect of the whole incident which turned it into a miracle. Otherwise any man with stronger will-power could have directly frustrated the efforts of the magicians. No one could judge better than the magicians themselves, who were in a position to realize that it had to be the Hand of God working on the side of Moses[as]. They had witnessed Moses[as] to have fallen under their sway like all other spectators. How then could his mind liberate itself as well as the minds of the spectators from the magicians' spell? Incidentally, this verse also lifts the veil from the so-called mysteries of magic. What the magicians produced were not real serpents made out of ropes and sticks, but only an illusion created by their psychic power.

Revelation is just another name for the product of human psyche but only when commanded and controlled from on high by God Himself. We can reasonably conclude therefore, that God must have created such a highly advanced and intricate receptive system within the human mind for the ultimate purpose of communicating with Him. Divine revelation therefore has nothing of the bizarre and unnatural about it.

Every human mind is provided with the aptitude to communicate with other human beings through this extrasensory means of perception. It is important to warn the reader that the refined built-in apparatus we are talking about works with reliability and dependability in proportion to the quality of the truth of the person involved. A false man's imagination can run wild with the images of unreal and unsubstantial things. His wishful thinking can create for him false dreams, a mere product of his psyche. But the person who is habitually straightforward, honest and true is very unlikely to let his imagination run riot and produce chaotic visions and sounds. That is why the apostle chosen by God to deliver His message to mankind has to be absolutely true, honest and trustworthy. It is his integrity which vouches for the unadulterated purity of the message. Hence the truth of the recipient plays the most vital role in guarding and protecting the purity of the revelation. No wonder that in all Divine books, all prophets are described as truth personified. The truth is the most authentic proof of the genuineness of their claim and the validity of the message they deliver.

Sometimes an intuitive experience, without sound or vision, may in reality be a type of external revelation. Many a saintly person describes such experiences of losing his awareness of the world around him and sinking into a state of inner consciousness. He returns to the surface of the outer realities at last, carrying a message like a pearl diver breaks surface with a handful of pearls. Seemingly the subject in this case has an inner experience of something which at its source is without words or images. It is just an intense, ecstatic experience which begins to wear robes of words as it emerges. Yet the impact on him is so powerful as though he had heard someone speak to him directly and clearly during his conscious hours of wakefulness. But the external revelation cannot be identified merely by the impression of the receiver or the manner in which he describes that experience. The only dependable criterion apart from the verified, well-established truthfulness of the person, is the nature of the contents. It is not enough for the receiver to be true, but the contents of the revelation must also bear an internal testimony of their truthfulness.

The distinction mentioned above, between psychic experiences and a genuine revelation from on high, may not be clearly understood by the unfamiliar. Yet the person involved often recognizes it to be a message from on high because the nature of the message is totally unrelated to his personal knowledge and psychic experience.

But the genuineness of revelation is more reliably identified by outsiders with the help of external evidence. The external evidence may be available to contemporary people, or it may not be available because it may emerge later in time with the emergence of things which are predicted. None could have imagined them because they belong to a future era of knowledge and discovery. The truth of such revelations are in fact meant to convince the people of later ages whose advanced knowledge testifies to the truth of Divine revelations of the past. Hence it is not at all difficult, for the observers as well, to distinguish between psychic experiences on the one hand, and genuine communication from God on the other.

Now we turn to a prophecy based on Divine revelation which, though addressed to the contemporary generations, had an element of surprise for the people of the future as well.

The case in point can be illustrated with reference to a famous dream of a king of Egypt, which was later interpreted by Prophet Joseph[as]. According to the Quran, this dream was narrated to Joseph[as], while he was serving a prison sentence under a false charge. It was a strange dream, which had baffled the great sages of the king's court, but did not present any difficulty to Joseph[as] who rightly discerned its underlying message. It was this wise and masterly interpretation by him which was completely supported and testified by the events of subsequent years.

In his dream the king had seen seven healthy, green ears of corn, and seven dried ones, carrying hardly any seed. He also saw seven lean cows devouring seven others who were strong and fat. When he related this dream to his courtiers demanding an interpretation, they dismissed it as mere subconscious ravings of his mind, carrying no significance.

Now it so happened that a servant of the king who had served a term with Joseph[as] in the same prison was present at this occasion. He too had seen a strange dream while in prison, which Joseph[as] had correctly interpreted, indicating that he would soon gain his freedom and return to serve his master, the king, once again. Hoping that Joseph[as] might possibly interpret the dream of the king as well, he suggested that he should be sent to meet him.

Having obtained permission, he visited Joseph[as] in prison and related the king's dream to him. Joseph[as] immediately grasped its significance and explained it so logically that there was no ambiguity left.

Upon his return to the king, the servant related Josephs'[as] interpretation which ran as follows:

In the seven years which would commence from the time of the dream, God would shower His blessings upon Egypt in the form of abundant rains, resulting in bountiful crops and fruits. After these seven years of bumper harvests, seven lean years would follow bringing drought in their wake. These years would result in disastrous famine unless crops from the previous seven years were saved and stored to compensate for the loss of the drought years.

This interpretation impressed the king so profoundly that he issued orders for the immediate release of Joseph[as] who, opted instead to remain in prison until a fair enquiry was held and the false charges against him were dropped. It was after he was honourably acquitted and the real culprit confessed her crime, that he agreed to be released. He was exceptionally honoured by the king and was appointed minister of finance and economic affairs in his government.

To the surprise of all, the events foretold in the dream came to pass exactly as interpreted by Joseph[as] which not only saved the people of Egypt from disaster but also benefited the nomadic tribes and the populace of neighbouring countries. The same events also resulted in reuniting Joseph[as] with his family.

A dream like this with its subsequent fulfilment could in no way be dismissed as a glutton's overfed fancy. But it took a Joseph[as] to interpret it. This should suffice to illustrate how the internal psychic mechanism is activated by God with a purpose. Thus, a definite meaningful message is delivered by Him and a portion from the realm of the unseen is transferred to that of the seen. However, it should be remembered here that the psychic mechanism under discussion is not exclusively employed by God or the subconscious mind.

There is a third possibility also mentioned in the Holy Quran:

هَلْ اُنَبِّئُكُمْ عَلَى مَنْ تَنَزَّلُ الشَّيْطِيْنُ* تَنَزَّلُ عَلَى كُلِّ اَفَّاكٍ اَثِيْمٍ*
يُّلْقُوْنَ السَّمْعَ وَاَكْثَرُهُمْ كٰذِبُوْنَ * 26:222-224

Shall I inform you on whom the evil ones descend?
They descend on every lying sinner.
They strain their ears *towards heaven*, and most of them are liars.[3]

According to these verses, the false people and habitual liars may have this mechanism activated by their satanic disposition and as such their falsehood disguised as revelation misleads them, and those who follow them. This is a third category of the functioning of the psychic mechanism. The decisive factor will always be the truth or falsehood of the person who is subjected to such experiences. The false people will have false revelations. Hence in the final analysis the revelation of the untrue can always be recognized by the satanic element it contains and the false promises delivered therein.

REFERENCES

1. Translation of 7:117-119 by Maulawi Sher Ali.
2. Translation of 20:67-69 by the author.
3. Translation of 26:222-224 by the author.

DIVINE REVELATION
AND RATIONALITY

IN another chapter we briefly covered the progress of Muslim thought and intellectual pursuits in many areas of human interest. During that period, although Muslim enquiry was predominantly influenced by Quranic teachings and the traditions of the Holy Prophet[sa], it could not be entirely qualified as Islamic. There was a rapid proliferation of academic growth in all directions. Many new philosophies and sciences were acquired from past eras of secular, academic and scientific achievements. Also, many a new branch of religious and secular knowledge was pioneered by some outstanding Muslim thinkers. Thus, religion and rationality went hand in hand. They drew their thrust largely from the emphasis on the pursuit of knowledge laid in the Quran and the instructions of the Holy Prophet[sa]. The role of rationality was so powerfully highlighted that religious belief and rationality became synonymous. The proclamation by the Quran that Muhammad[sa] is a universal Prophet with a universal message, is in itself tantamount to declaring that the religion of Islam is founded on rationality. No religion with any element of irrationality can be acceptable to the universal conscience of man:

وَمَآ اَرْسَلْنٰكَ اِلَّا كَآفَّةً لِّلنَّاسِ بَشِيْرًا وَّنَذِيْرًا وَّلٰكِنَّ اَكْثَرَ النَّاسِ لَا يَعْلَمُوْنَ* 34:29

And We have not sent thee but as a bearer of glad tidings and a Warner, for all mankind, but most men know not.[1]

Again, the Quran demonstrates the universality of its teachings by addressing all human, moral, social and religious problems of man, irrespective of race, colour, creed or nationality. It is necessary therefore, that Islamic teachings should have the potential of global application with an appeal to universal human nature. But this is not the only reason why we draw this conclusion.

The Quran manifestly acknowledges the role of rationality for the attainment of truth without drawing any separating line between religious or secular truths. Truth is the religion of Islam, Islam is the religion of Truth. The truth requires no compulsion for the transmission of its message, the only instrument it needs is rationality. As such, Islam invokes human intellect to investigate the truth of the Quranic teachings with reference to the study of human nature, history and rationality. It arouses the human faculties of reasoning and deduction, not only for the pursuit of religious investigation, but also for the attainment of secular knowledge. Impressed by this outstanding emphasis by the Quran on the quest for knowledge, Professor Dr Abdus Salam*, the renowned Nobel Laureate was invoked to study the impact of this enlightning attitude on the Muslim thought of the early period. In one of his articles on this subject, he observes:

> 'According to Dr Mohammed Aijazul Khatib of Damascus University, nothing could emphasize the importance of sciences more than the remark that "in contrast to 250 verses which are legislative, some 750 verses of the Holy Quran — almost one-eighth of it — exhort the believers to study Nature — to reflect, to make the best use of reason and to

---

* Sadly, Professor Dr Abdus Salam passed away before the publication of this book.

make the scientific enterprise an integral part of the community's life". The Holy Prophet of Islam — peace be upon him — said that it was the "bounden duty of every muslim — man and woman — to acquire knowledge".[2]

The enquiry by itself is not sufficient, however, warns the Quran. The inner truth of man is a prerequisite for him to draw right conclusions from it. This principle of fundamental importance is dictated in the very beginning in the Surah *Al-Baqarah*. It should be remembered that though *Al-Baqarah* is formally counted as the second after Surah *Al-Fātiḥah* which contains the gist of the entire Quran, in effect it could be treated as an introductory Surah. Thus *Al-Baqarah* may be counted as the first Surah with which the full text begins. *Al-Baqarah* begins with the following opening statement:

بِسْمِ اللهِ الرَّحْمٰنِ الرَّحِيمِ * الٓمٓ * ذٰلِكَ الْكِتٰبُ لَا رَيْبَ فِيهِ
هُدًى لِّلْمُتَّقِيْنَ * 3-1:2

In the name of Allah, the Most Gracious, Ever Merciful.
I am Allah, the Most Knowledgeable.
This is that perfect Book; there is no doubt in it; a guidance for the righteous (muttaqi).[3]

This profound declaration, simple as it may appear, demands special attention for the comprehension of its underlying message. The Divine teachings are obviously expected to guide the unrighteous to the right path. What, then, is the significance of the claim that this book can guide only those who are already righteous? What the Quran implies is simply this that the seeker after truth must necessarily be true himself or his inquiry will prove futile.

The discovery of truth according to this declaration depends essentially on the honesty of the enquirer's intent. A profound wisdom is reflected in this short simple statement:

$$2:3 \quad * \quad هُدًى لِّلْمُتَّقِينَ$$

... a guidance for the righteous.[4]

The same principle often applies to the realm of secular enquiry as well. Every enquiry made with a biased mind will often lose credibility. Attention is drawn to the fact that an honest, healthy mind is a prerequisite for every true meaningful enquiry. A mind bonded to prejudice cannot draw unbiased conclusions. An observer with a squint in his eye cannot see straight. Hence, no guidance is in itself sufficient to lead one to truth. It takes a sound, unbiased, healthy, honest mind to benefit from it. It is here that one problem is resolved but another begins.

Contrary to what one may expect in the realm of religious controversies, little inner truth is displayed by most of the warring religious factions in the world today. One would normally expect that the religious should adhere more strongly to truth than the secular. In reality however, we find the opposite to be true in the later stages of every religion. In the beginning of religions it is invariably the religious who are unbiased and uncompromisingly committed to truth rather than the rest of the society, be it secular or avowedly religious. The graph of rationality, reason and truth touches its highest peak at a time when the religious founders are themselves alive.

Returning to the verses under discussion, we find that in them God is introduced as the Knower of all things to the point of absolute precision. Thus the knowledge that He bestows has to be perfect and most reliable. Yet the recipient of that knowledge may fail to benefit from it if he lacks the quality of inner truth.

If we replace the idea of God with that of rationality, for the convenience of the non-believer, the statement would read as follows:

That which is absolutely rational cannot lead anyone to the truth except those who possess a quality of righteousness or inner truth within them. This provides the most essential prerequisite for the attainment of reliable knowledge, be it religious or secular. Both the source of information and the recipient of information must be true.

SO FAR SO GOOD, but this is not the end of the road. In fact it is from here that the more difficult part of the journey begins. Who can adjudge the quality of another person's inner truth? Everyone has a right to claim that he is absolutely true in his inner bearing. Hence whatever he believes is true. How does the Quran resolve this problem, is the question. Merely by pronouncing that 'Allah knows best', this problem cannot be resolved at the human level. But this is not the solution which the Quran proposes. According to the Quran the measure and quality of anyone's inner truth can be reliably adjudged by reference to his visible conduct in everyday life. If he is habitually true in his ordinary daily bearing then his inner invisible self can also be adjudged as true. By the same criterion the truth of prophets is also judged. Although it is not impossible for a habitual liar to be occasionally true, both in his expressed word and unexpressed intentions, it is next to impossible for him to be consistently true. Hence it is absolutely rational for the prophets to argue that a society which could never blame them, prior to their claim, for even a semblance of a lie, had no justification whatsoever in blaming them for fabricating lies against God and calling it revelation.

This method of measuring the inner truth may work with unfaltering reliability in the case of prophets, who consistently display exemplary conduct throughout their lives. But it cannot be applied with equal certainty to other humans less than prophets. The situations vary widely from person to person, the vantage points differ, the faculty of comprehension and the ability to draw the right conclusions are not equally shared. Everyone is not gifted with the rare ability of penetrating across the façade of words or false portrayals. The interplay between the faculties of the observer and the one who is observed leads to innumerable possibilities. Some can conceal their hidden intentions almost to the point of perfection, while there are those who are less competent to deceive. With what measure of reliability therefore, can a human observer pass judgement on the inner quality of truth or falsehood of another? The problem deepens further when it comes to the matter of faith and belief. Even if one holds the maddest of beliefs and dogmas, and there is no dearth of such people in the realm of religion today, they cannot be blamed with any finality of being consciously untrue. They may be too naive or too stupid to identify their folly which may be manifestly evident to others. Yet they have every right to believe or claim that they are right. They, in turn, can condemn the beliefs of others to be false, however sound and rational they may appear to the holders of such beliefs.

The only unfaltering answer to this dilemma is the one proposed by the Quran. It grants every human the fundamental right to believe in whatever he may and to claim that his beliefs are true. Yet it does not, in any way, permit him to impose his personal convictions on others, nor does it grant him any right to punish others for the crime of their wrong beliefs (as he judges them). Man is only answerable to God, and it is He alone Who knows the hidden intricacies of the human mind and heart. Again it is not the failure to recognize truth which is punishable. What is punishable is the falsehood of the person who rejects truth knowing deep within that he is wrong. Evidently the detection of this hidden crime lies beyond the reach of human investigation. The decisive factor is always the criminal failure and not the failure itself. The only reliable vantage point is that of God the All-Knowing, the Omnipresent, the Unchanging, the All-Wise. That indeed is the most important factor of which the Holy Quran reminds the reader so emphatically and repeatedly. In the area of religious beliefs and modes of worship, man is specifically warned not to combine in himself the role of a judge and that of an executioner. Even the Holy Founder of Islam[sa] is reminded:

$$\text{88:22-23} \quad * \text{ لَسْتَ عَلَيْهِمْ بِمُصَيْطِرٍ } * \text{ اِنَّمَا اَنْتَ مُذَكِّرٌ }$$

... you are merely an admonisher,
You are not a magistrate over them.[5]

It is forbidden even to abuse the imaginary gods of idolaters which are a mere concoction of their fancy:

$$\text{ وَلَا تَسُبُّوا الَّذِينَ يَدْعُونَ مِنْ دُونِ اللهِ فَيَسُبُّوا اللهَ عَدْوًا بِغَيْرِ عِلْمٍ }$$
$$\text{ كَذٰلِكَ زَيَّنَّا لِكُلِّ اُمَّةٍ عَمَلَهُمْ ثُمَّ اِلٰى رَبِّهِمْ مَرْجِعُهُمْ فَيُنَبِّئُهُمْ بِمَا }$$
$$\text{ كَانُوا يَعْمَلُونَ } * \text{ 6:109 }$$

Do not abuse those whom they worship besides Allah, lest in retaliation they are driven to abuse Allah (the only true God). So have We made the practice of everyone to appear to be attractive in their view. Then their return will be to their Lord who will then inform them of what they had been really doing.[6]

This, however, does not obviate the vital need for recognizing and acquiring truth before one breathes one's last. To possess the right to believe in whatever one may is one thing, but to escape the consequences of one's belief is quite another. The fundamental right and freedom to hold any belief is not a license to violate the sanctity of truth. It is provided only to protect the freedom of human conscience to act as it may deem fit. Had this freedom in matters of faith not been granted, anyone could have felt at liberty to forcibly change an other's views and beliefs in the name of truth. His perverted logic would convince him that as no one is entitled to hold false beliefs, everyone with right beliefs is authorized to forcibly change them in accordance with his own. Again this freedom of belief does not, in any way, override the principle of accountability. The right of freedom can be correctly understood only when it is coupled with this principle. If a group of mountaineers are told to follow whatever trail they may choose in whatever direction they please, but are also warned that some trails could lead them to the precipice of annihilation, they would certainly watch their steps with every caution at their command. Yet such daredevils as are blind to their own interest may altogether ignore the warning and exercise their right of freedom to their own ultimate destruction. This is the meaning of freedom of faith and freedom of choice in the Quranic terms:

لَآ اِكْرَاهَ فِى الدِّيْنِ قَدْ تَّبَيَّنَ الرُّشْدُ مِنَ الْغَـــيِّ فَمَـــنْ يَّكْفُـــرْ بِالطَّاغُوْتِ وَيُؤْمِنْ بِاللهِ فَقَدِ اسْتَمْسَكَ بِالْعُرْوَةِ الْوُثْقٰى لَا انْفِصَامَ لَهَا ۗ وَاللهُ سَمِيْعٌ عَلِيْمٌ* 2:257

There is no compulsion in religion. Surely, the right way has become distinct from error; so whosoever refuses to be led by those who transgress, and believes in Allah, has surely grasped a strong handle which knows no breaking. And Allah is All-Hearing, All-Knowing.[7]

All the same, the categoric prohibition to change another person's faith by force does not deprive anyone of his right to change others through persuasive arguments and dialogues, so long as it is free from even a whisper of threat. Let alone permission, it is the bounden duty of every believer to invite mankind to the path of God with wisdom and goodly persuasion:

$$ اُدْعُ اِلٰى سَبِيْلِ رَبِّكَ بِالْحِكْمَةِ وَالْمَوْعِظَةِ الْحَسَـــنَةِ وَجَادِلْـــهُمْ $$
$$ بِالَّتِىْ هِىَ اَحْسَنُ \quad 16:126 $$

Invite to the path of thy Lord with wisdom and comely admonishment and dispute with them in the best of manners...[8]

THIS IS the Divine global plan for the conquest of human ideas and ideologies by Islam. Can anyone detect even a particle of irrationality therein? The steaming stinking breath of the fundamentalist, as he exhorts the sentiments of the Muslim masses and stirs them up to wage bloody wars against the non-believers has never been observed in the conduct of prophets and those who follow them. He draws his authority entirely from his own distorted vision. His attitude is as alien to the Quran as disease is to cure and venom is to elixir. The number of verses exhorting Muslims to make the best use of reason, rationality and scientific investigation as mentioned by Dr Mohammad A'ijāzul Khatīb of Damascus adds up to 750.

As against this, there is not a single verse in the entire Quran advocating irrational dogmatic invasion of the world of ideas. To conclude, we quote just a few of the verses to give the reader a taste of how the Holy Quran emphasizes the role of reason, rationality and solid evidence in the realm of ideas and beliefs.

اَتَأْمُرُوْنَ النَّاسَ بِالْبِرِّ وَتَنْسَوْنَ اَنْفُسَكُمْ وَاَنْتُمْ تَتْلُوْنَ الْكِتٰبَ اَفَلَا تَعْقِلُوْنَ* 2:45

Do you enjoin others to do what is good and forget your own selves, while you read the Book? Will you not then understand?[9]

وَاِذَا لَقُوا الَّذِيْنَ اٰمَنُوْا قَالُوْۤا اٰمَنَّا وَاِذَا خَلَا بَعْضُهُمْ اِلٰى بَعْضٍ قَالُوْۤا اَتُحَدِّثُوْنَهُمْ بِمَا فَتَحَ اللّٰهُ عَلَيْكُمْ لِيُحَآجُّوْكُمْ بِهٖ عِنْدَ رَبِّكُمْ اَفَلَا تَعْقِلُوْنَ* 2:77

And when they meet those who believe, they say: 'We believe,' and when they meet one another in private, they say: 'Do you inform them of what Allah has unfolded to you, that they may thereby argue with you before your Lord? Will you not then understand?'[10]

وَقَالُوْا لَنْ يَّدْخُلَ الْجَنَّةَ اِلَّا مَنْ كَانَ هُوْدًا اَوْ نَصٰرٰى تِلْكَ اَمَانِيُّهُمْ قُلْ هَاتُوْا بُرْهَانَكُمْ اِنْ كُنْتُمْ صٰدِقِيْنَ* 2:112

And they say, 'None shall ever enter Heaven unless he be a Jew or a Christian.' These are their vain desires. Say, 'Produce your proof, if you are truthful.'[11]

يَا أَيُّهَا النَّاسُ قَدْ جَاءَكُمْ بُرْهَانٌ مِّنْ رَّبِّكُمْ وَأَنْزَلْنَا إِلَيْكُمْ نُـــوْرًا

مُّبِيْنًا* 4:175

O ye people, a manifest proof has indeed come to
you from your Lord, and We have sent down to you
a clear light.[12]

وَمَا الْحَيْوةُ الدُّنْيَا إِلَّا لَعِبٌ وَّلَهْوٌ وَّلَلدَّارُ الْاٰخِرَةُ خَـــيْرٌ لِّلَّذِيْـــنَ

يَتَّقُوْنَ اَفَلَا تَعْقِلُوْنَ* 6:33

And worldly life is nothing but a sport and pastime.
And surely the abode of the Hereafter is better for
those who are righteous. Will you not then
understand?[13]

قُلْ لَّا اَقُوْلُ لَكُمْ عِنْدِىْ خَزَآئِنُ اللهِ وَلَا اَعْلَمُ الْغَيْبَ وَلَا اَقُـــوْلُ

لَكُمْ اِنِّىْ مَلَكٌ اِنْ اَتَّبِعُ اِلَّا مَا يُوْحٰى اِلَىَّ قُلْ هَلْ يَسْتَوِى الْاَعْمٰى

وَالْبَصِيْرُ اَفَلَا تَتَفَكَّرُوْنَ* 6:51

Say, "I do not say to you: 'I possess the treasures of
Allah', nor do I know the unseen; nor do I say to
you: 'I am an angel.' I follow only that which is
revealed to me." Say: 'Can a blind man and one who
sees be alike?' Will you not then reflect?[14]

قُلْ هُوَ الْقَادِرُ عَلٰى اَنْ يَّبْعَثَ عَلَيْكُمْ عَذَابًا مِّنْ فَوْقِكُمْ اَوْ مِـــنْ

تَحْتِ اَرْجُلِكُمْ اَوْ يَلْبِسَكُمْ شِيَعًا وَّيُذِيْقَ بَعْضَكُمْ بَأْسَ بَعْــــضٍ

اُنْظُرْ كَيْفَ نُصَرِّفُ الْاٰيٰتِ لَعَلَّهُمْ يَفْقَهُوْنَ* 6:66

Say, 'He has power to send punishment upon you from above you or from beneath your feet, or to confound you by *splitting you into* sects and make you taste the violence of one another.' See how We expound the Signs in various ways that they may understand![15]

قُلْ لَّوْ شَآءَ اللهُ مَا تَلَوْتُهُ عَلَيْكُمْ وَلَآ اَدْرٰىكُمْ بِهِۖ فَقَدْ لَبِثْتُ فِيْكُمْ عُمُرًا مِّنْ قَبْلِهِۗ اَفَلَا تَعْقِلُوْنَ* 10:17

Say, 'If Allah had *so* willed, I should not have recited it to you nor would He have made it known to you. I have indeed lived among you a *whole* lifetime before this. Will you not then understand?'[16]

يٰقَوْمِ لَآ اَسْـَٔلُكُمْ عَلَيْهِ اَجْرًاۗ اِنْ اَجْرِيَ اِلَّا عَلَــى الَّــذِيْ فَطَرَنِيْۗ اَفَلَا تَعْقِلُوْنَ* 11:52

'O my people, I do not ask of you any reward therefore. My reward is not due except from Him Who created me. Will you not then understand?'[17]

اَمِ اتَّخَذُوْا مِنْ دُوْنِهٖٓ اٰلِهَةًۗ قُلْ هَاتُوْا بُرْهَانَكُمْۖ هٰذَا ذِكْرُ مَنْ مَّعِيَ وَذِكْرُ مَنْ قَبْلِيْۗ بَلْ اَكْثَرُهُمْ لَا يَعْلَمُوْنَۙ الْحَقَّ فَهُمْ مُّعْرِضُـــوْنَ* 21:25

Have they taken gods beside Him? Say, 'Bring forth your proof. Here is the Book of those with me, and the Book of those before me.' Nay, most of them know not the truth, and so they turn away.[18]

وَهُوَ الَّذِىْ يُحْىِ وَيُمِيْتُ وَلَهُ اخْتِلَافُ الَّيْــلِ وَالنَّــهَارِ اَفَــلَا
تَعْقِلُوْنَ * 23:81

And He it is Who gives life and causes death, and in His Hands is the alteration of night and day. Will you not then understand?[19]

وَمَنْ يَّدْعُ مَعَ اللهِ الـهًا اخَرَ لَا بُرْهَانَ لَهُ بِهٖ فَاِنَّمَا حِسَابُهُ عِنْدَ
رَبِّهٖ اِنَّهُ لَا يُفْلِحُ الْكٰفِرُوْنَ * 23:118

And he who calls on another god along with Allah, for which he has no proof, shall have to render an account to his Lord. Certainly the disbelievers will not prosper.[20]

ءَاِلٰهٌ مَّعَ اللهِ قُلْ هَاتُوْا بُرْهَانَكُمْ اِنْ كُنْتُمْ صٰدِقِيْنَ * 27:65

… Is there a God besides Allah? Say, 'Bring forward your proof if you are truthful.'[21]

وَمَآ اُوْتِيْتُمْ مِّنْ شَىْءٍ فَمَتَاعُ الْحَيٰوةِ الدُّنْيَا وَزِيْنَتُهَا وَمَا عِنْدَ اللهِ
خَيْرٌ وَّاَبْقٰى اَفَلَا تَعْقِلُوْنَ * 28:61

And whatever of the things *of this world* you are given is only a temporary enjoyment of the present life and an adornment thereof; and that which is with Allah is better and more lasting. Will you not then understand?[22]

وَنَزَعْنَا مِنْ كُلِّ اُمَّةٍ شَهِيْدًا فَقُلْنَا هَاتُوْا بُرْهَانَكُمْ فَعَلِمُوْٓا اَنَّ الْحَقَّ لِلّٰهِ وَضَلَّ عَنْهُمْ مَّا كَانُوْا يَفْتَرُوْنَ* 28:76

And We shall draw from every people a witness and We shall say, 'Bring your proof.' Then they will know that the truth belongs to Allah. And that which they used to forge will be lost unto them.[23]

وَلَقَدْ اَضَلَّ مِنْكُمْ جِبِلًّا كَثِيْرًا اَفَلَمْ تَكُوْنُوْا تَعْقِلُوْنَ* 36:63

And he did lead astray a great multitude of you. Why did you not then understand?[24]

لَوْ اَنْزَلْنَا هٰذَا الْقُرْاٰنَ عَلٰى جَبَلٍ لَّرَاَيْتَهٗ خَاشِعًا مُّتَصَدِّعًا مِّنْ خَشْيَةِ اللّٰهِ وَتِلْكَ الْاَمْثَالُ نَضْرِبُهَا لِلنَّاسِ لَعَلَّهُمْ يَتَفَكَّرُوْنَ* 59:22

If We had sent down this Quran on a mountain, thou wouldst certainly have seen it humbled and rent asunder for fear of Allah. And these are similitudes that We set forth for mankind that they may reflect.[25]

REFERENCES

1. Translation of 34:29 by Maulawi Sher Ali.
2. LAI, C.H., KIDWAI, A (1989) *Ideals and Realities. Selected Essays of Abdus Salam.* 3rd ed. World Scientific Publishing Co. London, pp.343-344
3. Translation of 2:1-3 by the author.
4. Translation of 2:3 by the author.
5. Translation of 88:22-23 by the author.
6. Translation of 6:109 by the author.
7. Translation of 2:257 by the author.
8. Translation of 16:126 by the author.
9. Translation of 2:45 by Maulawi Sher Ali.
10. Translation of 2:77 by Maulawi Sher Ali.
11. Translation of 2:112 by Maulawi Sher Ali.
12. Translation of 4:175 by Maulawi Sher Ali.
13. Translation of 6:33 by Maulawi Sher Ali.
14. Translation of 6:51 by Maulawi Sher Ali.
15. Translation of 6:66 by Maulawi Sher Ali.
16. Translation of 10:17 by Maulawi Sher Ali.
17. Translation of 11:52 by Maulawi Sher Ali.
18. Translation of 21:25 by Maulawi Sher Ali.
19. Translation of 23:81 by Maulawi Sher Ali.
20. Translation of 23:118 by Maulawi Sher Ali.
21. Translation of 27:65 by Maulawi Sher Ali.
22. Translation of 28:61 by Maulawi Sher Ali.
23. Translation of 28:76 by Maulawi Sher Ali.
24. Translation of 36:63 by Maulawi Sher Ali.
25. Translation of 59:22 by Maulawi Sher Ali.

BELIEF IN THE UNSEEN

هُدًى لِّلْمُتَّقِيْنَ ۙ الَّذِيْنَ يُؤْمِنُوْنَ بِالْغَيْبِ 2:3-4

... *it is* a guidance for the righteous,
Who believe in the unseen...[1]

TO BELIEVE IN THE 'UNSEEN' is a fundamental constituent of the Muslim faith as mentioned in the verse quoted above. But as has been well demonstrated in the previous chapter, the Quran is a book of reason and rationality which roundly condemns coercion or threat in any form to change human ideas. Thus to interpret this verse to indicate that it promotes blind faith by requiring man to believe in the 'unseen' would stand counter to this Quranic emphasis. Quite to the contrary, to believe in the spurious without evidence and solid justification is what the Quran attributes to the non-believers. It further condemns them for attempting to change the views of the believers by sheer brutality. What then, does the phrase 'Belief in the Unseen' mean? This is the important question which needs to be fully addressed.

One must make an in-depth study of this phrase as a specific term coined by the Quran. The failure to grasp its true meaning may result in serious consequences as happened in the medieval ages during the scholastic debates between different Muslim schools of thought. Some rigid and uncompromising Muslim scholars disallow the use of rationality altogether in matters of faith. They state that the revealed truth by itself is all-sufficient and as such it should be accepted without any rational investigation. Others who oppose this view quote many Quranic verses requiring everyone to abide invariably by the dictates of reason at

271

every stage of decision making and give priority to rationality over blind faith.

But what is faith? How can one have faith without satisfying one's sense of inquiry? Is it not a reality that the majority of common people belonging to all religions believe without actually comprehending the meaning of their belief? They just happen to believe and that is all there is to it.

This is the dilemma which necessarily requires one to address the issue of faith versus reason, and the need to determine the nature of their interrelationship becomes all the more important. As this question is sufficiently covered in the chapter entitled *European Philosophy*, we shall endeavour not to unnecessarily repeat what has already been covered therein. What is left therefore is to acquire a more elaborate understanding of the term 'unseen'.

To begin with, let us point out that the lack of knowledge about things does not necessarily mean that they do not exist. They may exist, but lie hidden behind the veil of the unknown. Later, either through the course of human investigation or through the agency of Divine revelation, they emerge from the realm of the unseen to that of the seen.

The term 'unseen' in its wider application is employed to cover everything which is not directly visible or audible. Likewise it also covers all that is not directly accessible through other human sensory faculties. In this respect we may also define the unseen as a domain which covers all forms of existence which lie beyond the direct access of the five senses. The things which belong to this category do not remain permanently inaccessible. They are inaccessible only with reference to a given period in time.

All hidden knowledge of perceivable things, whether it pertains to the past, the present or the future, lies within the scope of this category. In other words, we are required to believe in the existence of things which are not known at a given point in time, but do exist and may become known at another point in time. This belief cannot be dubbed as blind faith. The Quran does not require the believers to have faith in anything which is not supported by irrefutable arguments. Hence the unseen covers only such things as may become accessible through the instruments of reason, rationality and deductive logic. The point to be noted here is that the unseen as defined, though not directly perceivable by the senses, is yet verifiable. The rationale of this Quranic injunction is fully supported by human experience.

OF THE MATERIAL FORMS of existence, there are many categories which defy direct examination. The knowledge of their existence and that of their physical properties can only be gained through logical deduction, or with the help of sophisticated electronic devices, which make them accessible to the senses, indirectly. What are neutrinos and anti-neutrinos? What is matter and antimatter? What are bosons and anti-bosons? The answer to these questions cannot be obtained through any direct means of examination, yet their unseen world has become a universally accepted reality. It should be remembered here that the mind is the ultimate entity of life, which receives and computes all messages transmitted to it by the senses through the computer of the human brain. Mind is not just another name for the brain. It transcends the brain and manipulates its operation.

The mind is the ultimate seat of consciousness. Deductive logic is the most amazing faculty of mind. Even when there are no facts fed to it, it may continue to operate with hypothetical data. It can also operate by ruminating over the previously stored data. All decision making is done at the level of the mind, while the brain is merely a material hardware, a storehouse of memory. Moreover, the mind has the power to contemplate upon metaphysical and conceptual issues like infinity and eternity. It endeavours to resolve the enigma of a seemingly endless chain of cause and effect. Where did a certain thing begin and what lies beyond every beginning? Was there a first cause preceding all other causes? If so, was that first cause living and conscious, or was it dead and mindless? The only rational conclusion the mind can draw is that the first cause could not be unconscious and dead.

Again the question as to whether death can create life, and unconsciousness give birth to consciousness, is a subject fit only to be explored by the mind and not by the mere brain mass itself. Thus, sometimes the mind learns to believe in the unseen entirely through hypothetical exercises, while at other times it examines and sifts material data and draws logical conclusions from them. It can visualize all forms of radiation which coexist with us, but man can learn of their presence neither through sight, hearing, taste or smell nor through the sense of touch. They can be seen and heard of course by means of radio and television, but only when they are transformed into visible and audible pulses. Even then it is only the faculty of mind which is responsible in the final analysis for decoding these electrical vibrations into sounds and pictures and lifelike phenomena. The images which the mind creates are not merely those seen by the eye on the flat surface of television. There is more to them than meets the eye. Many an unseen meaning is added to the visible scene by the mind, before it is finally developed into a meaningful concept.

But the hidden knowledge within the realm of the unseen is also accessible through revelation in addition to the instruments just discussed. Thus the faculty of mind which is the final recipient of all impressions can be fed both through the sensory organs and the phenomenon of revelation. Both can work independently or jointly, one helping the other. For instance, revelation can help provide a better understanding of things which are observed through sensory organs by illuminating the human faculties to a much higher and more refined order of perception. It helps the mind decipher the message of sensory organs with such clarity and precision as could not have been possible otherwise. The sensory organs in their turn also help the recipient of revelation to understand its message better, with the help of the data stored in its memory banks, without reference to which no meaningful perception is possible anyway. However, for man to reach beyond his physical limitations even without any direct help from revelation, is neither impossible nor rare. But the faculty of mind has its own limitations too. The domain of God's knowledge transcends time and space but that of human knowledge cannot. Hence all such knowledge as lies beyond the reach of human faculties can only be obtained by means of Divine revelation bestowed upon whomsoever He desires. Thus the Quran states:

$$\text{72:27-28} \quad \text{فَلَا يُظْهِرُ عَلَى غَيْبِهِ أَحَدًا}^{*} \text{ اِلَّا مَنِ ارْتَضَى مِنْ رَّسُوْلٍ}$$

... He does not grant ascendancy to anyone over His domain of the unseen,
Except to him whom He selects as *His* messenger...[2]

It should be clearly understood that the second verse does not rule out the possibility of non-prophets witnessing the unseen through Divine dreams, visions or even verbal revelations. What is denied is the possibility of people, other than the messengers of God, gaining ascendancy over any area of God's knowledge. What is asserted is the fact that the knowledge granted to the non-messengers, even through revelation, can in no way be matched in clarity, certainty and perfection with that bestowed upon the messengers of God.

Again, this exclusiveness of transcendent knowledge granted to the prophets relates largely to the field of spiritual knowledge and to the knowledge about life after death. There are many areas of mundane knowledge however, which are also covered by some Divine revelations, but this is done only incidentally to strengthen the faith of the believers in the truth of the prophets and in the existence of an All-Knowledgeable God. In all areas of secular research, man is generally left free to investigate into the realm of the unknown without being directly aided by Divine revelation. What the Quran categorically rejects is the human potential to completely encompass even a small portion of God's knowledge without His aid and permission:

$$ \text{وَلَا يُحِيطُونَ بِشَىْءٍ مِّنْ عِلْمِهِ إِلَّا بِمَا شَآءَ} \quad 2:256 $$

... and they encompass nothing of His knowledge except what He pleases...[3]

THE MESSAGE is obvious that humans can have access to the realm of the unknown, but only to the extent that He allows. This also implies that the so-called secular research and exploration is not entirely secular after all. Every era, which opens up a new vista of knowledge, is in accordance with the Divine plan and design. This interpretation is further supported by the verse:

وَاِنْ مِّنْ شَیْءٍ اِلَّا عِنْدَنَا خَزَآئِنُهُ وَمَا نُنَزِّلُهَ اِلَّا بِقَـدَرٍ مَّعْلُـوْمٍ*
15:22

We possess inexhaustible treasures of everything,
but We do not cause them to descend except in well-
defined and calculated measure.[4]

The most wonderful message delivered by the verse
just quoted is that the world of the unknown is boundless
and fathomless, yet man will always be permitted access to
it, but in measured portions which will be estimated by God
in accordance with the requirements and dictates of the
time. Thus, the Quranic terms of 'the unknown' and 'the
unseen' do not in any way encourage blind faith and
ignorance. On the contrary, they promote perpetual
investigation by assuring man that what he knows and
observes as reality is but infinitesimally small in proportion
to what he knows not. Hence man's quest for knowledge
must always continue because the ocean of the secrets of
nature is inexhaustible.

For rational decision making the only tools at the
disposal of human intellect are its subjective and objective
impressions. Hence, even if the integrity of the decision
maker is beyond question, his decisions could still be
wrong because of such factors as are not within his control.
Misinformation, misunderstanding, deception and
inadequacy of mental faculties can adversely influence the
quality of his decision making. Again, as the vantage points
of different observers are most often diverse, so also the
nature of their observations vary. Despite these inherent
flaws and possible margins of error, it cannot be denied that
the human faculty of rationality has been largely
responsible for guiding his steps, age after age, from eras of
darkness to eras of comparative light.

Can it be proved with certainty that the Holy Quran is true in its claim that God reveals some aspects of the unseen to those whom He chooses? Can it be shown to the sceptic that the faith in the unseen is not merely an illusion or wishful thinking, but is founded on reality and can be rationally demonstrated? Answers to these questions have to be fully supported by factual and scientific evidence. This exactly is the purpose of this treatise and the reader will find ample proof of the validity of revelation as a dependable means of the transfer of knowledge in the following chapters.

In accordance with the message delivered in Surah *Al-Ḥijr* verse 22 (Chapter 15), man's horizon is forever expanding; the unknown is forever being transferred into the known. This realization creates an unquenchable thirst for the quest of knowledge. It is a message of hope and pride, as well as a lesson in humility.

The message of humility relates to the ever-growing awareness of man of his knowledge being so small by comparison to what he does not know, as though it were a mere dot or less than that on the endlessly vast canvas of eternity. What we know today is perhaps a billion times more than what we knew a thousand years ago. What we shall know a thousand years from now, may well be a billion times greater than what we know today. Yet even that would be insignificantly small when compared to the limitless unseen treasure-house of God's knowledge.

As the voyage of discovery accelerates its pace, the limitations of the five senses become more apparent. Vast spectra of life and sound exist beyond the reach of our normal perception. If we could improve our ability to perceive them, we would see many new colours and hear many new sounds. Again the colours and shapes of things we see are viewed very differently by some other animals.

The vision of the material world, the perception of colour, smell and taste, differ so much from species to species that every reality turns into a relative reality. This does not, however, result in functional failure in the vast animal kingdom. Perceptional differences promote life and its functions at all levels, rather than impede them. The different visual perceptions of vultures, honey-bees and squids are perfectly suited to their respective requirements. Squids and insects see things in different configurations as compared to humans, because it is essential for their survival to perceive them as either much bigger or much smaller than they actually are. So the faculty of perception varies from species to species. But the human eye does not remain confined within its potentials. Aided by the most advanced electronic devices, man's perception has advanced by astronomical proportions.

WHEN Galileo (c.1600 AD), saw the universe with his elementary telescope, he was so impressed with his discovery that he proudly announced that he had increased the horizon of human vision by a hundredfold. Little did he know that not far from his time, a day would dawn when man would perceive the universe enlarged a hundred thousand, nay a hundred million times greater and vaster than what he observed. He could compare his discoveries and inventions only in relation to the past from his vantage point. But how transitory man's exultations over his achievements so often prove.

The tragedy of Galileo's last days, which ended in total blindness, is a sad illustration to prove the point. In one of his letters written to a close friend he laments the fact that he, the inventor of the first telescope, who had 'broadened the horizon of the universe' as he thought 'a hundredfold', was himself reduced to the mere confines of his own body.

This lay heavy on his heart and embittered his life unbearably. This poignant expression of frustration by Galileo leads us to another aspect of the unseen. If Galileo had not been familiar with the faculty of sight prior to his blindness, it would have been impossible for him to visualize what lay beyond the earth he trod. Nor could he have ever distinguished between light and darkness. The best he could do was to have faith in what he heard of the reality of light, but that too only in an obscure indescribable way. Although, in matters of colours and light he could not have ascertained by any direct measure the truth of his faith, yet it could not have been dismissed as unreal, merely for the reason of it being hearsay. The illustration we have given above is only applicable to a specific context. We are visualizing the dilemma of a blind man surrounded by those who are gifted with the faculty of sight. He has at least something to go upon, on which to build his faith. But visualize a society of men who are all blind. Could they also have faith in the existence of light and the faculty of sight? Most certainly not. It takes a seeing man to try to help the blind to perceive the existence of things which lie beyond the reach of their senses. It is here that the supremacy of revelation over the secular quest of knowledge can be demonstrated effectively.

Man with his limited number of senses, however wise and enlightened he may be, cannot overstep the boundaries of his senses. Yet the possibility of there being more senses cannot be ruled out. It is God alone who can inform man about the realities which lie beyond his scope.

THE NATURE OF the Hereafter which the Holy Quran attempts to portray belongs to just that area of the unknowable which has been referred to. With reference to it, the Quran has coined a charming phrase expressing the hopelessness of the situation. After mentioning such subjects as are in reality incomprehensible for man, it ends with this expression of exasperation: *whatever can make you (O man), understand what it really is?* Following are a few more illustrations of the same:

$$\text{وَمَآ اَدْرٰىكَ مَا يَوْمُ الدِّيْنِ ثُمَّ مَآ اَدْرٰىكَ مَا يَوْمُ الدِّيْنِ } \quad 82:18\text{-}19$$

And what should make thee know what the Day of Judgement is!
Again, what should make thee know what the Day of Judgement is![5]

$$\text{اَلْحَآقَّةُ مَا الْحَآقَّةُ وَمَآ اَدْرٰىكَ مَا الْحَآقَّةُ } \quad 69:2\text{-}4$$

The Inevitable!
What is the Inevitable?
And what should make thee know what the Inevitable is?[6]

$$\text{سَاُصْلِيْهِ سَقَرَ وَمَآ اَدْرٰىكَ مَا سَقَرُ } \quad 74:27\text{-}28$$

Him shall I cast into the Hellfire.
But what can make thee understand *O man*, what the Hellfire is?[7]

In fact the problem does not relate as much to God's inability as it does to the limitation of human senses. Naturally anyone who is deficient in one or two of the five senses can by no means grasp the true nature of anything which pertains to the missing senses. The deaf cannot grasp the idea of sound and the blind cannot visualize what sight is. Yet others who can hear and see do make attempts to help them grope for the idea which for them is ever elusive.

Likewise when the Quran speaks of the hereafter and warns man that he cannot truly understand the nature of what is being described, it is the inadequacy of man and not that of God which is being highlighted. The implication is loud and clear. There have to be some new senses added in the hereafter to the senses we possess here on earth. All our present knowledge of the hereafter, therefore, is at best a shadowy vision of some unknown realities like that of a blind man who has some concept at least of what colour and light may have been. *What can really make you understand (O man) what it really is?*

The broadening of our senses, whenever it will take place, will perhaps completely transform beyond recognition the perception of what we seemed to have already experienced here on earth. We think we know what love is and we think we are familiar with suffering but what love would be in the hereafter and what suffering would be, one shudders to visualize. No wonder that the Quran reminds us that despite the vivid picture of heaven it portrays, no eye has ever seen and no ear has ever heard the like of it. So also, despite clearly describing the chastisement of hell, it hastens to warn 'but what can make thee understand *O man*, what the Hellfire is?' The more one ponders over the meaning of the unseen, the more avenues of undreamt of possibilities begin to loom before one's vision. But to grasp what lies beyond in the unexplored avenues of hidden realities, man shall always stand in need of Divine revelation. The limitation of our perception, however, is not the only hindrance which impedes our enquiry. Even within the domain of our senses what lies hidden from us is far more than what we see. Whatever the belief in the unseen is, it is certainly not a belief in nothingness. A belief in nothingness is only a rejection of the belief in the unseen.

The journey of the believers is enlightened with the wisdom of this verse which leads them on to an endless voyage of discovery. For them there is no void, no emptiness, but just curtains waiting to be lifted from the limitless treasure-houses of knowledge.

However much pride we may take in the small knowledge we possess, by comparison it is as insignificant as a molehill by the side of a vast lofty mountain range. But the mountain ranges we know here on earth are not endless and infinite. The mountain ranges of knowledge that we are talking about extend into the limitless expanse of eternity with no beginning and no end.

There is no element of discouragement for the explorers in this declaration. It implies that whatever knowledge man gains, seemingly through his personal effort alone, is in reality made possible because of Divine will and blessing. Independent of the will and pleasure of God, human enquiry and labour could bear no fruit. The human quest for knowledge is only rewarded in appropriate measure at appropriate times in accordance with the Divine plan of creation. Although the achievement of knowledge by man in the area of secular research is not directly through the instrument of Divine revelation, it nonetheless carries the mark of His approval and design. The faculties of the five senses bestowed upon him and the opportunity granted to him to employ them to his best advantage are but by the grace of God to enable him to acquire knowledge.

IT IS THE ALL-POWERFUL CREATOR who has pressed into man's service all the known or latent properties of the Universe. It is God again Who foresaw all the possible requirements man could ever need during all the ages of his spiritual, material, scientific, economic and cultural advancement:

وَسَخَّرَ لَكُمْ مَّا فِى السَّمٰوٰتِ وَمَا فِى ٱلْأَرْضِ جَمِيْعًا مِّنْهُ ٱِنَّ فِىْ
ذٰلِكَ لَأٰيٰتٍ لِّقَوْمٍ يَّتَفَكَّرُوْنَ * 45:14

And He has pressed into your service whatever is in
the heavens and whatever is in the earth, all of it
entirely. In that there are Signs surely for a people
who reflect.[8]

A more wonderful gesture of encouragement for
limitless exploration could not be conceived. It is
underwritten that everything that man would discover
would be of service to him. But that is not all. The
following verse speaks not only of the visible heavens and
earth but also of that something which fills the space
between the two – the heavens and the earth – to be of
benefit to man. The Quran made this amazing disclosure as
early as fourteen hundred years ago. The message is clear
that the apparent void in the interstellar space is in reality
filled with some form of existence of which man has no
knowledge:

وَمَا خَلَقْنَا السَّمٰوٰتِ وَٱلْأَرْضَ وَمَا بَيْنَهُمَآ ٱِلَّا بِالْحَقِّ 15:86

We have created the heavens and the earth, and
whatever lies between the two, according to the
requirements of truth and wisdom...[9]

What is it that exists between the two and how can
that be pressed into the service of man, are questions as yet
unanswered. The Quran is speaking of such vastness as lies
beyond the grasp of human imagination. Perhaps it is the
dark matter which is being referred to, or something of
which we have no knowledge so far. This spectacular
disclosure by the Quran implies, that one day man will be

able to share and utilize some of the secrets to which this verse refers.

The circumference of the earth is merely twenty-five thousand miles, but the vastness of which the Holy Quran is speaking stretches some eighteen or twenty billion light years across from end to end and continues to expand further at an amazing speed. This means that if a space traveller begins his journey today from one edge of the universe to the other at the speed of light (186,000 miles per second), he could possibly reach the other edge after travelling for eighteen to twenty billion years, provided that the universe were stationary – which it is not. Now one may try to grasp the meaning of the Holy Quran, when it declares that in all the vastness of space there is not a single bubble of emptiness, not an inch, not a millimetre, not a nanometre or the tiniest of tiny dots.

The verse under review has also another important significance worthy of note. Even without the employment of natural means of enquiry, God the All-Knowing can reveal some of His secrets to whomsoever He pleases. Hence any mention in the Divine scripture of the mysteries of nature, before they are discovered by scientific exploration, presents a powerful evidence in favour of the existence of an All-Knowing Supreme Creator of the Universe. It is He alone, Who possesses the full knowledge of the realms of the seen and the unseen (عٰـلِمُ الْغَيْبِ وَالشَّهَادَة).

The knowledge gained through revelation is quite a different story from that of the knowledge gained through secular scientific investigation. The Divine scriptures are not textbooks of science, hence any reference therein to scientific subjects could not be merely incidental. The main purpose is to establish the unity of source; to prove that the material world and the spiritual world are both the work of the same Creator. Remember that the Founder[sa] of Islam, the recipient of the Holy Quran, was an unlettered person, born in an unlettered society. His birth and upbringing took place in a land flanked on its eastern and western frontiers by two great civilizations of that time, the Roman and Persian empires.

The desert of Arabia lay trapped in the middle as a wasteland of darkness and ignorance. Would it not be extraordinary for a person born there in AD 600, to so vividly talk of the vastness of the universe and the secrets it contains, secrets which are only now beginning to emerge like the twinkling of dimly lit stars seen through the hazy light of dusk. It is incredible for such a person to speak of things unknown to the greatest scholars of his time anywhere in the world, and yet be proved right under the scrutiny of the scientific examination of the twentieth century. How right he must have been when he declared that whatever knowledge he transmitted to the world was not of his own making, but came from a Supreme, All-Knowing Eternal source of Absolute Wisdom!

Impressed by the same, Dr Maurice Bucaille, a reputable French author, expresses his wonder at some length in his book, *The Bible, The Qur'an And Science*.[10] He gathered material from the Bible and the Quran and subjected both to an impartial scrutiny by comparing them with universally accepted contemporary scientific knowledge. To discover the Quran to be right every time is the last thing he expected his enquiry to reveal. The full report of his investigation was published in the first French edition in 1976. Nothing that the Quran had observed was found to be at variance with the scientific knowledge of the twentieth century.

Here it would be appropriate to also mention the name of a renowned Canadian Professor of anatomy, Keith L. Moore, Chairman of the Department of the Faculty of

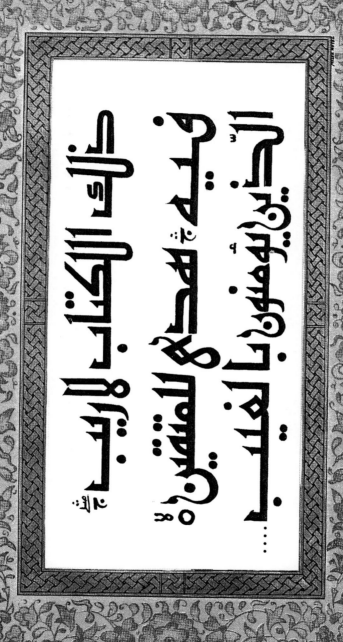

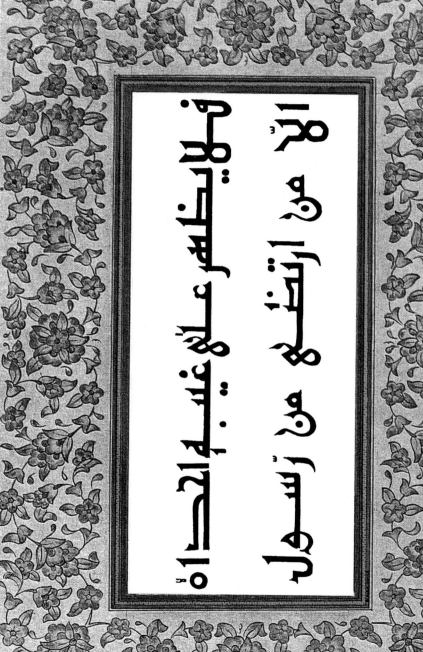

لَقَدْ جَاءَكُمْ رَسُولٌ مِنْ أَنْفُسِكُمْ عَزِيزٌ عَلَيْهِ مَا عَنِتُّمْ حَرِيصٌ عَلَيْكُم بِالْمُؤْمِنِينَ رَؤُوفٌ رَحِيمٌ

Medicine, University of Toronto, who has critically examined the question of the Holy Quran and embryology.[11,12] In addition to the Quran, he also quotes some relevant traditions of the Holy Prophet, may peace and blessings of Allah be upon him. Encouraged by his research he testifies to the truth of Quranic revelation with amazing boldness and clarity.

How far we can trust the conclusions drawn from such comparisons between scriptural observations and known scientific facts, is the question which must be addressed here. Time continues to refine the conceptual faculties of man, forever widening the horizon of his awareness. Hence man's understanding of things is subject to constant change. How then can one rely on the verdict of any given scientific era and accept it as final? Take for instance the case of the natural laws which are unanimously accepted as universal and unchanging. Yet it cannot be said that they were understood alike by the philosophers and scientists of all ages. In view of this, will not the scientific testimony of the contemporary age in favour of Quranic revelation lose some of its dependability? Can one rely with absolute certainty on the finality of this verdict? Will it not be justified to suggest that the universally accepted concepts of today may be put to question by the advanced intellectual enlightenment of tomorrow?

To raise such questions is justified indeed but only partially so. All the concepts of the past have not necessarily changed in subsequent ages. There are countless cases of human understanding of things which, after undergoing some change for a period of time, became stabilized ultimately. There is many a law of nature which having been once accepted as universal truth, always remained so without further debate. There may occur some minor adjustments but in general their understanding remains unaltered. No intricate philosophical or scientific discussion is required any more to prove their validity. At the elementary level of water, fire, air and earth, their properties are better understood with the passage of time of course, but no change has ever occurred in the understanding of their fundamental nature. Fire still burns as it always did, water still extinguishes as it has done in the past. They have become fundamental truths belonging to all times, hence no one in his senses can ever predict that water will one day begin to burn and will feed the flames of fire. Yet in the domain of Divine prophecies some predictions are made which are no less startling by virtue of their being so different from the well-established human knowledge. For instance, in the past ages it would take only a prophet to make a prediction so bizarre as to prophesy that a day would dawn when water would also be observed to burn in addition to its extinguishing properties. That would be some prophecy indeed! If later on the existence and the properties of sodium are discovered to exactly correspond to the prophecy, no one has a right to dismiss such a prophecy as a soothsayer's vain babble. Once discovered, however, this unusual behaviour of sodium will be counted among the unchangeable universal laws. No one can suspect that a day may dawn when water would cease to ignite sodium. Yet if man looks around with awareness he will be amazed to find how much of his knowledge has already come to stay as unchangeable realities.

The same is true of human sensory perceptions. Their scope may widen but their recognition of the sweet, the bitter, the savoury, the unsavoury, heat and cold, noise and silence, comfort and discomfort, pain and pleasure and a myriad of other similar sensory stimulators will not undergo any change. Stability of concepts such as these can be classified as the primary stage of certainty. A comparatively higher stage of certainty belongs to the area of scientific enquiry. There too, we can find examples of complete agreement among scientists on many a concept which has come to stay and as such is accepted as universal. For instance, about the chemical composition of water there are no two opinions. One cannot suggest that with the passage of time its formula will change and a new formula may be discovered to replace it, such as H_3O_5 instead of H_2O.

Evidently there are limitations to the possibilities of change in the human understanding of things. The main body of scientific knowledge, once established and stabilized, remains essentially the same except for some fine modifications in the fringe area. How atoms are bonded to atoms and molecules to molecules, which bonds are weak and which are stronger, and how to utilize this knowledge to synthesize new chemicals, are matters which are well-understood. The continuous flow of new information does not alter their established patterns of behaviour. The knowledge of man in this area of research grows without challenging the universally accepted fundamentals. It becomes evident from this that the truth of any scriptural observation can indeed be verified to a large measure of certainty when compared with such secular knowledge as has stood the test of time, age after age.

Again, there are things which become certainties, not because they have been tested over a long period of time, but because their truth is universally demonstrable. All new ideas and discoveries pertaining to natural laws and behaviour of matter fall into this category when proved through experimentation in different laboratories of the world. It is to such established truths that we refer when we testify the truths of spiritual claims by applying them to the touchstone of scientific discoveries.

Subject to this explanation, Quranic revelations have always been proved right; and once proved right they have never been proved wrong. This role of the Quranic revelation, with regard to the transfer of knowledge from the realm of the unseen to the seen, is remarkable and will be further elaborated under various categories in the following chapters.

FOR THE PRESENT, we return to the general discussion concerning the phenomenon of the broadening of human knowledge, and the stages through which a new idea passes before reaching the stage of absolute truth. When a new idea emerges from the realm of the unseen, it is always put to the test of rational scrutiny or experimental trial whenever possible. Having survived this scrutiny, age after age, it can be categorized as absolute truth.

This is a universal phenomenon which continues to work uninterrupted in every area of human experience. We are not talking here of theses and antitheses, the two philosophical terms employed by Kant to such great ideas as are of global importance; we are talking of an ongoing, all-comprehensive phenomenon which relates to human experiences, impressions and perceptions of everyday life. It is a comprehensive continuous process like evolution. Layer upon layer of such well testified, established facts continue to raise the level of dependable human knowledge and widen the human grasp of surrounding realities. It is this all-pervasive phenomenon which continues to convert doubts into plausibilities, plausibilities into probabilities, and probabilities into certainties and established facts. If the truth of Divine revelation is objectively testified by such reliable human knowledge, there is no justification for subjecting it to further doubt.

The unseen belongs to all ages – the past, the present and the future alike. The Quran does not keep itself confined to any one of these in disclosing its secrets. It covers all ages with equal clarity, as though no dividing line separates the past from the present and the present from the future. Events as ancient as the birth of the universe are resurrected before human vision, as though they were contemporary events. And things as distant as the sinking of the universe into yet another black hole, are described as though they were taking place while the Quran was revealed.

With the same exactitude and precision, the secrets of the creation of life and its ultimate destiny are revealed. The Quran recounts the history of man and records the stage by stage journey of human progress and achievements from the beginning to the end. It does so with such perfect clarity and dexterity, as though the pen that wrote the Quran was held in the hand of the Beholder who wrote what He saw etched across the vast canvas of eternity. This is what the import of our book is all about.

But before we proceed further to demonstrate how Quranic truth is testified by the post-Quranic era of scientific, social and political advancement of man, we should like to draw the attention of the reader to the important fact that the validity of Divine revelation does not essentially depend on subjective secular evidence alone. Among all the Divinely revealed facts there is a category which stands out above all others styled as *Al-Bayyinah*. To this we shall turn our attention in the following chapter.

REFERENCES

1. Translation of 2:3-4 by Maulawi Sher Ali.
2. Translation of 72:27-28 by the author.
3. Translation of 2:256 by Maulawi Sher Ali.
4. Translation of 15:22 by the author.
5. Translation of 82:18-19 by Maulawi Sher Ali.
6. Translation of 69:2-4 by Maulawi Sher Ali.
7. Translation of 74:27-28 by the author.
8. Translation of 45:14 by the author.
9. Translation of 15:86 by the author.
10. BUCAILLE, M. (1979) *The Bible, The Qur'an and Science.* BB Books & Books, Lahore.
11. MOORE, K. L., PERSAUD T.V.N. (1993) *The Developing Human: Clinically Oriented Embryology.* 5th ed., W.B. Saunders Company, Philadelphia.
12. MOORE, K.L. (1986) *A Scientists Interpretation of References to Embryology in the Holy Quran.* Journal Islamic Medical Association of the United States and Canada. 19:15-16

AL-BAYYINAH –
A MANIFEST PRINCIPLE AND
AL-QAYYIMAH –
AN EVERLASTING TEACHING

L-BAYYINAH, a Quranic term, applies to such manifest truth as is outstanding in its quality of dazzling brilliance, as though the sun had risen and the night dispelled. It appears with the appearance of all Divine messengers who usher in a new era of light. It does not relate to the beginning of Islam alone; it relates to the beginning of all Divine manifestations. When a messenger comes to revolutionize a society, he personifies *Al-Bayyinah* of which he himself is the harbinger.

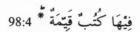

98:4 فِيْهَا كُتُبٌ قَيِّمَةٌ *

Therein are everlasting teachings.[1]

L-QAYYIMAH (ٱلْقَيِّمَة) is another term which signifies that part of a prophet's teachings which makes the central core of every religion. It has a quality of permanence about it which defies change. All prophets according to the pronouncement of Surah *Al-Bayyinah* (Chapter 98), essentially bring the same message in fundamentals. This means that Adam[as], the first messenger of God, was no different in this respect from any other prophet who followed him. *Al-Qayyimah* provides the binding link between all Divinely revealed religions. According to this declaration the religion of Adam[as], the first prophet, and that of Hazrat Muhammad[sa], the last of all the law-bearing prophets, have to be the same in bare essentials. Despite this similarity, there may be vast differences in the teachings of the earlier religions and those of the more evolved ones of subsequent ages. To produce dissimilarity in detail despite similarity in the fundamentals is in fact an intrinsic character of evolution. The term 'mammal' for instance is a term applied to all warm-blooded animals who possess vertebral columns and limbs but they are not exactly alike. Sheep differ so much from humans, and cats from monkeys, despite the fact that they belong to the same order of mammals. Hence, as religions continue to evolve, they appear with new titles and names without becoming different in fundamentals. *Al-Qayyimah* remains their permanent binding link.

The *Bayyinah* as explained above, is not only the quality of the truth a prophet brings but it is also the quality of his personal character. His truth is so manifest that prior to his claim of Divine representation, the entire society in which he is born and raised testifies to it with unanimous accord. But *Al-Bayyinah* is not that alone! The truth of a prophet, when further supported by heavenly signs, becomes so evident that there is no genuine excuse whatsoever for the society to deny it. It is this same irrefutable manifestation of his Divine origin which ironically becomes responsible for the extreme hostility and antagonism displayed against him, particularly by the old order religious clergy of the time. They reject him only because they recognize in him the dawn of a new day of truth. This rise of a new dawn, if permitted, would break their hegemony over the ignorant masses and destroy the old order of their religious hierarchy. It is this potent threat to their survival as a class which compels them to forget their mutual differences and put up a joint front of

I.7

resistance with no holds barred. When all their baboonish noises and threats fail to intimidate the prophet, the only option they are left with is a desperate recourse to violence. But it is far beyond their united might to defeat *Al-Bayyinah*. Its winning potential lies not merely in the quality of its truth but more than that it lies in the support that God lends it. *Al-Bayyinah* thus aided by destiny transcends time and space, and always emerges as the dominant principle. To be on the right side of *Al-Bayyinah* is to survive, to be on the left is to perish.

Al-Bayyinah does not belong to that category of absolute truth which makes the subject of philosophical discussions. Nor is it similar to the emergence of absolute ideas which gradually develop after successfully meeting the challenges of successive eras. The quality of brilliance it displays is lent to it by Divine revelation from its very inception.

The term *Al-Bayyinah* also comprises other connotations. It works as a motive phenomenon which advances faith and spiritual evolution. It is not inert, but is more like the domineering principle of evolution. All prophetic movements emanate from *Al-Bayyinah*. The word is derived from an infinitive which has the root meaning of differentiation and discrimination, a meaning it shares with another Quranic term, '*Al-Bayān*'. *Al-Bayān* (اَلْبَيَان) is the faculty of speech which has the power to differentiate between two meanings and to define human thought into clear expressions. It should be noted that like the '*Bayyinah*', *Al-Bayān* (اَلْبَيَان) also is described by the Quran to have a Divine origin as mentioned in the following verse:

$$ \text{خَلَقَ الْإِنْسَانَ * عَلَّمَهُ الْبَيَانَ * } 55:4\text{-}5 $$

295

He created man;
And taught him how to express himself and differentiate.[2]

Hence, the faculty of speech is clearly claimed to have been bestowed by God upon man, which leads to the inevitable conclusion that the first language taught to him was taught by God Himself. In the light of this, the enigma of the human faculty of speech does not remain as incomprehensible as it would otherwise be. The faculty of speech separates man from the rest of the animal kingdom by such a wide margin as cannot be explained by the doctrine of evolution alone, however much it may be extended. Hence, *Al-Bayān*, the faculty of speech has to be a gift of Divine revelation.

Thus both the *Bayān* and the *Bayyinah* have the same common origin and both possess the same quality of differentiation. Despite this similarity however, there is a characteristic difference between the two. While *Al-Bayān* is intrinsically bonded to verbal expressions, *Al-Bayyinah* is not confined to this alone. It may at times carry verbal pronouncements, but at others it may manifest itself without the medium of speech. This silent display of *Al-Bayyinah* is like the radiance of a midday sun in which all ever-lasting Divine teachings bask. While on the one hand it draws its strength from God, on the other it lends support to those who lean on it.

"*Al-Qayyimah*", the other term, applies to all such fundamental teachings as have a quality of permanence about them. It is there that the two terms seem to merge together into one. The philosophical terms of absoluteness or universality of values can also fully apply to the values which are expressed by the religious term *Al-Qayyimah*. But whether there can be any ideas or values which can in reality be described as absolute or universal is the question which we must examine now purely from the secular angle. Almost all the prominent thinkers belonging to the school of scientific socialism reject the absoluteness of ideas or values categorically. They only do so because of the incompatibility of absoluteness with the Marxist vision of dialectical materialism. But their encounter with the day-to-day realities of the surrounding material world leaves them no justification for their total rejection of the idea of absoluteness.

Night follows day and day follows night. Fire burns and water extinguishes. Our sense of heat and cold, of sorrow and pleasure, our awareness of appetite and satiation, our concept of thirst and its slaking and a myriad of other similar perceptions do not require a scientist to prove their validity. They simply exist without change, without question, requiring no advocate to prove their validity. All the same their absoluteness is inseparably linked with the quality of human perception. The concept of night and day requires the faculty of sight. But what of those whose vision is impaired? Their perception of things will be relatively different from that of those who are gifted with a better quality of sight. This raises the doubt that even what we categorize as elementary perceptions may only be relative in nature. There is a wide spectrum between the extreme edge of doubt and that of absolute certainty. Both may shift in any direction along the spectrum depending on the clarity of the observer's sight and that of the available light. But such doubts are raised only with reference to exceptional cases and situations. Compared to the universal human experience at large, they make only a very small and insignificant minority, which cannot alter the consensus of the universal human experience.

Again it is not just in relation to these elementary concepts that man has reached a stage of certainty; there are other far more complex and intricate issues which can yet be safely described as absolute. Most of our advanced knowledge of chemistry and physics today belongs to this category. It continues to grow, no doubt, but most often without contradicting the previously held views based on universal human observation. The alterations and amendments take place only in the peripheral areas. The uncertainty factor does not cast shadow of doubt over the main body of proven facts; it does so only in relation to a few limited and confined areas of advanced research. Hence, one can safely conclude that at least in the secular field of human experience, the concept of absoluteness is not merely valid, it is certainly an ongoing progressive reality. But in the matter of faith and belief the same cannot be claimed with any justification. It is extremely difficult for believers, if not impossible, to draw a clear line between the facts and fantasies of their beliefs. Most often they are raised as children in the cradle of faith and, before they ever become capable of judging the truth or falsehood of their beliefs, they already become an integral part of their system. The few who awaken from their mental state of lethargy and oblivion do so at the cost of their religion but seldom admit this fact publicly. They keep wearing the same garb under the same title so that despite the loss of faith their religion continues to survive merely as a symbol of identity. This, unfortunately, is the fate of all religions which deny rationality any instrumental role in judging the validity of their beliefs.

Returning to the discussion of the progressive transformation of uncertainties into certainties and certainties into absolute truth, we must admit that the same universal trend of change leads some philosophers to regret the very concept of absoluteness altogether. No perception can ever be absolutely free from the influence of ever-changing time and the variant faculties of the beholder. If their logic is accepted, one is left with no choice but to reject everything as possibly untrue and believe in nothing. But in everyday life a philosophy such as this would lead to utter disaster. With what measure of dependability can one decide whether the precipice one sees at the edge of a lofty rock is really a precipice? By what criterion can one become absolutely sure that the deadly viper blocking one's path is actually what it appears to be? In all such encounters with threats to life, even the most sceptical would accept the verdict of the common human experience. It is this common human experience which is most steadily moving in the direction of absoluteness of knowledge. At every cross-section of time this verdict must be accepted. Call it probability if not absoluteness but remember that it is this probability which commands the human destiny with absolute firmness. One cannot deny a seeming reality lest it should prove to be false in future.

All said and done, in the evolution of human knowledge most concepts do mature to a fullness which cannot be further touched by the hand of change or doubt. Similarly, the behaviour of many physical and chemical laws once understood continues to remain the same. Our ignorance of some of their operations does not invalidate the knowledge that we have already gained in most areas of their operation. Despite the fact that the dynamics of the heavenly bodies and the laws of gravitation are now perceived with a minute variation of perception, the Newtonian understanding of them is still valid within its context. Thus the laws of motion of the heavenly bodies are as absolute as they ever were within their respective field of operation. The laws of motion of the subatomic particles are also absolute within the domain of their miniature universe. Hence there is no discrepancy or contradiction between the laws which govern the cosmos and the laws which govern the subatomic world. Their field is different and the context in which they operate is not the same either. What man has discovered is only the fact that Newton's laws of dynamics are applicable only to the cosmos. Both categories of the laws are absolute and exist independently of man's ability or inability to understand them. Thus, absolute truth is not just a product of the human mind. It must exist independently.

Returning to the Quranic pronouncements, on the subject of rationality and its bearing on religious truths, the reader's attention is drawn to the following verses of the Holy Quran which rule out the possibility of any contradiction in the universe created by God:

مَا تَرَى فِىْ خَلْقِ الرَّحْمٰنِ مِنْ تَفٰوُتٍ فَارْجِعِ الْبَصَرَ هَلْ تَرٰى مِنْ
فُطُوْرٍ ۞ ثُمَّ ارْجِعِ الْبَصَرَ كَرَّتَيْنِ يَنْقَلِبْ اِلَيْكَ الْبَصَرُ خَاسِئًا وَّهُوَ
حَسِيْرٌ ۞   67:4-5

… No incongruity can you see in the creation of the Gracious God. Then look again: Do you see any flaw?
Aye, look again, and yet again, your sight will *only* return to you tired and fatigued.[3]

THE QURAN FURTHER stipulates that likewise there can be no contradiction within the scriptural universe which is the Word of God (4:83, 21:23). Both the Word of God which is revealed truth and the Work of God which is material universe, must be in perfect unison with each other. Thus Divine revelation can never be at odds with the laws of nature, both sharing the same Fountainhead of Eternal Wisdom. This categorical denial of contradiction is yet another way of endorsing the inviolable principle of rationality.

Thus, whenever and in whatever area the scientists' understanding of the material world is correct, it is impossible for the Word of God to contradict it. The converse is also true. As such whenever we witness a perfect accord between the two, the quality of their absolute truth becomes par-absolute.

In the light of what has passed, we are ready now to undertake the issue of Quranic revelation and examine its validity on the touchstone of rationality and reason, category by category.

REFERENCES

1. Translation of 98:4 by the author.
2. Translation of 55:4-5 by the author.
3. Translation of 67:4-5 by the author.

THE QURAN AND COSMOLOGY

*A*T the time the Holy Quran was revealed, the human understanding of the nature of the cosmos and the movement or the stillness of the heavenly bodies was extremely primitive and obscure. This is no longer the case, as our knowledge of the universe has considerably advanced and expanded by the present age.

Some of the theories relating to the creation of the universe have been verified as facts, whereas some others are still being explored. The concept of the expanding universe belongs to the former category, and has been universally accepted by the scientific community as 'fact'. This discovery was first made by Edwin Hubble in the 1920s. Yet some thirteen centuries before this, it was clearly mentioned in the Quran:

وَالسَّمَآءَ بَنَيْنٰهَا بِاَيْدٍ وَّاِنَّا لَمُوْسِعُوْنَ* 51:48

And the heaven We built with *Our own* powers (aydin) and indeed We go on expanding it (musi'ūn).[1]

It should be remembered that the concept of the continuous expansion of the universe is exclusive to the Quran. No other Divine scriptures even remotely hint at it. The discovery that the universe is constantly expanding is of prime significance to scientists, because it helps create a better understanding of how the universe was initially created. It clearly explains the stage by stage process of creation, in a manner which perfectly falls into step with the theory of the Big Bang. The Quran goes further and describes the entire cycle of the beginning, the end and the return again to a similar beginning. The first step of creation as related in the Quran accurately describes the event of the Big Bang in the following words:

$$اَوَلَمْ يَرَ الَّذِيْنَ كَفَرُوْۤا اَنَّ السَّمٰوٰتِ وَالْاَرْضَ كَانَتَا رَتْقًا فَفَتَقْنٰهُمَا$$
$$وَجَعَلْنَا مِنَ الْمَآءِ كُلَّ شَىْءٍ حَيٍّ ۖ اَفَلَا يُؤْمِنُوْنَ ۝ 21:31$$

Do not the unbelievers see that the heavens and the earth were *a* closed-up *mass* (ratqan), then We clove them asunder (fataqnā)? And We made from water every living thing. Will they not then believe?[2]

It is significant that this verse is specifically addressed to non-believers, implying perhaps, that the unveiling of the secret mentioned in this verse would be made by the non-believers, a sign for them of the truth of the Quran.

In this verse the words *ratqan* (closed-up mass), and *fataqnā* (We clove them asunder), carry the basic message of the whole verse. Authentic Arabic lexicons[3] give two meanings of *ratqan*, that have great relevance to the topic under discussion. One meaning is 'the coming together of something and the consequent infusion into a single entity' and the second meaning is 'total darkness'. Both these meanings are significantly applicable. Taken together, they offer an apt description of the singularity of a black hole.

A BLACK HOLE is a gravitationally collapsed mass of colossal size. It begins with the collapse of such massive stars as are 15 or more times the size of the sun. The immensity of their inward gravitational pull causes the stars to collapse into a much smaller size. The gravitational pull is further concentrated and results in the further collapse of the entire mass into a supernova. At this stage the basic bricks of matter such as molecules, atoms etc. begin to be crushed into a nondescript mass of energy. Thus that moment in space-time is created which is called *event horizon*. The inward gravitational pull of that something becomes so powerful that all forms of radiation are pulled back so that even light cannot escape. A resultant total darkness ensues which earns it the name *black hole,* reminding one of the word *ratqan* used by the Quran indicating total darkness. This is called *singularity* which lies beyond the event horizon.

A black hole once created grows rapidly because even distant stars begin to be pulled in with the progressive concentration of gravitational energy. It is estimated that the mass of a black hole could grow as large as a hundred million times the mass of the sun. As its gravitational field widens, more material from space is drawn in at a speed close to that of light. In 1997 there was observational evidence suggesting that in our galaxy a black hole of 2,000,000 solar masses existed. But other calculations show that in our universe there could be many black holes as big as 3,000,000,000 solar masses.[4] At that concentration of gravitational pull even distant stars would stagger and lose their mooring to be devoured by a glutton of such magnitude. Thus the process of *ratqan* is completed resulting into that singularity which is both completely closed as well as comprising total darkness. In answer to the question as to how the universe was initially created, the two most recent theories are both Big Bang theories. They claim that it was initiated from a singularity which suddenly erupted releasing the trapped mass leading yet again into the creation of a new universe through the event horizon. This dawn of light sprouting from the event horizon is called the *white hole*[5,6]. One of the two theories relating to the expansion predicts that the universe thus created will carry on expanding forever. The other claims that the expansion of the universe will, at some time, be reversed because the inward gravitational pull will ultimately prevail. Eventually, all matter will be pulled back again to form perhaps another gigantic black hole. This latter view appears to be supported by the Quran.

Whilst speaking of the first creation of the universe, the Quran clearly describes its ending into yet another black hole, connecting the end to the beginning, thus completing the full circle of the story of cosmos. The Quran declares:

يَوْمَ نَطْوِى السَّمَآءَ كَطَيِّ السِّجِلِّ لِلْكُتُبِ 21:105

Remember the day when We shall roll up the heavens like the rolling up of scrolls ...[7]

The clear message of this verse is that the universe is not eternal. It speaks of a future when the heavens will be rolled up, in a manner similar to the rolling up of a scroll. Scientific descriptions illustrating the making of a black hole, very closely resemble what the Quran describes in the above verse. (See plate 1).

A mass of accretion from space falling into a black hole, as described above, would be pressed into a sheet under the enormous pressure created by the gravitational and electromagnetic forces. As the centre of the black hole is constantly revolving around itself, this sheet – as it approaches – will begin to be wrapped around it, before disappearing into the realm of the unknown at last.

The verse continues:

كَمَا بَدَأْنَآ أَوَّلَ خَلْقٍ نُّعِيدُهُ وَعْدًا عَلَيْنَا إِنَّا كُنَّا فَٰعِلِينَ 21:105 *

... As We began the first creation, so shall We repeat it; a promise *binding* on Us; that We shall certainly fulfil.[7]

Following the eventual collapse of the universe into a black hole, here we have the promise of a new beginning. God will recreate the universe, as He had done before. The collapsed universe will re-emerge from its darkness and the whole process of creation will start yet again (see plate 2). This wrapping up and unfolding of the universe appears to be an ongoing phenomenon, according to the Holy Quran.

This Quranic concept of the beginning and the end of the creation is undoubtedly extraordinary. It would not have been less amazing if it had been revealed to a highly educated person of our contemporary age, but one is wonder-struck by the fact that this most advanced knowledge, regarding the perpetually repeating phenomenon of creation, was revealed more than fourteen hundred years ago to an unlettered dweller of the Arabian desert.

The Quran and the Heavenly Bodies

Now we turn to another aspect of the description of the cosmos which relates to the motion of the heavenly bodies. The most striking feature of this description relates to the way the motion of the earth is described without glaringly contradicting the popular view prevailing in that age. All the scholars and sages of that time were unanimous in their belief that the earth is stationary while other heavenly bodies like the sun and the moon are constantly revolving around it. In view of this, the motion of the earth as described by the Quran may not be apparent to the casual reader, but to a careful student the message is loud and clear. If the Quran had described the earth as stationary and the heavenly bodies as revolving around it, then although the people of that time might have been satisfied with this description, the people of the later ages would have treated that statement as a proof of the ignorance of the Quran's author. Such a statement, they would emphasize, could not have been made by an All-Knowing, Supreme Being.

Rather than literally comparing the motion of the earth to that of other heavenly bodies, the Quran makes the following statement:

$$وَتَرَى الْجِبَالَ تَحْسَبُهَا جَامِدَةً وَّهِيَ تَمُرُّ مَرَّ السَّحَابِ صُنْعَ اللهِ$$
$$الَّذِيْ اَتْقَنَ كُلَّ شَيْءٍ 27:89$$

> The mountains that you see, you think they are
> stationary while they are constantly floating like the
> floating of clouds. Such is the work of Allah Who
> made everything firm and strong...[8]

If the mountains are declared to be in constant motion, then the only logical inference to be drawn from this would be that the earth is also rotating along with them. But thanks to the masterly language of the Quran this observation went unnoticed. They had the impression, shared with the rest of mankind, that the earth was stationary and it was this false impression that was not obtrusively challenged. If they had read with care the end of the same verse they would have been left with no room for any misunderstanding. It ends with a lasting tribute to the creative faculty of God, Who has created all things with such firmness that they cannot be dislodged. Anything which cannot be dislodged can never be catapulted out of the earth, to fly alone, leaving the earth behind.

Again, in many other verses the Quran refers to the mountains as *ravāsiya* which means 'firmly rooted in the earth':

$$\text{خَلَقَ السَّمٰوٰتِ بِغَيْرِ عَمَدٍ تَرَوْنَهَا وَأَلْقٰى فِى الْأَرْضِ رَوَاسِىَ أَنْ}$$
$$\text{تَمِيدَ بِكُمْ وَبَثَّ فِيهَا مِنْ كُلِّ دَآبَّةٍ وَأَنْزَلْنَا مِنَ السَّمَآءِ مَـآءً}$$
$$\text{فَأَنْبَتْنَا فِيهَا مِنْ كُلِّ زَوْجٍ كَرِيْمٍ * 31:11}$$

He has created the heavens without any pillars that you can see, and He has placed in the earth firm mountains that it may not quake with you, and He has scattered therein all kinds of creatures; and We have sent down water from the clouds, and caused to grow therein every noble species.[9]

Also:

$$\text{وَجَعَلْنَا فِى الْأَرْضِ رَوَاسِىَ أَنْ تَمِيدَ بِهِمْ وَجَعَلْنَا فِيهَا فِجَاجًـا}$$
$$\text{سُبُلاً لَّعَلَّهُمْ يَهْتَدُوْنَ * 21:32}$$

And We have made in the earth firm mountains, that they may provide them *humans* food, and We have made therein wide pathways that they may be rightly guided.[10]

and,

$$\text{وَأَلْقٰى فِى الْأَرْضِ رَوَاسِىَ أَنْ تَمِيدَ بِكُمْ وَأَنْهٰـرًا وَّسُبُلاً لَّعَلَّكُمْ}$$
$$\text{تَهْتَدُوْنَ * 16:16}$$

And He has placed in the earth firm mountains that they may provide you food, and rivers and routes that you may be guided.[11]

Thus, the Holy Quran exquisitely succeeds in making this revelation in a manner that the prevalent knowledge of that time is not too loudly challenged. It is likely that the people may have believed verse 89 of Surah *Al-Naml*, referred to a future event associated with Doomsday. But as has been demonstrated, this misinterpretation would be absolutely unacceptable for the following reasons:

1) The verse clearly speaks in the present tense and not in the future tense. The letter (و) *vaow* used here can literally be translated as 'while' instead of 'and', so the meaning could be, *'you think the mountains are stationary, while they are moving'*. To refer this part of the statement to the future is impermissible.

2) If they, the mountains, were to fly in the future then how could man, even if he were perched at a safe distance on another planet, believe them to be stationary despite watching them flying in space? Hence such a translation is out of the question. Also, to translate this verse to indicate that though humans today consider the mountains to be stationary, they are not so because in future they will fly, would be evidently wrong. If the mountains are stationary today the humans would certainly see them to be stationary. It is not a question of their *thinking* them to be stationary. The Quran would have said *'You know them to be stationary and so they are but in future they will no longer be so'*. This is not what the Quran says at all.

3) At the end of the same verse, a tribute to the firmness of God's creation is the last clinching proof that the mountains, despite flying, are firmly entrenched.

It is noteworthy that the early commentaries maintain silence on the true meaning of this verse which suggests that it was too difficult for them to interpret.

The Holy Quran also pronounces that all heavenly bodies are in a constant state of motion; none of them is stationary:

$$ \text{كُلٌّ فِىْ فَلَكٍ يَّسْبَحُوْنَ} * 21:34 $$

... everything is gliding along smoothly in *its* orbit.[12]

This all-embracing statement covers the entire universe, our solar system being no exception. In addition to this, there are many other verses which mention the elliptical movement of all the heavenly bodies. But they also speak of their movement towards their destined time of death. Following are some of the verses which cover both subjects:

$$ \text{اَللّٰهُ الَّذِىْ رَفَعَ السَّمٰوٰتِ بِغَيْرِ عَمَدٍ تَرَوْنَهَا ثُمَّ اسْتَوٰى عَلَى الْعَرْشِ وَسَخَّرَ الشَّمْسَ وَالْقَمَرَ كُلٌّ يَّجْرِىْ لِاَجَلٍ مُّسَمًّى يُدَبِّرُ الْاَمْرَ يُفَصِّلُ الْاٰيٰتِ لَعَلَّكُمْ بِلِقَآءِ رَبِّكُمْ تُوْقِنُوْنَ} * 13:3 $$

Allah is He Who raised up the heavens without any pillars that you can see. Then He settled Himself on the Throne. And He pressed the sun and the moon into service. All pursue their course until an appointed time. He regulates it all. He clearly explains the Signs, that you may have a firm belief in the meeting with your Lord.[13]

$$ \text{اَلَمْ تَرَ اَنَّ اللّٰهَ يُوْلِجُ الَّيْلَ فِى النَّهَارِ وَيُوْلِجُ النَّهَارَ فِى الَّيْلِ وَسَخَّرَ الشَّمْسَ وَالْقَمَرَ كُلٌّ يَّجْرِىْ اِلٰى اَجَلٍ مُّسَمًّى وَّ اَنَّ اللّٰهَ بِمَا تَعْمَلُوْنَ خَبِيْرٌ} * 31:30 $$

Hast thou not seen that Allah makes the night pass into the day, and makes the day pass into the night, and He has pressed the sun and the moon into service; all pursuing their course till an appointed term, and Allah is well aware of what you do?[14]

يُوْلِجُ الَّيْلَ فِى النَّهَارِ وَيُوْلِجُ النَّهَارَ فِى الَّيْلِ وَسَخَّرَ الشَّمْـسَ وَالْقَمَرَ كُلٌّ يَّجْرِئ لِاَجَلٍ مُّسَمًّى ذلِكُمُ اللهُ رَبُّكُمْ لَهُ الْمُلْـكُ وَالَّذِيْنَ تَدْعُوْنَ مِنْ دُوْنِهِ مَا يَمْلِكُوْنَ مِنْ قِطْمِيْرٍ* 35:14

He merges the night into the day, and He merges the day into the night. And He has pressed into service the sun and the moon; each one runs *its* course to an appointed term. Such is Allah, your Lord; His is the kingdom, and those whom you call upon beside Allah own not even a whit.[15]

خَلَقَ السَّمُوْتِ وَالْاَرْضَ بِالْحَقِّ يُكَوِّرُ الَّيْلَ عَلَى النَّهَارِ وَيُكَوِّرُ النَّهَارَ عَلَى الَّيْلِ وَسَخَّرَ الشَّمْسَ وَالْقَمَرَ كُلٌّ يَّجْـرِئ لِـاَجَلٍ مُّسَمًّى اَلَا هُوَ الْعَزِيْزُ الْغَفَّارُ* 39:6

He created the heavens and earth in accordance with the requirements of wisdom. He makes the night to cover the day, and He makes the day to cover the night; and He has pressed the sun and the moon into service; each pursues *its* course until an appointed time. Hearken, *it is* He *alone Who* is the Mighty, the Great Forgiver.[16]

𝓝 ow we turn to another amazing revelation of the Quran regarding a specific motion of the sun which is mentioned nowhere else. This verse 36:39, pronounces,

وَالشَّمْسُ تَجْرِى لِمُسْتَقَرٍّ لَّهَا ذَلِكَ تَقْدِيرُ الْعَزِيزِ الْعَلِيمِ* 36:39

And the sun is constantly moving in the direction of
its ultimate abode of rest. This is the decree of the
Almighty, the All-Knowing.[17]

It clearly speaks of a point in space to be the sun's
final resting place. Despite the fact that it is only the sun
which is mentioned, the verses which immediately follow
bind the entire universe to the movement of the sun in the
same specific direction:

وَالشَّمْسُ تَجْرِى لِمُسْتَقَرٍّ لَّهَا ذَلِكَ تَقْدِيرُ الْعَزِيزِ الْعَلِيمِ * وَالْقَمَرَ
قَدَّرْنَـٰهُ مَنَازِلَ حَتَّىٰ عَادَ كَالْعُرْجُونِ الْقَدِيمِ * لَا الشَّمْـسُ
يَنبَغِى لَهَا أَن تُدْرِكَ الْقَمَرَ وَلَا الَّيْلُ سَابِقُ النَّهَارِ 36:39-41

And the sun is constantly moving in the direction of
its ultimate abode of rest. This is the decree of the
Almighty, the All-Knowing.
And for the moon We have regulated stages until it
looks like a thin branch of an old palm tree.
Nor does it behove for the sun to overtake the moon
nor for the night to overtake the day ...[18]

If it were only the sun which was moving in a fixed
direction, the verse which follows this statement would not
have proclaimed that the sun and the moon strictly maintain
their mutual distance; they will never be able to gain or
move away from each other, an unchangeable destiny till
their appointed time. This clearly shows that in whatever
direction the sun is moving, the moon is also moving.

But it is not only the question of the sun and the
moon. All the heavenly bodies are described in the Quran
as soundlessly floating. Again there are numerous verses in

the Quran which describe the heavenly bodies bound together with invisible links. Hence if one of them moves in a direction other than its orbital and elliptical motion, all the other heavenly bodies must also move along to maintain their mutual balance.

وَهُوَ الَّذِيْ خَلَقَ الَّيْلَ وَالنَّهَارَ وَالشَّمْسَ وَالْقَمَرَ كُلٌّ فِيْ فَلَــكٍ يَّسْبَحُوْنَ* 21:34

And He it is Who created the night and the day, and the sun and the moon; everything gliding along in orbit.[19]

لَا الشَّمْسُ يَنْبَغِيْ لَهَآ اَنْ تُدْرِكَ الْقَمَرَ وَلَا الَّيْلُ سَــابِقُ النَّــهَارِ وَكُلٌّ فِيْ فَلَكٍ يَّسْبَحُوْنَ* 36:41

It is not for the sun to overtake the moon, nor can the night outstrip the day. All float in an orbit.[20]

This is a unique style of the Quran also employed for indicating the movement of the earth upon its axis. The people of the time of both these revelations could not clearly grasp the underlying idea. If the mountains are moving the earth must also move along, but this is not what the people of that age inferred. Nor could they grasp the idea that if the sun is moving in the direction of a specific space, the entire universe must also be moving along with it to the same destination. This vision of the entire universe drifting away in space is an idea which perhaps has not as yet been conceived by contemporary scientists. Yet it can be implied from an in-depth study of the Quran that the entire cosmos is moving towards some point in space. If that implication is true then one is left with no choice but to visualize all 180 billion or more galaxies, of which our planetary system is but a tiny dot, to be moving along with the sun in a set direction.

Elsewhere in the chapter we have suggested the possibility of an all-consuming gigantic black hole which may pull back the entire universal mass into its singularity.

As such, we have concluded that according to the Quran the case of the universe is an open and shut case. At the moment of the Big Bang it began to expand almost at the speed of light. At the end it will once again be drawn back into the abyss which we refer to as a black hole.

As far as the concept of a single universal black hole is concerned, it is based on the Big Bang theory which is fully supported by the Quran. Some scientists however, propose the case of an open universe. They believe that the universe will continue to expand forever and ever until the spacial matter becomes too thin and sparse, and extends beyond the gravitational pull of the centre of the universe. This scenario leaves no room for the universe to be reassembled and recreated. The Quran categorically rejects this open concept. It is loud, clear and specific that from a singularity the universe erupted, and back into another singularity it will sink again. The Unity of God and its creative outburst and the return of the creation again to the Unity of God could not have been better expressed than:

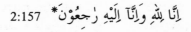

2:157 اِنَّا لِلّٰهِ وَاِنَّآ اِلَيْهِ رٰجِعُوْنَ*

... to God we belong and to Him shall we return.[21]

REFERENCES

1. Translation of 51:48 by the author.
2. Translation of 21:31 by the author.
3. LANE, E.W. (1984) *Arabic — English Lexicon*. Islamic Text Society, William & Norgate, Cambridge.
4. Space Telescope Science Institute. (1997) Press release no. STScI-PR97-01, Baltimore, Maryland, USA.
5. RONAN, C. A. (1991) *The Natural History of the Universe*. Transworld Publishers Ltd., London.
6. *Reader's Digest Universal Dictionary*. (1987) The Reader's Digest Association Limited. London.
7. Translation of 21:105 by the author.
8. Translation of 27:89 by the author.
9. Translation of 31:11 by Maulawi Sher Ali.
10. Translation of 21:32 by the author.
11. Translation of 16:16 by the author.
12. Translation of 21:34 by the author.
13. Translation of 13:3 by the author.
14. Translation of 31:30 by Maulawi Sher Ali.
15. Translation of 35:14 by Maulawi Sher Ali.
16. Translation of 39:6 by Maulawi Sher Ali.
17. Translation of 36:39 by the author.
18. Translation of 36:39-41 by the author.
19. Translation of 21:34 by the author.
20. Translation of 36:41 by the author.
21. Translation of 2:157 by the author.

Plate 1.

THE DROWNING UNIVERSE

يوم نطوى السَّمَاءَ كَطَىِّ السِّجِلِّ لِلْكُتُبِ

Remember the day when We shall roll up the heavens like the rolling up of scrolls . . . (21:105)

The ultimate black hole as presented
in a pictorial illustration.

The image on this page presents the scientific vision of how the ultimate black hole may have devoured whatever was left of the universe. Excretion from all around, as it approaches the event horizon, is compressed into a ribbon-like form which before sinking into the pit revolves round it because the pit itself is revolving. This ressurects in one's mind the image of a scribe rolling his scroll, as mentioned in the above quoted verse.

Plate 2.

THE RE-EMERGING UNIVERSE

. . . As We began the first creation, so shall We repeat it; a promise *binding* on Us; that We shall certainly fulfil. (21:105)

In the remaining part of the verse quoted overleaf, God proclaims that the universe which sank into the black hole would most certainly be made to re-emerge. The image on this page attempts to create a pictorial impression of how the universe will re-emerge through a white hole, breaking into a new day. White hole is a scientific term applied to just such an event. (RONAN, C.A., (1991) The Natural History of The Universe. Transworld Publishers Ltd., London.)

It may not be considered an accurate scientific presentation but to project the idea of a new emergent universe we have presented this pictorial display.

ENTROPY
AND THE FINITE UNIVERSE

IT HAS BEEN clearly demonstrated that the entire universe would be drawn back into a black hole, which later on would explode into another Big Bang releasing its entrapped mass once again. From this the reader may be misled to believe that the universe, thus appearing and disappearing periodically, will live on and on forever. What follows will eliminate any such misconception of a never-ending universe.

It can be mathematically proved that this universe which we occupy can never be eternal in relation to its past, nor can it be eternal in relation to its future. To elaborate this point further we need to explain the scientific definition of the term 'entropy'. Entropy simply means that the material universe, in whatever form it exists, continuously loses an infinitesimal part of its mass in the form of escaped energy which can never be retrieved again.

All things that exist interact with each other under certain conditions. For hydrogen and oxygen to produce water is one of the simplest examples of elemental interaction. When a molecule of water is created by mixing hydrogen and oxygen, it releases part of the energy which had gone into its making.

If hydrogen is made to burn in a jar full of oxygen by blowing a jet of burning hydrogen into it, it will burn only till the time that the oxygen is exhausted. What is left into the bargain is water. While this chemical reaction takes place, it releases energy. To convert water again into hydrogen and oxygen can only be possible if the amount of energy which was released during the synthesis of water is re-supplied to separate the constituents of water, i.e. oxygen and hydrogen, once again.

In all these cases there is no permanent loss of energy. This is not what is referred to as the loss of energy through entropy. The long and short of this is that every chemical reaction either releases energy or absorbs it, and all such exchanges of energy do not produce any permanent waste. But there is some loss of energy which is constant and irreversible. It has nothing to do with normal chemical reactions. Instead of going into the scientific complexities of how this happens, the reader is advised to visualize a hot body gradually cooling off. If it cools to the level of the ambient temperature of the atmosphere, a state of equilibrium will be reached. The flow of heat from the hot body to the cool atmosphere cannot reverse itself. It is always heat which flows in the direction of cold. When at last the entire heat of the universe would have thus exhausted itself reaching a state of equilibrium, no further exchange of heat would remain possible and no chemical reaction could be visualized. It is this to which scientists refer as the 'heat death' of the universe.

The quantum of the consumed energy of the universe continues to rise and the quantum of the consumable energy of the entire universe continues to fall. Hence a time may come, however remote, when the entire universe will ultimately sink into an inert state which could never be revitalized into its previous form of material existence. No action would ever take place, no reaction would ever be possible. This is another name for absolute death or nothingness.

To have an idea of how infinitesimal this loss of energy is, the reader should remember that even scientists have to estimate it with the help of complex mathematics. For them the universe remains practically the same in weight and mass as it was twenty billion years ago. The escaped energy can be measured with reference to the ambient temperature of the universe, which is a mere 4°K up to this point in time. This means that there is no space in the knowable universe which has a temperature lower that 4°K. So energy that would flow in the direction of this lowest temperature, would become a part of it and could never be lifted up again to higher degree of existence. Whether one is able to understand this mathematical jargon or not, of this one must be certain that the universe is constantly losing something which can never be recycled. It can never be added back to the mass of the universe again.

HAVING EXPLAINED entropy enough for the purpose of this book, we now draw the attention of the reader to its inevitable conclusion. Prior to the full comprehension of entropy, the majority of scientists had believed that there was no need for a Creator because all forms of existence continued to exist eternally. Now a better understanding of entropy has revolutionized this view of at least some of the members of the scientific community. The rest somehow avoid confronting the problem. Eternity can be examined in its relation to the past as well as to that of its future. The scientists who believe matter to be eternal, believe it to be eternal with reference to both its past and its future. This means that when we look back, no point can be conceived as the beginning of anything that exists. Eternity has no beginning nor has it an end.

Thus the scientific myth of the eternity of matter has been exploded out of existence by the discovery of the principle of entropy. Even if this universe were somehow conceived to be eternal, it would continue to lose its mass incessantly under the effect of entropy. Logically this can only mean that it should become non-existent at a time eternally remote from us. Looking back at the past from any point in time, eternity will appear as endless as it would appear when viewed from another point in time. In other words, eternity can never be chased to any moment in time beyond which it does not exist. Anyone can imagine himself chasing eternity backwards in time. Even if he travels in the direction of the past for trillions times trillions times trillions of years, sitting on the shoulders of light, he could never find its other end. If he did he should rest assured he was barking up the wrong tree — it was not eternity he was chasing!

Now imagine him once again, travelling backwards in search of a universe. If he ever finds one, eternity would snatch it away from his hand and shove it back onto the path of endlessness yet again. A difficult idea to conceive but in reality it is quite simple and easy to understand. If such a hypothetical traveller in time finds any trace of the universe, he should inquire from himself as to why this universe had not dwindled out of existence long before he had caught up with it. The traveller could easily work out that beyond that point in time, entropy had enough time left to swallow an endless number of such universes.

Imagine a colossal figure big enough to accommodate a myriad of gigantic time steps and try to fill eternity with them. The figure will, most certainly, come to an end but not eternity. Even if entropy required a trillion raised to the power of a trillion years to bring about the 'heat death' of the universe, it would still be inevitable. Now return from this hypothetical pursuit into the past to the present and enquire from yourself why does this universe around you exist at this point in time? Should it not have been completely destroyed by entropy so that it could not have continued to escape detection during its flight into the endless past?

Yet there is another point to be borne in mind. Entropy or no entropy, the theoretical scientists who once believed that protons were ageless, have reached a consensus of opinion that protons too have a definite span of age which they cannot transcend. Whether their age is 10^{32} or 10^{34} years is immaterial; even if it were estimated to be one hundred thousand raised to the power of one hundred thousand, if they were ever created, they would still come to an end at last. If they were never created however – and existed eternally – then the hand of entropy should have annihilated them an endless number of years before.

Wastefulness and eternity cannot go hand in hand. Everything wasteful must come to an end. But lo! We are here, both the writer of these words and the reader at this moment in time. The universe which gave birth to us has no right to occupy this point in time along with all the inanimate forms of existence, if it were eternal.

Some may find it perplexing but it is a simple question of a mathematical equation. A wasteful body cannot be eternal. If it is eternal, it cannot be wasteful. The only option left to us is to believe in an Eternal Creator Who is beyond and above the reach of entropy and wastefulness. Surprisingly, this is the same inescapable conclusion which was drawn by Aristotle two thousand and four hundred years before us. It remains as valid today as it was during his time.

For the sake of further elucidation, we return to the scenario of the Big Bang perpetually giving birth to a new universe after it has swallowed the previous one. The point to be emphasized is simply this: every time a gigantic black hole pulls back the universe into its abysmal depths, it cannot pull back that quantum of energy which has been thrown out of circulation by entropy prior to this event. Nor can it feed back to the universe at the time of its explosion the same amount of mass it had swallowed. The unbelievably large forces at work beyond the event horizon accelerate the rate of loss by entropy by the same proportion. So the emerging mass from the event horizon on a new day of the creation of the universe would be certainly less in mass than that which had sunk into it. That portion of it having been devoured by entropy is forever lost. Hence, at every new eruption of the universe from a new black hole, the universe thus created has to be smaller than the preceding one. Evidently this phenomenon cannot go on repeating itself endlessly. It will be reduced to a size, at long last, which may not have sufficient mass left for it to collapse into another black hole.

Will that tiny leftover continue to exist eternally? Certainly not, is the answer. All that is left of anything would be finally finished off by entropy. It would happen thus because if there is no Creator, no beginning of the universe can ever be visualized. If no beginning for it can be visualized, then it has to have existed eternally. But the factors mentioned above would have completely annihilated it forever before this moment in time. Every finite thing has an end and should have disappeared into the bottomless pit of eternal nothingness. If so, there is no justification for the existence of anything today. How could we have survived the all-smiting hand of entropy which spares naught? If annihilated once, how would we materialize yet again from the limitless void of nothingness? It is the Eternal Creator alone Whom the hand of entropy can never touch. His form of existence has to be completely different from that of everything else which He has created or will ever create. The moment He is conceived to have created any substance like unto Him, His substantial existence cannot be proclaimed as eternal.

Hence when we talk of black holes or entropy, we talk only of the creation and not of the Creator. Whatever is created cannot make the Creator. He has to be the Prime Cause of every finite creation.

The event of the ultimate black hole exploding asunder into yet another universe requires the scenario of a 'shut' universe. According to this, the universe continues to expand not limitlessly, but up to a point in time when the centrifugal force which is throwing the universe apart is ultimately offset by the mightier centripetal gravitational pull.

Scientists who reject this 'shut' scenario of the universe believe in the 'open' universe, which means that the mass of the universe will continue to expand until it scatters out far too thinly to be attracted back by any central gravitational force. This will sap the concentration of energy per space unit to a degree that the creation of a new black hole would become impossible. Even if this 'open' image of the universe is accepted, entropy cannot be done away with. However scattered the universe may become and whatever unimaginably long period it may take, entropy would ultimately catch up with it, because wherever matter exists it still remains subjected to the influence of entropy. Hence, whatever the mode of the universe, 'open' or 'shut', it cannot be eternal. Thus the Quranic statement:

$$\text{بَدِيْعُ السَّمٰوٰتِ وَالْأَرْضِ } 2:118$$

He is the Prime Cause of creation, Who created the heavens and the earth...[1]

Everything which began from Him must come to an end but not He.

كُلُّ مَنْ عَلَيْهَا فَانٍ ۞ وَيَبْقَى وَجْهُ رَبِّكَ ذُو الْجَلَـــالِ وَالْإِكْرَامِ ۞

55:27-28

All that exists upon this *earth* is to perish,
Except for the countenance of thy Lord, the
Possessor of Glory, the Possessor of Honour.[2]

The dilemma of entropy as against the existence of the universe, can only be resolved by the solution that the Quran offered fourteen hundred years ago. It is not just a repeating universe that is being created from what is left of the previous universe. Each time it is created anew by the same Creator, Who brings it to an end after it has served the purpose for which it was designed. Amazingly the Holy Quran made this pronouncement during an age of utter ignorance. It is statements like these which illustrate how the realm of the unknown is being constantly transformed to that of the known. Though unnoticed and unappreciated for more than a thousand years, they suddenly seem to have come to life in our modern age of exploration and discovery, as if it was here that they had always belonged.

Another interesting point to note is that despite the great advancement of science in the last few hundred years, even by the turn of this century, scientists continued to believe in the indestructibility of the atom. This remained so until the current century advanced and scientists were able to split the atom. With the consequent nuclear holocausts the myth of the indestructibility of the atom was exploded once and for all. But even after that, the destructibility of protons began to emerge merely as a mathematical probability. Some meagre evidence has just started to trickle through the highly costly deep subterranean experimental tunnels.

Huge, extremely expensive experiments are being carried out to observe the possible decay of protons and it is considered only a matter of time before scientists are able to finally demonstrate their destructibility and estimate their age. In what form they decay and whether that decayed matter will be recyclable or not, are issues for the future generations of scientists to decide. Hence protons are not as immortal, after all, as they were once thought to be.

As for the Quran, this issue was categorically settled fourteen hundred years ago. Everything which is created must have an age and must come to an end. It is God alone Who creates from nothing and returns to nothing whatever He creates, if and when He so desires.

It is one of the fascinating styles of the Quran that it employs terminology and expressions far ahead of the time that they were coined by humans. In the modern world, everyone is familiar with the scientific practice of showing the date of expiry of many things which are manufactured, built or prepared. For instance, when bridges are built, even before their inauguration, their age is predetermined by the engineers who built them and often etched upon their pillars. This also is the case for automobiles, railway engines, tracks and the paraphernalia that goes with them. In fact, everything that man wears or consumes has an age which can be scientifically predetermined. Nowadays, even food sold in cans, cartons or bottles, shows the date of its expiry.

No wonder therefore that the Creator of the universe should know the intricacies of His creation. The style and terminology of the Quran seems so fresh and contemporary. In short, the inviolable principle of the finiteness of the universe is proclaimed that whatever begins must come to an end. Whatever is created must decay into nothingness at last. The beginning and the end of everything is already recorded in the Book of the grand plan of creation.

يَوْمَ نَطْوِى السَّمَاءَ كَطَيِّ السِّجِلِّ لِلْكُتُبِ ۚ كَمَا بَدَأْنَآ اَوَّلَ خَلْقٍ
نُّعِيْدُهٗ ۚ وَعْدًا عَلَيْنَا ۚ اِنَّا كُنَّا فٰعِلِيْنَ ٭21:105

Remember the day when We shall roll up the heavens like the rolling up of written scrolls by a scribe. As We began the first creation, so shall We repeat it – a promise *binding* upon Us; We shall certainly perform *it*.[3]

*N*ow we quote some eminent scientists in support of what we have claimed in the foregoing passages. Paul Davies, Professor of Natural Philosophy at the University of Adelaide, and winner of the prestigious Templeton Prize states:

'These problems began to force themselves on scientists during the mid-nineteenth century. Until then the physicists had dealt with laws that are symmetric in time, displaying no favoritism between past and future. Then the investigation of the thermodynamic processes changed that for good. At the heart of thermodynamics lies the second law, which forbids heat to flow spontaneously from cold to hot bodies, while allowing it to flow from hot to cold. This law is therefore not reversible: it imprints upon the universe an arrow of time, pointing the way of unidirectional change. Scientists were quick to draw the conclusion that the universe is engaged in a one-way slide toward a state of thermodynamic equilibrium. This tendency toward uniformity, wherein temperatures even out and the universe settles into a stable state, became known as the "heat death." It represents a state of maximum molecular disorder, or entropy. The fact that the universe has not yet so died — that is, it is still in a state of less-than-maximum entropy — implies that it cannot have endured for all eternity.'[4]

Also in the book *God and the New Physics*, he writes:

'Physicists have invented a mathematical quantity called entropy to quantify disorder, and many careful experiments verify that the total entropy in a system never decreases.'[5]

'If the universe has a finite stock of order, and is changing irreversibly towards disorder – ultimately to thermodynamic equilibrium – two very deep inferences follow immediately. The first is that the universe will eventually die, wallowing, as it were, in its own entropy. This is known among physicists as the "heat death" of the universe. The second is that the universe cannot have existed for ever, otherwise it would have reached its equilibrium end state an infinite time ago. Conclusion: the universe did not always exist.'[6]

Professor Edward Kessel, Chairman of the University of San Francisco writes:

'... life is still going on, and chemical and physical processes are still in progress, it is evident that our universe could not have existed from eternity, else it would have long since run out of useful energy and ground to a halt. Therefore, quite un-intentionally, science proves that our universe had a beginning. And in so doing it proves the reality of God, for whatever had a beginning did not begin of itself but demands a Prime Mover, a Creator, a God.'[7]

From the above-quoted excerpt it becomes quite clear that on the issue of the existence of God, there is sound scientific evidence to support belief in Him. This contention is securely based on the very information the so-called non-committed scientists have revealed after thorough investigation. It is up to them to willfully shut their eyes to the only conclusion which can be drawn from it:

There has to be a Creator of this universe or nothing including ourselves can exist at any point in time.

REFERENCES

1. Translation of 2:118 by the author.
2. Translation of 55:27-28 by the author.
3. Translation of 21:105 by Maulawi Sher Ali.
4. DAVIES, P. (1992) *The Mind of God: Science and The Search for the Ultimate Meaning.* Penguin Books Ltd., England, p.47
5. DAVIES, P. (1990) *God and the New Physics.* Penguin Books Ltd., England, p.10
6. DAVIES, P. (1990) *God and the New Physics.* Penguin Books Ltd., England, p.11
7. KESSEL, E.L. (1968) *Lets Look at Facts, without Bent or Bias.* In: The Evidence of God in an Expanding Universe by Monsma, J.C. Thomas Samuel Publishers, India, p.51

THE QURAN AND EXTRATERRESTRIAL LIFE

THE vision of the universe that the Quran presents is poles apart from the one held by the philosophers and sages of all the past ages. At the time of the Quranic revelation, it was Greek astronomy which dominated the minds of men everywhere in the world and all civilizations seemed to have been influenced by the same. This domination continued uninterrupted until the time of Copernicus. It was universally believed that the heavens consisted of layer upon layer of some transparent plastic material, studded with bright heavenly bodies we know as stars. To be more specific, the following was the sum total of the entire knowledge of the people of that age:

1) The earth was composed of a mass of dust, rock, water, air and minerals. It was a stationary mass, with a near flat surface neither rotating around itself nor revolving around any other heavenly body.

2) The earth occupied a unique position in the cosmos, the like of which did not exist anywhere else in space. It remained fixed and stationary in its mooring while the Heavens perpetually revolved around it.

Evidently, this concept of the universe eliminated the possibility of the existence of life elsewhere. The only habitat for life the people of that age knew, was this earth – suspended as they thought it was in mid-space. Contrary to this, the Quran admits neither the uniqueness of the earth nor its being stationary. On the issue of the number of earths, it declares:

اَللّٰهُ الَّذِىْ خَلَقَ سَبْعَ سَمٰوٰتٍ وَّمِنَ الْاَرْضِ مِثْلَهُنَّ 65:13

Allah is He Who created seven heavens, and of the earth the like thereof...[1]

It needs to be explained here that the figure 'seven' can be treated as a specific term of the Quran in this verse and many other similar ones. As such it would mean that the universe comprises many units of heavens, each divided into groups of seven (a perfect number), each having at least one earth to it which will be supported by the entire system of that heaven (galaxy). Referring to that system in general, a more specific verse on the existence of extraterrestrial life runs life as follows:

وَمِنْ اٰيٰتِهٖ خَلْقُ السَّمٰوٰتِ وَالْاَرْضِ وَمَا بَثَّ فِيْهِمَا مِنْ دَآبَّةٍ
42:30

And among His Signs is the creation of the heavens and the earth, and *of* whatever living creatures (da'bbah) He has spread forth in both...[2]

Da'bbah covers all animals which creep or move along the surface of the earth. It does not apply to animals which fly or swim. It is certainly not applicable to any form of spiritual life. In Arabic a ghost will never be referred to as *da'bbah*, nor an angel for that matter. The second part of the same verse speaks not only of the possibility of extraterrestrial life, but it categorically declares that it does exist — a claim which even the most modern scientific researchers have not been able to make so far with any measure of certainty. Yet, this is not all that this verse reveals. Wonder upon wonder is added when we read at the end of this verse, that He (Allah) will bring together the life in the heavenly bodies and the life on earth when He so pleases:

$$\text{وَهُوَ عَلَىٰ جَمْعِهِمْ اِذَا يَشَآءُ قَدِيرٌ} \quad \text{42:30}$$

...And He has the power to gather them together (jam-'i-him) when He will so please.[3]

Jam-'i-him is the Arabic expression in this verse which specifically speaks of bringing together of life on earth and the life elsewhere. When this meeting of the two will take place is not specified, nor is it mentioned whether it will happen here on earth or elsewhere. One thing however, is definitely stated: this event will most certainly come to pass whenever God so desires. It should be kept in mind that the word *jama'* can imply either a physical contact or a contact through communication. Only the future will tell how and when this contact will take place, but the very fact that more than fourteen hundred years ago such a possibility was even predicted is miraculous in itself.

This revelation of the Quran was made at a time when cosmology as a science was not yet born. A different age of conjectural visualization prevailed which had to go a long way before it could contemplate the existence of extraterrestrial life. Even today such claims are only found in science fiction.

Scientists have still not been able to completely shake off their earlier scepticism regarding the existence of life in space. No definitive evidence has as yet been discovered in its support. Scientists are still talking of only 'chances'.

Professor Archibald Roy of the University of Glasgow is one of the many prominent enthusiasts deeply committed to probing into the possibilities of intelligent life forms on celestial bodies. He writes:

'At various international conferences on the problem of extraterrestrial life, the question has been discussed and it has become clear that not only is there a chance of recognizing that a signal is of intelligent origin but it would also be possible to enter into communication with the intelligent species and exchange information.'[4]

Not everyone shares Professor Roy's enthusiasm on this subject. Dr Frank Tipler of Tulane University, New Orleans, can be counted amongst the sceptics. He bases his pessimism on mathematical calculations. To him the appearance of intelligent beings elsewhere in the universe through the blind processes of material evolution defy the law of large numbers. The evolution of life here on earth is dilemma enough for scientists to resolve. For it to repeat itself through a collusion of such an enormous number of chances as defy human calculations is a mathematical impossibility. Dr Tipler states:

'... extraterrestrial intelligences are not here. We just have to interpret this fact. Most astronomers cling to a belief in extraterrestrial intelligence against the evidence because of a philosophical principle: the copernican idea that our place in the cosmos must be completely typical. But we know this idea is false. The Universe is evolving: the cosmic radiation shows that there was once a time when no life existed because it was too hot. Thus, our place is atypical in time. In particular there must be a first civilization, and it happens to be ours.'[5]

Dr Tony Martin, former vice-president of the British Interplanetary Society, holds similar sceptical views. Yet, despite all this opposition, Dr Roy's scientific dream seems, at least partly, to have come within reach of realization. In the United States, NASA has already secured governmental approval for a major search for extraterrestrial intelligence. Other scientists of international fame like Professor Sagan, are also strong supporters of this cause.[6]

*A*MAZING IS IT NOT that what the Quran asserted as a fact, around fourteen hundred years ago, is just beginning to appear as a feasible reality to the scientists of today! The Quran goes a step further when it predicts that man shall one day make contact with extraterrestrial life.

The time for the full realization of this prophecy has not yet arrived, but its signs are appearing on the horizon. This demonstrates that the prophecies of the Quran run ahead of human scientific progress. Every new era witnesses the fulfilment of some more revelations which previous eras had no means to testify. Hence it should be clearly understood here that Quranic prophecies are intrinsically different in nature from those implied in science fiction.

It has never been uncommon for human fancy to take flight from the springboard of the known facts of nature in the direction of things to be. But seldom does the future testify to the predictions implied in such fictional flights. Moreover, all works of fiction invariably remain confined to the possibilities created by the knowledge of the age. Fiction writers always take their cue from current knowledge to visualize what may emerge tomorrow. Most often however, their guesses prove to be as wild as wild can be. The future as it is carved, does not follow the dictates of their vision. This can only lead to the inevitable conclusion that the exercise of human imagination in relation to the unknown has its limitations.

To illustrate the limitation of any particular era with regard to its imaginative scope, the genius of Leonardo da Vinci can be quoted as a befitting example. He attempted to visualize the possibility of human flight but could only conceive it in relation to the then available knowledge. Science and technology had not, until then, advanced to a stage where the human mind could envisage the image of man flying with the help of machines driven by fire. Thus, to visualize even a rudimentary aeroplane lay beyond the limits of Leonardo's potential.

The case of the Divine scriptures, however, is a different matter altogether and the knowledge expressed in them cannot be confined to any particular era. Moreover, chance has no role to play in their fulfilment. The scientific discoveries of subsequent ages have never proved any Quranic prophecy to be wrong.

So we must look forward with well-founded hope for the realization of even such prophecies as rest with the future to decide. The prophecy about the meeting of life here and the life elsewhere belongs to the same category which remains as yet unfulfilled. May we live long enough to witness the glorious day when life on earth will establish some sort of communion with life in space.

REFERENCES

1. Translation of 65:13 by Maulawi Sher Ali.
2. Translation of 42:30 by Maulawi Sher Ali.
   (Note: The word 'da'bbah' in brackets has been added by the author).
3. Translation of 42:30 by the author.
4. ROY, A. E., CLARKE, D. (1989) *Astronomy: Structure of the Universe*. Adam Hilger Ltd., Bristol, p.270
5. TIPLER, F. (November, 1991) *Alien Life*. Nature: 354:334-335
6. Mc KIE, R. (September, 1985) *Calling Outer Space: Is Anybody There?* Readers Digest:31-35

PART V

LIFE IN THE PERSPECTIVE OF QURANIC REVELATIONS
— A BRIEF INTRODUCTORY CHAPTER

*T*HE HOLY QURAN makes a wide range of observations covering the entire span of creative processes pertaining to both the evolution of life and the preparatory stages preceding it. Some of the observations have set landmarks of unique character and it is to them that we propose to draw the attention of the reader.

However, it should be kept in mind that the brief introductory passages which follow, comprise discussions which are fully elaborated in the relevant chapters.

Of prime importance to note are the guiding principles mentioned in the following verse:

تَبَـٰرَكَ الَّذِىْ بِيَدِهِ الْمُلْكُ ۖ وَهُوَ عَلَىٰ كُلِّ شَىْءٍ قَدِيْرٌ ۙ إِلَّـذِىْ خَلَقَ الْمَوْتَ وَالْحَيٰوةَ لِيَبْلُوَكُمْ أَيُّكُمْ أَحْسَنُ عَمَلًا ۚ وَهُوَ الْعَزِيْـزُ الْغَفُوْرُ ۙ الَّذِىْ خَلَقَ سَبْعَ سَمٰوٰتٍ طِبَاقًا ۖ مَا تَرٰى فِـىْ خَلْـقِ الرَّحْمٰنِ مِنْ تَفٰوُتٍ ۖ فَارْجِعِ الْبَصَرَ ۙ هَلْ تَرٰى مِنْ فُطُوْرٍ ۙ 67:2-4

Blessed is He in Whose hand is the kingdom, and He has power over all things;
It is He Who has created death and life that He might try you — which of you is best in deeds; and He is the Mighty, the Most Forgiving,
The Same **Who has created seven heavens in stages (Ṭibāqan). No incongruity can you see in the creation of the Gracious God. Then look again: Do you see any flaw?**[1]

This is the principle verse which speaks of the plan of things covering the entire universe. The two fundamentals highlighted in this verse are as follows: a total absence of contradiction in the entire universe created by God and a stage by stage development of all that has been created. The latter is further elaborated in an attribute of God which is extensively used in the Holy Quran in relation to all creative processes. The word (رَبّ) (*Rabb* — *a* in this word is pronounced like *u* in *but*) invariably means someone who continues to evolve something from a lower to a higher stage. When a foal, for instance, is raised to the state of a fully grown horse — with special care taken to improve its potential qualities — the Arabs use the expression رَبُّ الفُلُوّ (Rabb-al-Fuluwwa) meaning that someone has brought up and trained the foal excellently. Similarly, the same attribute (الرَّبّ) *Al-Rabb* is often translated as 'The Provident'. This indicates that God the Creator also provides for all the subsequent stages of development of His creation. This leaves no doubt whatsoever as to the fact that the Quran speaks of creation only in step by step progressive stages which are well provided for, categorically rejecting the concept of spontaneous generation. Spontaneous generation is further rejected by the Quran because it violates the dignity of God. Thus the following verses enquire from man remonstratively:

$$\text{مَا لَكُمْ لَا تَرْجُوْنَ لِلّٰهِ وَقَارًا * وَقَدْ خَلَقَكُمْ اَطْوَارًا * 71:14-15}$$

What is the matter with you that you expect not wisdom and staidness from Allah?
While He has created you in *different* forms and ever *varying* states?[2]

340

The following verse from Surah *Al-Inshiqāq* addressing humans, promises them that theirs is a continuous journey of moving on from stage to stage:

$$\text{لَتَرْكَبُنَّ طَبَقًا عَنْ طَبَقٍ} * \text{ 84:20}$$

That you shall assuredly pass on from one stage to another.[3]

This is the all-embracing plan of Creation. At different stages of evolution, the processes that governed and shaped life were different but their direction remained the same – always pointing at man.

This is an important topic which has been the subject of much debate amongst various scientists and religious scholars who seek to unravel the mysteries of the origin of life. Various scenarios have been proposed and experiments carried out which attempt to simulate the conditions resulting in the creation of organisms billions of years ago from an entirely lifeless earth. To that we shall return later. Presently we propose to confine ourselves to a brief account of the Quranic concept of how life originated and evolved on earth. Some observations relevant to this subject have been gathered from various verses of the Holy Quran. This serves the double purpose of illustrating the role of the Quran in transferring parts of the 'unknown' to the realm of the known and to assist the specialists in this field of knowledge to benefit from Quranic guidance.

We shall begin by noting that many a time when the Quran speaks of some earlier forms of creation, it refers to them as the creation of man while whatever was created at that time had no semblance to him. In fact, all the landmarks of creation have been likewise referred to as human creations because right from the beginning it was man alone who was the ultimate object and purpose of the entire exercise of creation.

By way of example, we may consider the construction of an aeroplane for which many thousands of stages and processes are required. The designer while planning its production treats every component nuts, bolts, wings, seats and all — as the building of the aeroplane itself, which is the real object of this exercise. Nuts and bolts also have an independent purpose to serve other than just being the components of the plane. As such all the earlier stages are treated as merely preparatory to the consummation of the ultimate purpose. This aspect is highly essential to note because it is here that the Quran parts company with the biologists who believe in a haphazard evolution without a pre-set design. To these biologists the origin and evolution of life appear to have neither purpose nor design, nor a well-calculated plan of execution.

These various stages as mentioned in the Holy Quran shall now be introduced only briefly point by point but a fuller discussion will follow in the relevant chapters.

The Creation of Ancient Organisms

We begin with the most ancient creative phenomenon which existed prior to the biotic evolution as mentioned in the Quran. It is with reference to this age that it employs a specific term, the *jinn*. But in this context it is certainly not applicable to the word *genie* to which ordinarily the readers relate it.

Their concept of jinn (genie) as a ghostlike creature is largely superstitious. Such superstitions would have us believe that the jinn possess a mixture of part human and part hobgoblin characteristics, which can adopt as many shapes and forms as they please. They are particularly prone to haunt and possess women and the weak. They can be mastered by the so-called divines who enjoy the knowledge of such verses from various scriptures as press the jinn into their service. Once subjugated, the jinn can perform fantastic tasks at their command such as materializing anything they like out of thin air. Through the jinn they can gain control over their loved ones or acquire power to annihilate their enemies. The Quran most certainly does not speak of this superstitious human fantasy when it speaks of the pre-biotic age with reference to the jinn. Of that the reader will be given a full account in the chapter *The Jinn*.

The Role of Clay

In the Quran, dry dust or wet clay are also repeatedly mentioned as stages through which life passed in ancient times. In Surah *Āl-'Imrān*, it states:

$$\text{خَلَقَهُ مِنْ تُرَابٍ} \quad 3:60$$

... He created him (Adam) out of dust (*turāb*)...[4]

On the same subject we read the following:

$$\text{خَلَقَكُم مِّنْ طِينٍ} \quad 6:3$$

... He created you from clay (humid or moist earth)...[5]

Clay is also mentioned in Surah *Al-Raḥmān*, but this time it is not wet clay which is referred to for it is clearly stated:

$$\text{خَلَقَ الْإِنسَانَ مِنْ صَلْصَالٍ كَالْفَخَّارِ} * \quad 55:15$$

He created man from dry ringing clay like pieces of pottery.[6]

Here its quality is described as having a plate-like appearance dry enough to create ringing sounds, like broken pieces of pottery. Again in Surah *Al-Ḥijr*, clay is mentioned three times with the added qualification that man is created from dry ringing clay, formed out of dark fermenting mud.*

The overall scenario as presented by the Holy Quran envisions life as having been advanced step by step from dust, from water, from clay and also from fermenting blackish mud which subsequently turned into dry, ringing clay. These last two stages attract particular attention. No man of the era when the Quran was revealed could even remotely relate the creation of man to dry ringing clay made out of stagnant mud.*

Later on we shall present a brief account of what scientists say in relation to this subject. The reader is at liberty to draw his own conclusions regarding the compatibility of Quranic statements with the outcome of contemporary research. One is the scenario presented by the Quran based entirely on Divine revelation; the other is the scenario composed of various theories, claims and assertions made by many scientists who have devoted their lives to the study of the origin of life entirely on the basis of scientific investigation. Everytime the conclusions of scientists are found to be well-established, the reader will also find them to be in perfect agreement with Quranic statements. This will be so despite the fact that, at the time of the Quranic revelation, science had not yet advanced enough to investigate the mysteries of life and its origin. The purpose of such verses is to particularly address man of

---

* The Holy Quran 15:27,29,34

a later scientific age, so that his belief in the existence of an All-Knowing Supreme Creator is aided by the knowledge he has gained.

Survival by Accident or Design?

On the issue of survival the Quranic view is diametrically opposed to that of the naturalist's. According to the Quran accidents play no major role in the survival of species or individuals. Not only species but also individuals are well protected from a host of impending dangers, constantly surrounding them, threatening extinction at every moment of their lives. Hence their survival is in no way accidental. Instead it is a well-chalked out, well-preserved and well-implemented protective design which is in operation throughout the history of life. Among many relevant Quranic verses we choose the following to illustrate the case in point:

اَللّٰهُ يَعْلَمُ مَا تَحْمِلُ كُلُّ اُنْثٰى وَمَا تَغِيضُ الْاَرْحَامُ وَمَا تَـــزْدَادُ وَكُلُّ شَىْءٍ عِنْدَهُ بِمِقْدَارٍ* عٰـلِمُ الْغَيْبِ وَالشَّـــهَادَةِ الْكَبِـــيْرُ الْمُتَعَالِ* سَوَآءٌ مِّنْكُمْ مَّنْ اَسَرَّ الْقَوْلَ وَمَنْ جَهَرَ بِهٖ وَمَنْ هُـــوَ مُسْتَخْفٍ بِالَّيْلِ وَسَارِبٌ بِالنَّهَارِ* لَهُ مُعَقِّـــبٰتٌ مِّنْ بَيْنِ يَدَيْـــهِ وَمِنْ خَلْفِهٖ يَحْفَظُوْنَهُ مِنْ اَمْرِ اللّٰهِ 13:9-12

Allah knows what each female womb bears and whatever they secrete and reject therefrom and whatever they fostered to grow. And with Him everything has a *proper* measure.

He is the Knower of the unseen and the seen, the Incomparably Great, the Most High.

Equal are *in His sight* those of you who speak secretly and those who speak up aloud. Also those who move about under the cover of night and those who walk *openly* during the day.

For each of them there are sentinels in front of him
and behind him, to protect him by the command of
Allah ...[7]

Sidedness or Chirality in Nature

Among all the scriptures, the Quran is unique in
highlighting the issue of sidedness in relation to
socio-religious behaviour. One is surprised to read any
significance attached to the right or the left. The same is
observed in the conduct and instructions of the Holy
Prophet[sa], where the right and left are each portrayed as
playing a specialized role in a Muslim's conduct. For
instance, the right hand is selected for all good things and
clean acts; one should eat with the right hand, one should
start serving from the right side, one should not touch any
filthy object with the right hand etc. The opposite applies to
the left hand. Incidentally, when one shakes hands with a
Muslim, he should be confident that he is shaking a hand
which is clean. In the comparative fuller discussions of
sidedness and chirality, the reader will come across
amazing disclosures regarding the phenomenon of
sidedness as observed in nature. The reader should bear in
mind that this is strongly suggestive of the sameness of the
Author of the Quran and the Creator of the universe.

The expression 'partiality' is generally used to
indicate that a choice is made without specific reasons
leading to that choice. However, in application to God,
one's lack of knowledge as to why God is partial to
sidedness does not necessarily mean that there is no hidden
reason for His selective behaviour.

As science continues to delve deeper and deeper into
the understanding of the chain of cause and effect, many
hitherto inexplicable patterns of natural behaviour are being
understood.

Natural Selection and Survival of the Fittest

Without ambiguity the Quran repeatedly declares that at every step of creation choices had to be made and each time the selector was not the blind operator of natural selection, but the hand of God, the All-Seeing, the All-Knowing. Again it is specifically and categorically declared:

$$وَرَبُّكَ يَخْلُقُ مَا يَشَآءُ وَيَخْتَارُ مَا كَانَ لَهُمُ الْخِيَرَةُ سُبْحَٰنَ اللّٰهِ وَتَعَٰلَى عَمَّا يُشْرِكُونَ \quad 28:69$$

And thy Lord creates whatever He pleases and chooses *whomsoever He pleases*. It is not for them to choose. Glorified be Allah, and far is He above all that they associate *with Him*.[8]

The same assertion runs through the following verses:

$$نَحْنُ خَلَقْنَٰكُمْ فَلَوْلَا تُصَدِّقُونَ * أَفَرَءَيْتُم مَّا تُمْنُونَ * ءَ أَنتُمْ تَخْلُقُونَهُ أَمْ نَحْنُ الْخَٰلِقُونَ * نَحْنُ قَدَّرْنَا بَيْنَكُمُ الْمَوْتَ وَمَا نَحْنُ بِمَسْبُوقِينَ * عَلَى أَن نُّبَدِّلَ أَمْثَٰلَكُمْ وَنُنشِئَكُمْ فِى مَا لَا تَعْلَمُونَ * وَلَقَدْ عَلِمْتُمُ النَّشْأَةَ الْأُولَىٰ فَلَوْلَا تَذَكَّرُونَ * أَفَرَءَيْتُم مَّا تَحْرُثُونَ * ءَ أَنتُمْ تَزْرَعُونَهُ أَمْ نَحْنُ الزَّٰرِعُونَ * لَوْ نَشَآءُ لَجَعَلْنَٰهُ حُطَٰمًا فَظَلْتُمْ تَفَكَّهُونَ * اِنَّا لَمُغْرَمُونَ * بَلْ نَحْنُ مَحْرُومُونَ * أَفَرَءَيْتُمُ الْمَآءَ الَّذِى تَشْرَبُونَ * ءَ أَنتُمْ أَنزَلْتُمُوهُ مِنَ الْمُزْنِ أَمْ نَحْنُ الْمُنزِلُونَ * لَوْ نَشَآءُ جَعَلْنَٰهُ أُجَاجًا فَلَوْلَا تَشْكُرُونَ * أَفَرَءَيْتُمُ النَّارَ الَّتِى تُورُونَ * ءَ أَنتُمْ أَنشَأْتُمْ شَجَرَتَهَآ أَمْ نَحْنُ الْمُنشِئُونَ * نَحْنُ جَعَلْنَٰهَا تَذْكِرَةً وَمَتَٰعًا لِّلْمُقْوِينَ \quad 56:58-74$$

We have created you. Why, then, do you not accept
the truth?
What think you *of the sperm-drop* that you emit?
Is it you who created it or are We the Creator?
We have ordained death for *all of* you; and We
cannot be prevented.
From bringing in your place others like you, and
from developing you into a form which *at present*
you know not.
And you have certainly known the first creation.
Why then, do you not reflect?
Do you see what you sow?
Is it you who grow it or are We the Grower?
If We *so* pleased, We could reduce it all to broken
pieces, then you would keep lamenting:
'We are ruined!
'Nay, we are deprived *of everything.*'
Do you see the water which you drink?
Is it you who send it down from the clouds, or are
We the Sender?
If We *so* pleased, We could make it bitter. Why,
then, are you not grateful?
Do you see the fire which you kindle?
Is it you who produce the tree for it, or are We the
Producer?
We have made it a reminder and a benefit for the
wayfarers.[9]

These verses draw the attention of man repeatedly and
emphatically to the fact that it is God Who is the Creator,
and it is He alone Who makes choices. The decision
making is not left to chance, nor to the things which are
themselves being created. At every such moment it is God
Who makes the choice and operates as the Supreme
Selector.

There is no blind haphazard selection of characters as
life evolves. It is God who through the trials between life

and death makes it possible for life to evolve in its character, design, style and mode of survival. In this grand scheme of things there is no flaw whatsoever because it is He who governs from the seat of His majesty with absolute wisdom. Nowhere in His creation can one find any flaw or contradiction. The import of these verses is manifestly clear.

In the Darwinian hypothesis of *The Survival of the Fittest* as we shall discuss later, there is no guarantee for a flawless operation which must always result in the survival of the fittest. On the contrary, some of those animals which may survive in the struggle may be fit only to survive that particular challenge. As far as the more evolved qualities of life are concerned however, the mere survival of an animal in a given situation certainly does not offer a guarantee that with it these qualities will also be preserved. This is so because there is no room for a Conscious Selector in that scheme, capable of invariably choosing better characters emerging during the struggle between life and death. The Quranic vision of creation speaks of a universally flawless operative system, controlled to its finest detail so there is not the least chance of flaws and defects stealing their way into this scheme of things:

تَبَـٰرَكَ الَّذِىٔ بِيَدِهِ الْمُلْكُ ُوَهُوَ عَلَىٰ كُلِّ شَىْءٍ قَدِيْرٌ * إِلَّـٰـذِىٔ خَلَقَ الْمَوْتَ وَالْحَيَـٰوةَ لِيَبْلُوَكُمْ أَيُّكُمْ أَحْسَنُ عَمَلًا ُوَهُوَ الْعَزِيْزُ الْغَفُوْرُ * الَّذِىٔ خَلَقَ سَبْعَ سَمٰوٰتٍ طِبَاقًا ُمَا تَرَىٰ فِـــىٔ خَلْـــقِ الرَّحْمٰنِ مِنْ تَفَـٰـوُتٍ فَارْجِعِ الْبَصَرَ ُهَلْ تَرَىٰ مِنْ فُطُورٍ * ثُـــمَّ ارْجِعِ الْبَصَرَ كَرَّتَيْنِ يَنْقَلِبْ اِلَيْكَ الْبَصَرُ خَاسِئًا وَّهُوَ حَسِـــــيْرٌ *

67:2-5

Blessed is He in Whose hand is the kingdom, and He has power over all things;

It is He Who has created death and life that He might try you — which of you is best in deeds; and He is the Mighty, the Most Forgiving,
The Same Who has created seven heavens in stages. No incongruity can you see in the creation of the Gracious God. Then look again: Do you see any flaw?
Aye, look again, and yet again, your sight will *only* return to you tired and fatigued.[10]

A Game of Chess or a Game of Chance!
Some of the verses mentioned above, deal with the same subject creating the scenario of a guiding hand of a planner who plans and executes with absolute adroitness and dexterity. Each creature on the vast chequer-board of creation is moved square after square to a predetermined destination. This vision of creation leaves no room for an ungoverned and unguided course of evolution. In fact the entire scheme of things, both biotic and pre-biotic, is sketched by the Holy Quran as a coherent plan of order completely devoid of chaos.

Building the same theme of universal order, the Quran rejects the possibility of there being another God who would certainly have clashed with his adversary turning the order we observe into disorder.

So far the discussion has been introductory, now we are ready for a detailed examination of the same subjects, chapter by chapter and category by category.

REFERENCES

1. Translation of 67:2-4 by the author.
2. Translation of 71:14-15 by the author.
3. Translation of 84:20 by Maulawi Sher Ali.
4. Translation of 3:60 by the author.
5. Translation of 6:3 by the author.
6. Translation of 55:15 by the author.
7. Translation of 13:9-12 by the author.
8. Translation of 28:69 by Maulawi Sher Ali.
9. Translation of 56:58-74 by Maulawi Sher Ali.
10. Translation of 67:2-5 by the author.

ORIGIN OF LIFE
— DIFFERENT THEORIES AND PROPOSITIONS

FOR AEONS, philosophers have been attempting to solve the riddle of existence and origin of the universe. In the current era, their attention has been particularly focused on the origin of life. The dilemma they face is the question of who preceded whom — was it the chicken which laid the egg, or the egg which hatched the chicken? The most difficult challenge they face is about the creation of organic material. Organic material is a product of life and life itself is a product of organic material. How did inorganic chemicals convert into organic chemicals before the creation of life?

The problem which confronted researchers was evidently of a paradoxical nature. Every problem solved gave birth to many others perhaps more difficult to resolve. Every question that was answered led to a chain of other unanswerable questions, or, so it seemed. As the research proceeded, with a growing number of participating scientists, sometimes it appeared as if some of the researchers had at last struck bonanza. Such discoveries created great excitement among some who were inclined to make tall claims at every breakthrough that favoured their conception of how things might have been. There were others however, who were far more cautious and kept warning their fellow scientists not to be overzealous in drawing conclusions. The search for such clues as could scientifically satisfy their inquiry was set in motion in every direction. To date, none of the proposed solutions have found unanimous acceptance in the scientific community. Different scientists have reacted differently to different theories. Some have rejected them entirely, propounding their own propositions instead, while some have accepted them but only partially. Yet as a whole, the general direction of the overall research has begun to emerge, becoming clearer with the passage of time. Evidence is being discovered which lends new support to some of the propositions which are finding greater favour among the scientific community.

The purpose of this exercise is not to bother the reader with overmuch scientific jargon but some of it is unavoidable, otherwise we shall fail to achieve the object of co-relating the scientific data with the relevant Quranic verses. As much as the subject would allow, care is taken to simplify the language so that even the ordinary reader, unfamiliar with science, could keep up with us provided he makes a special effort to remain alert. A difficult task indeed, but not altogether impossible we hope!

This study will help the reader to realize that none of the Quranic declarations relating to the origin of life and its consequent evolution have ever been proved wrong. On the contrary, the general trend of the research continues to support the scenario of the creation of life as presented by them. We believe this will lead the reader to a world of wonders, far more intriguing than the story of Alice in Wonderland. The wonders of Alice's dreamland were fictional after all, but the journey we propose to undertake into our ancient past is on the wings of Divine revelation supported by scientific evidence. This is no fiction. It is a real land of wonders and mysteries of the creation of God, the Unique, the Peerless.

Origin of Life Theories

Let us visualize with the help of scientific investigation, the image of the environment and the atmosphere around the earth as it existed for three and a half billion years before the origin of life. The atmosphere at that time is believed to be anoxic — lacking free unlocked oxygen. No form of life which depends on metabolism for the release of energy through oxidation could have survived in such an atmosphere. In fact the absence of oxygen was an essential prerequisite for the synthesis of organic material from inorganic chemicals. Hence by design, as we believe, or by accident as the secular scientist will have it, it so happened that during the first three and a half billion years of the age of the earth, the atmosphere remained oxygen-free. There was no protective ozone layer in the stratosphere either. The chemical materials which must have been the precursors to stable forms of organic chemicals had to evolve without oxygen:

> 'J.B.S. Haldane, the British biochemist, seems to have been the first to appreciate that a reducing atmosphere one with no free oxygen, was a requirement for the evolution of life from nonliving organic matter.'[1]

The absence of an ozone layer must have facilitated the high energy radiation blasts from the cosmos to reach the earth and ocean surfaces uninterrupted. The bombardment of this intense cosmic energy became largely instrumental in the creation of pre-biotic organisms which helped the transfer of material from inorganic to organic. The synthesis from inorganic chemicals in the oceans into preliminary organic chemicals such as amino acids was initially triggered off by the cosmic radiation in an anoxic atmosphere. This chemical reaction started from simple inorganic molecules such as water, carbon dioxide and ammonia. As this process advanced, according to Haldane, the primitive oceans reached the consistency of a hot, dilute soup (primordial soup).[2]

The outcome of Haldane's research was published in 1929 in the *Rationalist Annual* but no serious note was taken of it in scientific circles. A few years before Haldane, A.I. Oparin, a Soviet scientist, had also published a small monograph in Russia in 1924, proposing similar ideas concerning the origin of life. This article too was met with no better fate. Both had simultaneously and independently worked on the problem of how organic material could have been synthesized from inorganic material before the beginning of biotic evolution.

A New Landmark

After Oparin and Haldane, other scientists rose to fame by taking up the same inquiry all over again. During this period, it was undoubtedly Harold C. Urey of the American University of Chicago, who made the greatest theoretical contribution in this field. He restated the Oparin-Haldane thesis in his book *The Planets*[3] and resurrected the interest of the scientists in their pioneer research concerning the issue of the origin of life. In practical research however, it was Stanley L. Miller, a pupil of Urey, who stole the limelight in 1953. He, in accordance with Urey's theory recreated the atmospheric semblance of the primitive earth in a sealed glass apparatus. He filled it with a few litres of methane, ammonia and hydrogen gases, representing the atmosphere which scientists thought had then existed. To this mixture he added some water. A spark discharge device simulated lightning while a heated coil kept the water bubbling. Within a few days a reddish precipitate began to stain the glass which on analysis, to the utter delight of Miller, was found rich in amino acids.[4] It is amino acids, one should remember, which link up together to form proteins, the building material from which the bricks of life are made.

At that time, the outcome of this experiment was considered the most stunning evidence that the prerequisite organic material for building the bricks of life could originate from natural atmospheric interaction with sea water, producing the 'primordial soup'. Soon, scientific fiction began to take root in this discovery. Many a scientist, in a highly excited state of mind, began to predict that it would not be long before life itself could be conjured up in test tubes. Many years later, however, Miller himself had quite a different gloomy confession to make:

> 'The problem of the origin of life has turned out to be much more difficult than I, and most other people, envisioned.'[5]

His epoch-making experiment was performed in 1953 when he was a mere twenty-three year old undergraduate at the University of Chicago. Coincidentally, it was in the same year that another highly important research was successfully carried out, which was profoundly linked with the same issue. It related to the deciphering for the first time, by Watson and Crick, of the structure of deoxyribonucleic acid (DNA). DNA together with RNA, constitute the fundamental bricks of life. This led to a much bigger challenge of envisioning how life could have resulted from some primitive forms of organic material, accidentally created as scientists believed, into such profoundly complex material.

The problems were manifold. Of the many questions raised, one was how and by what game of chance, inorganic material could convert into the preliminary organic material which is a prerequisite for building the bricks of life. Returning to the early experiments of Urey, the first samples of laboratory test tube experiments were critically re-examined by many scientists. Some of them discovered grave flaws in Miller's experiment, taking some lustre off the hitherto much glorified exercise.

One major objection levelled at his experiment was that it was carried out in a simple flask and test-tube apparatus. The water substituting sea water was kept at boiling temperature while the natural conditions could not have admitted to such a proposition. This should have required the constantly controlled boiling of sea water over billions of years.

Some scientists would much rather have a cold start for the synthesis of life than the wet start proposed by Miller. They were inclined towards favouring the synthesis of organic material based on solid state chemistry rather than on the boiling water scenario.

Some went even further to suggest that the preliminary organic chemicals need not have been created here on earth. To support this view, they referred to the study of meteoritic rocks some of which are known to have contained many amino acids. In fact, the controlled experiment of Miller could produce only thirty-five amino acids as against the fifty-two counted during the analytical study of material from space. But those in favour of a 'wet start', originating in the sea water, raised many counter-objections against this proposition. One such objection relates to the well-known phenomenon of atmospheric friction which must have generated an immense amount of heat as the meteorites entered the earth's atmosphere. Such friction can raise the temperature of the intruding rocks so high as to set them ablaze. Hence all organic material carried by the burning rock should have disintegrated in mid-air before reaching the earth. The evidence of amino acids found in meteoric rock, according to the critics, could have indicated only the contamination it must have received after reaching the earth and cooling down. Those who insisted that it is possible for the organic material to have reached the earth safely from space, without confronting frictional heat, proposed another mode of transport which would be free from this flaw. It was suggested that the organic material might have been carried by small particles enwrapped in protective layers of icy covers such as found in the tails of comets. They could have softly alighted upon the earth like dew.

Returning once again to the epoch-making experiment performed by Miller, and the storm it raised, it did not take very long for its dust to settle down. In the calm that ensued, many a cool-minded reappraisal was conducted by some scientists.

One most eminent scholar R.E. Dickerson, in his excellent article *Chemical Evolution and the Origin of Life*, has critically examined at length the inferences drawn from Millers' experiment, in a detached, unbiased study. One thing that emerges predominantly from his review is that all the facts and experimental data relating to the Miller experiment were not included in the early reports.

Dickerson deemed it essential to point out:

'Although the simulations yield many of the amino acids found in the proteins of living organisms, they also yield at least as many related molecules that are not present.'[6]

Experiments, simulating Miller's pioneer work, carried out by other scientists, revealed that out of three isomeric forms of an amino acid produced during these experiments 'only valine appears in proteins today'. None of the seven amino acid isomers, created during spark-discharge experiments has been 'disignated as a protein constituent' by the universal code of life on earth. He further observes:

> '...why the present set of 20 amino acids was chosen. Were there false starts, with genetic codes that specified different sets of amino acids, in lines of development that died out without a trace because they could not compete with the lines that survived?'[6]

The task of creating the most highly complex and precisely sequenced proteins, the essential material for building the bricks of life — DNA/RNA, out of the simple amino acids synthesized by Miller is a 'mission impossible'. Even if conceded that due to the interplay of limitless chances the molecules of DNA/RNA were finally synthesized, the dilemma remains far from being resolved.

Dickerson quotes the British scientist, J.D. Bernal to emphasize the problem at hand, by suggesting that the scenario of a single molecule of DNA, created by chance,

> '... generating the rest of life was put forward with slightly less plausibility than that of Adam and Eve in the Garden.'[7]

Dickerson, during his summarization of the attendant problem highlights the difficulties inherent in the proposed solutions and suggests that the theorists actually rely on a wild, fantastic game of chance. But to that we shall return later.

REFERENCES

1. DICKERSON, R.E. (September, 1978) *Chemical Evolution and The Origin of Life*. Scientific American, p.70
2. DICKERSON, R.E. (September, 1978) *Chemical Evolution and The Origin of Life*. Scientific American, p.71
3. UREY, H.C. (1952) *The Planets*. Yale University Press, New Haven.
4. MILLER, S.L. (1955) *Production of Some Organic Compounds under Possible Primitive Earth Conditions*. Journal of The American Chemical Society: 77:2351-2361
5. HORGAN, J. (February, 1991) *In The Beginning*. Scientific American, p.117
6. DICKERSON, R.E. (September, 1978) *Chemical Evolution and The Origin of Life*. Scientific American, pp.75-76
7. DICKERSON, R.E. (September, 1978) *Chemical Evolution and The Origin of Life*. Scientific American, p.73

THE JINN

PREPARE NOW to undertake a journey upon the wings of scientific vision into the ancient past to explore the nature and identity of the jinn. The Quranic concept of jinn has been briefly discussed before in *Life in the Perspective of Quranic Revelations*. Arabic lexicon mentions the following as the possible meanings of the word jinn. It literally means anything which has the connotation of concealment, invisibility, seclusion and remoteness. It also has the connotation of thick shades and dark shadows. That is why the word *'jannah'* (from the same root word) is employed by the Quran to denote paradise, which would be full of thick, heavily shaded gardens. The word jinn is also applicable to snakes which habitually remain hidden from common view and live a life secluded from other animals in rock crevices and earthen holes. It is also applied to women who observe segregation and to such chieftains as keep their distance from the common people. The inhabitants of remote, inaccessible mountains are likewise referred to as jinn. Hence, anything which lies beyond the reach of common sight or is invisible to the unaided naked eye, could well be described by this word.

This proposition is fully endorsed by a tradition of the Holy Prophet^{sa} in which he strongly admonishes people not to use dried up lumps of dung or bones of dead animals for cleaning themselves after attending to the call of nature because they are food for the jinn. As we use toilet paper now, at that time people used lumps of earth, stones or any dry article close at hand to clean themselves. We can safely infer therefore, that what he referred to as jinn was nothing other than some invisible organisms, which feed on rotting bones, dung etc. Remember that the concept of bacteria and viruses was not till then born. No man had even the vaguest idea about the existence of such invisible tiny creatures. Amazingly it is to these that the Holy Prophet[sa] referred. The Arabic language could offer him no better, more appropriate expression than the word jinn.

Another important observation made by the Quran is in relation to the creation of the jinn. They are described as having been born out of blasts of fire (from the cosmos).

15:28 * وَالْجَآنَّ خَلَقْنَـٰهُ مِنْ قَبْلُ مِنْ نَّارِ السَّمُوْمِ

And the Jinn We created before that (the creation of man) from blasts of fire (ñaris-samūm).[1]

Here the adjective used to describe the nature of the particular fire from which the jinn were created is *Samūm*, which means a blazing fire or a blast that has no smoke.[2] We find a similar statement in another Quranic verse:

55:16 * وَخَلَقَ الْجَآنَّ مِنْ مَّارِجٍ مِّنْ نَّارٍ

And the Jinn He created from the flame of fire.[3]

Having established that the word jinn applies here to some type of bacterial organisms, let us again turn our attention to the verses quoted above that speak of the jinn as having been created out of fire. The prime candidates for the application of these verses seem to be such minute organisms as drew the energy for their existence directly from hot blazes of lightning — *Samūm* — and cosmic radiation.

364

Dickerson inadvertently agrees with the Quranic view when he observes that the most ancient organisms:-

'... would have lived on the energy of lightning and ultraviolet radiation ...'[4]

This scenario of cosmic radiation is not specifically mentioned in the work of other scientists in their search for the pre-biotic organisms. But they too have corroborated the idea that whatever organisms existed before biotic evolution must have drawn their energy directly from heat. Of all the categories of bacteria classified as the most ancient only 'prokaryotes' and 'eukaryotes' were mentioned by previous generations of scientists. However, that conclusion proved to be a hastily drawn one, according to Karl R. Woese and his colleagues. They observed:

'Simply because there are two types of cells at the microscopic level it does not follow that there must be only two types at the molecular level.'[5]

For the benefit of the lay reader the difference between the two bacteria, known as the prokaryotes and eukaryotes, is explained in terms as simple as possible. It relates to the presence or absence of a nucleus in them. The prokaryote type of bacteria, despite having a well-defined cell membrane, have no distinct nucleus. The eukaryotes on the other hand, possess well-defined and well-developed nuclei occupying the centre of each cell.

It was considered that these were the only two ancient forms of bacteria which gave birth to others and evolved into organisms which could be referred to as the ancestors of life. However, Woese published the findings of his pioneer research in *Scientific American,* June 1981, claiming that archaebacteria, could be rightly considered as the earliest form of organisms. He and his colleagues informed the scientific community that they were a third distinct line which preceded all others. Thus it is they who should be entitled as the most ancient ancestors of life. Woese and his collaborators continued to pour strong evidence into this discovery and as the ice began to thaw, according to Woese:

'Although a few biologists still dispute our interpretation, the idea that archaebacteria represent a separate grouping at the highest level is becoming generally accepted.'[6]

Again he writes:

'This implies that the methanogens are as old as or older than any other bacterial group.'[6]

According to *The Hutchinson Dictionary of Science:*

'... the archaebacteria are related to the earliest life forms, which appeared about 4 billion years ago, when there was little oxygen in the Earth's atmosphere.'[7]

But the author of *Genetics a Molecular Approach* states:

'Since 1977 more and more differences between archaebacteria and other prokaryotes have been found, so much so that microbiologists now favour the term archaea, to emphasize that these organisms are distinct from bacteria.'[8]

THE ORGANISMS REFERRED TO AS JINN in the Quran seem to fit the above description. But, though scientists unanimously describe these bacteria as possessing the potential of drawing their energy from heat, they are not mentioned as having been originally created directly by the cosmic rays and blasts of lightning by any scientist other than Dickerson. The rest however, continue to unveil more mysteries with further research.

'... in undersea vents, hot springs, the Dead Sea, and salt pans, and have even adapted to refuse tips.'[9]

On the issue of antiquity, though Woese and his colleagues have no doubt that the archaebacteria are the prime claimants. According to some scientists they may have evolved from some unknown parenthood simultaneously.

But these are issues which fall outside the domain of this exercise. Whether the other bacteria evolved out of them or not is irrelevant to the discussion. The relevant point is that all forms of most ancient bacteria draw their energy directly from heat. This is a tribute of no small magnitude to the Quranic declaration made over fourteen hundred years ago:

$$ \text{15:28} \quad * \text{وَالْجَانَّ خَلَقْنَـٰهُ مِنْ قَبْلُ مِنْ نَّارِ السَّمُومِ} $$

And the Jinn We created before that from blasts of fire (nāris-samūm).[10]

According to the accepted scientific studies, direct heat from fire had to play a vital role in the creation and maintenance of pre-biotic organisms. This, in fact was the only mode of transfer of energy for the consumption of organized forms of existence during this era. As they multiplied during their uninterrupted proliferation lasting over billions of years, their death must have polluted the oceans while they decayed and fermented turning the oceans into the primordial soup. This will be discussed at greater length in the following chapter.

REFERENCES

1. Translation of 15:28 by the author.
2. LANE, E.W. (1984) *Arabic-English Lexicon*. Islamic Text Society, William & Norgate. Cambridge.
3. Translation of 55:16 by Maulawi Sher Ali.
4. DICKERSON, R.E. (September 1978) *Chemical Evolution and the Origin of Life*. Scientific American, p.80
5. WOESE, C.R. (June, 1981) *Archaebacteria*. Scientific American, p.104
6. WOESE, C.R. (June, 1981) *Archaebacteria*. Scientific American, p.114
7. *The Hutchinson Dictionary of Science* (1993) Helicon Publishing Ltd. Oxford. p.37
8. BROWN, T.A. (1992) *Genetics A Molecular Approach*. Chapman & Hall. London, p.245
9. *The Hutchinson Dictionary of Science* (1993) Helicon Publishing Ltd. Oxford. p.37
10. Translation of 15:28 by the author.

THE ESSENTIAL ROLE OF CLAY
AND PHOTOSYNTHESIS
IN EVOLUTION

ENOUGH OF FIRE. Let us now turn our gaze upon water — its opposite number, and the role it played in the creation of life.

The era of the jinn comes to a close and a completely different phase begins which intermediates between this phase and the final act of photosynthesis. This intermediary phase can be referred to as the preparatory stage for the synthesis of material which was prerequisite for the creation of the living. A careful study of the following will be helpful for correctly visualizing all that transpired during this period.

Chemistry is largely divided into two major branches — inorganic chemistry and organic chemistry. Inorganic chemistry relates to compounds which are mineral in nature and are not the product of life. The mere presence of carbon does not entitle them to be called organic. Water, sodium chloride and potassium are inorganic because they are also widely found outside living cells. However, carbon dioxide is considered inorganic, despite the fact that it is manufactured by living organisms during respiration.

Except for carbon dioxide which is inorganic, carbon is found in all organic compounds which are not necessarily the product of living things.

This chapter deals with all the preparatory steps which were needed before the creation of bio-units. We briefly quote the Quranic account in our words of what happened during this critical intermediary phase: after the end of the most ancient period of jinn, water played a vital role for the preparation of material needed for moulding the living. This material consisted of organic compounds mentioned as stagnant mud.

SOME outstanding scientists have attempted to resolve the riddle of the preparation of organic compounds prior to the beginning of life on earth. The essence of the problem was that all organic compounds were a product of the living. How could they have been prepared in sea or dry land while, during that period, only inorganic compounds were known to have existed? There were no advanced chemical laboratories which could synthesize organic compounds from the inorganic, like we find today in the modern pharmaceutical industry. Great pioneer work has already been carried out by Bernal, Haldane, Dickerson, Miller, Urey, Cairns-Smith, Oparin and many others. It is a great tribute to their genius that they have attempted to rebuild this amazing story of how organic compounds could have been synthesized from the inorganic without controlled laboratory conditions. Following is the amazing story of their success and failure. This failure they themselves confess, but this confession is another tribute to their greatness. This chapter entirely deals with how various attempts were made to solve this riddle and how various solutions were suggested during this period of research. It is not just an exercise in presenting the great works of biochemistry to which we draw the attention of our reader. We draw the attention of the reader to the fact that the Quranic account to which we referred above is fully corroborated by the most advanced scientific research on this matter.

The scientific exploration revolves around the preparation of organic material for life. They mostly remain confined to prove a watery beginning. In this much they agree with the Quran. But the Quran additionally mentions a separate earlier beginning on dry land.

The crux of the matter is simply this, that although organic chemicals could have been synthesized in a watery solution of prehistoric oceans, they must have reverted to their original elementary form by the influence of hydrolysis. It was a challenge to propose how this threat could be avoided and a more advanced organic material could be prepared which would not revert to its elementary form. This means that as long as this preliminary organic material remained in water, the transfer of a hydrogen atom to the newly born chemicals would have broken them into their earlier, simpler forms perpetually. This must have resulted in a vicious circle by which no sooner was the organic material gained than it was lost. For the benefit of such readers as would demand a more scientific description of this account, we venture to present the following:

All the amino acids needed by the bricks of life are formed from aldehydes by a well known mechanism known as the Strecker Synthesis. The Strecker Synthesis of amino acids is a two-step sequence. The first step is the reaction of an aldehyde with a mixture of ammonia and HCN to yield an aminonitrile. Further hydrolysis of the aminonitrile results in the amino acid.

But the problem is that the two steps involved in the Strecker Synthesis are reversible. How the evolution of these unstable elementary compounds could become possible, is the major challenge which scientists confront. Various solutions have been proposed but they raise many more questions than they answer.

There is a growing consensus among the scientific community that somehow a dry stage has to be envisioned, whereby the elementary unstable organic chemicals in the primordial soup could be given a chance to develop into

371

more advanced irreversible organic compounds. Moreover the formation of proteins and nucleic acids from the elementary amino acids, inevitably requires the elimination of a molecule of water from every couple of amino acid molecules and nucleotides. This is called polymerisation. But the problem is that despite the fact that it occurred in sea water, the presence of water should certainly have reversed this reaction. Hence all this polymerisation would be depolymerised.

It means that in the primitive solution each molecule had to be dehydrated within water, an extremely complicated and difficult, if not impossible, task. Most condensation reactions in the laboratory invariably give better results when the mixture is allowed to dry. This suggests that the evaporation of primitive solutions must have taken place after it was splashed on rocks, mud and beaches. This may well have been an essential stage between the rudimentary compounds created in water and the more highly evolved ones which would no longer remain reversible to their elementary forms.

OF ALL THE THEORIES tackling this problem, the most interesting and probable are those which present the scenario of surface catalysts, like silica and clay, to have played their part in this process. This was first pointed out by John Bernal in 1951. He writes in his book *The Physical Basis of Life*:

> '…the adsorption of clays, muds and inorganic crystals are powerful means to concentrate and polymerize organic molecules…'[1]

The idea has not lost its appeal ever since.

> '… Sidney, W. Fox showed that amino acids were capable of polymerizing fairly easily to yeild polypeptides under various conditions simulating

those which may have prevailed on the primitive Earth. This polymerization may have been induced by electrical discharges, by heat (geothermal energy for example) or by contact with certain types of clay and polyphosphates.'[2]

Cairns-Smith took this idea even further. While Bernal had proposed that not only clay, but also silicon was necessary to help the formation of organic molecules, Cairns-Smith suggested that clays were the material, perhaps the sole material, out of which the necessary organic compounds were made. His theory was vividly summarized in the opening statement of his 1966 paper.

Some scientists however, insist that the evolution of organic material did not have a wet start, which, because of the constant threat of hydrolysis, could not carry the reactions beyond a reversible vicious circle. They insist that it is solid state chemistry we should be looking for.

Despite the differences of opinion as to how the problem of hydrolysis was finally overcome, one thing is certain that no scientific theory of chemical evolution is conceivable without proposing an initial or intermediary dry stage. This stage was reached when the oceanic pre-biotic soup was concentrated and dried in the form of laminated micro-thin layers of clay. The Quran is evidently on the side of those who support a wet beginning with an intermediary stage of dryness where concentrated primordial soup was moulded into plates like dry ringing clay, such as broken pieces of earthenware.

The research of Noam Lahav, David White and Sherwood Chang further illustrates the importance of clay as playing a pivotal role in the synthesis of organic material. They showed how clays subjected to cycles of wetting and drying can link molecules of the amino acid known as glycine. The cycling transfers energy from the environment to the organic molecule.[3]

Their proposed solution was very close to the one presented by the Quran but it was Cairns-Smith who even more clearly and unreservedly supported the Quran while he was absolutely unaware of any Quranic statement on this subject.

THE relevant verses of the Quran are repeated below:

$$ \text{21:31} \quad وَجَعَلْنَا مِنَ الْمَاءِ كُلَّ شَيْءٍ حَيٍّ $$

… With water did We create every living thing …[4]

$$ \text{55:15} * خَلَقَ الْاِنْسَانَ مِنْ صَلْصَالٍ كَالْفَخَّارِ $$

He created man from dry ringing clay like pieces of pottery.[5]

$$ \text{15:27} * وَلَقَدْ خَلَقْنَا الْاِنْسَانَ مِنْ صَلْصَالٍ مِّنْ حَمَإٍ مَّسْنُوْنٍ $$

And, surely, We created man from dry ringing clay made from stagnant blackish mud.[6]

It is worthy of note here that these verses clearly state that the material used for the making of pottery-like plates was decayed organic matter — stagnant blackish mud.

As the translators could not visualize how man could have been moulded out of pottery, they inferred that the pottery was only mentioned because pieces of pottery struck against other pieces of pottery would emit a ringing sound. Thus they thought that the relevant verse hinted at the human faculty of speech. This is a very far-fetched interpretation which twists the word *al-fakhkhār* beyond recognition. Now when we begin to understand the nature of the intermediary preparatory stages which synthesized the material for building, it has become within our grasp to understand this term better. This is the true significance of the word *al-fakhkhār*.

The scientists believe that upon further drying, the clay must have crystallized asymmetrically thus becoming laminated into extremely thin layers, set one upon the other, to form plates resembling pieces of pottery. It should be noted with interest that this thin lamination also serves another very important purpose — that of enlarging the area of reaction. Micas and clays comprise laminated sheets of silicate with layers of water molecules separating these sheets. They are only 0.71 nanometres apart (a nanometre is ten-millionth of a centimetre). This increases the surface area for adsorbing molecules enormously. Hence a cube of dry clay of this formation, as small as one centimetre on each side, can provide a total surface area of around two thousand eight hundred square metres — about three-quarters of an acre.

A brief account of what scientists have been engaged in during their search for clues leading to the creation of material required for life has already been given. What happened from then on till the end of their journey is produced below with reference to Coyne's profound research on this subject.

Coyne, University of California, discussing the role of kaolinite clays in the early stages of chemical evolution, argues that they can gather energy from the environment, (by radioactive processes), store it, and then release it when the clay is suitably disturbed, by repeated wetting and drying.[7]

375

The journey of exploration is far from over. In fact, the entire research of scientists and their efforts to unravel the riddle of the origin of life are no more advanced than the very primordial organic soup, the mysteries of which they are attempting to fathom. What happened and how it happened, during the misty dawn of creation in the primordial soup of the oceans, is as yet a study at its nascent stage.

Having examined the amazing significance of dry ringing clay at the preparatory stages of biotic evolution, let us pause and wonder for a while at the dazzling brilliance of the Quranic claim made over fourteen hundred years ago. The idea of the participation of dry ringing clay in the creation of man is so bizarre and unique, and is diametrically opposed to the then prevalent popular tale of the genesis of Adam. One can easily understand the workings of a simple mind, under the influence of such popular tales, to think of God as mixing earth with water, drying it up to a degree, until it achieved the consistency of modelling clay. What remained to be done was the simple exercise of moulding it into the shape of man. And Lo! Adam is raised from dust, complete with all his organic constituents! In that instant sprang into being the entire complex of his body cells furnished with DNA, RNA, chromosomes, genes, somatic cells, reproductive cells etc. Ears, nose and eyes were formed, blood vessels were created, and heart and lungs with all their complexities were completed and set in place. Also, of course, the central nervous and immune systems were completed that instant!

All that miracle was created, according to some naive readers of the scriptures, within the space of a single breath of life which, as they understand, the Creator blew into the statue of clay which He had moulded as Adam. This belief is as devoid of brain as blind evolution is devoid of sight. The evolutionists who believe in creation without a God, without a Conscious Supermind, may scorn at the naivety of those who take the account of the Old Testament over-literally. They forget however, that their stance is equally lamentable. If the scripture scenario is literally accepted, then the only conclusion one can draw is that God the Creator is Almighty, but not All-Wise! An All-Wise God could not have conceived such a brainless scheme of creation, in which even a skilful potter could beat Him at His own game!

The plan of evolution which antecedes the creation of man is a masterpiece of creative wonders and a work of beauty which knows no parallel. For such a Creator to have forgotten altogether the intricate laws of nature which He Himself had framed, and the bricks of life which He had so dextrously designed and moulded, and the profound wonders He packed into their tiny cells, is absolutely inconceivable. How could He have forgotten a billion years of the history of the evolution of life? Little did *he* remember, as *he* was engaged so seriously in shaping another Adam out of clay, all anew, that *he* had already created and perfected him a hundred thousand years before in a far more sensible manner. The earth was already abounding in Homo sapiens — and with what amazement they must have watched *him* engaged in this futile exercise in the garden of Eden!

However disdainfully one may reject this naive vision of the creation of man, as held by religious zealots, the case of the secular scientists is no less deplorable. They know full well the limitless intricacies involved in the scheme of creation and the most exquisitely executed plan of evolution. All the same they attribute this most wonderful masterpiece merely to 'chance' who is not only brainless,

377

but is also blind, deaf and dumb! Little does it behove them to laugh and scorn at the religious zealots. The vision of their god, however senile he may have become — after executing his tremendous plan of creation — is out of all proportion superior to the evolutionist's concept of the creative force at work. The most exquisite and unimaginably intricate plan of creation, they believe, was conceived and executed merely by a sightless brainless fashioner of man, the ancient thrower of dice.

The image of God as emerges from the Book of Genesis, when taken literally, presents Him no doubt as a doting senile but what the scientists would have us believe is even more exasperating. All through the journey of a billion years of biotic evolution, only a brainless phantom of chance occupied the driving seat, the naturalists insist, steering the wagon of evolution through the uncountable number of twists and turns it took before reaching its ultimate goal.

But unfortunately all their profound search for truth comes to a naught when they reach the point where life should begin to emerge in an oxygen-free atmosphere, which then existed, according to Haldane. In agreement with his theory, the scientists believe that a transformation did take place from a non-biotic era to a biotic era despite the absence of oxygen. We believe, on the other hand, that despite their denial of the existence of free oxygen, one must visualize its presence in the atmosphere somehow to the degree that it could support life. For this we have no alternative mechanism to suggest, but our failure to do so does not prove that it did not happen.

There are many examples of unresolved mysteries of a certain age which in the light of discoveries of later ages became understandable. A specific example can be quoted in relation to the rapid extinction of dinosaurs. This problem remained unresolved for a very long time. Scientists could not understand why dinosaurs disappeared at all while other much weaker species of life continued to evolve uninterrupted. Finally, this mystery was resolved when they discovered that the impact from a fairly large asteroid hitting the ocean some sixty-five million years ago disrupted the entire life system of the planet, particularly to the disadvantage of dinosaurs. Under the changed environmental conditions it became progressively harder for them to survive. Until this knowledge was gained, there was no satisfactory explanation as to why the era of the dinosaurs came to such a swift end.

The transformation of an atmosphere devoid of free oxygen into the one comparatively rich in it, could as well be a case similar to that of the extinction of dinosaurs. But only the future will tell how far we are wrong, if the scientists are right. If they are right, then the problems which will emerge will be so enormous as to put to doubt the very existence of the new era of photosynthesis.

We must clearly visualize what may have happened at the time of transition when the age of photosynthesis had just dawned. All oxygen was found bonded to inorganic materials like carbon dioxide (CO_2), water (H_2O) and silicon dioxide (SiO_2) according to the prevailing scientific opinion. In other words, the emergent bio-units must have manufactured oxygen themselves for their own consumption. After presenting the unrealistic manner in which this is supposed to have happened — but could not have happened, we will return to a more serious discussion on the nature of photosynthesis and that of chlorophyll, and the immense problems attendant upon the complexities of chlorophyll.

Imagine the scenario of a few pioneer biotic molecules suddenly emerging on the primitive seashore of evolution in an atmosphere totally devoid of oxygen to become the ancestors of all forms of life to come. It is an idea as beautiful as it is bizarre! There are many inherent problems and mysteries which remain unsolved. Their survival could not be possible merely because of photosynthesis. The energy converted from sunlight had to be stored and utilized by catabolism which was dependent in turn upon the availability of free oxygen, which during the said period was not available, or was extremely hard to come by. It was a period of storms and chaotic atmospheric conditions. How could the newly emergent life generate the oxygen itself and chase it to reabsorb it into its system for catabolism to work. How on earth, therefore, could our ancient ancestors begin their journey of life? The only supply of oxygen on which their survival depended had to be created by them themselves through photosynthesis. It is indeed a strange idea to visualize them springing into life and maintaining it without oxygen, as though they held their first breath till the time they were capable of producing the vitally needed oxygen — and catching it back from the air!

This means that if they were luckily ushered into life on a bright sunny morning, only then could photosynthesis start functioning, leading to steps which could produce oxygen. But that was not sufficient either. It was essential that the newly released oxygen should have remained within the easy reach of the bio-units for immediate consumption. In the most stormy and violent atmospheric conditions which then prevailed, it is most unlikely that the minute trickle of oxygen which they had just started producing, would remain hovering around them until it was consumed through respiration.

Every atom that was synthesized must have been carried away faster than it was produced on the wings of tempestuous winds. Can anyone imagine the utter dismay with which the bio-units must have watched that oxygen drift away before they could jump into the air to catch their first breath of life? But that is not all. The day must have ended at last, however bright, sunny and calm it might have been.

On the issue of prehistoric days and nights, let us turn to the Old Testament to catch a glimpse through Divine Scriptures as to what was happening in that remote period:

'And the earth was without form, and void; and darkness *was* upon the face of the deep. And the spirit of God moved upon the face of the waters.
And God said, Let there be light: and there was light. And God saw the light, that *it was* good: and God divided the light from the darkness.
And God called the light Day, and the darkness he called Night. And the evening and the morning were the first day'.[8]

It must have been a bright day, like the one described, during which the early bio-units emerged for the first time with a fighting chance for them to survive on earth. But that day must have ended at last and, before the beginning of the second day, photosynthesis must have ceased altogether.

How could the poor bio-units completely destitute in the supply of oxygen have survived the first night of their precarious existence? Even the most competent yogis cannot hold their breath for that long. For the poor bio-units it was not the sun of light, but the sun of life which must have set!

Different scenarios are proposed indeed and natural selection is casually mentioned while no practical solution is offered. Natural selection has become a cliché for the scientists who want to escape into obscurism when confronted with the challenge of explaining how by chance complex things took place in precise sequence. Dickerson has enumerated some of the problems confronting them, which they have not as yet been able to resolve.

We present, in our own words, the five stages mentioned by Dickerson.

1. The formation of the planet, with gases in the atmosphere that could serve as raw material for life is not as simple as it appears to be.

The formation of gases in their right proportion throughout the early history of the planet Earth in itself comprises many problems which demand particular attention. But that is not all. In every change of atmospheric complexion and proportion of the gases, the question of the how and the why arises. For the earth's atmosphere to remain oxygen-free for around three and a half billion years, cannot be dismissed as merely accidental. Add to that the constant bombardment of the earth by powerful radioactive blasts from the cosmos and their devastating effect on early organisms, the problems contingent upon that would become clear. Unless countermeasures were taken against this threat no ancient organisms could survive on earth.

2. The synthesis of biological monomers such as amino acids, sugars and organic bases took place for around five hundred million years. All that occurred during this phase was actually fraught with enormous problems.

3. The polymerization of such monomers into primitive protein and nucleic acid chains in an aqueous environment is a very crucial stage in the early years of the preparation of life. This stage in itself would require generations of scientists to spend many a lifetime to fully comprehend all the intricacies involved in this seemingly simple proposition. Despite more than fifty years of exploration and in-depth research, scientists have not yet

been able to settle even the elementary chicken and egg problem in relation to the evolution of proteins.

4. The segregation of Haldane's soup into protobionts with a chemistry and an identity of their own during the early period of life in the making, was again a gigantic problem.

5. Last but not least, is the challenge of conceiving how the development of some kind of reproductive machinery took place when the first bricks of life evolved. This was highly essential for the daughter cells to have all the chemical and metabolic capabilities of the parent cells.

Before closing this chapter, we should like to add a few more examples of how scientists are baffled by the dilemma of life as though originating by itself. There are millions of stages involved, of tiny invisible steps, through which the chemical evolution must have carved its course. It is not just the enormity of the challenge to comprehend how these chemical steps were taken in a certain direction and under what natural influences. There are also immense problems to visualize and discover the rationale of how these steps were sequenced in a well-designed and worked out chain — linking each ring with the other at the right place — the only place where it should have been linked. How easy it sounds for a scientist to declare that the age of bionts, drawing their energy from fermentation, came to an end and at that point began the new era of photosynthesis. But how difficult indeed it is to visualize and solve the problems attendant upon this transition from one age to another.

The presence of phosphorus in every living cell must also be justified in view of the fact that phosphorus is a rare element. Add to this the case of molybdenum and some other even rarer elements, essentially used in life building processes, and the dilemma is further compounded. Some scientists attempting to explain this have even been driven to believe that life must have come from the cosmos, because phosphorus and molybdenum are found in comparative abundance there. But they still cannot answer the question as to how life, having been shaped and designed in outer space, once transported to the planet Earth could continue to be uniformly fed by phosphorus and molybdenum all over the globe. How could it continue to prosper unhindered in an unfriendly climate where phosphorus and molybdenum, the two essentials, were no longer freely available?

Another intriguing problem confronting the scientists relates to two coexisting phenomena responsible for the maintenance and continuity of life. A living cell has two central talents — a capacity for metabolism and a capacity for reproduction. But the problem is that the nucleic acid cannot replicate without enzymes and enzymes cannot be made without nucleic acid. According to Watson and Crick, DNA cannot do its work, including forming more DNA, without catalytic proteins or enzymes. In short, proteins cannot form without DNA but neither can DNA form without proteins. To those pondering over the origin of life, it is another classic chicken and egg problem — which came first the proteins or the DNA?

To wriggle out of this dilemma some propose that both DNA and proteins developed separately, in parallel, until somehow they started a new phase of interdependence. A brilliant stroke of genius it seems, to some, but when examined more closely they will find neither an element of brilliance nor a trace of genius in this proposition. They shut their eyes to the question of how they could have developed and run parallel to each other while at every step their survival depended on the other.

384

It could not have happened merely by the chance interplay of all the necessary factors which could make this apparent impossibility possible without the supervision of experienced scientists. Such scientists needed a most advanced laboratory apparatus without which they could not have achieved any success, while the paradox quoted above is known to have happened outside any controlled conditions. Those who conducted the said experiments did so with reference to a similar paradox, which concerns self-replication of RNA without the essential presence of proteins and enzymes which it has to produce itself. But they had to admit that their success was no success indeed, in relation to the paradox which they attempted to resolve. Horgan confesses that these scientific experiments are too complicated to represent a plausible scenario for the origin of life.

> 'You have to get an awful lot of things right and nothing wrong'[9]

is the admission of Orgel who conducted these experiments. What he and Horgan agree upon is that their success under strict laboratory conditions does not prove anything happening under open conditions which prevailed before the origin of life. J. Szostak separately conducted similar experiments successfully but again under strictly controlled laboratory conditions.

Harold P. Klein of Santa Clara University expresses his doubt in the following words:

> '... it is almost impossible to imagine how it happened.'[10]

We only object to the word *almost*. Instead he should have clearly confessed it was *absolutely* impossible without the existence of God.

According to Dickerson existence of mutual recognition is most essential. Mentioning many attempts to find a complimentary process between protein sequences and nucleic acid sequences he admits that none of them have been satisfactory.

Further elaborating the complexities of a coexistence of two parallel mechanisms in which each gives birth to the other, he again likens this impossible situation to the chicken-and-egg paradox. But the solution he proposes to solve this problem is absolutely untenable. He proposes that both egg and chicken should have separately developed and evolved independent of each other.

All those who hold Dickerson in high esteem for his priceless pioneering work in attempting to solve the riddle of life would certainly be astounded by this naive statement. The only concession one can give Dickerson is that he must have been dead tired after his long laborious pursuits to find a way out of this dilemma without admitting to the existence of God. But there is no way out for anyone without Him! With Him at the command of things, there is no paradox in nature. The omission of scientists to see the hand of the Supreme, All-Knowing, All-Powerful Creator behind the intricacies of creation is un-understandable without suggesting they are wilfully turning a blind eye to manifest realities. The so-called paradoxes become unreal when one admits the existence of God.

So declares the Quran:

ٱلَّذِىْ خَلَقَ سَبْعَ سَمٰوٰتٍ طِبَاقًا ۖ مَا تَرٰى فِىْ خَلْقِ الرَّحْمٰنِ مِـــنْ تَفٰـــوُتٍ ۖ فَارْجِعِ الْبَصَرَ ۙ هَلْ تَرٰى مِنْ فُطُوْرٍ * ثُمَّ ارْجِعِ الْبَصَرَ كَرَّتَيْنِ يَنْقَلِبْ اِلَيْكَ الْبَصَرُ خَاسِئًا وَّهُوَ حَسِيْرٌ * 67:4-5

Who has created seven heavens in stages. No
incongruity can you see in the creation of the
Gracious God. Then look again: Do you see any
flaw?
Aye, look again, and yet again, your sight will *only*
return to you tired and fatigued.[11]

The problem with Dickerson and other scientists who
take pride in their secular stance is simply their
determination never to permit God to play any creative role
in the scheme of things. Of course there is no dilemma in
nature. But the dilemma begins the moment the idea of God
is tossed out of the realms of His own creation. An example
of the exasperation that naturally follows can be found in
the solution hinted by Dickerson mentioned above. This in
reality is tantamount to the admission of utter frustration.

We repeat that RNA molecules are understood to
work as messengers for the transfer of information and
instructions given by DNA to be carried across to other
specific intended sites where the command is precisely
delivered and responded to. When scientists endeavour to
unveil the methodology adopted by nature for the
performance of this task, they are not only amazed at the
complexity of the exercise but also find themselves facing
another paradox. A charging enzyme is required to attach a
specific amino acid to a transfer RNA molecule, which
must be received at the other end by an anticodon. But the
problem is that the charging enzyme which triggers off this
translation mechanism is itself synthesized by the very
mechanism it produces — another egg and chicken
paradox.

A perusal of the above would imply that DNA is the
mother of RNA. The replication of RNA is encoded in the
genetics of DNA yet scientists are positive that in some
cases, at least, RNA proceeded DNA. Call it yet another

chicken and egg problem, call it by any name, the existence of RNA prior to the existence of DNA will always remain an enigma.

Thus every avenue the scientists explore leads them to the same age-old dilemma. It seems as if a stone wall is obstructing the passage of research from any further development beyond it. Dickerson, however, has attempted to extricate himself out of this tight corner by suggesting that both must have developed in parallel. If so, then we shall have to envisage a scenario of eggs giving birth to eggs and chickens giving birth to chicks separately on parallel lines for millions of years. Thus they lived on without interdependence, when one fine morning the chicken thought of laying eggs instead, and the eggs decided to break open into chicks and so the story came to a mutually advantageous conclusion. Together they both lived happily ever after, producing each other!

We profoundly respect Dickerson for his tremendous service in the cause of science and laud him for his balanced unbiased attitude in resolving scientific problems. Yet for Dickerson to suggest this, leaves one absolutely astounded! Perhaps it was not a well-calculated conclusion of the scientist but merely a cry of an anguished soul that Dickerson possessed, frustrated by the impossibility of a situation which could only be resolved by paying homage to the existence of God.

WE have just mentioned the confession of great scientists that despite their best efforts they have not been able to resolve the enigma of life. But nowhere will the reader find any reference by them to the complexities of chlorophyll which they simply dismiss by referring to it as 'a green pigment'. Nor has ever an attempt been made to visualize its evolution like they have visualized the evolution of complex organic compounds. It is so because chlorophyll never evolved. Not a trace of its evolution can be detected on land, air or sea.

As life began on earth, all vegetative growth which contains a green pigmented material — chlorophyll — entrapped the incident sunlight, converting it to chemical energy to synthesize organic compounds from inorganic compounds. During this process they manufactured carbohydrates from carbon dioxide and water releasing oxygen simultaneously:

$$6CO_2 + 6H_2O \xrightarrow{\text{LIGHT ENERGY}} C_6H_{12}O_6 + 6O_2$$

Chlorophyll is of two types, chlorophyll a ($C_{55}H_{72}MgN_4O_5$) and chlorophyll b ($C_{55}H_{70}MgN_4O_6$). The composition of these formulae has the exact placing of each element in a certain sequence which is reminiscent of the composition of haemoglobin — being no less wonderful in its complexity. Thus writes Steven Rose in his book *The Chemistry of Life*:

'Although chlorophyll is by no means the only photosynthetic pigment, it is the only essential one. ... The polar head part of the molecule is in fact very similar in design to that of the haem of the cytochromes and haemoglobin. Like haem it consists of a linked series of four carbon-and-nitrogen containing rings ('pyrrole rings') joined together to form a sort of doughnut with a hole in the middle. This hole is filled in haem by the metal iron: in chlorophyll on the other hand the jam in the doughnut is made of magnesium. The ring structures contain a series of alternating double and single bonds, and the absorption of a given small amount of light (a quantum) of a particular wavelength causes a sort of vibration, or resonance around these bonds. Because of the close packing and stable orientation of the pigment molecules within the lamellae, this resonance energy can be transferred from one pigment molecule to another until it is eventually channelled into a slightly different chlorophyll molecule from which it cannot escape. This final energy-trapping type of chlorophyll can receive an input from as many as 300 of the standard chlorophyll molecules. The energy from the light is thus very highly concentrated at a single site, giving the second molecule the ability to transfer an electron to a non-pigment receptor which in turn passes it, via an intermediate set of carriers, to NADP...

But **the essential point to note** is that, **with the exception of** the chlorophyll-containing apparatus responsible for the splitting of water and hence providing the primary energy source, all the reactions of photosynthesis, fixation of carbon dioxide, and synthesis of sugars follow pathways with which we are already familiar in the biochemistry of the animal cell.'[12]

In the most complicated huge molecule of chlorophyll, there is an immensely long chain of atoms precisely arranged in a sequence which if altered, at even a single link, will completely destroy the very function and significance of chlorophyll. Life in every form owes its existence to this fundamental trap of energy, but carbohydrates thus produced cannot be utilized by life directly. The chain of all chemical reactions that follow depend on ATP and ADP, chemicals which essentially contain three or two phosphate groups. In both these chemicals the phosphorus groups play the central role. It is this most important ingredient which is present in every living cell of both plants and animals. It runs the immensely vast factory which provides a multitude of organic chemicals needed by the living.

In the preceding discussion we have in fact touched upon three mysteries of creation which the routinely familiar eyes of the scientists do not register. But all the great scientists who have tried to unravel the mysteries of the origin of life register these facts and attempt to resolve them. Chlorophyll is an exception to the rule. Instead of attempting to solve the enigma presented by this pigment, they bypass the issue altogether and proceed on to discuss some other hurdles regarding which they have at least some partial solutions to offer.

They bypass the issue of chlorophyll because they must have fully realized that this extremely complex pigment could not have suddenly jumped into existence out of nowhere. If on the other hand it had evolved, it must have left behind a very long trail of its evolution. Most certainly it should not have begun to exist out of nothing. But it does exist, and hurls a challenge to all the atheists, philosophers and scientists to explain its sudden emergence and existence. It is easier to conceive the haemoglobin to have evolved. But it is next to impossible to justify the existence of this little pigment.

REFERENCES

1. BARBIERI, M. (1985) *The Semantic Theory of Evolution*. Harwood Academic Publishers: p.86
2. OLOMUCKI, M. (1993) *The Chemistry of Life*. McGraw-Hill, Inc. France, p.55
3. CARINS-SMITH, A.G. (June, 1985) *The First Organisms*. Scientific American: p.100
4. Translation of 21:31 by the author.
5. Translation of 55:15 by the author.
6. Translation of 15:27 by the author.
7. CARINS-SMITH, A.G. (June, 1985) *The First Organisms*. Scientific American: p.100
8. *The Holy Bible* (1900) King James, Eyre and Spottiswoode Ltd., London, Genesis 1:2-5
9. HORGAN, J. (February, 1991) *In The Beginning*. Scientific American: p.119
10. HORGAN, J. (February, 1991) *In The Beginning*. Scientific American: p. 120
11. Translation of 67:4-5 by the author.
12. ROSE, S. (1991) *The Chemistry of Life*. Penguin Books Ltd., London, pp.353-355

SURVIVAL
BY ACCIDENT OR DESIGN?

*T*HE ISSUE of the survival of all living creatures is not as easy and simple as normally understood by the Darwinian cliché of the 'Survival of the Fittest'. This term can only be understood in depth when applied to specific, concrete examples. Otherwise there is a danger that this popular cliché will mislead people rather than lead them to the truth. The snag lies in the word 'fittest'. Without defining what it means, one cannot put this claim to test. As to its role in advancing life, invariably from lower forms to higher forms, it is certainly likely to fail the test.

To declare a character of life to be better than another is a complex problem which may vary from situation to situation. Many a time it happens that a superior, far more highly placed species of life is far less capable of surviving the challenge of a given crisis than a species of life which is placed at a much lower order. As such, nature would automatically give its verdict in favour of the latter at the hour of struggle and inclement conditions.

At the time of a severe drought, many animal species of the lower order survive easily, while man perishes unable to withstand the pressures. Natural calamities such as sudden unexpected changes in temperature, volcanic eruptions, tornadoes and typhoons, wild fires, floods and earthquakes are seldom partial in their treatment to various species of life.

It is not at all unlikely for them to take away in a few seconds, minutes or hours what it took hundreds of millions of years for evolution to create. Yet, under the same devastating conditions many lower forms of life will flourish and multiply unhindered. The question as to who is the fittest and by what yardstick it could be declared the fittest, remains unanswered.

It is a simple case of survival and no more. It is not the fittest who always survive and whoever survives is not always the fittest. All that we can sensibly conclude is that there are certain species of life that are fittest to survive under certain conditions, and there are some other species of life which are fittest to survive under essentially different conditions. Hence mere survival is no competitive test between the species for judging their respective values. Now we analyse the case of struggle for existence which occurs within a species when members of the same species are put to various trials of natural calamities. Many of them are eliminated, overwhelmed by the dangers they confront. Many others display an innate strength against the befalling calamities; some fare so well as to treat them with scant respect. They happily outlive such trials as had destroyed their fellow members. Consider for example a severe epidemic of dysentery. It is likely for it to kill an eminent naturalist while it may altogether spare a farm labourer with only strong guts to his credit, without any other faculties of head and heart to be proud of. Again the same people who survive a specific epidemic may not be able to survive other contagious diseases. Some may die during a spread of cholera while survivors from it may be despatched to death by the yearly recurring disease of influenza or even lesser diseases.

Such are the trials of life. The survival is only relative to the context of a precise situation which does not always adjudge the survivors to be fittest in all qualities of life. The real reasons why natural selection prefers some animals as against others who are apparently doomed by it are unknown to scientists. There is no single yardstick by which every case can be equitably adjudged. Unconscious natural selection could not take into account all the positive and negative points before it could pass judgement in favour of some or against some others. The most important thing to note is that the laws of life and death are not directly governed by natural selection in the ordinary course of the phenomenon of survival and destruction. The final outcome is influenced by innumerable factors which spare or kill an animal for reasons which are in fact governed by a universal Divine scheme of things. This scheme of things could not have served the cause of evolution without the conscious role played by a Supreme All-Knowing Creator Who governs everything in accordance with His Divine Plan. Those who deny this have to be predetermined in their denial. It is tantamount to the denial of evolution itself, if they honestly recognize the problems involved in believing in evolution without believing in the Creator.

As we study life at all stages from its beginning to its ultimate culmination when humans were formed, what we observe is that survival is an exception, and the rule is death. But the factors which cause death are innumerable and very often go hand in hand with the factor of chance. These factors, if identified and located, would make life miserable if not impossible. The living would have to suffer through a state of fear and terror constantly hovering over them. Fortunately death moves stealthily and man remains most often forgetful of its impending threat. But for his propensity to live in a state of oblivion to the inevitable decree of death, man's life would turn into a perpetual nightmare.

If bacteria of which drinking water is seldom free, were visible to man, to quench one's thirst would become a punishment rather than a pleasure. If we begin to see what living organisms we inhale with each breath of air we take, breathing would become a torture.

If we could somehow see with the naked eye the creatures which jump into the air with every step we take upon a well cleaned Persian rug, for many, the ordinary process of breathing would become a torture. Little do people know that the common household mite in carpets, if magnified to visible proportions, would appear more horrendous than the ugliest of the dinosaurs that ever grazed upon planet earth.

The air we breathe abounds in so many different forms of bacteria which, if they happen to take root in our system, could cause tuberculosis, pneumonia, lung cancer, liver cancer, all forms of dysentery, diarrhoea, septicaemia, eczema and other deadly diseases related to all major human organs. Yet we inhale them and most often do not fall prey to them. There has to be a protective system to keep them at bay from us without their free unrestricted access to our inner organs. This is fitness which is precisely designed to safeguard survival – survival is not a chance product of fitness.

There is far more to it than we have briefly indicated. Each movement we make, each thought that crosses our mind bequeaths to our nervous system a waste residual of consumed energy which, if not immediately taken care of could cause instantaneous death. Hence, during every fraction of our living seconds we confront and survive death. This is the true meaning of the survival of the fittest. And this fitness is not a product of a mere game of chance.

At every step, highly intricate and complex measures are taken which must be well-designed to ensure protection to life from the innumerable threats surrounding it. The case of the role of oxygen in plant and animal metabolism presents an ideal example to help understand this phenomenon.

The term metabolism is subdivided into two categories, anabolism and catabolism. Anabolism is instrumental in building new living tissues out of available nutrients. It is also responsible for the storage of extra energy in the form of fats. Catabolism is the opposite of anabolism. It breaks down complex molecules into simpler ones with the consequent release of energy.

Complex molecules which are rich in calories, when broken down into smaller constituents release energy, a process during which the sum total of their mass and weight is reduced and the apparent loss is gained in the form of energy which the living organisms utilize for their survival. Although catabolism is referred to as destructive metabolism, it is highly essential for the maintenance of life, because it is through this process that all the daily needs of energy are met. All physical movements, emotional agitation and mental processes require energy. It is catabolism which provides this vital need.

All lower forms of biotic organisms, even those which have neither lungs nor blood vessels, have somehow been provided with an alternative arrangement for respiration. Hence their need of oxygen is also met with in a manner similar to the animals which possess lungs.

The mere availability of nutrients is useless without catabolism. The importance of catabolism is apparent in the daily human experience. Man can live without food for weeks and without water for days but without breathing he cannot survive even for a few minutes. The moment the supply of oxygen is cut off, catabolic activity ceases forthwith and all living cells begin to die — the first to be hit is the brain.

Before we begin to discuss the extremely harmful effects of oxygen and describe how highly effective protective measures are taken against them we would like to remind the reader that oxygen is vitally essential for life in every sphere of its activity. This presents the fantastic measures adopted by nature to create balances. Everything which is beneficial may also have harmful effects to a degree that if not kept at bay they will entirely wipe out the beneficial effects. This paradox, paradox as it is, is still highly essential for the existence of life on earth. This is the story of creation which is repeated on and on limitlessly. Not a single faltering step can be heard even by the keenest ear of a merciless critic. The subject of oxygen will be discussed at greater length later on.

At present we should like to draw the attention of the reader to an allotropic form of oxygen called ozone. Ozone (O_3) is the only gas among gases which possesses a molecule with three atoms — a unique property which is not shared by any other gas. This is a most highly needed life supporting element which at the same time is most lethal against it. This is another example to illustrate that the survival of life on earth is not left to chance, but adequate and precise measures are taken, not only to support life, but also to protect it from the very factors which are required to support it.

There was once a time when the atmosphere close to the earth was kept free from unlocked available oxygen. This has become common knowledge now, but when Haldane first bought it to light it created a great stir of excitement among scientists who were searching for clues which could resolve the mystery of the beginning of life. An extremely long time had elapsed prior to the beginning of biotic evolution which kept confronting scientists with a most puzzling enigma. If the atmosphere, as it then prevailed, had any freely available oxygen, the type of organisms which must have preceded biotic evolution should have been completely destroyed by their interaction with oxygen. If precise steps were not taken to protect them from oxygen, no organism could survive on earth. The discovery that during that period there was no free oxygen was, therefore, an epoch-making discovery. To conceive the surrounding atmosphere close to earth as completely empty of free oxygen was a great breakthrough. Yet at the same time other problems arose out of this solution which were even more puzzling.

The solution suggested by Haldane took care of unlocked oxygen roaming about freely in the atmosphere close to earth. But what of the preventive measures against constant bombardment of cosmic rays, a problem which was further highlighted by the absence of free oxygen. How could they be taken care of? The cosmic radiation could only be prevented from destroying organisms on earth if free oxygen had existed in the earth's atmosphere. This presents an apparently insoluble paradox. The choice is simple but lethal either way. If you decide to protect organisms by removing free oxygen altogether from the atmosphere this will naturally result in their being destroyed by lethal cosmic rays instead.

As will be presently shown, it is the presence of free oxygen in the atmosphere which becomes indirectly instrumental in preventing destructive cosmic rays to reach the earth. It should also be remembered that like all other gases oxygen contains only two atoms to each molecule — being lighter by one atom to its allotrope ozone. One should normally expect that, being heavier, ozone should be close to earth, while oxygen, even if present, being 'lighter' should have been hurled to the higher stratosphere. That is one dilemma, but another even more perplexing is the fact that if there was no free oxygen at all, how could it give birth to its child ozone and toss it up to the very top of the stratosphere where it was so direly needed? Riddle as it is, it is also a joke. In the Punjabi language they say:

ماں جمّی نئیں تے پُت کوٹھے تے

'Man jammi naeen, te put kothe te'.

This literally means that the mother is not yet born while the son is already running about on the top of the roof. In Punjabi it is an unrealistic joke indeed, which highlights the impossibility of an opponents proposition. But here we face a proposition which is impossible, yet exists according to scientists. This problem could not have been resolved without a set purpose and creative design. During the period we are discussing, oxygen, the mother of ozone, was not yet born but its child ozone was running about at the top of the stratosphere.

It is of special interest to note, here, that ozone is not permitted to destroy ultraviolet rays altogether. At their broadest wavelength, the ultraviolet rays are permitted to pass through the ozone barrier and reach close to the global surface because at this wavelength they do not pose any threat to the dwellers of earth. On the contrary at this wavelength, they are beneficial being largely responsible for the synthesis of vitamin D in mammals including human beings. One really wonders as to how many billions of chaotic chances must have colluded to create this wonder, and how? Everything is so precisely calculated, so superbly designed and so dextrously executed!

The scenario of natural selection as against the scenario of purposeful design, would require hundreds of thousands of variant atmospheres, accidentally created by the interplay of billions of chances over millions of earths, of which only one could be rightly proportioned to support life on earth. Another interesting aspect of ozone relates to its synthesis. Ozone is created by intense ultraviolet rays striking at oxygen. As they do so, the oxygen molecule is split into its ionic form — that is atomic oxygen. The free atoms of oxygen then merge with each other creating a molecule of O_3 which is ozone. While ozone is synthesized by the direct effect of ultraviolet rays on oxygen, the ozone in turn destroys its benefactor — ultraviolet rays — in the process. What a fantastic scheme indeed, to make the two prime enemies of life come to grips with each other and get locked in a grim battle of mutual destruction while neither can gain supremacy over the other — an amazing parity is maintained.

Returning to the scenario of the pre-biotic age when life was just about beginning to take shape, the absence of the ozone layer must have created an enormous problem. An uninterrupted bombardment of cosmic radiation must have constantly kept destroying pre-biotic organisms. Hence some ozone had to be formed in the upper stratosphere before the beginning of biotic activities. That must have been, but how, is the question which is conveniently avoided. This brings us to the conclusion that life is indeed surrounded by diametrically opposed forces which are simultaneously friendly and inimical. Yet the presence of both is essential for life, so somehow it must have been carried across these hazards in the lap of Divine protection.

سَوَآءٌ مِّنكُم مَّنْ اَسَرَّ الْقَوْلَ وَمَنْ جَهَرَ بِهِ وَمَنْ هُوَ مُسْتَخْفٍ
بِالَّيْلِ وَسَارِبٌ بِالنَّهَارِ * لَهُ مُعَقِّبَـاتٌ مِّنْ بَيْنِ يَدَيْهِ وَمِنْ خَلْفِـهِ
يَحْفَظُونَهُ مِنْ اَمْرِ اللهِ 13:11-12

401

> He among you who conceals *his* word or pronounces
> it loudly and he who hides himself under the cover
> of night or walks openly during the day, each one is
> equal *in the sight of God*.
> For each there are those who constantly move along
> in front of him and behind him protecting him by the
> decree of God...[1]

There are many other similar verses in the Quran to the same effect that life has to be protected by God, every moment of its existence, or it will cease to be.

If man looks down from the dizzy heights he occupies on the ladder of life, at the innumerable steps below him in the chain of evolution, seldom will he realize that for him to have survived the hazards he faced at each of these steps, was no less than a grand miracle. We owe gratitude to the many generations of dedicated biologists who with their hard work have helped us to understand, to some degree, the inexhaustible mysteries of life! But alas, few among those who themselves unravel the mysteries ever realize how much they owe to the infinite mercy of God and His limitless creative Wisdom.

To further illustrate the case in point, once again we invite the attention of the reader to the extreme intricacies of human physiology. In fact every human is a microuniverse in himself. This microuniverse does not survive by itself, but requires millions of protective, well-designed, precise measures at every level of its existence.

Physiologists have discovered a host of factors within the human system which could severally or collectively cause spontaneous death, if countermeasures had not been designed. These difficulties and challenges are, in fact, oversimplified. To devise and implement a plan to take countermeasures against all the hazards confronting life is an immensely formidable challenge which requires many a lifetime of research on the part of future generations of scientists.

TAKE FOR EXAMPLE the impending dangers to the inner chambers of every living cell from the surrounding liquid in which it is suspended in the form of colloidal solution. Nature has worked out plans to the minutest detail to save the nucleus from random adsorption of water through osmotic pressure which could prove fatal. Also, it has devised an exquisite plan to transport into the inner chamber, the much needed sugar along with the required amount of insulin. Again, it has perfectly designed the system for the excretion of waste material which occurs during the continuous chemical reactions within these cells.

It should be clearly understood that the watery solution of the blood in which the cells are suspended, can cause their instantaneous death if it is permitted to penetrate into their inner chambers. To eliminate the threat of stray entry of water molecules into the cellular chambers, a double cover of lipids are created with a masterly design. They can prevent unwanted material entering the cells with perfect efficiency. Yet they do not obstruct the passage of the required food supply etc., which has to be constantly transported across the lipid covers into the inner chambers. But this defensive step in itself poses other very serious problems. If the double protective layer of lipids will not permit any liquid to penetrate, how can sugar and oxygen be transported into the cell where they are vitally needed is the most crucial question which arises here. In each millisecond of their existence, cells require a constant supply of sugar, insulin, oxygen and other essential salts for their survival. Considering the extremely minute size of the blood cell and the paradoxical nature of the problems involved, it requires a profound knowledge of the laws of nature and highly advanced technical know-how to successfully meet this challenge.

On the one hand the nuclei and the protoplasm in the cellular chambers are fortified by this impervious double protective layer of lipids against the possible penetration of the surrounding plasma. On the other hand they need a constant supply of energy to be transported across the lipid covers. To meet this essential requirement, the measures taken by nature are so amazingly profound and intricate as boggles the mind.

It is inconceivable for these measures to have been planned and executed by a mere blind collusion of chances. In fact, the intricate internal structure and order of arrangement of the transporter protein, which delivers glucose molecules to the cells, had to be exactly designed to do the needful. Again, complementary measures had to be taken for each recipient cell to harmonize perfectly with the working of the transporter protein. As some readers unfamiliar with scientific terminology may find it difficult to keep track of this subject, every effort is being made to make it generally comprehensible even for the lay reader.

This system of transportation is such a masterpiece of scientific designing and structuring as to keep complete silence over it may indeed be unfair. The Creator has specifically designed this system so that each transporter protein is interwoven in the lipid covers and consists of a chain of 492 amino acids which are arranged in 25 segments. Thirteen of these segments are hydrophilic which means that they have a special affinity for water. The remaining 12 are hydrophobic, which means that they detest and repel watery solutions. The hydrophilic segments promote the absorption of liquid and welcome the outer watery surroundings, while the hydrophobic segments repulse water and prefer the inner cellular environment.

Together both are organized to weave back and forth twelve times[2] within the space of two lipids changing their conformation, during which whatever proteins, sugars etc. they carry are delivered first into the protoplasm across the membrane through a special porous arrangement. Then whatever is to be transferred from the protoplasm to the outer bloodstream is done through this spiral conformation which transfers the specific material from the protoplasm to the outer lipid wall which through another complex porous arrangement delivers the material to the bloodstream. Thus the transporter oscillator:

> '... shifts the binding pocket for glucose between opposite sides of the membrane. Kinetic studies, including several performed at Dartmouth Medical School... indicate that such oscillation is extraordinarily rapid... When glucose is bound to the transporter, the rate is even greater, about 900 times per second.' [3]

Without a Perfect Knowledgeable Organizer, whose existence they do not recognize, this scheme of 'hows' could not be designed and precisely executed by itself. Spectroscopic evidence has established that the entire protein is coiled into a helix, and in this helical-cylindrical arrangement the hydrophilic segments are arranged on one side of the cylinder and hydrophobic segments on the other. The methodology of this exercise is highly intriguing and fascinating! This complex mechanism is by no means a product of chance, but had to be purpose-built.

Apart from the energy requirement of the cell, there is an additional problem of maintenance of the ratio of salts inside and outside the cellular chambers. The essential salts present in the cell have to maintain a certain proportion. This ratio is different by a large margin from the one found in the electrolyte solutions surrounding the cell. Sodium ions, for example, are ten times more concentrated outside than inside the cell. If a simple open pore arrangement were made for the transportation of glucose into the cell it would simultaneously promote the free access of sodium ions as well, thereby disturbing the ratio by a factor of ten, which could prove disastrous. A constantly controlled supply of sodium ions is also essential for the survival of the cell which is well taken care of — a technological miracle of no small magnitude! Special inlet valves are created in the lipid covers, which when opened, permit about ten million sodium ions per second across the cell membrane. This is one hundred thousand times faster than the glucose transportation.[4] Some speed indeed! And the story is not over as yet.

IT becomes manifestly clear from this study that life, even at its most rudimentary level, needs to be constantly protected. In another area of operation of natural laws, however, we observe a different design to serve the same purpose. There, death is repeatedly employed to serve the cause of life in an entirely different manner. Here, death outnumbers survival by enormously large proportions. This apparently is the opposite of what we have discussed above, but in reality it further supports the contention that in the story of life nothing is left to chance or accident.

Every law which is created, every process that is designed, is to support life in one way or another. What we have in mind here is the Darwinian principle of the 'Survival of the Fittest'. According to this principle, for the advancement of the quality of life, nature has worked out an automatic method of sifting. This slow continuous process of selection becomes pronounced when a species confronts challenges to its survival. It works in every area of animal activity. The predators, when they chase their prey in air or on land, continue to eliminate the weaker and less capable of survival among them. Of course they do not discriminate intentionally, but the stronger, the faster and also the comparatively more clever members of the species naturally stand a better chance of escape.

Likewise, in the area of reproduction, the stronger and more powerful male members of a species at a time of mating, stand a much higher chance of succeeding than those who are weaker or suffer from other disadvantages. Hence, in the ultimate analysis, it is the hand of death which serves the cause of life. At this level this phenomenon is easy to observe and natural to operate, requiring no specific design for it to prevail. But this principle is not only at work in relation to the competition between members of different species; it also operates more subtly and far less perceivably in an inner area of the functions of life.

For every child which is conceived by a mother, billions upon billions of chances of conception are sacrificed. Most people do not know the fact that every healthy male has been gifted with a reproductive potential capable of producing billions of offspring during an average life span. But it is only a few sperm during the entire lifetime of a man which are fortunate to succeed in fertilizing a female ovum which results in the possible birth of a child. Even if a man can boast of having produced a hundred offspring in a primitive society, where unrestricted polygamy is practised, the number of his reproductive sperm, potentially capable of fertilizing a female egg, outnumber the actual conceptions by an enormously large proportion. But even the billions of sperms which fail the test of natural selection, do not die in vain. Their death guarantees that only the most competitive and the most worthy of survival is ushered into the next generation of species. Incidentally, it leaves one to wonder by what stroke of chance only one ovum is created in the female instead of billions, like the sperms created in the male. If it had so happened, the number of offspring which every married or unmarried couple would gift to the world would have created some problems for the already overburdened economics of the world, struggling hard for their survival in the modern competitive world.

Hence, in the course of the struggle for existence, a very large number of contestants had to be sacrificed for the sake of every small gain in the quality of life. Yet, once the threshold of death is crossed successfully, it is not the end at all. Every living moment of their lives, those who pass the test of survival once, continue to face death. It is this perpetually impending danger from which the Quran declares that the living are saved consciously at the command of God by the angels of life. Hence, neither death is accidental, nor life. They go side by side like night and day to weave the yarn of conscious existence.

The protective system which we are discussing covers the entire span of the operation of life, both at its visible outer level as well as the invisible deep recesses. This complementary design of advancement and protection along the course of evolution is an all-pervasive law covering the entire scheme of things. As we look back at the journey of life from the time of its origin to the present day, we observe it to have travelled through many a different unfriendly, even hostile, terrain. It could also be portrayed as attempting to move across a large expanse of quicksand with stepping stones at convenient distances. If the traveller was a blind, senseless creature, how many chances, if at all any, would one give him to move safely across, step by step, in the right direction, without wavering and without making a single *faux pas*? If the distance to be covered is a billion steps across this lethal journey — where every stepping stone is surrounded by the quicksand of death — who would bet on him reaching safely across to the shore of his ultimate destination? Always stepping in the right direction, never failing to plant his feet firmly on the next pedestal of survival has to be the greatest miracle performed by the ancient blind traveller of chance.

It is evolution of course, but not blind evolution. At every cross-section of their journey, it was never the living who made their choices as to the bearing they should take. There was no fixed destination, if there was no conscious Designer and Creator of life. Hence, every step which life took, could have moved in any direction. A single step to be taken in the right direction is an outside chance. For each step to move invariably in the right direction, a billion times over and to pursue unfalteringly the course which could only lead to the creation of man, is something so bizarre and unreal that even the phantom figures of fairy tales would not believe in it. Yet, there are *some* scientists who do!

If God is removed from this intricate scheme of things the only identity which remains to be fixed is that of the Creator. Let alone the mysteries of the inanimate universe, the living wonders of the tiny planet Earth will cry out for the Hand that shaped them and filled their existence with fathomless intricacies. Rule God out and their cries will forever remain unheard, unanswered. Man can only be sure of one thing, that Life did not create itself, and Death could not create Life.

REFERENCES

1. Translation of 13:11-12 by the author.
2. LIENHARD, G.E., SLOT, J.W., JAMES, D.E., MUECKLER, M.M. (January, 1992) *How Cells Absorb Glucose*. Scientific American: p.34
3. LIENHARD, G.E., SLOT, J.W., JAMES, D.E., MUECKLER, M.M. (January, 1992) *How Cells Absorb Glucose*. Scientific American: pp.36-37
4. LIENHARD, G.E., SLOT, J.W., JAMES, D.E., MUECKLER, M.M. (January, 1992) *How Cells Absorb Glucose*. Scientific American: p.37

CHIRALITY
OR SIDEDNESS IN NATURE

WHAT IS SIDEDNESS, what significance does it possess if any and why sidedness at all, are the questions to which we shall presently turn our attention. When moving in circles whether we begin to turn from right to left, or left to right, the quality of this exercise is not in the least altered in whichever direction we initiate the turn. If we pick up an object with our right hand or pick it up with our left, so long as it is lifted the question of right or left loses significance. The question of right or left will acquire significance only if we understand its underlying wisdom. But surprisingly, both in Islamic teachings and in some manifestations of natural laws, sidedness seems to be rigidly enforced without any apparent reason for its preference. In the chapter *Life in the Perspective of Quranic Revelation* we briefly mentioned that many verses of the Holy Quran speak of sidedness with a religious significance. This Quranic attitude is further elaborated to some detail in many traditions of the Holy Prophet[sa] which instruct the believers as to how they should conduct themselves in their everyday social and religious practices. They display a decided trend in favour of the right over the left.

Why such partiality in matters so trivial, as the mere preference of one side over the other, is a question intriguing enough in its application to religious teachings. But when addressed to a similar universal phenomenon of sidedness in nature, the enigma assumes astronomical proportions. Religious instructions are invariably dictated by a conscious human mind, or Divine teachings. No such Conscious Creator is recognized by the secular scientists to have designed any code of natural conduct. Why then this intriguing similarity between religion and nature in the area of sidedness? If not due to a common origin, could it be reasonably dismissed as mere coincidence? But that is not all. The more we study the manifestations of sidedness in nature, the more we are overwhelmed by the element of wonder it generates. There is no known scientific rationale for its existence. Why nature should display such selective propensity of preferring one side over the other is a question which has not been answered until now and may yet remain unanswered for many a decade to come.

It should be worthy of note here, that according to the Quran every natural behaviour should be rationally explainable. The Quran categorically rules out any scenario of creation which is haphazard, disorderly or accidental. Hence, if not today, the dawn of that tomorrow may not be too far away when scientists will be able to fathom the deep underlying reasons beneath all expressions of sidedness in nature, however shallow they may appear at present.

Before proceeding further, it seems appropriate to explain at some length the phenomenon of sidedness, or chirality, as found operative in nature. It can easily be understood with reference to some group displays of children which highlight the excellence of their physical training. Children of some groups organized in circles of equal number are required to run clockwise while those of some other groups are instructed to run counterclockwise. To enhance the spectacular effect they are generally so paired that if one of the pairs runs in one direction, then the other runs in the opposite one. Visualize just such a pair and you will grasp the meaning of sidedness or chirality in scientific terms. Although similar in all other respects, the

CHIRALITY OR SIDEDNESS IN NATURE

image of the group moving from right to left cannot be superimposed on the group moving from left to right because of the opposite direction of their movement. Likewise, though all molecules spin, all do not spin in the same direction. Some move from right to left, while others do so from left to right. Some compounds of exactly the same chemical formula may contain both the right spinning and the left spinning molecules suspended together in a single solution; while some others are composed only of such molecules as move in just one direction. But chirality is not confined to the molecular level alone, even the tiniest of subatomic particles display chirality.

THE EVIDENCE of chirality in nature came to light only some one hundred and fifty years ago. It was Louis Pasteur, the great French scientist who discovered chirality in the spin of molecules in 1848. It is a great tribute to his exceptional intelligence and keen observation that while

LOUIS PASTEUR

examining a certain salt of tartaric acid he noticed that there were two types of crystals, each a mirror image of the other. He carefully separated the two, dissolved them in water and made a beam of light pass through the solution. He was surprised to discover that the polarized light was rotated differently by the two specimens. One was rotated clockwise and the other anticlockwise. This clearly meant that the molecules of the two separated specimens of tartaric acid were either spinning to the right or to the left — neither could be superimposed on the other. This was the first ever case of chirality observed by scientists at the elemental level.[1]

Another singularly significant discovery in the same field was made yet again by Pasteur in 1857. One day he noticed the growth of a mould in a chemical solution lying in a jar. Instead of throwing away the solution as contaminated, he made a beam of light pass through it to examine the effect, if any, of that mould on the solution. He was astounded to discover that the solution, though inactive in relation to light prior to its contamination, had suddenly become active and started polarizing light. It was inactive in relation to light for the simple reason that it was composed of an equal number of right spinning and left spinning molecules each neutralizing the other's effect on light. Hence the polarity displayed by the contaminated specimen could only mean that the mould had eaten up only such molecules as spun in the same direction and left completely untouched those which spun in the opposite. One mystery was thus resolved but only after having given birth to another much more complex one. How could a mere mould detect the spin of molecules with such unfailing exactness and why was it at all partial to the molecules spinning in any specific direction? These were the questions which baffled the mind of Pasteur then and still baffle the minds of scientists today. For how long they remain unanswered, the scientists know not. The magnitude of the dilemma is enormous. The molecules of any element or compound, right spinning or left spinning, share exactly the same chemical and physical properties. What or who dictates their propensity to spin in any particular direction is a brain-twister enough, but when it comes to the most uncanny ability of life to detect which molecules are spinning in which direction, the question acquires bizarre astronomical proportions. None of the five senses bestowed to man are equipped with any known mechanism which can determine the spin of molecules. The spinning molecules leave no imprint on the property of matter to become detectable through human sensory organs. But what of moulds which have no known sensory organs; all they have is a diffused sense of awareness?

This amazing tale of chirality in nature does not end here. It just begins. Since the time of Pasteur, research on chirality has made tremendous progress and many more extremely perplexing examples have come to light testifying that chirality can be unmistakably detected by different species of life.

By now chirality is discovered to operate at every level of material existence. Yet the manner of how and why it so behaves is far from understood. Until 1957 it was believed that the four fundamental forces which govern the interaction of elementary particles were parity conserving. This simply means that all particles at elementary level had chiral-symmetry. However, in 1957 Chien-Shiung Wu and her colleagues at Columbia University discovered that beta particles emitted from radioactive nuclei did not display chiral-symmetry. The left-handed electrons far outnumbered the right-handed ones. It was further discovered that the tiniest subatomic particles, neutrinos and anti-neutrinos, which are electrically neutral and move at the speed of light, also display a certain spin. But unlike electrons which predominantly prefer left-handed spin, anti-neutrinos are always partial to the right-hand. The contrary is not found in nature. No one knows why chiral-asymmetry exists at such fundamental levels of existence at all.

Many hypotheses are being presented but most are found to be simply preposterous when examined more minutely. However, there is one suggestion which seems to have provided scientists with a clue to the factor possibly at work at the most rudimentary level of chirality in nature. Yet at this level, it is too ethereal to be demonstrated or verified. It is related to a theory which unifies the weak and electromagnetic forces first propounded by Dr Abdus Salam, Steven Weinberg and Sheldon Glashow in 1960. That theory predicted a new electroweak force which does not conserve parity. This disparity according to scientists could possibly be responsible for the right-handed spin of anti-neutrinos and left-handed spin of neutrinos, as well as that of electrons. But this weak electric force cannot be contemplated as the causative factor to produce the right sided or left sided behaviours at all other levels of chirality. The behavioural difference between the two sometimes perplexes scientists, particularly in relation to the role they play in biotic evolution. The problem is further compounded when we observe that the two right sided and left sided components of exactly the same chemical formula exert a completely different influence on life in odd ways. The following are some fascinating examples:

Limonene is a compound found both in lemons and oranges. There is not the slightest difference in their chemical formula, yet the spin of limonene molecules in lemons is invariably opposite to the molecular spin of limonene found in oranges. Limonene in lemons is always right spinning while in oranges it is always left spinning. How on earth could lemons and oranges always pick the limonene of a specific spin for their consumption while the difference between their limonene is merely that of molecular spin? It needs to be emphasized yet again that both the right sided and left sided specimens of limonene contain exactly the same chemical and physical properties. How the olfactory glands of the human nose can ever detect the difference of the spin in oranges and lemons and ascribe to them completely different smells is absolutely astounding. Of course there has to be some reason but as yet we cannot identify it.

Another example relates to the influence of chirality on life of a rather sinister nature. This came to light in 1963 when a drug, thalidomide, was introduced by a pharmaceutical company for the cure of morning sickness in pregnant women. Many were cured, but for many others it proved disastrous. Horrible congenital defects were found in the babies born to some mothers treated by the same drug. A subsequent intensive research revealed that the pharmaceutical company which manufactured thalidomide had inadvertently manufactured two types of thalidomide compounds of the same formula. While the molecules of one type spun in one direction, those of the second type spun in the other. While one type cured morning sickness without producing any adverse effect on the embryo, the other type produced the most horrible congenital deformities instead of curing the morning sickness. The most profound side-effect was the deformities of the lower limbs among the infants born under its influence.

Another intriguing case of the detection of the spin and the preference of one spin over the other is found at the most fundamental level of life. Although there were several hundred amino acids freely available in the primordial soup from which such proteins were created as made the fundamental bricks of life (DNA and RNA), 'nature' selected only twenty amino acids out of them and they were all left spinning!

In the case of selecting molecules for building sugars however, the choice was reversed. The molecules of all the four different forms of sugars responsible for the provision of energy to all forms of life are, without exception, right spinning. This means that all natural sources of sugar available to life, like sugar cane, beet root, fruit, etc., manufacture sugar consisting only of right spinning molecules.

Nevertheless, a successful experiment was conducted a few years ago for synthesizing sugar comprising only left spinning molecules. It was discovered that this artificially synthesized sugar, though exactly the same in taste, chemical properties and cooking behaviour, was totally rejected by the human digestive system. Not a molecule was assimilated. This gave rise to the bizarre idea of manufacturing sugar consisting of only left spinning molecules on a commercial scale, not only for the benefit of diabetics but also for the pleasure of gourmands and gluttons. They could consume mountains of sugar without the fear of accumulating even a molehill of fat. The only snag is that, at present, the cost of manufacturing left spinning synthetic sugar is prohibitive. A mountain of money would be needed to produce a mere molehill of such sugar. Perhaps only the royal highnesses of oil rich monarchies sitting upon mountains of oil wealth could afford this luxury.

The apparently arbitrary preference for right or left also manifests itself in many other ways. Most humans are right-handed and the arrangement of the heart and liver is universally left sided and right sided respectively, barring a few rare individual exceptions of course. Roger A. Hegstrom and Dillip K. Kondepudi in their jointly authored article *The Handedness of the Universe* published in *Scientific American,* January 1990, present many examples of handedness in nature without any apparent reason for preference. While observing that most people are right-handed, they fail to recognize any reason

'...why right- and left-handed persons are not born in equal numbers.'[2]

But it is not a prerogative of the human race alone to display definite trends with regards to handedness.

418

On partiality to sidedness as found in the animal kingdom and vegetative behaviour, they write:

'Right-handed or dextral shells dominate-on both sides of the Equator. Among these right-dominated animals, left-handed individuals exist only as a result of mutations, which appear with a frequency ranging from about one in hundreds to one in millions, depending on the species.'[3]

right sided grooves

left sided grooves

In contrast to them, the lightning-whelk of the Atlantic coast are predominantly left-handed. In plants, the

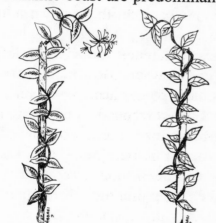

honeysuckle winds around its support in a left-handed helix while the bindweed prefers winding from right to left. Even in bacteria some of their colonies spiral from right to left yet as the temperature increases they reverse the spiral direction to left-handed turns.[3]

These are but a few cases. At every level of evolution we find many other outstanding examples of how life displays partiality to the spin of molecules. Their study excites wonderment and leaves one bewildered. There has to be a Conscious All-Wise Supreme Selector who made choices at every stage of decision making or one has to ascribe this role to the haphazard vagaries of blind nature!

WE FEEL that at the end, the purpose of this exercise needs to be emphasized once again. The basic issue of discussion is whether revelation can play any role in transferring information from the realm of the unknown to the realm of the known. Every discussion under different titles in this treatise is invariably related to this issue. In this chapter the relevance may not have been clearly understood, hence the need for further elaboration of this point. We have already pointed out that in the entire comity of religions Islam stands out in its emphasis on sidedness in religious behaviour and conduct. We respectfully draw the attention of the reader that in all other religions the opposite number of right is wrong, not left.

IN ISLAM however, the word 'right' is not employed exclusively to indicate goodness, it is also employed to indicate 'the side' literally. As such, in this context the term 'right' is not used against 'wrong'; it is used against 'left'. This is clearly sidedness. In many Quranic verses right is decidedly mentioned in its preference over the left. It is these verses which must have provided the guidelines for the Holy Prophet[sa] to direct the believers to prefer right over left in day-to-day religious conduct. His established practice was to always commence good things from his right side or by his right hand. The believers are told to perform ablution, for instance, with the right hand first. When they wear their shoes, they should insert the right foot first. In the seating arrangements at a table, the guest of honour is seated on the right side of the host. At the birth of a child in Islam, the Muslim call for prayer (Azān) should be whispered into the right ear before whispering Al-Takbir in the left. Such instructions were not accidental but were specific down to the minutest detail. According to his instructions and his own personal consistent example, the

Muslims are required to always use the right hand for touching and holding clean things, while the rest are left to the left hand. Hence when a Muslim shakes hands with others he is expected to do so with full confidence that he is offering a clean hand.

Instructions such as these clearly indicate that the concept of sidedness in religious and social behaviour were purposefully incorporated in Islam. It is also in this sense that the prophecies concerning the future of mankind use the terms 'rightist' and 'leftist'. Hence the political and economic division in the contemporary age, based on the rightist philosophy or the leftist philosophy, tally clearly with the Quranic prophecies regarding the future of mankind.

Why is it that it is Islam alone which emphasizes sidedness so strongly while other Divinely revealed religions do not even mention it?

In answer to this question, it should be well understood that according to the Quran, the age of all other religions had come to an end with the dawn of Islam. Polarity and sidedness are the trends which had not yet been born in human affairs in the age prior to it. It was only Islam which was to address the people of an age where polarity and sidedness were to become common coinage in matters of expression.

Looking at it from this angle, the evidence of sidedness in day-to-day behavioural matters was in a way prophetic, that man was about to be ushered into that advanced age when sidedness would acquire new depths and new dimensions. This is exactly what has come to pass. Little did the man of that age know that not only in matters of political and economic divisions, but also in the domain of science, sidedness would acquire such importance as could never be imagined in any previous era.

REFERENCES

1. FESSENDEN, R.J., FESSENDEN, J.S. (1982) *Organic Chemistry.* 2nd ed. PWS Publishers. Willard Grant Press. Massachusetts, p.139
2. HEGSTROM, R.A., KONDEPUDI, D.K. (January, 1990) *The Handedness of The Universe.* Scientific American: pp.98-99
3. HEGSTROM, R.A., KONDEPUDI, D.K. (January, 1990) *The Handedness of The Universe.* Scientific American: p.99

NATURAL SELECTION AND SURVIVAL OF THE FITTEST

ANSWERING the question as to who has been responsible, throughout the ages, for taking important decisions, which had to be taken at every step of evolutionary advancement, the Quran pronounces the following:

تَبَـٰرَكَ الَّذِیْ بِیَدِهِ الْمُلْكُ وَهُوَ عَلیٰ كُلِّ شَیْءٍ قَدِیْرٌ * إِلَّـٰـذِیْ خَلَقَ الْمَوْتَ وَالْحَیَـٰوةَ لِیَبْلُوَكُمْ أَیُّـٰكُمْ أَحْسَنُ عَمَلًا ٱوَهُـٰوَ الْعَزِیْزُ الْغَفُوْرُ * الَّذِیْ خَلَقَ سَبْعَ سَمٰوٰتٍ طِبَاقًا مَّا تَـٰرىٰ فِـٰیْ خَلْقِ الرَّحْمٰنِ مِنْ تَفَـٰوُتٍ فَارْجِعِ الْبَصَرَ هَلْ تَرىٰ مِنْ فُطُوْرٍ * ثُمَّ ارْجِعِ الْبَصَرَ كَرَّتَیْنِ یَنْقَلِبْ إِلَیْكَ الْبَصَرُ خَاسِئًا وَّهُوَ حَسِیْرٌ* 67:2-5

Blessed is He in Whose hand is the kingdom, and He has power over all things;
It is He Who has created death and life that He might try you — which of you is best in deeds; and He is the Mighty, the Most Forgiving,
The Same Who has created seven heavens in stages (طِبَاقًا). No incongruity can you see in the creation of the Gracious God. Then look again: Do you see any flaw?
Aye, look again, and yet again, your sight will *only* return to you tired and fatigued.[1]

In the absence of God, life could not have travelled on a purpose-built path following a single direction throughout. At every step there was a wide aimless expanse of possibilities stretched before it, riddled with difficulties through which it had to carve its path. There were countless options which could potentially have changed the course and direction of evolution at every such critical moment in time. The question arises as to why life pursued a definite evolutionary course in a single direction as though none else was available.

The only explanation offered by scientists relates to the role of natural selection. Though they fully recognize the dimension and the gravity of the problem, they would have us believe that at every crucial point of decision making it was natural selection which took the decision, always making the right choices out of a countless number of available options.

Ever since Darwin coined the phrase 'Natural Selection', it has served as a magic wand for the scientists who probe into the mysteries of nature. In relation to events which appear to present evidence of the role of a wilful Conscious Creator as the choice maker, they seek protection behind the mist of

DARWIN

this vague term which is mostly incorrectly understood. Every step forward in the path of evolution is inadvertently attributed by them to innumerable chances having created a host of options for natural selection to choose from. But this choice, on the part of natural selection, they agree, is not conscious. When different characters and species struggle for survival in a competitive situation, it is quite natural for some to survive at the cost of others if they happen to possess greater potential for survival.

Here we may also mention another hackneyed phrase of Darwinian terminology 'The Survival of the Fittest' which is so extensively used by the naturalists. This phrase is coined on the presumption that natural selection, however blind it may be, would always go for the right choice and only the fittest would survive in a competitive world. Whatever is inferior in the struggle for existence is doomed to become extinct. Darwin's principle is perhaps misinterpreted to a degree that the very principle becomes questionable. We have irrefutable evidence spread all over the globe that even the most inferior character bearing species and the most ill-equipped animals at the lowest rung of evolution are still found to have survived. The extinction of some, as against the others, only takes place when the contest for survival is extremely severe and mutually confrontational. Then too, it does not invariably lead to the survival of the fittest in its absolute sense. Survival of the fittest in its absolute sense, though possible, is yet unlikely to occur in the case of every struggle for existence. The fittest at such outcomes would only be the fittest in relation to that particular challenge. The unfortunate who may not survive these moments of trials may otherwise possess many more highly advanced qualities of life which may adjudge them to be the fittest in some other contexts.

ET US elaborate this further by visualizing the scenario of a grave famine resulting from a rare spell of drought covering an entire continent. Such a famine, if it persists for too long, is likely to bring to extinction a large number of species. The issue of extinction or survival would hang on the respective compatibility of the species in the given situation.

In a famine as severe as the one we are visualizing, almost all shrubs, bushes, trees and grasses with short roots, would be completely annihilated. The obvious reason for this is that the water level sinks lower and lower as the famine strikes deeper and deeper, until with the total dryness of the upper soil, the shorter roots are completely dehydrated. But this may not be the fate of some trees with very long, deeply entrenched roots. Such roots are known to have reached astounding depths during long-lasting spells of severe droughts. There are many caves in mountains that have been explored by archaeologists which bear witness to this fact. Some roots of trees which stood right on the top of a mountain appear to have chased the water as it sank to amazingly low depths. Similarly, despite periodic long spells of droughts in deserts, the secret of the survival of an oasis lies in this ability of the roots of some trees to chase water.

In the scenario under study, one can reasonably expect all the short root shrubbery, bushes, trees and grasses etc., to have been completely wiped out, whereas some tall trees with tapering, long embedded roots could withstand even worse droughts.

Let us now visualize what would happen to life in general upon such a continent during this period of extreme trial. Most of the grazing animals with shorter legs and necks would most certainly be starved or dehydrated to death. So also the carnivores among the animals would not survive much longer after their food supply had dwindled out of existence.

Maybe the only survivors would be those who could survive on very little water such as worms, scorpions, and millipedes and those animals which take their daily need of water by feeding on them with relish. Among them, meerkats are known to possess exceptional qualities to survive in such hostile environments. Some sorts of rodents could perhaps also share a fighting chance to crawl across an overly extended drought.

Among tall vertebrates however, there is one likely candidate who could have an outside chance to survive. For giraffes with exceptionally long necks and tall forequarters, it is not impossible to reach the green foliage on the tops of

An Artist's Vision of a Severe Drought   I.8

I.9   **A Giraffe during a Drought**

tall deep-rooted trees while all other species of grazing animals would be starving to death all around them.

There are also other factors which have to be brought to the focus of attention. There are animals which can run fast for long distances in search of whatever water holes remain available, and there are slow moving animals as well, at evident disadvantage. There are others better equipped with the sense of detecting water at long distances, and there are those who must find water right under their noses. We have also to include in the picture the role of the beasts of the jungle who must thrive on the flesh of grazing animals, and follow them wherever they go. They too, in turn however, need water for their survival. It is painful to visualize at what tragic moment the curtain of this bizarre drama will fall at last. They must depart this stage fatigued and starved one after the other. Maybe the only spectators left behind will be some giraffes, some vermin, some meerkats, in the vast empty amphitheatre of this continent where this ghastly drama is playing its last act. Maybe the only applause that will be heard would be the tiny clapping of the meerkats, or the neighing of the giraffes — if they have any neighing strength left in them — applauding their own survival!

Is this the survival of the fittest? Is this what the scientists clamour about? Is this what they mean by natural selection at work? Do the qualities of the giraffes and the meerkats, not to mention those of a few species of vermin which survived, really represent the ultimate evolutionary preferences?

In a billion years, hundreds of such alternating waves of drastic fluctuations in the climate can be realistically estimated. There would have been times when life was threatened with excessive cold or with excessive heat. There would have been times when life was threatened with excessive drought or excessive rains; there would also have been many scores of diseases attendant upon all such climatic changes. Whatever may have survived during the periods of these varying trials would not always be the giraffes and the meerkats, or the vermin for that matter.

In every changed context, the principle of the survival of the fittest would favour the survival of different contestants. Every calamity would have its own preferences. Looking at the issue of survival in relation to varying threats and challenges to life as it hazards its journey through a billion years of evolution, it is hard to visualize any survival at all. Little chance, if any, can be envisaged for the survival of all the forms of life, because different crises will have their own favourite targets which most often will not be the same. The poison for one category of life would be the meat for another. So the law of random selection would choose at random and continue to reject all that cross its path.

WE HOPE that by now the reader will have fully comprehended the nature and dimension of the problems involved in the operation of the survival of the fittest and natural selection. It should be remembered here that the term 'Natural Selection' is not being comprehensively examined in all its areas of application. We have only specifically taken up one of its many aspects to suit this context.

In Darwin's theory of biological evolution, as observed in comparatively more advanced species of life, the role of natural selection can be more easily discerned. But there also, it is found to be inadequate in accepting the right values and discarding the wrong ones.

Again, it should be emphasized here that the phenomenon of natural selection under changing environments does not possess any instrument of effecting internal cellular changes to suit the external requirements. The chromosomes and the character bearing genes lie far beyond the reach of chaotic external changes. The natural laws which govern them are insulated from the whims of cold and heat, or dryness and humidity. They are two absolutely unrelated phenomena.

Natural selection becomes operative only after a host of variants are created through progressive or random genetic changes. In the competitive world of the variants, thus created by 'chance', only those are able to survive which are proved fittest in relation to the given challenges. With a change in the nature and character of challenges, the definition of preferred characters would also change. Hence, this misconception that natural selection would always favour the best characters in all varying situations should be dispelled once and for all. Occasionally it may do so, but most often it does not. The term is largely relative and rarely definitive regarding its choices. The competition for survival can be between members of the same species, or between different species. It is only the chance outcome of a given situation which decides the quality of the surviving factors. Blind struggle for existence cannot always aim at the right qualities. Whatever emerges, bad or good, must be accepted as the fittest. A particular species could be adjudged as champion with regards to its potential for survival in a specific situation. The species that becomes extinct could have possessed more advanced qualities and characters in other regards.

Consider for example the case of a solitary gorilla left stranded in a hostile arctic environment. In comparison to it, the polar bear and foxes stand far greater chances of survival in the same habitat. In that particular case the gorilla, despite its comparative evolutionary advancement, would be condemned to extinction by the instrument of natural selection as a worthless thing in comparison to the polar bear and the arctic foxes. Replace the gorilla with a human in the same hypothetical situation, the condemnation of him to death by the principle of survival of the fittest will be speedier than in the case of the gorilla. Hence it is wrong to believe that natural selection goes for quality as such. In the barest terms, natural selection can at best be described as 'might is right'; even when might is vicious, distorted, oppressive and merciless, might will always emerge victorious in the sight of natural selection.

If we undertake the work of tracing the history of evolution in relation to all the various forms of life and try to determine how the principles of natural selection and survival of the fittest actually work, it would exhaust voluminous books running into hundreds of thousands of pages or more. It would take many generations of future scientists to pursue this task.

However, we must draw the attention of the reader to the fact that if one visualizes all the possible options at work, progressive selection would become impossible. At every such occasion where this discrimination is needed, it may take millions of chances to collude for the selection of a single superior character. The converse should also be seriously considered.

For haphazard mutations to jump in any direction, is not controversial, but for them to always jump in the right direction, to advance the cause of evolution towards a definite goal, is next to impossible. Hence, in a game of chance, as indeed it is a game of chance, is highly implausible for it to always take the stride in the right direction as needed by the dictates of evolutionary requirements at that point in time. It is unfortunate however, that most scientists shut their eyes to the inevitability of the Hand of a Conscious Wise Selector Who will always take the right decisions at the right moment and will not leave them to the throw of a dice.

HOW CAN IT be possible for evolution to continuously march forward in the direction of man while at each moment the possibilities of its taking the wrong steps backwards are overwhelmingly larger? The only possible solution to this otherwise insoluble dilemma would be to follow the backward escape route envisaged by a boy during a rainy day. Once, it is said, a boy reached his school very late. When severely reprimanded by his teacher, he offered the excuse that the road to school was so muddy and slippery that as he took one step forward in the direction of the school, he slipped back two steps.

'How on earth did you reach the school at all?' shouted the angry teacher.

'Excuse me, sir,' was the apologetic reply of the boy, 'It struck me rather late, that I should start walking in the direction of my house instead of that of the school. The moment I did it, I began to slide backwards towards the school at an even faster speed than I ordinarily maintain. And here I am sir, hitting the back of my head against the school wall, such was my haste to reach here, backwards all the way.'

The dilemma that life faces, if left entirely to the mercy of chance, is far more exasperating than the case of that boy. At each step forward, evolution driven by chance should have slipped a hundred thousand steps backwards. But for life with no prefixed direction, as some naturalists believe, the concept of a step forward simply does not arise. Forward in which direction and to what end, are the questions which can never be answered in relation to chance being its creator. Every step it took could be in any direction. Hence even turning the journey of life backwards could not resolve the problem. Man not being the ultimate goal of evolution, life would lose its bearing in the wilderness of chaos, squandering each quality it had gained, by chance, to the stormy aimless winds of annihilation.

Whatever the mutative changes might have gained, they may lose by other leaps in wrong directions. Let us apply the same logic to the creation of eyes and examine how blind mutative changes could have succeeded in manufacturing even a most rudimentary eye which could see and transmit what it saw to the brain behind. It is far more likely for mutation, or gradual cellular development, to disorganize what it has created itself, than for it to organize the surrounding confusion with the passage of time. The haphazard mutative changes created only by chance could actually play havoc with the orderly shape and design of life. It could change, for instance, the positioning of the eye, the nose, the ear, the mouth, the tongue and their sensory buds. Maybe in a few subsequent generations some species could have eyes shifted to the back of their heads instead, or upon their stomachs, or one each under their armpits! Who can stay or discipline the hand of chance? Again, it is not unlikely that the ears could begin to see, the nose could talk and the tongue could hear, ankles could grow with buds of taste and smell! Different animals, at least some of them, should have exhibited such freaks of nature without a purpose to serve. But wherever in nature we find a shifting of the ear or the eye from their normally expected position, it is always done purposefully, being of advantage to the animal concerned rather than of disadvantage. But these are exceptions. The rule that governs millions of species dictates a universal design. When we observe chance at work it behaves differently; babies are born with congenital disorders, alas never to their advantage. Who knows? A game of chance is a game of chance.

The task of examining the evolutionary processes which led to the making of an eye require a thorough, in-depth study. Also, the evolution of all animal organs, which make complex, yet perfect little worlds of their own need to be examined in depth.

It is intended, therefore, to add a separate chapter on the creative processes which resulted in the creation of complete organic units, eyes being central to the discussion.

Unfortunately, the physical features of species as they evolve have been far more emphasized by naturalists than their sensory organs. However, mere physical changes in a certain direction are of no significance compared to the advancement of awareness and consciousness in the grand scheme of the evolutionary spiral. What is Life after all, if it is not awareness, as against the absolute unawareness of Death?

The most dramatic miracle does not take place on the plane of mere cellular changes and complexities of molecules at the level of proteins. The miracle of the origin of life lies in the sudden dawn of consciousness upon the horizon of the dead universe that preceded it. Ever since that happened it continues to grow from weakness to strength, from a lone beginning to diversity. The meaning of evolution can in no way be understood by confining oneself to the Darwinian principle of haphazard physical changes being selected and grouped together by the hand of natural selection. It can only be comprehended by gaining a better understanding of the five senses which ultimately evolved after the hazardous journey of life during its last billion years.

Man can look down from his vantage point at whatever lies behind him and below him. Only then will he realize the meaning of life and the meaning of evolution — bit by bit, nanometre by nanometre; the senses once born climbed through the spiralling path of endless evolution. The purpose and philosophy of evolution is doubtlessly the creation and promotion of the five senses. The creation of five senses, each of which in itself is a masterpiece of creative wonders, stands witness to a well-executed design at the grandest scale, where harmony rules supreme. No wonder then, that the Holy Quran repeatedly sums up the outcome of evolution in just three simple terms: the creation and perfection of the faculty of hearing, seeing and understanding.

وَاللهُ اَخْرَجَكُمْ مِّنْ بُطُوْنِ اُمَّهٰتِكُمْ لَا تَعْلَمُوْنَ شَيْئًا وَّجَعَـــلَ
لَكُمُ السَّمْعَ وَالْاَبْصَارَ وَالْاَفْئِدَةَ لَعَلَّكُمْ تَشْكُرُوْنَ * 16:79

And Allah brought you forth from the wombs of
your mothers while you knew nothing, and gave you
ears and eyes and hearts, that you might be grateful.[2]

To return to the main subject of discussion, let us emphasize once again that mutative changes could go far more often wrong than right, leaving little room, if any, for natural selection to choose from, for the betterment of life. But this is not all we observe in the grand panorama of evolution at play on the stage of life.

To pursue the point further, let us focus our gaze here upon the arctic habitat. The naturalist's understanding of physical evolution can specifically be put to test there with the characteristic study of polar bears and arctic foxes. Polar bears differ in shape from brown and black bears. Their hindquarters are set higher than their forequarters so that they can run faster in pursuit of prey, while their elongated necks give them a more streamlined shape for swimming. Other bears can also swim, but polar bears can swim comparatively much faster and cover much longer distances, a competence direly needed for their survival in the arctic environment.

Polar bears can weigh as much as 800 kilograms and measure 3.0 metres. Their size is both a protection against the cold and a necessary factor in their ability to hunt and kill. Incidentally, the cubs born to a mother bear are amazingly small, they weigh a mere 500 grams, just a fraction of the weight of a human baby. Their black skin is covered with thick white fur, thus nature provides them with a perfect camouflage throughout the year. Their coats take a yellowish tinge only briefly in summer, matching perfectly with the melting ice. The polar bear's dense fur and an exceptionally thick layer of fat under its skin protect it against the freezing temperatures of the habitat.[3] The fat is particularly important when the bear is swimming, because the fur cannot retain the insulating air trapped in it. When dry, the white fur reflects the heat it receives from the sun's rays back to the body. The hairs are hollow, so that ultraviolet rays from the sun can pass through them and be absorbed by the black skin beneath.

Another striking feature of the polar bear is the relatively large size of its paws. They are very wide and armed with sharp claws for tearing its prey and for gripping the ice. The soles of its feet are covered with the same thick, creamy white fur as covers its body providing them a better grip on icy surfaces and much needed insulation. Amazingly, polar bears can run as fast on ice as the fastest dog on firm ground. During the exceptionally long spells of night in the polar winter, it is almost impossible for the polar bear to perceive and reach the open water pools where seals are found. Thanks to its extra sharp faculty of smell, darkness offers no hindrance, so it can smell seals, meat or carrion even from as far as 20 kilometres, according to naturalists. In sharpness, its eyesight matches its sense of smell, which is keener than that of most other bears. During daylight they can locate seals from a considerably long distance. Having spotted the seal, the patience with which they stalk them is amazing, they creep upon them with bodies flattened to the ice, forefeet doubled under them and only the hind feet providing propulsion. They possess the artifice for contriving excellent camouflage. Sometimes they push a small heap of ice in front of them to camouflage their dark muzzles, or cover their noses with their white paws to avoid detection.

Much of a polar bear's time is spent in water. It possesses some unique features to correspond to this situation. The usage of limbs in water is reversed in comparison to the bear's behaviour when it stalks seals on pack ice. Instead of hind legs, which are now used as rudders, it uses only its forequarters for propulsion. In addition to their exceptionally large size, the front paws have the added advantage of being partially webbed. Another exceptional feature which makes the polar bear perfectly adapted to the polar habitat, is its ability to swim under water with eyes fully open and nostrils closed.[3] Although some scientists try to explain away these unique features of the polar bear by simply referring them to be a product of evolution, there are other naturalists however who remind them that it would take millions of years of evolution to create the specific features that separate polar bears from the bear family in general.

In adaptability to the polar climate, the arctic fox does not lag far behind the polar bear. In winter it grows a dense white fur to keep it warm and to provide it with camouflage. Little of its body heat is lost through its small, furry and rounded ears, so different from the ears of the foxes found elsewhere. Again in comparison to other foxes, the arctic fox has a short muzzle and legs, which also help it to conserve heat. Like the polar bear, the arctic fox also has thick fur under the soles of its paws, which provides it with excellent insulation against extreme cold. Surprisingly, the only other fox which shares the fur under the sole with the arctic fox is the desert fox. Obviously, there it needs this fur for insulation against heat. White arctic foxes are hard to see in the snow but their white fur could become a disadvantage in other habitats. For instance, in islands and in the coasts of the arctic ocean where there is less snow, they need a camouflage of a different colour. A bluish-grey colour seems to be ideally suited and it is exactly that which their coats turn into.[4]

This leads us back to the all-important question of the role of natural selection in the origin of species. If it took some millions of years for the polar bear to be equipped with such exceptional features, as are essential for its survival in the arctic climate, the same time-scale would show no partiality to the fox either. The question arises as to how many thousands of generations of bears and foxes must have perished in vain before they could have evolved the changes in their anatomy, vitally essential for their survival.

Again, if they had survived as they must have survived for millions of years, even without the advantage of these exceptional features which make them perfectly adapted to the arctic climate, where was the need for any adaptation at all? Why all the fuss about genetic changes and chance mutations colluding for that long to provide the opportunity for natural selection to approve of a choice which, in fact, was imposed upon it.

Moreover, if ordinary bears and foxes as found elsewhere in the world were to be dumped into the arctic region today, while polar bears and artic foxes are removed from the arena, the question would arise as to whether they would have any chance of survival in that hostile climate, continuously, generation after generation, without becoming extinct. If they could do so with a fair guarantee for the survival of the species, the evolutionary exercise of the polar bears would be rendered superfluous and the characteristic changes brought about in features could no longer be considered as necessary.

Now we look at the same scenario from a slightly different angle. It is impossible for the extremely inhospitable environment, such as obtains in the arctic region, to work causatively for bringing about appropriate changes to the biochemistry of cells. Yet, without such profound changes in the character bearing genes, no gradual or mutative changes can be visualized. White fur upon black skin, taller hindquarters and shorter forequarters, tiny rounded ears, an exceptionally sharp sense of smell and vision, thick fur under the soles of their paws, change of coats in accordance with environmental dictates and layer upon layer of fat under the skin, cannot be made to order by the climatic conditions prevailing in the arctic habitat of the polar bears and foxes. Chance must continue to play its role separately and blindly in the cellular chemistry to add variety to characters and to bring about spontaneous changes in animal features, haphazardly in every direction.

Natural selection must wait for these painstakingly slow changes to provide a large variety of options for it to choose from. For instance, if random changes in the cellular chemistry can suddenly alter the colour of hair from black to white, with a thick layer of white fur added on top of that, why cannot they change the colour of the hair from black to blue or red or crimson or violet or green or deep yellow or saffron for that matter? How did cellular chemistry know that what was needed in the arctic climate was only white? Yet it failed to learn that the skin underneath the white fur would remain black. Why did the same cellular changes leave the skin alone and think only of changing the colour of the fur — a novel idea indeed to grow white fur on black skin! Hence, each of the specific features mentioned in relation to polar bears and foxes would evidently require a host of other options to have been created by chance.

According to the Darwinian theory of the origin of species, one should expect a wide variety of polar bears and foxes with a host of different features, to have been created by chance before natural selection could come into play. The fossil record of the arctic region should testify to the earlier chance creation of red bears, blue bears, saffron bears and pink bears. But evolution, in relation to its effect on polar bears, seems to be colour-blind, capable only of recognizing black or white. Moreover, the bears should also come in all shapes and sizes. There should be tiny polar bears, giant polar bears, heavyweights, middle weights, lightweights, flyweights, bantamweights and featherweights etc. Some should be born with taller forequarters and shorter hindquarters, some with dim vision and diminished sense of smell. Why should the creative factors, whatever they were, provide only single options in the polar habitat and let natural selection sit idly by? There was nothing for it to choose from.

Some polar bears should again, have been accidentally born with a sense of utter distaste for the flesh of seals, and abhor it to the degree that they would rather die of starvation than to venture upon a mouthful of it. The very sight of it should have made them vomit and retch miserably for hours. It should be of no surprise if some among them were shabby swimmers and tardy runners.

If so, the Darwinian naturalist would have some right to make us believe that it was only random creation which took care of the evolutionary processes in that specific region. Subsequently however, the inevitable law of the survival of the fittest and natural selection must have wiped out the unwanted and incompatible specimens of polar bears. All that was left to survive was the polar bear in its present form.

But where did those polar bears, whom survival of the fittest had condemned to extinction, disappear? We are not talking of a tropical environment. What we are talking about is the extremely cold habitat of the arctic. In a climate such as this, some of the corpses of different polar bears which became extinct must have been perfectly preserved as fossil records. One should remember that some animals which existed hundreds of thousands of years ago have been found buried in the arctic deep freeze, so completely unchanged that their flesh was edible, as if they had been buried yesterday; such is the case of a mammoth elephant discovered in Siberia not so long ago.

The same random cellular changes resulting in the creation of a host of variants among animal species should also be found operative in non-polar climates and habitats. At least some of their fossil records should have been found in the archives of nature.

Let us travel now from the arctic to the non-arctic regions of the world. By comparison to the massive polar bears, the study of a tiny spider presents a fascinating contrast.

SPIDERS are found virtually everywhere except in the arctic climate. In tropical forests, however, they abound and flourish like nowhere else. Rain forests

1.10

HYPOTHETICAL

A polar bear stalking seals 30 km away.

A polar bear chasing seals underwater.

An Arctic Scene

A tiny rat size cub born to a 200 kg polar bear.

For description, see page 429.

I.11   **A Scene of Tropical Forest**

are not their only habitat. Their ability to survive extreme climates is amazing. They survive on mountain tops as well as in deep canyons and caves.

There are at least thirty thousand known species of spiders, but some estimate the number to be twice as much.[5] All spiders are not weavers of webs. About half of them weave webs and the other half, despite the fact that they also produce silky threads, hunt their prey by directly attacking it and leaping upon it with amazing speed and precision. The cobweb weavers invariably go for insects alone, while other spiders can attack and kill comparatively much bigger animals.

Incidentally, in the last century, one naturalist estimated that the number of insects devoured by spiders was more than the total weight of the human population.[5] Returning to the main discussion, we should like to remind the reader that the greater the difference between the lifestyle of different species, the more challenging it becomes for the evolutionist to trace back the evolutionary history of each species. What natural factors guided their steps and how, over millions of years? Each of them seems to have accidentally reached the stage in which they are found today.

For the interest of the reader, we just quote a few examples of how vastly spiders vary from species to species. There are wolf spiders, which hunt with the ferocity of a wolf and there are huntsman spiders which move at amazingly fast speeds and there are bird-eating spiders, also known as tarantulas. They are exceptionally large in size by comparison to other spiders. Even small vertebrates appear diminutive by their side. Under extreme provocation they will not hesitate to attack humans. Their staple food consists of small roosting birds, reptiles, amphibians, beetles, moths, grasshoppers and also when needs be, they devour other spiders.

Again there are ant-eating spiders which are mere dwarfs as compared to the tarantulas. They are no bigger than the size of the ordinary ants they hunt. The Creator has provided them with such perfect camouflage as the ants never suspect the presence of these deadly aliens among them. They look like ants, they act like ants, they move like ants and the adage 'when in Rome do as the Romans do', applies to them most befittingly. Only, they do not think like ants. How could this amazing camouflage evolve by a mere collusion of blind chances and how long did it take for aimless mutative changes to perfect this wonder? These are some questions for the evolutionist to answer.

Of course one would also expect some explanation as to how natural selection might have worked in relation to the ant-hunters. How many millions of generations of imperfect hunters must have been created and wiped out before the most perfect hunter was finally evolved by the aimless meanderings of the so-called evolutionary factors!

Another mysterious species of spiders is known as Atypus. Ever since they were discovered by W.E. Leach in 1816, they have continued to arouse widespread interest amongst zoologists. Long before sealed room mysteries were invented by detective story writers, Nature had created a living model of the sealed room mystery by designing and perfecting a female species known as 'the trapdoor spider'. Naturalists had long been puzzled as to how she could keep herself alive closeted in a long silk tube sealed at both ends. It took F. Enoch to finally provide the solution to this baffling problem during his work between 1885 to 1892. The silken tube in which Atypus locks herself is usually eight to nine inches in length. Of this all but two to three inches pass steeply down into the ground while the remaining portion juts out of the ground like an inflated finger of a glove. In the middle, the tube is more spacious to provide the spider room to turn and manoeuvre. The mastermind of blind evolution takes care that during the winter, when the spiders hibernate, the aerial portion is collapsed. At other times they are easily mistaken for roots protruding from soil. The silk is intermixed with earth or sand grains by the spiders to make it appear inconspicuous. The way in which an insect is seized can be watched by tickling the tube with a grass stem. Suddenly two shining curved fangs are violently protruded through the web and it can be seen from their position that the spider strikes in a shark-like manner with its lower side uppermost. If a buzzing fly is held against the tube the fangs pierce its body and hold it like fish hooks. After a certain amount of tugging and jerking a slit appears in the tube wall through which the insect is pulled in. Before retiring to the inner chamber with the prey to enjoy the fruit of her labour, the spider returns to the upper portion of the tube to repair and reseal it.[6]

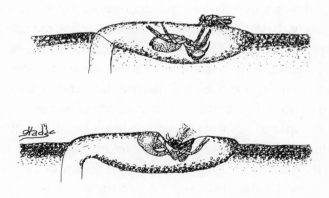

The trapdoor spider waiting in its tube, about to seize its prey.

How the Darwinian principle of 'Survival of the Fittest', aided only by mutative changes, could conceive, design and execute the creative plan of trapdoor spiders, is a mystery which perhaps only the elite among the naturalists can understand to their satisfaction.

Finally, we conclude this discussion by taking up the case of weaver spiders which make almost half of all the spider species. So tiny, so fragile, so delicately built, they all the same possess the surprising faculty and know-how to build intricate contraptions for catching flying insects. It is an intriguing case study because as we move from one type of weavers to another, the whole complexion of their style, strategy and weaving skills change dramatically. Let us visualize how blind chance might have endowed the spider to turn his salivary glands into a highly efficient mill for spinning yarn.

Of course it could not have happened overnight by an explosion of mutative changes. If we reconstruct the entire process bit by bit and stage by stage, then perhaps we can visualize to some degree what aimless evolution could have done for the spider.

Perhaps the story began with the salivary glands of the spider suddenly becoming over-sensitised due to some accidental factors. Then, maybe during the next one or two million years, an interplay of a host of chances taught its saliva to harden into strands the moment it was ejected into the air. But these fine fragile looking threads were simultaneously bestowed with a tensile strength greater than that of steel for the same body weight.

These exasperatingly long unmanageable threads must have scattered all over the place, entwining the spider's legs, entrapping it itself as a sitting duck for its predators. How long this might have gone on perhaps the evolutionists could visualize better. But as a layman's guess, we suggest that after a million or two years, a mentally more advanced spider was basking in the sun, lamenting its sorry state. At that rare moment rushed to its aid at last, a configuration of mutative changes which endowed its tiny spot of a brain with the skill to turn its disadvantage to advantage. In that flash of a moment, a new era began in the lifestyle of spiders which has no parallel in the entire animal kingdom.

It set itself immediately to the task of learning the art of weaving cobwebs as snares. How long it might have taken it to bring this exercise to a successful conclusion is indeed hard to visualize. In keeping with the pace of evolution it should not be surprising if it took the spider another couple of million years to perfect this art.

The most intricate and fascinating patterns of different types of webs that the spider weaves are not only wonderful to look at but are also precision-made to serve a set purpose. They never obstruct the movement of the spider's feet which dances along, light-footed, like the most skilful ballet dancer, and puts to shame the proudest of tightrope walkers. Never taking a false step, never faltering, never needing a balancing rod, never hesitating in a state of indecision as to how and where it should fix the next string as it proceeds to complete the task of constructing its meticulously designed cobweb to the finish. Thus the story of a spider learning to manufacture yarn and weave it into such perfect traps comes to a happy ending. Even the most vicious of wasps which prey upon it would think twice before venturing to attack it as it sits safely entrenched in its spidery castle.

So far so good, but suddenly a disturbing thought passes one's mind as to what, after all, was the purpose of this exercise. Why was blind evolution driven towards this goal without a conscious pre-design and without a purpose? The only purpose one can think of is to provide the spider with the much needed food which was so essential for its survival.

The poor spider was only bestowed by nature with some twisted shabby looking legs. Before its skill to weave cobweb snares was perfected, it must have continued to survive on some food, generation after generation, for millions of years. Flies may be stupid, but they are not stupid enough to head straight for the spider's mouth without a cobweb to trap them. Yet, with or without this fly-meal, the spiders continued to survive over a long period of their existence. Where was the need for the entire exercise of spinning a yarn and weaving a web and all the evolutionary requirements concomitant upon them?

It is indeed difficult for the uninitiated to visualize the challenges of a tremendously long period of transition from one manner to another. How many generations of spiders must have aimlessly perished during these challenges one wonders!

When we suggested earlier that perhaps the spider was suddenly taught the art of weaving a web for procuring food, by a configuration of mutative changes, we only did it to highlight the absurdity of this idea. Mutative changes do not occur simultaneously in perfectly organized purpose-built packages. It would require hundreds of thousands of chances to manipulate a meaningful sequence of mutative changes to be encoded in the character bearing genes of life, to bring about such dramatic changes as these in the lifestyle of any animal species.

THE CASE OF the delicate carnivorous aqueous plants is no less wondrous by any means. The simplest of these is complex enough to defy human attempts to demonstrate how a procession of blind chances in the right order could, over millions of years, create such perfect trapping machines. We begin by presenting the case of the marsh pitcher which, according to experts, belongs to the simplest category of carnivorous plants. It comprises leaves about a foot in length, which are bonded together at the seam to make a funnel. Each of these funnels is visible in its entire length as it protrudes above the water surface. The funnel tops are hooded by conspicuous reddish rims which are generously studded with nectar producing glands. Abundant rains in the tropical regions where they grow, keep the funnels filled with water, yet they neither burst nor topple down under their weight. This is made possible in two ways:

(a) The leaves are bonded all the way, but for an inch or two at the top. They are left unjoined, leaving enough opening for the extra water to be drained out.

(b) A ring of small holes is provided at the right place just below the upper margin so that the right level of water is always maintained.

Insects are attracted by the colour as well as the sweet scent of the nectar exuding from the glands. As they hop around in search of more nectar, they slip down the funnel which is cropped with downward pointing slippery hairs which do not permit them to climb back up again. Down they go until they reach the lowest part of the funnel which has no hairs. In that enclosed pit they finally die and disintegrate enriching the water with proteins, salts etc. This food is assimilated by the plant for its survival. How many sightless attempts by nature must have been frustrated before it could finally perfect this well-coordinated trapping machine, is hard to estimate.

Now we present another example of how nature has turned the tables against the animal kingdom in favour of the vegetative life. The trumpet pitchers are provided with such waxy scales on the surface of their traps as would stick to the exploring animals' feet and loosen their hold.

'Having lost their balance, down they tumble into the water-filled pit. The vibration thus caused stimulates the digestive glands of the funnel which immediately begin to exude a strong digestive juice. By this the fallen midgets can be completely dissolved in a few hours time, while flies may last for a day or two. It is not merely these insects which are devoured by these carnivorous plants. The 'rajah' among the trumpets can even dissolve and devour scorpions and mice.

The case of the Venus's fly-trap (see plate 3) is even more complicated as it is electrically operated. The mystery of how this electric current is produced, and what governs the operation of this mechanism, has so far baffled all attempts by scientists.

We can only invite the attention of Darwinian evolutionists to these amazing contrivances and most humbly require that they should explain how they must have evolved. How many generations of unsuccessful attempts must have perished before the final successful experiments by evolution to create a carnivorous plant with all its necessary trapping gadgets and digestive enzymes? Until ordinary green plants were finally transformed into formidable hunting machines they simply could not have started this completely different phase of their lives. The difference between the two is immeasurable. To have started supplementing their diet with animal enzymes and proteins was impossible until this transformation was completed. How many millions of years were required for this through an ordinary course of evolution governed by the Darwinian principle of natural selection is inconceivable.

It simply could not have happened, because no naturalist can even suggest a bit by bit transformation of ordinary green plants into carnivorous plants (see plate 4).

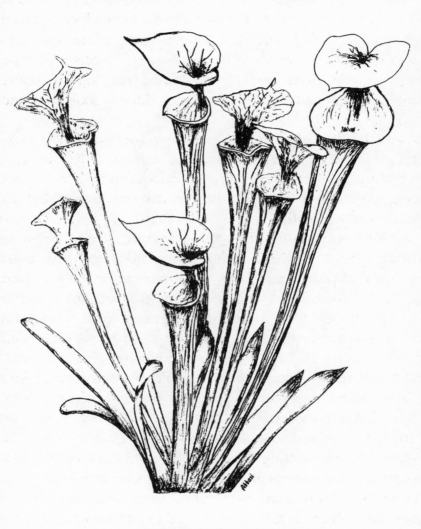

THE TRUMPET PITCHER PLANT

Plant provided by courtesy of *Marston Exotics*.

THE SUNDEW

Plant provided by courtesy of *Marston Exotics*.

I.13

The transformation has to be completed before they could start functioning.

We have yet to come across an attempt by naturalists to trace the evolutionary course of carnivorous plants bit by bit, organ by organ, back to their origin. Even the smallest insect eating plants pose extremely big problems when we examine them in depth and bring to the focus of our attention the intricacies of their coherent organic identity. Each part has to be purpose-built and specifically designed into a composite organic entity.

Last but not least, there was no impelling reason why they should have suddenly abandoned the most profitable lifestyle of their ancestors, who were well taken care of by photosynthesis, providing them with a glorious start in their struggle for existence. The Darwinian principle 'Survival of the Fittest' could not have played any role in their so-called evolution, adjudging them to be the fittest to survive. If it were so the entire dry land and all watery habitats should have become their prime territory. Evidently they were just made fit to survive without any history of evolution preceding that fitness.

Moreover, though it is understandable according to the evolutionary principles for any plant or animal to shift from a hostile environment to a hospitable one, the converse is never heard of. But, if the naturalists are to be taken seriously, their story runs counter to this phenomenon in the case of the Sundew and Venus's fly-trap.

Imagine a Sundew plant growing luxuriously by the side of a stagnant puddle, staring with abhorrence at what it observed in its middle. No plant could survive there because of most hostile environments. If the Sundew had an invisible brain while watching that puddle, with eyes that did not visibly exist, it should have been horrified at what it observed and leapt away from it were it not firmly rooted in the soil. But the naturalists have a completely different vision of what happened. According to them, it is the same Sundew — naturally and healthily growing by the side of that puddle — which got transformed into a fly-trap which we find flourishing undeterred in that hostile surrounding. It is inconceivable for it to survive there without having previously evolved to meet the new challenges. This could only happen if all the necessary changes had been brought about while it was still on dry land. Without having completed its transformation outside that environment, it could not have survived there for a single moment.

This is the dilemma which the scientists confront and must explain in sensible and logical terms. Two vital points need to be registered here.

1) The Sundew, which scientists believe to be the forefather of Venus's fly-trap is in itself an enigma. It has no traceable history of having evolved from ordinary green foliage

2) Venus's fly-trap must have evolved to its final minutest detail on dry soil outside the puddle without any evolutionary compulsion.

We rest our case here and expect the naturalists to take over from this point. Their explanation is most eagerly sought for.

We have specially highlighted the case of the Venus's fly-trap because it possesses a highly sophisticated, intricately designed and electrically operated mechanism which even advanced scientists fail to understand. As has been described above, in its finished form Venus's fly-trap is completely different from the anatomical composition of its so-called ancestors. Hence, it is not to impossible for the naturalists to try to fill this vast gap by suggesting a countless number of small evolutionary steps, which could appropriately fill this immense blank. In the absence of this material, it is impossible to conceive natural selection to work on something which does not exist. To further highlight the absurdity of the naturalists' contention, they seem to believe in the birth of a child to a non-existent mother. Is this the picture of evolution which the survival of the fittest presents? What survival, what fitness? Where is the competition? If scientists have any professional ethics which they ordinarily do, let them apply their ethics to the case of all carnivorous plants which were already fully equipped with their hunting gears before entering the realm of natural selection! If this is 'Natural Selection', then what else is the mockery of common sense, one wonders!

The Case of Mosquitoes

Consider now for instance, the case of a mosquito. There is so much in it to be explained logically and convincingly, that it would require generations of scientists to unfold each mystery attendant upon the exquisite and precise mechanism of all its organs and their constituents. Such a study would remain inexhaustive, because as they reach one level of understanding there would appear yet another level waiting for them to unravel its mysteries.

No wonder therefore, that the Holy Quran singles out this small miracle of God's creation to make people see the greatness of His creative wonders. Even in the modelling of a mosquito, which the humans look down upon as a small insignificant thing, there is nothing for the Creator to be ashamed of. Let us build this theme further and share with the reader the intricacies of this flying machine, which may put to shame even the best achievements of the most advanced masters of technology.

Let us begin with the Quranic account of a mosquito which is so different from that of all other animals. It is the only animal which is mentioned with an emphatic denial that its creation could present any cause for embarrassment to its Creator. Thus declares the Quran:

إِنَّ اللهَ لاَ يَسْتَحْيِ أَنْ يَّضْرِبَ مَثَلًا مَّا بَعُوْضَةً فَمَا فَوْقَهَا 2:27

> Allah does not feel shy (or embarrassed) at mentioning the example of a mosquito because of what is carried above it . . .[7]

Here the word (فَوْق) *fauq* literally means 'above'.* Yet other translators have not employed its literal meaning. The evident reason why they did not do so is because they had no knowledge that mosquitoes do carry things above them.

The following are some of the questions which stir the reader's mind. At least the author has always been intrigued by the implied message of this verse.

The very first question which stirs the mind is why should God deny any cause to be ashamed of for creating mosquitoes. Nowhere else in the Quran is such a denial made in relation to any other creation; everywhere it is mentioned with pride. Is the exceptional treatment of the mosquito's creation, as found in this verse, indicative of the fact that the Quran draws the attention of the reader to the apparent worthlessness of the mosquito? The denial of an element of shame or embarrassment related to the creation of a worthless thing is in fact a denial of worthlessness itself. The denial invites the attention of man to reconsider

---

*   See Al-Munjad and Al-Mufradāt Lil-Rāghib

his attitude towards mosquitoes. It indicates the following implied statements:

> (a) the mosquitoes are not worthless and insignificant as commonly understood, and
>
> (b) they play an important role which is not as yet fully understood and needs to be further investigated.

When investigated, it is admitted, the role of the mosquito will emerge to be extremely harmful and horrendous. Yet despite this admission, the element of shame related to this harmful creation is emphatically denied. It is denied because to perform this negative role mosquitoes had to be built precisely to be able to fulfil this purpose. Secondly the mosquito's function, though negative in character, must have played a vital role in the scheme of creation. As such the inevitability of the mosquito's creation and the perfection with which it is accomplished has to be understood as a mark of pride rather than a mark of shame for its Creator. The inference we have drawn can only be proved right if mosquitoes display some exceptional constructional beauty which is even more wonderful than that found in the creation of other forms of life. And again, the role of mosquitoes in the general scheme of life and its evolution has to be that of a blessing in disguise – a discovery yet to be made by scientists. Presently, we can only suggest that mosquitoes may have played a vital role in developing and perfecting our immune system – a role which it still continues to play.

The possibility of all the above-mentioned implications of this verse to be simultaneously correct led the author to an in-depth study of mosquitoes, their anatomy and the role they perform in the animal kingdom — a task which is far more complex and difficult than it had appeared in the beginning. Most of the available literature on mosquitoes fails to explain the evolution of its organs – an omission which has especially attracted the author's attention. In many other cases, the results of their excellent study are available which describe the evolution of animal parts with minute attention. We have relied heavily on this material in the following discourse which testifies to the truth of the Quranic claim that mosquitoes are no ordinary things. Further research into the evolutionary aspect of the mosquito's creation is already taken up by a competent team of Ahmadi scholars from America and Canada. This, however, is a time-consuming process and as the publication of this book cannot wait till then, we have decided to finish this work with the help of whatever material is available.

The apparently insignificant minute mosquito is perhaps the most important insect in relation to man and other forms of life. Mosquitoes are thought to have originated in the Cretaceous period (65-140 millions years ago)[8], when most of the modern taxonomic group of insects co-evolved with the origin of flowering plants. It is also speculated that mosquitoes may have originated in the Jurassic period (136-190 million years ago). As mammals were not created till then they must have sucked blood from reptiles, amphibians, primitive forms of mammals, or even perhaps from dinosaurs. This urge for blood, as conceived by the naturalist to have occurred during such a remote period of their creation raises many questions. Why had they developed this urge at all, when even without it they had survived for a very long period merely on vegetable produce? There were no flowering plants in that period so they may have fed mainly on honeydew.[9]

Mosquitoes are small two-winged insects belonging to the family Culicidae of the order of Diptera (two-winged flies). They essentially differ from all other flies by a long

Plate 3.   Venus's fly-trap.

Plate 4. Ordinary flora of photosynthetic plants.
(Photographed by: Hadi Ali Chaudhary)

No evolutionary history from these plants to carnivorous plants
has ever been presented.

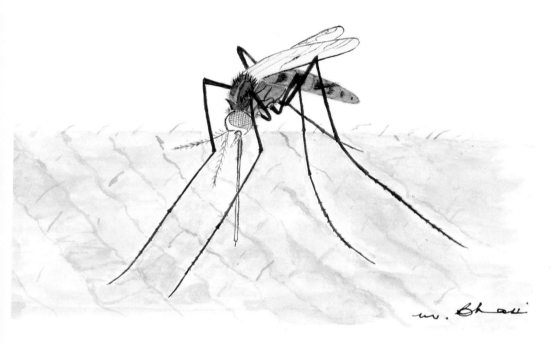

Plate 5.   A female mosquito about to pierce through the skin of her human victim with her proboscis.

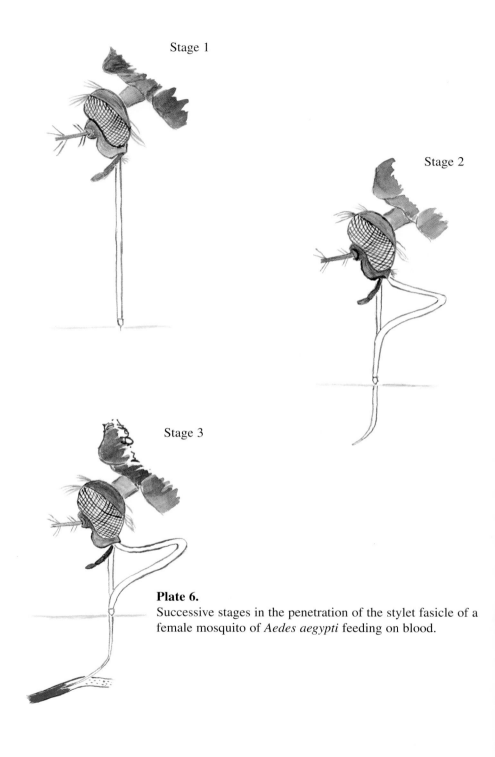

Stage 1

Stage 2

Stage 3

Plate 6.
Successive stages in the penetration of the stylet fasicle of a
female mosquito of *Aedes aegypti* feeding on blood.

proboscis projecting from the head and some other features which are unique to them – like the presence of scales on the wing veins, a fringe of scales along the posterior margin of wings, and a characteristic venation whereby the second, the fourth, and the fifth longitudinal veins are branched.

Like other Diptera they undergo a complete metamorphosis during their reproduction, but many features of their metamorphosis are strikingly different from other flies. An active larva hatches from a passive egg bearing no resemblance to its parents, fully adapted to living and feeding in water.

It is amazing how all the highly competent authorities on mosquitoes, though thoroughly proficient in the knowledge of their anatomy and morphological cycles, do not present any sensible, logically acceptable scenario of natural selection playing any part in the design and manufacture of this tiny wonder of creation.

To modify a non blood-sucking mosquito into a blood-sucking one requires such changes as would take an interminably long period of time if left to chance. For them to develop patiently, bit by bit, each part developing separately yet simultaneously, in perfect coordination with each other, is an amazing proposition. Particularly when one considers that this bit by bit organic development could serve no purpose in the life of a mosquito until it had culminated into its final completely organized and fully developed form. Take for instance the need of the mosquito to find and locate blood. When scientists study this small requirement they discover a complex support system to justify its existence.

The anatomical, sensory and physiological changes needed in a mosquito just for the act of finding a suitable host on which it will feed are tremendous. The mosquito faces the routine task of finding a suitable protein source amidst all the extraneous stimuli with which the environment bombards it. Scientists say the strategy that they have evolved is to:

> '...respond to visual cues, heat, and emanations such as carbon dioxide, lactic acid, and volatile fatty acids that are typical of those organisms that contain blood.'[10]

A further difficulty faced by the mosquito is the fact that chemical odour emanations are dispersed through air currents. Thus the mosquito must navigate an indirect route to the host. As the mosquito comes closer to the host, heat is used by it to home in on the host. During this chain of events in the mosquito's behaviour, a stimulus-response mechanism has to be perfected within it. The mosquito is not consciously seeking a host, but rather responding to stimuli for which it has been pre-programmed. Further complicating the issue is the fact that most mosquitoes are species-specific in their host seeking behaviour. For example, a certain species of mosquito may respond only to the stimuli of a cow and yet not respond to those of a human.

Scientists speculate this behaviour evolved in the Mesozoic era (over sixty-five millions years ago) with

> '...the establishment of regular terrestrial dwellings (nests) by reptiles, birds, and mammals...'[11]

It is suggested by some scientists that the emergence of parental care in birds, mammals and dinosaurs further promoted associations with mosquitoes by providing them well protected and secure habitats. They felt at an advantage in and around nests where the young of the birds were kept. The same applied to the dens of the beasts of the jungle and the habitats of the dinosaurs where they reared their young. This, they suggest, presented opportunities for the mosquitoes to suck the blood of the animals whenever they liked, undisturbed. An amazing suggestion indeed if they mean that this caused the development of the blood-sucking proboscis among female mosquitoes. It can only be taken seriously if it implies that female mosquitoes had already turned into blood-sucking machines before they began to seek easy targets. Either way this conjecture does not serve to provide any methodology which may have been responsible for the evolution of blood-sucking female mosquitoes. It has been observed that if a human host moves within five seconds of the female mosquito landing on it, she will fly off. (See plate 5). Considering the complex chain of instinctive behaviour involved just in the act of locating a host, the chances of an accidental switch to blood feeding seem highly remote.

A female blood-sucking mosquito did not require only some complementary changes in its system for finding blood on a host. It also required suitable instruments for piercing skin and locating vessels, and a transport system for the blood to be carried to its storage reservoir which had to be a sac different from the one to which plant nectars are carried — a staple source of nourishment for all mosquitoes, even for the blood-sucking females who need blood only during specific periods. (See plate 6).

As mentioned before, the scientific literature on the issue of mosquito evolution is largely silent. Scientists discussing the origin of various insects, point out that

> '...some of the better known groups are highly evolved — parasitic forms such as the Culicidae [mosquitoes] — whose evolutionary origins are obscure.'[12]

The cause of this obscurity, they say, is the insufficient fossil record, but that is no justification. They could and should have followed Darwin who studied the living finches of the Galapagos islands and not their fossil record in developing his theory of evolution. Likewise, it should have been possible to analyse the process of mosquito evolution even in the absence of a complete, detailed fossil history. The characteristics of modern mosquitoes as compared to other insects, or of the female mosquito in comparison to the male of the same species, can be studied to determine what steps in evolution must have occurred for the mosquito to have assumed its present form.

Before analyzing the unique characteristics of the mosquito let us very briefly examine the probable scenario for mosquito evolution presently put forth by scientists. They suggest that the mosquito progenitors prior to their feeding on vertebrate blood must have fed on soft-bodied insects. Later on, at some point in their evolutionary history, the adults switched to feeding on vertebrate blood.[13] According to this view, the progenitors' mouthparts had already developed similarities to the finally evolved form of mosquito mouthparts. However, it is known that at the larval stage (analogous to the caterpillar stage of a butterfly's life cycle) these insects do not have dependence or association with vertebrate hosts that would have facilitated an evolution toward a blood requirement. Additionally, if dinosaurs were indeed among the very first mosquito hosts, a serendipitous switch from feeding on soft-bodied insects to a feeding behaviour that involved penetration of dinosaur skin would seem all the more improbable. Scientists themselves admit that this process of evolution would have required 'adaptations leading to a radical switch'[14] from feeding on insects to feeding on blood. The explanation presented by them in support of this theory is a mere conjecture that these progenitors accidentally started feeding on hosts that frequented their damp, recessed habitats. As will be demonstrated below, the process of blood-sucking requires multiple specializations within the mosquito. In light of all of these interdependent adaptations, it is difficult to conceive of an 'accidental' switch in the feeding behaviour of mosquitoes.

It should be remembered that three major aspects of the female mosquito had to be adapted to the specialized task of feeding on vertebrate blood. Feeding on blood requires adaptations of anatomy and form,

> '...such as a development of mouthparts able to penetrate skin; physiological adaptations, such as the proteolytic enzymes for blood digestion; and behavioural adaptations, such as the abilities to find objects that have blood and distinguish them from those that do not.'[15]

All this requires immense scientific knowledge and technical know-how.

The blood-sucking ability of a female mosquito, apart from its inbred system of locating the host and homing in on it, requires a host of other highly specialized precision instruments such as the proboscis. In itself the proboscis of a female mosquito is far more wonderful than the seven wonders of the world. It is a masterpiece of an artifact. The entire digestive system of a mosquito in fact, is to be keenly studied to realize that it is no product of the blind forces that model and shape the evolution of life. Returning to the proboscis, even a cursory examination of its construction should be sufficient to dispel the notion that it could have been constructed by natural selection, working patiently at it for over a million or so years. In adult females a proboscis, which is the apparatus for piercing and sucking blood, consists of six elongated parts enclosed in a flexible sheath.

The six include mandibles for cutting through the host's skin. They are blade-like tips which are enclosed within the proboscis and are protruded to its tip only when the mosquito requires a blood meal. Only then are they protruded through the outer tube to make a sharp surgical incision.

THE MOUTHPARTS OF A FEMALE MOSQUITO

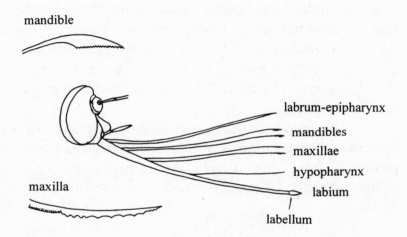

mandible

labrum-epipharynx

mandibles

maxillae

hypopharynx

maxilla

labium

labellum

Then there is the labrum-epipharynx which during the act of biting, becomes a complete tube called the food canal through which blood is drawn. Whenever the mosquito bites, its saliva is transferred to the wound through the hypopharynx.

There is also a pump to suck and transport the blood into a sort of stomach and to channel the plant nectars separately to the gut.

Expert naturalists maintain that by the selective action of the Cardia, a thickened portion at the anterior end of the mid-gut, blood is admitted directly into the mid-gut. The remaining food such as vegetative juices are led into the diverticula and held there for a while.

The unique salivary glands embedded in the proboscis present a wonder not to be witnessed elsewhere in the entire animal kingdom. But for these glands the entire blood-sucking exercise of a mosquito would have come to naught. In the saliva produced by them is a rare chemical of anticoagulant qualities. Typically, when a blood vessel is ruptured, platelets in the blood rush within a few seconds to start the process of clotting to close the leak. In order to make possible the process of feeding on blood, the female mosquito has within its saliva an enzyme known as apyrase. Apyrase is rare in animal tissues, but the mosquito salivary glands are rich in this enzyme. This chemical counteracts the fast acting chemical response in blood that leads to platelet coagulation.

Even more amazing is the fact that the digestive system of the mosquito and its blood stream is completely protected from this singularly dangerous enzyme. It is utilized exactly where it is needed — just at the point of incision.

Yet it is present in the saliva which is extensively used by a mosquito when it dissolves dried-up plant juice or nectar to render it suckable. It is said that almost a continuous stream of saliva flows from the mouth of a mosquito to facilitate this task, yet apyrase in the saliva is not utilized at all because there is no blood in the juices. All this unutilized apyrase is digested by the mosquito without doing any harm to its own blood circulation. Anyone can see from this that it is not just a game of chance creation on which natural selection is dependent, it is a case of wilful design. The entire negative role that the mosquito plays in the animal kingdom depends just on this factor. If the spitting of saliva containing apyrase into the host bloodstream was not made intuitively essential for female mosquitoes, the immense negative role of spreading disease worldwide among a variety of animals could not be made possible. The entire anatomy of the mosquito seems purpose-built to achieve that objective.

Of the five hundred or so viruses so far known to scientists, almost half that number are found in mosquitoes and about one hundred of them are responsible for spreading disease among humans alone. Some mosquitoes are host-specific for other animal species, yet they too carry viruses which may cause diseases which can also be shared by humans. There are some viruses for instance, which transfer from monkeys to man or vice versa by mosquitoes which feed on both. Mosquitoes may not necessarily be carriers of only one virus, they can carry many simultaneously. Again, they can be strong active vectors in one area while in other areas they may remain idle.

Among the major mosquito-conducted diseases which may be universal or regional, malaria leads them all. Then there are other widely known diseases like filariasis, yellow fever, dengue and encephalitis. The damage done to humans alone, over and above the vast damage caused to other animals, is horrendous. Malaria does not always kill directly but prepares the soil for so many dangerous diseases by disturbing the physiological economy of malarial patients.

The largest killer in the world, malaria is not always identified for the deaths it causes. Many malarial deaths are either not registered at all in Third World countries or not identified as malarial deaths. Many malarial patients die of diseases which result from malarial effects like tuberculosis and pneumonia commonly prevalent in malarial districts. Likewise there are many other diseases which actually relate to malaria because it damages the vital organs of the host resulting in a number of different diseases.

Two species of filariasis are widely transmitted by mosquitoes. Prolonged infection by them may cause elephantiasis both among humans and domestic animals.

Yellow fever, another mosquito transmitted disease, comprises both urban and jungle forms of yellow fever. The latter is transferable from animals to humans or humans to animals by the mosquito vector. The horrors which yellow fever has spelled in human history are but common knowledge. West Africa was called the white man's grave, solely for the presence of yellow fever there.

The colossal worldwide damage done by mosquitoes is not limited to the immense loss of human or animal life alone. The adverse influence of mosquitoes on human economy varies widely from a great loss of working hours in offices, factories or fields to a depression in prices of lands because of their nearness to mosquito habitats. Limitations are also imposed on residential areas in many ways. The history of World War II proves that many important battles were lost or won or the progress of war was seriously hampered because of this tiny, apparently insignificant, animal.

Returning to the subject of natural selection having played any role in this grand, yet bizarre scheme of things, we beg the naturalists to readjust their position regarding the factors which evolved and modelled life. It could be an eye-opener for them to concentrate on just one enzyme called apyrase. What mechanism or creative potential of natural selection could manage to produce this enzyme in the saliva of only female mosquitoes to the exclusion of the males? Again, they are respectfully requested to quote one good reason why and how natural selection could compel female mosquitoes to add a blood meal to their customary vegetable diet. Why, again, is it only the female mosquitoes which feed on the blood of hosts while both male and female feed on nectar and other plant sugars as a common source of their survival? Is it not because the female mosquito requires the protein found in the blood of its hosts only in order to synthesize yolk and develop its eggs — a task certainly not needed by the male mosquito? How could natural selection teach only the female members of the species that protein is good for their reproductive organs so they must evolve a most complex system of blood-sucking? Why did the mosquitoes survive long before this female urge to seek more readily available protein from blood? How long did it take the female to bring about all the essential fundamental changes in its anatomy and synthesize the wonder drug apyrase to transfer to a new mode of survival without which it had already survived for hundreds of thousands of years?

The only sensible answer to this question is that it was purposefully designed and could not accidentally be created by natural selection. Evidently, the negative yet essential role which the mosquitoes were designed to play in the scheme of life must have necessitated the mosquito's propensity towards animal blood. The bloodsucking capability of female mosquitoes remarkably illustrates design in the process of evolution.

Evolutionists consider natural selection to somehow invariably take the right decisions and preserve only that which is good for life. Is the mosquito – the greatest threat to life – really the choice and product of natural selection?

According to the Quran, on the other hand, the threat to life created through the mosquito was intended and planned to serve a wide purpose.

The masterly perfection and exquisite implementation of this design has already been discussed above. Now we should like to point out that the Quranic verse on this subject is itself a miracle of literary excellence. Of particular note is the expression *and what is carried above it* (فَمَا فَوْقَهَا) (2:27). It can be translated to indicate the creation of similar living things beyond mosquitoes, but the evident literal meaning of *Fauq* which has eluded translators in the past, is: *and what it — the mosquito — carries.* When the Quran speaks of the Earth and all that it bears, it uses the same word *Fauq* (فَوْق). *Wa Mā fauq-al-Arḍ* means whatever is upon the earth.

Now when one re-translates the verse in question literally, it will read as follows: 'God does not feel shy of quoting the example of a mosquito and whatever is on it or whatever it carries.'

Now we know better why the previous generation of scholars failed to grasp its evident meaning. They had no idea that mosquitoes do carry viruses invisible to the naked eye.

Why God is not embarrassed of creating a disease carrier of such high magnitude is because it was intended and purposefully done to create balances in the grand scheme of life. Also it may be so because the very construction of this fantastic flying machine is in itself a grand tribute to its Creator. We also propose that mosquitoes must have played a most vital role in promoting the immune system in life. One example of this function we already know relates to the sickle-cell anaemia, which largely prevails among the Gambians. The presence of this anaemia creates resistance against even the most deadly forms of malaria. It is not at all unlikely therefore, that apart from some as yet unknown purposes which mosquito related diseases serve in the scheme of life, they may also have served the purpose of promoting and evolving the immune system. That may or may not be so, but the general declaration of the Quran is undeniable that the factors which lead to life and those which lead to death are both integral to the plan of creation.

Another rather strange fact which has to be noted is that mosquitoes carry hundreds of disease sources without ever being inflicted by them. No naturalist can ever recall a mosquito trembling with pre-malarial chills. Nor can he ever locate a mosquito suffering itself from any disease which it carries for others, within its own system, and not upon its feet or wings. The virus of elephantiasis that it carries has never stricken its own proboscis enlarging it to the size of a baby elephant's trunk.

So much scientific knowledge goes into the making of the mosquito and such complex technology is required, that even today man cannot manufacture the mere proboscis of a mosquito. The mosquito can buzz the challenge into the ears of the most sophisticated and adroit modern genetic engineer to come and get him if he may and make him if he can. But, alas, all the mosquitoes in the world cannot bite an atheist enough to stir him out of his atheistic slumber! Let them fly away singing their mosquito songs! The deaf will never hear, the blind shall not see!

TO RECAPITULATE, we again emphasize the characters and features of all animal species which present a systematic unfolding of precisely encoded messages in their cellular genetic symbols. The proteins of the cellular content are the guardian angels of their destiny. The character bearing strands, which make the DNA, RNA, somatic and reproductive cells of all living organisms, are totally independent of the outer environments and their influences upon them. The mindless environment has no mechanism to dictate terms to the genetic custodians of life, and the genetic custodians of life could not have designed themselves nor could they have set the precise sequence of amino acids within them which, if disturbed at any of their links and positioning, would rob the fundamental bricks of life of all their purpose and creative potential. That is why many a scientist has calculated that chance could certainly not have moulded them into shape even if it had worked upon them for trillions of years. Yet they are created somehow, having a world of their own, completely independent of climatic and environmental influences.

If God is removed from this intricate scheme of things, another creator must be found to replace Him. Let alone the mysteries of the inanimate universe, the living wonders which occupy the planet Earth will cry out for the Hand which shaped them and filled their existence with fathomless intricacies. Rule God out and their cries will forever remain unheard and unanswered. Man can only be sure of one thing: that Life did not create itself, and Death did not create Life. Natural selection is neither conscious nor alive. It is no more than a dead phenomenon like gravity. It can pull a rock deep into a ravine without ever realizing whether it fell upon a deer or a porcupine.

REFERENCES

1. Translation of 67:2-5 by the author.
2. Translation of 16:79 by Maulawi Sher Ali.
3. THEODOROU, R., TELFORD, C. (1996) *Polar Bear & Grizzly Bear.* Heinemann Publishers, Oxford.
4. HARPER, D. (1995) *Polar Animals.* Ladybird Books Ltd., Leicestershire.
5. O'TOOLE, C. (1986) *The Encyclopaedia of Insects.* George Allen & Unwin, London, p.134
6. BRISTOWE, W.S. (1958) *The World of Spiders.* Collins, London, pp.70-75
7. Translation of 2:27 by the author.
8. LANE, R.P., CROSSKEY, R.W. (1993) *Medical Insects and Arachnids.* Chapman & Hall, London, p.120
9. DOWNES, W.L., DANLEM, G.A. (1987) *Key to the Evolution of Diptera: Role of Homoptera.* Environmental Entomology: 16:852-853
10. KLOWDEN, M.J. (1995) *Blood, Sex and the Mosquito.* Bioscience: 45:327
11. WAAGE, J.K. (November 1979) *The Evolution of Insect/Vertebrate Associations.* Biological Journal of the Linnean Society: 12:216
12. WAAGE, J.K. (November 1979) *The Evolution of Insect/Vertebrate Associations.* Biological Journal of the Linnean Society: 12:188
13. KLOWDEN, M.J. (1995) *Blood, Sex and the Mosquito.* Bioscience: 45:326
14. WAAGE, J.K. (November 1979) *The Evolution of Insect/Vertebrate Associations.* Biological Journal of the Linnean Society: 12:195
15. KLOWDEN, M.J. (1995) *Blood, Sex and the Mosquito.* Bioscience: 45:327

بِسْمِ اللّٰهِ الرَّحْمٰنِ الرَّحِيْمِ

تَبٰرَكَ الَّذِىْ بِيَدِهِ الْمُلْكُ ۖ

وَهُوَ عَلٰى كُلِّ شَىْءٍ قَدِيْرُ ۙ الَّذِىْ خَلَقَ

الْمَوْتَ وَالْحَيٰوةَ لِيَبْلُوَكُمْ اَيُّكُمْ اَحْسَنُ عَمَلًا ۗ

وَهُوَ الْعَزِيْزُ الْغَفُوْرُ ۙ الَّذِىْ خَلَقَ

سَبْعَ سَمٰوٰتٍ طِبَاقًا ۗ مَا تَرٰى فِىْ

خَلْقِ الرَّحْمٰنِ مِنْ تَفٰوُتٍ ۗ فَارْجِعِ الْبَصَرَ ۙ

هَلْ تَرٰى مِنْ فُطُوْرٍ ۞ ثُمَّ ارْجِعِ الْبَصَرَ

كَرَّتَيْنِ يَنْقَلِبْ اِلَيْكَ الْبَصَرُ خَاسِئًا

وَّهُوَ حَسِيْرُ ۖ الْمُلْك

A GAME OF CHESS
OR A GAME OF CHANCE!

'The Ball no question makes of Ayes and Noes
But Here or There as strikes the Player goes;
And He that toss'd you down into the Field,
He knows about it all — HE knows — HE knows!' [1]

'But helpless Pieces of the Game He plays
Upon this Chequer-board of Night and Days;
Hither and thither moves, and checks, and slays,
And one by one back in the Closet lays.' [2]

VISUALIZE the drama of life and death as staged, act by act, from the beginning of evolution to the present time. As the curtain lifts, does it lift from the vision of a mindless universe endlessly engaged in the casting of dice, or does it lift from a completely different scenario? The drama, it should be noted, remains the same, as also the actors who play their part. The vision alters only in relation to the viewer. If the viewer sees it through the coloured glass of deep-seated, preconceived, atheistic prejudices then of course he will view nothing but chaos wedded to chaos, giving birth to a brood of meticulously shaped and well-disciplined offspring. This happens generation after generation after generation. Each generation invariably recedes yet again into a world of utter chaos, continuously giving birth to order and discipline without exception, without fail. So the drama of evolution moves on from chaos to order without an orderly disciplined mind to command it. Despite this, however, order always emerges out of disorder, until man the masterpiece of evolution is created – the ultimate child of compounded chaos and confusion.

If, on the other hand the viewer is an unbiased observer of what he sees and permits his vision to be led to whichever direction the scheme of creation leads him, then of course the same drama will take on a completely different complexion. At each replication of life into more complex and more organized entities of higher order and at each step forward on the evolutionary journey, he will perceive the guiding hand of the Supreme Creator. If the former scenario can be likened to a game of roulette, the latter perhaps would be more aptly described as a game of chess where every pawn, king, queen, bishop, castle etc., is moved by the hand of a Prime Mover. Evidently the perplexities and the problems that we are discussing can only be resolved if the invisible hand of a Conscious All-Wise Operator is contemplated to be at play. As if an astoundingly vast chequer-board of chess were spread out from end to end over the entire expanse of the globe, over dry land and water, over hills and dales, over highs and lows; such is the vastness of the arena in which countless actors played the drama of the synthesis of life from nothingness. All they had to work on was a state of stark death which prevailed over the entire planet Earth some 4.5 billion years ago.

*W*AS IT REALLY A game of chess being played with a Prime Mover representing order, wisdom, design, foresight, command and patience on the one hand and vast limitless chaos on the other? Or was it a mere game of roulette contested between chaos on the one hand and chaos on the other? An all-encompassing confusion of the grandest scale was locked in a battle of life and death with its opposite number, a vast unruly disorder blowing across the face of earth in every direction from

every direction. There were no rules of the game, no purpose, no set design, yet it was *hoped* without awareness by the mindless cosmos that neither of the giants of chaos would win. Both would end up in mutual destruction or commit suicide in utter frustration, hopelessness, despondency and despair. A grandiose display of hara-kiri indeed! For the proponents of chaos versus chaos giving birth to a child of perfect order, it is here in hara-kiri perhaps that the solution lies. This is the only advanced mathematical absurdity which they can think of to advocate their cause. What homage to the goddess of chaos by her devotees! Evidently if chaos is destroyed at the hand of chaos or through an act of self-demolition, whatever is left is either nothing or order. Hence no dilemma, no riddle, no mystery is left to be resolved. Good riddance!

So far in the previous discussions we have attempted to draw some logically inevitable conclusions. But in the final analysis it is after all no more than the word of an outsider against the word of a constellation of eminent secular scholars. To lend our inferences some additional support, we have decided to bring this subject to a close by quoting some competent scientists who had to confess that the only solution to the problem of creation lies in the admission that there does exist a Supreme Creator. It was He who created options at every creative step and it was He Himself who selected the right option to usher the creation into a higher order of existence. Hence, stage after stage it was He who made choices with purpose, design and direction.

Frank Allen, Professor of Biophysics, University of Manitoba, Canada and recipient of the Tory Gold Medal, Royal Society of Canada writes:

> 'The adjustments of the earth for life are far too numerous to be accounted for by chance.' [3]

What he evidently means is that in the long journey of evolution we find design, order and harmony which cannot be ascribed to chance.

Commenting on the complexity of proteins and the manner in which they play the essential role of building, supporting and advancing life, Allen categorically rejects the idea of attributing this to chance.

Also for a single protein molecule to be formed out of chance would require 10^{248} years! As far as the known span of evolution is concerned, for it to accommodate all the figures as have been mentioned, is as impossible as impossible can be. All the amazing steps of creation only took 4.5 billion years!

Scientists conduct their experiments in precisely controlled laboratory conditions. A chance spillage or leakage would ruin an experiment; the apparatus would have to be reorganized, and the experiment repeated in order to negate the effects of the mistake. A conscious mind has to supervise what is going on and make sure nothing goes wrong by chance.

The conditions prevailing at the time of some of the major stages in evolution were far from favourable. It has in fact been described by John Horgan that:

'... life evolved and survived under unpleasant — and periodically even hellish-circumstances.'[4]

For special favourable conditions to prevail uninterrupted over an exceptionally long period of time is not by itself sufficient to evolve and fix a new character in the evolving species. Time is not a creator; it is just a neutral span, like a vast cauldron, in which any constructive or destructive interaction takes place. If different elements are shoved into a cauldron haphazardly without purpose or design, time by itself, however long, cannot organize ingredients into any meaningful product.

SCIENTISTS who try to simulate the creative phenomenon in nature, in carefully controlled laboratory conditions, fully realize that the whole process has to be precisely monitored and guided step after step to achieve the intended purpose. Yet they are frustrated despite the fact that the entire exercise is pre-planned and consciously masterminded by highly knowledgeable scientists. Leave the laboratory at the mercy of time alone and return to it after a lapse of some fifty or more years and observe the disorder time created and the ruin to which it has led whatever it comprised.

Given time, order turns into chaos if no countermeasures are consciously designed to protect it.

William Krantz, Kevin J. Gleason and Nelson Caine in their article, *Patterned Ground* write:

'Order in nature would appear to be the exception, not the rule. The regularity of the solar system, the complex organization of living things and the lattice of a crystal are all transient patterns in a grand dissolution into chaos. The prevailing theme of the universe is one of increasing entropy. All the more wondrous, then, are the examples of order in nature.'[5]

There are many other scientists who having pondered over the issue of the origin of creation and of life in relation to time and chance, have drawn the inevitable conclusion that there has to be an Omniscient, Omnipotent, Omnipresent Supreme Intelligence to design, organize and govern creative phenomena. Without Him, the beginning of creation and evolution of life are mathematically inconceivable.

Horgan in his article *In the Beginning* quotes Crick's observation:

'The origin of life appears to be almost a miracle, so many are the conditions which have had to be satisfied to get it going.'[6]

But why 'almost' one may ask, it is indeed a miracle! Horgan goes on to say:

'Some scientists have argued that, given enough time, even apparently miraculous events become possible — such as the spontaneous emergence of a single-cell organism from the random couplings of chemicals.'[7]

But how many chances of random couplings would be needed for the creation of life is the very question which has been answered by Fred Hoyle, the renowned British astronomer, in the following words:

'... such an occurrence is about as likely as the assemblage of a 747 by a tornado whirling through a junkyard.'[7]

Professor Edwin Conklin, an eminent biologist at Princeton University, puts it like this:

'The probability of life originating from accident is comparable to the probability of the Unabridged Dictionary resulting from an explosion in a printing shop.'[8]

Dr Winchester, another great biologist, admitted that:

'. . . after many years of study and work in the fields of science, my faith in God, rather than being shaken, has become much stronger and acquired a firmer foundation than heretofore. Science brings about an insight into the majesty and omnipotence of the Supreme Being which grows stronger with each new discovery.'[9]

The time scale required for evolution, if haphazard blind brainless chance were to be its creator, is so enormously large that it boggles the mind of even the most expert mathematician. No human expression can describe it, no human mind can grasp the immensity of the figures involved.

As mentioned earlier, Allen estimated the time needed for the chance synthesis of the complex proteins to be 10^{248} years. The entire span of evolution however requires a much larger slice of time than the mere production of proteins to which Allen refers.

To help the unfamiliar reader visualize this mathematical concept, we would like to remind him that the total age of the universe since the Big Bang is only eighteen to twenty billion years. No name has been ever invented or will ever be invented to denote the astronomical figure Professor Frank Allen has worked out. Perhaps eternity is the nearest name to it.

To CUT A LONG STORY SHORT, we request the reader to realize that even if the creation of the universe and the subsequent evolution of life had actually started a trillion multiplied by a trillion years ago, it would still be mathematically impossible for evolution to reach the stage of man.

This simply means that both the author of this treatise and the reader who is holding this book in his hand, are neither here nor there. The pen shall never be created nor the hand which holds it. The eye that reads it and the mind that struggles to grasp what the pen has drawn have not even been conceived by the blind creator — chance. Who am I, O reader, and who are you? What is the quarrel about? Let us slump into a restful slumber until that remote time when mindless, sightless chance would have consummated the plan of evolution that it never conceived. For each chance step that it will take in the right direction, it will have to blunder into millions upon millions of steps in the wrong direction. But by that time, alas, entropy would have left nothing of the universe to evolve into anything, nor of the blind creator itself. Chance will cease to play any role whatsoever in the inert state of an all-pervading death. The figure 10^{248} is most certainly larger than the time needed for entropy to finish off everything.

Evidently it takes a very determined person who is otherwise sane to believe in such insanity. Yet many sane, highly intellectual scientists do believe in it. Their case is like that of a religious fanatic, who in ordinary affairs of life appears quite normal, but when it comes to matters of faith and belief, shuts himself off completely from the light of rationality and common sense into a cocoon of mindless prejudice. It is amazing how the human mind is capable of withdrawing itself into a midsummer night's dream in broad daylight. Perhaps it is more realistic to say that he continues to live in two different worlds of reality and fantasy simultaneously. Only death can liberate man from his bondage to a life of make-believe.

REFERENCES

1. HERON-ALLEN, E. (1899) *Edward Fitzgeralds Rubâiyāt of 'Omar Khayyām*. H.S. Nicholas Ltd., London, p.104

2. HERON-ALLEN, E. (1899) *Edward Fitzgeralds Rubâiyāt of 'Omar Khayyām*. H.S. Nicholas Ltd., London, p.102

3. ALLEN, F. (1968). *The Origin of The World — By Chance or Design?* In: The Evidence of God in An Expanding Universe, by Monsma, J.C. Thomas Samuel Publishers, Bombay, p.20

4. HORGAN, J. (February, 1991) *In the Beginning*. Scientific American: p.121

5. KRANTZ, W.B., GLEASON, K.J., CAINE, N. (1988) *Patterned Ground*. Scientific American: p.68

6. HORGAN, J. (February, 1991) *In the Beginning*. Scientific American: p.125

7. HORGAN, J. (February, 1991) *In the Beginning*. Scientific American: p.118

8. KORNTELD, E.C. (1968) *God — Alpha and Omega*. In: The Evidence of God in An Expanding Universe, by Monsma, J.C. Thomas Samuel Publishers, Bombay, p.174

9. WINCHESTER, A.M. (1968) *Science Undergirded my Faith*. In: The Evidence of God in An Expanding Universe, by Monsma, J.C. Thomas Samuel Publishers, Bombay, p.165

THE FUTURE OF LIFE ON EARTH

DOES MAN represent the final stage of development or will there be another creation after man? Is there any possibility of a new species evolving from Homo sapiens with improved or added senses, that is able to perceive new dimensions with the capacity to develop a higher intelligence? Again, could it be possible for that new species to appear in a completely different form and shape with an entirely new life pattern? To the best of our knowledge, these questions have not been examined as such by any religion other than Islam.

For the philosophers or scholars of previous ages, this was entirely beyond the scope of their intellect. Even modern science can only discuss this issue in a vague way. No serious methodology within a scholastic framework has been developed to examine these possibilities.

It is an amazing distinction of the Holy Quran that it raises and resolves such questions and predicts such possibilities. The issue of life after death is different, discussed traditionally by almost all major religions. None, however, has even hypothetically examined the possibility of other forms of life here on earth evolving before or after Doomsday.

Having said that, we beg to remind the reader that although other scriptures also share the description of Doomsday, the Quranic terminology is much wider and varied in its application. There are many prophecies in the Quran regarding some epoch-making future events like great revolutions and upheavals. All these are referred to by the same term *Al-Qiyāmah* (الْقِيَامَة), or its synonym *Al-sā'ah* (اَلسَّاعَة). All the same, these terms also cover that

which is commonly understood by the expression
'Doomsday' which indicates the coming to an end of the
entire mankind. It is this meaning which is shared by the
other scriptures when they speak of Doomsday.

But although the term 'Doomsday' is generally
interpreted by the adherents of these religions to be the be-
all and end-all of the universe, the Holy Quran does not
employ the term entirely in the same sense. The earth
according to it, is a small part of the vast universe. A great
upheaval of gigantic global dimension can create vast
destruction, wiping out all life from the face of the earth.
Yet, it does not imply that the entire earth itself will be
completely annihilated nor can it result in the total
annihilation of the entire universe.

BEFORE PROCEEDING FURTHER, let us give an outline of
what is to come in this chapter in relation to the
future of man here on earth, or elsewhere in the
otherworldly existence, according to the Quranic teachings.
There are some verses which speak of events to take place
in this world, beyond the occurrence of Doomsday. These
mention the changing of man's form into something
different after death as he is raised into a new life. Then
there are verses distinctly apart from them which speak of a
future beyond Doomsday, but not in the Hereafter. They
clearly present the scenario of continuous evolution here on
earth, resulting in the creation of a species belonging to an
order higher than man. This latter concept is not to be
confused with, or linked to the former, i.e. resurrection after
death.

Let us begin with the study of the verses relating to
the Hereafter, other than those which discuss the possibility
of a completely new form of intellectual life here on earth.
Addressing those who are sceptical to the idea of life after
death, the Quran reminds them that they should be more

sceptical of their own existence here on earth than their life after death. One thing which they most certainly know is that they came from nowhere. It was non-existence which preceded them. Having been created from nothing, why should they doubt that they may be created again from something which they now are. The proposition of their being re-born out of what they are today, is evidently far more logical than the proposition of their materializing out of nothing. This is the import of many verses of the Quran on the subject of man's scepticism regarding life after death, but it is merely like the opening of a door for further investigation. In itself, it is never meant to be an argument to prove the existence of life in the hereafter: it is only meant to disprove the justification of scepticism. The Quran further reminds man that the high level of consciousness which he has gained should have been a source of light for him rather than that of darkness. His awareness of his surroundings and what lies beyond should have convinced him of the existence of his Creator to whom he raises his head in defiance instead. Yet if he believes in Him his denial of the hereafter could have sprung merely from his amazement – it is far too wonderful to be true. In reality however, his first creation is far more amazing and unbelievable than his second creation.

TURNING TO A DEDUCTIVE ARGUMENT, the Quran first lays its foundation by declaring that no direct witnessing of the hereafter is possible for humans on earth. Beyond the end of his life, from man's vantage point, nothing can be seen but utter void and emptiness. Look at the wisdom of man: he believes himself to be born out of this total void and does not raise an eyebrow in incredulity. Yet, when he is told that he will rise again after death, he refuses to accept this suggestion as absolutely absurd and senseless. The comparison is so powerful that it does not require a great philosopher to comprehend the strength of this argument.

No better witness therefore, than man himself, can be brought to testify against his own denial. The Holy Quran in dealing with this subject first builds precisely and accurately, the viewpoints of the disbelievers in the clearest terms, then it turns to their rebuttal. The following are some of the relevant verses:

وَقَالُوا مَا هِيَ اِلَّا حَيَاتُنَا الدُّنْيَا نَمُوتُ وَنَحْيَا وَمَا يُـــهْلِكُنَا اِلَّا
الدَّهْرُ وَمَا لَهُمْ بِذَٰلِكَ مِنْ عِلْمٍ اِنْ هُمْ اِلَّا يَظُنُّونَ * 45:25

And they say, 'There is nothing but this our present life; we die and we live *here*; and nothing but Time destroys us.' But they have no knowledge of that; they do but conjecture.[1]

اَيَعِدُكُمْ اَنَّكُمْ اِذَا مِتُّمْ وَكُنْتُمْ تُرَابًا وَّعِظَامًا اَنَّكُمْ مُّخْرَجُــونَ *
هَيْهَاتَ هَيْهَاتَ لِمَا تُوعَدُونَ * اِنْ هِيَ اِلَّا حَيَــاتُنَا الــــدُّنْيَا
نَمُوتُ وَنَحْيَا وَمَا نَحْنُ بِمَبْعُوثِينَ* 23:36-38

Does he promise you that when you are dead and have become dust and bones, you will be brought forth *again*?
Far, far *from truth* is that which you are promised.
There is no life other than our present life; we were lifeless and *now* we live, but we shall not be raised up again.[2]

وَيَقُولُ الْاِنْسَانُ ءَاِذَا مَا مِتُّ لَسَوْفَ اُخْرَجُ حَـيًّا* 19:67

And says man, 'What! When I am dead, shall I be brought forth alive?'[3]

وَأَقْسَمُوا بِاللهِ جَهْدَ أَيْمَانِهِمْ لَا يَبْعَثُ اللهُ مَنْ يَّمُوتُ بَلَى وَعْدًا عَلَيْهِ حَقًّا وَّلَكِنَّ أَكْثَرَ النَّاسِ لَا يَعْلَمُونَ لِيُبَيِّنَ لَهُمُ الَّذِى يَخْتَلِفُونَ فِيهِ وَلِيَعْلَمَ الَّذِينَ كَفَرُوا أَنَّهُمْ كَانُوا كَاذِبِينَ* 16:39-40

And they swear by Allah their strongest oaths that Allah will not raise up those who die. Nay, *He will certainly raise them up* – a promise *He has made binding on Himself*, but most people know not.
He will raise them up that He may make clear to them that wherein they differed, and that those who disbelieved may know that they were liars.[4]

وَضَرَبَ لَنَا مَثَلًا وَّنَسِىَ خَلْقَهُ قَالَ مَنْ يُّحْيِ الْعِظَامَ وَهِىَ رَمِيمٌ*
36:79

And he coins similitudes for Us and forgets his own creation. He says, 'Who can quicken the bones when they are decayed?'[5]

أَفَعَيِينَا بِالْخَلْقِ الْأَوَّلِ بَلْ هُمْ فِى لَبْسٍ مِّنْ خَلْقٍ جَدِيدٍ* 50:16

Have We then become weary with the first creation? Nay, but they are in confusion about the new creation.[6]

وَكَانُوا يَقُولُونَ أَإِذَا مِتْنَا وَكُنَّا تُرَابًا وَّعِظَامًا ءَ إِنَّا لَمَبْعُوثُونَ*
أَوَ ابَآؤُنَا الْأَوَّلُونَ* 56:48-49

And they were wont to say, 'What! when we are dead and have become dust and bones, shall we indeed be raised again,
'And our fathers of yore too?'[7]

نَحْنُ قَدَّرْنَا بَيْنَكُمُ الْمَوْتَ وَمَا نَحْنُ بِمَسْبُوقِيْنَ * عَلَى اَنْ

نُّبَدِّلَ اَمْثَالَكُمْ وَنُنْشِئَكُمْ فِىْ مَا لَا تَعْلَمُوْنَ * وَلَقَدْ عَلِمْتُمُ

النَّشْأَةَ الْأُوْلَى فَلَوْلَا تَذَكَّرُوْنَ* 56:61-63

We ordained death for you and We shall not be prevented.
From changing your forms altogether and raise you unto something of which you have no knowledge.
And you have certainly learnt as to how you were raised during your first creation, why then do you not contemplate? [8]

Thus the Quran facilitates for man his belief in the hereafter, but that is not all the argument there is to it:

مَا خَلْقُكُمْ وَلَا بَعْثُكُمْ اِلَّا كَنَفْسٍ وَّاحِدَةٍ ط اِنَّ اللهَ سَمِيْعٌ بَصِيْرٌ *
31:29

Your creation and your resurrection are only like *the creation and resurrection of* a single self. Verily Allah is All-Hearing, All-Seeing.[9]

This is the verse which builds the subject further and opens up a new vista for man's understanding of the life after death.

The phenomenon of resurrection is related to the phenomenon of the birth of each individual. If one visualizes the initial embryonic stage of the fusion of the sperm with the ovum and tries to conceive from that vantage point the end product — the birth of a fully developed child, it would seem impossible to believe that it would happen. Imagine the gigantic transformation from that insignificant fertilized egg into the live and kicking wonder of a baby, delivered at the end of nine months. A viewer who has not witnessed this transformation repeatedly could not at all imagine it to have happened just by looking at the first few stages of fused embryonic cells. Life after death is likened to this amazing process — a transformation from almost nothing to a highly developed and organized form of life.

The difference between the origin of man as a mere bio-unit to what he has become, is a fantastic transformation. It is impossible for the rudimentary life forms to envision the future of evolution culminating in man, even if granted the sense to do so. Their awareness of what they are is so insignificant, that it is extremely difficult for humans to refer to it as awareness. This is a profound statement, so short yet so far-reaching, covering the entire span of evolution from end to end. The message given here is that between you as you exist now, and you at the time of resurrection, the difference will be as vast as the difference between the origin of life on earth and you in your present form. The transformation will be colossal. It is impossible for you to comprehend the nature of what you may be raised into after death. Yet, you can in no way escape the inevitable conclusion that your first creation is far more unbelievable than the second one that you reject. Perhaps it will take a billion years or so for the resurrected soul to reach its final perfected form of spiritual evolution. We draw this inference because the resurrection is likened unto the first phase of human creation from nothingness. We know now that it took at least one billion years, if not more, for man to evolve from his first ancestral elementary form of life. Hence, if this phase of his creation is similar to the second phase of his resurrection, it is not unlikely that the similarity may also cover the span of time between the first and the second creation.

To prove the point further the Holy Quran enters a unique style of deductive logic. We do not plan to fully

485

illustrate this point here with reference to the relevant verses because many of them have already been discussed in other chapters. Here we only want to explain the style of this argument. Speaking of some future events of this world at a time when no human could envisage them, the Quran simultaneously begins to speak of the life after death, sometimes in a language which has two concurrent meanings. The prophecies contained in these verses can be read as applicable to here as well as to the Hereafter. When the events of this world, mentioned therein, clearly and irrefutably become realized, the fulfilment of the events of the Hereafter becomes only a matter of time. The same superhuman agency which is proved right with the unfolding of the events of this world must also be trusted concerning that which remains to be fulfilled in matters pertaining to the Hereafter. This is as far as any argument can go regarding the life to come, otherwise it is impossible to prove by any other means before death.

Having discussed the possibility of an evolved form of existence after death, some verses of the Quran clearly depict the appearance of a new form of life here on earth, replacing humans and distinctly different from them.

اَلَمْ تَرَ اَنَّ اللهَ خَلَقَ السَّمٰوٰتِ وَالْاَرْضَ بِالْحَقِّ اِنْ يَّشَاْ يُذْهِبْكُمْ

وَيَاْتِ بِخَلْقٍ جَدِيْدٍ * وَّمَا ذٰلِكَ عَلَى اللهِ بِعَزِيْزٍ * 14:20-21

Seest thou not that Allah created the heavens and the earth in accordance with the requirements of truth (Ḥaq)? If (اِنْ) He so pleases, He can remove you and put in your place a new creation (خَلْق). And that is not *at all* hard for Allah.[10]

These verses simply cannot be applied to the case of life after death. The use of the conditional preposition *in*

(اِنْ) which means *if,* clearly implies that life after death is not intended otherwise this condition would put to doubt the definite existence of the hereafter – while the entire Quran speaks of it as an absolute unconditional reality. The verse under discussion does not speak of replacing man with others like him. It clearly mentions the bringing into being of a new creation, *khalq* (خَلْق) and speaks of the whole of mankind to be changed into a different entity.

The whole universe is built with The Truth, so also is the creation of man — the very summit of creation. Quite distinct from the subject of life after death, the Holy Quran also speaks of a different form here on earth which will supersede humans:

$$نَحْنُ خَلَقْنَٰهُمْ وَشَدَدْنَآ اَسْرَهُمْ ۖ وَاِذَا شِئْنَا بَدَّلْنَآ اَمْثَالَهُمْ$$
$$تَبْدِيلًا ۞ \quad 76:29$$

We created them and strengthened their make; and when We will so decide, We will change their form to something completely different.[11]

And again:

$$فَلَآ اُقْسِمُ بِرَبِّ الْمَشَٰرِقِ وَالْمَغَٰرِبِ اِنَّا لَقَٰدِرُوْنَ ۞ عَلَىٰٓ$$
$$اَنْ نُّبَدِّلَ خَيْرًا مِّنْهُمْ ۙ وَمَا نَحْنُ بِمَسْبُوْقِيْنَ ۞ \quad 70:41-42$$

But nay! I swear by the Lord of the easts and of the wests, that We have the power
To substitute in their place others better than they, and We cannot be frustrated *in Our plans.*[12]

The substitute creation is not mentioned as another nation *qaum* (قَوْم) nor as another generation of humans. The conditional use of *if* implies that *if* man reforms himself and begins to behave properly, he may not necessarily be wiped out as a species to make room for another better one.

Thus, the Quran raises the possibility of more advanced forms of creation developing, with superior sensory faculties or even new senses in addition to our five. Although the Quran does not state that this will definitely happen, yet it affirms God's power to produce such changes as are within His plan. It does not present an idea of blind evolution based on accidental events. This possibility of continuous evolution, as mentioned here, is one of the greatest tributes to the Wisdom and Knowledge of the Quran's Author. It further proves that all that has been attributed to the Quran in the previous chapters concerning the evolution of life must have been true. Otherwise, it could not have mentioned the possibility of man evolving into another species – a subject not discussed in any other secular or religious literature. Such statements could only be made from a platform of absolute knowledge and certainty.

We may not yet completely grasp the possibilities of our continuing evolution or that of a completely new chain of evolution beginning with a fresh start. Our understanding can only reach the periphery of present knowledge and for us it remains a part of the unseen. However, the unknown is constantly being transformed into that which is known or understood. This is the natural process of education. God is the Lord of all that is seen and all that is unseen. Gradually He broadens our horizons so that our vision is constantly enlarged with the coming into view of that which previously lay beyond the curtain of darkness.

REFERENCES

1. Translation of 45:25 by Maulawi Sher Ali.
2. Translation of 23:36-38 by Maulawi Sher Ali.
3. Translation of 19:67 by Maulawi Sher Ali.
4. Translation of 16:39-40 by Maulawi Sher Ali.
5. Translation of 36:79 by Maulawi Sher Ali.
6. Translation of 50:16 by Maulawi Sher Ali.
7. Translation of 56:48-49 by Maulawi Sher Ali.
8. Translation of 56:61-63 by the author.
9. Translation of 31:29 by the author.
10. Translation of 14:20-21 by the author.
11. Translation of 76:29 by the author.
12. Translation of 70:41-42 by Maulawi Sher Ali.
   (Note: the words 'to bring' have been replaced by the words 'to substitute' by the author)

ORGANIC SYSTEMS
AND EVOLUTION

AN ORGAN, in medical terms, is defined as any differentiated part devoted to a specific function. There are many organs in the human body which need to be studied in-depth to determine whether they evolved gradually over a very long period of time, or were created spontaneously in their finished form as some of the clergy believe. They defy the evolutionary theory of Darwin in its specifics, yet, we insist here that they do not defy evolution itself.

It is a complete misunderstanding on the part of the naturalists that the divide between them and the creationists is the real contention. The religious clergy they often allude to is the extremist faction among the Christian scholars who deny evolution at all levels and believe in spontaneity instead. Spontaneity means that each animal was created separately in its finished form with all the organs it contains. This is certainly not the Quranic concept of creation which we have been explaining throughout the book. It is completely different from the creationist's view found among the Christians. As such we should not be misunderstood and confused with the creationist when we discuss the creation and development of organs. One thing, however, is certain about the organic systems that even at their most rudimentary stage, they displayed four things simultaneously:

1.   The creation of an outer component which in itself is entitled to be called an organ.

2.   The creation of a transmission system like nerve cords which carry the information gathered by the outer organ.

3.   The creation of an internal highly complicated recognition system which we refer to as a specific part of the brain. It is designed to receive the information and break it into components and to visualize the central message correctly.

4.   Having done that, the brain centre has to transmit all the gathered information to a great number of other centres in the brain which take care of recording and re-distributing them to similar nerve centres in other parts of the body.

The purposefulness and design in the making of every organ which makes a component of this extremely complex organic system are but evident.

OUR CONTENTION IS that eyes and ears etc. are erroneously described as single organs which can perform a meaningful function by themselves. As single organs they do not mean anything. They only begin to mean something when they are viewed as integral parts of the whole system to which they belong. Again, when minutely examined within their own confines, they reveal that they themselves are sub-systems comprising many smaller organs within them. Thus in their totality they acquire a relative role of sub-systems. Even at the rudimentary stages such organs are split into components which perfectly accord with the above description. The mechanism of sight, for instance, found among animals which existed hundreds of millions of years before humans were born, show the same complexity of well-organized systems. Their visual system also is composed of many organs. By what logic can this be attributed to natural selection or any other Darwinian principle is completely beyond human understanding.

We also intend to present to the reader the example of not just one sort of eye that we are familiar with, but some differently constructed eyes which serve the same purpose of connecting the outer world with the inner universe of the living. There is no exception to this universal rule. Again, it is our purpose to demonstrate to every sensible reader that in all these cases the structural details could not have been possible without pre-design and without the complete scientific know-how of a designer who conceived them. It should be remembered that each component comprises sub-components which themselves are highly complex and need a lot of explanation with regard to their internal composition and the nature of the material they are made of.

THE TWO MOST VITAL ORGANS which separate the living from the dead are the ears along with the auditory system they belong to, and the eyes as part of the optic system. We begin with the faculty of hearing in sequence as in the following verse of the Holy Quran:

وَاللهُ اَخْرَجَكُمْ مِّنْ بُطُوْنِ اُمَّهَـٰتِـكُمْ لَا تَعْلَمُوْنَ شَيْئًا وَّجَعَلَ
لَكُمُ السَّمْعَ وَالْاَبْصَارَ وَالْاَفْئِدَةَ لَعَلَّكُمْ تَشْكُرُوْنَ * 16:79

And Allah brought you forth from the wombs of your mothers while you knew nothing, and gave you ears and eyes and hearts, that you might be grateful.[1]

The reader should be reminded that the Arabic word (الفُؤَاد) (al-Fuad) which is translated here as *heart* in fact always refers to the final seat of human understanding and not the physical heart. Many verses of the Quran strongly support this contention. For instance,

مَا كَذَبَ الْفُؤَادُ مَا رَاٰى * 53:12

> The heart *of the Prophet* was not untrue to that which he saw.[2]

This verse refers to the vision of God's attributes by Prophet Muhammad[sa]. Evidently the translation 'heart' is a figure of speech which customarily refers to mind because it is not the physical heart which envisions the attributes of God, it is the human mind which does so. With this brief essential remark we return to the preceding discussion and demonstrate the anatomy of the human ear.

THE visible external part of the ear is called the auricle (pinna), slightly differently shaped in different individuals, some having big pinnas and some tiny ones. The purpose remains the same – to enlarge the catchment area of sound waves which are directed towards the outer opening. This makes the beginning of the external auditory canal. It extends into a tube about one inch long lined with skin which secretes some soft wax and is connected with the tympanic membrane (tympanum or the eardrum). Here ends the external ear. The tympanic membrane marks the boundary between the external and the middle ear. The air pressure on both sides is kept equal by means of a special tube, called the eustachian tube, which connects the middle ear cavity and the throat (pharynx). This mechanism is highly essential because it permits the eardrum to vibrate freely in both directions.

The middle ear is a slit-like cavity located between the external auditory canal and the internal ear. It contains air and three ossicles, or small bones, which are connected so that they amplify and transmit sound waves from the tympanic membrane to the inner ear. The three bones in the chain are called the malleus, the incus and the stapes. The American counterpart of this terminology is the hammer, the anvil and the stirrup. The first of these connects with the tympanic membrane and the second is joined to the first and the third ossicle. The third (stapes or stirrup) connects with the membrane of the oval window which in turn vibrates and transmits the vibration to the fluid in the internal ear.

The internal ear is a series of sacs and ducts which together perform the function of hearing and balance. This is the most complicated part of the whole ear comprising three separate spaces hollowed out inside the temporal bone. These spaces make up the bony labyrinth, comprising the vestibule, the cochlea and the semicircular canals, all filled with a fluid called perilymph. The membranes are lined with nerve endings extremely sensitive to the movement of fluid. In the fluid of the bony semicircular canals are the membranous canals which contain another fluid called endolymph. In a similar fashion, a membranous cochlea is situated in the perilymph of the bony cochlea and it is also filled with endolymph. The sound waves cause the tympanic membrane to vibrate as they strike it. These vibrations are enormously amplified by the ossicles and transmitted by them to the perilymph. The perilymph conducts them through the membrane to the endolymph. The waves of the endolymph are transmitted to tiny hair-like receptors which are stimulated and conduct nerve impulses through the nerve fibres to the brain centre (cerebrum).

The function of balance is performed by the three loop shaped tubes of the semicircular canals which lie at right angles to one another in three different planes. The fluid within them rocks when the head is turned, even slightly, in any of the three planes. The signals are constantly transmitted to the cerebrum through nerves and are interpreted there. By this interpretation we learn which way we are positioned and in which direction our position is changing. Right, left, front, back, above and below are all precisely covered. The slightest change in one direction to another is recorded and a corresponding awareness is created in the brain.[3] A sketch of the ear is presented in plate 7 to help the reader to visualize what has been described above.

We have briefly outlined the shape and the functions of parts of the ear. This description could be further elaborated with reference to the cells and tissues which constitute the parts and their internal complexities. Whatever we have described is quite sufficient to prove the point that the outer ear is an organ which defies all evolutionary theory for its gradual sequenced construction, slowly and bit by bit. Each part of this organ is essential for hearing, which if diseased, can either damage or render it completely out of order. We invite the attention of all who depend entirely on Darwinian principles as causative and commanding factors of evolution and request them to explain how such a perfect artifact of science and technology could have been created step by step in a billion or even a trillion years under the influence of the said principles. Can scientists, with all their advanced knowledge of the mechanisms of life, physics or advanced chemistry, design even the structure of this organ to make hearing possible? Now that they know the complexities of the hollowed temporal bone through which this labyrinth passes, can they copy and reconstruct it with a suitable material which they have synthesized themselves? Could they honestly believe that such a wonder could have ever been created without a purpose and without a functional design, precise to its minutest detail, merely under the mindless influence of natural selection? The greater the time span taken by the blind forces of nature to create such a wonder as the human ear, the more impossible it becomes to organize, bit by bit, its constituent parts into a meaningful sequence. There has to be a conscious operator with perfect knowledge of natural laws which could be pressed into service to create a human ear.

BUT the outer organ we have discussed is not the only problem blind evolutionists will have to face and resolve. Now let us return to the nerve cords which transmit the pulses received by the ear. The making of these nerves in itself is an impossible task without there consciously being a design. Suitable material for their making has also to be synthesized and the electrical currents have to be provided to them in a precisely controlled manner. The nerve coatings have to be prepared from a special material which should insulate each nerve from its outer surroundings and protect it from the danger of short circuiting. This nerve must be attached in the right place to the inner ear while the other end needs to be connected to the precise spot in the cerebrum for it to deliver even the minutest vibrations, which when read together by the cerebrum make a complete message. We do not intend to explain the cerebrum itself, a task which lies beyond the scope of even the most knowledgeable scientists. The complexities of how it is made, how it performs all its functions and how it precisely transmits a meaningful message, which it has itself deciphered in the language of pulses, transmitted to the whole of the brain and further to the entire living body is impossible to have happened by itself. How the memory of that message is separately stored and preserved in the relevant receptacles, which may run into billions, and how the instant a particular message is required to be brought to the surface of our awareness, it is suddenly done without any apparent delay is yet another impossibility to have happened without having been specifically designed. For each such message to be brought back to the awareness requires an efficient computer far greater and more complex than any computer so far built by humans.

Let us visualize some moment of our childhood when we laughed at a sound created by an animal or a human around us. It is quite possible that even seventy years later we hear a similar sound and it tickles the stored up sounds of seventy years ago instantaneously and makes us smile again. This system of similar sounds is so minutely and precisely designed that it baffles the most advanced experts who excel in the science of acoustics. Can any devotee of Darwin ever believe that all these complexities of the hearing system could have been created by the blind hand of natural selection? But we are not talking simply of their separate individual creation. The most exasperating part of this exercise relates to their simultaneous coordinated development, completely independent, yet most perfectly corresponding with each other. As the outer ear began to grow, at that very moment, by chance, a nerve must have started to grow by itself and by the same forces their counterpart in the plane must also have begun to be shaped. Each totally unaware of each other, each totally incapable of designing itself, each having no purpose or design, yet each serving a grand scheme and collective purpose. This is the multiple dilemma we face, which relates only to a single organ or a combination of organs, each of which is essential for the sense of hearing.

What we promised, however, was not only to discuss the human ear and its complex organic system but also to discuss some other ears in the animal kingdom whose complexities are fathomless. Some of these still pose a challenge to the specialists to design on their drawing boards such animal ears with the same singular faculties.

LET US BEGIN WITH THE OWL, the symbol of wisdom in the West and that of utter stupidity in the East. Wise he may be but even the wisest among them could not have designed any auditory system let alone his own, and the most exquisite functional mechanism of his ears. To highlight its unique features we advise the reader to compare it with the human auditory system. The human ear, as in most animals, is divided into two receptacles. In most animals of advanced species they are similar and serve the same purpose. The information collected by both ears is harmonized by the brain as single sound yet it informs us with regard to the direction and location of the sound. Those who are hard of hearing in one ear always find it difficult to locate a sound. The separate placing of the two ears in itself pays great homage to their designer. But the naturalists refuse the existence of any design pertaining to this most masterly product of acoustic engineering. Yet if one suggests that this was neither wilfully designed nor created but must have happened under the influence of a non-creative mindless principle, how happily they would break into a smile and say *yes, now you have got the point!* Could a wise owl's smile be essentially different from theirs at such moments? But here we do not intend to elaborate this point further.

The ears of the owl are not only in line with an overall complicated design but they also stand out among all animal ears. The right and left outer ears in an owl are directed slightly differently in bearing to each other. This difference in their orientation is so well-measured and precisely designed as to serve a specific purpose. The slightest random variation in this intricate design could have rendered them useless. The sounds they emit to the internal ear are transmitted to the brain which deciphers them perfectly despite their complexity. The whole system

The ears of the owl are not only in line with an overall complicated design but they also stand out among all animal ears. The right and left outer ears in an owl are directed slightly differently in bearing to each other.

is so unique and precise in its intricacies as enables the owl to hunt for its prey in absolute darkness without ever making a mistake.

Intrigued by this uncanny ability of the owl, the scientific community of the world has performed the fantastic task of exactly defining the owl's hearing system with the most sophisticated electronic devices. To our knowledge the greatest work on this was carried out by Masakazu Konishi, Bing Professor of Behavioural Biology at the California Institute of Technology and his colleagues. Their work was published in *Scientific American*, April 1993.[4] Although we bank largely on this article for the following information our brief description does not do justice to the great intricate work. Anyone interested in more scientific and mathematical data would be amply rewarded by reading that great scholarly thesis.

The unique auditory mechanism enables the owl to detect the feeblest sound emitted by the flutter of a mouse beneath fallen leaves in the dead of night. He knows

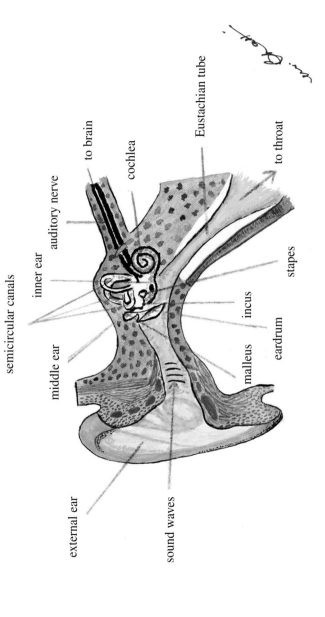

semicircular canals

to brain

auditory nerve

cochlea

inner ear

Eustachian tube

middle ear

stapes

incus

malleus

to throat

eardrum

external ear

sound waves

Plate 7. The human ear.

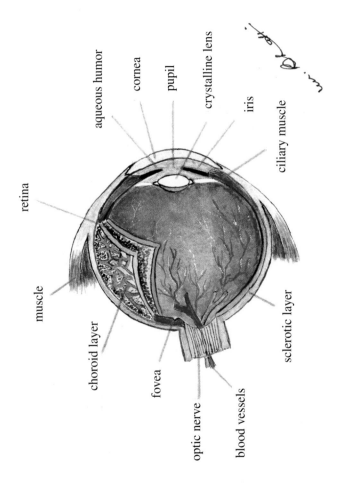

aqueous humor

cornea

pupil

crystalline lens

iris

ciliary muscle

retina

muscle

choroid layer

fovea

sclerotic layer

optic nerve

blood vessels

Plate 8. The human eye.

Because of the twist in the owl's ears, the owl can measure the exact distance between it and the prey. In total darkness, the owl can swoop down on the prey, picking it up without disturbing the soil underneath.

I.16

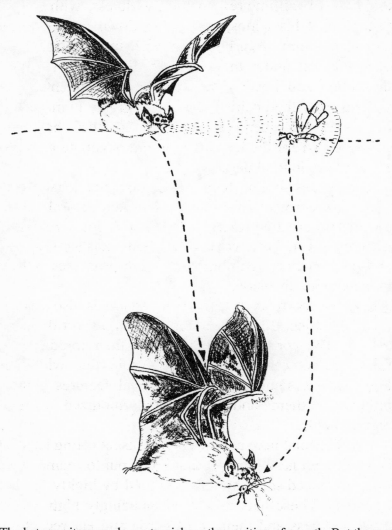

The bat uses its sonar beam to pick up the position of a moth. But the moth has its own defence mechanism and makes a weak sonar image. It abruptly changes its path to avoid attack but the bat anticipating the moth's evasive action moves into position and catches the moth.

I.17

exactly how far, in which direction, and at what spot the mouse is hiding. He correctly reads the distance down to the scale of millimetres. In total darkness, with soundless fluttering of his wings, he swoops down upon the mouse and scoops him up in his claws with such precision as not even the soil under the mouse is disturbed. Who shaped these ears and how? Can even the most talented plastic surgeon alter the position and shape of any human ear of a blind person, ever so slightly, so that he can be compensated for his loss of sight and negotiate as freely as an owl does in total darkness?

Blind evolution, they tell us however, chanced upon such a masterpiece of craftsmanship and natural selection, playing no creative role, just selected it for survival. How naturalists can keep calm over their exasperating beliefs and contradictory realities of creative processes is beyond human comprehension.

THE ANATOMY OF THE EAR OF THE BAT is also a complex subject difficult to compress in a short description. The constructional detail of their middle ear and their internal ear, though generally in line with that of humans, has some specific additional features which are unique to them and perfectly harmonized with their requirements.

Of special note are the ears of insect eating bats. Their sonar system is so intricate that it can put to shame even the most advanced sonar system designed by highly competent scientists. These bats can fly at amazingly high speeds in pitch darkness and their vocal cords and ear receptors are perfectly harmonized to the environment. An insect eating bat can chuckle at staggeringly fast speeds at such high pitch that if a perfect protective system had not been devised, the sounds it emits could damage its own ears. This problem is resolved by the creation of the stapedius muscle in the middle ear attached to three tiny bones, the malleus, the incus and the stapes, which are responsible for transmitting the sound waves to the internal ear. At each click the bat emits, this muscle pulls aside the stapes which touches the eardrum; hence, no sound of the click is directly transmitted to the internal ear. The frequency of clicks and such momentary breaks of contact is a make and break system which never fails despite its high frequency. Such bats are known to emit these sounds more than 200 times per second and this muscle can keep pace with these rapid variations. Yet when the sound strikes against a solid object and returns to the ear, the contact of the bone with the drum is immediately renewed so that no echo is ever missed by the bat during the innumerable intervals of disconnection.[5] How it can perform this magic beats comprehension. Imagine, 200 sounds per second with not a ripple transmitted to the internal ear and yet it connects 200 times again in order not to miss a single echo of the returning sound signals. The bat's ear does it in an amazingly complex world of sound and echoes which are delivered in different pitches with different frequencies. Thousands of bats flying in a small chamber in total darkness continue to click at different pitches. The bats do not interfere with each others' signals as if each sound is tagged with a different frequency that is recognized by every bat.

The conscious command of frequency is the most amazing part of the system. The faster the clicks are emitted, the faster information is updated in fractions of seconds, so that bats can negotiate with perfect ease every interfering object, be it another bat or a physical obstruction. They can safely negotiate through innumerable branches in the lush growth of dark forests without striking against any of them. In the bat caves they can manoeuvre

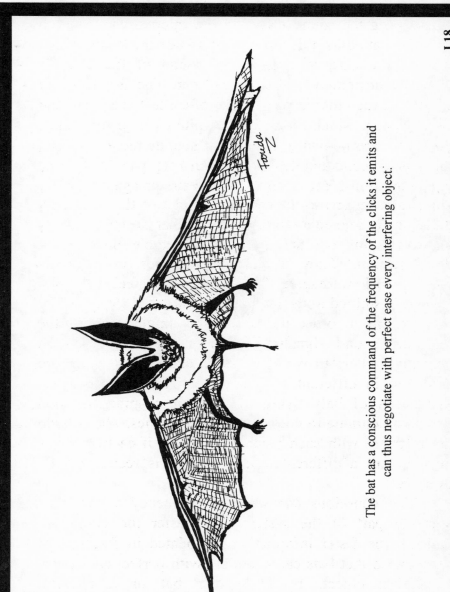

The bat has a conscious command of the frequency of the clicks it emits and can thus negotiate with perfect ease every interfering object.

THE INTERNAL AUDITORY SYSTEM OF THE BAT'S EAR

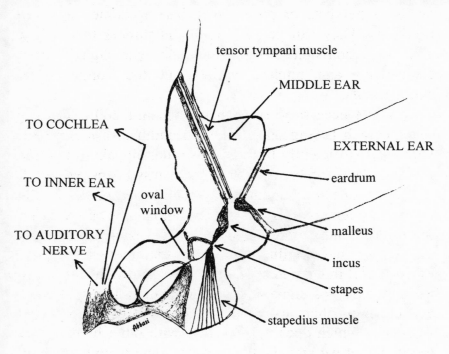

tensor tympani muscle

MIDDLE EAR

TO COCHLEA

EXTERNAL EAR

TO INNER EAR

eardrum

oval
window

TO AUDITORY
NERVE

malleus

incus

stapes

stapedius muscle

I.19

An insect eating bat can chuckle at staggeringly fast speeds at such high pitch that if a perfect protective system had not been devised, the sounds it emits could damage its own ears. This problem is resolved by the creation of the stapedius muscle in the middle ear attached to three tiny bones, the malleus, the incus and the stapes, which are responsible for transmitting the sound waves to the internal ear. At each click the bat emits, this muscle pulls aside the stapes which touches the eardrum; hence, no sound of the click is directly transmitted to the internal ear. The frequency of clicks and such momentary breaks of contact is a make and break system which never fails despite its high frequency. Such bats are known to emit these sounds more than 200 times per second and this muscle can keep pace with these rapid variations. Yet when the sound strikes against a solid object and returns to the ear, the contact of the bone with the drum is immediately rehabilitated so that no echo is ever missed by the bat during the innumerable intervals of disconnection.

their flight in accordance with the contours, or rocks and their undulating surfaces. They never strike their heads against other bats or protrusions, barring some very rare accidents. They can perceive a thread thinner than a hair and avoid collision. All this is done with signals, their frequencies and pitches, entirely at the command of acoustic bats.

When necessary, some bats can emit 200 clicks per second, each lasting only one thousandth of a second but kept apart sufficiently from other similar signals so that the internal make and break system constantly keeps pace with it. Within one thousandth of a second the contact of the bone, the counterpart of ossicles in humans, is broken from the eardrum and before the signal arrives back as echo it is made again, never failing within this extremely short space of time.[5] All this is intentional. The bat knows how to raise the frequency of signals, fully commanding their pitches and changing them exactly, as needed. It can choose the frequency which does not interfere with other hundreds of thousands of bat signals. One really wonders how the hand of natural selection could have shaped the ears, the throats and the brains of the bats with such profound precision and such complete harmony. If a man happens to be there, the clicks may not be heard by him at all. Most of them are at a pitch which cannot be heard by human ears. All this profusion of sound signals if audible to man would explode his eardrums, yet luckily, all that he perceives is perfect silence in a jungle full of bats.

The disuse of eyes over a very long period of time has a shrivelling effect, like a human limb when it is not used for years is rendered useless. Prolonged effect of disuse will always continue to shrivel an organ until it becomes smaller and smaller, and may finally become obliterated. This phenomenon is common to life and spares nothing. Thus the eyes of the insect eating bats are also reduced to such a miniature size as to appear like mere holes to an observer. The fruit eating bats however have large beautiful eyes which can see, discern and locate. Returning to the construction of the bat's ear, over and above what we have said about the complexity of the human ear, the extra muscle which works as a most precise make and break machine offers an unanswerable challenge to the evolutionists. Remove the specific function of the tiny muscle, which it performs only in the case of bats, and the whole hearing system of the insect eating bats would become totally ineffective. How could natural selection have played any role in the creation and selection of that muscle? Its precise construction and location can certainly not be attributed to it. The only part natural selection could have played was to wait until random and mutational changes had created so many possible variations of this muscle from which it could finally choose. But it is impossible to visualize that this specific muscle with its specific functions could have been created by the random creative forces of life at work, without design, perfect know-how and precise technology. Made-to-measure precise instruments such as these are created to perform specific tasks in specific contexts and cannot be dismissed as random.

INCIDENTALLY, there is another similar example from among the birds which is also singular and precisely tailor-made. It saves the animal from the ill effects of its own functional ability — an ability unique in the entire animal kingdom.

The beak of the woodpecker rapidly strikes at such points upon the trunks of trees where it locates the presence of worms by acutely listening to their crawling movements. It begins to strike so rapidly that hundreds of strikes are

THE WOODPECKER

The system is exceptional and unique which protects the brain of the woodpecker from being damaged by the impact of the extremely powerful shock waves produced by the rapid striking of its beak.

I.20

THE DOLPHIN

The bulge at the front of the dolphin's head contains a fat-packed melon which acts as a fantastic sonar navigation system. There are also special passages and sinuses in its head that powerfully compresses a current of air which strikes against the top of its head.

I.21

powerfully made in a second which scare the worms out of their hideout for the woodpecker to scoop them up with its long elastic tongue. It is so fast that humans cannot distinguish between different strikes which appear to them as a single blur. That functional availability is exceptional among birds. More exceptional and unique is the system which protects the brain of the woodpecker from being damaged by the impact of extremely powerful shock waves produced by the striking beak.

Between the beak and the brain there is a separating impact absorbing tissue which prevents the shock waves reaching the brain directly. No other bird can strike at such a rate and no other bird is provided with such a protective device. This is another example of how animals are protected against the possible harm of their own specialized functional abilities. We wonder if any naturalist could suggest any random methodology to explain how natural selection could have chanced upon this.

Let us now return to the main topic of discussion on the ear, sound waves and sonar devices. From the birds of darkness in the air let us delve deep to the bottom of the muddy seas and rivers such as the Indus, the Ganges and the Amazon and see how animals confronting such murky habitats can shift and negotiate.

DOLPHINS are provided with a fantastic sonar device which they employ to their advantage both in the open seas and thick muddy bottoms of oceans and rivers. The thick stagnant mud would not permit them to see what lies even a few inches in front of them. What they need is not merely their eyes but a complete sonar system with which all dolphins are equipped. This system is so complex and interdependent as requires a special study. Special passages and sinuses are created in its head through which it most powerfully compresses a current of air which strikes against the top. There happens to be on the forehead of these dolphins a large fat-packed, oval shaped organ called a melon. The compressed air, when it strikes against the melon, activates it to initiate a strange incomprehensible phenomenon. That lump of fat immediately turns into a fantastic sonar station. It works like a sound lens that emits a sonic searchlight which can move ahead uninterrupted by the turbid waters or mud.

The dolphin can emit 700 such sonar signals per second which are echoed back when they strike against any solid object. The echoes are perfectly calculated by the dolphin's brain to indicate to it the exact distance between the dolphin and the object, and also the precise nature of that obstruction. It can perceive a small metallic object at some distance and know exactly whether it is filled or empty. It can distinguish between living and non-living objects. The dolphin employs the same device in the open seas to detect fish even miles ahead. Aided by the same sonar device, it rapidly homes in on them constantly calculating how close it has reached the shoal before it begins to rapidly swallow them up, one after the other.[6] Could natural selection create this complex sonar system with an exactly corresponding receptive apparatus in the brain which could precisely decipher the echoes? Can any naturalist create a similar bulk of fat to produce a well-directed sonar beam? Whatever modern technology he may employ, let him try his hand at producing even a single sonar wave from such a fatty bulk. Yet a dolphin's melon can somehow produce 700 such waves per second.

The great brainwave of Darwin, which the naturalists believed solved the riddle of life, could only produce three dead principles: struggle for existence, survival of the fittest and natural selection to carve and modulate life. The naturalists prefer to forget that all these three principles are dead, deaf, dumb and sightless. They are not creative principles. They only operate when some creator has already produced something for them to work upon. The naturalist has to demonstrate first the creative processes of the dolphin's hearing system, only then can they talk of what natural selection might have done to them. We only demand from them not to confuse the two issues of natural selection and creative factors. How and which creative processes were at work in the case of the dolphin, or the bat for that matter, and how did they gradually begin to develop these systems to perfection? How did Darwinian principles aid the anonymous creator at each creative step before they were finally consummated into their present form?

Now, we shall move on to discuss the faculty of sight and commence with a brief overview of the human eye.

THE EYE, as we shall demonstrate, is a very delicate and intricate organ. As such it is carefully and naturally protected. The dorsal part, or the back half of the eyeball, is protected by the skull bones while the eyelids and eyelashes aid in protecting the anterior part, or the front half of the eye.

A sac separates the anterior part of the eye from the eyeball itself and is lined with an epithelial membrane which aids in the destruction of some pathogenic bacteria that may enter from the outside.

Should any small foreign object enter the lid area the natural defence system is immediately activated. Swift eyelid movement and tears released by the tear glands, containing an antibacterial enzyme, try to wash it away. These tears then drain away into tear ducts located in the lower corners of the sockets and leading to the nasal cavity. The eyeball itself rests against protective cushions of fat within its socket, and is attached by pairs of muscles

507

extending from the inside of the socket to the eyeball. These are the muscles which move the eye.

The eye (see plate 8) has an almost spherical shape. The wall of the eyeball consists of three layers:

1. The sclera: the outermost layer made of tough white connective tissue, commonly known as the white of the eye. It bulges and is transparent at its front, forming the cornea.

2. The choroid layer: the middle layer made of a delicate network of connective tissue and richly supplied with blood vessels. This layer completely surrounds the eye except for the pupil which is a small opening at the front of the eye, directly behind the cornea. Around the pupil the choroid layer is pigmented, known as the iris, giving eyes their different colours, either brown, blue, green, hazel or a combination of these. It is the pupil which controls the amount of light entering the eye onto the convex crystalline lens attached to the choroid layer by ciliary muscles. These muscles, when they contract, allow the eye to focus on objects whether they are near or far. The aqueous humor is a watery fluid filling the area between the cornea and the lens and helps to maintain the forward curve of the cornea. Behind the lens, the entire space is filled with a thicker transparent substance, the vitreous humor, which is necessary to keep the eyeball firm and in its spherical shape.[7]

3. The retina: the innermost and perceptive layer *less than a millimetre thick*. It includes some 10 different layers of cells known as the receptors, ganglia and nerve fibres.[8] The receptors, better referred to as photoreceptors, are of two types: cones and rods. There are about 130 million rod cells for black and white vision and only 7 million cone cells for colour vision in

the human eye.[9] Cones are conical in shape. The light which is focused on the retina stimulates the cones and rods. The cones perform the major function of splitting the light into various colours. If defective, the person would become colour-blind. During the full light of day the cones are sufficient to perform all the functions of sight. Rods are rendered useless yet they have their own importance in dim or night vision. In dim light, or total darkness, it is the rods which perform the function of vision but they can only differentiate between black and white. Cones cannot work at all under such conditions. During very dim light, colours become faded or totally disappear. When a person moves from a brightly lit place to a dark room the time he takes to begin to see things again is the time taken by the rods to become fully reactivated. The cones and rods transfer their stimulation to the ganglia which are situated near the front of the retina. When stimulated, they start impulses which stimulate the ganglia in front. From the ganglia more than half a million nerve fibres carry the impulses to a large cranial nerve called the optic nerve. The spot where the optic nerve joins the retina is called the blind spot because there are no cones and rods there.

FROM THE BACK of each eyeball, separate optic nerves take up the function of transmission of sight to the occipital lobe of the cerebrum which make the centre of vision. This centre is divided into two lobes, one for each eye. Some of the optic fibres cross from the right eyeball to the left, and from the left to the right. Thus what one sees with each eye is interpreted in both lobes.[10] The image formed by the retina is inverted but the centre of vision re-erects it. The centre of vision performs other fantastic things as well. The image is in fact very tiny but is enlarged

509

to life-size and what we see enlarged is sometimes a hundred thousand times or billions of times greater than the original image. Cast a glance towards the stars. The vision of vast space which fills the tiny spot in the brain is many trillions of times greater than the original image cast on the retina. This act of wonder is performed not by the organ, the eyeball alone, but by the entire visual system of the three major organs involved. However, the grandest display of resultant imagery is performed by the centre of vision in the brain.

The retina also does some other wondrous things. It works as a film that captures visions, washes them instantly and new visions replace the previous ones; a task which is impossible to be performed by man-made films and videotapes. Far more amazing things are done by the centre of vision. It immediately preserves the image in life-size somewhere in the intricate filing system of the brain. Billions of such images can be recorded and preserved during the lifetime of a person. A man with a healthy mind can, in an instant, invoke an image cast during his early childhood with the same colour, environment and lifelike size. Again, the stimuli which are related to a particular image, however remote they may have been in time, are also invoked with the resurrection of the image. Thus, the brain makes the third organ of the organic system of sight.

PROFOUND scientific research has been made on the fear stimuli in various animals and their effect on the receptive organ of sound and vision referred to as the brain. They have discovered that the imprint of fear on the relevant brain tissue, whether caused by sound or sight, is permanent. Its response can be subdued or erased by psychiatric or medical treatment but the image itself remains permanent. The whole optic system frustrates all attempts by the modern scientists to fully understand it. No man-made optic or auditory system comprising the three organs we have discussed can ever match the intricacies of these amazing coordinating machines. This should have been the area of the naturalists research to discover which forces play a creative harmonious role. That is what they do not attempt, perhaps because evidently the fingers of these composite systems would be raised in the direction of God and not in the direction of Darwin. We are talking here of internal biology and mechanisms of life, not of the external forces which blindly operate and have nothing to do with the mechanisms just described.

As we have suggested in this book before, the beginning of vision does not begin with the creation of eyes. It is a composite sense of awareness which grows in an animal resulting in organic development. Recent, intense scientifically controlled tests have been carried out in the dark underwater world, hundreds of metres below the sea surface and the research is being extended beyond to the sea bed several kilometres below. At around 200 metres, light practically disappears. During this probe, it was discovered that the dark underworld of oceans presents some completely eyeless animals who show reaction to the weak glimmer of light emitted by phosphorescent animals. This discovery was made with the help of a highly advanced electronic machine called the Ventana. It carries no pilot and is remotely controlled via cables which also guarantees a constant supply of electricity to the Ventana. The same cables carry the information back to the scientists sitting in the ships above, closely watching the experiment day and night. A fascinating report of this experiment was published in *Scientific American,* July 1995.[11] Among so many other amazing things it shows that Medusa, a jellyfish, possesses no eyes whatsoever yet showed a reaction to the robots' light by sinking deeper. This is exactly what we claimed earlier, that it is the diffused awareness of the living at the lowest level of their existence which is employed by the Creator to give birth to the sensory organs. Every beginning is often a tiny beginning yet it is likely to grow to higher stages of fascinating developments. The next step to this general awareness, as explicitly displayed by Medusae, has to be an eye like a pinhole camera without lenses and this is exactly what we find in nature. But even this pinhole eye cannot be modelled by any Darwinian principle because even at this rudimentary stage it presents a full optic system and not a casual hole. These animals have two pinholes instead of one, converging a mutually coordinated information to a receptacle behind, which in turn passes it on to an inner sense of awareness that can be referred to as a sort of elementary brain. Moreover, the system we observe in humans is also found as fully developed in the optic organs of ancient animals which lived many hundreds of millions of years before. It remarkably reduces the time left at the disposal of blind evolution from the beginning to the creation of such animals. Most insects are found with complete optic systems and some fish fossils in Australia have been dated as five hundred million years old, with holes indicating large eyes.[12] This further reduces the time for bit by bit development of animals' eyes to a mere five hundred million years which is incredibly small for their evolution to take place. Take note that this expanse of five hundred million years has to be divided further into subsections, a portion of which has to be employed for the creation of the bricks of life. However, the entire time available from the beginning to the end of the ultimate consummation of life is in itself far too short – as though it were a mere tiny speck compared to what was needed. The building of the bricks of life alone requires a time unimaginably greater than the entire time spent on evolution, yet that too has to be accommodated within this short period. This is the magnitude of the dilemma the scientists face. Whether to weep at them or to laugh is the dilemma for the rest of the world to resolve.

All eyes, wherever they are found in the animal kingdom, perform a scientific function for which they are perfectly designed. They are completely harmonious with their surroundings. Purposelessness negates the existence of an instrument which performs any function. If even a rudimentary instrument is created before it is put to some function, that function has to be presupposed. This is the simple logic of the realities of life.

Man began to work with stones. These stones were apparently without a purpose but the moment we see them shaped into axes with a handle attached, no sane man can declare that even this rudimentary machine was created by chance without purpose. What life offers is billions of times more complex. Each creation of life serves a purpose and is exactly designed to serve it. To call it a purposeless creative journey is blindness supreme.

REFERENCES

1. Translation of 16:79 by Maulawi Sher Ali.
2. Translation of 53:12 by Maulawi Sher Ali.
3. Anatomy Notes (details not listed).
4. KONISHI, M. (April, 1993) *Listening with Two Ears*. Scientific American, pp.34-41
5. DAWKINS, R. (1996) *The Blind Watchmaker*. Penguin Books Ltd, England, pp.27-29
6. DAWKINS, R. (1996) *The Blind Watchmaker*. Penguin Books Ltd, England, pp.96-97
7. Anatomy Notes (details not listed).
8. OTTO, J.H., TOWLE, A. (1977) *Modern Biology*. Holt, Rinehart and Winston, Publishers. USA, p.592
9. *The Hutchinson Dictionary of Science* (1993) Helicon Publishing Ltd. London, p.224
10. OTTO, J.H., TOWLE, A. (1977) *Modern Biology*. Holt, Rinehart and Winston, Publishers. USA, pp.593-595
11. ROBISON, B.H. (July, 1995) *Light In The Ocean's Midwaters*. Scientific American, pp.51-56
12. LONG, JOHN A. (1995) *The Rise of Fishes 500 million years of Evolution*. University of New South Wales Press, Australia.
    (Also worthy of study are his other works on fishes like *The Rise of Fishes* (1957)).

I.22

*And thy Lord creates
whatever He pleases and selects.*

THE 'BLIND WATCHMAKER'
WHO IS ALSO DEAF AND DUMB

IN KEEPING with the promise made in our introductory remarks we now turn to the book entitled *The Blind Watchmaker*[1] by Richard Dawkins — now Professor Dawkins.

At first it was rather discomforting to read through the said book because Professor Dawkins seems to avoid confronting the real problems of life despite knowing them and admitting their existence. He loses no time in hiding his theories behind a smokescreen of grandiose confusion of his own creation. It is impossible to take up all the points he has made because most of them are irrelevant and unrelated. However, when he writes of real life and the mysteries it possesses, he does so purely as a scientist and does not interfere with realities to gain any ulterior motive. Here Dawkins is at his best. But the problem is that when he is at his best, he is at his worst in relation to the cause of natural selection. No honest treatment of the realities of life can lead to the idea of life having been created with all its complexities without a preceding conscious creator, which natural selection is not. It is to avoid this inevitable logical conclusion that he hastens to escape into an unreal phantom world of his own creation — a land of computer games and biomorphs. Then, he attempts to draw a line between the complexities of man-made machines and the apparent complexities of nature. He attempts to mislead the reader by claiming that the complexities of man-made wonders are real, purposeful and well-designed but the complexities of nature, though they far exceed in the element of wonder they contain, lack purpose and design. He would have the reader believe that it is only his impression that they are complex and pre-designed with a goal to achieve. Here he confuses the mind of the unwary reader by taking him to and fro, from hindsight to foresight, from foresight to hindsight – an amazing attempt at deceit. He would have the world believe that all man-made products are made with foresight, thus they must have purpose, design and complexity which are the work of a conscious mind. When turning to nature, he has to admit that in the products of nature the element of wonder is greater by thousands of factors than in the man-made products. Yet he insists that because we are accustomed to attribute design to human products, our hindsight, when we look at natural products, creates in us an illusion of purpose and design. Thus we are tricked into believing that they too must also have a conscious designer. Evidently, he has no argument to support this illusion theory except his authoritative word for it. On the contrary, whatever illustrations he chooses from real life most powerfully contradict his conclusion and prove the converse.

Take for instance his scholarly work on bats. As we have already discussed bats and some of the wonders related to them, we shall only refer to some of the observations made by Dawkins on this subject and remind him of his promise made on the first page of the preface of his book that:

'...having built up the mystery, my other main aim is to remove it again by explaining the solution.'[2]

Regrettably, this is a promise he does not keep.

To bats he devotes the better part of the chapter *Good Design*. He writes:

'Their brains are delicately tuned packages of miniaturized electronic wizardry, programmed with the elaborate software necessary to decode a world of echoes in real time. Their faces are often distorted into gargoyle shapes that appear hideous to us until we see them for what they are, exquisitely fashioned instruments for beaming ultrasound in desired directions.'[3]

So ably does he sum up the mystery. Further enlarging upon it, he pays the unique compliment to the bat's ability of being a past master on sonar. He states:

'When a little brown bat detects an insect and starts to move in on an interception course, its click rate goes up. Faster than a machine gun, it can reach peak rates of 200 pulses per second as the bat finally closes in on the moving target.'[4]

Having raised the questions,

'If bats are capable of boosting their sampling rates to 200 pulses per second, why don't they keep this up all the time? Since they evidently have a rate control 'knob' on their 'stroboscope', why don't they turn it permanently to maximum, thereby keeping their perception of the world at its most acute, all the time, to meet any emergency?'[4]

he answers, informing the readers,

'One reason is that these high rates are suitable only for near targets. If a pulse follows too hard on the heels of its predecessor it gets mixed up with the echo of its predecessor returning from a distant target.'[5]

He goes on to speak of amazing wonders about the bats' aeronautical and sonar potentials, and concludes by affirming:

'... we can only understand it at a level of artificial instrumentation, and mathematical calculations on paper, we find it hard to imagine a little animal doing it in its head.'[6]

Speaking of the complexities of similar but less complex man-made machines, he observes:

'Of course, a sophisticated conscious brain did the wiring up (or at least designed the wiring diagram), but no conscious brain is involved in the moment-to-moment working of the box.'[7]

'... our experience of technology also prepares us to see the mind of a conscious and purposeful designer in the genesis of sophisticated machinery.'[8]

From here the conclusive absurdity begins because he claims that the designer is the unconscious natural selection, *the blind watchmaker*. Regarding the impossibility of a blind know-nothing Darwinian principle having created the living wonder of the bats' auditory system, he addresses the question:

'How could an organ so complex evolve?'

The answer he gives is:

'This is not an argument, it is simply an affirmation of incredulity.'[9]

If Dawkins is told that the 64 kilobyte computer he claims to have worked upon is not the creation of a conscious mind nor does it have any design whatsoever, will he readily agree with the suggestion? He will certainly not, despite the fact that his elementary computer is far less complicated than a bats' auditory system.

If he refuses to agree with the suggestion that any computer could have been built without a competent conscious designer, he must honestly examine himself to discover the reason for his refusal to believe in a creator of life. The only answer he can find will be that he does so because of the computer's complicated design and orderly construction which could not have happened by itself. Yet when it comes to life, he completely transforms his attitude, as though he had undergone a metamorphosis. Being a biologist he must realize that, as against a computer, life is far more complex. The figure of a trillion raised to the power of a trillion is a mere nothing by comparison. If the enormous complexity of life is an illusion then a computer has a far greater right to be dismissed as one. How can Dawkins forget, even for a moment, that if his verdict is correct, his own mind with all its intricacies must itself be described as an illusion. We do not want to be impolite to him, so let him speak for himself. Which of the two will he choose? Will he prefer his mind to be described as a mere illusion of a disorganized mass of grey cells, or will he rather dismiss his own theories as hallucinations of a healthy mind. However much we may desire, we see no third option for him. If the human mind is an illusion then all its products must also be an illusion multiplied by itself, like a profusion of dreams created by the dreams of a madman, or hallucinations giving birth to hallucinations. The great scholar that he is, with a perfectly organized intellect, we are loathed to refer to his mind as an illusion. It is here that Dawkins begins to display his jugglery with words. Life is not complex, will be his simple answer. It is the illusion of those who behold it to be so. Hence, not being complex, it can be created by itself. To call the complexity of life an illusion and the mechanism of a computer a complexity is tantamount to turning reason upside down. To call the day night, and the night day, is less bereft of sense than Dawkins' somersault. Incredulity is the crux of the matter. Evidently it is incredible for Dawkins to believe the construction of a mere Boeing 747 by itself yet it is not incredible for him that far greater

519

complexities in nature have erupted into being without a creator. To dismiss this dilemma and to hide his prejudice against God he refers to the complexities of nature as illusions of an over-credulous religious people. But before this, he has to dismiss the existence of the builders of the Boeing 747 as an illusion of his own mind. The same arguments he uses against the believers in God can apply with even greater force to him. If a simple computer cannot be justified to have been built by itself, the building of a Boeing 747 becomes far more impossible. Yet Dawkins believes in these impossibilities. He only believes in them because he insists that they present complexity of design which demand the pre-existence of a conscious mind. When it comes to nature, to escape belief in a pre-existing mind, he simply dismisses nature's complexities as an illusion. If the coming into being of a Boeing 747 by itself is incredulous for Dawkins to believe, the creation of life by itself should have been far more impossible. This attitude only exposes his predetermination not to believe in God.

Dawkins has to explain and differentiate between his assertion and that of others who confront him with the type of logic he employs to suit himself. The only argument he builds in his defence comprises the following:

> '... we have no intuitive grasp of the immensities of time available for evolutionary change.'[9]

By this he means that we do possess the intuitive grasp of the changes during the time taken for the building of a Boeing 747. But we can demonstrate that his argument of time is irrelevant. The shortness or longevity of time simply does not apply. In the case of a Boeing 747 he knows that a conscious human mind was at work prior to its construction. That is the only reason why he believes in pre-design and purpose. Hypothetically, it can be proved that time is absolutely irrelevant to his argument. If any part of this machine was discovered from the archives of nature, to have been buried there for half a billion years, would he then believe that time could have shaped it? Most certainly not! He would have to believe in an unknown creator with a conscious mind. Dawkins may extend the time to any impossible number but he cannot himself believe that even the wheel of a Boeing 747 could have been created bit by bit. Life or no life is irrelevant to the issue. Complexity, design and mechanical wonder are the issues involved.

Again to insist that the bat was created by the unconscious blind forces of nature is only an attempt to replace an unknown conscious creator with an unconscious blind principle of Darwinism. Only those scholars can agree with this proposition who, despite their great knowledge and dedication to rationality, set them aside momentarily to escape the reality of God.

The main service Dawkins has done to Darwinism lies in his ingenious device to rebut a common objection against the principle of natural selection which rejects the proposition that natural selection has any role to play in the internal intricate workings of genes. This in fact is the main thrust of his approach to biology. He proposes a completely new idea of the interrelationship between natural selection and genes. He does not deny attributing the role of development and mutative changes to genes at all. He does not apparently claim that these changes are directly subservient to natural selection. All he claims is simply that whatever bodily changes are brought about by genes are governed by natural selection. When natural selection approves of such changes in bodies as are worthy of survival, this approval is also automatically extended to the genes which brought them about. But that is what he has already done with the help of the science of chance. Referring to the possibility of the haemoglobin's creation, merely by factors of chance, he most emphatically declares that it is impossible. On page 45 he further elaborates this improbability. He writes of four chains of amino acids twisted together comprising 146 amino acids in a single haemoglobin cell. From here he starts a rather complicated mathematical calculation and concludes that for a haemoglobin to have been created merely by a game of chance is next to impossible. In his own words:

> 'This is a staggeringly large number. A million is a 1 with 6 noughts after it. A billion (1,000 million) is a 1 with 9 noughts after it. The number we seek, the 'haemoglobin number', is (near enough) a 1 with 190 noughts after it! This is the chance against happening to hit upon haemoglobin by luck. And a haemoglobin molecule has only a **minute fraction of the complexity of a living body.**'[10]

It is an ingenious argument which for him is mainly responsible for solving the riddle of life by the application of Darwinian principles, which evidently it does not. The genes along with the haemoglobin which contain them are in this way dismissed by the above argument as impossible to exist. This is what we have understood from our in-depth study of Dawkins' relevant chapter. In fact, it is this brainwave of his which is largely responsible for influencing the younger generation of natural scientists today. But we shall presently demonstrate that this is only an illusion created by him because the realities of nature do not support his theory.

WE draw the attention of the reader to the fact that approval or disapproval of environmental factors do not in any way alter, command, or influence the activities of genes, despite the fact that the bodies which contain them themselves lie at the mercy of environmental factors.

As we are convinced that this is the most important argument which Dawkins has managed to contrive, we should explain our position more elaborately. In fact we have already discussed the evolutionary processes in our book in a pre-emptive manner so that Darwinian principles cannot be misapplied. We hope that the students of natural science will find this work helpful in their re-evaluation of the concept of evolution. Our approach is radically different from that of other religious and scientific scholars who have specifically written against Darwinism. The present work is based entirely on our study of general scientific literature. Despite the fact that we have not read the books written against Darwinism, how can we claim that our work to be radically different from theirs? It is so because throughout this work we have been taking our guidance from the Holy Quran which they unfortunately could not have done.

Returning to Dawkins' revolutionary approach, it should be remembered that the activities of genes are governed by laws inbred into them by forces unknown to him. Genes work without any reference to environmental changes. When the principle of natural selection approves some bodily features of the living, it still does not command and direct the activities of genes within those bodies. Again when natural selection disapproves of certain bodily features, with reference to their quality of survival in a competitive world, it still has no influence on their genes. This is absolutely evident from the study of evolution from beginning to end. The primitive organisms, like the amoebas and other elementary species of life which followed them on the rising ladder of evolution, were created by cellular activities commanded by genes. All these apparently inadequately equipped organisms and animals have survived the entire span of evolution along with the genes they contain.

Finally, man appeared at the pinnacle of evolution. Between the animal kingdom and man the difference is so vast and varied that no scientist in truth can envision any bit by bit progressive changes which can fill this vastness. We are not talking of simple physical similarities of which Darwin has taken note of. The evolutionists talk of a missing link which may have been a chimpanzee according to some or a gorilla according to others. Of course a tail is missing in some species of apes, but for a tail to be or not to be is not the question. The question is how the great void can be explained between man and animals in their behavioural patterns and mental potentials? Which animal has learnt to read and write, and to express himself in languages as sophisticated as human languages? A comparison between humans and animals in all these fields will show that human potential is many billion times greater than that of the animals. This is a conservative estimate when we turn to the realities. Look at all the libraries of the world and what they contain. Can a scientist show even a tiny library of the most elementary things in the cave of a gorilla or the private home of a chimpanzee? Show us a page authored by either of the two, dearly preserved upon their library shelves and we shall admit that our statement was rather exaggerated. They talk of animal languages of course but they also talk of those languages as expressions not consciously created. They even talk of dolphins mimicking human language, even uttering a word or two, but nowhere in the animal kingdom can they demonstrate such languages as humans have coined with such immense variety.

Perhaps Dawkins' imaginary monkey could write a line of Shakespeare on Dawkins' computer by randomly pressing any keys on the board but the time needed for that chance single sentence of Shakespeare's drama is not only remote, it is impossible. It is incomprehensible why Dawkins should have employed a hypothetical monkey while real monkeys were easily available. He should have employed a real monkey for the task without training him to press the keys. All he should have done was to tie a monkey in the vicinity of the computer. Next morning if he had returned to watch what the computer had produced with the help of that monkey he would be far more likely to see the computer shattered into pieces instead of discovering a single word of Shakespeare. But we know the time is too short. Each day a new computer should have to be bought and left at his disposal, and on the day the monkey breathes his last, the room would have been turned into a junkyard of shattered computers with not a trace of Shakespeare to be found anywhere, not even over the body of the deceased. Still, time may be far too short if measured

by Darwinian standards. But did the apes not exist and evolve for 5-8 million years before man? Is it not enough time for the bit by bit building of a Shakespeare among them? After all, the difference in brain between them and man is just a single, though long, leap.

TURNING to the question of haemoglobin once again, if godhead were to be attributed to anyone other than God, it must have been attributed to haemoglobin and not to the blind, dumb and deaf principle of natural selection. Whatever follows in the making of life up to the creation of the human body – which according to him is far more impossible to be created by chance – must be accredited to haemoglobin and not to Darwinism. Thus Professor Dawkins seems to identify his god, yet denies him. He must admit that haemoglobin is the god of all creation, yet there has to a God of haemoglobin. That god according to him is a fabulous number of chances, a number which certainly does not exist.

The sum total of his argument therefore, is that haemoglobin could not exist because the number of chances needed to create it are impossible. The next logical step for him should have been to explain why haemoglobin exists while it just could not have existed. The only inevitable answer to this dilemma is that its very existence rules out the game of chance being its creator. However, its immense intricacies and complexities of design cry out for another Creator to replace chance. Professor Dawkins has simply no third option. Either he should put his foot in the boat which cannot exist, or in the boat which will willy-nilly carry him to the presence of God the Creator. This is when he may have come nearest to God. But the moment he realizes his unavoidable folly, he immediately flies away from Him in the direction of Darwinism, his pseudo-god, which he knows full well had no hand to play in the creation of haemoglobin. He has no right whatsoever to attribute the cellular wonders created in the human body to Darwinism without first explaining how their creator, the haemoglobin itself, came into being. What factors, other than chance, must have shaped the basic cells of life is the real question he must answer. Hence all his clever contrivances to subjugate genes to environmental factors are absolutely meaningless and as we have shown they are in fact counterproductive. This is the main problem of Professor Dawkins — avoiding the real issues and diverting the attention of the reader to issues that are imaginary.

In the light of this analysis, all his attempts of employing computers and his theory of bit by bit cumulative factors are rendered useless. The shortage of time or its longevity has never been a problem. He himself informs us that the time needed for the cumulative bit by bit creation of even the first bricks of life is trillions into trillions of times greater than the real available time. When he again informs us that the time needed for the creation of living bodies is far greater by comparison, he is left with no right whatsoever to discuss his cumulative bit by bit theories. It is absolutely a sheer waste of his time and that of his readers because what he wants to pack into a mere one billion years – 1 with 9 noughts written on its right side if taken as an American billion, or 1 with 12 noughts as the British write it – could not have been packed by nature in a much larger number of years. In truth, the figure which has to be available for life with its cumulative bit by bit production could be as great as 1 with 1000 noughts written on its right side which in reality amounts to a total denial of existence. The reality of existence must therefore be dismissed by Professor Dawkins as a mere illusion.

THE FINAL ANALYSIS Professor Dawkins has made in his concluding chapter relates to a choice between the belief in a deity and a belief in natural selection. Who is the creator, that is to be identified. Whether he can discover Him or not, he certainly has no right to replace God with natural selection. Natural selection cannot be referred to as a creator, because it does not create but only works on whatever has already been created. It is exasperating to find Professor Dawkins pointing his finger at a mere principle, without a personal identity, to be the deity — a principle which is deaf, dumb and blind, and has no physical or spiritual existence. That most certainly is not the creator. If Professor Dawkins persists in denying the existence of any Creator, while he has no right to replace him with a principle, he once again has only two logical options. Either he should admit that creation exists, yet he has failed to identify the creator; or he should proclaim that there is no Creator yet the creation exists. This would be tantamount to saying that there is the book *The Blind Watchmaker* but there has never been a Professor Dawkins who penned it!

In our previous chapter we have described the anatomy of an eye and the whole optic system. When we read Professor Dawkins' remarks on the creation of the eye, they appeared so trivial and deficient in a sense that we are deeply disappointed. He has depended entirely on his cumulative bit by bit theory to be at work, a theory which we have roundly rejected in accordance with his own admissions. Still we should like to draw his attention to the fact that to treat the eyeball as an independent organ is wrong. It is an interdependent part of a full optic system otherwise it ceases to play any role in the faculty of sight. Just to indulge in the futile exercise of proving that a small percentage of vision is better than no vision at all does not serve any purpose. To prove that vision is possible even without a lens is just as meaningless. We have described the human optic system with scientific details provided by scientists. It is to this system that his bit by bit theory should be attempted to be applied – an exercise which he manages to avoid.

Let him begin for instance with the retina and inform the world how the rods and cones it contains evolved bit by bit and nanometre by nanometre to ultimately begin to recognize colours, light and darkness. Their recognition, if confined to themselves, could not have served any purpose. He should begin to apply his bit by bit theory to all the components of the system which play a collective role in realizing what rods and cones have achieved. A rudimentary weak eye with a mere 1% vision is still a weak eye but half an eye is no eye at all. Retina, rods, cones, the ganglia and the sequence in which they are placed, are essential for conveying the pulses to the brain. Many more such things about their complexities defy the wisdom of Professor Dawkins' theory. We have every right to request Professor Dawkins to suggest how, and for how long, the retina waited for its completion? If cones were not pre-designed with all their amazing potential, if rods were not preconceived with the fascinating scientific know-how which is visible in them, how could they have ever created themselves falling into step with each other in perfect harmony far more exquisitely than the best orchestral symphony ever conceived by man? Even the minutest constituents of this grand organ require an in-depth study in their own right. How they developed slowly and gradually into meaningful components, completely synchronized to become an eyeball, to begin to perform the functions which are bred into them is incomprehensible. These are just a few questions but there are hundreds and hundreds of questions which have to be answered by godless naturalists. The entire eyeball, including all the delicate and complex features it contains has to be explained in the light of his bit by bit theory. The optic system is far more complex and harmonized than any layman can ever understand. Even Professor Dawkins, a great naturalist that he is, is only hovering above its surface. But to cover the surfaces alone is a supreme task. So he has a lot more work to do in the same field. There are so many other illustrations from the sensory systems in animal life, which despite being hundreds of million years remote from us, present the same fundamental structural design. The differences are only peripheral but they too are precisely designed for the specific requirements of the animals which possess them.

ANIMALS other than bats, owls and dolphins are also provided with a highly sophisticated mechanism to hear and see in total darkness. Apart from that, the following are some examples of mechanisms of awareness which in their narrow field far exceed that of humans and man-made machines.

A most fascinating example is that of some snakes which are entirely guided by ultraviolet heat rays providing them with an extremely sensitive awareness, albeit narrowly confined to a specific task. They are fully equipped with the most advanced ultrasonic and infrared devices. A certain species of snakes is provided with an extremely sensitive receptacle between his eyes and nostrils which transmit to it infrared stimuli through an opening like a pinhole camera. This opening – only a few millimetres in size – transmits infrared rays to the receptacle which is so sensitive as it can detect changes in temperature as small as 0.003°C. To such changes the snake can respond as rapidly as within thirty-five milliseconds, a speed which is hundreds of times faster than any similar device made by humans with modern technology.[11]

Cockroaches are so sensitive to vibration that they can detect movements so small that they can only be measured in units appropriate to gauge molecular distances. They can detect movement a mere two thousand times the size of a hydrogen atom.[12] For a mere cockroach to detect a movement so infinitesimally small is absolutely mind-boggling. The human eye can only detect the size of a hydrogen atom if it is enlarged by a factor of approximately 400,000,000,000,000,000,000,000. Any reader who would like to read this figure is reminded that a trillion is only one, with eighteen zeroes on its right side. Anyone who attempts to read this figure is reminded that this would be an exercise in futility.

Scientists have now accomplished the gigantic and most complicated task of mapping and charting the magnetic variations which naturally occur across oceans. Whales employ them for correctly navigating their movements in the sea. So far the scientists have not understood how whales can detect and employ these variations to their advantage. Perhaps Dawkins could explain to them how elementary the solution would become if the Darwinian principle of natural selection could be employed. But the scientists will have to be patient with him because his bit by bit explanation may take as long as a lifetime, yet most probably it will remain as unsatisfactory at the end as it was in the beginning.

A duck-billed platypus is so sensitive to electricity that it can detect field strengths of five hundred millionth of a volt per centimetre – a performance that can outpace by a large margin the most sophisticated electrical devices. For it to detect a mere one thousandth of a volt per centimetre generated by the flick of a shrimp's tail is no problem at all.

Sharks and rays are known to even detect stationary prey as they can detect the electricity made by the preys muscles as it breathes, even if it's hiding in sediments on the ocean floor.[13]

Birds of prey have two circular fovea and a strip in each eye. Its structure and positioning enables it to function as a telephoto lens, magnifying images by an amazing number. Vultures can reach heights of 2000m or more and can survey the land for many kilometres around it for prey – which is often camouflaged![14]

The crustacean Copilia possesses a pair of the most fabulous eyes. It forms an image using its lens, which is scanned by a second mobile lens and retina.

'The retina contains only nine light detectors, but by scanning the image up to ten times each second it is able to build up some kind of picture.'[15]

'The tail of the electric eel contains 10,000 tiny electric organs, arranged in 70 columns, and over half of the fish is given over to electricity production. This allows it to generate an incredible 550 volts. In fact, such voltages can even kill a person.'[16]

WE most respectfully draw the scholarly attention of Dawkins to these realities which are just a few among thousands so far known to the scientists. We beg him not to waste his time and that of the reader by fiddling with childish computer games. Why does he not apply his theories to real life? It would have been far more sensible and convincing if he had taken up the case of all these freaks of nature as mentioned above with reference to their most complex mechanism. He does not have to search for the fossil records or the sequence of living animals which may have preceded them. We spare him that onerous task and require him only to concentrate his attention upon the eight living wonders quoted above and the amazing tasks they perform.

Let him demonstrate to the world how their complicated components and parts were assembled in such a complex sequence. Every step has to be justified with reference to the application of blind Darwinian principles. Having done that he would still have quite a task ahead. Each component would demand a similar treatment because each would be further subdivided into a variety of sub-parts and the material they are made of – each playing a collective and individual role in the making of the finished product.

In the end, the availability and the nature of the material necessary for their making has to be attended to in its own right. Who manufactured that material aimlessly? How was it manufactured without an appropriate factory? Who created that complicated factory with extremely delicate know-how? How did such factories survive uninterrupted and undisturbed in the wide open nature of winds and sea storms? How did that material offer itself at the right moment to be pressed into service? It is a very plain and realistic exercise which Dawkins is requested to perform. He should confront the realities of biological mysteries which are so real yet far more mysterious than any biomorphic world can be. Dawkins will be well-advised to resolve the riddles of life with reference to life itself as it exists. We suggest he should begin this exercise with the electric fish, which we briefly listed as the eighth wonder.

ELECTRIC FISH make use of their electric fields as navigation aids. These fish have an invisible, continuous field of electricity which surrounds the entire fish. On approaching an object, changes occur in its surrounding current which alters its voltage and aids direction. With this amazing navigation system the fish can distinguish between obstacles, predator or prey. As long as it does not confront any object its voltage is in a relaxed state. No extra burden causes any waste of energy. The moment it confronts an object, somehow a signal is sent to its voltmeters to immediately increase its voltage to such a high intensity that it can kill a man, or knock out a horse, in shallow waters.

Dawkins fails to realize that it is impossible for this complex, intricate system to arise from natural selection or the bit by bit development theory that he is so fond of. Does he not stop to think where these bits originate from? How could alien minor changes survive in an organism which has not the facilities to cater for it? A study of electric fishes provides an excellent proof of the existence of a Conscious Creator. Such a Creator must possess a profound knowledge of how electricity is generated and works. We ask where would the first change occur to accommodate the idea of electric currents in water and more intriguingly, how? How do the muscles of the fish, arrayed in series, suddenly become tense, each generating electricity like a highly sophisticated electrical device joining their currents at the ends to a level of very high voltage? Incidentally, this saves every muscle the damage which may have been caused by high voltage electricity if they had been connected in parallel. According to Dawkins:

> 'It is very important that the fish's own body is kept absolutely rigid. The computer in the head couldn't cope with the extra distortions that would be introduced if the fish's body were bending and twisting like an ordinary fish.'[17]

Logic and common sense raise a key question here, that if the fish couldn't cope with the changes then why was it making the change in the first place? However he goes on to add:

'. . . but they have had to pay a price: they have had to give up the normal, highly efficient, fish method of swimming, throwing the whole body into serpentine waves. They have solved the problem by keeping the body stiff as a poker...'[18]

Who 'they' are, who have solved the problem, Dawkins has avoided to mention. Did the fish do it themselves? If not, who did it for them? As we envision the initial making of the electric fish, in accordance with the bit by bit theory, the entire system seems to begin with the portholes.

Dawkins explains:

'The fish has what amounts to a tiny voltmeter monitoring the voltage at each "porthole"... if some obstacle appears in the vicinity, say a rock or an item of food, the lines of current that happen to hit the obstacle will be changed. This will change the voltage at any porthole whose current line is affected, and the appropriate voltmeter will register the fact. So in theory a computer, by comparing the pattern of voltages registered by the voltmeters at all the portholes, could calculate the pattern of obstacles around the fish. **This is apparently what the fish brain does**.'[19]

Why should the fish brain appear to perform this unique feat of electronic engineering? If one is totally convinced that the fish brain has no real wilfully created organization or complexity of design nor has it any capability of conscious operation itself as Dawkins asserts, then to allude to it as a *masterpiece* of electronic engineering is either extreme naivety or an inadvertent attempt to mislead others. In answer to this evident problem he immediately has this to say:

> 'Once again, this doesn't have to mean that the fish are clever mathematicians. They have an apparatus that solves the necessary equations, just as our brains unconsciously solve equations every time we catch a ball.'[19]

Thus, inadvertently, he has added another problem to the one he is already confronted with. Let alone the human brain and how it manages to compute the catching of a ball, turn back to the brain of that fish which unconsciously and automatically resolves a highly complicated mathematical problem. After this admission, we naturally expected him to turn to his cumulative bit by bit theory and show us how it applies to the electric fish he has described. He should have explained how these electrical portholes evolved piecemeal. How the issue of befitting voltage required by every specific situation was resolved, how this most fascinating electrical machine with all its portholes and their precisely controlled voltage automatically evolved, faultlessly following the unconscious bidding of the electric fish, remain the questions unresolved!

Once again, we spare Dawkins the laborious problem of tracing a long line of less competent fish which gradually evolved into this perfect machine. Evidently they have disappeared from the plan of existence. Let them be gone. What he has before him to support his theory of bit by bit construction is this fish, with all its complicated mechanisms which he has to admit excels all similar man-made devices. Dawkins should have leapt upon this opportunity to prove the point that the fish's brain could have created this fish unconsciously, directed only by the

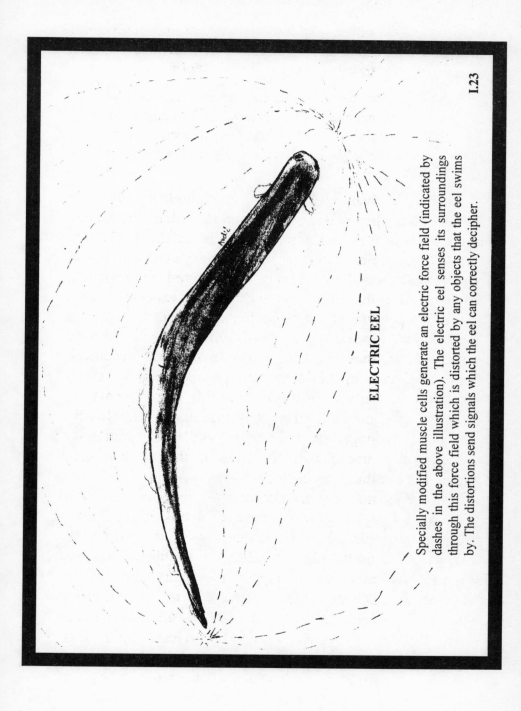

ELECTRIC EEL

Specially modified muscle cells generate an electric force field (indicated by dashes in the above illustration). The electric eel senses its surroundings through this force field which is distorted by any objects that the eel swims by. The distortions send signals which the eel can correctly decipher.

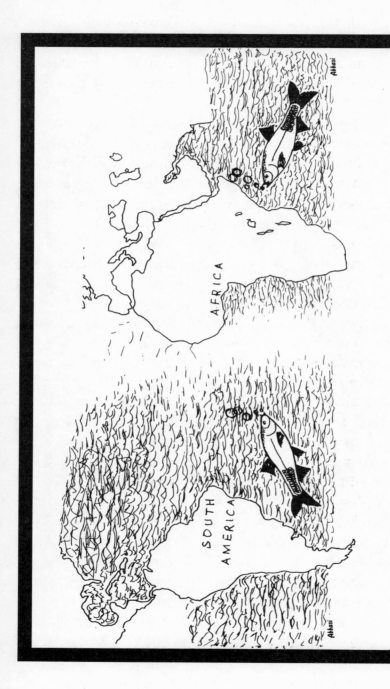

The highly sophisticated electric generator found in both the South American and the African weakly fish is exactly similar. They developed so many miles apart in waters that never met. Neither fish has left any evolutionary trail of how the generator developed bit by bit.

genes it carried. The genes themselves, Dawkins should not forget, are mindless unconscious things. Forget the fish for a while, let him explain how he himself could have devised and constructed such a fish with all the modern scientific know-how at his service!

Visualizing how this highly sophisticated electrical device was constructed in the sea, without purpose, without design and without a knowledge of how electricity works, one is only left with the scenario that one day in the remote past, an ordinary fish might have been surprised with the bizarre chance appearance of some portholes in its belly. All we can do is to sympathize at its exasperation while waiting for this most complicated electronic generative system to evolve into a meaningful device. Some internal disturbance indeed for the fish because as yet it could not have understood any useful purpose for this rigmarole. How long it could have taken in terms of Darwinian time, Dawkins understands better. Then, somewhere else in the body, the voltmeter began to appear with connecting wires to the tiny brain of the fish, and some fantastic physical changes were followed by a new arrangement of each muscle with special alignment and phenomenal qualities. The unknown maker, whoever it was, had thus created a masterpiece of an electric generator. Was it the know-nothing formless mindless principle of natural selection? Was it the brain of the fish which was not even aware of its own functional abilities? Was it the almighty gene which without possessing a conscious brain occupied the command centre to perfectly operate a system which had to be operated by a highly competent scientist?

Dawkins also avoids many other key issues. He provides no clear logical solution for the question as to why two such electric fish species, the South American and African weakly electric fish, are quite unrelated to each other and how both could be developing independently in different geographical locations, with a similar functional design.

He further elaborates this separated yet convergent evolution in the following words,

> 'Electric fish have, at least twice independently, hit upon this ingenious method of navigation...'[20]

and again,

> 'Fascinatingly, the South American electric fish have hit upon almost exactly the same solution as the African ones...'[21]

How these fish unanimously 'hit upon the same idea' is a most intriguing question. Moreover, how could they have hit upon an idea so complicated and problematic which they could not even contemplate, let alone resolve. This would also imply that different animals all over the world are hitting upon ideas to simultaneously develop bit by bit. The polar bear has hit upon the idea of being white in the Arctic whereas the polar bear in Canada hit upon the idea of being brown — all independently! This positively indicates purpose and design. The fact is that fish do not hit upon ideas nor does any other animal for that matter. Though Dawkins himself has provided all the necessary data for proof of a Great Conscious Designer, he fails to make the correct analysis of his hard labour. It is because of his greatly flawed theory that he has resorted to giving up and claiming that:

> 'The physical principle that they exploit – electric fields in water – is even more alien to our consciousness than that of bats and dolphins.'[22]

On this point of wonderment, which he is emphasising, we have made preceding observations previously in this chapter. The purpose of the preceding passage is to prove that Dawkins is definitely wrong in his previous assertions that the living do not present any purpose. All the paths of evolution which he describes, though having no relationship with each other, arrive at the same point of culmination independently. What made them converge to that point while pursuing a completely different and alien journey which had no destination? If different people begin their journey, without purpose and without aim, in directions which they do not choose, how can they meet exactly at the same spot which invariably suits them individually and collectively? Let Dawkins think this over calmly. Let him reconsider his theory of purposelessness in view of the testimony of his own scholarly writings.

HIS LACK OF DESIGN THEORY is also strongly rebutted by the coordinated development of animals and plants. There are thousands of such examples some of which we have already discussed in our book. Here we quote just one such example with reference to Darwin himself. Darwin has discussed the coexistence of many species of animal and vegetative life evolving together complementarily. Worms, insects and birds, on the one hand, go on evolving exactly in accordance with the evolution of plants. The nature and shape of the flowers and fruits on the other hand, remain exactly harmonized with animals which evolve separately. We can quote hundreds of such examples where it is impossible to suggest a blind mutual cooperation of the two entirely governed by natural selection.

Here we refer to the discovery of Madagascan orchid, *Angracecum*. The biologists refer to an episode in relation to this plant which had a star-shaped snow-white flower from which descended a foot long curved tubular structure into the ovarian chamber. Only a half-inch of this chamber was filled with nectar. When it was enquired from Darwin how this plant could have been pollinated, he suggested that there must exist a counterpart of this plant in the form of a moth which should have a corresponding foot long curved proboscis which could reach the nectar along this path. This is exactly what was discovered later on. It paid a tribute to Darwin's genius but not to his principle of natural selection. By the mere operation of natural selection, both the plant and the moth could not have evolved separately, yet together, in perfect harmony.

The question arose as to how this flower could have survived without its reproductive system being operative. If there was a bit by bit evolutionary process involved, why did it begin to evolve into an impossible situation? Why grow an exceptionally long curved tube and hide its nectar beneath it? Why obstruct any bird or insect from reaching the nectar at the bottom for the sake of pollination so that its reproductive organs could be activated? Two separate, yet simultaneous courses of evolution, one occurring in the plant and the other in the animal, are impossible to explain away by the mere factor of chance.

Can Professor Dawkins suggest some solution applicable to the problem quoted above? How did that flower evolve bit by bit simultaneously with the hawk-moth possessing that extraordinary proboscis? Do moths ever have such a long curved proboscis? How many varieties of moths must have been created and destroyed before natural selection could begin its work upon them. Both must have started their beginnings from a most trivial state. They had to remain constantly aware of what was happening on the other side so that they could precisely correspond to each other's shape and design perfectly. They both must have been interlocked into a single entity as though their separate identities as an animal and a vegetable had ceased to exist.

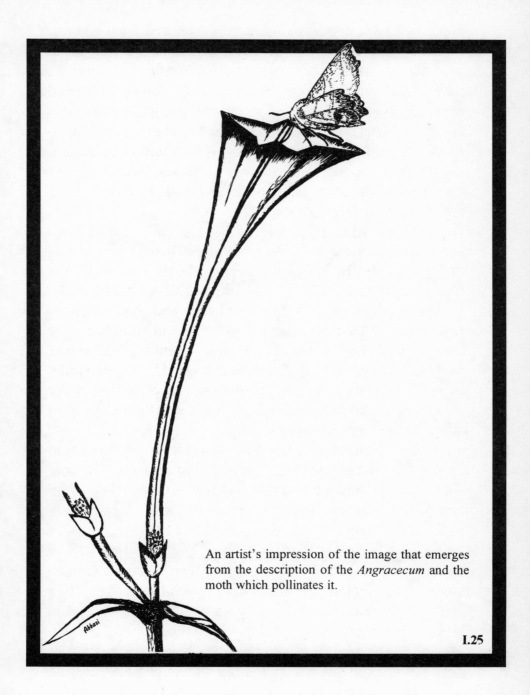

An artist's impression of the image that emerges from the description of the *Angracecum* and the moth which pollinates it.

I.25

The Hummingbird is one of hundreds of examples
created in parallel with the flora on which they flourish.

Having done that, Dawkins is required to throw light on the forces which throughout governed this separate, yet powerful development. What hand of blind selection could have achieved it? At each of millions of little steps they must have separately taken, the number of steps which must have gone wrong would be enormous, in accordance with the mathematics of chance. The blind hand of natural selection had a prodigal task of choosing and rejecting from among them. Yet the ultimate choice of natural selection went absolutely wrong. A flower was created which was almost impossible to be pollinated – a moth evolved which could only survive on the ultimate completion of that particular flower.

Here at least Dawkins must admit that natural selection worked against itself in creating enormous difficulties for the survival of species. The evolution of the two depended entirely on the coordinated moves of the species we have mentioned above. This by itself is impossible without a conscious and an extremely knowledgeable mind to govern it — a mind which natural selection does not possess. Neither of the two parallel evolutions should have survived to reach their culmination if there were no controller guiding their separate steps to remain exactly complimentary to each other. There are many other factors in the grand scheme of things as created by God which are beyond the dominion of natural selection. If those specifically designed factors were not brought into play, and evolution of the living were left entirely at the mercy of natural selection, life would have completely lost its bearing.

The list of the many specific measures taken by God during the evolution of life, which had nothing to do with natural selection, is too long to be reproduced here. One of them, for instance, relates to the extinction of dinosaurs and the profound objective this served in the scheme of creation. Why a massive meteorite should have brought about the end of the age of the dinosaurs precisely at the time when this end was needed? If predesigned by God, as we believe, one purpose it could and did serve was to give other forms of life a chance to develop their evolutionary potentials to the maximum limits, undeterred by dinosaurs. The second highly essential purpose it served, but was understood much later in time, was to bury dinosaurs deep down by the sea shore to gradually convert them to oil, which man of that age would have so direly needed. Such is the work of an All-Knowing Creator. None can attribute this perfect exercise to mere chance. It is impossible for it to have happened accidentally, while now we can clearly read a perfect well-coordinated design in this entire exercise, serving at least two essential purposes in the scheme of things. How on earth could this be the work of natural selection!

HOW WE WISH Dawkins had applied his all-pervasive theory to the real mysteries of nature which he so competently describes instead of the phantom games his mind creates. Incidentally, we draw his attention to figure 5 on page 61 of his book, which he has presented to justify his theory of *accumulating small change*. Each figure shown there, starting with the one resembling a swallowtail, could have at random created any other figure shown in this group of seventeen. This is a deliberate attempt to mislead the innocent computer which is only attuned to his master's voice. What concept of genes was fed into that will ever remain a mystery because the behaviour of genes is unpredictable and they do not work in a two-dimensional world of lines and figures. The world of genes is far more complex than the land of biomorphs where evidently the figures at every generation are doctored by a brain which genes do not possess. Again the figures are concocted by a brain which operated the computer, while it can never claim to know all the intracacies of the world of genes. The childlike figures which his computer has drawn could as well have been sketched by a toddler on a piece of paper, lacking meaning and reality as much as the figures produced by his computer do. Could figures such as these ever be the creation of genes? Genes do not possess minds but the complex work they produce cannot be created by a mindless thing. They work as though they possess the most advanced mind and are capable of implementing their intricate decisions. No comparison whatsoever can be drawn between these computer figures and real living things. But let us suppose for a while that this model is really representative. If so, any figure among the seventeen could give birth to any other figure by cellular development or random mutations of genes.

If such computations as Dawkins has done could be found in nature, a swallowtail could give birth to a 'man in hat', or an extremely surprised 'man in hat' could give birth to a scorpion. A frog could be born out of a spitfire giving birth to a fox which could lay a litter of beautiful lamps, out of which emerge jumping spiders or bats rapidly fluttering away to their caves of darkness. This is how his computer game works in a single plane of straight or twisted lines. Why not start an analytical study of a real man wearing a hat and show us how natural selection could have built such a person, with or without the hat? Why pull a bat out of the hat of his computer images? Why not turn to the bats whom he has so aptly described and begin to show how they could they have evolved bit by bit. There he should have paused and demonstrated how natural selection could have created even the wing of the bat.

Incidentally, talking of wings, we are amazed to read his suggestion that amphibians could have turned into flying birds bit by bit just by flapping their arms. If anyone knows, he should have known that wings cannot be created by the flapping or twisting of arms. Such flapping or twisting could go on for billions of years yet would fail to create a wing.

The anatomy of a flying bird is far more complex. If moving arms up and down could create the internal and anatomical changes which could carve the breast bone of a bird, only then perhaps could we entertain this absurd suggestion. But the entire frame of the light hollow bones which a bird possesses are a prerequisite for the possibility of flight. Again feathers are not born with the up and down physical exercise of arms. They may go on till eternity but not the ghost of a feather would grow out of their movements. We have yet to see a physical trainer with his arms covered with tiny feather-like growth which could bit by bit turn into feathers. A naturalist could object to this suggestion by reminding us that the lifetime of a physical instructor is too short to produce such anatomical changes. He should remember that the class of mammals have been in existence for around three hundred million years. All mammals move their limbs, all try to scale as much height as they can by jumping, but feathers they never grow! Is that a prerogative of amphibians alone? But feathers or no feathers, the amphibians could never have built their internal mechanism into that of even the most rudimentary of birds. We know Darwin has suggested this but his suggestions can never alter the realities of life. Amphibians or no amphibians, Dawkins must project his mind five hundred million years into the past when the entire earth was buzzing with flying insects. How did they develop their wings bit by bit with all the cellular and anatomical features which go into the making of a flying insect?

Turning once again to the computer images of Dawkins, which seem to be so popular with him, he has taken only twenty-nine steps, while for a realistic vision of what happens within the genes and how they work, enormously large number of computations were required. Moreover genes according to his admission have no mind and no computer to work upon — while he has a mind and a computer and the know-how to manipulate the computer to his own advantage. Not only this, he also admits that he selected some specific figures out of every generation of computer images to be re-fed into the computer for creating the next generation. He has also disregarded the important factor that no human can visualize when genes should mutate or should not mutate. No scientist's brain, no matter how clever he might be, can project itself into the cellular universe. Thus any computer model proposed by the most knowledgeable scientist based on his estimation of when and how the genes should spurt into activity, interplaying with a myriad of other internal factors, is fiction not reality.

Enough of computer games! Now we take up the case of the **honey-bee**. How by the application of Darwinian principles could the internal mechanism of the honey-bee have been conceived without a designer with any specific purpose in mind? How genes could have fashioned and created the honey-bee with all its fantastic behavioural wonders is equally incomprehensible. Can any scientist explain how this internal mechanism gradually evolved with all its functional abilities? The way it sees, the way its eyes and vision are modelled in perfect unison with its outer world of flowers and fruits is, in itself, a grave challenge to the naturalists who deny design. What forces, if any, shape them and how could they have slowly unfolded into existence by themselves? That is not all there is to it. The manner it builds its honeycomb and collects material for it also requires a lot of explaining on the part of the naturalists. Just to find material is common to all living animals but to create that material to suit a precise purpose is rare. This is exactly what the honey-bee does.

> 'Flakes of wax are removed by the enlarged first tarsal joint of the hind leg from four paired glands on the underside of the abdomen and passed forward for construction manipulations by the front legs and mandibles ... The wax is mixed with saliva and kneaded to the proper consistency and degree of plasticity at which it can best be molded.'[23]

Why should an insect with a mind which cannot conceive the scientific intricacies of the material world suddenly begin to employ them to its own advantage? Thus a slow, gradual building of the honey-bee's mind as well as its intuitive knowledge of how it should build its dwelling and what material has to be employed, must have been ciphered into it by someone who knew. But there is far more to this than meets the eye. The cells of which the honeycomb is constructed are all hexagonal with walls which meet at exactly 120 degrees.

> 'The comb itself is one of the marvels of animal architecture. It consists of a regular back-to-back array of hexagonal cells, arranged in parallel series, each comb a precise distance from its neighbor.'[24]

Bees display fantastic engineering skills and their building gives the impression that they have been equipped with most sophisticated measuring instruments:

'The precision and strength of the newly built comb is remarkable. For example, cell wall thickness is 0.073 ± 0.002 mm, the angle between adjacent cell walls is an exact 120°, and each comb is generally constructed 0.95 cm from its neighbor.'[25]

Born out of similar eggs, the offspring are divided into three different professional groups; the queens, the workers and the drones. The queen is capable of laying thousands of eggs in a day.

'The aptly named queen reigns over the nest, surrounded by attendants and fed the rich food she requires to perform her few but crucial tasks in the colony. Her slim lines hide the huge ovaries which make her an extraordinary egg-laying machine, capable of laying thousands of eggs a day, and her calm behaviour masks her powerful pheromones, chemical signals to recipient workers which control many of their behaviours and provide part of the social glue which holds honey bee life together.'[26]

The drones who are also specially fed by the worker bees have strong masculine bodies. They only perform one function — mating with the queen, after which they die.

The main body of the colony consists of worker bees who collect pollen and make honey. They also array themselves around the rim, always watchful, always ready to defend the colony. Their functional ability to fly at an instant's notice depends however on their body temperature which must be maintained at 35°C. Temperature is no problem in the centre of the honeycomb which is protected from all sides but at the rim their temperature begins to fall because of the effects of the open air. They counter this problem by fanning their wings from time to time to build frictional energy.

The bees' nest, when built in the hollows of trees or in narrow caves, has a single entrance so air cannot ventilate it and the level of carbon dioxide and other gases in the air cannot be automatically maintained. Carbon dioxide tends to increase in proportion threatening the survival of the bees. To offset this danger, worker honey-bees keep moving, group by group, to the exit and sit there in a position with tails directed outwards. In that position they rapidly fan their wings so that fresh air wafts the stale air out. They do this for 10 seconds and are replaced by another batch of workers if needs be. They repeat the same feat when the temperature rises higher than 35°C. The well-maintained fanning at such times largely succeeds in controlling the temperature. They begin fanning simultaneously and stop simultaneously. In addition to fanning, they haul water instead of nectar into the honeycomb and deposit it around the cells which contain larvae sensitive to heat.

The honey-bees' choice of diet, the way each drop of honey is created from floral nectar, how the saliva must be mixed with it to provide it the viscosity it requires to become honey, is a marvel in itself. With every tiny spot of this mixture on their tongue, they have to stick it out repeatedly to finally mature it. For each drop of honey thus created, they have to make repeated sorties to the field in search of nectar. This goes on day in and day out until they fill the section of the honeycomb which is specifically reserved for this purpose. Somehow they know how to differentiate between ordinary honey and royal jelly which they manufacture entirely for the queen to be fed upon. Royal jelly has that special quality which provides the queen the reproductive energy for the rapid laying of eggs. Each day the queen can lay eggs equal to her body weight which is much more than the body weight of ordinary honey-bees. Again, royal jelly has the uncanny quality of increasing the age of the queen a hundred times longer than that of ordinary bees. The entire colony of some eighty thousand individuals are the queens' subjects. No better discipline can ever be displayed by human monarchies.

Apart from the tasks mentioned above there has to be a surveillance system, with competent workers, to find suitable new sites for the next colony to be built when the old colony is to be abandoned. The surveyor honey-bees who perform this task and the manner in which they do so are to be counted among the greatest wonders of life's behaviour. They span out in search of suitable well-protected sites which should also be close to some rich fields of nectar. Such sites may be situated at different distances from the floral fields and may be comparatively less or better suited for the new colony to be built. Comparing and analyzing all the information brought in by different surveyor bees has somehow to be done by the queen to judge the comparative merits of the site of her next colony. This information is conveyed to the queen by the surveyor bees in a manner which completely defeats comprehension. In fact the whole exercise is unique in the entire animal kingdom. It should have baffled the minds of the most advanced natural scientists as to how this strange communicative system could have come into existence without a designer and an executor. But do they ever ponder over these things, one wonders! Each surveyor when it returns to the colony performs a fantastic dance. Aligning itself in a precise direction it begins to dance and conveys all these messages through that dance and its directional posture to the queen. The information the dance communicates could not be conveyed better or more precisely in human language. It tells the queen what it has seen, where it has seen it, how far it is situated and how far from that site is an adequate floral field. It conveys the distance involved from the colony to the new site and from the new site to the floral field. It also describes the site itself in perfect detail, how well it is protected from natural interference, whether it is a hollow of a tree, a crevice in a rock or a spot on the stem of a tree well-surrounded by protective branches. Each surveyor takes its turn and the queen waits till all have finished. Only then does she decide what to do and takes flight in the exact direction of the site she has chosen. How the transfer is finalized and a new colony is finally built is another fantastic story.

At the end we must mention how honey-bees and honeycombs are hygienically maintained in a manner which puts to shame modern hospitals and clinics. In sharp contrast to the mosquito, the notorious carrier of viruses and germs, the honey-bee was discovered by researchers to carry no viruses or germs on its body. Having been utterly surprised they launched a new research programme to discover why this was so. This revealed an amazing story of how the bees manufacture their own disinfectant material by collecting it from certain resins of plants, now known as propolis. This material has the amazing quality of destroying all bacteria and viruses. The honey-bees having built their combs, paste this material on the rim of the entire comb. Each bee when it returns to the comb, steps first on that rim so that all viruses and bacteria which may have adhered to its tiny feet are destroyed by the propolis before it enters the colony.

We have discussed the honey-bee in some detail here while in the reference to the eight fantastic animals mentioned earlier we did not enter into an elaborate discussion. We have done so mainly because the Holy Quran specifically mentions the honey-bee in a manner which should resolve the riddle of life for naturalists. We have selected the case of the honey-bee for them to ponder and search far and wide to identify the creative forces which modelled them. Of course, the naturalists who specialize in this subject know far more than we do about the honey-bee and its complex world. To be quite honest, we doubt if they could lightly dismiss the case of the honey-bee and the wonders related to it merely to chance.

Let them lay down their arms and admit that there has to be a Creator. In the Holy Quran it is that Creator Who speaks and resolves the mysteries of life once and for all. With reference to the honey-bee the following is the Quranic statement:

وَاَوْحَى رَبُّكَ اِلَى النَّحْلِ اَنِ اتَّخِذِيْ مِنَ الْجِبَالِ بُيُوْتًا وَّمِـنَ الشَّجَرِ وَمِمَّا يَعْرِشُوْنَ * ثُمَّ كُلِيْ مِنْ كُلِّ الثَّمَــرَاتِ فَاسْلُكِيْ سُبُلَ رَبِّكِ ذُلُلًا يَخْرُجُ مِنْ بُطُوْنِهَا شَرَابٌ مُّخْتَلِفٌ اَلْوَانُهُ فِيْـهِ شِفَآءٌ لِّلنَّاسِ اِنَّ فِيْ ذٰلِكَ لَاٰيَةً لِّقَوْمٍ يَّتَفَكَّرُوْنَ * 16:69-70

And thy Lord has inspired the bee, *saying,* 'Make thou houses in the hills and in the trees and in the trellises which they build.
'Then eat of every *kind of* fruit, and follow the ways of thy Lord *that have been* made easy *for thee.*'
There comes forth from their bellies a drink of varying hues. Therein is cure for men. Surely, in that is a Sign for a people who reflect.[27]

Of all the insects which pervade the world, God has picked just this one to demonstrate that when He communicates with an animal belonging to an ordinary species, how its status is lifted beyond comparison to that of the other members of the same species. What is a honey-bee after all, but a fly. Yet what a fly! It is only after the message is delivered to the honey-bee at the earliest stage of its creation and is imprinted in an intuitive language upon its genes that it begins to function as it does. It does not have to perform its functions consciously with a conscious control of its mind. The genes that teach it what to do have no mind of their own. But He who has created them has a mind and the genes simply function as slaves to His command. He has spoken Himself to demonstrate to the world that when He specifically chooses even an insignificant insect, it becomes supreme in the entire world of insects. It becomes a source of healing and cure, unlike other insects which carry and spread disease. They are poles apart in their function of life.

As far as the curative properties of honey are concerned, this is an ongoing research and the researchers who have already discovered some wonderful things about it are expecting far more yet to be revealed. Whatever medical science has identified so far is summed up in the following:

> 'Currently, honey treatment is used for gastrointestinal, some cardiovascular, pulmonary, renal, skin, and neural diseases of the oral cavity, ear, throat, nose inflammatory affection of female genitals, and of the cervix of the uterus.'[28]

One healing quality of honey which British scientists have discovered to their amazement is its ability to cure such eye sores as were otherwise considered incurable. Many a patient has been saved from total blindness by its application.

> 'Patients with ulcerous blepharitis and blepharo-conjunctivitis, under the influence of honey

experienced that the itch and a sensation of sand in the eye disappeared; reddening of conjunctivas reduced or disappeared, ulcers of eye-lids edges, epithelisation of erosions and ulcers reduced in the duration of the treatment. With patients suffering from ray dystrophic processes, as a result of honey treatment, corneal epithelisation improved, photophobia disappeared and sight improved.'[28]

Is there not a message in this for the naturalists to reflect upon? How we wonder, hoping against hope!

To CONCLUDE our discussion, we reaffirm that the naturalists' denial of purpose in the design of the living is only because it would invariably lead to God. They would much rather prefer a deaf, dumb and blind agent to have created everything. They are purposefully deceitful because the blind principles of Darwinism are not creators. These principles only begin to operate when the creation is performed by other hands. They are powerful principles like the laws of physics. Yet all the laws of physics, chemistry and dynamics put together could not have created even a single poor man's shack complete with plumbing, a small kitchen and a toilet. Of course these laws are employed for such construction, but the employer has to be a conscious person with a brain. The brain is the master which employs the laws of nature.

The blind step forward theory can only work in some limited cases and they have to be critically examined to remove the confusion they could cause. The creation of coral islands is just the case in point. The death of each coral, out of trillions upon trillions of them, does not show any purpose. Yet when they pile up one upon the other, maybe in millions of years, the progressive enlargement of their mass ultimately creates coral islands. If we look back at how the process began and was completed, we may allude to it a purpose which apparently it does not possess. One could envisage mountains being built in the middle of the oceans so patiently, bit by bit, over aeons. They do not come to the notice of those living on land until they break to the surface. Then they begin to serve a purpose which we may read into their making when they become coral islands. They serve and support life in so many wonderful ways. This is the case of random bit by bit creation of things in whose creation a preceding purpose is not traceable. It may not have been there at all, yet their usefulness cannot be denied.

The laws of nature run independently if there is no mind to operate them. It is they who operate and govern everything that exists. The living are not exempt from this all-pervasive principle. The absence of a conscious mind to manipulate these laws completely does away with the imaginary line which is said to separate the living from the dead. If the brain of the living cannot design itself and cannot play any conscious role in the making of the body which possesses it, then the living and the dead are governed exactly alike by the same laws of nature. It has to be only these mindless laws which are responsible for the cumulative building of the bricks of life. If they are capable of building the bricks of life, they are far more likely to build a mere Empire State Building through the same cumulative bit by bit process. Yet the naturalists contradict themselves and refuse to believe the bit by bit piling up of the Empire State Building by cumulative random steps, however small tiny and insignificant they may have been. Here they artificially create a divide between the laws of nature at work on dead matter and the laws of nature at work on the living. In reality no such divide should exist if there is no conscious operator of natural laws on either side. Naturalists confess that there is no conscious operator in the case of the living, hence they must admit there is no difference between the living and the dead. All that remain are the free laws of nature, working on the living as well as the dead. If they by themselves could create things as complex as the bricks of life, then for them to create the Empire State Building should have been much less difficult than the building of a molehill by a mole. The only objection, which in fact is no objection at all, may relate to the time available. But the time available to nature at work on the dead is far greater than that available in relation to the evolution of life. Forget for a while the existing Empire State Building because it is a known fact that it was created by a conscious mind. Visualize instead the possibility of hundreds of thousands of far loftier and more complex skyscrapers created merely by the physical laws of nature during the last fifteen billion years or so. Remember that the laws remain exactly the same in the case of the living as well as the dead, and remember that the existence of a conscious mind is ruled out by naturalists in both cases. Hence no divide between the two can exist if sanity must prevail. As such, the bit by bit creation of complexities and order must be evident in both cases alike. Hence any person who believes in the creation of life without a mind preceding it has every hypothetical right to jump to the top of the Empire State Building and pronounce from its loftiness: *this building is the work of trillions of piled up random chances. There is no design and no conscious preceding mind which perceived it. It is only a delusion entertained by some stupid religious people who are over-impressed by the exquisiteness of the finished work.* The same pronouncement should also apply with equal force to the evolutionists who deny purpose and design in the evolution of life. They stand at the pinnacle of evolution where it culminated in man. Looking down from their vantage point, the Empire State Building should have appeared as the tiniest of spots somewhere on the planet Earth. Yet they shout at the top of their voices: *there is no design, no purpose to our creation, we are impossible to exist, yet we appear to exist. All the world is an illusion. You think that we exist and we have the illusion that you also exist. Thus the whole universe is a chain of illusions like those entertained by subjective philosophers. To dispel the illusion of existence, think once again of the haemoglobin number and vanish into nothingness!*

By denying the existence of a Creator who has to be a person with a conscious mind and all the powers to implement His decisions, they try to replace Him with a formless idea. It is this absurdity, to attribute the process of creation or selection to a mindless idea, which is categorically rejected in the following verse of the Holy Quran:

اَلَهُمْ اَرْجُلٌ يَّمْشُوْنَ بِهَآ اَمْ لَهُمْ اَيْدٍ يَّبْطِشُوْنَ بِهَآ اَمْ لَهُمْ اَعْيُـنٌ يُّبْصِرُوْنَ بِهَآ اَمْ لَهُمْ اٰذَانٌ يَّسْمَعُوْنَ بِهَا قُلِ ادْعُوْا شُرَكَآءَكُمْ ثُمَّ كِيْدُوْنِ فَلَا تُنْظِرُوْنِ 7:196 *

Have they feet wherewith they walk, or have they hands wherewith they hold, or have they eyes wherewith they see, or have they ears wherewith they hear? Say, 'Call upon the partners you associate *with God*, then contrive *ye all* against me, and give me no time'.[29]

This Quranic statement is evidently addressed to the idolaters of that age and reminds them that though they believe that their gods are living persons possessing human forms, yet they are mere formless ideas. The statement should have ended here and the question of time should not have been raised as it is raised. The last part of this verse clearly implies that mere ideas cannot create, though they may have as much time as possible at their disposal. God on the other hand is not dependent on any vast expanse of time for His creative faculties. In its entirety, the verse can only apply to the modern idea of natural selection which is claimed to be responsible for the evolution of life provided it is given enough time. The factor of time in the context of natural selection is fundamentally essential. A limbless, armless, mindless vague idea is proposed to work in the frame of an enormous time to suit the theory of bit by bit evolution. Squeeze the time to a mere billion years and the theory immediately begins to crack and fall apart. This leaves no doubt that it is time which is all-important to them in the creative processes of life. This is exactly what the Quran denies in effect when it says: *Formless ideas can have as much time as they may, but God with His creative faculties can create in practically no time.*

This factor of time has only gained importance in the modern age, in relation to Darwinian principles. One may have doubts that this verse was intended to apply to this modern concept but the fact that the whole idea of the verse is so perfectly applicable to it can in no way be denied. Intended or not intended the theory of natural selection could not have been criticized in better words.

Naturalists claim that both the function of creation and the function of selection are performed by forces which are separate yet work in perfect unison. They would have us believe that the mindless genes create, and a formless, impersonal law of natural selection selects. At the same time however, they dismiss the issue of genes as though taken for granted and subjugate them to the authority of natural selection. Thus they unite the two functions which have to be treated as separate, combining them in a most absurd manner. If genes recede into an inconspicuous position as creators, what is left into the bargain is merely a selector which admittedly has no mind with a conscious decision-making faculty. Genes thus pushed aside, natural selection is the only factor which remains in the field. In this sense the separate functions of creation and selection are moulded, without justification, into one. However, no scientist with the slightest idea of what Darwin propounds can attribute to him the claim that natural selection could also directly create. There has to be some creation before natural selection can begin to work. It is this dilemma which the proponents of natural selection can never resolve.

THE HOLY QURAN presents a completely different picture fitting perfectly into the slot of the problem. The Quran declares that the realities of evolution require that the creator and the selector cannot be two separate persons. Whoever creates, it is only He Who can select from His own creative works. What He does not select as the next advanced character is not wiped out of existence but remains to widen the base of His creation at every such level playing a meaningful role in the scheme of things. Thus every time a step forward in evolution is taken, the base of evolution is simultaneously broadened to support what has been added to its rising column.

According to the Quran, man could not have occupied the lofty position he occupies and maintained it without the ecosystem which the lower order of animal life provides. To this the following verse specifically refers:

وَلَوْ يُؤَاخِذُ اللهُ النَّاسَ بِظُلْمِهِمْ مَّا تَرَكَ عَلَيْهَا مِنْ دَآبَّةٍ وَّلٰكِـــنْ يُؤَخِّرُهُمْ اِلٰى أَجَلٍ مُّسَمًّى فَاذَا جَآءَ أَجَلُهُمْ لَا يَسْتَأْخِرُوْنَ سَاعَةً وَّلَا يَسْتَقْدِمُوْنَ * 16:62

And if Allah were to punish men for their wrongdoing, He would not leave thereon any animal, but He gives them respite till an appointed term; and when their term is come, they cannot remain behind a single hour, nor can they go ahead *of it*.[30]

The most significant point to be noted is that it is the entire animal life which would be wiped out if man is to be punished. It is evident that the entire lower order of life serves no purpose other than to maintain the human life above. If that goes, they all go.

Thus the final all-important question which has to be raised and answered by philosophers, scientists and those who believe that natural selection virtually plays both the role of a selector and a creator in the scheme of things, is precisely the following:

They must somehow be combined in the person of the creator and not in that of a selector who cannot create. This is the only logical conclusion which anyone can draw. But this can only lead to God, which the naturalist would struggle hard to avoid. It was to eliminate this inevitable conclusion that Darwin attempted to attribute both these functions to natural selection in an indirect manner. *Did Darwin ever present the idea that natural selection could also create?* To the best of our knowledge, he never did so. He knew, like any intelligent man should have known that the role of selection and that of creation are two separate functions. It would be far more logical if he who performed the function of creation should also have performed the function of selection out of his own creation. This could not suit the blind theory of evolution, hence all the hectic effort to eliminate a conscious creator who could also be the selector. However, it is impossible to conceive a separate plan of selection and a separate plan of creation, both unconscious, yet moving forward hand in hand. Darwin seems to have resolved this problem by suggesting that since natural selection approves the bodies created by genes, so in a manner of speaking, natural selection also acquires the role of a creator in an indirect way.

WE have written elsewhere at length, rejecting the proposition that the products of genes can be accredited to natural selection directly or indirectly. But here we wish to point out that to attribute creative factors to genes and to simultaneously deprive them of conscious know-how is inherently contradictory. It is absurdity supreme to begin the evolutionary journey from genes without resolving the factors which created genes themselves. It is impossible for a proponent of Darwinism to demonstrate how natural selection could have played any role in the creation of genes. How and why genes create without possessing the creative faculties of a conscious mind is the question which should have been addressed first. In a nutshell, a conscious creator of genes has to be identified or it has to be admitted that unconscious genes created themselves as though they were highly competent and conscious creative faculties. It is intriguing to visualize any mindless thing creating itself with masterly dexterity. The naturalists begin their journey without investigating this most essential prerequisite. Their failure to address this question is because it is impossible for them to answer it without disrupting their own evolutionary scheme. The Holy Quran has a straightforward answer to resolve this riddle by declaring:

وَرَبُّكَ يَخْلُقُ مَا يَشَآءُ وَيَخْتَارُ مَا كَانَ لَهُمُ الْخِيَرَةُ سُبْحَـٰنَ اللهِ وَتَعَـٰلَىٰ عَمَّا يُشْرِكُوْنَ*69:28

And thy Lord creates whatever He pleases and selects. It is not for them to select. Glorified be Allah, and far is He above all that they associate.[31]

The main thrust of this verse is that the task of selection is primarily the prerogative of the Creator and the two cannot be separated.

God proclaims Himself to be that Creator Who selects from His own creation. This is how it should be and this is exactly what it is. No naturalist can alter this and replace Him with a mindless Creator of his own choice. In a desperate attempt to do so, they try to combine in natural selection the additional role of a creator. Thus they would much rather believe in a know-nothing mindless principle both as a selector and a creator — lacking consciousness either way. They prefer to be fathered by a mere nothingness.

All they are left with is a mindless, non-personal, deaf, dumb and blind principle which they believe must have created them. Incidentally, this brings to mind the saying: *like father, like son.* They may take pride in this, but we beg to strongly differ. We much rather prefer to be the work of a Creator Who possesses a supreme mind and the power to implement what He designs. We have to believe in Him or we must deny ourselves the faculties of head and heart which we seem to own. If the non-believers have any option to select, it is here they must exercise that option. Which of the two creators will they select for themselves, is a matter for them to decide.

وَرَبُّكَ
يَخْلُقُ مَا يَشَاءُ وَيَخْتَارُ

And thy Lord creates
whatever He pleases and selects.

I.27

REFERENCES

1. DAWKINS, R. (1986) *The Blind Watchmaker*. Penguin Books Ltd, England.

2. DAWKINS, R. (1986) *The Blind Watchmaker*. Penguin Books Ltd, England, p.xiii

3. DAWKINS, R. (1986) *The Blind Watchmaker*. Penguin Books Ltd, England, p.24

4. DAWKINS, R. (1986) *The Blind Watchmaker*. Penguin Books Ltd, England, p.25

5. DAWKINS, R. (1986) *The Blind Watchmaker*. Penguin Books Ltd, England, pp.25-26

6. DAWKINS, R. (1986) *The Blind Watchmaker*. Penguin Books Ltd, England, p.35

7. DAWKINS, R. (1986) *The Blind Watchmaker*. Penguin Books Ltd, England, p.36

8. DAWKINS, R. (1986) *The Blind Watchmaker*. Penguin Books Ltd, England, p.37

9. DAWKINS, R. (1986) *The Blind Watchmaker*. Penguin Books Ltd, England, p.39

10. DAWKINS, R. (1986) *The Blind Watchmaker*. Penguin Books Ltd, England, p.45

11. DOWNER, J. (1988) *Supersense*. Perception In The Animal World. BBC Books, London, pp.12-13

12. DOWNER, J. (1988) *Supersense*. Perception In The Animal World. BBC Books, London, p.16

13. DOWNER, J. (1988) *Supersense*. Perception In The Animal World. BBC Books, London, p.29

14. DOWNER, J. (1988) *Supersense*. Perception In The Animal World. BBC Books, London, pp.48-49

15. DOWNER, J. (1988) *Supersense*. Perception In The Animal World. BBC Books, London, p.64

16. DOWNER, J. (1988) *Supersense*. Perception In The Animal World. BBC Books, London, p.32

17. DAWKINS, R. (1986) *The Blind Watchmaker*. Penguin Books Ltd, England, p.98

18. DAWKINS, R. (1986) *The Blind Watchmaker*. Penguin Books Ltd, England, p.99

19. DAWKINS, R. (1986) *The Blind Watchmaker*. Penguin Books Ltd, England, p.98

20. DAWKINS, R. (1986) *The Blind Watchmaker*. Penguin Books Ltd, England, pp.98-99
21. DAWKINS, R. (1986) *The Blind Watchmaker*. Penguin Books Ltd, England, p.99
22. DAWKINS, R. (1986) *The Blind Watchmaker*. Penguin Books Ltd, England, p.97
23. WINSTON, M.L., (1991) *The Biology of the Honey Bee*. Harvard University Press, London, p.83
24. WINSTON, M.L., (1991) *The Biology of the Honey Bee*. Harvard University Press, London, p.81
25. WINSTON, M.L., (1991) *The Biology of the Honey Bee*. Harvard University Press, London, p.83
26. WINSTON, M.L., (1991) *The Biology of the Honey Bee*. Harvard University Press, London, p.1
27. Translation of 16:69-70 by Maulawi Sher Ali.
28. MOZHERENKOV, V.P., SHUBINA, L.F. (1982) *Use of Honey In Treating Eye Diseases* — Translation of Russian Article: Feldsher Akush.
29. Translation of 7:196 by Maulawi Sher Ali.
30. Translation of 16:62 by the author.
31. Translation of 28:69 by the author.

PART VI

UNVEILING OF THE 'UNSEEN'
BY THE QURAN
— A HISTORIC PERSPECTIVE

HUMAN KNOWLEDGE is surrounded on all sides by a limitless expanse of the 'unseen'. What man knows of his past, present and future is like a tiny spot of light no bigger than the pulsating tail of a firefly hung in the midst of a vast ocean of utter darkness. Although he seems to have extended the horizon of his knowledge to the very edges of the universe with the help of astrophysics and higher mathematics, the factual evidence that has just started to reach him from the edge of the universe is through signals which were emitted around eighteen to twenty billion light years ago. What may have happened there since or what may be happening there now, is only a matter of conjecture.

Let alone the past and the future, even the knowledge of the present lies mostly beyond the scope of human awareness. What does man truly know of the events taking place beyond his house, his street, his township and the country where he resides? All the news media put together cannot convey to him even a billionth of what is going on in the world around him. But that is not all. What does man really know of the people he seems to know among his friends and closest relatives? To penetrate across the human visage and to read what actually lies behind, is sometimes a more difficult exercise than watching the surface of a muddy pond in an attempt to see what hides beneath. In both cases, one merely sees the images reflected on the surface, the difference being that ponds cannot act, they cannot pose, they cannot wilfully create unreal impressions.

Depending on the weather and the day of the year, ponds are almost monotype; humans are not. The complications of human psyche, the vagaries of human moods and conduct, varying standards of morality and personal philosophies, the aptitudes and different qualities of head and heart, the depth or the shallowness of their conduct are some of the innumerable variables which are not shared by ponds. Even what passes within humans themselves lies very often beyond the reach of their own grasp. Yet few among men learn the lesson in humility. Seldom do they realize that the ultimate source of Truth and the fountainhead of Absolute Knowledge can only be the Creator. It is He alone Who knows the secrets of His own creation. It is He alone Who is All-Seeing, All-Knowing, the Great, the Supreme.

Knowledge is the most essential prerequisite of creation, be it Divine or human, great or little. Without an in-depth knowledge of what is intended to be created, no creative objective can be achieved. Hence no one knows the intricacies and complexities of creation like the Creator Himself and this is why Omniscience is a prerogative of God. A perfect all-embracing knowledge of things is termed Omniscience with reference to God to the exclusion of all others.

If it is the same Omniscient, Omnipresent God who authored the Quran, then all Quranic revelations with reference to the past, the present and the future must invariably be affirmed by verified facts when they come to light. It is exactly this that the following exercise is all about. With the help of incontrovertible facts, we strongly hope to prove the case in point.

We have already discussed at some length the role of the Quranic revelation in bringing to light some of the most ancient events of creation. It begins with the beginning of the time when the universe suddenly erupted from a black hole. According to the Quran it only split asunder at the command of an Almighty Creator. The Quranic coverage of the history of creation ends with the end of time when the universe will plunge once again into yet another black hole.

As for the origin of life, the Quranic account is likewise amazingly comprehensive and precise. It covers all the important stages of organic and biotic evolution of 4.5 billion years of evolution's history until the time when it culminated in the creation of man. From that point onwards the Quran takes up the account of human history in relation to the development of society, religion and civilization. It also mentions the possibility of the ultimate extinction of the human species which may be replaced by a better and more highly evolved form of life.

All that we have briefly mentioned above has been elaborately discussed in the relevant chapters of this book, demonstrating how Divine revelation can effectively transfer parts of the unknown into the realm of the known. Now in this chapter we shall demonstrate how the Quran unveils some of the important events of history which lay buried in an obscure past. We shall also demonstrate how it reveals many future events to which no one during the age of Quranic revelations could have had any access. We shall specifically illustrate how the Quran precisely predicts great future scientific achievements of man destined to transform the entire style of human life.

WE BEGIN HERE with the account of an event of great historical importance with a religious significance of common interest to Jews, Christians and Muslims. It relates to the Exodus of Moses[as] and what happened to the pursuing army of Pharaoh and his hosts when Moses[as] and his people had safely waded across the treacherous delta of the Nile.

There are many other examples of the Judaeo-Christian history of the same period covered by the Old Testament, the New Testament and the Holy Quran. But we have carefully selected only the event of the Exodus for the present discussion because it concisely demonstrates the Divine nature of Quranic revelation.

The Biblical account, though it records contemporary history, is evidently shallow and superficial by comparison. From the vantage point of a follower of the camp of Moses[as], the most that he could observe and record was the drowning of Pharaoh and his host, quashed between two mountain-like waves inundating them. What happened to Pharaoh himself before he was drowned? What passed between Pharaoh and God during his drowning moments? What was it he begged of Him, if anything at all, during his dying moments? These are things which lie absolutely beyond the reach of any human observer looking across from the dry shore. Hence, all that the Bible mentions of Pharaoh and his pursuing army is that each of them was drowned without exception.

> 'Then the waters returned and covered the chariots, the horsemen, *and* all the army of Pharaoh that came into the sea after them. Not so much as one of them remained.
> But the children of Israel had walked on dry *land* in the midst of the sea...'[1]

Evidently, according to this Biblical statement, all bodies were claimed by the sea, Pharaoh being no exception. The rout was total. As against this, the following is the statement of the Quran referring to the same event. The difference is so obvious:

وَجَــاوَزْنَا بِبَنِيّ اِسْرَآءِيْلَ الْبَحْرَ فَاَتْبَعَهُمْ فِرْعَوْنُ وَجُنُوْدُهٗ بَغْيًـــا

وَّعَدْوًا ۖ حَتّٰى اِذَآ اَدْرَكَهُ الْغَرَقُ ۙ قَالَ اٰمَنْتُ اَنَّهٗ لَآ اِلٰهَ اِلَّا الَّـــذِيّ

اٰمَنَتْ بِهٖ بَنُوٓا اِسْرَآءِیْلَ وَاَنَا مِنَ الْمُسْلِمِیْنَ * آٰلْئٰنَ وَقَدْ عَصَیْــتَ

قَبْلُ وَكُنْتَ مِنَ الْمُفْسِدِیْنَ * فَالْیَوْمَ نُنَجِّیْكَ بِبَدَنِكَ لِتَكُوْنَ لِمَنْ

خَلْفَكَ اٰیَةً ؕ وَاِنَّ كَثِیْرًا مِّنَ النَّاسِ عَنْ اٰیٰــتِنَا لَغٰفِلُوْنَ * 10:91-93

And We brought the children of Israel across the sea;
and Pharaoh and his hosts pursued them wrongfully
and aggressively, till, when *the calamity of* drowning
overtook him, he said, 'I believe that there is no God
but He in Whom the children of Israel believe, and I
am of those who submit *to Him.*'
What! Now! While thou wast disobedient before *this*
and wast of those who create disorder.
So this day We will save thee in thy body *alone* that
thou mayest be a Sign to those *who come* after thee.
And surely, many of mankind are heedless of Our
Signs.[2]

It should be especially noted here that contrary to this
Quranic statement, the Biblical account does not as much as
hint at the possibility of the retrieval of Pharaoh's body: '…
not so much as one of them remained.'

Hence, till the time the Quran mentions the saving of
Pharaoh's body with the purpose that the posterity may
learn their lesson from it, no human source of history had
ever referred to it.

When the Quran was revealed, the tombs of the
Egyptian kings lay buried deep under layer upon layer of
desert sand. Little was known of the science of
mummification to the people of that age, certainly not to
the Arabs. No books or tradition, religious or otherwise,
had ever hinted at the rescue of Pharaoh's body let alone
mention its subsequent preservation. This account of the
Quran is unique also in the sense that it does not merely
reveal some past events which were till then unknown to
the rest of the world, but it also prophesises that the future

would testify to the truth of the Quranic statement. It was implausible enough to conceive that the body of Pharaoh having drowned in the conditions described by the Bible, could be retrieved. The phenomenon of such a body, even if retrieved, would present no small problem for the purpose of mummification.

Yet, this is what the Quran claims. No man could have dreamt of making such a statement contrary to the available historical evidence at the time of the revelation of the Quran. All that man knew was that the body of Pharaoh had been devoured by the sea, lost forever. Even the Egyptian plunderers of the tombs had no notion whatsoever as to which, if any, of the Pharaohs were buried in the Valley of the Kings. What made the Prophet[sa] of Islam make this unique statement if he were the author of the Quran? It could serve him no purpose anyway; if anything it could be counter-productive. If challenged, the Prophet[sa] could not have produced any evidence to support his contentions. The only purpose it would serve was to compromise the truth of the Quran. It was many centuries after the revelation of the Quran that the earth began to throw up its secrets. The mummified bodies of all the Pharaohs which can claim to be the Pharaohs of the time of Moses[as] have been retrieved.

Whether it was Rameses II or another Pharaoh is a question still debated, but the fact that one of the mummies recovered from the Valley of the Kings is that of the Pharaoh who confronted Moses is no longer debatable. The only conclusion therefore, one is left to draw, is that against the verdict of the entire world history it is the verdict of the Quranic revelation alone which is proved correct: So this day We will save thee in thy body *alone*...[3] فَالْيَوْمَ نُنَجِّيكَ بِبَدَنِكَ . This is the verdict of the Quran which has now become the verdict of world history.

572

One possible meaning of this address by God to Pharaoh is that the time for saving his life was over, hence it would be only his dead body which would be saved. The other possible meaning would be that the time for the acceptance of his faith had expired, hence his soul would not be redeemed. In this case, only his body would be saved to live on like that of a zombie without a soul. To our understanding it is the latter meaning which is intended by the Quran. To support our inference further, we cite the Quranic style in which this episode is narrated. Of particular interest is the expression: We will save thee in thy body alone.[3] نُنَجِّيْكَ بِبَدَنِكَ

Now Pharaoh was evidently concerned for his survival here on earth, rather than the retrieval of his corpse. If neither his spiritual nor his physical life was to be saved, what would this promise mean? Evidently Pharaoh was not praying for the rescue of his dead body.

If his prayer was accepted even partially, as is evident from the Quran, then to cause him to die both physically and spiritually seems out of the question. It is tantamount to a total denial of what he begged for. His profession of faith in the God of Israel must have been made for fear of his life. Hence it was justifiably rejected as meaningless. All that is promised is that only his body would be redeemed but not his soul. But most Muslim scholars insist that his plea was totally rejected and the promise of saving the body referred only to the recovery of his corpse from the sea.

That too, according to them, is no small miracle under the conditions described both in the Bible and the Quran. Even the promise of the retrieval of his corpse was in fact a great favour to the drowning Pharaoh.

The Pharaohs, they argue, were an extremely proud dynasty. Even the mere assurance that his body would be preserved must have brought some comfort to his dying moments. The purpose of God, however, was not to satisfy his vanity alone. The real purpose was to provide posterity with a great sign of multiple significance from which they could possibly benefit.

Whatever the outcome of this controversy — whether it is established that the Pharaoh in question died from drowning, only his body being retrieved, or whether he was rescued from a state of near death while drowning, the miracle of the Quranic statement is in no way obscured. The body of that Pharaoh was indeed preserved and this fact was brought to the knowledge of posterity exactly as the Quran had predicted.

Incidentally the scholars who believe that Pharaoh was already dead when his body was retrieved, also believe that it was Merneptah, the successor of Rameses II and not Rameses himself. This implies that Moses[as] lived under the reign of two Pharaohs instead of one. He was born while Rameses II was already a king and was raised in his palace by one of his God-fearing wives, who they believe was the youngest. As she had no issue herself, her desire to adopt a son is understandable. If this proposition is accepted then Moses[as] must have left Midian to return to Egypt after the death of Rameses II when Merneptah had already been enthroned. They quote the Bible in their support that Moses[as] was informed by God during his exile in Midian that the Pharaoh in whose reign he had committed manslaughter was dead.

This scenario seems to be logical and acceptable but only apparently. The death of a king does not absolve anyone of any crime he may have committed. There is no logic in that whatsoever. That is why God does not even remotely hint at the death of any Pharaoh to dispel Moses'[as] fears. Instead he is told not to fear because God would protect him and his brother. This is far more sensible.

Again the problem is that according to the archaeological evidence of his mummy's condition, Rameses II who died at the ripe old age of ninety years had spent the last thirty years of his life as a bedridden, senile, tottering old man probably suffering from an extreme case of arteriosclerosis. This state could be a direct consequence of his near-drowning, resulting in an insufficient supply of oxygen to the brain for an extended period.

Now the exile of Moses[as] to Midian and his entire stay there lasted only eight to ten years by the end of which period Rameses II could not be more than forty to fifty years old. Hence, the Biblical statement that God was only waiting for Pharaoh's death to commission Moses[as] as a prophet and command him to return to Egypt is unacceptable. Incidentally according to the Quran, the Pharaoh to whom Moses[as] returned did accuse him of murder but appeared to be hesitant to take action against him because of the Divine signs which Moses[as] had displayed. Evidently, his escape from punishment was certainly not due to the death of one Pharaoh and the enthronement of another.

Again the life of Moses[as] and Aaron[as] after their return to Egypt is described by the Quran and the Bible as very eventful and their confrontation with Pharaoh seems so drawn out that it must have taken a decade or so to come to its final conclusion. All the signs narrated could not have been packed in the mere short space of a year or two. As against this the historians estimate that the entire reign of Merneptah from the day of his crowning to the day of his death is reported to have lasted only eight years or less.

Moreover, history describes Merneptah as a warrior king who repeatedly attacked the Palestinians year after year, while both the Quran and the Bible are absolutely silent about the Pharaoh of Moses[as] having carried out such expeditions into the land of Israelites. But this is not the place perhaps for a full in-depth discussion on the issue. Nor is it necessary in any way to prove which of the two Pharaohs, Rameses II or Merneptah was the one who was the Pharaoh of the Exodus. As long as their mummies remain preserved, either of the two will always testify to the truth of the Quranic prophecy. Their names are of no real consequence.

The Prophecies Relating to the Immediate or Distant Future

Having dealt at some length with certain important events of Egyptian history during the age of Moses[as] which had remained concealed until the revelation of the Quran, we now turn to some prophetic Quranic revelations in relation to many other events. They relate to different areas of human interest comprising social, religious and political developments as well as epoch-making scientific advancements which were to change the face of the earth.

Some of these prophecies also cover significant ecological and environmental changes to be brought about by future scientific inventions and proliferation of industry. There is a long list of such prophecies contained mostly in the last few Surahs of the Holy Quran but not exclusively so. The discussion is by no means exhaustive. Some of these Quranic prophecies have been explained and enlarged upon by many traditions of the Holy Prophet[sa]. We have only selected some specimen prophecies belonging to different categories. The prophecies relating to the new modes of travel and their wide impact will be discussed at the end of the chapter at some greater length because of their global importance.

To maintain chronological order we begin with the prophecies which were fulfilled within the lifetime of the

Holy Prophet[sa]. A few of them relate to his return to Mecca after his forced exile. All such verses were revealed even before his migration to Medina thus simultaneously prophesying both his departure and subsequent return. The following verse belongs to a Surah (*Al-Qaṣaṣ*) which was revealed before Hijra (the Prophet's[sa] migration from Mecca to Medina).

اِنَّ الَّذِیْ فَرَضَ عَلَیْكَ الْقُرْاٰنَ لَرَآدُّكَ الـٰی مَعَادٍ قُلْ رَّبِّیْ اَعْلَمُ

مَنْ جَآءَ بِالْهُدٰی وَمَنْ هُوَ فِیْ ضَلـٰلٍ مُّبِیْنٍ * 28:86

Most surely He Who had made *the teaching of* the Quran binding on thee will bring thee back to *thy* place of return. Say, 'My Lord knows best who brings the guidance, and who is in manifest error.'[4]

To predict his return to Mecca before his migration to Medina is in fact a twofold prophecy. In view of the constantly worsening situation which made life progressively impossible for him and his followers in Mecca, migration may seem to some readers a mere logical conclusion. But it should not be forgotten that the element of surprise and wonder in this part of the prophecy is not about the suggestion of migration. The element of wonder is in the open defiance to the will and might of the Meccans who would not permit the predicted migration to take place. Again the ever hardening determination of the Meccans not to permit the Prophet[sa] to escape are the factors which highlight the unlikelihood of such a prophecy to have been made by the Prophet[sa] himself in his state of utter helplessness.

Another Divine promise that he would most certainly return to Mecca with manifest truth was vouched to him in the following verse:

$$\text{وَقُلْ رَّبِّ اَدْخِلْنِيْ مُدْخَلَ صِدْقٍ وَّاَخْرِجْنِيْ مُخْـــرَجَ صِـــدْقٍ}$$

17:81

And say, 'O my Lord, make my entry a good entry and *then* make me come forth with a good forthcoming...'[5]

The third example of how his ultimate victorious return to Mecca was predicted even before the actual migration took place, is taken from the first few verses of Surah *Al-Rūm* (Chapter 30), which by the unanimous verdict of scholars was revealed before Hijra:

$$\text{غُلِبَتِ الرُّوْمُ * فِيْ اَدْنَى الْاَرْضِ وَهُمْ مِنْ بَعْدِ غَلَبِهِمْ سَيَغْلِبُوْنَ *}$$
$$\text{فِيْ بِضْعِ سِنِيْنَ ؕ لِلّٰهِ الْاَمْرُ مِنْ قَبْلُ وَمِنْ بَعْدُ ؕ وَيَوْمَئِذٍ يَّفْرَحُ}$$
$$\text{الْمُؤْمِنُوْنَ * بِنَصْرِ اللّٰهِ ؕ يَنْصُرُ مَنْ يَّشَاءُ ؕ وَهُوَ الْعَزِيْـــزُ الرَّحِيْـــمُ *}$$

30:3-6

The Romans have been defeated,
In the land nearby, and they, after their defeat, will emerge victorious.
(This will happen) within a few years. And to Allah belongs the command before and after *that*. And that will be the day when the believers will rejoice,
With the succour from Allah. He helps whomsoever He pleases; and He is the Mighty the Merciful.[6]

These verses refer to a partial territorial defeat which the Romans suffered at the hands of the Persians. The verses clearly prophesied that the Persian victory would prove only short-lived and in a few years' time the defeat of the Romans will turn into victory. *'That will be the day when the believers will (also) rejoice with the succour they would receive from Allah.'* The implication of this prophecy in relation to the fate of the believers was all too obvious. When shortly after this revelation the Muslims lost their homes and property to the idolaters of Mecca, like the Romans had done to the idol worshippers of Persia, the consensus among the companions was that soon after the Romans' victory, the Muslims would also regain their territory – Mecca. This understanding was unanimous among all the companions of the Holy Prophet[sa]. The only difference was regarding the period in which the prophecy would be fulfilled. This controversy stemmed from the expression *'bid'ai Sineen'* بِضْعِ سِنِيْنَ . Literally, it means a period extending from three to nine years. Some companions of the Holy Prophet[sa] in their eagerness bet with some others that they would certainly return soon after the expiry of three years. But others reminded them that their return could be delayed by as much as nine years which is the upper limit of the term *'bid'ai Sineen'* بِضْعِ سِنِيْنَ. The events as they unfolded themselves, proved the latter opinion to be right. Thus, in this sense both the promises were fulfilled in letter and in spirit. First it was the Romans who regained their lost territory within the prescribed limit and then it was the turn of the Muslims to return to Mecca in glory before the end of the eighth year.

Another category of the prophecies which was manifestly fulfilled during the lifetime of the Holy Prophet[sa] relates to the repeated attacks on the Muslims in Medina by the Meccans and their confederates from among the nomad tribes.

The first of these prophecies as mentioned in the following verses clearly portrayed the events of the Battle of Badr. During this first serious encounter of the Muslims with a formidable, professionally organized army of Meccans, the invading hosts were completely routed and put to a most humiliating flight by a comparatively much smaller body of Muslim defenders.

اَمْ يَقُوْلُوْنَ نَحْنُ جَمِيْعٌ مُّنْتَصِرٌ * سَيُهْزَمُ الْجَمْعُ وَيُوَلُّوْنَ الدُّبُرَ *

بَلِ السَّاعَةُ مَوْعِدُهُمْ وَالسَّاعَةُ اَدْهٰى وَاَمَرُّ * 54:45-47

Do they say, 'We are a victorious host?'
The hosts shall soon be routed and will turn their
backs *in flight.*
Aye, the Hour is their appointed time; and the Hour
will be most calamitous and most bitter.[7]

The devastating defeat inflicted upon the Meccan
army was clearly predicted in the verses quoted above. The
last of these verses highlights for them the bitterness of the
Hour.

The very pick of the chieftains, the sworn enemies of
Islam, who were also renowned for their hatred of the Holy
Prophet[sa], fell one after the other and were made to bite the
dust in the field of Badr.

Abu-Jahl was slain by two young Muslim lads, so also
Shaibah and 'Utbah met their fated hour and were put to
sword within a few hours. The night fell upon the gloomy
hearts of the Meccans like Doomsday. They were put to
flight in utter disarray. It is this humiliating defeat which is
referred to in the following verse of Surah *Al-Anfāl:*

وَاِذْ يَعِدُكُمُ اللّٰهُ اِحْدَى الطَّآئِفَتَيْنِ اَنَّهَا لَكُمْ وَتَـوَدُّوْنَ اَنَّ غَـيْرَ

ذَاتِ الشَّوْكَةِ تَكُوْنُ لَكُمْ وَيُرِيْدُ اللّٰهُ اَنْ يُّحِقَّ الْحَقَّ بِكَلِمٰـتِهٖ

وَيَقْطَعَ دَابِرَ الْكٰـفِرِيْنَ * 8:8

And *remember the time* when Allah promised you
one of the two parties that it should be yours, and
you wished that one without sting should be yours,
but Allah desired to establish the truth by His words
and to cut off the root of the disbelievers.[8]

580

The Battle of The Ditch

Among other encounters with the enemies of Islam which occurred precisely as they were foretold, the Battle of the Ditch غزوة الخندق is of outstanding importance. It was during this battle that some other great historic victories were also predicted at a time when the very survival of the Muslims themselves was at stake.

The prediction of the Battle of the Ditch was first made in Surah *Ṣād* which was definitely revealed in Mecca and according to most scholars, during the early period of the Prophet's[sa] ministry. Following is the verse:

$$ 38:12 \quad * \text{ جُنْدٌ مَّا هُنَالِكَ مَهْزُومٌ مِّنَ الْأَحْزَابِ } $$

They are a host of the confederates *which shall be* routed here.[9]

It is to this prophecy that the Holy Quran refers:

$$ \text{ وَلَمَّا رَاَ الْمُؤْمِنُوْنَ الْاَحْزَابَ قَالُوْا هٰذَا مَا وَعَدَنَا اللهُ وَرَسُوْلُهُ } $$
$$ 33:23 \quad * \text{ وَصَدَقَ اللهُ وَرَسُوْلُهُ ؗوَمَا زَادَهُمْ اِلَّاۤ اِيْمَانًا وَّتَسْلِيْمًا } $$

And when the believers saw the confederates, they said, 'This is what Allah and His Messenger promised us; and Allah and His Messenger spoke the truth.' And it only added to their faith and submission.[10]

Of all the battles fought during the lifetime of the Holy Prophet[sa] of Islam, the Battle of the Ditch stands out for the maximum possible dangers and extreme trials of adversity which it brought to the Muslims in Medina. There was many a time when the odds were heavy against the survival of the Muslims. The Quran describes their state as follows:

اِذْ جَاءُوْكُمْ مِّنْ فَوْقِكُمْ وَمِنْ اَسْفَلَ مِنْكُمْ وَاِذْ زَاغَتِ الْاَبْصَارُ
وَبَلَغَتِ الْقُلُوْبُ الْحَنَاجِرَ وَتَظُنُّوْنَ بِاللهِ الظُّنُوْنَا * هُنَالِكَ ابْتُلِـــيَ
الْمُؤْمِنُوْنَ وَزُلْزِلُوْا زِلْزَالًا شَدِيْدًا * وَاِذْ يَقُـــوْلُ الْمُنٰـــفِقُوْنَ
وَالَّذِيْنَ فِىْ قُلُوْبِهِمْ مَّرَضٌ مَّا وَعَدَنَا اللهُ وَرَسُوْلُهٗٓ اِلَّا غُـــرُوْرًا *
وَاِذْ قَالَتْ طَّائِفَةٌ مِّنْهُمْ يٰـــاَهْلَ يَثْرِبَ لَا مُقَامَ لَكُـــمْ فَـــارْجِعُوْا
وَيَسْتَأْذِنُ فَرِيْقٌ مِّنْهُمُ النَّبِىَّ يَقُوْلُوْنَ اِنَّ بُيُوْتَنَا عَوْرَةٌ ؁وَمَـــا هِـــىَ
بِعَوْرَةٍ؁اِنْ يُّرِيْدُوْنَ اِلَّا فِرَارًا * 33:11-14

When they came upon you from above you, and from below you, and when *your* eyes became distracted, and *your* hearts reached to the throats, and you thought *diverse* thoughts about Allah.
There *and then* were the believers *sorely* tried, and they were shaken with a violent shaking.
And when the hypocrites and those in whose hearts was a disease said, 'Allah and His Messenger promised us nothing but a delusion.'
And when a party of them said, 'O people of Yathrib (Medina), you have *possibly* no stand *against the enemy*, therefore turn back.' And a section of them *even* asked leave of the Prophet, saying, 'Our houses are exposed *and defenceless.*' And they were *in truth* not exposed. They only sought to flee away.[11]

This battle has earned the title The Battle of the Ditch, because when the news reached Prophet Muhammad[sa] that almost all the Arab tribes had colluded to invade Medina for a final conclusive encounter to finish off Islam once and for all, the building of a barrier on the open side of Medina became an absolute must. The number of Muslims in Medina at that time, by comparison to the invading hosts, was so small that it was absolutely impossible for them to prevent the enemy from entering Medina in an open battle.

Hence, after consultation it was decided that the digging of a ditch was the only option. A one mile long ditch was required to be dug in extremely difficult rocky terrain.

The estimate as to the number of Muslims involved in this task differ. The minimum mentioned is seven hundred and the maximum three thousand. According to our estimate it was around one thousand eight hundred at the most, because the one thing on which the authorities are agreed is that to every group of ten persons, ten yards of the ditch were allocated. As it was not longer than one mile, the number of Muslims could not have been more than one thousand seven hundred and sixty. The task was hard and exacting. An overall state of poverty and deprivation further compounded the problems of the Muslim camp. At times they had to work for days an end on empty stomachs.

It was during this state of extreme adversity that the Holy Prophet[sa] was once informed that despite the best efforts of the sappers, a hard rock stubbornly refused to yield. The Prophet[sa] proceeded forthwith to visit the troubled spot. Having reached there he took up the pickaxe in his own hands and struck the rock three times before it yielded and broke into fragments. Each time he struck, sparks flew from the rock and he exclaimed out loud *Allah-o-Akbar!* (Allah is the Greatest). At the end the Companions inquired from him why he had shouted *Allah-o-Akbar!* with such a triumphant note. The Holy Prophet[sa] answered: 'In the sparks which flew at the first strike, I saw the Syrian palaces of the Byzantine Empire and their key was given to me. The second time I was shown the illuminated palaces of Persia at Madain and to me the key was handed. Again I was granted the key of the palaces of San'a as they appeared in the sparks when I struck the rock for the third time.' History bears witness that this is exactly what followed but the wonder lies not in their fulfilment alone. The very making of these prophecies at the time they were made is in itself a miracle.[12]

Seldom can history present such examples of a defending few, as powerless and vulnerable as the Muslims were while they were engaged in the digging of the trench, day in and day out, borne down with hunger and fatigue. That was the time when the adversity of the Muslim cause could sink no further. It was then that Muhammad[sa] spoke the historic words which history could not create, they created history.

To predict such victories at a time such as this could either be the ravings of a madman or the proclamation of God from the lips of a great Prophet[sa]. He was the wisest of all the wise that ever lived, 'mad' he was certainly not. If ever a prophet was blessed to be a Divine oracle, it was he. His was the mouth and his were the lips which shaped destinies and pronounced decrees as God spoke to him and he spoke for God.

As has been pointed out earlier the purpose of this exercise is not to present an exhaustive study of all the prophecies of the Holy Quran and the Holy Prophet[sa]. We are only attempting to present to the reader some specific prophecies with wider impact. Having discussed some of them which related to the lifetime of the Holy Prophet[sa] and the period which immediately followed, we now turn to another category of prophecies which relate to a comparatively distant future. It is difficult to decide where to begin but perhaps it would not be inappropriate to begin with the discovery of the Americas and the extension of the known world. The following are the relevant verses:

وَإِذَا الْأَرْضُ مُدَّتْ ۞ وَأَلْقَتْ مَا فِيهَا وَتَخَلَّتْ ۞ وَأَذِنَتْ لِرَبِّهَا
وَحُقَّتْ ۞ 84:4-6

And when the earth will spread out,
And will cast out *all* that she contains and become
empty;
And will give ear to her Lord — and *this* will be
incumbent upon her.[13]

The prophecy contained in verse 4 above was
manifestly realized with the discovery of the 'New World'
by the end of the fifteenth century, when on 12 October
1492, Christopher Columbus landed on an island in the
Bahamas.

That was the beginning of the end for the native
Americans. But a new seemingly endless beginning was
made for the Americans to rise and dominate the rest of the
old world. This is clearly implied in the prophecy contained
in the next verse which speaks of the earth throwing up all
its secrets and emptying itself.

The same issue is taken up again and further
elaborated in some other chapters as well. For instance,
verses 2 and 3 of Surah *Al-Zilzāl* read:

إِذَا زُلْزِلَتِ الْاَرْضُ زِلْزَالَهَا * وَاَخْرَجَتِ الْاَرْضُ اَثْقَالَهَا* 99:2-3

When the earth is shaken with her *violent* shaking,
And the earth throws up her burdens.[14]

It is predicted that the earth will go through a mighty
shaking and will throw up its heavy metals and man will
begin to wonder what indeed is happening to it.

The word *athqāl* (اَثْقَال) refers to everything which
is heavy, so the throwing up by the earth of its heavy metals
will not be a forced extension of its meaning. Again it can
also be translated as 'the earth will throw up its hidden
treasures'. The tremendous scientific advancements which
we have witnessed in this age could not become possible

without the discovery of new minerals which the earth has thrown up as predicted. Count them out and the wheel of scientific advancement will turn back a full circle. No modern invention of any significance can be conceived without the discovery of coal, petroleum, uranium, plutonium etc.

The chronological order of the two prophecies mentioned above also has a message to deliver. The prophecy of the extension of the old world is followed immediately by the discovery of new minerals and this is exactly the sequence in which the prophecies were fulfilled.

The Prophecy About Archaeological Exploration

وَإِذَا الْقُبُورُ بُعْثِرَتْ * 82:5

And when the graves will be laid open.[15]

While the verse of *Al-Zilzāl* clearly refers to the throwing up by the earth of its hidden treasures, this verse of Surah *Al-Infiṭār* is evidently speaking of archaeology.

But this is not the only verse which does that. We have selected this because of its prophetic nature, otherwise there are many other verses in the Quran which draw the attention of man repeatedly and directly to many a buried township and civilization of earlier people. They exhort man to dig up their remains and study the factors which brought about their ultimate ruin.

THE FOLLOWING TWO OPENING VERSES OF SURAH *AL-TAKWĪR* predict that Islam will already have gone into decline before the dawn of the new age:

إِذَا الشَّمْسُ كُوِّرَتْ * وَإِذَا النُّجُومُ انْكَدَرَتْ * 81:2-3

When the sun is wrapped up,
And when the stars are obscured.[16]

It should be borne in mind that the sun and the stars as mentioned in these verses refer symbolically to Islam and Muslim divines. The Quran refers to the Holy Prophet[sa] as *Sirājan-munira* سِرَاجًا مُّنِيْرًا which literally means the 'radiant sun' and the Holy Prophet[sa] refers to the company of the pious people who borrowed from his light as shining stars, who in the absence of the sun still emit enough light to guide the wayward:

أصحابى كالنجوم فبأيّهم اقتديتم اهتديتم

My Companions are like the guiding stars; whomsoever you follow, you will be led to the right path.[17]

When the sun is described as having ceased to shed light it clearly speaks of the decline of Islam, because the Holy Prophet[sa] was its living symbol. The obscurity of stars by the same logic refers to an age when the Muslim divines would cease to reflect the light of Islam. This inference is fully supported by the contents of the verses which follow. They all invariably speak of an age of great scientific, political and social advancement which evidently is a tribute to the age. If the opening statement of this Surah as quoted above applies to these revolutionary changes, the discord between the two would be too jarring. What a dismal compliment it would become. That brilliant age of exceptional advancement in knowledge would be described as if the sun had been wrapped up and the stars had ceased to shed light. They are two different things applicable to different areas of future developments. Hence, if the main contents of this chapter refer to the material rise of the

Christian world which was to follow the discovery of the Americas, the first two verses must be understood by way of contrast to apply to the fate of Islam. What had happened to Islam to earn this gloomy description by the year the Americas were discovered? If we find the answer to this question no further proof would be needed to support our interpretation of the said verses. The year 1492 as we have pointed out before is the most outstanding landmark which separates the old world from the new. Can we prove that the downfall of Islam did reach its nadir in the same year so that any reader could easily recognise a clear link between the two? Yes we can and the verdict is not ours nor that of any other Muslim. The verdict is that of history evidenced by Christian historians themselves. The *Chronicle of the World* has the following to say about the most distinctive feature of that year in relation to Islam:

> 'After a ten-year campaign Granada, the only remaining Moslem state in Spain, has fallen to the Castilian army. The surrender of the city is being hailed by Christians as the "most signal and blessed day there has ever been in Spain". Moslems are describing it as one of the most terrible catastrophes ever to befall Islam.'[18]

> 'Ferdinand and Isabella take Granada, the last Moslem kingdom in Spain, which had resisted Christian conquest for two centuries'[18].

This brought to end the unbroken rule of Spain by the Muslims for seven hundred years.

After the termination of the Muslim political rule in 1492, there began an organized campaign by the Church to murder Islam. Though the Muslim domination had come to an abrupt end after an extended rule of more than five hundred years, the influence which Islam had built over the previous five centuries could not have been done away within a year or two. There was a large number of Moors who were scattered all over the southern hilly terrain of Andalusia providing strong isolated pockets for Islam. There was an even larger number of Spanish converts to Islam who were no less sincere and devout in practising Islam than their conquerors from Arabia and Africa. It was they, more than any other reminder of their faith, who proved an intolerable irritant to the Christian clergy which had grown desperate over the years to destroy them or their religion.

It was Ximenes (pronounced Khemenies), the loudest apostle of the Church Militant who,

> '... would have the souls of these "infidels" saved from the hell fire whether they liked it or no.'[19]

He imprinted in 'Isabella's holy mind the pernicious doctrine that to keep faith with infidels was breaking faith with God.'[19] He was

> '... not a man to be easily deterred from his purpose. He induced the queen to promulgate a decree by which the Moors were given their choice to baptism or exile. They were reminded that their ancestors had once been Christian, and that by descent they themselves were born in the Church, and must naturally profess her doctrine'.[20]

Thus began the beginning of the end for Islam in Spain which took two hundred years to run its deathly course.

> 'The mosques were closed, the countless manuscripts that contained the results of ages of Moorish learning were burnt by the ruthless Cardinal, and the unhappy "infidels" were threatened and beaten into the Gospel of Peace and

Goodwill after the manner already approved by their Catholic Majesties in respect of the no less miserable Jews. The majority of course yielded, finding it easier to spare their religion than their homes; but a spark of the old Moorish spirit remained burning bright among the hillmen of the Alpuxarras...'[21]

'... the rulers of Spain were neither wise nor honest in their dealings with the Moriscos, and as time went on they became more and more cruel and false. The "infidels" were ordered to abandon their native and picturesque costume, and to assume the hats and breeches of the Christians; to give up bathing, and adopt the dirt of their conquerors; to renounce their language, their customs and ceremonies, even their very names, and to speak Spanish, behave Spanishly, and re-name themselves Spaniards.'[22]

'It was reserved for Philip II. to carry into practical effect the tyrannical law which his father had prudently left alone. In 1567 he enforced the odious regulations about language, customs, and the like, and, to secure the validity of the prohibition of cleanliness, began by pulling down the beautiful baths of the Alhambra.'[22]

'In the winter of 1569-70 he (Don John) began his campaign, and in May the terms of surrender had been arranged. The months between had been stained with a crimson river of blood. Don John's motto was "no quarter"; men, women, and children were butchered by his order and under his own eye; the villages of Alpuxarras were turned into human shambles.'[23]

'Many hapless exiles died by the way, from want, fatigue, and exposure; others reached Africa, where they might beg a daily pittance, but could find no soil to till...'[24]

AL-HAMBRA IN SPAIN

I.28

THE CORDOBA MOSQUE IN SPAIN
Now it contains Christian images and is used as a church.

I.29

'It is stated that no less than three million of Moors were banished between the fall of Granada and the first decade of the 17th century. The Arab chronicler mournfully records the *coup-de-grâce:* "The Almighty was not pleased to grant them victory, so they were overcome and slain on all sides, till at last they were driven forth from the land of Andalusia, the which calamity came to pass in our own days, in the year of the Flight, 1017. Verily to God belong lands and dominions, and He giveth them to whom He doth will." '[24]

'The Moors were banished; for a while Christian Spain shone, like the moon, with a borrowed light; then came the eclipse, and in that darkness Spain has grovelled ever since.'[25]

Thus concludes Stanley Lane-Poole in his history of *The Moors in Spain.* The sun of the Muslim political domination of Spain which had set in 1492, left behind, it seems, a gory dusk which took two centuries to finally dissipate the light of Islam from the sky of Spain, and turn it into a starless night.

As for the secular enlightenment brought to Spain by the outgoing Muslim civilization, it did not take that long to follow.

Thus the year 1492 opened two gates at once. Out of one the future of the Christian domination of the world marched in with such majestic glory. Out of the other departed all the past glories of Islam with heads hung low, each aching step inflicting unbearable agony.

The fourth verse speaks of mountains being moved from one place to another:

$$\text{وَإِذَا الْجِبَالُ سُيِّرَتْ} * \text{ 81:4}$$

591

And when the mountains will be made to move.[26]

Mountains in Islamic terminology mean great worldly powers. There are many verses in the Holy Quran which mention mountains with the same connotation. So the third verse which speaks of the mountains is in fact the verse with which we begin our study to understand what would happen in the latter days. After the initial decline of Islam, a starless night would fall to be followed by the dawn of a day which would not to be the dawn of Islam. Great material powers would not only rise but move their influence widely from territory to territory, from continent to continent and bring under their domination country after country. That is how mountains in their sense can move and they did move. The moving of the mountains can also be understood in other ways, a discussion to which we shall turn later. Now that we have begun to re-visualize the great changes which according to this Surah of the Quran were destined to take place in that age, we take up the subject bit by bit and category by category in accordance with the verses as they follow.

While on the subject of movements, the implication of the fifth verse can be easily understood. It reads:

$$\text{وَإِذَا الْعِشَارُ عُطِّلَتْ} \; * \; 81\text{:}5$$

… when the ten month pregnant she-camels will be abandoned.[27]

In this context the prophecy of the she-camels being abandoned can evidently be understood to mean that better, faster and more powerful means of transport will have been invented. The scenario of the mountains moving from place to place, great powers spreading their influence from continent to continent is directly related to the issue of the she-camels being abandoned.

It should be kept in mind that the movement of the mountains can be interpreted as transportation of immense loads as well as the spread of influence of mighty political powers. Both of these definitely require more advanced and powerful means of transport than she-camels. Unless such new means had become available to man it would be sheer madness on his part to abandon whatever poor means he already had available. He would certainly not abandon the she-camel and start carrying mountain-like loads on his bare back!

The inevitable conclusion one is left to draw from this verse is that far more powerful and swifter mechanical means would be invented which would render animal modes as insignificant and obsolete.

The she-camel, it should be remembered, can only symbolically represent such modes of transport as move on land surfaces. One wonders about boats and ships etc., and why have they not been mentioned and what breakthrough does the Quran predict in the area of marine transport? To this we shall return later. Presently we would like to take up the next verse which speaks of the gathering of all sorts of animals.

$$\text{81:6 } * \text{ وَإِذَا الْوُحُوشُ حُشِرَتْ}$$

And when the wild animals will be gathered together.[28]

The shift from the abandonment of she-camels to the gathering of animals is quite intriguing. This provides another proof that she-camels will not be left alone despite their usefulness. The mention of wild animals being gathered together in fact further advances the same idea of the invention of revolutionary means of transport. Of course all sorts of wild animals cannot be transported from place to place merely on the backs of camels. None can imagine elephants, rhinoceroses, hippopotamuses, giraffes, crocodiles, blue whales and giant octopuses enjoying camel rides! Their transportation could only become possible by the modes of transport invented in our age.

The verse which follows is still on the subject of transport:

$$\text{وَاِذَا الْبِحَارُ سُجِّرَتْ} * \quad 81:7$$

And when the seas are made to flow forth *one into the other*.[29]

The word *Sujjirat* (سُجِّرَتْ) according to Lane can be translated into the following three concurrent meanings:

1. *And when the seas shall be filled.*
2. *And when the seas shall flow forth one into another.*
3. *And when the seas will be set on fire.*

As for the first possible meaning the filling of the seas naturally creates the vision of the sea filled with plying vessels. Thus this verse too remains primarily occupied with the same discussion as in the preceding verses. This interpretation will be further corroborated when we return to this subject once again.

Presently we take up the second of the three possible meanings which speak of the joining of the seas. This prophecy is further elaborated in the following two verses of the Quran:

$$\text{مَرَجَ الْبَحْرَيْنِ يَلْتَقِيَانِ} * \text{بَيْنَهُمَا بَرْزَخٌ لَّا يَبْغِيَانِ} * \quad 55:20\text{-}21$$

He has made the two bodies of water flow. They will
one day meet.
Between them there is a barrier *now* which neither
can trespass in an act of defiance.[30]

وَهُوَ الَّذِىْ مَرَجَ الْبَحْرَيْنِ هٰذَا عَذْبٌ فُرَاتٌ وَّهٰذَا مِلْحٌ اُجَـــاجٌ

وَجَعَلَ بَيْنَهُمَا بَرْزَخًا وَّحِجْرًا مَّحْجُوْرًا * 25:54

And He it is Who shall merge the two seas together.
This palatable *and* sweet, that saltish *and* bitter. And
between them He has *(presently)* placed a barrier and
a massive partition.[31]

The two verses quoted above are taken from two
different Surahs of the Holy Quran. Each predicts a
separate event of the joining of two different seas together.
This is exactly what happened in modern times. In the
digging of the Suez Canal during 1859-1869 and that of the
Panama Canal during 1903-1914, the world has already
witnessed the fulfilment of these prophecies in a manner
that could not have been even vaguely visualized by man
during the age of the Holy Prophet[sa].

The third concurrent meaning which presents the
scenario of the seas put on fire is no less bizarre than the
first one, hence as unlikely to be conceived by the human
mind fourteen hundred years ago. It is an idea which can
only be born during the age of naval warfare with
exchanges of intense firepower. Incidentally the huge
number of ships involved in modern naval warfare covers
such large areas of the sea as justify our interpretation that
by the filling of the seas it is primarily meant that the seas
would be filled with plying vessels.

Again the third concurrent meaning portraying the
seas as set ablaze is an idea which belongs to the age of

huge oil spills such as occur in our time. They are often ignited to minimize the horrendous threat they pose to marine life. At such times even hundreds of thousands of square miles of sea can be observed as literally set on fire.

The next verse from Surah *Al-Takwīr* advances the same idea still further. Instead of the gathering of animals, it is humans who would be gathered together is the central message of this verse:

$$81:8 \text{ * } \text{وَإِذَا النُّفُوسُ زُوِّجَتْ}$$

And when people are brought together.[32]

This too can be translated simultaneously into three different meanings as follows:
1. When people will be linked together by mutually binding ties.
2. When people from all over the world will be merged together.
3. When the meeting of people together will be facilitated by means of much faster modes of transport.

Each of the three interpretations mentioned above has clearly come true. Ours is an age when international treaties bind practically all the nations of the world without exception. Hence, this interpretation has evidently come true and needs no further elaboration.

Likewise the founding of the League of Nations which was replaced later by the United Nations has evidently advanced the ultimate unification of the world a step further as predicted.

As for the fulfilment of the third prophecy implied in the same verse, we have already observed the distances to be virtually so reduced by the new modes of travel as to create the impression that the whole world is squeezed into one community of a single township.

Before proceeding further it would be appropriate to mention another prophecy which also relates to the subject of the bringing together of people. That prophecy speaks of the return of the Children of Israel to the Promised Land in the latter days:

وَقُلْنَا مِنْ بَعْدِهِ لِبَنِيٓ اِسْرَآءِيْلَ اسْكُنُوا الْاَرْضَ فَاِذَا جَآءَ وَعْـــدُ
الْاٰخِرَةِ جِئْنَا بِكُمْ لَفِيْفًا 17:105*

And after him We said to the children of Israel, 'Dwell ye in the land; and when *the time of* the promise of the latter days comes, We shall bring you together *out of various peoples.*'[33]

The destruction of Jerusalem in AD 70, by the Romans tolled the bell for the death of the Jewish state. From then on the Jews were scattered throughout the world moving on from country to country. It is this state of ultimate diaspora to which the above verse refers when it declares that one day the Jews will be gathered from all over the world and once again they will be assembled in the Holy Land. It is a covenant of God which shall be fulfilled. We have already seen the fulfilment of this promise on such a wide scale as has never been witnessed by man before. Never in the history of the Jewish people after any diaspora were they brought back from all the countries of the world as it happened in the recent past after the creation of the state of Israel.

Returning to Surah *Al-Takwīr* from which we digressed for a while, let us now take up verse 9 which follows. This verse as well as the next, describe the same age to which all previous verses refer to from different angles.

$$\text{81:9-10 * قُتِلَتْ ذَنْبٍ بِاَىّ * سُئِلَتْ دَةُ الْمَوْءُ وَإِذَا}$$

And when the girl-child buried alive is questioned about,
'For what offence has she been put to death?'[34]

In their ignorance some Arabs felt extremely insulted when a daughter was born to them and out of shame might even bury her alive. Society had no right to interfere in such matters as though the fathers owned their children like property.

That age would be the age of the strict rule of law is the evident message. This message however, is delivered particularly with reference to the rights of women. Otherwise a simple statement concerning law and order could as well have been made. In the light of this, one simply cannot fail to register this significance. No longer will men be able to trifle with the rights of women, is the powerful import of this verse. Never in any age did the rights of women acquire such importance as in contemporary times.

All the features of the latter days which the verses of this Quranic Surah develop systematically with a progressive sequence, carry the subject forward from one feature to another like the brush of a master painter. The scientific development which is throughout implied is continuously interwoven with the political and social aspects. In verse 8 the bonding together of man is predicted in more than one way. The same subject is taken up again in verse 11 after the mention of social and political developments. The idea is introduced with reference to the most powerful means of joining people together which is through wider extensive publication of literature, newspapers, magazines etc. All the modes of transport referred to above have played their part in uniting the people of the world, but the role of the press can never be overshadowed or replaced by any other measure of uniting man. Take the role of the wide distribution of printed literature away from this age and mankind, despite the distances being reduced, will suddenly appear to fall apart once again. The people will become disjointed and isolated from each other. It was this modern state of the news media and the extensive publication of literature which is mentioned in the verse under discussion:

$$ \text{81:11} \quad {}^{*}\text{وَإِذَا الصُّحُفُ نُشِرَتْ} $$

And when the books will be extensively published and spread.[35]

Also implied in this prophecy is the invention of the modern press, otherwise it would not be possible for handwritten manuscripts to be extensively published and widely distributed.

An age of large-scale publication is also bound to be an age of intense proliferation of knowledge, research and investigation. The Holy Quran emphasizes the role of the pen so powerfully that it directly attributes to God the act of teaching humans how to write.

The following verses which are taken from Surah *Al-'Alaq,* the very first Chapter revealed to the Holy Prophet[sa] emphatically pronounce:

$$ \text{اِقْرَأْ وَرَبُّكَ الْأَكْرَمُ * الَّذِيْ عَلَّمَ بِالْقَلَمِ * عَلَّمَ الْإِنْسَانَ مَا لَـــمْ} $$

$$ \text{96:4-6} \quad {}^{*}\text{يَعْلَمْ} $$

599

Read! And your Lord is the Most Honourable.
Who taught by the pen.
He taught man what he knew not.[36]

These verses when read in conjunction with the verse under study clearly emphasize the character of the age as highly advanced in knowledge. During that age, the spread of educational institutions such as schools, colleges and universities also seems to be implied.

The very first verse which makes the opening statement introduces God as Most Honourable because He has taught with the pen. It is obviously implied that the pen will be the source of all knowledge and knowledge would be the source of all greatness and honour. Incidentally one should not forget that these revelations were vouched to one who himself had never learnt to hold a pen in his hand. It was the pen of God which authored the Quran and not the pen of Muhammad[sa]. Another implication of the verse is that knowledge would become the means of gaining power and the pen shall emerge as mightier than the sword.

The next verse advancing the same theme further pronounces that the sky will be the limit of man's knowledge:

$$ \text{وَإِذَا السَّمَآءُ كُشِطَتْ} \text{ * } 81:12 $$

And when the heaven will be peeled off (laid bare).[37]

This verse presents a tragic comparison between the state of Islam in that age and the rise of the worldly Christian powers when the light of the sun of Islam will be wrapped up and the stars of the Muslim heaven will cease to shed light. The non-Muslim materialistic world will begin to scale the heavenly heights to learn the secrets of space.

This scenario brings to mind some other verses of the Holy Quran which also predict an era of space and air travel. The following are the relevant verses:

وَالسَّمَآءِ ذَاتِ الْحُبُكِ * 51:8

And by the heaven *full* of tracks.[38]

وَالْمُرْسَلَٰتِ عُرْفًا * فَالْعَٰصِفَٰتِ عَصْفًا * وَّالنَّٰشِرَٰتِ
نَشْرًا * فَالْفَٰرِقَٰتِ فَرْقًا* 77:2-5

And by those who are sent forth with specific tasks,
And by those who move like the moving of fast winds,
And by those who propagate a goodly propaganda,
And by those who distinguish and discriminate *between friends and foes.*[39]

These and many other similar verses repeatedly draw the picture of a sky which is extensively used for air travel. It is charted into tracks, messengers fly to and fro, airborne propaganda is carried out extensively and it has become possible at last for man to fly on the wings of air. Having fulfilled his dream to fly, man would begin to entertain loftier ambitions. He would begin to discern the secrets of the heavens and the heavenly bodies. He would peel off the covers which enwrap them to unveil their mysteries. He would set space stations and posts to watch and monitor what passes in the heavens above him. The following verse clearly illustrates this phase of human advancement in science and technology which would make it literally possible for him to probe into the vast expanse of the universe.

$$لَا يَسَّمَّعُوْنَ اِلَى الْمَلَاِ الْاَعْلٰى وَيُقْذَفُوْنَ مِنْ كُـلِّ جَـانِبٍ *$$

$$دُحُوْرًا وَّلَهُمْ عَذَابٌ وَّاصِبٌ * 37:9-10$$

However much they strain their ears to eavesdrop on whatever passes in the lofty celestial chambers, they will not be able to do so without being pelted from all sides.
Repulsed! And for them will be a perpetual punishment.[40]

Concerning the ambition of man to conquer space physically to its very limits, the following is the challenge which the Quran throws to all who seek the conquest of space, be they high or low.

Before we quote the relevant verse, it is essential to clarify the nature of its address. The translation: *'the company of the jinn and the company of the men'* does not do full justice to the message implied. The word *'jinn'* (جِنّ) does not indicate here a ghostlike existence different from humans. Instead as also mentioned earlier it is frequently employed to indicate big people as against the common people who are referred to as *An-Nās* (اَلنَّاس). Hence, the true import of this address would perhaps be better understood if it were translated as: *'O company of the capitalist powers and O company of the proletariat.'*

Now we quote the verse and its translation taken from Maulawi Sher Ali:

$$يٰـمَعْشَرَ الْجِنِّ وَالْاِنْسِ اِنِ اسْتَطَعْتُمْ اَنْ تَنْفُذُوْا مِـــنْ اَقْطَارِ$$

$$السَّمٰـــوٰتِ وَالْاَرْضِ فَانْفُذُوْا طَلَا تَنْفُذُوْنَ اِلَّا بِسُلْطٰـنٍ * 55:34$$

O company of Jinn and men! if you have power to
go beyond the confines of the heavens and the earth,
then do go. But you cannot go save with authority.[41]

We humbly suggest that a more appropriate
translation in this context should have been 'Except with
the help of most powerful deductive logic'. This means that
although physically unable to transcend the boundaries of
the universe, man would still be able to reach the limits of
the universe as far as the extension of his knowledge is
concerned. We have the following reasons to support this
inference:

The translation *'Save with authority'* can in fact create
the opposite impression to what the Quran actually intends
to convey which is a categorical denial of the possibility of
physical conquest of space by man to its outer limits.
Authority is not the only meaning of the word *Al-Sultān*. It
can be simultaneously translated as a mighty monarch, a
powerful argument or strong deductive logic. Hence it may
signify that man will still be able to reach across the
boundaries of the universe through powerful logical
deduction.

What is clearly denied is not just a short hop or two
into space. What is denied is the ability of man to reach the
limits of the universe with his physical body. Incidentally
the hazards attending upon space flights are also mentioned
as follows:

يُرْسَلُ عَلَيْكُمَا شُوَاظٌ مِنْ نَّارٍ وَّنُحَاسٌ فَلَا تَنتَصِرَانِ * 55:36

There shall be sent against you blasts of fire, and
smoke; and you shall not be able to help
yourselves.[42]

This verse in fact draws a clear picture of cosmic rays rather than that of ordinary flames of fire.

Having elaborated the implied meanings of verse 12 of Surah *Al-Takwīr,* with the help of the above quoted verses of Surah *Al-Raḥmān* (Chapter 55), we now return to *Al-Takwīr* from where we left off.

It is a strange coincidence that we finished our comments on the verses of Surah *Al-Raḥmān* with the warning of perpetual punishment by fire. This exactly is the subject of discussion of verse 13 of Surah *Al-Takwīr* which we intend to elaborate now:

$$ \text{81:13} \quad * \quad \text{وَإِذَا الْجَحِيْمُ سُعِّرَتْ} $$

And when the hellfire will be made to rage.[43]

Here the expression hellfire refers to such wars as would create the impression that all hell has broken loose. Hence, this is the warning delivered in this verse. This is the only feasible interpretation in the context of the preceding prophecies which speak without exception of the events of this world. It would appear very odd indeed if man is told that at some time while these events are taking place here on earth, hellfire would be raging above in an otherworldly space.

The sequence of prophecies thus reaches its logical conclusion. Material progress however massive it may be cannot be of any avail to man if he gains his worldly ambitions at the cost of God's pleasure. The hour of punishment must arrive and strike man down despite all his material might. But no calamity will befall him from on high as such. He will build his own hellfire himself and his selfishness will create such global tensions as are bound to culminate in hellish wars. Looking back at the history of the two World Wars this interpretation no longer remains an academic exercise but acquires a substantial threat. This exercise so far has brought to bold relief the contrast between the tragic decline of Islam and the rise of the non-Muslim powers. The verse under study clearly depicts that the global domination of materialism will not last perpetually. The downfall of the materialistic powers will begin with growing mutual enmities which will culminate in horrendous catastrophes of their own making. Wars will follow one after the other. They will be re-kindled and quenched yet again leaving behind the ashes of the mighty powers which will incinerate themselves. The two global wars have already dented the unchallenged might of the superpowers while the weaker and the poorer nations have relatively emerged with a sense of having gained some measure of their lost dignity. The balance is far from tilted as yet to have reached a critical stage, but though slowly, time is certainly moving in the direction of a global revolution. It is that revolution which is predicted in the Quran to be the ultimate revolution of Islam. Lest it should seem an over-generalized, unsubstantiated statement, we shall produce in the following chapter some sound concomitant evidence to dispel such doubts.

Based on the direct messages contained in many a verse of the Quran, the Holy Prophet[sa] has clearly predicted the ultimate outcome of the global conflict during the latter days. This he has done with reference to the advent of the anti-Christ. But it should be clarified at the outset that his image as it arises from the traditions of the Holy Prophet[sa] is not in reality as freakish as might appear on the surface. It refers to the anti-Christ in a manner that seems to combine in him the power and might of immensely powerful nations. In fact the entire age of the latter days is mentioned by the Holy Prophet[sa] as the age of the anti-

Christ. All signs of the age are mentioned with reference to him. Among the signs which assist his identification is a category devoted specifically to the new modes of travel of which man had no experience before. A detailed account of what the anti-Christ would be and how he would dominate the world leaves no shadow of doubt in the mind of any unbiased reader that it is not a single person to whom these prophecies refer. The term 'anti-Christ' as used by the Holy Prophet[sa] is only symbolic. He would be a symbol of the mighty powers of his age and his exploits would in fact be the exploits of many highly advanced and powerful Christian nations of the world. But their supremacy would not last forever. The ultimate downfall of the anti-Christ who symbolizes them is also predicted in no uncertain terms. From the ruins of materialism would rise once again the sun of Islam unveiling its radiant beauty as it casts away the covers of doubt and suspicion which had enwrapped it for many a dismal century.

Now we take up the discussion of the revolutionary mode of travel once again but this time we refer to the traditions of the Holy Prophet[sa]. As for the remaining signs of the anti-Christ, particularly those which have religious significance, we shall discuss them separately at some greater length in another chapter.

Modes of travel on land, sea and air are all described without exception in a manner that fully endorses the interpretation of many a Quranic verse which we have presented earlier. Even the issue of the movement of mountains is explained so that the memory of the relevant verses is effortlessly resurrected. The Holy Prophet's[sa] elaboration of the anti-Christ and the unique donkey he would ride must have seemed extremely odd to the people of his time. It had to appear odd because despite the fact that he continually refers to that mount as a donkey, none of the known characteristics of a donkey are ascribed to that oddity. However all the modern modes of transport answer to this description perfectly.

They have one common feature about them; they are all propelled by combustion engines drawing their energy from fire. Even the external combustion engines like those of locomotives driven by steam are dependant on fire. This is the sharp separating line between the earlier modes of animal transport and the revolutionary new modes of transport in the age of the anti-Christ which would reveal him to be not an animal but an inanimate object. We refer to him as 'he' only because in the prophecy he is literally spoken of as an animal. In fact he could be identified by this distinctive mark alone. Recognize the donkey of the anti-Christ and you will recognize in him the modern modes of transport. Fail to recognize him if you so choose and travel back to the age of donkeys.

Some other novel features of this symbolic donkey of the anti-Christ are described in great detail in various books of traditions. The following is a composite presentation of the information derived from them:

1.   Like his donkey the anti-Christ himself would be so massive and gigantic that a monster like unto him has not even been heard of in the most bizarre tales of fantasy. He would be so tall that his head would seem to disappear beyond the clouds. He will be so immensely powerful that he would conquer the whole world single-handedly. [44]

2.   Despite all these physical advantages the one blemish that he would be blighted with would be the total loss of one eye, the right eye for that matter.[45]

3.   This donkey would not merely be a personal mount of the anti-Christ, but would also be made freely available as a means of public transport. People will

climb into his belly from the openings on his side provided specifically for this purpose. [46]

4.   The belly will be well lighted within and equipped with comfortable seats. [46]

5.   The donkey would move at exceptionally fast speeds covering long distances in a matter of days or hours which ordinary animal mounts take months to cover. [47]

6.   He would have regular stoppages on its way. At every stoppage the public would be invited to come and be seated before he resumes his journey and every departure would be loudly announced. Thus the metaphorical donkey would continuously travel from place to place providing people with a fast, convenient and comfortable means of transport. [48]

7.   The passengers travelling in the belly would in no way be scorched by the fire he had eaten indicating that the seating compartment in his belly would be fully insulated from the fire chamber. [48]

8.   This donkey will also be able to travel by sea and move from continent to continent riding the ocean waves. [49]

9.   During his journey by sea he would somehow swell to a much larger size. Thus he will be able to transport mountains of food upon his back across the oceans. Many a time he will be employed to deliver these enormous food supplies to such poor nations as abjectly bow to the will of the anti-Christ. The transportation of mountain-loads of food is a figurative expression reminiscent of the one contained in another previously quoted verse which predicted such times when mountains will be made to move. [50]

10. The amazing donkey would also know how to fly because some of his gigantic leaps are described to cover distances between East and West. It is said that

one foot of the beast will be in the East and the other in the West. This is indicative of the size of his leap meaning that he would take off from one continent and land in another. [51]

11. In the air he will move above the level of the clouds. [52]

12. On his forehead he would carry the moon. Apparently the moon refers to the headlights which most modern vehicles are equipped with. [52]

After reading this vivid description of the donkey of the anti-Christ which he would use for his world conquest, we wonder if the reader really needs further assistance to recognize him.

Obviously such great Christian powers are mentioned under the title *Dajjāl*[53] as were destined one day to command the entire world. The fire-driven donkey which acquires the changeable roles of aeroplanes, ships or trains moving at exceptionally fast speeds was to play the most formative and crucial role in the conquest of the world by the Christian powers. Apart from emphasizing the advantage of higher speeds, the advantage of weightier possessions is also specifically mentioned in the global conflict for supremacy:

فَأَمَّا مَنْ ثَقُلَتْ مَوَازِيْنُهُ * فَهُوَ فِىْ عِيْشَةٍ رَّاضِيَةٍ * 101:7-8

Then, as for him whose scales are heavy,
he will have a pleasant life. [54]

The weightier they are in their possession and the faster in their speeds, the more inevitable would become the supremacy of the world powers. The mass and the speed at which he moves is what matters on the road to victory.

These prophecies are so unique that it is hard to find their equal in the realm of Divine prophecies elsewhere.

The description is so vivid and precise that one has the impression that like a painter who captures with his brush what he sees, the Holy Prophet[sa] was moulding into picturesque words what he observed unfolding before his eyes.

With this we bring to a close the discussion on the series of the prophecies contained in the Surah *Al-Takwīr*. Now we plan to present to the reader some other highly important prophecies which describe some other important features of the same age. Each of the following prophecies deals with different specific topics. They are dextrously encapsulated in various other Surahs of the Quran.

REFERENCES

1. *The Holy Bible* (1982) The New King James Version. Thomas Nelson Publishers, Nashville, Exodus 14:28-29
2. Translation of 10:91-93 by Maulawi Sher Ali.
3. Translation of 10:93 by Maulawi Sher Ali.
4. Translation of 28:86 by Maulawi Sher Ali.
5. Translation of 17:81 by Maulawi Sher Ali.
6. Translation of 30:3-6 by the author.
7. Translation of 54:45-47 by Maulawi Sher Ali.
8. Translation of 8:8 by Maulawi Sher Ali.
9. Translation of 38:12 by the author.
10. Translation of 33:23 by Maulawi Sher Ali.
11. Translation of 33:11-14 by Maulawi Sher Ali. (Note: We have added 'Medına' in brackets).
12. *Fat-ḥul-Bārī* — The Commentary of Saḥiḥ Al-Bukhārī by Hāfiz Ahmad bin 'Ali Hajar Al-'Asqalāni (773-852). Kitāb Al-Maghāzī Babo Ghazwah Al-Khandaq Al-Aḥzāb. Vol.VII p.397.
13. Translation of 84:4-6 by the author.
14. Translation of 99:2-3 by the author.
15. Translation of 82:5 by the author.
16. Translation of 81:2-3 by Maulawi Sher Ali.
17. *Miṣhkāt-ul-Masābih.* Vol.I, Chapter III. Kitāb Al-Manāqib. Babo Manāqib Al-Ṣahabah. Publisher: Al-Maktab Al-Islāmi, Beirut.
18. *Chronicle of the World.* (1989) Chronicle Communications Ltd and Longman Group UK Ltd., London, p.436
19. LANE-POOLE, S. (1888) *The Moors in Spain.* 8th ed., T. Fisher Unwin, London, p.270
20. LANE-POOLE, S. (1888) *The Moors in Spain.* 8th ed., T. Fisher Unwin, London, pp.270-271
21. LANE-POOLE, S. (1888) *The Moors in Spain.* 8th ed., T. Fisher Unwin, London, p.271
22. LANE-POOLE, S. (1888) *The Moors in Spain.* 8th ed., T. Fisher Unwin, London, p.273
23. LANE-POOLE, S. (1888) *The Moors in Spain.* 8th ed., T. Fisher Unwin, London, p.278
24. LANE-POOLE, S. (1888) *The Moors in Spain.* 8th ed., T. Fisher Unwin, London, p.279
25. LANE-POOLE, S. (1888) *The Moors in Spain.* 8th ed., T. Fisher Unwin, London, p.280

26. Translation of 81:4 by the author.
27. Translation of 81:5 by the author.
28. Translation of 81:6 by the author.
29. Translation of 81:7 by Maulawi Sher Ali.
30. Translation of 55:20-21 by the author.
31. Translation of 25:54 by the author.
32. Translation of 81:8 by the author.
33. Translation of 17:105 by Maulawi Sher Ali.
34. Translation of 81:9-10 by the author.
35. Translation of 81:11 by the author.
36. Translation of 96:4-6 by the author.
37. Translation of 81:12 by the author.
38. Translation of 51:8 by Maulawi Sher Ali.
39. Translation of 77:2-5 by the author.
40. Translation of 37:9-10 by the author.
41. Translation of 55:34 by Maulawi Sher Ali.
42. Translation of 55:36 by the author.
43. Translation of 81:13 by the author.
44. 'ALLAMAH 'ALA-UD-DIN 'ALI AL-MUTTAQI. *Kanz-ul-'ummāl* vol:14 p.604 & 613 (1979), Beirut.
45. IMAM MUSLIM BIN AL-ḤAJJĀJ BIN MUSLIM AL-QASHIRĪ AL-NAISAPŪRĪ. *Saḥiḥ Muslim,* Kitābul-Fitan, Babo Zikrid-Dajjāl wa Sifātehī Wa ma ma'ahū.
46. 'ALLAMAH MUHAMMAD BĀQIR AL-MAJLISĪ. *Bihārul-Anwār,* Babo 'Alāmāte Zohurihī Alaihis-salām min Al-sufyāni wad-Dajjāl.
47. 'ABDUR-REḤMĀN AL-SAFŪRĪ. *Nuzhat-ul-Majālis,* vol:1 p.109. Maimaniyyah Press, Egypt.
48. 'ALLĀMAH MUHAMMAD BĀQIR AL-MAJLISĪ. *Bihārul-Anwār,* Babo 'Alāmāte Zohurihī Alaihis-salām min Al-sufyani wad-Dajjāl.
49. 'ABDUR-REḤMAN AL-SAFŪRĪ. *Nuzhat-ul-Majālis,* vol:1 p.109. Maimaniyyah Press, Egypt.
50. *Saḥīḥ Al-Bukhārī.* Kitāb-ul-Fitan, Babo Zikrid-Dajjāl.
51. 'ABDUR-REḤMĀN AL-SAFŪRĪ. *Nuzhat-ul-Majālis,* vol:1 p.109. Maimaniyyah Press, Egypt.
52. 'ALLĀMAH 'ALĀ-UD-DĪN 'ALI AL-MUTTAQĪ. *Kanz-ul-'ummāl* vol:14 p.613 (1979), Beirut.
53. *Saḥiḥ Muslim,* Kitāb-ul-Fitan. Babo Zikrid-Dajjāl wa Sifato wa Ma Ma'ahū.
54. Translation of 101:7-8 by Maulawi Sher Ali.

NUCLEAR HOLOCAUST

AMONG THE QURANIC PROPHECIES relating to events and inventions of our age, there are some which are of outstanding importance and great global significance. One such prophecy relates to the impending danger of a nuclear holocaust.

This prophecy was made at a time when man could not entertain the idea of an atomic explosion by any stretch of his imagination. But as we will presently illustrate, there are certain verses of the Holy Quran which clearly speak of tiny insignificant particles which are described as storehouses of immense energy, as though the fire of hell was locked within them. Amazing as it may seem, this is exactly what is literally described in the following verses.

وَيْلٌ لِّكُلِّ هُمَزَةٍ لُّمَزَةٍ * الَّذِى جَمَعَ مَالًا وَّعَدَّدَهُ * يَحْسَبُ اَنَّ مَالَهُ اَخْلَدَهُ * كَلَّا لَيُنْبَذَنَّ فِى الْحُطَمَةِ * وَمَا اَدْرَاكَ مَا الْحُطَمَةُ * نَارُ اللهِ الْمُوْقَدَةُ * الَّتِىْ تَطَّلِعُ عَلَى الْاَفْئِدَةِ * اِنَّهَا عَلَيْهِمْ مُّؤْصَدَةٌ * فِىْ عَمَدٍ مُّمَدَّدَةٍ * 104:2-10

Woe to every backbiter, slanderer,
Who amasses wealth and counts it over and over.
He imagines that his wealth will make him immortal.
Nay! he shall surely be cast into the "hotamah".
And what should make thee know what the "hotamah" is?
Allah's fire as preserved fuel,
Which will leap suddenly on to the hearts.
It is locked up in outstretched pillars to be used against them.[1]

This short Quranic Chapter is densely packed with astounding statements which lie far beyond the reach of the people of that age. Strange is it not, to read that the sinful people of a certain description would be cast into the *ḥoṭamah,* which means the tiniest of particles, such as we see floating in a beam of light which passes through a poorly lit room.

Authentic Arabic lexicons describe *ḥoṭamah* as possessing two root meanings; first *ḥaṭamah,* which means 'to pound' or 'pulverize into extremely small particles', and the second *ḥiṭmah,* which means 'the smallest insignificant particle'. Thus *ḥiṭmah* is the result obtained by breaking something down to its smallest constituents.

The two meanings just mentioned can rightfully be applied to any extremely minute particle which has reached the limits of its divisible potential. As the concept of the atom had not been born fourteen hundred years ago, the nearest substitute to it could only be *ḥoṭamah* which also sounds intriguingly close to atom. One hardly recovers from the shock of the claim that a time would come when man would be cast in the *ḥoṭamah* when another claim, even more bizarre, comes in its wake.

Explaining the word *ḥoṭamah,* the Holy Quran speaks of a blazing fire built within it and confined in extended columns. It goes on to declare that when man will be cast into it, this fire will directly leap upon his heart as though no intervening rib cage existed. This can only mean that this fire would be of a completely different nature which could directly kill the heart before it could scorch the body. Certainly no fire known to man of that age could be described as such.

These however are not the only elements of surprise about this description; what follows is even more astonishing. This fire is mentioned as having been locked

THE CANOPY OF FIRE LIKE A HUGE MUSHROOM
IN A NUCLEAR EXPLOSION

wind 40 m.p.h.

3 miles high

damaged buildings

3 miles wide

damaged buildings

37 seconds after detonation

12 miles high

12 miles wide

10 minutes after detonation

I.30

The wreck of a concrete building in Hiroshima after the explosion.

I.31

up in outstretched columns waiting to leap upon man till such time as it is destined to be unleashed.

WONDER UPON WONDER is heaped in such a short space of a few simple statements. First the declaration that the time would come when man would be cast into the smallest particle, then the description of that smallest particle and what it contains. It contains a type of fire which is kept confined in some tiny vessels which could appear like extended columns.

The casting of man into this minute particle does not mean that a single man will be cast into it. Man is mentioned as a generic name and the casting indicates his subjection to that affliction to which he will be doomed. This has only become conceivable in the contemporary age when man has discovered the secret of the atoms and the immense stores of energy which they contain. This is the age when the fire contained in the smallest particles leaps out and engulfs large areas extending to thousands of square miles. Everything that lies within its range is engulfed, man and all. Hence, what seemed so unrealistic fourteen hundred years ago, has become a commonplace reality which even young children can understand.

The most hyperbolical expression of wonder fails to do justice to the greatness of this prophecy. No less wonderful is the fact that the people of that age failed to recognize the import of this short Surah *Al-Humazah;* or it would have leapt upon their beliefs and faith, rather than upon their hearts. How these amazing statements escaped their notice and went unchallenged defies logic. Perhaps they sought refuge in the belief that these verses do not apply to the events of this world, but relate to the mysterious realm of the unknown in the hereafter. Many a commentator simply avoided even an attempt to explain these verses. A few who took up the challenge, unburdened themselves by arbitrarily relegating the contents of these verses to the time of resurrection. Thus, not comprehending their meaning, they tossed them lock, stock and barrel over to the unknown.

Among the Western orientalists, Sale faced the same dilemma of how to translate the word *hotamah* literally. He simply mentioned a large number of people to be thrust into the *hotamah* without translating *Al-hotamah* at all. This left no danger for the English speaking people to express their incredulance at the impossibility of people being cast into a tiny particle. As they would have no idea what *hotamah* is, they would be free to imagine a vast hall of burning fire called the *hotamah* (the smallest particle). This strategy of Sale saved him from the embarrassment of this translation. Yet, at the same time, he failed to do justice to this amazing prophecy.

The fire described in this verse, whether it is a conflagration here upon earth or a raging fire in the hereafter, could in no way be pressed into the tiny space of the minutest of particles. But that is not the only dilemma which must have confronted Sale and other earlier commentators. What about the fire which is packed into tiny extended columns, a scenario altogether impossible to conceive until the dawn of the atomic era? Now the jigsaw puzzle appears to be finally resolved, with every piece settling into its right place.

Unless one is familiar with the scientific description of how an atomic explosion takes place and what changes are brought about within the nuclear mass, one cannot fully comprehend the meaning of the Quranic expression of 'extended columns'. Nuclear experts describe the state of a critical mass which is about to explode, as something elongating and pulsating with the immense pressure built within it. This pressure is caused by the elongation of the nuclei before they burst and in that process an element of high atomic weight is split into two elements of lesser atomic weight. The sum total of the atomic weight of the newly formed elements is less than the atomic weight of the original parent element, normally referred to as a heavy metal. The small portion of the atomic weight which is lost in this process is turned into energy. This is not the only model of a nuclear bomb but we have chosen this simple one to describe the process of the extended columns.

TURNING TO the issue of how this fire could leap directly upon the hearts, the scientific description is given below:

At the instant of explosion, large quantities of gamma rays, neutrons and x-rays are immediately released. The x-rays raise the temperature immediately to meteoric heights creating a great ball of fire rising rapidly, riding the extremely hot atomic blast. This is the canopy of fire like a huge mushroom which is seen from far and wide.

The x-rays also travel sideways in all directions along with the neutrons, causing immense heat which burns everything on its way. The speed at which this heat front moves is many times the speed of sound which also creates shockwaves. But much faster and more penetrating than this are the gamma rays which outpace the heat front by leaping forward at the speed of light. They are so immensely vibrant that by the sheer force of their vibration they strike the hearts dead. So death is not caused by the intense heat generated by x-rays, it is the tremendous energy of the gamma rays which inflicts instantaneous death. This is exactly how the Holy Quran describes it.

Again in Surah *Al-Dukhān* (The Smoke), the Quran describes a lethal cloud which comprises a deadly radiant smoke:

فَارْتَقِبْ يَوْمَ تَأْتِى السَّمَآءُ بِدُخَانٍ مُّبِينٍ * يَّغْشَى النَّاسَ هَـــذَا
عَذَابٌ اَلِيْمٌ * 44:11-12

Then watch for the day when the sky will bring forth
a manifest smoke,
That will cast a shadow upon people. This will be a
painful suffering.[2]

The nature of this cloud is further qualified by the
following verses:

انْطَلِقُوٓا الَـى مَا كُنتُمْ بِهِ تُكَذِّبُوْنَ * انْطَلِقُوٓا الَـى ظِـلٍّ ذِىْ
ثَلٰــثِ شُعَبَ * لَّا ظَلِيلٍ وَّلاَ يُغْنِىْ مِنَ اللَّهَبِ * اِنَّهَا تَرْمِـــىْ
بِشَرَرٍ كَالْقَصْرِ * كَاَنَّهُ جِمٰــلَتٌ صُفْرٌ * 77:30-34

'Now move towards what you have been denying,
'Move on towards a three-pronged shadow,
'Neither affording shade, nor protecting from the
blaze.'
It throws up flames like *huge* castles,
As though the castles were dusky yellow camels.[3]

The words 'move towards' indicate that mankind will
be gradually carried into an era where it will confront this
calamity of a tormenting cloud which offers no shade or
protection. Shadows provide relief and shelter. The clouds
stand between us and the blazing heat of the sun. In the
above verse no sun is mentioned, just a fire, from whose
blaze this shadow affords no protection. Rather, the shadow
of this cloud becomes a means of transmitting the torment
of the fire which emits it. Nothing under its shade is safe.
This clearly is the description of a radioactive cloud. The
event being described will throw up huge flames of a dusky
yellow appearance, flames that are likened to castles and

also have the appearance of camels. Perhaps, here it is not only the likeness to the colour of the camel, but also the shape of its hump which is highlighted.

People of the seventh century would not have been able to understand the significance of such a deadly cloud or smoke. It would have been beyond their comprehension. However, today we know of atomic explosions and can understand the images of radioactive clouds they produce.

This fateful description is also referred to in another verse of the Quran which reads as follows:

$$ \text{77:16}^* \quad \text{وَيْلٌ يَّوْمَئِذٍ لِّلْمُكَذِّبِينَ} $$

Woe on that day unto those who deny.[4]

'That day' (يَوْمَئِذٍ) can refer to the day of judgement, but it also refers to a time here on earth, when those who refuse to believe in the signs (اَلْمُكَذِّبِينَ) will be tormented by a smoke that casts a deadly shadow over whatever lies beneath. It will be a shadow which will move on, from land to land, bringing no relief, but only a shade full of agony. That will be the age when having witnessed this Divine punishment of colossal dimensions, man would at last turn to God beseeching His favour to rescue him from this unbearable chastisement. But when the wrath of Allah overtakes people, the time for forgiveness and deliverance is already over. Thus the Holy Quran explains:

$$ \text{أَنَّى لَهُمُ الذِّكْرٰى وَقَدْ جَآءَهُمْ رَسُولٌ مُّبِينٌ}^* \quad \text{ثُمَّ تَوَلَّوْا عَنْهُ} $$
$$ \text{44:14-15}^* \quad \text{وَقَالُوْا مُعَلَّمٌ مَّجْنُوْنٌ} $$

How shall a message be effectual for them, since a messenger has already come to them, explaining things clearly?

Yet they turn away from him, saying, 'He is tutored,
a man possessed.'[5]

PROPHETIC WARNINGS are only delivered to awaken man
to the danger of calamities which are but the
consequence of his own folly. The prophecies
mentioned above clearly relate to our age. They speak of
events which were completely unknown to the people of
earlier ages. One wonders if the full implications of all such
prophecies were revealed by God to the Holy Prophet[sa] in
every detail. But the clarity with which he describes future
events leaves a strong impression as if he were beholding
them like a prophetic puppet show being staged in the hall
of destiny. Yet mankind had to wait for more than a
thousand years before these prophecies would begin to be
realized. Hence, the real transfer of these events from the
realm of the unseen to that of the seen, could only become
possible in the nuclear age.

The enormity of the atomic catastrophe is horrendous,
yet little attention is paid by man to investigate and identify
the underlying roots of this evil. The sight of man seldom
penetrates beyond the surfaces he scans. Few among them
can introspect themselves to discover the hidden face of
their evil intentions. This is a sort of blindness which is
specifically related to the crookedness in man. Whenever
he himself is responsible for causing suffering and
spreading evil around him, he will not identify his own
hand behind them.

Such is the chain of catastrophes of global impact we
are examining. A scientist explains the underlying
phenomenon of nuclear explosions only to the extent of
material and physical causes. But when such enormously
destructive devices are employed to play havoc with the
peace of man, it is not the scientists who created them who
should be blamed. The root cause lies elsewhere. It is the

great world powers which are invariably responsible for such cruel and senseless decisions of global magnitude. Yet despite their greatness they are no more than mere pawns in the hands of the utterly selfish collective will of the masses.

The Holy Quran, though speaking of scientific events with great precision, does not assume the role of a mere scientific instructor. Rather it is the immoral causes of distorted human behaviour to which it draws our attention. It explains the phenomenon of a trigger indeed, but focuses our attention not on the trigger but upon the finger that pulls it. This is the purpose of Quranic warnings. As such, it repeatedly pronounces that for all the ugliness done to man, it is man himself who is to blame. Thus the preventive measures, according to the Quran, relate to the reformation of human character. It states that if people change their conduct and reform themselves in accordance with Divine guidance, this would create the healthy climate necessary for the survival of justice and fair play.

The lighthouse of the Quranic prophecies clearly shows what rocks to avoid and what channels to follow. Yet how unlikely it is for those who command the ship of human affairs to heed the warning and steer the ship across the impending hazards to the safe haven of peace. It is herein that the ultimate cause of disaster lies. Without a critical and realistic analysis of human behaviour at every level of its activity, no sound workable solution can be conceived of problems which confront man today. In simplest terms, it lies in the rehabilitation of basic human values such as truth, honesty, integrity, justice, fair play, concern for others, sensibility to the sufferings of people even when they are unrelated, and an overall commitment to goodness. Remove them as factors from human relationships and wait for the catastrophe to overtake you. It is the only logical conclusion.

Surah *Al-Qamar* (Chapter 54), explains this with reference to the history of earlier peoples who did not take heed of the warnings delivered to them by the Divine messengers of their time. As a consequence they, one and all, witnessed the tragic end that was promised to them, and their belated repentance was of no avail. The only purpose served by the warning is for the future generations to take heed. The Holy Quran thus points its finger at their tragedy so that the generations to follow may learn the art of life from the death of those who preceded them.

وَلَقَدْ جَآءَهُمْ مِنَ الْأَ نْبَآءِ مَا فِيهِ مُزْدَجَرٌ ۞ حِكْمَةٌ ۢبَالِغَةٌ فَمَا تُغْنِ النُّذُرُ ۞ 54:5-6

And there has already come to them the great news wherein is a warning—
Consummate wisdom; but the warnings profit them not.[6]

If a people do not draw their lesson, then it is only they who are to be blamed for the disastrous consequences which await them.

The atomic holocaust to which we refer is also discussed in Surah *Ṭā Hā* (Chapter 20) in relation to its ultimate consequences. By implication, the verse also makes it clear that it would be the pride and arrogance of the great world powers of the time which will be broken, mankind as such will not be wiped out.

The relevant verse clearly predicts that this will not be a point of termination for mankind as such. It will be only the might of the arrogant political powers that will be shattered and laid low. From their graves will rise the new world order. The mountain-like superpowers will be pulverized and levelled as though into a vast expanse of sand. You will not detect any highs or lows, or aboves and belows in their contour.

وَيَسْـَٔلُوْنَكَ عَنِ الْجِبَالِ فَقُلْ يَنْسِفُهَا رَبِّيْ نَسْفًا * فَيَذَرُهَا قَاعًا صَفْصَفًا * لَّا تَرٰى فِيْهَا عِوَجًا وَّلَآ اَمْتًا * يَوْمَئِذٍ يَّتَّبِعُوْنَ الدَّاعِيَ لَا عِوَجَ لَهٗ ۚ وَخَشَعَتِ الْاَصْوَاتُ لِلرَّحْمٰنِ فَلَا تَسْمَعُ اِلَّا هَمْسًا*

20:106-109

And they ask thee concerning the mountains. Say, 'My Lord will break them into pieces and scatter them as dust.
'And He will leave them as a barren, level plain,
'Wherein thou wilt see no depression, or elevation.'
On that day they will follow the Caller *straight*, there being no deviation therefrom; and *all* voices shall be hushed before the Gracious *God* and thou shalt not hear but a subdued sound of footsteps.[7]

It will be God, the Perfect Leveller, Whose hand will bring about this amazing transformation. The mountains are mere figures of speech, indicating powerful states, nations and people. The Quran predicts that once their pride is shattered and they are finally humbled and straightened, only then will they be fit to respond to the humblest of callers unto God, who has no crookedness about him. Such destruction as described could only result from a holocaust of the magnitude of hundreds of nuclear explosions, which implies that man will not learn his lesson and the head of his arrogance will have to be bent by the sheer weight of this enormity. Along with this grim message of warning there is also a glorious message of hope that mankind will ultimately survive and be ushered into a new era of light. Man will learn to mend his ways — if not before, at least after tasting some of the fruits of his follies and defiance to God.

In another Surah, the Quran speaks of cardinal geographic and climatic changes of such horrendous nature as would render the face of many tracts of land, countries and continents entirely desolate. This perhaps is related to the aftermath of the holocaust we have just discussed. Before that, the same lands were counted among the most scenic and beautiful parts of the world, uniquely rich in dazzling beauty. How we wish that of all the Quranic prophecies, this one at least will not have to be realized. This wish is certainly not a sign of disrespect to the prophetic Quranic warnings. It only springs from our unshakeable faith in the all-embracing graciousness of God — the All-Merciful, the All-Beneficent. All warnings, however categoric they may sound, are conditional to the response of man. The example of the people of Jonah[as], who were spared the destined wrath of God after they turned to Him with profound repentance, kindles the flame of hope for us today. Despite the fact that there is no genuine justification for optimism in view of the consistent decline in human moral values, it is the only hope after all to which one may cling. The rest is a fearsome night of utter despair. But the cure for their deep-seated maladies no longer lies in the hands of godless messiahs. It lies in the hands of God alone — but only if our hands are raised in prayer before Him. Perhaps we are talking a language hard for contemporary man to understand. It runs counter to what his ears are attuned to hear. Allah knows best!

REFERENCES

1. Translation of 104:2-10 by the author.
2. Translation of 44:11-12 by the author.
3. Translation of 77:30-34 by the author.
4. Translation of 77:16 by the author.
5. Translation of 44:14-15 by the author.
6. Translation of 54:5-6 by Maulawi Sher Ali.
7. Translation of 20:106-109 by Maulawi Sher Ali.

GENETIC ENGINEERING

IN THE FIELD OF GENETIC ENGINEERING, it has today become possible to change certain features of life. But in the age when the following verse was revealed, no one could imagine such a thing in his wildest fancy. Below is the relevant verse and its translation:

وَقَالَ لَأَتَّخِذَنَّ مِنْ عِبَادِكَ نَصِيبًا مَّفْرُوضًا * وَّلَأُضِلَّـــنَّهُمْ
وَلَأُمَنِّـــيَنَّهُمْ وَلَآمُـــرَنَّهُمْ فَلَيُبَـــتِّكُنَّ اذَانَ الْأَنْعَامِ 4:119-120

... And he (Satan) said, 'I will assuredly take a fixed portion from Thy servants;
'And assuredly I will lead them astray and assuredly I will excite in them vain desires, and assuredly I will incite them and they will cut the ears of cattle...'[1]

The idea of mutilation of animals by chopping off their tails or slitting their ears is not what is meant here by the Quran. It simply refers to the common practice among the Arabs in pre-Islamic times to make incisions in the ears of animals marked for sacrifice to various gods. However, what follows in the same verse is of a far more dramatic and revolutionary nature. The verse ends by attributing to Satan another malevolent intention, to incite mankind to bring about changes in the pattern of God's creation. The verse continues:

وَلَآمُرَنَّهُمْ فَلَيُغَـــيِّرُنَّ خَلْقَ اللّهِ وَمَنْ يَّتَّخِذِ الشَّيْطَنَ وَلِيًّا مِّنْ دُوْنِ
اللّهِ فَقَدْ خَسِرَ خُسْرَانًا مُّبِيْنًا* 4:120

... 'and assuredly I will incite them and they will effect a change in the creation of Allah.' And he who takes Satan as a friend besides Allah has certainly suffered a manifest loss.[2]

The possibility of changing the nature of God's creation was not an idea that people of earlier times could have entertained. Clearly the verse is speaking of possibilities that had not yet dawned on the horizon of earlier eras. To inflict superficial injuries or to make small changes, through incisions for example, is quite a simple process and lies within the reach of man of all ages. However, the possibility of man bringing about substantial changes in God's creation has always been beyond the reach of human imagination, prior to the most recent times. The addition of genetic engineering as a new branch of scientific study is only a decade or two old. Yet this branch of science is moving rapidly to the stage against which a clear warning had been delivered by the Quran fourteen hundred years ago. Man has already started interfering with the plan of creation and to some measure has succeeded in altering the forms of life at the level of bacteria, insects etc. A few steps further and it may spell disaster. Some scientists have already started sounding the alarm. But unfortunately, to reverse the wheel of experimentation in this field already seems to be beyond their power.

Scholars are divided in two camps regarding the very ethics of genetic engineering. Some are throwing up their hands in alarm, whilst others argue that we should develop this field to its fullest extent so that we may discover the secrets of creation. They believe that technological developments in this field will brighten the future of man.

In America the debates are ferociously raging between the two camps which approve or disapprove of genetic engineering. Some legal suits and litigations against the unrestricted experiments of genetic engineering are pending in the courts of the United States. It is argued that already the experiments have defied the scientific expectations of what should have resulted from the transfer of genes from one species to another. In some cases the deviation from the expected course is surprisingly greater than even the sceptics could suspect. Until now, however, things have not gone completely out of hand. The experiments carried out on certain strains of bacteria and crops are proving beneficial for enhancing agricultural produce and protecting it from certain diseases. But it is far too early indeed to exult in these small transient gains.

What ultimate effects the new synthetic strains or altered species will have on the ecology in the future, cannot be assessed until the behaviour of the altered strains is closely and minutely monitored for a few successive generations. The danger of the disaster which they may spell is, however, real and substantial. If not strictly monitored, injudicious experimentation with genetic engineering could let loose some unpredictable form of life which may defy human control. The certainty with which the Quran has warned against the punishment of meddling with the creation of God bodes ill for the future of life on earth. Allah knows best if man will ever cease to play God. Can any measure, short of extinction, teach him the lesson in humility?

IT IS WRONG however to infer that this verse condemns all possible usage of genetic engineering. Any branch of science which is pressed into the service of His creation and employed to protect, rather than change it, is certainly not discouraged. If for instance genetic engineering is employed to correct faults in genetic codes caused by accidents, this can in no way be dubbed as interference with the Divine scheme of things. Again, if damage to genetic codes by disease or imprudent medication is attempted to be corrected through genetic engineering, this is certainly not what is condemned in the above verse.

All said and done, it cannot be overemphasized that scientists should not be given a free hand to trifle with the grand scheme of Divine Creation. They must thank their lucky stars if grave accidents have not already happened. They will have none to thank but themselves if they do. We do hope that the world governments will keep a strict watch over the trends and scope of experimentation in the field of genetic engineering. What hangs in the balance is the honour and dignity of the human species within the animal kingdom. We do hope and pray that mankind will be spared the torment of haplessly watching the day when it will be mastered by the synthetic slaves of its own creation.

REFERENCES

1. Translation of 4:119-120 by Maulawi Sher Ali.
   (Note: The word 'Satan' in brackets has been added by the author).
2. Translation of 4:120 by the author.

THE PLAGUE

THE WORLD WE KNOW TODAY is so different from that of a mere hundred years ago. The age of air travel had not yet dawned. The fledgling flight of the Wright brothers was to remain, for many more years, a dream to be realized. Massive ships towering high like mountains were not yet built and the era of submarines was not as yet afloat. Nevertheless, there was a stir in the air, like that at the early break of dawn. A dazzling new day of revolutionary scientific inventions was breaking.

The air in the realm of religion was also vibrant with an expectancy of a different nature. There was talk in every religion of the near advent of a Divine Reformer of global dimensions. Who would come and where, was the most hotly debated question. The air was tense with claims and counterclaims. But nowhere was the tension of inter-religious debate so intense as in the subcontinent of India.

Christians and Muslims were awaiting the arrival of the Messiah among them. The Hindus were no less enthusiastic about the manifestation of their Lord Krishna. The Buddhists did not lag behind either, in hoping for the re-advent of Buddha.

In that atmosphere of multi-religious conflict, a voice was heard loud and clear, from a person of humble origin by the name of Mirza Ghulam Ahmad[as] of Qadian. He electrified the atmosphere with his outstanding advocacy of the supremacy of Islam over all other faiths. He threw challenges on behalf of Islam in every direction with such powerful arguments based on scriptural and logical evidence as compelled the champions of other religions to take serious note of him. 'A new warrior has risen for the defence of Islam,' was the clamour everywhere.

The Muslims of the subcontinent were astir with joy and hope. Till the entry into the arena of this new champion of the Muslim cause, Islam was the least ably defended of all the combatant religions. Meteoric was his rise to fame among the Indian Muslims when the first few volumes of his monumental work *Brahin-e-Ahmadiyyah* were published. Glowing tributes were paid to him by eminent Muslim scholars of that time. Leading articles were published in his praise by the Muslim press. But it was not to last long.

The situation changed dramatically when he pronounced, one day, that God had revealed to him that Jesus[as], son of Mary, was dead. He died many long years after his deliverance from the cross like any other human prophet. In his name and in his spirit and style it was he, Mirza Ghulam Ahmad[as] who had been raised as the Messiah of the latter days, to fulfil the prophecies of the second advent of Jesus[as]. A fuller discussion on this will follow in Part VII. For the present it should suffice that his fame had reached heavenly heights before he made this claim. But the first thing that claim cost him was that fame which turned overnight into notoriety. His name was still known from end to end in the vast subcontinent of India among the people of Islam, but no longer with honour and dignity and with hopes and aspirations. The hunter of the enemies of Islam became the most hunted person by the very Muslims whose battles he had fought. All his friends turned into foes, all his well-wishers wished him dead rather than accept the death of Jesus Christ[as] and his spiritual rebirth among the Muslims. He was maligned and vilified and abused and opposed with such frenzy as the subcontinent of India had not witnessed before. It was at this moment of total betrayal by the world of Islam, and undisguised hostility by the rest of the religions, that he was reassured by God that He would not abandon him. Many prophetic warnings were vouched to him concerning the Divine chastisement for those who led campaigns of bitter antagonism against him. Many Divine warnings were bestowed to him regarding heavenly punishments of a much wider application, so that the people at large might draw their lesson from them, but they heeded not. He was falsified. But his prophetic warnings of Divine chastisement could not be falsified.

ONE SUCH WARNING related to the impending epidemic of the plague which was to play exceptional havoc in the Punjab, the province of India to which he belonged. The most emphatic warning delivered by him to the world was bestowed upon him in the words of the following Divine revelation:

دنیا میں ایک نذیر آیا پر دنیا نے اس کو قبول نہ کیا لیکن خدا اسے قبول کرے گا اور بڑے زور آور حملوں سے اس کی سچائی ظاہر کر دے گا۔[1]

'A Warner came unto the world, but the world accepted him not; yet God shall manifest His favour and demonstrate his truth with powerful assaults.'

Plague, as we have already mentioned, was just one of the many punitive signs which he prophesied. But it was so great a sign of extraordinary import that we have specifically selected it as a category by itself. It was not just a sign of the truth of the Promised Messiah[as], it was a sign of the truth of the Quran and the Bearer[sa] of the Quran. Again it manifestly proved the claim that revelation is a most reliable means of transferring knowledge from the realm of the unknown to that of the known. The visitation of the plague which was revealed to the Promised Messiah[as] was in fact a Quranic prophecy reasserted during his time, because his was the age when it was destined to be realized.

$$وَاِذَا وَقَعَ الْقَوْلُ عَلَيْهِمْ اَخْرَجْنَا لَهُمْ دَآبَّةً مِّنَ الْاَرْضِ تُكَلِّمُهُمْ$$
$$اَنَّ النَّاسَ كَانُوْا بِاٰيٰتِـنَا لَا يُوْقِنُوْنَ* 27:83$$

And when the sentence is passed against them, We shall bring forth for them an insect (Da'bbah) out of the earth, which shall wound them (Tukallemo) because people did not believe in Our Signs.[2]

The word *da'bbah* as used by the Quran has already been defined with reference to another verse discussed earlier. It applies to all animals, from the tiniest to the most massive ones, which move along earth surfaces with a locomotive mechanism.[3]

It is highly important to understand the significance of this prophecy, which has a very potent message for the people of this age. Many a past Muslim scholar and commentator of the Quran has related this prophecy to the age when the Mahdi and the Messiah would appear. Although they could not fathom the entire import of the message, they still came surprisingly close. 'Allamah Isma'il Haqqi Al-Buruswi (d. AH 1137) commentating on the above verse in *Rūhul Bayān* wrote that the Mahdi would come and then the Dajjāl (anti-Christ) would appear followed by the Messiah. During this time *da'bbah* will emerge and after that the sun will rise from the West.

The Shi'a scholar, Mullāh Fath-Ullāh Kāshānī (d. AH 988), in his commentary *Minhāj-us Sādiqīn*, has made the following comments:

'According to some of our friends this verse (i.e. relating to the emergence of *da'bbah*) points to the advent of the Divine authority who is the Mahdi of the Muslim people *(Ummah)*.'

This is as far as these commentators could go from their study of Hadith in conjunction with the above Quranic verse. They did not offer any explanation as to the nature of *da'bbah*. It was left to Hazrat Mirza Ghulam Ahmad[as], in his capacity as the reformer of the latter days to further elaborate and explain the true implication of this prophecy in the light of the Divine revelations and visions bestowed upon him.

In February 1898, Hazrat Ahmad[as] received revelations about an impending plague, and he immediately published this important warning through newspapers and pamphlets to the world at large. He explained that the plague of which he had foretold was the same calamity implied in the verse relating to the appearance of *al-da'bbah* (الدَّآبَّة)

He further observed that the word *tukallemo* (تُكَلِّمُ) mentioned in the verse has two basic meanings. One is to wound and the other is to speak. The context in which this verse is set clearly relates to an animal of a sort which would bite the people for having rejected the signs of the Lord. The alternative meaning requires the *da'bbah* to speak to the people. This he does by implication indicating that this punitive measure is a result of their denial. Thus he speaks as he wounds by discriminating between good and bad.

After this initial warning, many others followed, further elaborating the nature of the impending plague and the manner in which it would strike. The Promised Messiah[as] was told in no uncertain terms that this plague would devastate large areas in the Punjab, and village after village would be emptied of life. Death would knock at every door and strike the townships from end to end leaving a trail of horror behind as it went. Qadian, the township where he himself dwelled, would be no exception, he declared, but the plague there would be employed to further enhance the sign of his truth. It would strike all around his house but would not be permitted to step within its four walls.

إِنِّى اُحَافِظُ كُلَّ مَنْ فِي الدَّار

'I will save all who dwell in the House.'[4]

For those who sought and cared for his shelter, he made it clear that this promise of security would not be confined only to such as occupy his house physically but would also cover those who dwell in his spiritual home — the Ahmadiyya Muslim Community. Thus he delivered manifest warnings to all who rejected him and gave glad tidings of miraculous protection to all who believed.

When he mentioned that the Ahmadis would be miraculously saved from this affliction, he made it clear at the same time that in exceptional cases, the Ahmadis who were Ahmadis in name only may also suffer. But by and large, they would be saved in such outstanding proportion as would leave no doubt in the mind of the observer that this protection was in no way accidental.

THE TALE OF THE PLAGUE in the Punjab is an amazing tale indeed. It testifies to the truth of the Promised Messiah[as] in letter and spirit. How could a man claim protection even from the common cold as a sign of his truth? To speak of the plague to show distinct partiality to his followers was too tall a claim to be made by an ordinary mortal if God Himself had not vouchsafed it to him. It was an exceptionally tall claim indeed that all who would sincerely submit to his authority as the Divinely appointed Imam of the age would be spared the agony of the plague.

When finally the hour struck, it struck to toll the bell over the funeral of his sworn enemies. Many among them had publicly vowed that it would be Mirza Ghulam Ahmad[as] himself who would die of the plague. But it was they themselves who were stricken by the plague along with their families, one after the other, until none were left to mourn their death. It did spare, as was promised, his followers, by an outstandingly large margin. A margin which could not be explained away by any factor of chance or accident. No earthly logic could account for the distinct partiality with which the plague treated the Ahmadis in hundreds of villages of mixed population. This miracle repeated itself everywhere with such brilliance as even the blind could see. And the blind did see and rushed towards the safe haven of Ahmadiyyat in such numbers as had never happened before. And lo, they were saved. But alas for those who possessed the faculty of sight that they were blinded by its dazzling brilliance. There were villages where no one was left to carry the coffins of the victims of the plague to the nearby graveyards, except the followers of Mirza Ghulam Ahmad[as]. They carried the corpses of the disbelievers on their shoulders to the burial ground without the least fear of contracting the plague.

Returning to Qadian from an overview of the Punjab, let us see what was happening there. Everything went according to the prophecy, but for an incident or two which appeared odd and discordant. It so happened that a prominent follower of the Promised Messiah, Maulawi Mohammad Ali by name, suffered from a very intense fever with all the symptoms resembling the plague. Even the glands under his armpits had swelled threateningly, causing severe pain and distress. The best available medical aid was provided, but without avail. His agony did not abate. He just could not reconcile himself to the fact that he, a companion of the Messiah[as], should meet such an end, contrary to the Divine promise. The agony of the plague in itself was unbearable, add to this the torture of conscience which might have tormented him, lest in the sight of God he was counted out of His true servants.

Thus he tossed in his bed and cried and wailed that someone should hasten to the Promised Messiah[as] to inform him of his miserable plight and urge him to visit him and bless him. This is what the Promised Messiah[as] did forthwith. It did not perturb him in the least that the patient was medically declared to be suffering from plague. He went to his bedside and put his hand on the forehead of Maulawi Sahib, speaking words of solace and comfort, reassuring him that as certainly as he was the true Messiah, Maulawi Sahib would not die of plague. It did not take Maulawi Sahib long to watch these prophetic words fulfilled. As the Promised Messiah[as] stood talking to him, his hand still resting on his forehead, his temperature subsided rapidly, leaving no sign of the fever or the plague behind. He sat up and touched himself here and there, bewildered at the rapidity with which the fever had vanished. So also were bewildered those who sat around awaiting his death but were destined instead to watch the miracle of his survival. He lived many long years after that before he died in Lahore in 1951, at the ripe old age of 77.

HOW COULD the plague differentiate between people who believed in the Promised Messiah and those who did not will always remain a mystery, but not for those who believe in the limitless attributes of the Omnipotent God.

A genuine question arises here as to what solid evidence can be presented for the satisfaction of neutral enquiry in support of whatever has been recorded in this chapter as facts. The problem is that the only direct evidence which can be produced is internal. The witnesses are all Ahmadis or those who converted to Ahmadiyyat after watching this miracle. There is no external evidence except that which is indirect and implied, yet it is powerful because it stems from hostile witnesses. The major problem is that no independent enquiry was constituted at that time by any neutral authority. There were only two parties, Ahmadis and non-Ahmadis. Of all the facts and figures in relation to the behavioural pattern of the plague, the only record available is from the archives of whatever was published in contemporary newspapers, magazines, pamphlets, posters and books. The only scrutiny regarding the reliability of this material which can be made is circumstantial.

The most important factor worthy of note here is that a strong vibrant interest had been created in the nature, claims and activities of the Ahmadiyya Jamaat in the period under review. An exceptionally hostile, strong non-Ahmadi press was giving sharp, pungent, negative coverage to whatever was happening in the newly emergent world of the Ahmadiyya Jamaat. Whatever was said or done by Mirza Ghulam Ahmad[as] of Qadian and whatever happened to him was keenly observed and eagerly recorded by his opponents. A full and rather overexcited coverage was given to anything and everything which could be turned against him. This hostile coverage was not confined merely to the non-Ahmadi Muslim press, but the Christian and the Hindu press did not miss the least opportunity either to censure him and bring him to disrepute at the slightest excuse. Had the coverage of the Ahmadiyya press on the issue of the plague been ever so slightly wrong, it would be impossible for the bitterly critical non-Ahmadiyya press to ignore it.

All through the period of seven years, or thereabouts, that the plague remained active in the Punjab, Mirza Ghulam Ahmad[as], the Promised Messiah would never let the public interest in the outcome of the plague in relation to the Ahmadis wane or die. Many of his well-known adversaries were locked with him in spiritual duels and every now and then claims and counterclaims were published regarding which of the two would die smitten down by the plague, as a sign of God's wrath. Many of his adversaries began to die one after the other and the remaining waited in suspense and fear. But the plague touched him not. It touched neither him nor his wife, none of his sons or daughters were afflicted by the plague either. Not even a mouse was ever found having died of plague within the four walls of his house.

He published these facts repeatedly adding fuel to the fire, invoking the hatred of his enemies and causing them to pray against him more than ever before to bring the curse of the plague upon him. But all in vain. Nothing happened to him and to those who lived within the boundaries of his physical and spiritual abode of peace and security. Can anyone produce a single line ever published in any newspaper or magazine or book of his time which falsified his claims by listing the names of any victims of the plague who belonged to his family or dwelled in his house?

The same goes for the overall publications of the Ahmadiyya press in those days which became conspicuous by their silence on such mishaps. No death is recorded by them in the family of the Promised Messiah[as] nor among those who lived around him. It is worthy of note that the Ahmadiyya Press routinely covered all incidents even remotely related to the Promised Messiah[as].

As far as the members of the Community outside Qadian were concerned, they were spared by the plague in an outstandingly large proportion. The death rate among the non-Ahmadis who died of the plague stood far higher by comparison to the very rare cases of Ahmadi deaths in the same villages.

Had this claim of the Ahmadiyya Press been wrong, the antagonist press must have played it up and capitalized on it. That it did not happen should be reasonably treated as strong indirect external evidence, by default.

Another irrefutable proof in favour of the Ahmadiyya claim is the fact of exceptionally accelerated growth of Ahmadiyyat during the years of the plague. The figures which were regularly published in the Ahmadiyya organ *Al-Ḥakam*, presented an enormous rise in the rate of conversion to Ahmadiyyat during this critical period. No denial of these figures was ever made by the non-Ahmadiyya press. They were figures of real people occupying real villages and towns. Why did not any section of the antagonist press give *Al-Ḥakam* the lie and publish counter evidence? Such are the times when silence speaks louder than words.

The fact that Ahmadiyyat spread far more rapidly during 1898-1906, the years of the plague in the Punjab, is indelible. According to the periodically published data in *Al-Ḥakam*, by the year 1902, the number of Ahmadis had risen from some tens of thousand to a hundred thousand. By the year 1904 the Ahmadi population had swelled to two hundred thousand. By 1906, the year when the plague finally beat a retreat, the number of Ahmadis had risen to four hundred thousand plus.

IN VIEW OF THE ABOVE, it should be borne in mind that had the prophecy of the Promised Messiah[as] been proved wrong, Ahmadiyyat must have been wiped out from the face of the earth. After the plague had taken its full toll, whatever number of Ahmadis were spared must have been stricken by the 'exposure of Mirza Ghulam Ahmad's[as] falsehood'. But that was not so. As the number of hostile opponents of Ahmadiyyat was counted down by the plague, the number of Ahmadis grew and swelled. Ahmadiyyat marched forward in leaps and bounds.

$$\text{اِنَّ فِىْ ذٰلِكَ لَاٰيٰتٍ لِّقَوْمٍ يَّتَفَكَّرُوْنَ} \quad 30{:}22$$

… In that surely are Signs for a people who reflect.[5]

Concerning the verse of the Quran upon which this entire prophecy is based, let us draw the reader's attention to the fact that this verse in itself is a miracle. To capture its miraculous beauty, the reader must be assisted to fully admire its fascinating subtleties. In the following passage, we have attempted to achieve this purpose. The following points need to be emphasized:

At the time of the Quranic revelation, the reasons for the spread of the bubonic plague were not known. No knowledge existed about the manner in which rats might have played a part in infecting others. It was certainly not their bites which did so. It was also not known that there existed a tiny wingless insect — the flea, which was the carrier of this fatal disease. Nor was it known that it was the bite of this flea which injected the plague virus into the bloodstream of its victims. If the Quran had been authored by a human, he could never have predicted the spread of the plague by the bite of an animal classified as the *da'bbah*.

Now we know that the animal which spreads the plague is an insect. Now we also know that an overwhelmingly large proportion of insects is winged, and those which are wingless are infinitesimally fewer by comparison, such as the lice, the silverfish and the non reproductive termites. And finally, it is now that we have come to know that the flea, despite being an insect, is also a *da'bbah* by virtue of its being wingless. It is this exceptional quality of the flea which rightfully entitles it to be called *da'bbah,* or the relevant Quranic verse could be censured as definitely wrong.

We humbly invite the attention of naturalists to this unique example and beg them to search their minds and hearts. Can they really dismiss this exception as a mere accident?

REFERENCES

1. *Nozūl-ul-Masīh* — Rūhānī Khazā'en (1984) Vol.18 pp.466-467
2. Translation of 27:83 by the author.
3. LANE, E.W. (1984) *Arabic-English Lexicon.* Islamic Text Society, William & Norgate. Cambridge.
4. *Tazkirah* — Collection of the Revelations and Dreams of the Promised Messiah — HAZRAT MIRZA GHULAM AHMAD OF QADIAN. (1969) Published by Al-Shirkatul Islāmiyyah Ltd. p. 428
5. Translation of 30:22 by Maulawi Sher Ali.

THE AIDS VIRUS

AZRAT MIRZA GHULAM AHMAD[as] also prophesied about another type of plague to appear later in some other parts of the world. In 1907, after the end of the plague in India, he received a revelation informing him of a type of plague to also appear in the future:

یورپ اور دوسرے عیسائی ملکوں میں ایک قسم کی طاعون پھیلے گی جو بہت ہی سخت ہو گی۔[1]

'A type of plague will spread in Europe and other Christian countries, which will be very severe.'

What is meant by the term 'a type of plague' and why should it particularly strike Europe and other Christian countries? A clue to this is found in a hadith* of the Holy Prophet[sa] of Islam in an observation he made almost thirteen hundred years before the time of the Promised Messiah. According to this tradition reported by Ibn-e-Majah's *Kitāb-ul-Fitan*, the Holy Prophet[sa] states:

لَمْ تَظْهَرِ الْفَاحِشَةُ فِي قَوْمٍ قَطُّ حَتَّى يُعْلِنُوا بِهَا إِلَّا فَشَا فِيهِمُ الطَّاعُونُ وَالْأَوْجَاعُ الَّتِي لَمْ تَكُنْ مَضَتْ فِي أَسْلَافِهِمُ الَّذِينَ مَضَوْا[2]

It never happens that permissiveness *(faḥshā)* overwhelms a people to the extent that they display their acts of sex shamelessly and they are not uniquely punished by God. Among them, invariably,

---

* The word of the Holy Prophet[sa] is termed *hadith* which is translated into English as tradition. But as the word tradition has many other connotations as well, the English reader may find it confusing at times. For this reason we shall refer to the Holy Prophet's[sa] word as hadith which is the correct technical term.

pestilence is made to spread and such other diseases, the like of which have never been witnessed by their forefathers.

The word *faḥshā* means 'permissiveness' with the connotation of audacity and shamelessness, resulting in open display of sex. It should be noted that mere permissiveness does not warrant so severe a chastisement from Allah; but when it exceeds all bounds and is acknowledged as a commonly accepted social behaviour, then that society is affected with some completely new sex-related disease as a sign of God's displeasure.

The accusing finger of this hadith seems to be pointing at the sinfulness of the present age rather than that of any other. Such shamelessness as has been described in the hadith is displayed these days on television, in newspapers and in magazines, day in and day out, to the extent that it has never been witnessed before in human history. Consequently, absolute justice requires that the punishment must match the crime. Sensual indulgence with flagrant shameless display is central to the chastisement prescribed. The prophecy of the Promised Messiah[as] specifically picks out Europe and other Christian countries. The earlier prophecy of the Holy Founder[sa] of Islam does not mention people of any country or religion, but confines itself to the nature of the crime, warranting a corresponding punishment.

Both prophecies read together make up the whole story. Among Christian countries the United States of America answers the description perfectly. But according to the latest census, sub-Saharan Africa leads the world in this particular type of permissiveness, with the Caribbean lagging only a few lengths behind.[3] In the census we have referred to, it is the Christian African countries which lead in the AIDS figures far beyond the rest of the African countries.

The only issue which remains to be resolved is the identity of 'that sort of plague' as has been mentioned in prophecies. It seems quite justified to claim that it is AIDS which is that punishment. Eminent physicians refer to it as a type of pestilence. Like the plague, it too causes inflammation of some glands with a high burning fever. It is as ruthless a killer as the bubonic plague has ever been. Yet it has its own unique features which the bubonic plague lacked. AIDS is definitely sex-related while the bubonic plague is not. It is precisely designed to punish sexual transgressions.

The reader is reminded here that religious prophecies should not be treated over-literally. European and other Christian countries are mentioned only to help us to locate and identify the territories where this new type of plague will be most rampant. It does not mean that it will remain confined only to Europe and other Christian countries.

The prophecy of the Holy Founder[sa] of Islam clearly indicates the possibility of a much wider application because it binds this disease not to countries, but to a specific moral crime. Wherever that causative crime will spread, the punitive disease will follow. But it will only become epidemic in such countries as are excessively permissive. It matters not what the names of such countries are, nor does it matter much whether their population is predominantly Christian, or Hindu, or Muslim. The countries and religions are not causative. What is causative is permissiveness, hence wherever the cause is at work, the effect will certainly follow.

The reason why European and other Christian countries are specifically mentioned while others are not, is perhaps because permissiveness as a progressive social behaviour at the national level is not witnessed elsewhere in the world. One will not hear of homosexuality being legalized except in Western countries. You will not hear of homosexuality in any religious institutions except in Christianity.

But it should be remembered however, that these countries though Christian in name, are farthest from Christian values. Nor can the Muslim countries, for that matter, be rightly described as custodians of Islam.

Hence, if permissiveness and the unrestrained display of shameless conduct are found among Hindu or Muslim countries there is no reason why the same consequent disaster should not befall them.

THE AIDS EPIDEMIC has already reached all the continents of the world and there will be hardly anyone not familiar with the horrors of this disease. However, it would be naive to assume that the full dimensions of the horror have been properly realized. Nor is it right to assume that AIDS has already played its role and will soon be on its way out. Ill-advised indeed are those who entertain the hope that soon scientific research will find an effective antidote or prophylactic against the AIDS virus. We entertain no such optimism. On the contrary, we are afraid that the main thrust of the disease is yet to come. The observation that lends support to this view relates to a general similarity between the first advent of the Messiah in the form of Jesus[as] and his second advent in the person of Ahmad[as] of Qadian.

This is not the proper place to enter into an in-depth study of similitude between the old and the new Christ. However, as far as the sign of the plague is concerned, we must point out that the plague also appeared as a sign to punish the antagonists of Jesus Christ[as]. At the rejection of Jesus[as], the first epidemic of plague was recorded in AD 65.

By coincidence or design, this plague epidemic covered mainly the areas where the message of Christ had reached and been denied. The plague struck again about one hundred years later in AD 167, but this time it devastated a much larger and wider part of the world, extending over two continents from Asia Minor to Rome and beyond to Gaul and Egypt. In all these countries the message of Christ[as] had already been delivered and was rejected by the majority of the people.

If, as suggested, the similarity between the two periods repeats itself, it would not be unlikely for the new type of plague to reach its climax by the end of this century extending into the beginning of the next one. This calculation is our estimation based on the fact that during the time of the Promised Messiah[as] this is how the first plague struck, with exceptionally greater intensity during the period 1898-1904. God knows best how far He wills to repeat these similarities in every detail, yet we should be warned and prepared.

We pray that God may save mankind from this catastrophe of global dimensions by enabling people to reform. By mending his ways and true repentance, it is not at all unlikely for man to win pardon from Allah and escape the consequences of his sin. But what is unlikely, alas, is for man to repent and mend his ways. It is of no significance whether one is religious or irreligious, whether one believes in God or denies His existence. As far as human moral conduct is concerned it seems to be universal in its sinfulness. Those who claim to be religious are unfortunately no less immoral than the irreligious. The so-called believers in God are no longer clearly distinguishable from those who do not believe. It will be no exaggeration, therefore, to declare the entire age to be at loss. This is how the Holy Quran pronounces its judgement on the people of the latter days:

وَالْعَصْرِ * اِنَّ الْإِنْسَانَ لَفِيْ خُسْرٍ * اِلَّا الَّذِيْنَ اٰمَنُوْا وَعَمِلُـوا الصّٰـلِحٰتِ وَتَوَاصَوْا بِالْحَقِّ ۙ وَتَوَاصَوْا بِالصَّبْرِ * 103:2-4

We call that age to witness,
That man is most certainly at loss.
Save for those who believe and do good deeds and admonish righteousness by righteous means, and admonish patience with patience.[4]

The fortunate few who would exercise patience and act righteously are by comparison far too small to turn the tide. An odd blade of grass, or a twitter or two of a finch, cannot turn the desolation of autumn into the splendour of spring.

REFERENCES

1. *Tazkirah* (1969), Al-Shirkatul Islāmiyyah Ltd., Rabwah. Urdu edition, p.705
2. *Sunan Ibn-e-Mājah*. Kitābul-Fitan, Bābul-'Uqoobāt. Vol.II. Dār-ul-Fikr Al-'Arabi, p.1333
3. UNAIDS and WHO (December 1996) HIV/AIDS: The Global Epidemic. UN web site.
4. Translation of 103:2-4 by the author.

PART VII

FUTURE OF REVELATION

ANIMALS LIVE FROM DAY TO DAY with whatever life offers them. They do not seem to look back to their past nor to a dreamy future ahead of them. Man is an exception in the animal kingdom. Seldom is he content with his present. Either he lives lost in the memories of the past or sustains himself with the hope that there are better days to come. Such hopes generally pertain to his economic, political or religious future. It is to his religious hopes that we now turn our gaze.

All major religions promise the advent of a Divine personage who would usher in a new era of hope for mankind and unite them under one Divine flag. This is the promised land which one day they all aspire to reach, govern and command. This is utopia, the meeting point of the hopes of all religions and this too, alas, becomes the parting of their ways. Only the dreams are shared but not their realization. They are unanimous in their belief that one Divine personage will certainly come as the saviour of the human race, but when it comes to his identity they could not disagree more with each other. Will he be Lord Krishna or Jesus Christ? Will he be Zoroaster or Buddha, or Confucius or Lao-tzu for that matter? Each is expecting a different person, under a different name and title; each is expecting him to belong exclusively to their own religious order. It is here that the gates one finds left open for the advent of the saviour begin to be shut again. They are seen shut from the vantage point of those who consider all other religions to be false except their own. The only gate they see open is their own; while their gate, as seen by others, is also shut. All who had joined in the chorus, singing the songs of the advent of a universal Redeemer, begin to sing their separate songs when it comes to his identity. Either he must somehow materialize out of their dreams, or they will accept none other. Alas, the latter is the only fate which they have carved for themselves. Why should God care for their pleasure if they care not for His? Let them create their saviour themselves out of the nothingness of their wild irrational hopes.

It is so intriguing to watch this wrangle on a global scale. After the dust of claims and counterclaims settles down, the only agreement the proponents of different religions reach is to continue to disagree even more vehemently. The Reformer they will accept has to be of their own faith and brand, or none other. Their talk is idle, their hopes are vain, their saviours dwell only in their dreams.

Can the Redeemer, whenever he comes, fulfil the hopes of all religions or will he meet those of only one? To whom will he actually belong, whose aspirations will he fulfil while all will be chanting by the fountain of hope: *make them mine, make them mine, make them mine!* The question which finally emerges is whether a single person is promised or many, simultaneously. God has no contradiction in Him, hence He will either send one person with a single message, or none at all. What would happen to different warring factions of various religions at such a time, each holding views divergent from the other? It is to this inherent contradiction in their attitudes that we shall now turn our attention.

THE WAY THEY ALL ENVISION the realization of their hopes is an impossible task. Take for example the case of the Jewish people, who have long been yearning for the advent of the Christ. For thousands of years they have been striking their heads against the Wailing Wall and still do so, beseeching the Christ to come. Never do they realize that he has come and gone but not in the way they had expected, nor in the manner and style they had assigned to his advent. Thus the gate they thought they had kept open lay practically shut and locked. How tantalizing it must be that the guest one so dearly awaits does not come though one sees no hurdle obstructing his path. In reality, all those who await the coming of any Divine guest are themselves responsible for placing impassable obstructions in his way. But somehow they remain unaware of what they do. If they could only realize that their expectations are impossible to be fulfilled they could at least rest in the sort of peace which follows despondency. The barriers help to relinquish hope and extinguish the flame of expectancy but only if they are recognized. If some people are oblivious to their existence, it is they who are to be blamed for their frustration. The Jewish people, for example, who await the advent of the Christ have not understood this hard, simple reality despite their wisdom. For them there is nothing but to weep and wail beside a wall of stones, beseeching the advent of a Messiah who can never come. For them, none will ever come.

But they are not alone in this inconsistency of being stupid and wise all at once. The case of all other religions who expect an ultimate Redeemer is no different from theirs. The actors are different of course, the acts are played in different garb, yet the drama remains the same. A Christ should have come to the aid of the Jewish people and did come but it was not the same Christ they were awaiting, so they failed to recognize him. They expected him to appear with a crown over his head seated on a royal throne. He would be a warrior Messiah, they believed, who would successfully lead the armies of the Israelites against the despotic rule of the Roman Empire. Two thousand years have passed since their rejection of Jesus[as] as Messiah, yet no Messiah of their expectation has come. History has changed the political geography of the world and the prophecy of the coming of the Christ has lost all relevance. There is no Judea or Palestine under the yoke of a Roman Empire from which the Jewish people are to be liberated. In fact, that Roman Empire which once ruled half of the world has completely disappeared from the map of the world. We still hear of *deliverance*, but it is a deliverance from the Jews, not of the Jews.

Although there was nothing wrong in their belief that Christ would be born like any other human child to a human mother, yet they attached some supernatural preconditions to his birth which could not have been realized. Their belief about the bodily descent of Elijah[as] before the advent of the Messiah, is just the case in point which effectively blocked the passage of the Messiah they awaited. So the Jewish position, vis-à-vis the advent of a Messiah, in reality turns out to be a denial of his advent altogether.

TURNING OUR GAZE from the Jews to the Christians, we find a situation not too dissimilar to the one described above. Imagine a Christ paying a second visit to earth in the grand style envisaged by the Christians who still await his literal second coming. A son of God descending in glory from heaven in a human form is an idea fit only for fiction, yet it serves to keep hope, or shall we say blind faith, alive. Looking at it from the rational vantage point of the non-Christian, the absurdity becomes even more glaring. No non-Christian, be he religious or otherwise, can share this belief because it speaks of an outrageous wedlock between spirit and matter. Yet the Christians see no element of irrationality about it because dogma has blinded them.

The same anomaly of the Jews and the Christians applies to the unreal and supernatural expectations of the followers of all other religions. Even a speck of irrationality in the beliefs of others offends their sense of right and wrong, while they are totally blind to the presence of the same in their own, however preposterous it may be. They could not have failed to detect the squint of their own eyes, if only they had looked at themselves through the eyes of others. Rationality would have helped each of them to realize that the literal revisit to earth by any prophet or so-called god is illogical. Never has it taken place at any time, anywhere in the entire history of the world, nor can it ever take place in the future. Never was the founder of any religion sighted to have descended from on high; he always appeared through the normal course of human birth. Invariably, he launched a movement that had to strive hard for its survival against all odds. This is reality; any belief that does not conform to this must be relegated to the realms of fantasy. All such promises for the revival of religion must be rejected which offend rationality and have never before been employed by God in religious history.

The case of the Muslims seems to offer a rather strange exception to this general rule. Yet, on closer examination, one can discern practically no difference in their position and that of the others, except in the sequence. The Muslims begin by claiming that Prophet Muhammad[sa] is the last of all the prophets and his finality is absolute. The term *Khatme-Nabuwwat,* the finality of prophethood, is unanimously understood by all the mainstream Muslims to mean this. Despite this, they too await the descent of Jesus Christ[as], an old prophet of God. Will his advent not violate the finality of Prophet Muhammad[sa]? This is the most crucial question they must answer. In response to this evident contradiction, they propose that though a new prophet cannot be created, an old prophet can be brought back to fulfil new needs. By this strategy, they seem to have succeeded in keeping the door of prophethood (*Nabuwwat*) shut and sealed, while manoeuvring to furtively admit Jesus through the back door. The contemporary Muslims, whether they are Sunnites or Shi'ites, seem to share the same interpretation of finality (*Khatme-Nabuwwat*). All have faith in the re-advent of Jesus[as] as a prophet of God, whilst believing simultaneously in the absolute finality of Prophet Muhammad[sa].

The problem of inherent contradiction in their belief becomes even more pronounced when it comes to the prophesied advent of Al-Imam Al-Mahdi. As an Imam he is to be directly commissioned by God, and as such it should be incumbent upon every Muslim to believe in him. This aspect of his office will be further elaborated later on. It is briefly mentioned here only to emphasize that the office of Al-Imam Al-Mahdi, despite not possessing the title, holds the prerequisites of a prophet all the same. Having said that we must return now to the likelihood of the re-advent of Jesus Christ[as] and the form in which this may take place. The Ahmadiyya belief differs from the mainstream Muslims only in form and not in the act of his re-advent. The question is whether the form will be literal or metaphorical. Will he be the same person, or will another person be born reminiscent of the old one? Will he appear as a Christian prophet turned Muslim, or a Muslim prophet turned into the metaphorical image of Jesus Christ[as]? What will be his relationship to all other religions? These are the intriguing questions which must be fully addressed.

THE STANCE of the Ahmadiyya Muslim Jamaat is singularly rational. In principle it accepts the claims of all religions who promise the advent of a universal Divine Reformer in the latter days. When the Hindus talk of the re-advent of Krishna, their claim has as much right to be accepted as that of the Christians when they speak of the second coming of Jesus Christ[as]. Likewise the expectations of Zoroastrians concerning Zoroaster, if they too look forward to his re-advent, or the hopes of the Buddhists or Confucianists that a Buddha or a Confucius would reappear as the Promised Saviour should also be treated with equal respect. But the recognition of the truth of all such diverse and seemingly contradictory claims can only read sense if they are taken metaphorically and not literally. The only rational inference that can be drawn is that the Promised Reformer has to be a single person, embodying the advent of all. Otherwise, the literal fulfilment of all such prophecies is impossible because of the supernatural element intertwined with all of them. This is what the Founder[as] of the Ahmadiyya Jamaat put across to the people of the world with incontrovertible logic. The promise of the simultaneous advent of so many reformers could only be metaphorical and not corporeal. It was exactly in this sense that he claimed to have fulfilled the advent of Jesus[as] and the Mahdi as one person and also the advents of all others like Buddha[as], Krishna[as] and other promised reformers awaited anywhere on earth.

Leaving for a while the reaction this claim created among others, we begin with the account of the turmoil it created within the orthodoxy in Islam. They were not concerned with the re-advent of Buddha or Krishna or others in whom they did not believe but they were deeply concerned with Jesus[as], the prophet to the House of Israel. For anyone to claim to be the reborn image of Jesus[as] was far too much for them to digest. For the Jesus[as] of their dreams to be declared physically dead was an enormity absolute. For his likeness to be born among them was nauseatingly repulsive to the Muslims.

It should be remembered that prior to his above mentioned claim, the fame of Mirza Ghulam Ahmad[as] had spread far and wide in British India because of his book *Brahin-e-Ahmadiyyah*. Paying tribute to the author of this book, Maulawi Muhammad Hussain Batalvi, a renowned Muslim scholar of the Ahle-Hadith sect, has introduced the author of this book to be the best defender of Islam, since the demise of Prophet Muhammad[sa].[1] However in the midst of this popularity, when he suddenly pronounced Jesus[as], the prophet of Israel, to be dead instead of being alive in heaven, the position changed dramatically. The same scholars who had praised him with hyperbolical tributes changed their attitude diametrically. What was he as compared to their Lord Jesus Christ, the would-be Saviour of the world? Overnight his fame plummeted to earth from the celestial heights it had occupied. The image of Jesus had to be tossed back to heaven aloft; he who claimed to have come in his likeness should have been killed instead. The commotion stirred by Mirza Ghulam Ahmad[as] of Qadian was such as the like of which had never been seen before in the religious history of India. Against him, a pandemonium of abuse and vilification broke loose. The rising star of Muslim India, the most sought for leader of Islam, became the most hunted person, no longer deemed fit even to be called an ordinary Muslim. But it completely failed to cower him. Nothing could deter him from carrying forward the Divine task bestowed upon him.

The Christians did not lag far behind either in their hostile reaction. They left no stone unturned to destroy him and demolish his mission. Even fake charges of murder were pressed against him in the British Indian courts of law. But he remained completely unruffled, not in the least bit intimidated.

As though that was not enough, he further pronounced himself a manifestation of Krishna[as], the great Indian prophet who was idolized and worshipped as god incarnate. He personally antagonized the Arya Samaj, the most active and redoubtable sect of the Hindus, by launching a counteroffensive against their ferocious attacks on Islam and the Holy Prophet[sa]. He also invited their leaders to a spiritual duel with devastating effect upon those who accepted it. In short, he claimed that all the prophecies relating to the Reformers of the latter days were applicable to only one person. Different names and titles mentioned in different scriptures were of no significance. All that was significant was that the Reformer, whoever he may be, must be commissioned by God as the universal Reformer of the latter days. To those who were prisoners of prejudice, he and his claims meant nothing and it was largely by them that he was rejected with unyielding antagonism. He was rejected like all the servants of God before him and was most certainly supported by God as He has always supported His servants.

It is amazing how people keep forgetting that all prophets of God are treated alike by Him. They too show no difference in their complete submission to Him. Likewise, the universal Promised Reformer will belong exclusively to Him and not to the various religious denominations who expect him to support their distorted beliefs. He will represent God, not those who no longer represent Him. He will only belong to all His servants but not to the self-styled masters of His servants.

The Unity of God and the institution of prophethood from among humans are the two fundamentals which belong to every religion. Names and titles differ but they matter not. What matters is for the claimant to be from God. Mirza Ghulam Ahmad[as] never claimed that he had become different persons with different names and titles moulded into one. But most clergy feigned to misunderstand him in this regard and incited the ignorant masses to jeer and mock him telling them that he claimed to be all the promised prophets kneaded into one person. The masses were rudely shocked. How could a Krishna, a Jesus, a Mahdi and a Buddha all become a single person? 'The claimant has to be mad,' some shouted in scorn. The treatment meted out to him is reminiscent of the same treatment meted out to the Holy Founder[sa] of Islam when he claimed the uncompromising Unity of God. The idolatrous priesthood wilfully distorted his message and made the people believe that he had forged all their gods into a single one whom he styled as Allah.

اَجَعَلَ الْاٰلِهَةَ اِلٰـهًا وَّاحِدًا ۖ اِنَّ هٰذَا لَشَىْءٌ عُجَابٌ ۖ 38:6*

'What! Has he made all the gods into one God? This is indeed an astounding thing.'[2]

It should not be difficult for an unbiased investigator to see the wisdom of Mirza Ghulam Ahmad[as] during all his disputations with his opponents. His position was always that of a rational person. Were it not so he could easily be proved wrong in most of his beliefs and contentions by the same instrument of rationality.

If he were wrong each religion would be visited by a separate reformer holding a different name, title and ideology. This would open a Pandora's box of claims and counterclaims which once opened could never be shut again. Each claimant would proclaim himself to be the only true manifestation of the Promised Reformer. Each would invite all of mankind to himself as the only hope of their salvation. Each would declare all rivals to be mere hoaxes and impostors. The utter madness of this scenario is self-evident. No man with any element of sanity can believe in a God who would split humans into hundreds of conflicting schisms and factions in His own name, with His own authority.

WHAT MANNER OF GOD would it be who would make Jesus descend among the Christians, issuing a call for the conquest of the entire world in the name of the Trinity – God the Father, God the Son, and the Holy Ghost? Having done that, *He* would hasten to incarnate *Himself* in the form of Lord Krishna upon Indian soil, assuring the Indian people that *He* is neither one, nor two, nor three, *He* is a multitudinous god whose persons and manifestations are hard to count. *He* is to be worshipped as trees, as snakes, as scorpions, as elephants and as the deafening thunderstorms. *He* is to be worshipped as a moon gliding in the stillness of the night. It is *He* who is also the sun and a countless number of stars in the heavens. On the earth *He* can clearly be recognised as the cows, the monkeys, the bears, the hyenas, the tigers, the horses, the donkeys, and limitless forms of other animals dwelling in the sea, on land and in the air. *He* is also to be worshipped as ghosts and other ghostly forms of human fantasy. 'Run towards me', *He* would claim, 'and worship us'.

Before *His* voice is drowned in the tumult of chantings: 'O Lord Krishna, hare-Ram, hare-Ram, we worship you one and all', another voice would be heard gradually rising in crescendo as the voice of the Buddha. It would loudly reject the existence of all such godly figures as Lord Krishna had claimed. He would scorn at the very idea of the existence of God: 'I am Buddha', he would shout at the top of his voice. 'I am no God, neither is there

667

any God besides me. I am only the consummation of human wisdom. That is all you need to know on earth. Let us deny all gods together and celebrate our deliverance from the shackles of this human myth. I have come again to deliver you from God as I always did after every millennium, and there is none other besides me who can guide you as I can'.

Before he sinks into an all-pervasive silence and retreats into his inner void of eternal nothingness, another voice would rise loud and clear from the neighbouring country of Iran. It would be that of Ahura Mazda, the god of light, speaking through the mouth of Zoroaster. 'The voice you just heard', he would pronounce, 'O children of Bharat and Tibet and China, must have been the voice of Ahraman – the god of darkness, the only god besides me. It had to be he, because there is none other except he and I. Listen carefully O children of Adam: God is neither one nor three, nor four or five. It is a folly to believe in any number of multiple gods. We are neither one nor many, we are just two and the rest is fiction. There is me – the god of goodness, and he — the god of evil, whose voice you just heard impersonating Buddha. He is the god of darkness, while I am that of light. He always denies me, he always rejects me. He always dissuades my servants from worshipping me. He informs mankind that there is none worthy of worship other than man himself. He occupies the seat of each man's ego and in the name of that ego runs away with all the homage paid to it. Still god he is, I must admit, dark as the darkest night he may be. So bear with him, yet beware of him and worship only me'.

In the midst of the tumult created by the warring religious factions mentioned above, the world of Islam will also be stirred to action with the advent of the Mahdi. He will come brandishing his sword, if he is really as bloody as many of the mainstream clergy believe. He will issue the call for a Holy War fighting all the non-Islamic governments of the world.

In this paroxysm of religious madness, religion itself would become the ultimate target. Sanity would take flight from this arena of imbecility, beseeching God to rescue religion from the hands of its rescuers. Without urgent remedial measures by Him, the Hindu, the Christian, the Buddhist, the Zoroastrian, the Jew and the Muslim will all suffer alike.

No man with common sense would hold a brief for such senseless and irrational understanding of God's designs. Rationality and common sense must be granted their due role in the interpretation of religious prophecies and parables. The golden age of the ultimate unification of man could only be consummated if a single Reformer appeared in the name of God, in a single religion of His choice. This, the only rational solution of the problems confronting the religious world of the latter days, has been firmly rejected by the very people who needed it for their survival. They continue to cling, instead, to their empty vision of a golden age which is nothing but a mirage.

The above scenario is a genuine attempt to explain the self-contradictory position of each religion regarding the role it will play in the ultimate redemption of mankind. They open the doors of hope and shut them themselves. The case of the Muslims is only opposite in sequence. They begin to shut the doors by pronouncing the absolute finality of the Holy Prophet[sa] and no sooner have they done so than they begin to open them again. In reality, however, their stance remains unchanged. Hence the drama played on the Muslim stage is essentially no different from the one played on the stages of other world religions. Despite declaring the total uncompromising finality of the Holy Prophet[sa] they cling no less eagerly to the figure of Prophet Jesus[as]. They claim that he will certainly come after the Holy Prophet[sa] yet the manner they assign to his coming makes his coming impossible. Thus, for all practical purposes their position remains unaltered.

The Rationale of Finality

The finality of any prophet can be observed with reference to his message as well as with reference to his status. It is possible for a prophet to be final in his message and his status, yet it is also possible for another lesser prophet to come after him without violating his finality. It is this aspect of prophethood that we are going to thoroughly examine now.

The belief in the finality of the Quranic law and in the finality of the Prophet[sa] to whom this law was revealed, is unanimously held by all Muslims. The Quran — a complete code of life — claims for itself a promise of eternal Divine protection from interpolation by human hands. If this claim is right, as the Muslims believe and demonstrate it to be, the bearer of such a book must be accepted as the last law-bearing prophet. This is clearly understandable and is so endorsed by the entire world of Islam without exception. But from the non-Muslim vantage point, it is difficult to comprehend how any Book could fulfil the needs of all ages and defy the requirements for change during the times to come. Add to this the Quranic claim of universality and the problem will increase manifold. How can it be logically explained that any Divine Book could satisfactorily address the ethnic and parochial problems of all mankind alike? There are Europeans, Americans, Africans, Arabs, Russians, Israelis, and numerous people of Asian origin with different ethnic backgrounds and inherited cultures. Their political and social traditions also differ so widely that it is difficult to visualize how a single universal code of religious law could satisfy them with equal justice.

In answer to both these questions, the Quran claims that all its teachings are founded on the human psyche which is common to mankind and unchangeable in relation to time. Any teaching which perfectly corresponds to the human psyche becomes unchangeable. It is this principle that the Quran alludes to when it says:

$$\text{فَاَقِمْ وَجْهَكَ لِلدِّيْنِ حَنِيْفًا ۚ فِطْرَتَ اللّٰهِ الَّتِيْ فَطَرَ النَّاسَ عَلَيْهَا ۚ لَا}$$
$$\text{تَبْدِيْلَ لِخَلْقِ اللّٰهِ ۚ ذٰلِكَ الدِّيْنُ الْقَيِّمُ ۙ وَلٰكِنَّ اَكْـــثَرَ النَّـــاسِ لَا}$$
$$\text{يَعْلَمُوْنَ}^* \text{ 30:31}$$

So set thy face to *the service of* religion as one devoted *to God. And follow* the nature made by Allah – the nature in which He has created mankind. There is no altering the creation of God. That is the right religion. But most men know not.[3]

Indeed the nature created by God cannot be altered. Even the atheist must concede that human nature has remained universally unaltered since time immemorial. But a Book of Law corresponding to this unalterable nature can itself be changed all the same by the interference of humans. The Quran takes care of this danger by declaring it is a well-protected book.

$$\text{اِنَّا نَحْنُ نَزَّلْنَا الذِّكْرَ وَاِنَّا لَهٗ لَحٰـــفِظُوْنَ}^* \text{ 15:10}$$

Verily, it is We Who have sent down this Exhortation, and most surely We are its Guardian.[4]

History has proved this claim to be right. Hence the Prophet[sa] who was bestowed this Book has to be accepted as the last law-bearer. Nothing in this claim is irrational, but when it is suggested that even non-law-bearing prophets cannot come, the jurisdiction of finality is overextended without any rational justification. No sooner have they made this claim of absolute finality than they venture to demolish it themselves. The cracks begin to appear the moment they hasten to exempt Jesus[as] from this all-pervasive law of finality.

When confronted with this dilemma, they dismiss it with a mere wave of their hand as though it were no dilemma at all.

The reappearance of Jesus[as] as a prophet after Prophet Muhammad[sa], they argue, does not contradict his absolute finality on the following counts:

- Jesus would be brought back from a stock of prophets who had already been commissioned before the advent of Prophet Muhammad[sa]. Thus his finality will not be violated. It can only be violated if a prophet is raised after his advent even if that prophet brings no new law and is selected by God from within his own *Ummah* (people).
- Jesus' prophethood would be the one granted to him during his advent prior to Islam.
- Moreover because during his second advent he would be subordinated to the Holy Prophet[sa], he would no longer be held as independent.

Hence by being an older prophet and by becoming subordinated, he would not violate the seal of prophethood. As such, their concept of finality only means that new prophets cannot be commissioned while old prophets can be brought back; but this is sheer absurdity. What manner of an All-Wise God would He be who would pass the verdict of absolute finality in favour of anyone despite His knowledge that a prophet would certainly be needed after

672

him? The question of old or new is irrelevant. Central to the issue is the question of need.

The need for another prophet after the advent of the last is an intrinsically contradictory belief. Faced with this dilemma the Ulema always twist the issue by arguing that the need for the advent of a prophet may occur after the final prophet had come and gone. Yet, the absoluteness of his finality would remain intact as long as the new need is fulfilled by an old prophet. But anyone should be able to see through this transparent effort at cheating. The difference of old or new is just a childish attempt to confuse the issue. If Jesus[as] of Nazareth reappears and submits to the supremacy of Prophet Muhammad[sa], he would still be a prophet after him. To fulfil the new need by borrowing an old prophet from a bygone people is far worse than fulfilling the same need by raising a new prophet from within the people of Islam. If the former does not violate the Doctrine of Finality the latter most certainly cannot.

AL-Imam Al Mahdi (The Guided Leader)

We may now be permitted to deviate from the issue of Jesus'[as] re-advent, but only for a while, to turn our gaze upon the status of Al-Imam Al-Mahdi.

According to the prophecies of the Holy Prophet[sa], Jesus[as] does not seem to be the only one whose appearance is predicted in the latter days. One finds the repeated mention of another Divine Reformer, under the title of Al-Mahdi, which means 'The Guided One'. Most traditions speak of Isa[as] (Jesus) and Al-Mahdi (the Guided Imam) as two different persons. But there is one prominent exception. Ibn-e-Mājah — one of the six authentic books of tradition — creates a strong impression that the two Promised Reformers would in fact be one person, only holding two different titles. The exact words of the tradition run as follows:

$$\text{لَا الْمَهْدِىُّ إِلَّا عِيْسَى ابْنُ مَرْيَمَ}^{5}$$

There would be no Mahdi other than Isa (Jesus).

This can only mean that the promised Mahdi himself is referred to as Jesus[as]. However, Al-Mahdi is to be born within the *Ummah*, according to most traditions. How then, could he be the person of Jesus[as] if Jesus[as] is to descend from heaven after him? This can only happen if Jesus is a mere title which Al-Mahdi would possess together with his own so that no separate Jesus would descend from the heavens. His role will be performed by Al-Mahdi instead. It ensues that the prophet Jesus[as] would be born metaphorically, as Al-Imam Al-Mahdi within Islam. This leads us to the issue of determining the real status of Al-Mahdi. As will be shown presently, his status has to be that of a non-law-bearing subordinate prophet though the mainstream Ulema do not refer to him as such. In the case of Jesus[as], they can freely refer to him as a prophet because of the reasons mentioned above; but in the case of Al-Mahdi they cannot do so lest this admission should clearly clash with their Doctrine of Finality.

Their strategy regarding the Mahdi is completely different. For them, he will remain an uncrowned prophet to whom all attributes of a prophet are freely granted except for the title. It is like defining a man without calling him one, while calling him by any other name would not make him less than a man. The Ulema must realize that the status of Al-Mahdi must be determined by virtue of his attributes. His entitlement to the status of a prophet cannot be denied him as long as he functions as one. If the prerequisites of a prophet are combined in any person, then call him by whatever title you may, a prophet he would always remain. A denial of him, while he will be directly commissioned by God, will be tantamount to a denial of God. As such, whoever refuses to believe in Al-Mahdi as a subordinate prophet will lose his right to be counted among the true believers. Belief in him will be incumbent upon every Muslim, as admitted even by the orthodoxy. Thus he would enjoy a prerogative which is shared only by a prophet and by no one less than a prophet. The act of not granting Al-Mahdi the status he is entitled to enjoy can in no way deprive him of that right. The inconsistency in their beliefs will by no means become less glaring.

Non-law-bearing Prophets and Revelation

In Islam, the status of a prophet is the highest a man is granted. A prophet is not just a person who prophesies, he is the one who is specifically commissioned as such by God. All reformers are not essentially prophets but all prophets are essentially reformers. Revelation by itself does make one a prophet. Even non-prophets can be granted revelation and be blessed by communion with Him.

Revelation has a much wider field of application with many connotations such as dreams, visions, inspirations and even verbal addresses. As such it has never been denied by most scholars even in the medieval ages. The controversy only arose in relation to the institution of prophethood and it is this particular aspect of revelation that is being presently examined.

One can easily understand the wisdom behind the discontinuity of law-bearing prophets in the light of the foregoing discussion. The question which must be examined at length is, why should non-law-bearing prophets also be discontinued and why should the institution of prophethood in its entirety be brought to an abrupt end?

The history of religion proves beyond a shadow of doubt that it has never been essential for every prophet to bring a new law. There are many among them like Isaac[as], Jacob[as], Joseph[as], Lot[as] and Isaiah[as], who did not bring any new law. However, they shared with the prophets before them the distinction of having been commissioned by God as Divinely appointed spiritual leaders.

REFERENCES

1. BATALVI, MAULAWI MUHAMMAD HUSSAIN, *Ishā'at-us-Sunnah* (June/July/Aug, 1884) No.6. Vol.7. p.169
2. Translation of 38:6 by the author.
3. Translation of 30:31 by Maulawi Sher Ali.
   (Note: The author has replaced the word 'Allah' by 'God')
4. Translation of 15:10 by the author.
5. *Sunan Ibn-e-Mājah.* Kitābul-Fitan. Bābo Shiddatiz-Zamān

ATTEMPTS TO PHILOSOPHICALLY JUSTIFY THE FINALITY OF NON-LAW-BEARING PROPHETHOOD

TWO MAJOR ATTEMPTS have been made by Muslim theologians and thinkers to logically justify the cessation of even non-law-bearing prophets. The first relates to the issue of the need for a new teacher. The advent of a perfect teacher and a perfect book, it is argued, obviates the need of any other teacher to follow. Of course, if it can be proved that the presence of a perfect book and the appearance of a perfect teacher are sufficient guarantees against any future moral or spiritual decline, then there is no reason why, after this, another prophet should ever be raised again. Regrettably however, this proposition can neither be proved correct theoretically nor historically.

This contention is insupportable because the bringing of a book of law is not the only function performed by prophets. Prophethood is a thing of many splendours. After the death of a law-bearing prophet, the mere preservation of his book and his traditions cannot offer a sufficient substitute for prophethood itself. The case in point becomes amply clear when we examine the conduct of Muslims after the demise of the Holy Prophet^{sa}. The progressive deterioration of Muslim society should be sufficient to prove this point. The difference between their moral status during the lifetime of the Holy Prophet^{sa} and that of Muslims today defies comparison. The Book however remains the same perfect, unaltered, un-interpolated Book that it was fourteen hundred years ago.

THE SECOND justification in support of the Doctrine of Absolute Finality relates to the idea of the intellectual maturity of man. The chief proponent of this view is no less a person than 'Allāmah Iqbal claimed by some to be the greatest Muslim thinker of modern times. This doctrine of maturity is based on the assumption that the Holy Quran was revealed at a time when man had finally reached the ultimate stage of his mental and intellectual maturity. As such, he stood in no further need of day-to-day guidance by any Divine personage as did his ancestors of earlier ages. A beautiful philosophy but how hollow and empty of substance it turns out to be under closer scrutiny. The very premise that man has matured enough to be able to draw his own conclusions and chart his own course of conduct from the principle teachings of a perfect religion is challengeable on many counts.

It should not be forgotten that at every stage of man's progress, he always considered himself to be at the summit of intellectual maturity. At every point in history, the generation which occupied it also considered itself to be at the pinnacle of human progress. Looking back from their vantage point, all previous generations must have appeared less mature and less advanced by comparison. Yet at no stage in the past has man behaved wisely enough to guide himself. Heads such as that of the Pharaoh's were always raised in defiance of Divine guidance. All such rebels rejected the prophets of their time with the same inflated ideas of their own importance. All repeated the same claim over and over again that they had matured to take care of their own affairs. Nonetheless, history proves each of them to be wrong. It is so naive therefore, to consider the contemporary age as the only one in which man has finally become self-sufficient in every aspect of his moral and spiritual requirements.

As far as the concept of maturity is concerned, it is also falsified by the realities of history. After the passing away of prophets the division and multiplication of religious sects, based on doctrinal differences and varying interpretations, is a universal trend that has not spared the followers of any religion including Islam. Hence, it is not simply his intellectual maturity which helps man to draw right conclusions from the scriptures, he must also be Divinely guided.

If 'maturity of man' is taken to mean that he becomes independent in drawing his conclusions from the study of scriptures, then there must ensue a perfect unity of agreement on all the fundamental aspects of religious teachings. Alas, what we observe in real life fails miserably to support this view. Muslims, the proud recipients of the last perfect Book, are no less divided among themselves in the matter of interpretation than are the peoples of all other religions. To what avail therefore, is the so-called maturity of man? The history of religion proves that people once split into sects and schisms have never been reunified by human effort alone. The same inevitably applies to the Muslims today. Without the agency of a Divine Reformer, they cannot be assembled again under the single flag of Unity. But they have outrightly rejected this Divine measure, the only avenue of hope left open to them.

The existence of about seventy-two doctrinal divisions among them, despite a well-preserved book and a well-documented record of traditions, throws a dismal light on the Iqbalian philosophy of the maturity of man.

Their differences are not merely marginal. They are fundamental and deep-rooted, further multiplying and proliferating as time goes by. Add to this the moral destitution prevailing in the Muslim world and the tragedy of their lifeless existence becomes all the more pathetic. Commit their survival to the maturity of their intellect and perform ablution for their funeral rites, 'ashes to ashes, dust to dust and earth to earth — Amen!'

What misery! Why can modern intellectuals not understand that the purification of a religious society is a task which the mere existence of a Perfect Book cannot perform? Were it so, the followers of Islam must have retained an exemplary state of ideological unity. This unfortunately is farthest from the truth.

All that can be said here in defence of the late Dr 'Allāmah Sir Muhammad Iqbal is that the idea of blocking the passage of Heavenly light with this balderdash did not originate from him. His mistake was to copy, rather blindly one must say, the great German philosopher Nietzsche. It was Nietzsche who had first employed the idea of the maturity of human mind in the modern age against any need of guidance from God. In fact, Nietzsche coaxed man to come to age and utilize his own faculties of five senses. Overman, or superman, is Nietzsche's term for a man who reaches a stage of maturity where his senses are developed to the full. Such a man needs no God to guide him — a God which according to him is no more than a conjecture. Such conjectures were born out of an imperfect faculty of reasoning during an age when man had not yet matured enough to become his own master. Now that man had attained maturity, he concluded in his book *Thus spoke Zarathustra** — the symbolic oracle of the wisdom of Nietzsche that there was no more need for holding onto conjectures.

---

* see footnote on Zoroaster in *Zoroastrianism*.

'Once one said God when one looked upon distant seas; but now I have taught you to say: overman (superman).

'God is a conjecture; but I desire that your conjectures should not reach beyond your creative will.'[1]

'Could you *think* a god? But this is what the will to truth should mean to you: that everything be changed into what is thinkable for man, visible for man, feelable by man. You should think through your own senses to their consequences.'[2]

'God is a conjecture; but who could drain all the agony of this conjecture without dying?'[2]

The long and short of *Thus spoke Zarathustra* is a rebellion of Nietzsche against a conjectural god which in fact is the Christian idea of God, and to understand Zarathustra clearly as to why he rebelled against God, one must read the chapter *Retired.*[3] But for our purpose it should be sufficient to note that the oracle of Nietzsche's wisdom sets man free from being guided from on high. The maturity of his faculties is sufficient to guide him.

This exactly is the Iqbalian philosophy against the need of a prophet after man has matured to the maximum of his faculties. Instead of employing this borrowed philosophy for a categorical rejection of the need for God, 'Allāmah Iqbal neatly trimmed the maturity concept to suit his own purpose within the framework

NEITZSCHE

IQBAL

of Islam. He conceded that though man stands in need of a Perfect Master and a Perfect Book, once this objective is accomplished he requires no more to be badgered with any further interference from on high. But that is not all there is to it. The doctrine of maturity, as amended by Iqbal, does not merely do away with the need of prophethood, it does away altogether with the need for any communication from God even in the form of non-prophetic revelations. This has to be the only logical conclusion drawn from his doctrine of maturity. The maturity concept requires total independence of man from further Divine guidance in any form. He has become capable of taking all-important decisions for himself in the light of the guidance already vouchsafed to him. Man, Iqbal argued, is no longer a child to be walked with his little finger held in a prophet's hand. Has he not matured to full adulthood, to shift for himself? A sound healthy logic it seems, but just one glance at the spiritual decadence and utter moral destitution of man today is sufficient to dispel this argument as entirely fallacious and conjectural.

ENOUGH of Iqbal and his postulations. Let us now turn to Maudoodi, another renowned scholar of the mainstream Sunni Muslims. He pleads that the absolute cessation of prophethood after Prophet Muhammad[sa] has been a singular blessing of God upon mankind. It is a boon, especially for the Muslims, because it spares them the risk of rejecting a Divine messenger of God ever again. They are shielded from ever being accursed by God, as others before them were cursed, for committing the crime of rejecting the prophets of their time. Such a view deserves to be treated more by way of a joke rather than a legitimate argument.

Maudoodi's philosophy, if accepted, would imply that the very institution of prophethood is a curse indeed otherwise its cessation could not have been claimed to be a blessing. This appears to be more in line with the thinking of St. Paul, who branded the law of the Torah as a curse and believed Jesus to be the redeemer because he did away with that law. If there were no law to be broken, argued St. Paul, there would be no sin to be committed.

ST. PAUL

MAUDOODI

The aery Maudoodi philosophy however, does not seem to originate from St. Paul alone. It also resurrects the image of Bahāullah. What the Messiah had done by rejecting the law of the Torah, according to St. Paul, Bahāullah claimed to have done to the Quranic law. Thus he pronounced himself to be the liberator of mankind from the bondage of the Quran. Nonetheless he did not imitate St. Paul entirely because St. Paul had never claimed a role of God personified for himself. He assigned this role of godhead entirely to Jesus. Jesus to him, was in fact a liberator who had undone the blunder committed by 'God the Father' against mankind. The very promulgation of Divine law was tantamount to the creation of sin. Hence, by cancelling the Divine law, what Jesus actually achieved was to have destroyed the very soil from which sin sprouted. By the same act of redeeming mankind he appears to have simultaneously redeemed 'God the father' from the folly of creating sin.

Bahāullah applied this philosophy only partially and argued that the Quranic law being too heavy and cumbersome had lost its relevance to the people of the modern age. So by liberating mankind from this exacting

685

'burden' he feigned to set them free, but not entirely so. He betook for himself the role of a new 'Law-maker', after cancelling the previous Law. But in the final analysis Bahāullah succeeded only in making a mockery of God and himself. The shariah that Bahāullah dictated to replace the law of the Quran was no more and no less than a blatant affront to common sense, reason and rationality.

Between these two modern day disciples of St. Paul, i.e. Bahāullah and Maudoodi, nothing seems to have been left of the religion of Islam. As for the Quranic law, Bahāullah claimed to have done away with it in the name of emancipation. As for the institution of prophethood, Maudoodi ventured to abolish it by virtue of the same Pauline philosophy. Both failed to achieve their objectives in the sight of God. Both were applauded as great heroes in the sight of men who were already spiritually diseased.

But Maudoodi did not follow St. Paul entirely. He did not go as far as to suggest that the Quranic law should be annulled by God, lest the people should incur His wrath by failing to abide by it. He only applied the Pauline principle to the institution of prophethood. Even if non-law-bearing prophets are raised after the Holy Founder[sa] of Islam, they are likely to be rejected by the majority of Muslims as prophets have been rejected before them. Thus according to Maudoodi's logic, the threat of the curse would keep hanging over their heads like the sword of Damocles. In Maudoodi's estimation by altogether doing away with the institution of prophethood after the Holy Prophet Muhammad[sa], God has bestowed untold blessings upon mankind, particularly upon the Muslims.

If the institution of prophethood is finally brought to a close, lest people should be cursed, it is tantamount to pronouncing prophethood itself to be a curse. Thus, the neo-Pauline philosophy of Maudoodi would require God to do away with the curse of prophethood altogether. What deliverance! What redemption! Good riddance is the other name for it!

But it should be clearly understood that this logic is applicable as much to the past as it is to the future. Why was Jesus[as] sent by God before the Holy Prophet[sa]? Does not the Holy Quran categorically denounce the Jewish people as accursed for the crime of denying him? And what happened to earlier peoples? Did they not defy the Divine messengers sent to them and mock and ridicule them? A sad reflection on human arrogance indeed! Thus declares the Holy Quran:

$$ يٰحَسْرَةً عَلَى الْعِبَادِ مَا يَأْتِيهِمْ مِّنْ رَّسُوْلٍ اِلَّا كَانُوْا بِهٖ يَسْتَهْزِءُوْنَ * 36:31 $$

Woe to mankind. Never does a prophet come to them, but they scorn him and ridicule him![4]

It is amazing why God did not think of bringing this curse to an end earlier in time. What happened to the Jewish people throughout the long history of their encounters with the prophets? Were they not cursed at the tongue of David[as]? What happened to the people of the Book between the time of Moses[as] and Jesus Christ[as]?

Was this universal human trend of treating all messengers of God inhumanly not sufficient to make God realize that prophethood was more of a curse than a blessing? Why was Noah[as] sent and why Abraham[as] and why Lot[as]? Did their rejection not cause the wrath of Allah to befall upon their people? But for some insignificant few, were they not obliterated from the face of the earth? Still, the idea that struck Maudoodi did not strike God. Was it because it was Maudoodi's mind which had fabricated this myth of a god? Such infirmity of judgement behoves only a brainchild of his. God kept sending prophet after prophet but arrogant man continued to reject them, one after the other. The curse they thus earned cannot be blamed on the office of prophethood, they themselves are to blame.

Again, if this argument is accepted as valid at any particular point in time, it must also be accepted as valid at all times since the advent of Adam[as]. The fear of rejection of Adam[as] by his people, who would thus incur upon themselves the wrath of God, should have been enough justification for God never to have sent Adam[as] at all. If the fear that people should reject a lesser prophet from among the followers of Hazrat Muhammad[sa] is a legitimate reason for the cessation of prophethood altogether, then the same fear should have stood in the way of the advent of the Holy Founder[sa] of Islam even more powerfully. Is he not the best among all the prophets? Of course he is — as the entire world of Islam testifies. Being supreme among them, for him to be rejected was to earn the worst curse of God ever inflicted. Alas Maudoodi seems to have completely forgotten that not only was the Holy Prophet[sa] rejected by most of the world's population of his time, but also his truth is still denied by three-fourths of mankind today. At best, it is just one-fourth of the human population which can be described as believers in the Holy Prophet[sa]. But can they really be defined as Muslims? Is their faith in the Holy Founder[sa] of Islam genuine enough to include them among those who really believe? Maudoodi thinks otherwise. Out of the one billion population of the Muslims, nine hundred and ninety-nine in every one thousand are already condemned by him to be virtually non-Muslims:

یہ انبوہِ عظیم جس کو مسلمان قوم کہا جاتا ہے اس کا حال یہ ہے کہ اس کے

۹۹۹ فی ہزار افراد نہ اسلام کا علم رکھتے ہیں نہ حق اور باطل کی تمیز سے آشنا ہیں، نہ

ان کا اخلاقی نقطہ نظر اور ذہنی رویہ اسلام کے مطابق تبدیل ہوا ہے - باپ سے بیٹے
اور بیٹے سے پوتے کو بس مسلمان کا نام ملتا چلا آرہا ہے اس لئے یہ مسلمان ہیں -⁵

'This huge hotch potch body of the so-called
Muslims is such as nine hundred and ninety nine out
of every one thousand have no knowledge of Islam
whatsoever. They are incapable of distinguishing
right from wrong. Nor have their moral and mental
attitudes been in the least Islamicised. From father to
son, from grandfather to grandson, they have only
inherited a Muslim name and no more.'

From Maudoodi's account of the scheme of things,
God had better not send any Divine book or messenger lest
His poor creatures should be cursed forever.

Yet Maudoodi believes in the justification of God
sending all His prophets since the time of Adam[as] to the
time of the best among them. If their rejection brought a
curse from God on those who rejected them, what
exceptional harm would it do if one more like them is
added to the list. But the paradox in Maudoodi becomes
more of an eyesore when he is discovered to believe in the
re-advent of Jesus Christ[as] as a prophet of God.

If instead of the old Jesus[as], a new non-law-bearing
prophet was to be raised from among the people of Islam,
how could he in any way alter this eternal grand plan of
cursedness? Why should only his advent be objectionable
while all those before him since the time of Adam[as] served
the same Divine decree of a perpetual curse?

REFERENCES

1. KAUFMANN, W. (1976) *The Portable Nietzsche*. Penguin Books. England, p.197
2. KAUFMANN, W. (1976) *The Portable Nietzsche*. Penguin Books. England, p.198
3. KAUFMANN, W. (1976) *The Portable Nietzsche*. Penguin Books. England, p.370-375
4. Translation of 36:31 by the author.
5. MAUDOODI, SYED ABUL-A'ALA. *Musalmān Aur Maujoodah Siyasi Kashmakash*. 1st ed. Vol.III. Published by Maktabah Jama'at-i-Islāmi, Dār-ul-Islām, Jamālpur, Pathānkot, p.130

JESUS VERSUS FINALITY

THE BELIEF that the last prophet, Muhammad[sa], has already come and gone and the assertion that Jesus[as] would descend to earth as a prophet after him are so inconsistent that they cannot be owned simultaneously. In fact this cocktail of two unrelated issues was made by some Ulema of the late medieval times. At the time of the revelation of the Holy Quran any connection between the two was unthinkable.

For the sake of the unfamiliar non-Muslim reader we need to explain the historical background of this issue lest they should fail to understand what the row is all about. The verse خَاتَمَ النَّبِيّيْنَ *Khātamun-Nabiyyeen* is one of the most fundamental verses of the Quran which is profoundly rich in meaning and contains many possible connotations. But none of its connotations can even remotely be related to the so-called ascent of Jesus Christ[as]. Hence the Mullah's plea that Jesus[as] was lifted to the fourth heaven because this verse of finality was to be revealed by God is absolutely ridiculous and melodramatic. This so-called bodily ascent of Jesus has nothing to do with this verse nor with any verse in the Quran. The idea of raising Jesus Christ[as] to heaven had never occurred to God. The entire Quran and the traditions of the Holy Prophet[sa] absolve God of this absurdity by a total absence of any such reference to the ascent of Jesus[as]. For the Mullahs to maintain that God had lifted him to forestall the problem created by this verse is a blatant lie and an unfounded allegation against the Quran. Thus it is the Mullah who is creating the problem himself and resolving it in the name of God. To bind this unfounded conjecture to one of the most fundamental verses of the

Quran is an act of abomination. The reasons which motivate the medievalist clergy to do this and the deceptive manner in which they attempt to fuse these absolutely unrelated issues is the main subject of discussion here. Having familiarized the reader with the background, now we proceed to tell the tale of the Mullah's desperation. With this in mind we hope that the reader will fully understand that which follows.

DESPITE THE FACT that the imagined ascent or descent of Jesus^{as} has nothing to do with the independent declaration of the Holy Prophet's^{sa} finality, the clergy still assert that there is a definite link between the two. Prophet Jesus^{as}, son of Mary, they insist, will be personally brought back from the heavens because no new prophet can be raised after Prophet Muhammad^{sa}. This ingenious device of bringing an old prophet back to earth instead of raising one from the *Ummah* to meet the new need may seem highly laudable to the Muslim orthodoxy but their enthusiasm cannot be shared by ordinary humans. No one with an iota of common sense can attribute this cheap act of trickstering to God the Almighty, the All-Wise. Only the Mullahs can and this exactly is what they attempt to do. By connecting the return of Jesus^{as} with the finality of the Holy Prophet^{sa}, they think that they have rescued God from the consequences of a premature declaration of finality. Thus, the clergy believes that they have saved God from a grave dilemma of contradiction. This has to be the brainchild of a half-wit Mullah to whom it rightly belongs. The promise of finality to any prophet by God, despite His knowledge that it could not be kept, is inconceivable of Him. To make a show of keeping the promise by bringing an old prophet after the demise of the last one is sheer mockery. Thus, judging God by his own standards, the Mullah first attributes a shameful act of contradiction to Him, then comes forward to help Him save His face from it. This blatant attempt is not made without a purpose. To the Mullah it is a great idea having multiple advantages.

It saves the life of Jesus from an ignoble death upon the cross and frustrates his enemies' attempts to prove him false. Imagine their exasperation at finding Jesus escape their clutches by vanishing into thin air (if there is any air at all in the fourth heaven where he is assumed to have ascended). But this measure must also have created another small problem for God. When and why he should be brought back to earth must have been the question. After all he could not be left abandoned in his heavenly confine till Doomsday. As far as God is concerned the problem does not exist. As far as the Mullah is concerned the problem is created by him to hide his own contradiction of believing in the finality of the Holy Prophet[sa], as well as believing in the re-advent of Jesus[as] as a prophet after him. That is the only reason why he connects the verse of *Khātamun-Nabiyyeen* with the imaginary ascent of Jesus[as]. He does it with a cunning deceitfulness which cannot be detected by the ordinary Muslim masses. The following is the case he builds:

1. Jesus was lifted to heaven with a purpose and will be brought back finally to earth.

2. The coming of an old prophet after the last one had appeared would not break the seal of his finality.

3. The need for a new prophet in the latter days will be fulfilled without creating any dilemma of contradiction in God's Decree.

There are some who kill two birds with one stone but the orthodoxy seems to know how to kill three with one! In reality however, by shifting the twist of their own mind to that of God, they commit an unpardonable act of blasphemy.

We believe that by concocting this mindless exercise and spinning such a bizarre tale the most prominent advantage the Mullah gains, among others, is to escape the possibility of any Divine authority to be ever imposed upon him. Good riddance once and for all from the institution of prophethood and the danger of ever losing his absolute command over the ignorant Muslim masses. The belief that a two thousand year old prophet would come again has the inherent guarantee that no prophet would ever come again. Thus the Mullah's grip on Islam will be perpetuated and he will forever retain his despotic authority over the unsuspecting Muslim masses.

The dead never return from their otherworldly abode. Once departed, none has ever paid a second visit to begin mixing with the living. Never has God brought back any dwellers of the past. Those who literally await the return of Jesus may continue to do so till eternity. He will never come, nor will the Mullah ever quit his demagogic command over the Muslim world. Left forever at the mercy of the Mullah, who knows no mercy, the masses are duped to wait in vain for the return of Jesus[as] bearing a cup of elixir in his hand. Islam will continue to suffer year after year, century after century under the despotic rule of the Muslim clergy.

Looking yet again at the same question of Jesus versus finality, the solution proposed by the Mullah is untenable anyway. To borrow an old prophet from the bygone *Ummah* of Moses[as] for the completely different requirements of the Muslim *Ummah* of the latter days can in no way resolve their problems. A borrowed prophet, they fail to understand, will be the one who will violate the sanctity of the Holy Prophet's[sa] finality and not the one who is born and raised within his *Ummah* as his spiritual son.

Over and above what has been discussed, it must be noted that in the context of the present discussion mere chronology cannot determine whether a prophet is old or new. If a prophet comes again with exactly the same attributes which he had during his first advent then of course his visit could be treated as a repeat visit. But, if before his second advent, he has been radically changed in his physical characteristics and aptitudes and his attitude to his enemies has fundamentally changed, he can in no way be described as an old prophet come again. In addition, the spiritual status he holds, the message he delivers, the miracles he works and the authority he exercises over the whole of mankind has no similarity with the Jesus[as] of the New Testament. It is also worthy of note that the Jesus[as] whose advent was promised by the Holy Prophet[sa] has a completely different identity from that of the previous Jesus[as]. The promised Jesus[as] would not be a prophet of Israel any more. He will no longer be subordinate to the Torah, or to the Gospels he himself taught. Nor will he be confined to the domain of the House of Israel. If, despite all this, the Mullah must insist that the Promised Jesus[as] is the same Jesus[as] of Israel then they must admit that before being brought back to earth he would be completely reconditioned and recommissioned in all the essential features of his prophethood. If that is not the advent of a new prophet, what else is? No Mullah would concede that such a Jesus as the one described could ever be assimilated into Islam without compromising the principle of the Holy Prophet's[sa] finality. What remains for them is only to believe that Jesus[as] would return to earth without any change wrought in him. Once here, he would be budded onto the tree of Islam and re-grow as a reformer fit to be called a universal Muslim prophet. We should be permitted to draw the attention of the Mullah that even then, he will remain foreign to Islam, unable to shed his non-Muslim personality of an Israelite. His case would be like that of a bud from a tree of a different species grafted onto the stem of another. If a lotus can be grafted onto a cherry tree, or a blueberry to a pineapple bush, only then can one visualize a pre-Islamic prophet grafted onto Islam. But to what avail. The grafted stem can never lose its identity. What would grow out of Jesus [as] even when bonded to Islam, would still be a Jesus [as] of Israelitic identity.

JESUS[AS], THEREFORE, even if physically transferred to the world of Islam, can never change his true identity. The Quran will continue to describe him merely as a prophet to the children of Israel. Any infuriated Muslim divine could stand up to defy his claim on the basis of this Quranic injunction alone, if he ever returns. He will be roundly denounced as an impostor. By what authority, he will be questioned, did he abrogate the proclamation of the Quran that he was merely a prophet to the House of Israel? As long as the Quran defines him as such, his identity will never be changed; he was and will always remain a prophet to the House of Israel.

$$\ldots\ \text{رَسُوْلًا اِلـٰـى بَنِيْۤ اِسْرَآءِيْلَ}\ 3:50$$

... a Prophet to the children of Israel ... [1]

Ours is an age when the fundamentalists have overexcited the sensibility of the Muslim masses to the issue of blasphemy. Evidently, the life of Jesus will not be safer in the hands of Muslim fanatics than it was in the hands of the Jewish people. Moreover, he will have to face other multifarious dangers which he did not encounter during his first advent. The world of Islam is split into schisms far more sharply and intolerantly than the world of Judaism was at the time of Jesus Christ[as].

The threat to his life will be grave no matter where he lands in a Muslim state — if he ever lands! If his landing strip happens to be in Iran, evidently he will be subjected to a gruelling examination regarding his doctrinal position. Does he believe in the twelve Imams or does he reject them? Does he believe in the *Khilafat* of Abū Bakr, 'Umar and 'Uthmān or does he not? Does he believe in the unbroken continuity of succession of Hazrat 'Ali to the Holy Founder[sa] of Islam? If he conforms to the Shi'ite beliefs in answer to these questions, the threat to his life will still not be averted because of the additional problem of the disappearance of the twelfth Imam. It will be demanded of him as to how he dared return to earth alone while their *Holy* twelfth Imam (Al-Mahdi) is still in hiding somewhere in space. Without the personal testimony of that Imam to the truth of Jesus[as], he will most certainly be stigmatized and penalized for being false.

If he is found guilty of endorsing the right to *Khilafat* of the first three Caliphs, Hazrat Abū Bakr, Hazrat 'Umar and Hazrat 'Uthmān (may Allah be pleased with them), he will be denounced even more vehemently as an impostor. After this, his being condemned to death would be but a routine procedure of Shi'ite jurisprudence.

However, if he descends in a Sunni territory while holding Shi'ite views, no sooner will he land than be despatched back to heaven. If on the other hand he holds Sunni views, his life will still not be out of danger because each of the Sunni sects dwelling in that country would require him to testify to the truth of their beliefs, or be rejected as a liar. It is hard to conceive Jesus Christ[as] converting to the *Barelvi* faith or becoming a Wahhābī

697

fundamentalist the moment he touches down in their respective countries. Whichever of the two will he claim as his own? Either way it will be tantamount to bargaining for a death warrant issued by the clergy of the other.

The reason for this condemnation would not just be his belonging to a different sect; the reason for his condemnation to death would be his imposture as a true prophet of God. No true prophet of God can hold wrong religious views they will argue. Each sect would judge Jesus[as] by the testimony of their own beliefs; none will judge their beliefs by the testimony of Jesus[as].

There will also arise the question as to which school of jurisprudence he belongs. Will he belong to the school of Hazrat Imam Malik or that of Imam Abū Ḥanifā or Imam Shafe'ī or Imam Ahmad bin Hanbal? Having had no experience of such juristic wrangles, he will find himself helplessly trapped in the middle of this rigmarole. How he would wish that he had never ever returned to earth! Even if he is accepted by the sect whose garb he finally decides to wear, he will be strongly rejected by the remaining seventy-one sects. Over and above this will he not continue to confront the danger of rejection by all on the basis of the Quranic verse mentioned above, which declares him to be merely *a prophet to the House of Israel*?

The shout of 'Go back to where you really belong' may be heard from the mouth of any fanatic in the assembled crowd. 'Take off and re-route your flight to the State of Israel,' may well be curtly demanded of him. 'If you are man enough to face a retrial at their hands, go to the Jewish people and prove your true identity.'

What shall God do at this new turn of events one wonders. Will He command the angels to hasten to Jesus'[as] rescue once again, lifting him to the same remote celestial abode? Or will he be abandoned by God to shift for himself at the mercy of the Muslim or the Jewish clergy? Whether he will be re-crucified by Israelite soldiers in the state of Israel or whether he will be hung till death by a Muslim hangman, is a question which only the future will tell — if he ever visits this miserable world of ours again. Far more than his previous advent, he will find the new one to be a mission impossible.

ON A MORE SERIOUS NOTE, we beg to remind the reader that when religion is interpreted without rationality, when faith is divorced of reason, all that they give birth to are myths without legitimacy and legends without substance. Mindless trustees of faith succeed only in making a mockery of Divine wisdom.

The great scholars of medieval ages who failed to understand the true import of such prophecies can genuinely be excused. Theirs was a different age. Their understanding of the world and the cosmos around it was as yet merely conjectural. But the contemporary medievalists who are born and raised in this age of enlightenment have no justification for their gross misreading of Divine prophecies. The soul of holy Jesus[as], the true servant of God, has undoubtedly returned to Him to occupy the lofty station he is assigned. The Jesus they await is a mere fantasy of their own minds. What does one care therefore, if that phantom figure is crucified or stabbed to death or hung a thousand times! The whole episode of Jesus' bodily ascent and preservation somewhere in space, merely to fulfil the future need for a prophet, is so provocative to the human sense of propriety! Add to this the impunity of their attributing this nonsense to God and wonder what stuff their minds are made of !

Let the world of Islam get rid of this fantasy once and for all and let the clerics who nurture it get lost. The death of their age will usher in the age of the revival of Islam.

Last, but not least, there is yet another strong objection against the suggestion that a prophet of Israel could be somehow trimmed to fit into the robe of a Muslim prophet. How can the orthodox clergy forget that during his absence from earth the Holy Quran could not have been revealed to Jesus simultaneously with the Holy Prophet Muhammad[sa]. This angle of observation raises many difficult questions for the clergy to answer. The foremost among them is the issue of his conversion. When and from whom did he learn that the greatest of all the prophets had appeared down below on earth? Did he testify to his truth forthwith becoming a believer? If he did become one — the first ever in space — how did he learn to practice Islam without knowing anything of the Quran?

As such, whether the Quran was revealed to him directly by God through the Archangel Gabriel, is the highly crucial question which must be addressed and answered.

If the Quran was revealed to him while he was still in space, he would certainly have become a partner prophet to Prophet Muhammad[sa], like Aaron[as] was to Moses[as], both enjoying an almost similar status. If the Quran was not revealed directly to him through the archangel, what would be the nature of his faith before his return to earth? Had he remained a Judeo-Christian while Islam had been declared by God as the last universal religion of mankind? Was he treated as an exceptional case and allowed to remain a non-Muslim after the advent of the Holy Founder[sa] of Islam? If not, then one cannot escape the logical conclusion that the Quran must have been revealed to him somehow.

Will the Mullahs suggest that instead of the archangel, the Holy Prophet[sa] should himself have delivered the message to him? But the problem is that when the Holy Prophet[sa] delivered the message of the Quran to his

700

companions no intermediary agent was required. Whatever was revealed to him through the archangel, he directly passed it on to his companions. But Jesus, according to the medieval Mullahs, was sitting high above somewhere in the heavens with no possible direct link with the Holy Prophet[sa]. So there are only two options left. Either he should be considered as totally unaware of the revelation of the Quran till his eventual return to earth, or the Quran should only be revealed to Jesus as a message from the Holy Prophet[sa]. But how can this message be lifted to him while in space unless the archangel is again involved in this exercise? The scenario which develops is so insulting and so abhorrent that a true believer cannot entertain it even for a moment. Imagine the archangel delivering the Holy Quran to the Holy Prophet[sa] and then begging him to recite it back to him so that he could deliver it to Jesus as a message from the Holy Prophet[sa] and not from God.

Returning to the issue of Jesus' conversion to Islam, if the Quran was not revealed to Jesus at all, but he believed in the Holy Prophet[sa] in a vague nondescript manner, then at best he could be described as a non-practising Muslim with no knowledge of Quranic teachings. The common herd of Muslims anywhere on earth could claim a better status in Islam despite their ignorance. How would a Jesus such as this be welcomed back to earth by the great Muslim theologians and clerics of the time? To redress his ignorance will he be rushed to the presence of the Imam Al-Mahdi the instant he lands so that he could be initiated without further loss of time? No sooner than he accepts Islam, will he be offered the chair of judgement over all the conflicting Muslim sects? When and by whom will he be taught Islam fast enough to discharge such grave responsibilities with absolute precision and perfection?

701

If the clergy insist that he must have been recommissioned as a Muslim prophet, while still in space before his descent to earth, then how could he be treated as an old prophet of the pre-Islamic era?

To conclude, the borrowing of a prophet from a pre-Islamic era requires that either he is recommissioned in space as a new prophet in Islam after the advent of the last Prophet, or he is to be converted after his descent to earth and then recommissioned as a Muslim prophet.

However much this bizarre idea of inherent contradictions may appear devoid of all common sense to the rest of the world, the orthodox clergy is not perturbed in the least. Reason and rationality have no role to play in their understanding of Divine prophecies. They take them literally without ever realizing what damage this may do to the cause of Islam. It is this madness which is largely responsible for all the chaos we observe today prevailing in their perceptions, hopes and aspirations.

All said and done, the borrowing of a non-Muslim prophet from a pre-Islamic age does not transpire to be as profitable as it appeared to the clergy. It is a tribute to their relentless obstinacy that they would much rather have a convert prophet from space than a prophet born here on earth, within Islam. They do so because there are many more advantages from this fairy tale visit of Jesus to be gained. He, as a visitor from space, would not be the same ordinary human prophet as he was but would have amassed prodigal superhuman powers unheard of in the history of prophethood before his return to earth.

This mythical image of Jesus is evidently created by their same tendency to over-literalize prophecies. Evidently they do not care what price they have to pay for the folly of rejecting reason and rationality. To Jesus Christ they assign the task of salvaging whatever remains of the dignity and honour of Islam in the latter days. It will be he, they believe, who will launch a single-handed powerful offensive against the anti-Christ on a global scale. Having roundly defeated and destroyed the anti-Christ – the one-eyed monster, Jesus will hand over the keys of his world dominion to the people of Islam, and will also distribute the immense treasure and riches which he will have amassed. Thus all the spoils of his war against the anti-Christ will he lay at the feet of the Muslim *Ummah*.

The orthodoxy's vision of Jesus' re-advent when he will literally smash all the crosses in the world to smithereens.

HAVING RESOLVED their political and economic problems, he will turn his full attention to such prophecies as relate to religion. He will start by launching his campaign against Christianity. His strategy will be to break every cross in the world, whatever material it is made of. He will visit every cathedral, every monastery, every church, every temple, every Christian hermitage. He will walk every street of every township and stare at every passer-by in search of any cross. Ladies perhaps will become the prime object of his scrutiny because he will be aware of their despicable habit of having crosses engraved upon their jewellery and ornaments. He will take care of the fact that they also wear crosses hanging around their necks. Thus he will snatch away every bangle, every bracelet, every pendant and earring with the sign of the cross upon it. Woe to the ladies who dare to cross the path of that Jesus, but where can they escape and hide, the poor defenceless wretches? He will enter every house and search every cabinet and jewellery box. Every wall and every corner will be scanned. Crosses must be literally broken and wiped out from the face of earth. Until he has accomplished this task to the full he will not rest in peace. This is the vision of the Muslim orthodoxy of the mission of Jesus Christ if ever he returns to earth, but that is not all.

Having completely disposed of the symbol of Trinity, he would then turn to another task which prophecies assign to him, if they are taken literally. He will lose no time in beginning to kill every non-Muslim inhabiting the world. Either they must convert to Islam or they must die — these will be their only options. He will go about this slaughtering business in a rather unusual way. He will breathe fire like a mythical dragon, while no myth has ever presented such a dragon before, even in the wildest tales of fantasy. His blazing breath will scorch to death innumerable infidels even when they are miles away from him. Those within the reach of his sword, will have their heads stricken off and made to roll. He will identify them unmistakably because on the forehead of each non-believer would appear the imprint in bold: *Al-Kāfir*, the non-believer. Thus he will leave none alive except the Muslims, and the de-Christianized Christians of course, who will be left without a single cross to worship. Hence the curtain will fall upon this unique carnage by the imaginary Jesus, filling the entire earth with fetid odour, an obnoxious stench of rotting bodies, some slaughtered, some scorched to death. Hatred will generate more hatred, bloodshed will lead to more bloodshed.

Abbasi

The imaginary Jesus as painted by Christian artists, is shown in the vision of the Muslim orthodoxy as carrying a sword in hand during the carnage of the swine.

THE LAST GORY ACT of Jesus upon the earth will be to annihilate the species of swine. No quarter will be granted to pigs. All boars and all sows and all their brood will be put to the sword — each one of them. Hand on sword, fire in breath, Jesus will visit every township, every village, every street, every house, every shack and every sty in search of the hiding rascals. He will visit every wilderness, will thrash all the bushes of Africa, and will hunt for them in the rain-forests of South America. China will not be spared for that matter, nor will Japan. The islands of the South Pacific will also be combed where the flesh of pig is considered a highly prized delicacy.

Evidently no prophet of God in the entire history of mankind has ever performed such bloody, filthy feats as are attributed to the Jesus Christ envisioned by the Muslim orthodoxy. This is what the clergy in Islam have done to the profound wisdom of the Holy Prophet[sa]. They have failed to penetrate across the bodies of letters to reach the soul and spirit of the prophecy they contained.

The real task assigned to the Promised Christ in this prophecy was to purify the human society from inhuman behaviour and some evil habits which the swine symbolizes. There are many animals and birds which steal

705

the fruits of the farmer's labour for the sake of their survival but do not destroy the crops and trees just for the fun of it. The swine stands out among all the animals in this destructive tendency. The swine is also notorious for eating the corpses of its young ones. No other non-marine animals are known to devour their young ones when they die. A bloodthirsty lion, or even a ferocious wolf, will rather die of hunger, woefully sitting beside the dead bodies of their brood, than to even dream of eating their flesh. Dogs do not eat the corpses of their dead puppies either. Pigs and boars, it should be remembered, are vegetarians, yet by some devilish instinct they relish eating the corpses of their young ones. Evidently therefore, the message implied in this prophecy has to be to wage a Holy War against the perverted habit of humans to be inclined to genocide and to feel free to usurp the rights of the weak. The pig's habit of eating its own piglets could be likened to the child abuse of the modern age. Child abuse may be directed against one's own children or against the children of others, either way it is swinish in character. Recently it has become a subject of common talk in modern society, so needs no further elaboration. No other animal can match humans in this ugliness.

War against evil has always been the occupation of prophets. As such, Jesus Christ in his second advent would be no oddity among them if his second advent is understood to be metaphorical. But a Jesus such as the one who is idolized by the Muslim clergy — a literal murderer of the swine — is what they need and await to welcome. The moment this apple of their eyes arrives and discharges his task of eliminating the pig species from the animal kingdom, he must needs be applauded. So will he be applauded and befitting homage would be paid to his last glorious days spent on the planet earth.

G *lory be to Lord Jesus* will be chanted over sea, over land, over hill, over dale. The church bells will not toll for the carnage he will make but the minarets will resound with the shouts of the Muezzin heard far and wide, *Allah-O-Akbar, Allah-O-Akbar, God is the Greatest, God is the Greatest — and glory be to our saviour the Lord Jesus Christ.*

Lastly, before Jesus' departure from earth, there is yet another highly important business for him to conduct, but in this he must be assisted by the Mullah. Throughout it has been only Jesus Christ serving the cause of the Mullah. Let the Mullah serve his cause now, for once at least! All that Jesus would demand of the Mullahs after his global exploits would be to help him in the task of getting married. After the ruinous trail of rampage and bloodshed that he would have left behind, marriage would not be an unwelcome change for him.

If the Mullah has any serious regard for the literal fulfilment of prophecies he must find him a highly gifted young Muslim damsel who should not fail to bear him children. Christ is about to be married! Some great Mullah must be found to read his wedding sermon and enquire from the would be father-in-law of Christ if he consents to give the hand of his daughter to that of Jesus. After his consent would come the turn of Jesus, at last, to confirm the proposed marriage. What happy moments, what ecstasy! After a celibacy of two thousand years or more he would stand up and nod his head in affirmation *"Yes I do, O loving Mullah, yes I do"*. In what better manner could the exploits of Jesus Christ be celebrated than that! From North to South, from East to West, hymns will be sung in his praise and marriage songs will fill the air with their sweet melody. All that is left for him is to hopefully wait for the delivery of his blessed first-born with a holy string of other sons and daughters to follow. Thus by producing children at the ripe old age of two thousand years plus, he will create the greatest of all the miracles he had ever worked. His spirit has always been strong but the flesh too would not lag behind in strength it seems. What a miracle indeed that the passage of time makes him grow even stronger, while old age is left buried far behind in the land of his youthful first advent. Finally, the hour of death will arrive, but what a glorious enviable death it will be! Blessed be the day he was born and blessed be the way he will die.

This is the enchanting tale of Jesus which, if ever realised, the Mullahs will always tell their pupils in every *Madrasah* of Islamic instruction, year after year, generation after generation.

A MORE GRUESOME example is hard to find in the entire history of religion of how Divine prophecies are mutilated out of shape, by a mindless materialist clergy. But this is not a prerogative of the Muslim clergy alone. Whenever and wherever the priesthood takes over the command of religious orders they are likely to turn facts into fiction and realities into myths. This is the price man always pays for entrusting his faith to a hierarchy divested of common sense and reason, unable to distinguish between fair and foul. Whatever their business, rationality is not a commodity in which they trade.

The most tragic of all the religious leaders of the world is the case of the Muslim priesthood. The vain hopes they build for the ultimate victory of Islam are based utterly on misconstrued prophecies turned into mirages and illusions. They are no longer fit to lead any religious order, let alone Islam! They are no longer fit to follow any prophet of God, be he old or new.

Their vision of the final victory of Islam, attained entirely by the might of Jesus, absolves them of any role to play in the final struggle for the victory of Islam. In truth, what they need is not a prophet but an enslaved giant. They fail to realize that the type of Jesus for whom they aspire has never appeared in the entire comity of prophets before. No prophet is mentioned in the Quran or in any other scripture who would fight single-handedly for the supremacy of his people while they sit idly by. This is what the Jews demanded of Moses[as] and were denied. If the final victory of any religion can thus be achieved without blood, sweat or toil, where is there room for a prophet of God who invariably calls to the path of sacrifices? Their vision of a prodigal Jesus corresponds to a genie rather than that of a Divine Reformer. The real issue with them has never been a choice between an old prophet or a new one, it has always been between a genie and a prophet. Their attitude is reminiscent of a tale from the classic work of *A Thousand and One Nights*.

Once upon a time, so it is narrated, a magician in the guise of a vendor roamed the streets of Baghdad shouting at the top of his voice, 'Old lamps for new! Old lamps for new!' Many a housewife rushed to the door to have her old lamp swapped for the new ones he offered. A happy bargain indeed, they thought, and so it was. Yet there was one exception. Little did one of the housewives know that when she exchanged her old lamp for a new one offered by the swindler, the old lamp she was giving away had imprisoned in it a genie with almost unlimited powers. She had no idea that the owner of that lamp could also become the master of the genie. Hence, the interest of the swindler was in the prisoner of the lamp, not in the lamp itself. If that genie could be possessed by swapping a million new lamps for one that is old, no greater bargain could be conceived.

In reality the Mullahs are neither interested in a new lamp lit by the light of Muhammad[sa] nor are they interested in the old lamp of the *Ummah* of Moses[as]. All they are interested in is the prodigal Jesus of their fancy deemed to be trapped therein. No Divine torch of prophethood means anything to them. A prophet is not what they care for and a prophet is not what they require. All that they need is a giant slave who would lead them to all the worldly riches at their bidding.

Political and economic domination of the world is their only ambition for which they are most ill-equipped. All that they are trained for is the letting of Muslim blood at the hands of other Muslims butchered by the knives of others Muslims.

Any bloody revolution brought about by Mullahcracy in any Muslim country should not mislead others. In no way can it upset the balance of power in the world. To dream of world domination without scientific and technological advancement, to hope for tilting the existing balance of power without boosting their own economy and revolutionizing their industry; to challenge the might of great world powers without the capability of manufacturing highly advanced and sophisticated military hardware is ultimate madness. What little, one may ask, do they have to achieve their goal?

The Mullahs must realize that their blatant distortion of the great prophecies of the Holy Founder[sa] of Islam will not go unpunished. It will bring them and those whom they lead to nothing but utter ruin. This is the price they must pay for the crime of perverting the wisdom of God. Let them stand on a corner and watch the days and nights slip by. Let them watch the heavenly tracks and strain their ears to listen to the descending footsteps of their mythical saviour from the voids of space. Let them live on and on in hope, and perish again and again in despair, generation after generation after generation. None will ever come to rescue them from the entangled web of their own twisted vision and contradictions between their ideals and practice. Every moment that passes, every second that ticks by, the fear of God is fast vanishing from their daily life. Honesty, justice, selfless sacrifice, mutual brotherly love and respect for other's property have become values of the bygone days — still dearly remembered, but widely shunned. With what yearning they are talked about, with what love and tenderness they are treasured, but only in the storehouses of memories!

Theft, robbery, murder, child abuse, abduction, fornication, adultery, prostitution, fraud, and deceit are only registered by those whom they strike. Others live with them in an unholy alliance. Gang rapes committed in broad daylight by the very custodians of peace; bribery, corruption and brazen-faced violations of law by their lordships, who are supposed to be the defenders of justice —a society where the wardens of peace lynch and murder peace, a society where disorder is the only order of the day. Yet strangely enough, it is not altogether bereft of its sense of right and wrong. It hates the evil it generates itself, it abhors the horrors it commits. It is sick to death of the pollution it exhales. Everywhere, everyday the evils are decried by the very people who exude them. They are castigated, condemned and censured at such tempo as its resonance can be heard from one end to the other, from the lofty legislative chambers to the lowly shacks of the destitute. Yet how dearly they are embraced at the same time, how firmly clasped, how faithfully adhered to in everyday life at all tiers of society! Their deeds display what their mouths condemn. This is the lie they live or the death they daily die but call it life. Where are the custodians of Muslim values and where are the torch-bearers of decent conduct? Are there any who would lose a single moment of their sweet sleep over these bitter realities? Why should it matter anyway, and what do the Mullahs care! What difference could it make to a society which has been induced to believe that the hour of Divine Decree will finally strike and Jesus[as], son of Mary, will descend from his heavenly abode to raise Muslims such as these to the lofty chambers of command. It would be they who would carve and shape the destiny of the world. Thus the Mullahs lullaby the Muslim masses to sleep 'until such time as the Lord of the Christian West will desert their cause and rise in full glory as the Lord of the Muslim East'. Why then, should the Mullah ever bother about the moral destitution of the herds he leads? Why work for their reformation and strive hard needlessly to redeem them from their hopeless state of morbidity? Patience, patience, is the only panacea — just wait for the hour to strike!

*W*OE TO SUCH AN HOUR of destiny if it ever strikes! Damnation is the name for it. For the creatures of Allah to be subjected to the rule of the Mullah is sheer abomination. Jesus Christ! Could he ever permit himself to stoop so low! Could he ever be a party to such a blatant crime! No — not he! Jesus or no Jesus, no prophet of God would ever debase himself to champion the cause of a depraved people. It is a task fit only for a power-hungry demagogue who would not be reluctant even to become a king of beasts let alone of a beastly people. With or without the help of a Jesus he would not hesitate to step upon the shoulders of prophets to achieve his ambition.

The Mullahs' dreams are madder than those of a mad hatter's but how can they ever be realized? Mad dreams never turn darkness into light, nor do they ever break the dawn of a new day. It is always the dawn of a new day which breaks and shatters such dreams. Let the Mullah sleep forever. Let the empty chambers of his brain be filled with as many illusions as would feed upon his limitless craving for power. Let the people of Islam wake up and wish him to sink into a deep sleep till Doomsday. Let the sleeping Mullah lie and sink into a deeper sleep. And let him leave the *Ummah* of the Holy Prophet^{sa} alone to begin to see the light of the day.

REFERENCE

1. Translation of 3:50 by the author.

EPILOGUE

IN THE END, we turn to the issue of non-prophetic revelation. It is hard to entertain the idea that the phenomenon of non-prophetic revelation should also come to an end with the ending of prophethood. Continuity of Divine revelation is indispensable for supporting a profound unshakeable belief in God which cannot be attained with the help of rational investigation alone. Hence, revelation must always play a major role in strengthening belief in the existence of an Omniscient, Omnipotent God.

Revelation is not confined solely to the office of prophethood. It is simply a means of communion between God and man. It is a universally shared experience; to deny it is to deny the testimony of millions of people from all ages, all over the world.

It is mostly bestowed upon such servants of God as have attuned themselves to His will with unreserved dedication. Those who do not believe in God, or only believe in Him impersonally with just a vague notion of His existence, are least likely to be blessed with the honour of revelation. The same applies to the excessively sinful people, entirely given up to the vain pursuits of material gains and worldly pleasures. Yet even such as they are not altogether denied an occasional glimpse of His Grace. None can stop God from bestowing true dreams, visions and verbal revelations, whenever and to whomsoever He pleases.

Revelations are not always indicative of the piety of the person who receives them. They work sometimes as a reminder to humankind at large that God does exist and that He is free to communicate with whomsoever He pleases.

Such sample communication is not a prerogative of any particular religion or country or age. It is common to all. Had it not been so, the very faith in the existence of God and the institution of revelation would have faded out of existence. Specimen revelations are like odd, unexpected showers in the midst of a desert, creating life-supporting oases in the vast deathly expanse of a sandy wilderness.

Some non-believers however, dismiss this universal testimony as mere psychic illusion. Of course, psychic illusions cannot be ruled out, but the evidence of Divine revelation is so distinctly different from ordinary psychic ravings that one should not be confused with the other. The difference is as wide and clear as that between life and death or between light and darkness. However, it is also true that the evidence of genuine revelation becomes rarer to find as we move away from the age of a prophet. The growing influence of materialism acts upon the people as a poison which pollutes their minds and corrodes the purity of their hearts. Faith in Divine revelation dissipates by the same proportion. An ice-age of scepticism eventually sets in and an era of spiritual death begins. All that survives is falsehood and deception. Hypocrisy infiltrates and desecrates religions. Most believers are merely so-called; their way of life gives a lie to their faith. Truth practically vanishes from all spheres of human occupation. Doubt, even disbelief, begin to encroach upon the territories of faith. Godliness beats retreat. Yet the communion between God and man never ceases altogether. Revelation continues to resuscitate faith. As for those who glow with His love, even amidst total darkness, God reveals Himself to them with unmatched brilliance. The sample sprinkling of revelation upon an age of doubt and ignorance is not to be compared with the expression of love from God to His devoted servants. This is the consistent message of the Holy

Quran. It clearly promises the believer the blessings of Divine revelation unceasingly at all ages. It admonishes the Holy Prophet[sa] to proclaim:

قُلْ اِنَّمَآ اَنَا بَشَرٌ مِّثْلُكُمْ يُوْحٰى اِلَىَّ اَنَّمَآ اِلٰـهُكُمْ اِلٰـهٌ وَّاحِـدٌ ۚ فَمَنْ كَانَ يَرْجُوْا لِقَآءَ رَبِّهٖ فَلْيَعْمَلْ عَمَلًا صَالِحًـا وَّلَا يُشْـرِكْ بِعِبَادَةِ رَبِّهٖۤ اَحَدًا * 18:111

Say, I am but a man like yourselves, only I am recipient of revelation which admonishes that your God is only One God. Hence whoever among you desires to meet his Lord (as I have) then he too should perform righteous deeds and may not join partners in the worship of his Lord.[1]

The expression *desires to meet* is evidently linked to the preceding mention of revelation. But the decision concerning anyone's worthiness in this regard always lies with God and not with man.

The same promise of revelation is vouched even more clearly in other verses to all such believers as remain steadfast in their loyalty to God at times of trials:

اِنَّ الَّذِيْنَ قَالُوْا رَبُّنَا اللّٰهُ ثُمَّ اسْتَقَامُوْا تَتَنَزَّلُ عَلَيْهِمُ الْمَلٰـٓئِكَةُ اَلَّا تَخَافُوْا وَلَا تَحْزَنُوْا وَاَبْشِرُوْا بِالْجَنَّةِ الَّتِيْ كُنْتُمْ تُوْعَدُوْنَ * نَحْنُ اَوْلِيَـٰٓؤُكُمْ فِى الْحَيٰـوةِ الدُّنْيَا وَفِى الْاٰخِرَةِ 41:31-32

Verily those who proclaim that God is our Lord and then hold fast (to this claim), angels descend upon them incessantly *saying* 'Do not fear nor grieve; but rejoice in the Paradise you were promised.
We remain your friends in this life and in the life to come...'[2]

These verses leave no room for doubt on the issue of continuity of revelation. The Quran further states:

وَاِذَا سَاَلَكَ عِبَادِئْ عَنِّىْ فَاِنِّىْ قَرِيْبٌ ٱُجِيْبُ دَعْوَةَ الــــدَّاعِ اِذَا
دَعَانِ فَلْيَسْتَجِيْبُوْا لِىْ 2:187

When My servants ask thee about Me, *tell them*, I am close, I do answer the call of the caller when he seeks Me. So they too should respond to Me...[3]

ERE the promise of revelation is widened to include all servants of God who sincerely seek Him and submissively respond to His Call. This is a universal promise, not confined to any particular age or people.

Islam, in short, is a religion of eternal hope which does not relegate communion with God only to the past. His interest in human affairs as a Benign Mentor shall never cease. He is accessible when sought for and responds when prayed to. He is Eternal, none of His attributes will ever die.

Man shall always stand in need of Divine revelation. After the institution of prophethood, it is revelation which keeps the lamp of faith alight above all other means of rational and philosophical investigation. Through revelation, man is reassured of the existence of a Living God. He bestows such signs of nearness to Him as are not only subjective in their nature but are also objectively verifiable. Revelation builds faith on solid belief, dismissing all wavering doubts. The greatest tragedy of contemporary Islam is for it to fall under the ominous spell of medieval clergy and modern intellectuals. To the medievalists goes the lion's share of the kill but the great thinkers like 'Allamah Iqbal and theologians like Maudoodi are not far behind in vying for the leftovers. Iqbal as an able disciple of Nietzsche, forever does away with the need of Divine guidance. Maudoodi, a cross-breed of Pauline and Bahai wedlock, does away with prophethood lest its denial should make it a precursor to the curse of God. So between these two stalwarts nothing is left of prophethood or revelation leaving Islam emptied of all hope. The real import of their philosophy could not be summed up better than in the following words of Faiz Ahmad Faiz, one of the greatest Urdu poets of modern times:

اجنبی خاک نے دُھندلا دِئے قدموں کے سُراغ

گُل کرو شمعیں بڑھا دو ے و مینا و ایاغ

اپنے بے خواب کواڑوں کو مُقفل کر لو

اب یہاں کوئی نہیں ، کوئی نہیں آئے گا ⁴

Alien dust has obscured every footprint.
Extinguish the lamps and take away the goblets and pitchers of wine.
Shut your sleepless doors and lock them up.
None will come! No one will ever come!!

ALAS prophecy and revelation, the very soul and spirit of every living religion are thus expunged from the body of Islam. A zombie-like existence is all that is left into the bargain. An exasperating, meaningless semblance of life! Why can they not read the message writ large on the wall of history?

Remove revelation altogether from religious experience, and faith would be reduced to myths and legends. Do away with Divine revelation, and the spiritual life would forthwith lose its meaning, and religion its purpose.

Revelation enlightens belief, illuminates the soul and blows the breath of life into faith. In the pitch darkness of materialism, when despondency is compounded by atheism, it is revelation which sheds the light that turns despair into hope and the night of disbelief into a day of belief. What the sun is to the day, a prophet is to religion. What stars are to a moonless night, revelation is to the obscurities of faithlessness!

Bring to an end prophethood, block the passage of revelation, and call it a Doomsday! Nothing will remain but stark death!

Adieu!

REFERENCES

1. Translation of 18:111 by the author.
2. Translation of 41:31-32 by the author.
3. Translation of 2:187 by the author.
4. FAIZ AHMED FAIZ, *Nuskhah Hāi Wafā*, from poem 'Tanhāī'.

INDEX

Index of References to the Holy Quran

Subject Index

Name Index

List of Plates

List of Full-Page Illustrations

Index of References to the Holy Quran

Subject Index

A

Aaron[as]
 return to Egypt, 575
 partner of Moses, 700
Abhidhamma-Pitaka
 see *Tripitaka*
Aborigines
 author's personal experience with,
 223-227
 Christian influence on, 220
 concept of God, 217-230
 concept of paradise, 231-232
 concept of sacrifice, 223
 death in, 224-225
 independence of tribes, 218
 interpretation of dreams, 223-226
 magic and rituals, 224-225
 myths relating to God, 227-228
 reluctance to share knowledge, 226
 superstitions in, 224
 Unity of God, 219-220
 western scholars' view of, 220-221,
 226-228, 231
 worship among, 222-223
 concept of God, 217-234
Abraham[as], 51, 207-208, 687
Abu Jahl
 slaying of, 580
Acid
 tartaric, 413
Acoustics
 see *Hearing*
Adam[as], 688
 story of, 222
 prophethood of, 293, 688-689
 creation of, 343, 360, 376-377
ADP
 as energy of life, 390
Ahmad[as], Hazrat Mirza Ghulam
 as defender of Islam, 633-635
 family and followers safe from
 plague, 638, 642-643

opposition to claim of, 663-667
 prophecy of plague, 635, 637
 prophecy regarding AIDS, 647-649
 views on Buddha[as], 133
 defense against Arya Samaj, 665
 description of attributes of God,
 167
 press' hostility towards, 641-643
 reviews of his book,
 Brahin-e-Ahmadiyyah, 664
Ahmadiyyat
 concept of Promised Reformer,
 662-665
 growth of during time of plague,
 643
 opposition to, 663-667
Ahura Mazda
 speaking through Zoroaster[as], 668
AIDS, 647-652
 as punishment for sexual
 transgression, 647-650
 future of, 650-652
 prophecy of Hazrat Mirza Ghulam
 Ahmad[as], 647
 see also *virus*
Ál-Áshári, Imam, 21
 debate with Al-Jubbai, 22
 anthropomorphism and, 24
Al-Ḥallāj, Mansoor, 29
Al-Jubbāī, Imam, 21
 debate with Ál-Áshári, 22
Al-Bayyinah, 293-301
 manifest truth, 293
 origin of human speech, 296
 origin of word, 295
 permanence, 293
Al-fakhkhār, 375
Allah
 as *Rabb* (The Provident), 340
 as source of all knowledge, 568
 taught man to write, 599-600
 see also *God*
Al-Qayyimah, 293-301
 quality of permanence, 296

E

Fire
   punishment by, 604, 614
Fossils, 440
Fox, arctic 436-437
Freedom
   in Marxism, 64-66
   not found in Vedas, 120
   of belief in Islam, 262-263
   Sartre laments, 50-51
   vs. security, 14
Fu Hsi, 155, 165
   vision of, 155

G

Galileo, 279-280
Gamma rays, 617
Genes, 629
   independence from external factors, 429
   independent of environment, 466
   mutation of, 545
   not produced by Natural Selection, 560
   random changes in, 429
   role in evolution, 545, 557-558
   unaffected by external factors, 438, 522-524
   see also *genetic engineering*
Genesis, book of
   image of God, 377-378
Genetic Engineering, 627-630
   benefits and dangers of, 628-629
Geographic changes
   Quranic prophecy of, 624
Giraffe
   survival in drought, 426
Glucose
   see *sugar*
God
   Aborigines concept of, 217-234
   All-Knowing, 386-387
   All-Powerful, 386-387
   attributes of, 158
   Confucianism and concept of, 156
   Creator of life, 409, 467
   eternity of, 219

   existence of, 388
   fear of, 201
   belief in Unity of, 198
   Lord of Seen and Unseen, 488
   name of, Isana, 135
   name of, Shiv Devta, 135
   Protector of life, 408
   Rabb (The Provident), 340
   secular scholars on Aborigines view of, 229
   Source of All Knowledge, 568
   Teacher of man to write, 599-600
   thirst for in humans, 130
   Unity of, 198, 207, 212
   visions from, 242
   see also *Allah*
Golden Age
   of Rationalism, 33
Gorilla
   example of form fitting habitat, 429-430
   intellectual inferiority vs. humans, 524-525
Granada
   conquering of, 588
   Muslims surrender of, 588

H

Haemoglobin
   Dawkins' views on, 526-527
   evolution of, 522
   requires Creator, 526-527
Haldane, J.B.S.
   on anoxic atmosphere of early earth, 355
   on availability of oxygen in early atmosphere, 398-399
   on transformation from non-biotic to biotic era, 378
Hallucination, 243
   accusation of against Prophets, 97-98
Handedness, 418-20
   in heart and liver, 418
   see also *chirality, molecular spin, and sidedness.*

I

and Hegel, 46
and Socrates, 82, 86, 96
concept of Supreme Being, 74-76
Muslim propagation of views of,
35
on external reality, 29
rationality and, 74-76
Platypus, Duck Billed
use of electric fields, 531
Polar bear, 434-440
camouflage, 436
evolution of, 437
evolutionary distance from other
bears, 436
hunting by, 436
hypothetical extinction of, 440
in arctic habitat, 434
physical characteristics of, 435-436
swimming, 436
use of senses, 435-436
Polarization
of biological molecules, 413
Polytheism
Buddhism and, 139-142
coming after monotheism, 208
Press
hostility towards Promised
Messiah[as], 641
role of in bringing mankind
together, 599
Primordial soup, 367, 371-376
experimental production of, 356-
357
Prokaryotes, 365
see also *bacteria*
Promiscuity
consequences of sexual, 648
Promised Messiah[as]
see *Hazrat Mirza Ghulam Ahmad*[as]
and *Promised Reformer*
Promised Reformer
absurdity of multiple appearances,
666-669
advent of, 657-670
Christian interpretation of, 660-661
concept of in Ahmadiyyat,
662-667
Islamic interpretation of, 661-662
Jewish interpretation of, 658-660

literal vs. metaphorical
interpretation of, 662-663
reappearance in Islam, 702
Prophecies
of Muhammad[sa], see *Muhammad*[sa]
of Promised Messiah[as], see *Hazrat
Mirza Ghulam Ahmad*[as]
of Quran, see *Quranic prophecies*
Prophecy
vs. hallucination, 97
literal vs. metaphorical
interpretation, 702-703
misinterpretation of, 708
rationality in interpreting, 669
Prophethood
cessation of, 679-689
Divine dreams as part of, 227
finality of Holy Prophet[sa], 661-662,
670
non-law bearing, 675-676, 679-689
not a dictatorship, 65
rejection of, 205-206, 688
revelation and, 675
Prophets
characteristics of Divine, 205
characteristics of false claimants,
204
decadence of faith after demise of,
209
Divine attributes assigned to, 213
heavenly signs, 294
idolization of, 216
need for, 673, 679
not maligning other prophets, 212
not only recipients of revelation,
715
reappearance of, 695-696
status of, 675-676
see also *Aaron*[as], *Adam*[as], *Hazrat
Mirza Ghulam Ahmad*[as], *Buddha*[as],
Confucius[as], *Jesus*[as], *Moses*[as],
Muhammad[sa], *Yousef*[as], and
Zoroaster[as]
Propagation of faith
persuasion & dialogue needed for,
260-263
Protein
formation without DNA? 384
glucose transporter, 404-405

T

V

U

Name Index

List of Plates

List of Full-Page Illustrations

756